246

A History of
Public Education
in Georgia

1734 - 1976

Oscar H. Joiner, *General Editor*

James C. Bonner

H. S. Shearouse

T. E. Smith

Introduction and Epilogue by
Claude Purcell

Published by
THE R. L. BRYAN COMPANY
COLUMBIA, SOUTH CAROLINA

PRINTED AND BOUND IN THE UNITED STATES OF AMERICA

THE R. L. BRYAN COMPANY
COLUMBIA, SOUTH CAROLINA

Dedicated to

The Public School
Students
of Georgia

Table of Contents

Foreword

The history of education in Georgia is a history of the people of Georgia. In the more than two and one half centuries of Georgia's history, her people have been drawn from many groups—Indians and immigrants, slaves and landholders, farmers, soldiers, traders, merchants—and there has always been a direct correlation between the amount of education available to the people and how open, free and successful our society has been.

It has been said that education is life itself. When education was scarce, as in the early history of Georgia, only a select few could afford the luxury of a full life; in today's world, when everyone has the opportunity for an education, everyone also has the opportunity for a full and rewarding life. What good there has been in the world, the advances of civilization, the amazing technology of today, these are due not to military victories or narrow ideologies or political fortunes, but to the widespread availability of education to the people.

From Georgia's earliest old field schools to our modern, sophisticated system of public education today, the history of education in Georgia has been one of continual improvement. And the slow, sure advancement of education in the eighteenth and nineteenth centuries, the tremendous strides of the past few decades and the instances of enlightened leadership have cemented the fabric of that history together.

It is the purpose of a history such as this not only to preserve the facts of the past as accurately as possible, but also to prevent the regrettable errors of the past from recurring. Only by objectively reviewing the past can we keep the future positively in focus.

Oscar H. Joiner, retired associate superintendent of schools and principal editor and author of *A History of Education in Georgia*, has seen a great many of the positive educational changes in this century. Probably no one knows as much about the really striking educational innovations of the period as Mr. Joiner: wholesale changes such as the Smith-Hughes Act and the emergence of meaningful vocational education in the public schools; the Supreme Court decision of 1954 which led to the combining of the separate school systems of Georgia; the Minimum Foundation Program of Education Act of 1964 and later the Adequate Program of Education in Georgia Act of 1975, which led to comprehensive changes in public school funding and administration.

The people of Georgia owe a special thanks to the authors and editors of this history for the prodigious effort undertaken in researching, writing and publishing this book.

The initial work of research and writing was done by H. S. Shearouse, who wrote chapter one; James C. Bonner, who wrote chapter two; and T. E. Smith, who wrote chapters three and four. Mr. Joiner wrote chapters five and six, the curriculum sections for all chapters, the section on vocational rehabilitation and other sections. Research papers were contributed by Mamie Jo Jones on the program for exceptional children, Sarah Jones on school libraries, J. G. Bryant on vocational education, Mary Ellen Perkins on teacher education, Robert L. Cousins on Negro education, and Mr. Joiner on education finance. Retired State Superintendent Claude Purcell wrote the Introduction and the Epilogue.

The collection of historic photographs was compiled with the help of private citizens and representatives of public institutions. They are named and credited at the beginning of the illustrations section.

In addition, invaluable assistance in preparing the manuscript for publication was provided by Patricia D. Anderson, Stephen Edge, Leslie Friedman, Eleanor Gilmer, Steven B. Harvey, Jeanette A. Lloyd, Julia Martin, Glenn E. Oliver, William D. Osborne, Barbara Perkins, Anne S. Raymond, Lynn Roberts, Elizabeth G. Roe, Teresa Ross and Nancy G. Hall Shelton.

CHARLES MCDANIEL
State Superintendent of Schools
(1977-   )

Atlanta, Georgia
November, 1979

INTRODUCTION

A Chronological Digest of the Development of Public Schools

The First Schools

The establishment of public and private schools in Georgia has been a continuing act of faith by those who have led the way. Living in raw, hard, frontier conditions, the settlers in the early colonial period of Georgia were concerned primarily with survival. They had no time or desire to establish schools. Reflecting British attitudes, education in colonial Georgia was generally considered a privilege and not a right. The Salzburgers and the Moravians were among the first religious groups to organize schools for their children. These early schools taught religious beliefs first, with reading, writing and arithmetic as secondary objectives. In the approximately 25 communities that started small schools during the colonial years, none survived.

Provisions for Schools after 1776

Following the Declaration of Independence, Georgia adopted its first state constitution in 1777, which provided "schools shall be erected in each county and supported at the general expense of the state as the legislature shall hereafter point out and direct."

The first countywide school systems in Chatham, Richmond, Glynn and Bibb counties probably based their guidelines on this provision in the state constitution.

The second state constitution, adopted in 1789, omitted all references to public schools, while the third state constitution, in 1798, included an educational provision permitting rather than requiring the legislature to establish local schools. Based on this permissive legislation, the General Assembly issued charters for private academies in several counties. By 1850, Georgia had 219 chartered academies. The academies were not operated as free public schools. Only the children who lived nearby and whose parents were financially able to pay tuition attended these schools.

The state constitution has been revised by the people eight times, the first three times as outlined above, and again in 1861, 1865, 1968, 1877 and 1945.

Old Field Schools

The first Old Field School was a one room log building erected by a group of parents in an old, barren field. The seats were made from split logs with pegs inserted in the round side to add height. Sometimes plank seats were nailed to two walls of the room, with a fireplace and a door on the other two walls. The schoolmaster was usually a drifter who persuaded community parents to hire him as a teacher. During the two-month school term, children copied arithmetic problems on their slates and used blue-backed spellers.

Poor School Fund

In 1822 the state legislature agreed to divide its meager financial support between academies and a Poor School Fund to be used by counties for children who were unable to pay the tuition to private academies. A stigma attached to the pauper school funds lasted over 50 years. The poor people rejected with contempt the small pittance doled out for their children. In many counties these funds were turned over by local authorities to the academies.

First Public Schools

During most of Georgia's first 100 years as a state (1776-1872), public schools were mere charities. While the rich were educated in academies and private schools, the poor were given only the three R's, and most were denied even this opportunity.

The public school system as we know it today was established in the early 1870s. The legislature passed an act to establish a system of public instruction on October 13, 1870. This new public school system was officially opened in August 1871. Because of problems with state appropriated funds to operate schools, the first state school commissioner, John R. Lewis, resigned after little more than a year. At this time Governor James M. Smith and the citizens of Georgia regained control of the state's government. The new governor appointed Dr. Gustavus Orr as the second school commissioner.

In his 1873 report to the General Assembly, Orr stated, "There were no public schools in operation under the general school laws of the state in the year 1872." While the carpet-bag administration had attempted to make political gain from northern zeal for free education for the Negroes, Orr displayed a genuine personal concern for fair and equitable treatment of black children.

The Freedmens Bureau

Under the Freedmen's Bureau, which lasted five years following the Civil War, the federal government had spent approximately $6 million in staffing some 2,500 Negro schools in the South and providing a traditional education to 150,000 black children.

The Source of School Funds

Schools were funded during the 1870s primarily from rentals paid by the state-owned Western and Atlantic Railroad. In 1878 liquor tax revenues were added to the state school fund. Then came poll taxes and fees from the licensing of carnivals and shows.

The Establishment of Independent School Systems

By 1900 cities and towns, by revising or amending their charters, passed special legislation to support public schools by local tax levy. This continued until adoption of the 1945 constitution. The independent, or city, school systems were able to provide a higher quality education. With a greater taxable wealth, teachers were better qualified, were paid higher salaries for longer terms and remained for a longer tenure in the same schools. The larger school houses were better equipped. The quality of classroom instruction for children was better than that in the small rural schools. Because of these advantages, most of the sizable towns and cities established independent school systems.

Agricultural and Mechanical Schools

Governor Joseph M. Terrell in 1902 recommended that the General Assembly create agricultural schools in each of the 11 congressional districts. He felt that education should reflect Georgia's agricultural orientation. The Perry Bill created these district schools in August of 1906 with funding by fertilizer inspection fees. Nearby students commuted to the A & M schools, which provided dormitories for students who lived further away. The A & M schools operated for 25 years. Their courses in agriculture and homemaking as basic studies for Georgia youth influenced many public high schools to offer these two vocational subjects.

When the Board of Regents was established by Governor Richard B. Russell and the General Assembly, several A & M schools were converted to junior colleges, while the others were used by local school authorities to meet individual county needs.

Expenditure of State Funds Limited to Common Schools

Because the 1877 state constitution limited the operation and expenditure of school funds to the elementary grades, only the basic courses—reading, writing, arithmetic, grammar and spelling—could be taught. This constitution granted city and county authorities the right to levy taxes for common schools so long as the taxes were approved in a special election by a two-thirds vote. For many years legislators refused to pass enabling acts to permit a local school tax referendum.

Senator E. H. McMichael of Marion County introduced a constitutional amendment to simplify the manner of establishing local school tax districts. The amendment, ratified on October 5, 1904, empowered each county to organize board of education districts of 16 square miles, following lines of natural division such as streams, public roads, land-lot lines, militia district or county lines. The maximum tax rate levied on property was one-half of one percent, or five mills.

A school tax election could be called on petition of 25 percent of the voters in the district. At the same time three trustees would be elected for the district. A two-thirds majority vote was required.

This new law secured longer school terms and construction of new school buildings in the state. Community involvement in providing local school tax indicated that parents would continue to enthusiastically support better advantages for their children.

The Beginning of the Public High Schools

In 1911 the General Assembly proposed a constitutional amendment to delete the phrase, "in the elements of an English education only." When ratified by the voters, the 1912 legislation added free public high schools to Georgia education. From 1872 to 1945 the public schools were financed by placing state funds directly in the hands of local people. Parents and local school districts, towns and cities shared responsibility for education. Some local school systems, which were more committed to education than others, provided better schools. Leadership in local school systems had a great deal to do with the growth and development of good schools.

New School Laws of 1911

In 1911 the General Assembly made the following changes in existing school laws.

- The office of the state school commissioner became state superintendent of schools.
- Three state school supervisors and a state school auditor were hired.
- Provisions were made to recover any misapplied school funds.
- The position of county school commissioner became county school superintendent, whose responsibilities included school consolidation and arranging transportation for students living more than three miles from a newly consolidated school.
- Standards for awarding teaching certificates were changed.

Since 1911 the State Board of Education has prescribed standards and regulations for licensing teachers. The State Board of Education in 1912 adopted regulations for types and grades of teacher licenses. All teachers were required to pass Georgia history examinations. For the first time, recognition was given for special college subject areas and for completion of an approved normal school. The normal schools for teachers were usually four-year programs—two years of high school education and two college years in general and professional education.

Vocational Education

Vocational education had its start in the early 1900s. The Smith-Hughes Act passed by the U S. Congress in 1917 provided for a continuing appropriation of federal funds for vocational education in agriculture, trade and industry and home economics. Teacher salaries, teacher training and administration of the vocational education program were all federally funded. The Georgia legislature appropriated state funds for a state vocational education board.

Vocational education began slowly. At first, very few schools were ready to establish programs in agriculture, trade and industry and home economics. Local boards of education were unfamiliar with the purpose of the Smith-Hughes Act, and World War I affected the teacher supply.

Courses in agriculture and domestic science, which were instituted with federal funds, influenced local boards of education to begin purchasing equipment for commercial subjects. The colleges also began to prepare teachers for vocational instruction. The objectives of vocational education were quite different from those found in high school academic programs. Agriculture students, for example, completed six months of practical farm work in connection with the school curriculum. Home economics students completed home projects in cooking, garment making, planning and serving meals, interior decorating, home management and household accounts and child care.

The first vocational act passed by the U. S. Congress was sponsored by two Georgians, Representative Dudley Hughes and Senator Hoke Smith.

The Barrett-Rogers Act

In 1919 the General Assembly passed the Barrett-Rogers Act, which funded high school consolidation. It also encouraged the transfer of junior high schools to larger, four-year high schools. Counties with nonstandard high schools were offered $1,000 to consolidate. Consolidated elementary schools were awarded $500 grants. This act strengthened elementary and high schools in rural counties. During the first year there were 63 applications for Barrett-Rogers consolidation aid. The financial assistance also stimulated rural high schools which were initiating course work in agriculture and home economics at this time. The Barrett-Rogers Act, which was designed to encourage the consolidation of small schools, was most beneficial over a period of 20 years.

Legislation of 1919 assigned responsibility for tax support and school administration to the counties. Because independent city school systems within counties were exempt from the countywide school tax, people living in independent school districts were ineligible to vote for county school superintendents. County board of education members were required to live outside the area of independent school systems and were also required to reside in seperate militia districts.

Local revenue for schools in 1918 was $3,373,194. By 1921 it had increased to $6,686,408. The total amount of state appropriations for schools in 1921 was only $4,296,190.

State Equalization Fund

By 1925 disparities in tax support and wealth available for local school tax support became well known throughout the state. Gordon G. Singleton, a State Department of Education employee, analyzed the tax support programs in all school systems and concluded that, despite a five mill county tax levy, property in various counties was not assessed uniformly. For example, teachers' average salaries ranged from $292 to $1,418 annually. He suggested that the General Assembly allot additional state funds to equalize the poor counties. The state at that time allotted its school funds on a *pro rata* basis, with an equal amount per child going to each system. An equalization bill passed in the General Assembly in March 1926. Gasoline taxes were used to equalize educational opportunities in the poor districts. The State Board of Education became responsible for developing a formula by which these funds would be distributed.

Progress in the Late 1920s

The rural counties of Georgia continued to improve and equalize educational opportunities with state funds from the Barrett-Rogers Act and the Equalization Fund Act. About 3,500 small rural schools were consolidated into 900 larger, better equipped buildings, with longer terms and better trained faculties. A new campaign promoted adult education as a means of eradicating illiteracy in the state. The state school officials and college and university administrators cooperated to strengthen and improve the public schools.

Superintendent M. D. Collins

When campaigning for the Georgia state superintendency, Dr. M. D. Collins promised equalized opportunities for all children. He concluded that *pro rata* flat grants of state school funds on a per pupil basis were unfair. He pointed out the discrepancies in local taxable wealth in school districts, especially between rural and urban school districts, and the unequal resources in sub-tax districts within counties as well as from county to county.

Collins' first official act as state school superintendent was to cut his own salary. He and other staff members would not accept any salary increase until the salaries of rural teachers improved. He was convinced that educational opportunities and teacher salaries could be equalized in the entire state only with a greater appropriation of state school funds. His problem was to convince the voters to elect an education-oriented legislature.

The economic depression was keenly felt by all the school systems of Georgia. The collapse of local school support under the strain of the depression weighed heavily as an argument for more state support. In many communities bank failures, tax delinquencies, credit shortages and personal losses made the existing school support wholly inadequate and impossible. Local school systems were unable to handle the economic chaos. Money for school operations was the most immediate need at this time. Collins and a strong contingent of school leaders advocated shifting the tax load for supporting schools to the state.

A statewide campaign for a better school program began with all candidates for public office obliged to declare their stand on educational reforms. Their statements were given wide public notice. E. D. Rivers of Lakeland was elected governor.

Seven Months School Law

In 1936 school officials prepared three separate school bills for (1) a state-supported school term of seven months, (2) a state lay board of education and (3) free textbooks. Governor E. D. Rivers promised support and his full endorsement of these proposed bills.

The legislative enactment of 1937, providing for a state board of education composed of lay members, dissolved the previous board of professional school leaders and ex-officio members and created a nonprofessional board of 13 members. The new board included representatives from each of the 11 congressional districts appointed by the governor, with the governor as chief executive and the state school superintendent as executive secretary. Expanded board duties included matters formerly controlled by the legislature, such as administration, finance, teacher certification, authority in matters of curriculum, free textbook distribution and library administration. It also served as the state board for vocational education and as an appellate court for disagreements arising in school systems.

State Funds Run Short

This package of new school laws enacted in 1937 was perhaps the first major breakthrough in the field of education. Unfortunately, the legislature that made these benefits available failed to make adequate provision to finance them. Governor Rivers spent his second term in office struggling to finance legislation already on the statute books. In addition to education, health, welfare, highways, state highway patrol and homestead exemptions vied for state funds. By 1939 a financial crisis loomed large on the horizon.

J. Harold Saxon, executive secretary of the Georgia Education Association, along with school leaders and teachers, carefully planned a statewide publicity campaign to explain the public school crisis to the lay citizenry. A school policy statement called for adequate school support by making payments when due, funding the teacher salary schedule for seven months, funding the equalization law, furnishing students free textbooks, funding the university system and providing sufficient funds to operate properly the State Department of Education. The teachers association also called for retention of the 1937 laws relating to education. A questionnaire was sent to each candidate for state office requesting a statement on the proposed education policy. Replies were published in a special issue of the teacher education journal. A statewide effort to secure support of the education program was conducted by personal appeal to each legislative candidate.

Governor Eugene Talmadge returned to the capital January 14, 1941. In his inaugural address he pledged not to increase taxes, even though the state was about $32 million in debt, including $3.9 million to the local school systems. He pledged to pay teachers their back salaries by March 1, providing their schools had not closed early.

Works Progress Administration

During the economic depression of the 1930s, the Works Progress Administration provided new or rehabilitated school buildings for most local school systems. It also organized and maintained numerous courses in general and vocational education as well as in such special subjects as safety, first aid and special affairs. Vocational training included business, agriculture, domestic service, sewing, cooking, millinery and the native arts and crafts. Blacks received special attention in general and vocational instruction. The WPA teachers, who were 47 percent black, taught 78 percent of the reading and writing courses. This work provided employment for those in need of jobs and supplemented the public service programs in education.

M. D. Collins, state superintendent of schools, was successful in securing WPA financial assistance to keep the schools in many areas of Georgia operating when state and local funds gave out and teachers could not be paid. This was during the last term of Governor Rivers' administration, when many of the schools were forced to close due to lack of state funds.

Constitutional State Board of Education

When Ellis Arnall ran for governor in 1942, he advocated transforming the lay board of education into a constitutional board with the governor eliminated from its membership. An act providing for such a board was approved early in the 1943 legislative session and signed into law by Governor Arnall on February 4, 1943. By placing the state school system beyond the power of the governor, this provision for a constitutional board had certain advantages.

Wartime Measures Relating to Education

Georgia public education was of course affected by the long war which engaged every segment of the population and committed all its resources. At the request of the federal government, vocational teachers initiated an extensive training program for defense workers on July 1, 1940. This federally funded program provided vocational training for defense workers and rural defense training. About $1 million in training equipment was placed in vocational shops to train workers for defense employment. The rural defense training program was conducted in schools offering vocational agriculture. This was in addition to the regular program of instruction. About $300,000 in federal funds was spent for equipment for this program, which provided rural youth with basic training in farm equipment operation and maintenance. It also provided a general knowledge of tools.

High School Victory Corps

The High School Victory Corps was organized on a national basis in the fall of 1942 to mobilize high school students in a voluntary plan for participation in wartime service.

The School Lunch Program

Sponsored by the Works Progress Administration, the national school lunch program was highly popular in local communities. It employed women, helped farmers dispose of surplus produce and provided meals for many school children. The school lunch program began in 1935 and was terminated in 1943.

Teachers Retirement System

The Georgia Education Association actively secured passage of the teachers retirement system. Local superintendents Mark Smith of Bibb County and B. M. Grier of Athens were among the first school officials to call for retirement benefits in 1935. The General Assembly passed legislation in 1939 to provide retirement benefits to a few of the large school systems. The leaders who secured passage of a statewide teachers retirement system included Dr. Willis Sutton of Atlanta, Superintendent W. E. Knox of Jones County, Superintendent A. D. Copeland of Richmond County, Dr. Paul Munro of the College of Education, University of Georgia; Dr. J. I. Allman and State Superintendent M. D. Collins of the State Department of Education and Ralph Ramsey, secretary of the Georgia Education Association. It was decided early that the teacher, as beneficiary, and the state, as employer, should contribute on an equal basis toward the establishment of a retirement fund.

Membership in the retirement system was voluntary at first, but all newly employed teachers were required to become members. Those who joined paid in five percent of their salary, and the state matched this with six and one-quarter percent. The extra one and three-quarters percent paid by the state covered the costs of the prior years of teaching experience of those who were teaching. The retirement law has been amended many times, and both the state and participants have been required to pay into the system a larger percentage of their salaries as the benefits increased. The funds paid into the retirement system have been well managed. The benefits paid to retirees are exempt from state income tax.

The 1945 State Constitution

In 1945 the basic philosophy of school administration and financial support changed. The new state constitution, in Article 8, Section 1, provided that "an adequate education for the citizens will be a primary obligation of the state of Georgia, the expense of which shall be provided for by taxation." This provision of the constitution made the state of Georgia party of the first part in the field of education instead of second party, which had been the state's role since the inception of public schools in 1872.

Section 5 of the constitution stated that "authority is granted to the counties to establish and maintain public schools within their limits. Each county, exclusive of any independent school system now in existence shall compose one school district and shall be confined to the control and management of a county board of education."

More State Funds for Schools

Since 1945 the state has greatly increased its support of public schools. The state appropriation in 1945-46 was $21,-968,000. When the sales tax was passed in Georgia in 1951, the state appropriation for public schools for 1951-52 was increased to $86,863,804. A decade later, in 1961-62, it was $183,045,000. For 1971-72 it was $437,685,595.

New Foundation Program

The Minimum Foundation Program of Education was enacted in 1949 and financed with the passage of the sales tax in 1951. It marked a new day in education. This new educational program increased teacher salaries, funded the twelfth grade (25,000 pupils), expanded rural library services, provided special classes for exceptional children, expanded vocational rehabilitation, school lunch programs and veterans' education. It increased the textbook supply and provided more funds for operating school plants. It doubled the number of school buses.

Following the end of World War II, Georgia experienced a rapid birth rate. These "baby boom" children entered the first grade in 1952, with the growth continuing for 14 years. The school enrollment increased from 806,243 in 1951-52 to 1,161,148 in 1966-67. Additional classrooms, teachers, textbooks and other fixed costs had to be provided for a quarter million more children. While the rural counties lost population, the urban centers gained and were forced to absorb the additional children. This shift in population required more classrooms and teachers in the growing school systems. The problem was solved when the state legislature created the State School Building Authority.

Governor Herman Talmadge was responsible for the activation of the new Minimum Foundation Program of Education. The Honorable Fred Hand, speaker of the House of Representatives, was active in securing passage of the legislation. Roy Harris was retained by the Georgia Education Association as attorney to handle this bill in the House and Senate. M. D. Collins, state superintendent of schools, and Harold Saxon, executive secretary of the Georgia Education Association, were active in promoting a general understanding among the people for this new program of education.

Collins, during the last decade of his 25 years as state superintendent of schools, successfully persuaded the governors and members of the General Assembly to move public school education to the forefront of the state. He resigned his office in early January 1958, after serving longer than any chief state school officer.

Purcell Appointed Superintendent

In January 1958, Governor Marvin Griffin appointed Dr. Claude Purcell to succeed Collins as state superintendent of schools. For 15 years, Purcell had been exercising a leading role in the State Department of Education. During this time, he had served as liaison officer between the education agency and the General Assembly. Because of the confidence the governor and members of the General Assembly had in the new superintendent, Purcell was able to plan and put into effect many statewide improvements in public schools.

Area Vo-Tech Schools

Vocational education expanded in 1959, with post-high school centers serving large areas of students. These vocational-technical schools were jointly financed by state and local school systems. Located where industry could provide jobs for those who completed a year or more of training in specific skills, these schools served two purposes. They trained the non-college youth for jobs, and they provided a source of labor for the state's incoming and expanding industries. Each school had facilities and staff to train students for at least 20 different occupations. These schools provided day classes for full-time students and night classes for people interested in increasing their skills. Local school systems agreed to co-operate in sending students to an area vo-tech school. Twenty-five of these schools were established in the largest population centers. In the 1974 fiscal year, these schools had in attendance 24,900 full-time and 101,400 part-time students with a total operational expenditure of $20.6 million in state funds and $6.8 million in federal funds. Since construction began, a total of $59.4 million in state, local and federal funds has been spent for equipment and buildings, excluding the cost of land. These post secondary vocational-technical schools depart substantially from the traditionally academic college program. Federal funds first became available for these schools when Congress passed a new vocational education act in 1963. Since their beginning, vo-tech schools have operated with free tuition, though a small fee is charged for consumable materials used by some students. These schools have helped balance the state's economy between agriculture and industry.

Science Teachers Updated

Long before Sputnik was in orbit, the state moved to upgrade science teachers to the new demands of the jet age. Science teachers attended workshops in universities supported by $300 per teacher from state funds or payable after they returned to their classrooms in the fall. The $300 grant for summer study was eventually extended to other teaching areas in which there was a short supply of teachers.

Six-Year College Teaching Certificates

The State Board of Education established a sixth-year teaching certificate about 1959. This additional year of college beyond the master's degree developed educational specialists for the schools. The advanced certificate, based on 50 quarter hours of graduate scholarship concentrated in one work area, became the standard preparation for leadership positions. The state scale of pay provided $1,000 more in salary for the holders of the sixth-year college certificate.

Educational Television

In September 1960, the State Department of Education began broadcasting regular in-school telecourses, aired over WGTV, Athens, which was then the only state-owned educational television outlet. In February 1961, the State Board of Education was awarded a construction permit by the Federal Communications Commission to erect its first station. WXGA-TV is dedicated to former State Board of Education member Lonnie E. Sweat, who made the original motion to establish the Georgia Educational Television Network.

The State Board of Education in September 1963 activated WVAN-TV, whose call letters honor former Governor Ernest Vandiver.

WJSP-TV, named for James S. Peters, chairman of the State Board of Education, began service in May 1964. WCES-TV, which began operation in September 1966, was named for former Governor Carl E. Sanders.

In 1967, four additional stations were established. WABW-TV, which began transmitting in January, was named for State Board of Education Vice Chairman Robert (Bob) Wright. WCLP-TV, which started broadcasting in February, was named for former State Superintendent of Schools Claude L. Purcell. In March, WACS-TV was named for Associate State Superintendent of Schools Allen C. Smith, and construction was begun on WDCO-TV, named for M. D. Collins, former state superintendent of schools.

All state-owned educational television stations were interconnected in September 1965 to operate as the Georgia Educational Television Network.

The Governor's Honors Program

In the summer of 1964, the first Governor's Honors Program, designed to give new prestige to learning, was held on the campus of Wesleyan College in Macon, Georgia. Georgia was the second state to start such a program and first to finance it with state funds. The first honors program assembled 402 of the brightest Georgia high school juniors and seniors for eight free weeks of creative learning with a 40-member faculty of the state's ablest teachers. Of the 3,000 students recommended for participation, finalists were selected by test scores, grades, achievement and demonstrated skills. Governor Carl Sanders advocated establishing an honors program and the General Assembly appropriated funds. It has been conducted each year since 1964, stimulating higher levels of learning by recognizing the brightest minds among rising high school seniors.

The General Assembly Determines State School Funds

In the 1930s, '40s and '50s, the governor and the state auditor proposed the state appropriations. Generally, an all-inclusive, lump-sum amount of funds was granted to each state agency. As a rule, the wishes of the governor were carried out in the passage of appropriations. During Governor Vandiver's term in office, the General Assembly assumed greater control of state appropriations. After debate for weeks between the executive and legislative branches of state government, a line-item appropriation bill evolved for several state agencies, including the state education agency. The General Assembly finally passed the line item appropriation. Prior to this change, the governor and the state agency heads together decided on such things as salary raises, new or expanded programs and services, welfare payments, etc. But the line-item budget process had the effect of granting more financial decision-making to the legislative branch of government. Since that time, salary raises for teachers and expanded services have been finally set by the General Assembly. The governors recommend, through their budget message to the General Assembly and the proposed appropriation bill, their plans for the use of available state funds. The members of the General Assembly maintain their rights to determine the amount of state funds appropriated to each state agency. State Department of Education funds have been designated in this manner in the appropriation bill. This practice gives the General Assembly considerable responsibility for major improvements in public education financing.

Commission to Improve Education

In 1963, Governor Carl Sanders appointed a commission to improve education. After studying Georgia's population, economy and the present educational system, this commission listed objectives to improve education in Georgia. Among the objectives were provisions for more equitable educational opportunities, standards for schools, higher quality of instruction, upgraded teacher training, more efficient operation, educational television extended to all areas of the state, more planning and research in education and adequate financial support for these improvements. Following this study and report, Governor Sanders proposed a revision of the foundation program of education enacted in 1949. Georgia again became a pacesetter in enacting a new and improved foundation law for education. Designed to be used for a long period, the new law contained provisions for research, standards for schools, consumable teaching materials and free textbooks, requirements for more state and local school funds, the Governor's Honors Program, expansion of vo-tech schools and educational television, additional funds for increasing teachers' salaries and the construction of more school buildings.

Unique among the board of education standards for schools was a requirement that teachers in local school systems must teach in the field of their preparation and certification. This new requirement, designed to improve the quality of classroom instruction, was initiated first on a 75 percent basis and raised over a short period of years to a 95 percent level. There had been an oversupply of teachers in the depression years when married teachers who lived in the area of the school were given preferences in jobs without regard to their type of teaching certificate. During and after World War II, there was a scarcity of teachers, and school officials were begging people who were only partially qualified to take teaching jobs. By 1960, the supply of teachers had increased. This new standard requiring the employment of 95 percent of all teachers to work in school jobs for which they had been prepared and certified was finally accomplished.

Nix Appointed State Superintendent

Claude Purcell, state superintendent of schools, resigned effective January 1, 1966, and Governor Sanders appointed Jack P. Nix as successor. Early in his administration, Nix said, "Georgia is a national leader in many aspects of education. This is particularly true in vocational education. We are proud of the Georgia congressmen who introduced and secured the passage of nearly all national legislation in the field of vocational education. We will continue our efforts to improve all phases of the public school education program. In the next few years, I think we must begin the financing of a statewide public kindergarten program, and we must reduce the pupil-teacher ratio in the first two grades to 20-to-1. We will have to increase our teachers' salaries and provide more state funds for maintenance and operation of schools. We should also provide at least $3.00 per child for consumable supplies and materials in order to add quality to classroom instruction.

"As we go forward, we must think big, we must think new, and we must think ahead. We must work hard to provide the best possible education for our children."

The total expenditure per pupil in Georgia was $409.03 in 1965-66. It rose to $468.97 for 1967-68. Teachers received an average $1258 salary increase during this two-year period. Maintenance and operation funds under the foundation allotment rose from $850 to $1050 per state-allotted teacher.

U. S. Public Law 89-10

Title I of the Elementary and Secondary Education Act of 1965 (Public Law 89-10) provided for supplemental education services for educationally deprived (including handicapped) children who resided in low-income areas. This act was later amended to include handicapped children in institutions operated by state agencies.

About $35 million in federal funds financed supplemental school projects during the 1965-66 school year. These projects were developed by teachers and administrators in local school systems, then approved by the State Department of Education. Title I projects included program improvements in remedial reading, kindergarten, cultural experiences, summer school classes, curriculum materials centers, pupil personnel services, health and food services and enrichment in academic and humanity course offerings.

Expansion of Classes for Exceptional Children

In 1968 the General Assembly passed legislation and Governor Lester Maddox signed into law House Bill 453, which mandated that all school systems provide comprehensive and complete programming for all exceptional children by 1976. Special classes provide the services needed for children generally classified as handicapped with speech, vision or hearing impairments; those with multiple handicaps; the mentally retarded who are below normal intelligence, referred to as slow learners, and the severely retarded trainables who are taught basic living habits; those who are emotionally disturbed; and some who have inverted vision, delayed speech or the lack of speech. This program of special classes for exceptional children was started in the early 1950s under the direction of Dr. Mamie Jo Jones. Its development was slow because of the necessity of preparing qualified teachers. By 1972 there were 64,636 students, or about 53 percent of all handicapped children, in 2,583 special classes.

In addition to special classes offered in public schools, Georgia operates two residential institutions for handicapped children—the Georgia School for the Deaf at Cave Spring, where the state provides room, board and specialized teachers for 500 to 600 children in elementary and high school courses, and the Georgia Academy for the Blind at Macon, with 200 to 300 pupils in grades 1-12. The children in both these schools have first class buildings and equipment suitable to their use. There are appropriate vocational courses in both schools. Both schools are under the control and management of the State Board of Education and state school superintendent.

Not all blind or deaf children in Georgia attend the state residential schools in Macon and Cave Spring. In large population centers of the state, many blind and deaf children continue to live at home and go to public schools where special classes are conducted for them.

In the early 1970s, the Atlanta Area School for the Deaf was constructed in DeKalb County with state funds. This new school serves day students living in the Atlanta area.

Fifty Years of Rehabilitation

The rehabilitation of handicapped persons was for many years a vital service of Georgia education. In 1970, Georgia celebrated 50 years of rendering invaluable services to handicapped citizens of the state, enabling them to become self-sustaining and productive people. During this golden anniversary, the 150,000th client was rehabilitated in Georgia since the beginning of the program in 1920. The total number of citizens rehabilitated over the 50-year period was 150,022— a figure that represents 3,890 persons rehabilitated per 100,000 population over the half century. This is the highest rate of any state in the nation.

The Rehabilitation Act of Georgia passed soon after the national program was established on June 2, 1920. Only persons with physical infirmities were eligible for rehabilitation services when the program was first started. Federal support for the program was substantially expanded in 1935. During World War II, a drive was initiated to recruit physically handicapped persons for defense work. The federal law, as amended in 1943, authorized payments for physical restorations to reduce or eliminate disabilities as well as permit service to the emotionally and mentally ill. It was necessary that these services render a disabled individual fit to engage in a remunerative occupation.

Prison Schools

Through educational programs offered within the confines of correctional institutions, young people were trained in skills. Each offender was evaluated early after incarceration. Psychologists administered I.Q. tests and determined vocational preferences. The inmate was assigned a "work detail" suitable to individual abilities and vocational capacity.

The academic school taught elementary and high school level courses for regular credit. Hundreds of inmates graduated from high school at these institutions, and thousands of others made a smooth transition into local schools upon release. Some inmates successfully pursued college courses toward degrees.

The vocational school curriculum developed inmates' skills in auto body repair, auto mechanics, barbering, cooking and baking, masonry, plumbing, service station maintenance, sewing machine repair, small engine repair, upholstery, welding and woodworking.

These institutional schools made unique demands on the young offenders who had previously rejected the traditional public schools. These schools or skill centers until recently were managed directly under the supervision of the State Board of Education and state superintendent of schools.

Educating Migrant Children

The children of migrant farm workers face difficulty in attending school. Until recently, these children received little or no formal education. In the 1967-68 school year, Georgia received $438,418 to institute a migrant education program. Although the migrant workers usually move only within very restricted areas, when school district lines are crossed their children must change schools, often several times a year. Most migrant children are grouped in special classes and are given remedial instruction. Strengthening each child's self-awareness and confidence often is accomplished along with individualized reading, spelling, math and science instruction. In addition to classwork, the migrant education program provides lunchroom and health services at little or no cost to the students. Federal funds may be used to buy clothes for a boy too ashamed to attend school in rags or to send a girl suffering from abscessed teeth to the dentist.

In the 1971-72 school year, there were 27 school systems with migrant education classes with 2,100 elementary children enrolled. During the 1972-73 school year there were only 340 high school students enrolled from the families of migrant workers, and these were scattered all over the state.

With education extended to include children of migrant farm workers, all children in Georgia have an opportunity to attend school. In recent years, great strides have been made to reach all children regardless of their residence or financial circumstances.

Driver Education in High Schools

During the late 1960s, driver education became part of the high school curriculum. As the Georgia highway structure increased in complexity and as driving automobiles required more skill, educators recognized the need to teach safe driving habits to high school students. By 1970 about half the 476 schools had established driver training as an elective unit. The total amount of federally-shared funds made available for driver training during this year was $504,647. Since then, the program has been expanded to include more schools and a larger number of students.

Shared Services

Shared services emerged as one of the most promising improvements for small school systems in the late 1960s. Several small school systems in certain areas of the state agreed to share services which they could not afford alone. The size of the area and the extent of cooperation were the only significant limitations when school systems shared expensive services such as data processing, audiovisual equipment, special education consultants, language development, psychological testing and centralized purchasing.

Passage of the federal Elementary and Secondary Education Act of 1965 helped finance the shared service centers. Title III of the act authorized experimental education projects to test creative solutions to persistent educational problems. When federal funding ended on June 30, 1970, shared service centers were funded by state and local sources. During the 1970-71 school year, 116 of the state's 193 school systems were participating in these shared service projects. They were supported primarily by state and local matching funds. These centers expanded to include in-service training for teachers of math, history, art and science. Both college credit courses and non-credit workshops were conducted in the shared service areas.

By 1975, the state was spending $800,000, matched with local funds, to support shared services for school systems.

The Georgia Assessment Project (GAP)

The Georgia Assessment Project, financed with Title III federal funds in early 1970, studied the quality of teaching and learning in Georgia's public schools. Superintendent Nix said the project was perhaps "the most important step toward quality education Georgia has taken since the first MFPE law enacted in 1949." A commission of Georgians from many different walks of life was selected to determine goals for education during the next decade. This commission in their first report to the State Board of Education listed the following immediate goals.

- Statewide reorganization of school systems
- Establishment of a statewide kindergarten program
- Leadership and technical assistance to provide orderly transition to a unitary school system
- Adoption of minimum state standards for private schools.

The rationales concerning these four goals, as outlined by the commission, were as follows:

Reorganization	"Georgia has far too many school systems that cannot deliver an adequate program of education for all schools."
Kindergarten	"The early years of a child's life are crucial to development."
Unitary School System	"The preservation of the public school system may depend on satisfactory solution of the difficulties resulting from desegregation."
Regulation of Private Schools	"Many private schools are being established by individuals and groups seeking to avoid the racially integrated public schools. In many instances, buildings are inadequate, teachers are ill-prepared, library collections are insufficient, textbooks are lacking, and instructional equipment is nonexistent. Children and youth attending such are not receiving adequate educational experiences."

The commission also studied ways public education should prepare citizens for the future, targetting 1985. Now in its second phase, the assessment project is measuring how well public school students are attaining the most desirable goals identified by the commission.

Students Allowed to Cross County Lines

Following the passage of an amendment to the school laws, the State Board of Education in 1971 revised its policy concerning student transfers across boundary lines. The new policy allows parents and guardians to determine which school their children shall attend. This policy change had long been championed by James S. Peters, chairman of the State Board of Education.

During previous years, the State Board of Education had received many requests from parents to send their children to school systems other than the one in which they lived. The problem in the past had been that state funds for the child remained with the home system, unless there was an agreement between the home system and the system receiving the child.

The new policy adopted by the board stated that, "It is the position of the state board that any local system board of education is entitled to and shall receive state funds based on the attendance in that system of all pupil residents of the State of Georgia regardless of the place of residence of that pupil's parent or guardian; provided, however, that said guardian or parent is a bona fide resident of the State of Georgia." As noted, the receiving school system had authority to admit or reject the enrollment of students from other systems. This prevented the receiving system from being overflowed with pupils who lived outside the school area.

Where two or more systems entered into a 20-year written contract for certain children in a given area to attend school in another system, the receiving school system was eligible to receive state funds for the construction of classrooms for these children.

A New Blueprint for Education

The first minimum foundation program law for education began disbursing state funds in 1951. The new and improved foundation law was enacted by the General Assembly in 1964 and implemented by Governor Carl Sanders in the 1965 session of the legislature. It was expected to be used for a long period of years. Just a decade later, in 1974, a third foundation program law was passed by the General Assembly and given the

name "Adequate Program for Education in Georgia (APEG)."
It was signed into law by Governor Jimmy Carter and showed
promise of dramatic change in the state's schools.

Some portions of the new APEG law, which went into effect
on July 1, 1975, have not been fully financed because of the
reduction of state income from taxes.

The new APEG law will allow the city and county school
systems to move forward in the decade ahead toward a quality
program of education for all Georgians. The provisions of this
law are designed to bring about better classroom instruction
for both elementary and high school pupils.

Nix Elected Head of School Chiefs

Superintendent of Schools Jack P. Nix was named president
of the Council of Chief State School Officers at their November
meeting in 1974. The council is an independent organization
of state superintendents and commissioners of education whose
membership consists of the top educational officers of the 50
states and six outlying areas. In recent years, Nix had served
as national chairman of the Task Force on Career Education
and chaired the committee on federal-state relations. He represented the council on several occasions when the U. S. Congress
held hearings on pending legislation. Nix presided at the 1975
annual session in Atlanta where current national issues in
education were discussed.

Tri-County High School for Marion, Schley and Webster Counties

Marion County was the site of the first multicounty high
school built in Georgia. The $2.5 million complex, which houses
some 1,100 students from Marion, Schley and Webster counties, was dedicated by Governor George Busbee and State
Superintendent of Schools Nix on August 28, 1975.

Students coming from the three small school systems were
able to enroll in a much broader academic program at this
new Tri-County High School. The curriculum was strengthened
to more effectively prepare students for both college and vo-
cational/technical careers.

The new school operates as a joint venture among all three
counties. Superintendents L. K. Moss of Marion County,

Arthur T. Miller of Schley County and R. H. McDuffie of Webster County, together with their boards of education, proposed and planned the program of studies and the building facilities. Without a tax increase in the three counties, the school building has been financed primarily by state and federal funds. Other small school systems in Georgia are expected to establish similar schools in their districts.

Summary

The history of public eduaction in Georgia is told simply in the reports issued by the state superintendent of schools to the governor and General Assembly. The central themes recurring in these reports were these.

- The continuing struggle to build schools and pay teachers
- Efforts to upgrade teacher qualifications and retain teachers in their work
- Efforts to make public school education universal for all children
- Continued efforts of school leaders to improve and broaden classroom instruction to serve both college and employment bound youth
- The education of parents and legislators about educational inequities within and among the school systems and the need for corrective measures

Since public schools began in 1872, there has been a continuous effort to improve the quality of public school education. The financial support of schools has paralleled community earning ability and income. Georgians have been slow to realize that a higher level of educational achievement for all citizens results in greater earning ability and higher standards of living for all. But this attitude seems to be changing in the seventies.

Passage of the sales tax in Georgia in 1951 provided education with greater financial support. The state appropriation for public schools in 1950-51 school year was $50.3 million. Since then, the amount of state support has consistently increased for schools. In 1974-75, the state appropriated $605,-900,004 for public schools. During this 24-year period, public school enrollment increased by 50 percent while average daily attendance increased by 63 percent. The appropriations also increased teacher salaries and provided new standard classrooms and related facilities.

The prospects for continued public and legislative support, tempered by fluctuations in the state's economy, were bright at mid-decade.

Claude Purcell,
State Superintendent of
Schools, Retired

Atlanta, Georgia
November 1979

CHAPTER I

Beginning Efforts, Before 1867

Under The Trustees

The early settlers of Georgia came from England and the continent of Europe. The Europeans' general idea of education at the time was that a few members of the upper classes were to be educated, but the great majority of people were to remain uneducated. Whatever may have been the motivation of the first settlers, whether they sought to escape debt, to find religious refuge, to find personal freedom, adventure or monetary gain, they were primarily uneducated. Thus the settlers themselves could not be expected to have much interest in any educational enterprise. Had these people known what lay ahead—the difficult sea voyage and the harsh realities of becoming pioneers in an undeveloped country—quite likely many would have been deterred from the venture in the first place.

It is true that the passage of time tends to alter reality. The historian, looking back, often sees events in a much warmer light than actually existed. The very act of survival in their harsh environment was more than most of the early pioneers were able to attain. The 144 passengers of the "Ann," who first settled Georgia on February 12, 1733, had a very poor survival record. After 20 years, only 11 of these original settlers were known to be alive in Georgia; of the remainder, 60 were dead, of 19 there was no record, seven had gone to South Carolina, and 10 had returned to England.[1] Temple and Coleman say,

> The first and most obvious fact about life in Georgia in its first twenty years is that it was very hard. It could not have been otherwise. Frontier conditions are always hard, raw, and close to nature. Life had been hard in all the colonies settled before Georgia. The presence of the Spanish in Florida made for more strain than if a friendly people had been located there. The fact that so many of the colonists had had discouraging business experience

1

before they came to Georgia undoubtedly made life seem harder to them and achievement more difficult than it might have to people made hopeful by former success. People who had been artisans and tradesmen found the exertion of taming a wild unsettled country—clearing and planting land, building houses—much harder physically and psychologically than the activities of their former life.[2]

There were 160 Salzburger settlers at Ebenezer between the years of 1734 and 1735. As of May 1739, 55 of these persons had died.[3] George Fenwick Jones says,

A year and a half later, however, the awful truth could not long be denied, if for no other reason than that the appalling death rate gave the lie to all accounts of Georgia's salubrious climate. Most of the settlers had arrived with scurvy; various fevers such as typhoid and typhus. It was not a question of avoiding contagion, but merely of surviving it; and only those with the proper antibodies did so.[4]

The settlers' harsh background did not encourage a desire on their part to establish schools and institutions of learning. But even if they had wanted to, the situation was such that existence was the first order of the day. They had to clear forests, build roads, construct houses, plant and harvest crops. In general, the settlers were ill-prepared to be pioneers.

Nonetheless, some university graduates from European institutions were among the first persons who came to Georgia. A list of such people would include General James Oglethorpe, John Wesley, Charles Wesley, John Martin Bolzius, George Whitefield, Benjamin Ingham and Charles Delamotte. These men did give attention to schools for children, although the main thrust was in religious training. However, only John Martin Bolzius, the pastor of the Salzburger group, remained in Georgia. The first of four groups of Salzburgers, who had been driven from their homes in the Province of Salzburg for religious reasons, arrived at Savannah harbor on Sunday, March 10, 1734, almost exactly one year and one month after the first group on the "Ann," led by Oglethorpe, landed at the Savannah harbor. The Salzburgers camped in Savannah while a permanent place was being selected; then they were able to move to their new home.

The Trustees, who were concerned about education and active in its development, arranged for the first group of settlers, the Salzburgers, to come from England to Georgia under the leadership of General James Oglethorpe. Thus the first planning for a schoolmaster and instruction of children was done by the persons who arranged for the group of Salzburgers. The Reverend Samuel Urlsperger was responsible for organizing the group in Europe, and the Society for the Propagation of Christian Knowledge in London worked with the Trustees in helping support the Salzburgers who were going to Georgia.

Dr. Henry Walter Guerdes at New Broad Street, London, in a letter dated September 11, 1733, to Mr. Henry Newman (secretary of the Society for the Propagation of Christian Knowledge) wrote asking whether or not "a good sober and diligent man that could keep school both in English and in German is wanted or would be acceptable to the colony." He continued that he would like to recommend the person of Christopher Ortmann, who for many years had been keeping a charity school under Guerdes' inspection.[5]

Apparently, Ortmann was very much interested in this idea, because "as early as October 17, 1733, he (Christopher Ortmann) appeared before the Trustees and proposed to go to Georgia as a schoolmaster and parish clerk for the Salzburgers who were to settle there." [6] The Trustees must have been interested too, because the minutes of the Common Council for November 14, 1733, state, "that Mr. Vernon and Dr. Bundy be desired to propose to the Society for Promoting Christian Knowledge that on paying over three thousand pounds to the Trustees they will engage under their seal to pay three several salaries fifty, thirty, and ten pounds per annum to the minister, catechist, and the schoolmaster of the Salzburgers in Georgia." [7]

In a series of letters from Newman in London to Urlsperger in Augsburg, Newman says that the Ortmanns have visited the Society and have been accepted into its services. Also, he says that Mr. Ortmann is preparing himself to go to Rotterdam to meet the Salzburgers and act as interpreter to the English officers and sailors on board. He later tells Urlsperger that Ortmann has sailed.[8]

There is a letter from Benjamin Martyn, secretary of the Common Council of the Trustees, to Oglethorpe, dated November 24, 1733. It states, "Among the first rank is Mr. Phillip George Frederick de Reck their conductor, and Mr. Ortmann their Sent as a Schoolmaster to the Children, the Society in Bartlett's Buildings have engaged to pay to the Minister a Salary of 50 pounds a year and the Catechist 30 pounds a year and the Schoolmaster 10 pounds a year; And as a Schoolmaster's Salary is but small the Trustees think it right to allow him Twenty acres of Land for a House, Garden, and pasturage." [9] There are other letters concerning the schoolmaster Christopher Ortmann. However, these cited here plus the fact that he is listed by Carl Mauleshagen [10] and Coulter and Saye [11] as a member of the first group, will suffice to show Ortmann a member of the first group of Salzburgers to come to Georgia.

The Salzburgers arrived at Savannah March 10, 1734. The pastor, John Martin Bolzius, wrote on March 30, 1734, "Since God has brought us a calmer and more orderly life, we can give more serious attention to the Salzburgers' children. They come to our room several times a day, where we instruct and catechize them . . . As soon as we reach our destination we will also start with reading, writing, etc." [12]

Bolzius wrote in a letter dated May 15, 1734, "Since I have some tranquility, I have started, in the name of God, to hold school for the Salzburger children in Ebenezer. First I pray for them, then I recite some verses for them for our mutual awakening; afterwards I have them read and I finish up with more prayer." [13] Writing again on July 25, 1734, the Reverend Bolzius says, "Our school, which we hold in our little house every morning and afternoon, has become smaller again because two children have contracted dysentery."[14] Writing again February 9, 1735, the pastor says,

> Mr. Causton has promised to send some black slates for our pupils. As soon as they arrive, the bigger children, who are well founded in reading, will be started in writing and arithmetic. In order not to neglect the bigger ones for the smaller children, we have had to divide them into

two classes. All of the children are together in the two religious classes we have in the morning and in the afternoon. In all other lessons the smaller children are taught by Mr. Ortmann while the two of us continue with the bigger ones. The parents continue to send their children to school regularly, and the children themselves come to us eagerly and joyfully.[15]

At first, Bolzius apparently approved of the work done by Christopher Ortmann and his wife.[16] However, he did write concerning difficulty with the Ortmanns, especially a quarrel between the Ortmanns and Rheinlanders.[17] Also, Mrs. Ortmann took an English girl from Savannah to rear in her home but, apparently, she was very severe in punishment of the child, for which Bolzius rebuked her.[18]

The schoolmaster, Christopher Ortmann, had been part of the first group of Salzburgers to come to Georgia for the purpose of teaching the children English. He was a poor choice for this task, because he had little skill in the English tongue, poor pronunciation and, according to Bolzius, no skill in teaching children. He did instruct the small children in reading German.[19] After nine years, he was dismissed and was given a small pension by the trustees.[20]

The people who were responsible for this group of immigrants had made provisions for a schoolmaster. So from the beginning there was organized effort toward education. It is unfortunate that this person did not turn out well and that the school suffered because he was not able to teach English. In spite of the poor beginning, however, this school was established early and did continue. Strobel says,

> In every instance in which a pastor was sent over, a schoolmaster accompanied him, unless one was already provided. A fund, too, was subsequently created for his support . . . Thus we find that there was a regular school kept up during the lifetime of Mr. Bolzius and many years afterward, at Ebenezer, a school house was also erected, and a fund established for the support of the teacher.[21]

It is difficult to pinpoint exactly the types of instruction which occurred in this early school. However, it seems certain that while the main emphasis was on religious instruction, reading, writing and arithmetic were not overlooked. Brown says,

> After breakfast, they went to school until noon. We know they were given religious instruction and learned to read and write. We do not know if they all studied Latin, French, English, German, and mathematics as Governor (John Adam) Treutlen did under Mr. Bolzius. Another teacher gave them English lessons.[22]

It is known that Bolzius, the leader of the group, was an educated man and although he was the spiritual leader and pastor, he was also concerned with the education of the people. It is noteworthy that Bolzius came with the first group of Salzburgers and remained their leader until his death in 1765. He even had concern about people in the colony other than the Salzburgers. He wrote to General Oglethorpe about the future plan for their schools, saying they wanted to share with other children and other people in the colony, extending this invitation even to adults and native savages.[23] Bolzius and his assistant, The Reverend Israel Gronau, were both men of educational backgrounds. Bolzius was the superintendent of Francke's Latin School in the Orphan House at Halle, Germany, and Gronau was a tutor in the same school.[24]

The education of the Salzburgers was a threefold effort, first the orphan house, patterned after the Orphan House at Halle, Germany, of which Bolzius was superintendent; second, the parish school; and third, an instructor in the English language. The orphanage was supported by contributions from Europe and England and by the work of the children themselves and was the first institution of its type in the American colonies. The orphan house was discontinued as an institution among the Salzburgers after these families were able to take in orphans as helpers, primarily in field work.

The parish school was not the only parish school in America; German immigrants established similiar schools in other colonies. However, the parish school was strictly a German school, a community school centered around the church with the pastor as the director. As such it could not be successful in a plantation economy, and as the colony of Georgia evolved in that direction, the parish school finally disappeared. The

Salzburgers did, however maintain the parish school for a long period of time because they were slow to move to the plantation type social and economic organization.

The instructor in English for the Salzburgers really has no counterpart in early American education. The position was included because Bolzius and the people who were organizing the Salzburger immigration recognized the need for the German-speaking immigrants to learn English so they could function in an English colony. Because of the ineffectiveness of the several persons who were appointed as schoolmasters in English, it must be said that this phase of the education of the Salzburgers was largely a failure. McCaul says,

> The record of educational effort among the Salzburgers was a relatively bright one. For the Salzburgers there was a language barrier between themselves and the English inhabitants of the colony, but these German-speaking immigrants brought with them a tradition of education, the Lutheran conviction that every man should learn to read the Bible for himself, and they were led by men with university training and with teaching experience in an educational institution, August Hermann Francke's schools at Halle, famous throughout Europe.[25]

Also, McCaul says, "The first schoolmaster at Savannah was William Waterland who came to the colony in February, 1733. Waterland was a brother of the chaplain of the king, was a man of some culture, and the Trustees made him one of the bailiffs and conservators of the peace at Savannah. He was a drunkard, however, and within a few months he was removed from office for misbehavior." [26] There is no record that this man ever did any teaching in Savannah, although he may have come to the colony for that purpose. John Burnside, listed as a writing master, wrote to the Trustees asking that he be given permission to teach in Savannah.[27] Although he was issued a license "to instruct the youth of this province in writing and accounts and so forth," [28] there is nothing in the records to show that he ever taught school in Savannah.

A very short, but interesting, reference is made in a 1940 Georgia Supreme Court ruling pertaining to an early effort at public education in the colony. (Georgia Reports: Vol. 190

Case No. 13361. State Board of Education v. Richmond County Board of Education. pages 588-597. April Term. 1940). Briefly tracing pertinent educational milestones, the author states, ". . . While with the presentation of a thousand spelling books to James Edward Oglethorpe by James Leake, in 1732, the first step was taken towards public education in Georgia, and while many private mission schools were established and maintained by local support, education was a privilege limited to those who could afford it. . ." There are no records available indicating what use was made of the spelling books.

The next educational enterprise in Georgia was undertaken by a group of Moravians. These were German people from central Europe in the Province of Bohemia. Count Zinzendorf was the spiritual leader of this particular religious group, who came to Georgia as colonists and missionaries to the Indians. The first group consisted of 10 persons under the leadership of David Nitschumann entering the Savannah harbor April 6, 1735. Some of the group went to live with members of the Creek Indians so they might learn the language and the way of the Indians.[29]

The second group of Moravians was on the same vessel with General Oglethorpe, John and Charles Wesley, Benjamin Ingham and Charles Delamotte. Benjamin Ingham and John Wesley came to America as missionaries to the Indians. Charles Wesley, John's brother, came as Oglethorpe's secretary. Charles Delamotte, under the influence of the Wesleys shortly before they came to Georgia, decided to accompany them.[30]

This group of people arrived at Savannah on February 5, 1736. Benjamin Ingham soon associated himself with the Moravians who were working with the Indians as missionaries and were planning a school for Indian children. Oglethorpe agreed to build a school, and Ingham decided to become a teacher in the school. The building was to contain three rooms —one for Ingham, one for the Moravian missionaries and one to be used as the school. The structure was completed by September 20 and was the famous "Irene" School located on an island in the Savannah River about five miles above Savannah.[31] The enterprise showed promise, and Ingham went back to England in March 1737, to try and find some additional people to come and help in the work of the school and evangelism in the colony. He never returned, instead associating himself with the Moravians and their work in England.[32] Back in the colony, the Moravians would not agree to engage in conflict with the Spaniards and had a number of controversies with Oglethrope concerning this matter. In the end they left Georgia. Some returned to Europe, but the majority went to Pennsylvania. By 1740 they had all left.[33]

In the meantime Charles Delamotte had organized a school for the English children in Savannah. He became popular and

> during most of the day he taught thirty to forty children to read, write, and cast accounts. His teaching duties were of two kinds: secular and religious. Before school in the morning and after school in the afternoon he catechized the younger children, and in the evening, he instructed the older children.[34]

When John Wesley returned to England, Delamotte found himself in a difficult situation. He had been charging no fees for instructing the children. His subsistence had been received from Wesley, and now he had no way to get funds for his livelihood. When Whitefield came to Georgia in May 1738, Delamotte borrowed money from him to pay his debts and passage back to England.[35]

James Habersham, who had come with Whitefield to Georgia, became the schoolmaster when Delamotte left. He, too, did school work without remuneration. Although he received no salary from the Trustees, they did give him food and clothes.[36] He was more interested in Whitefield's orphan's home than in the school, and as soon as Whitefield's Bethesda Orphanage was established, he gave full time to its operation. The job of schoolmaster was taken over by John Dobell.

Dobell also had arrived in the colony with Habersham and Whitefield in May 1738. Like Habersham, he charged no fees and received no salary. He went back to England early in 1741 and secured from the Trustees an appointment as the regular teacher.[37] The appointment came December 5, 1741, with a salary of 10 pounds per year. In addition, he was appointed register of the province.

With the naming of Dobell, the Trustees had recognized their responsibility in the education of the children and had appointed a schoolmaster with a salary. In the beginning, the Trustees planned for the school to be free to those who were unable to pay tuition, with the schoolmaster collecting fees from those who had the ability to pay. It was found to be quite difficult to decide who was unable and who was able to pay. Finally, the Common Council, on April 18, 1743, decided to make the school free to all children of the colony irrespective of their ability to pay.[38] And so was established the Savannah Free School.

There are two very interesting and significant developments here; the first is the existence of a free school, and the second is the payment of the salary of the schoolmaster by Parliament through the Trustees. This situation continued into the period when Georgia became a royal colony and was no longer under the Trustees. Parliament paid the salaries of teachers at Savannah, at Vernonburg, and at Acton or Augusta. There is no parallel to this occurrence in American history; that is, the act of Parliament, through its constituted representatives, first the Trustees and later the Board of Trade and Royal Governor, paying the salaries of schoolmasters in the colonies. The Salzburger immigrants to the colony had a schoolmaster, and although his salary came through the Trustees, he was paid not by Parliament but by the sponsors of the immigrants —the German sponsors under Urlsperger and the English sponsors under the Society for the Propagation of Christian Knowledge. In both cases, this support continued until the Revolution. After the Revolution, the Society for the Propagation of Christian Knowledge withdrew its support.

When George Whitefield came to Georgia in May 1738, he quickly became concerned with organizing an orphan house. Upon a visit to the Salzburgers at Ebenezer, he was impressed with their orphan house and school and determined to organize and build one in Savannah along the same lines.[39] James Habersham soon was giving full time to the orphan house project of Whitefield, vacating the schoolmaster position. Whitefield's Bethesda Orphanage soon became a reality, and Habersham became the leading person in organizing and managing the orphanage and school. Whitefield spent the major part of his time soliciting funds for the venture throughout the colonies and in England.[40]

The early efforts at education by English settlers were an adjunct to religious emphasis, primarily by the Wesleys and

George Whitefield. The pattern of English educational thought must have influenced these beginnings,[41] but early educational activities were viewed as an aid to religion and not an end within themselves.

There were also some early efforts to educate Negroes in the colony, always coupled with religious efforts. Two years before the Trustees gave up their rule of the colony, they agreed to the persistent demands of a large segment of the colonists, particularly in the Savannah area, for slavery in the colony. However, they included in the Repealing Act of August 8, 1750, a stipulation obliging all masters to have their slaves taught the Christian religion.[42]

The Trustees appointed Joseph Ottolenghe as catechist for Negroes.[43] Although Ottolenghe was an Italian Jew, he had been converted to the Church of England. He came to the colony to help with the promotion of silk culture because he was knowledgeable of the Italian methods of processing silk.[44] Although he made some efforts, more and more of his time was taken with the silk culture project and, finally, he gave up his work with Negroes altogether.

When Ottolenghe first came to Georgia, he was advised and helped by James Habersham and the Reverend Bartholomew Zourberbuhler, the Church of England minister in Savannah.[45] Both Habersham and Zouberbuhler continued their interest in Negro education, even after Ottolenghe discontinued his efforts. Habersham taught some of his slaves to read and write,[46] although by act of March 7, 1755, the royal government of the colony placed severe legal restrictions on the instruction of Negroes. There was a fine of 15 pounds sterling for teaching Negroes to write.[47] The act of May 10, 1770, regarding the education of slaves is as follows.

> Whereas the having slaves taught to read or suffering them to be employed in writing may be attended with great inconvenience: BE IT THEREFORE ENACTED, that all and every person and persons whatsoever, who shall hereafter teach, or cause any slave or slaves to be taught to write or ready writing, or shall use or employ any slave as a scribe in any manner of writing whatsoever, every such person or persons shall, for every such offense, forfeit the sum of twenty pounds sterling.[48]

The Reverend Zouberbuhler left in his will a majority of his estate as a bequest for the education of Negroes. The executors of the will were directed to apply the profits and the produce of the plantation in "hiring and employing a person properly qualified for teaching and instructing Negroes in the principles of the Christian religion as held by the Church of England." [49]

Under the Royal Governors

The colony was governed by the Trustees during its first 20 years; however, the Trustees were in England, with an ocean between them and the Colony. It was not working, so a system of royal governors was initiated.

There were three royal governors during the period between the rule of the Trustees and the Revolution. Little can be said about education during this time, except that the school at Ebenezer operated by the Salzburgers continued, and Parliament continued to pay for two schoolmasters. There were many efforts by individuals to organize private schools of different kinds, primarily in Savannah and, to an extent, in Augusta. Advertisements were placed in the Savannah paper soliciting students for various private educational ventures.[50] Between 1763 and 1774, 21 people started schools in Savannah, but none survived.[51]

The Revolutionary Period

During its early years, the colony, although settled by diverse groups, was in organized communities making it possible even under frontier conditions to organize some kinds of schools. As slavery was permitted and the threat of attacks by the Spanish lessened, however, the plantation system began to emerge and people were dispersed on farms and plantations. It became more difficult for children of these families to have any kind of education through a community effort. More and more their education came from tutors and private boarding schools. During the Revolution, education came to a relative standstill. Coleman says,

> There was less educational than religious activity in Georgia during the war years, as had been the case in

the colonial period. Private schools continued in Savannah under whichever government controlled the city, but there seemed to have been fewer than formerly. Fees ranged from twenty shillings a quarter for reading and writing to ten pounds per year for Latin, Greek, French, or Mathematics. Not much is known about education outside Savannah, but it is extremely doubtful if there are many, if any, schools on plantations or in other towns after 1788. The parochial school at Ebenezer was abandoned when the British arrived, and there was no chance for any formal education in the upcountry.[52]

Georgia made some grand plans for an education system. However, during the critical time preceding the Revolution, during the war itself and the postwar period—a span of 40 to 50 years—there was little organized educational effort. Smith wrote, "There had been no possibilitty of carrying on any schools and those children who grew up during the war never entered a classroom."[53]

Even though there were some bright spots, up to and immediately following the Revolution, generally the story which must be related concerning education in Georgia for a very long period of time is a melancholy one, deriving from many circumstances. During this period there were almost two generations of people who literally had no chance at an education. The rise of the plantation system based on the institution of slavery did not stimulate any thinking concerning education for all people. The landed gentry could provide through tutors and private schools at home and abroad for whatever education they desired for their children, and generally that was not too much. It was against the law to provide any kind of education to the slaves, and the poor usually cared little about education for themselves.[54] The educational climate in Georgia was not promising as the colony entered the period when its schooling efforts were dominated by the "old field schools" and by the academies.

Early Legislation

Soon after the Declaration of Independence in 1777, Georgia adopted its first state constitution. It provided that "Schools shall be erected in each county and supported at the

general expense of the state as the Legislature shall hereafter point out and direct." [55]

Here was the groundwork for a state-supported system of
education. This was a grand concept for the framers of the
state constitution in the midst of the Revolutionary War. Dr.
Alonso Church, president of the University of Georgia, speaking before the Georgia Historical Society on February 12,
1845, recognized the potential of the idea, saying, ". . . (if)
we had carried out our dues of our early patriots, and the
framers of our first Constitution, Georgia would now have a
system of education, equal, if not superior, to that of any
State in the union." [56] But the grand concept was not soon to
be realized.

Georgia adopted constitutions in 1777, 1789, 1798, 1861,
1865, 1868, 1877 and 1945. The first constitution took notice of
education. The second constitution in 1789 had no education
provision; however, this constitution was adopted to conform to the new Federal Constitution of the United States.
The third constitution adopted in 1798 did have an educational provision. In Article IV, Section 13 it states,

> The arts and sciences shall be taught in one or more
> seminaries of learning and the legislature shall, as soon
> as conveniently may be, give such further donations and
> privileges, to those already established, as may be nec-
> essary to secure the object of their institution; and it
> shall be the duty of the General Assembly, at their next
> session, to provide effectual measures for the improve-
> ments of such institution. [57]

The earliest legislation passed in 1780 was local in nature,
designating a certain public lot in Augusta to be reserved for
public seminaries and schools. [58] The next legislation in July
of 1783 also included provisions of local application: the
town of Washington was to provide a free school from the
sale of town lots, and two academies were to be started, one in
Waynesboro and one in Augusta. The Waynesboro Academy
was to be established from the sale of town lots and was given
an endowment of 2,000 acres of land in the county; in Augusta the town commissioners were directed to lay out the reserve land in Augusta into acre lots and sell them. There was

further provision for the statewide application of the legislation, which empowered the governor to grant 1,000 acres of land for each free school in each county. [59] An act approved February 25, 1784, laid out two or more counties to the west, stating,

> That the county surveyors, immediately after passing of this act, shall proceed to lay out in each county, 20,000 acres of land of the first quality, in separate tracts of 5,000 acres each, for the endowment of a college or seminary of learning and which said land shall be vested in and granted in trust to His Honor the Governor for the time being.[60]

During the Revolution, considerable property was confiscated from the Tories and sympathizers to the crown. In 1792 legislation was passed giving permission to every county in the state to buy at a sale of confiscated property an amount of land not to exceed 1,000 pounds in value for use of an academy.[61]

The Academies

The term academy was first used in Georgia in its early laws. The origin of the word academy as an educational term, according to Cubberly, was as follows.

> Socrates' greatest disciple was a citizen of wealth by the name of Plato, who had abandoned a political career for the charms of philosophy, and to him we owe our chief information as to the work and aims of Socrates. In 386 B. C., he founded the Academy, where he passed almost forty years in lecturing and writing. His school, which formed a model for others, consisted of a union of teachers and students who possessed in common a chapel, library, lecturerooms, and livingrooms. Philosophy, mathematics, and science were taught, and women as well as men were admitted . . .

> The English named their classical schools after the chief subject of study, hence the English *grammar schools*. In 1638, Milton visited Italy, and was much entertained in Florence by members of the academy and university there. In 1644, he published his *Tractate on Education*, in which

he outlined his plan for a series of classical *academies* in England. Milton was a church reformer, as were the Puritans, and the Puritans, in settling America, brought first the term *grammar school,* and after the term *academy* to New England.[62]

The first academies were chartered by the legislature, apparently, in the following order.

Richmond Academy in Augusta—1783
Waynesboro Academy in Burke County—1783 [63]
Sunberry Academy in Liberty County—1788
Chatham Academy in Savannah—1788 [64]
Glynn Academy in Brunswick—1788 [65]
Louisville Academy in Jefferson County—1796 [66]
Green County Academy in Greensboro—1803
Washington County Academy in Sandersville—1803 [67]
The Oglethorpe Academy in Lexington—1807 [68]
The Effingham Academy in Springfield—1809 [69]
Mount Enon Academy—1810 [70]
Mount Zion Academy in Hancock County—1811
Powellton Academy in Hancock County—1811

The Richmond Academy is worthy of special note because it was authorized in 1783 and opened April 12, 1785. The academy closed in 1798 and opened again in 1802.[71] It has been in continuous operation since that time, except during the Civil War, when it was used by Confederate authorities as a hospital. The Sunberry Academy in Liberty County became famous because of the extraordinary man, the Reverend William McWhir, who was its celebrated headmaster. The Chatham Academy, although chartered in 1788, did not actually begin operation until some time in the next century.

The records of some of the academies are clear as to the time they were chartered, the time they began operation and some of the persons in charge For many of the academies, however, records are less clear. Boogher says,

Some academies were authorized, and Trustees appointed, and received grants of land, from the sale of which money was collected with which to start the school; yet these academies may never have been in operation. Other academy charters were granted, but when no work had been done toward erecting the schools, the charters were revoked, and the academy money given to conduct poor schools.[72]

That there were men of great vision in Georgia at this time is evident in an act of the legislature passed on January 27, 1785, creating a university, "An Act for the more full and complete establishment of a public seat of learning in the state." While this volume is not a history of higher education in the state, it should be noted that this act was an all encompassing scheme for education. The act created the Board of Visitors, vested with the power of visitation to see that the intent of the legislation was carried into effect. The Board of Trustees was vested with authority to manage property of the university other than to sell it. To sell property took the concurrence of both the Board of Visitors and the Board of Trustees, which together composed the Senatus Academicus of the University of Georgia.

The act also stated that all public schools supported by funds or public monies should be considered as parts or members of the university. The Senatus Academicus was given broad authority with respect to regulation of the schools in the state—the recommendation of schools and academies to be instituted, branches of education to be taught, examination and recommendation of instructors to be employed. Also, it required the president of the university to visit each school at least once a year to examine their order and their performance.[73]

It was a beautiful plan of education, but as Coulter says,

> This, then, was the theory, the well-planned system of education under which the statesmen of the day expected the people of Georgia to grow wise and prosperous. It was [too] good to be true in practice. Outside of theory and slight semblance, this system of education never entered into the life of Georgia. It failed to function properly from the very beginning. In the words of the Senatus Academicus itself, 'The plan marked out for the literary endowment of Georgia is beautiful in theory, and might be productive of the most useful results. But in practical utility

it has never yet met the reasonable expectations of the community.' [74]

The Senatus Academicus had more than enough to claim its attention with the management of the university, or, rather, getting the university organized and underway. In local communities schools were local enterprises if there were schools at all. Newly organized state government and county governments were certainly not efficiently operating units at this point. Then, too, communication was difficult to maintain. In retrospect, such an ambitious scheme was premature in Georgia's development and probably could not possibly have succeeded at that time. Kilpatrick says,

> The Constitution and Charter of the University opened up one of the most interesting bits of education in history to be found in the whole period of American life but the one 'general and complete establishment' never became a vital actuality. A frontier people were not ready for so high a degree of centralization.[75]

Dabney says,

> The University of Georgia was not only the first state university chartered; it was also the first one projected to direct and control an entire system of public education for a democratic state. It was a grand dream, an original, unique, bold plan, but it did not work.[76]

Although the university was chartered and some very fine academies were organized, the tragic fact is that the foundation upon which these institutions had to rest was thoroughly neglected so far as the state was concerned.

From the years 1790 to 1817, whatever funds were available from the state for public education went into the academies. After that time, the poor school fund was established; the pattern came to be that the proceeds from $500,000 was distributed by the state, with half going to the poor school fund and half to the academic fund or to the academies. An academy had to be chartered in order to receive funds from the academic fund, and many of these academies had the charter and a large board of trustees but lacked other features of a school

of high grade.[77] Boogher lists the growth of academies, some
of which were not chartered, in the state by decades.

1783-1799— 20 academies
1800-1809— 7 academies
1810-1819— 50 academies
1820-1829—108 academies
1830-1839—294 academies
1840-1849— 62 academies
1850-1860— 77 academies

Total   583 [78]

Stewart reports,

> In 1850 Georgia had 219 chartered academies, with 318
> teachers, 9,059 pupils, and incomes of $108,983. Only eight
> states had more academies at that time than Georgia;
> only eight states of the thirty-one had more students and
> only fifteen states spent more money on her academies
> than did Georgia. The greater part of this fund was re-
> ceived from tuition, $1,397 was from endowment and
> about $16,000 from state appropriation.[79]

The difference in the figures given by Boogher and Stewart is
explained by the fact that Boogher's figures are those chartered
and organized, while Stewart's figures are for academies in
operation at the time.

The academies were located in towns, and persons who lived
close enough could walk to attend. Other enrollees had to make
arrangements for board in the town.

> Even those of straightened means dwelling in a distance
> were able by some straining to meet the small expenses
> of board and tuition. The former, abundant and excellent,
> including lodging and laundering, was gotten for eight
> and ten dollars a month. Tuition was $8, $12, and $16
> for a term of twenty-two weeks, which was as sure to run
> through its whole lengths as the sun continued to give
> its light by day. A little more than one hundred dollars
> would carry a pupil even in classes most advanced,
> through the entire scholastic year of 44 weeks.[80]

Our place as we called it was located one mile north of Springfield, Georgia, the county seat of Effingham and near the road leading from Springfield to Sisters' Ferry on the Savannah River. Father often spoke of it as a poor place for a farm. His chief reason for remaining there as I have often heard him say was because the county academy was located in Springfield and he wanted his children to have advantage of a good school.[81]

Some of the academies had endowments.

Meson Academy at Lexington, Oglethorpe County, received from ten to fifteen thousand dollars, permanent endowment from the individual whose name it bears. The Burke County Academy has a permanent fund of more than $7,000, and within a few years the citizens of this county have given to other institutions probably over $20,000. The Richmond Academy has buildings and library apparatus worth probably $30,000 and annuity from real estate amounting to $16,000 and bank stock to the amount of $12,000, besides land which are rapidly increasing in value.[82]

The academy (Effingham) is richly endowed, with house for teachers, it had $15,000 twenty years ago.[83]

The curriculum of the academies, in general, could be called classical. Stress was placed on mathematics, English grammar, Latin and Greek.

Aurarians who contemplated entering the University as Freshmen 'must have a correct knowledge' of Cicero's Orations, Virgil, and Greek Testament, 'Jacob's Greek Reader, English Grammar, and Geography, and be well acquainted with Arithmetic.' . . . He must have that 'correct knowledge' of the ancient Latins and Greeks as well as of arithmetic and other subjects; and to get this instruction he must attend an academy. There was no such institution in Auraria, but not many miles away down in Clarkesville there was the Habersham County Academy, where the 'mode of teaching' was 'upon the new and most approved plan.' [84]

The term academy came to connote the school level which immediately preceded university education. Later this level of education came to be called the high school. There was, however, an elementary division in almost all of the early academies which persisted with many of them as they developed into predominantly high schools.

The following subjects were usually taught in the academies: Elementary—spelling, reading, writing, arithmetic, English grammar, and geography; High School—chemistry, logic, ethics or moral philosophy, psychology (called intellectual science), physics, astronomy, political economy, composition and rhetoric, Greek, Latin, French, algebra, geometry, trigonometry, mechanical drawing, analytical geometry and calculus (by request). In the female academies, drawing, painting, fine needlework, and music were always offered, the tuition being extra. All of these, of course, were not required; in fact, a student could take one or all of them as it suited him or his purse. The struggling country youth eager to acquire an education would take every course possible.[85]

Augustus Baldwin Longstreet, the author of *Georgia Scenes*, attended the Richmond Academy.

The boy (Augustus Longstreet) persisted in doing everything except keeping his mind on his books. He was doubtless often reminded that he should be more earnest, that his tuition alone cost his parents ten dollars a quarter, and that it was not every child who had opportunities equal to his mastering 'Latin, Greek, English, and the common, practical branches of arithmetic.' He knew well enough that he was a disappointment of his people, and had been cursed all too often by having pointed out for him the contrast between himself and the dutiful Mr. Augustus Baldwin, the first rector of the academy, for whom, in fond hope, he had been named.[86]

For a period his parents sent him to a school in South Carolina, then returned him to Richmond Academy.

Richmond Academy, the boy hoped would have changed beyond his recognition. Alas! He found teachers and textbooks just as they had been before. Very soon it was plain to everybody that Gus' absence had not helped him. He was still a dunce, or worse, a person who had sense enough to learn and was too lazy to do it. He did well enough in some studies for his teachers to know that he could learn anything if he only would. In all likelihood the boy was as greatly at fault as his teachers were, but he did not so regard himself, either then or sixty-five years later, when in setting down his reminiscences he still permitted himself to speak scathingly of the old Academy.[87]

It appears that the method of teaching was whatever type of instruction the teacher chose. In all probability, this was learning from a book, reciting to the teacher and passing an examination. "Material for a study on the methods of teaching used in academies is very scarce, it seems probable that in earlier years, teachers 'just taught' without any definite idea of method."[88]

Discipline in the academies was based on the rod. The schoolmaster who could control his students and maintain discipline was desired, and it was an accepted fact this could be done only by a stern application of the rod.

I shall devote a little space here to a description of some of the methods of Mr. Hawley. First his main reliance and discipline and for securing lessons was the rod which with him was a rule two inches wide and two feet long or whale bone the bow of an old fashioned umbrella. He had his own method too of administering the punishment. Generally, the culprit was required to stretch himself across the chair face downward and hold fast the lower round. Mr. Hawley stood in front of and held the chair with one foot elevated on a round, thus completely shutting off any attempts by the boy to rub the bruises or catch the whale bone with his hand.[89]

Johnston describes discipline in the academies of Powellton and Mount Zion as somewhat more moderate for girls than boys.[90] As Boogher says,

Discipline in the academies was a matter left generally to the master, though there must have been a policy of discipline supported by the governing boards of the various institutions. The earlier period was one of discipline by the rod, which seems to have been an accepted principal rather than a matter for discussion.[91]

The Old Field Schools

The old field school grew out of the time and situation.

> The name 'old field school' had its origin in the fact that the crude little schoolhouse was erected on an unproductive piece of land or field that had been exhausted and was no longer fertile. It was strictly a community enterprise, serving the children of the locality during its very short term each year. The boys and girls were taught the three R's with elocution added by an itinerant teacher whose qualifications were not necessarily very high. The only accrediting agency was the composite opinion of the persons who hired the teacher.[92]

The schoolmaster was usually a drifter who was able to persuade a group of parents in a community to employ him as a teacher of the school. "For these services a school teacher received the full payment of fifty cents per month, payable generally in provisions." [93] White describes the first teacher at the Goosepond School on the Broad River.

> The first teacher was a deserter from the British Navy, whose only qualification was, that he could write. He whipped according to Navy practice. On cold mornings, when fire could not be conveniently had, he made the children join hands and run around and around, whilst he hastened their speed by the free application of the switch. He was knowing in all sorts of rascality. He forced the locks of several of his employers, in search of money, was detected, and punished at the public whipping post.[94]

Coulter continues the description of some of the teachers at the Goosepond School.

> Another teacher who appeared in this neighborhood was a respectable man from North Carolina; however, he found someone he loved more than teaching school so he

married her, and quit. He was followed by a 'wandering, drunken Irishman', who 'knocked, kicked, cuffed, and whipped at a great rate.' Some of the boys he whipped as many as ten times a day. This Irishman gave way to a Virginia gentleman whose love of brandy was so great that on some days he would slip away to a brandy still, and then school would be out for those days. The next Goosepond schoolmaster on weekends incapacitated himself with drink whenever he could afford it; and after his tenure the Broad River people were done with ne'er-do-wells and began hiring their home grown schoolmasters.[95]

Clearly, these itinerant teachers usually were unfit in every respect as schoolmasters. In addition to this, the school year was so short that it would take several years for a student to have actually accumulated a full year of schooling. The building was the poorest kind of an affair. Sometimes it was put together by the community; sometimes it was an abandoned building which was put into use; but always it was one room made of logs. There was a clapboard window and door and a mud and stick chimney. The roof was also clapboard. The seats were split logs with no backs.[96] Smith gives a story of a Methodist minister, William J. Parks.

He had been reared in the back woods, and had no educational advantages save such as the old field school gave. He gave in his short autobiography an account of his first school. The teacher was an old drunkard. One day the boys turned him out, and after they had beaten him and tied him, and smeared him with mud, he surrendered, and gave the school a treat, which was a *gallon of whiskey,* which he drank with his scholars. He soon went as far as an old field school would allow, and then went to the new Methodist School at Salem to study grammar. Here he was licensed to preach.[97]

After the Revolution, those persons who had land and slaves continued their plantation operations, but there were many people in Georgia at that time who were not landed. Before the Revolution rice plantations had been established as the primary enterprise in the coastal area. After the Revolution there was an influx of people seeking new land, and they came primarily from Virginia and North Carolina into the upper part of the state. Georgia had plenty of land, or so it seemed at first. Many became large land owners and operated plantations with slave labor. Many more, however, became small land owners who lived at subsistence level. The few who could do so employed tutors or sent their children to private schools of the old field school type. There was no state or county support for these old field schools. Undoubtedly, there were quite a large number of children who did not go to school at all.

The Poor School Fund

From the time the first academies were authorized in 1783 until 1817, all money for education, from state or local effort or from whatever source, went into the academies. Actually, these academies were chartered and endowed with land and had opportunity to secure money from confiscated lands, and very few funds came from the legislature. The academies which were in operation charged tuition.

In 1817, the legislature passed an act to create and establish a fund for the support of free schools throughout the state.[98] The act provided that $250,000 should be set aside for the future establishment and support of free schools and that the governor, at a favorable opportunity, should invest this money in a bank or other profitable stock. In the land lottery act of 1818, the act prescribed that "lots number 10 and 100 shall be reserved and set apart, in each surveyor's district, and for the education of the poor children." [99] These acts spoke of the establishment and support of free schools, but there was no hint as to how this might be done. In 1819 an act required the governor to invest in the stock of the Darien Bank the sum of $100,000; also, he was required to invest $100,000 of the fund for the improvement of the internal navigation of the state.[100]

In 1821, the legislature passed an act "for the permanent endowment of county academies, and to increase the fund heretofore set apart for the encouragement and support of free schools, and for the internal improvement of the state." [101] The act says,

> The sum of $500,000, be and the same is hereby set apart, the one half for the support and encouragement of free

schools, and the other half for the permanent endowment
of county academies; and the further sum of $500,000 be
and the same is hereby set apart for the internal improvement of the state." These funds were to be invested and
the proceeds were to be used.

There was an act passed in 1822, "to dispose of and distribute
the bank dividends and other net proceeds of the Poor School
Fund among the different counties of the state." [102] Whether
or not it was the intent of the legislature in 1817 to really
establish free schools throughout the state, by 1822 it was
clear that these monies were to be used as a poor school
fund. The act required the governor to cause the sum of
$12,000 in bank dividends to be divided among the different
counties in proportion to their respective number of poor
children. The counties were to receive funds for children whose
parents could not pay tuition.

From this time until 1837, the state's support was about
evenly divided between funds to academies and to the counties
for poor children. This so-called Poor School Fund or Pauper
Fund had a long and undistinguished career. The legislature,
in fact, allowed many of the academies of the day to receive
the funds or allowed the counties themselves to receive the
funds with which they were supposed to provide schooling for
poor children.

A. D. Mayo says,

> Thus for fifty years or more, was the stigma of 'Pauper
> Schools' applied to the most central and vital institution
> of the Republic . . . The 'poor people' rejected with con-
> tempt the pittance doled out to their children. In 1845 only
> 53 of the 93 counties applied for their share of the fund.
> From 1817 to 1860 an annual distribution of $30,000 was
> the extent of the contribution of the state to the education
> of the people, in all $1,290,000.[103]

Legislative committees almost every year made recommendations looking toward a better use of the funds available and
more extensive programs for the state. (See Appendix I.)
Governor after governor made note of the poor situation.

Governor George Gilmer said,

> The proper application of the public money appropriated
> by the Legislature for the support of free schools, and
> the education of the poor, was a matter of a great diffi-
> culty when I was in the Executive Department. Society
> was so loosely organized, whilst the state was acquiring
> from time to time possession of its Indian territory, and
> its public lands settled upon with people from hither and
> thither without the knowledge of each other, or any
> principles of action in common, and the trial to educate
> the poor by the public money through the people of each
> neighborhood proved a wasteful expenditure.[104]

Dabney says,

> Georgia had made the public schools mere charities,
> miserable charities at that. It assumed that the children
> of the state belonged to two classes, the one rich, the
> other poor; that the rich had sufficient facilities for edu-
> cating their children in the academies and private schools;
> and that the poor children needed only the three R's. Even
> the three R's were denied to the majority of them.[105]

A. D. Mayo says, "These acts of the Legislature touched the
low water mark in Georgia . . . and account for all the obstacles
that hindered the development of the common school system." [106] "The poor school plan undoubtedly failed of its purpose. Unquestionably many a Georgian, poor but proud, let
his children grow up in illiteracy rather than set them apart in
the school as 'poor children.' " [107]

As the acts of the legislature are reviewed, many times the
phrase free schools is encountered. The phrase poor school
fund is another which occurs in the statutes time after time.
It is somewhat difficult to determine in each case what these
phrases mean, but in actual practice, it was most often a fund
to pay tuition for poor children. The act of 1822 required the
governor to set up $12,000 to be distributed through the poor
school fund, and the act of 1823, which increased this amount
to $20,000, also said that children could attend any school
convenient to them, that they had to be between the ages of
eight and 18, and that this fund would not pay for more than
three years of school. Further, it stated how records were to

be kept and how local counties were to secure their portion of the fund.[108]

In 1823 the legislature passed "An Act to authorize the citizens of Baldwin County to establish common schools." It authorized the county to be divided into school districts and to levy county taxes for the operation of the common schools, which would include all male white children seven to 18 years and all female white children six to 13 years. They "shall be entitled as a matter of right to equal participation in the advantages of the common school, in the district, in which they reside." [109] Milledgeville was designated as one district and the commissioners of the academy were designated as the trustees of that district. The act also provided for a referendum of the people of the county to decide whether or not they would put this into operation. There is no evidence that it was done. The act is notable because it appears to have been an attempt to set up common schools and it did provide for local taxation.

In 1836, the state received some surplus revenue from the federal government. By the act of 1836, the legislature "set apart, as a permanent free school and education fund" one-third of this surplus revenue. It also established a joint committee of five—two from the Senate and three from the House of Representatives, to make a report to the next session of the General Assembly on "information concerning education in the United States and especially in the New England states," and to recommend a plan for the state. [110] The committee's report to the 1837 legislature was long and comprehensive. It took into consideration educational systems in this country and foreign countries. The committee wrestled with the factors of a sparse and greatly spread population including the slaves, the lack of adequate funds, inadequate local subdivisions, and the differences between local communities and the state legislature. However, the conclusion was that there was need for a general system of education such as common schools.[111]

The 1837 act provided that the academic fund and the poor school fund be put together and be added to the one-third of the surplus revenue which had come from the United States government. However, it also provided that for 1837 and 1838 the academic fund and the poor school fund would be paid as before.[112] The act was to have become effective in 1840, but probably because of the great panic of 1837, it was rescinded by the legislature of 1840.[113] It is a fact that the banks suspended the payment of specie, the price of cotton declined and state revenue declined. In fact, there was panic.[114]

While this was not the greatest plan for a system of state public education, it certainly was for the time a progressive move in the direction of a state plan. The money was to have been distributed to the local units on the basis of the number of white school children between the ages of five and 15.

MANUAL LABOR SCHOOLS

In the late 1820s and early 1830s, there came into being in the United States a system of education known as the manual labor school.

> The manual labor movement originated in Europe and had become popular in the United States in the late 1820's. It began in Georgia as a church movement. The churches found themselves too poor to finance successfully the church schools that many felt were needed to provide an educated ministry and strengthen denominationalism. Therefore, they enthusiastically adopted the idea of having students bear a part of the burden of cost by working out a substantial part of their expenses. The experiment, however, proved to be a failure.[115]

The term manual labor schools is misleading, because it would appear these would be schools to teach manual arts or vocational education of some type; however, these schools had the regular classical educational program with all students working on a farm a certain period of time each day. The Baptist denomination, under the leadership of Adiel Sherwood, was the first to organize manual labor schools. Sherwood personally organized one near Eatonton as the first in the state.[116] "Of the 10 such schools established between 1834 and 1843, three became colleges: Oglethorpe, Presbyterian; Emory, Methodist; and Mercer, Baptist." [117]

Although the manual labor schools were church-related schools, there was discussion in the legislature concerning the state's giving them support. The idea of a young person working part time on a farm as he pursued his education seemed to be an excellent idea. Generally, people were highly in favor of the plan. An extended resolution in 1834 called on the legislature to provide aid to the church groups, namely the Baptists, Methodists and Presbyterians, in the establishment and operation of the manual labor schools.[118] Although there was considerable sentiment for state aid for these schools, during their existence they were private, denominational schools and not state schools.

The decade of the 1840s might be characterized as a period of confusion, low morale and generally a low water mark insofar as development of the public school system was concerned. The panic of 1837 in effect wiped out a very excellent period of planning and enactment of legislation which was progressive, forward looking and which, if it had succeeded, would have placed the state in a position of going forward in public education. Beyond doubt, one of the greatest contributing factors to the forward looking and progressive movements of the period in public education came from the organization known as the Teachers Society and Board of Education.[119] But this influence, too, failed at the time, primarily because of the financial panic.

Money for the Poor School Fund was virtually lost. As a matter of fact, because the fund was invested in bank stock, it was difficult for a time to determine what funds were available. The legislature of 1843 requested Governor George M. Crawford to determine the status of the school fund. During this period, some of the counties had not drawn their school money, and it had accumulated in the treasury in the amount of $49.43, according to the governor. He also said that the poor school fund for the years 1841 and 1842 was withheld from the counties, and this had accumulated. The 1841 and 1842 legislatures had authorized such action, and Governor Crawford said it was believed that the school fund had been applied in 1841 to the Western and Atlantic Railroad and to the Central Bank of Georgia.[120]

Toward A Public School System

The legislature of 1843 passed a new poor school law which was to take the place of the law passed in 1840. This act provided for a permanent fund of 1,744 shares of the capital stock of the Bank of the State of Georgia, 890 shares of the stock of the Bank of Augusta and the available assets of the Central Bank. At the local level, the management of the poor school fund was to be the responsibility of the justices of the inferior courts. If the grand jury so recommended, they (the justices of the inferior courts) were authorized to levy and collect an extra tax in each county to be added to the fund received from the state. The act also required the justices of the inferior court to determine the amount due teachers for the years 1842 and 1843 and to report this to the governor. The governor was to pay the teachers from proceeds of the sale of public lands that reverted to the state.[121] Toward the end of the decade, a number of bills were introduced into the legislature, all intending to bolster in some respect the poor school fund; however, none of these passed.

At almost every session of the legislature in the decades of the twenties, thirties, forties, committees on education were set up by resolution. (This practice still is utilized as a process in legislative actions. There have been some notable committees in the history of the state which were organized by resolution of the General Assembly.) The committee created by the General Assembly of 1836, noted earlier, accomplished a work of a very high caliber, and even though it did not always produce immediate results, some of the committee's work did have long range effect. Undoubtedly, many of the committees were simply a delaying device used by the legislature, enabling them to save face if they had just rejected some important legislation or deferred action in the hope that an issue would die.

After some legislation was defeated in the 1847 session of the General Assembly, W. H. Hunt, chairman of the Committee on Public Education and Free Schools, moved that a committee of three be appointed by the governor to recommend a plan for general education.[122] The quest for general education for all people would not die, but its time had not yet come.

The decade of the 1850s was marked by a stronger and more determined effort on the part of educational leaders in the state for a public school system. They could see the wretched illiteracy of most people of Georgia, and they realized this condition never could be remedied in the private and tuition academies. Also, they knew the pittance which the state allotted for the education of the poor through the poor school fund was, indeed, a farce. And although the politicians were not overtly against schools, the educational leaders saw that these politicians were subscribers to the political notion of paternalism, which caused them to oppose vigorously anything like a common school system.[123] There were 500 to 1,000 communities in the state without any school facilities. The census of 1850 showed 303,798 school children in the state; however, only 77,015 were in attendance in a school. Three-fourths of the children were growing up in illiteracy.[124]

A group of leaders in the state made a valiant effort during this decade to establish a public school system. Among these were Eugenius A. Nesbit; Joseph Lumpkin; Bishop Steven Elliott of the Episcopal church; George F. Pierce of the Methodist church; Thomas F. Scott of the Presbyterian church; Nathan Hoyt of the Presbyterian church; Dr. Alonzo Church, Presbyterian minister and president of the University of Georgia; Robert Toombs; Senator Davis A. Reese; and W. H. Stiles. A convention to develop a public school program to be presented to the Georgia Legislature was held in Marietta in 1851 with these men as the principal leaders.[125]

These leaders also felt they needed to organize teacher associations, and because the earlier efforts had failed, they thought they should start at the local level and organize associations in the several counties. Also, they felt a vehicle was needed to tell their story. The first association was organized in Muscogee County, but this one did not survive and other counties did not follow suit. One of the leaders, Thomas F. Scott, a Columbus clergyman, became the editor of a publication, *The Southern School Journal*. Issued monthly, this publication was to be very significant in this period.[126] Furthermore, these educational leaders at a meeting held in the Griffin Baptist Church organized a new teachers' organization known as the Georgia State Teachers Association.[127] It was never really strong and within three years had ceased to exist. With its demise, *The Southern School Journal* also became a casualty.[128]

The campaign waged by these outstanding leaders seems to have failed. The publication which they used to carry their message to the people failed. The professional organization which they established failed. There is no way to know how much of their effort was seed sown on good ground, but as Coulter says,

> . . . December 11, 1858, the legislature set aside one hundred thousand dollars annually from the rental on this road (Western and Atlantic Railroad) to be used in financing a public school system for the state, and increased the fund as the public debt should be paid off. No uniform plan of schools was formulated, but each county was left with power and resources sufficient to institute common free schools, and this a few did before the outbreak of the Civil War. The state was now starting on the road to redeem its name from the accusations so justly leveled against it, when the war came and prevented further educational progress for a decade.[129]

In 1858, the General Assembly passed an act which, although not creating a state system of education, was reaching toward this goal. It appropriated $100,000 of the net earnings of the Western and Atlantic Railroad annually for the purposes of education. It enabled the inferior court, upon recommendation of the grand jury, to assess a percentage of the state tax as it deemed right and proper. These provisions increased funds for education from the state and gave permission for the counties at the local level also to assess funds for education.[130] Some counties took advantage of this situation, notably, Bibb, Chatham, Glynn and Richmond. (See Appendix II.)

From the state's first constitution in 1777 until the time of the Civil War, there had been many ups and downs toward the establishment of a public school system in the state. Several times legislation was actually passed creating a public school system, but at no time did any of this legislation ever actually take effect. Instead, Georgia had old field schools, the tuition academies, the minimum kind of state support and the poor school fund or pauper fund. The poor school fund, intended by the state to pay the tuition of students whose parents were unable to pay, was poorly administered at both the state level and the local level. However, from the time it was passed early in the decade of the 1820s until the Civil War, this was the substance of the state program for public education.

The state then entered the decade of the 1860s with the Civil War and Reconstruction. There were no organized schools during the Civil War; whatever program of public and private education there was in the state came to a complete halt. After the war the state was destitute. Its economy had been destroyed; its social organization was completely changed; its manpower devastated; and its government in the hands of persons who had no background for government and persons from both the North and South with dubious motives. There quickly followed the period of Reconstruction, during which time the state was under military rule from the North.

Immediately after the war, Negro children of the state fared better educationally than did white children. The education of Negroes was left to the Freedmen's Bureau and northern philanthropy. For 1865 the Freedmen's Bureau reported 66 schools, 66 teachers and 3,500 pupils in Georgia.[131]

The legislature of 1866 passed "an act to provide for education and to establish a general system of Georgia schools." [132] This was a very comprehensive system of common schools. There was to be a state superintendent appointed by the governor, a commissioner for each county appointed by the grand jury of the superior court of the county, and three trustees in each district of the county elected by the qualifying voters in the district. Because the state did not have the funds with which to implement this program, the bill carried with it the proviso that the act would not go into effect until after January 1, 1868. Although this program of education was enacted by the General Assembly, it was never put into effect because in 1868 a constitutional convention changed the constitution of Georgia and rewrote the educational provisions.

In 1867, George Peabody made a gift of $1 million to promote educational opportunities in the South.[133] This was an extremely significant event because it greatly boosted the morale of school leaders in Georgia and other southern states. Georgia leaders went into action and banded together to organize the Georgia Teachers Association.[134] There had previously been a number of efforts in the state to organize for the promotion of education. In 1823 there was the Georgia Educational Society, in 1831 the Teachers Society and Board of Education of the State of Georgia, and later the Georgia State Teachers Association. None of these organizations lasted, but the Georgia Teachers Association, which was organized in 1867, has been in continuous operation since that time.

The persons who organized this association and did the early legislative work are among the most important and influential in the history of Georgia education. Among those present at the initial meeting of the Georgia Teachers Association were Henry Holcombe Tucker, Penfield; W. LeRoy Broun, University of Georgia; John Mitchell Bonnell, Wesleyan; W. R. Jones, Atlanta; T. J. Hill, Emory; D. Swope, Atlanta; Gustavus J. Orr, Covington; E. A. Ware, Atlanta; W. Baird, Jonesboro; J. A. Richardson, Atlanta; J. B. Randall, Americus; Thomas J. Dobbs, Atlanta; David W. Lewis, Washington; J. V. Bradford, Atlanta; Carlton Hillyer, University of Georgia; J. V. Connell, Atlanta; L. Carrington, Milledgeville; R. C. Ketchum, Atlanta; Joseph S. Stewart, Oxford; Barnard Mallon, Savannah; W. M. Bray, Atlanta; Simpson Fouche, Rome; T. H. Bonar, Atlanta; C. Schwartz, Wesleyan; W. M. Janes, Atlanta.[135]

The Georgia Teachers Association went to work immediately to make recommendations for a school system for the state. A meeting in Macon in 1868 was devoted largely to making plans for future action. The meeting in 1869 was held in Atlanta with 45 persons present. Some important people who were not at the first session were active at this meeting.

M. V. Calvin of Augusta made a speech entitled "Popular Education in Georgia," which emphasized several points— an enlightened common school law, a state educational fund, a progressive state school superintendent, county superintendents, boards of education in each county, teachers in deed and truth, and normal schools or normal departments in universities and colleges.

The paper by Calvin was the focal point of the meeting. After a full discussion, it was referred to a committee of five, composed of Orr, Calvin, Lewis, Mallon and Bonnell. Orr had introduced a resolution directing that the committee draft a bill to be submitted to the next annual meeting and then to the General Assembly. This committee functioned and presented to the meeting of the association in 1870 a proposed school law. This was adopted and was presented to the General Assembly of 1870, which did pass an act entitled, "An Act to Establish a System of Public Instruction." [136]

The Georgia Teachers Association could justly claim a great deal of credit for many provisions of the new law and for a statewide approach to a system of common schools. There had been many efforts prior to this time to establish a statewide system, and there had been laws passed which, if they had become effective, would have etstablished such a system. But this was the first time the legal structure for a system of public schools was put on the books and, in a measure at least, put into effect.

The leaders of the Georgia Teachers Association at this time were an enlightened and forward looking group of men. However, not all of the people in the state were in favor of a statewide system of education. Stewart said, "it met with violent opposition from the friends of private schools, from the friends of denominational schools, from those who opposed and those who did not believe that the Negro could be educated." [137]

The Curriculum

In Colonial Georgia the major efforts toward education were those of religious leaders. Ministers of the groups of Salzburgers, Moravians, Anglicans and dissenters taught in the early schools, and the curriculum consisted mostly of religion and the use of the English language. If the native language was not English, there was some instruction in the native tongue. Coleman says,

> Education, like religion, was supposed to be controlled and supervised by the Church of England, but the Church was little concerned with it. Two schoolmasters were paid out of the Parliamentary grant, but otherwise education was a private affair. Most clergymen, Anglican and dissenters alike, kept schools to supplement their income, and a schoolmaster was maintained by the Jerusalem Church of Ebenezer for the education of the young. The college of George Whitefield's dream never materialized at Bethesda, but both orphans and boarding students were

educated there. There were numerous private schools in Savannah at which one could take a variety of subjects including military drill and fencing, fancy work for girls, languages, mathematics, and scientific subjects. Classes were given day and night and private instruction could be arranged. Schools also existed in Georgia's other towns and on plantations, but with not so varied a curriculum as in Savannah. Education was available for those who wanted it and could afford to pay for it; few Georgians thought more was necessary.[138]

While the growth of these early schools fluctuated, there were incidents of enrichment courses being introduced, particularly in the private schools and through tutors paid for special lessons. Coleman cites some examples.

Music was not neglected by teachers and performers. A number of people advertised to teach instrumental and vocal music in schools or private homes during the day or evenings. In 1785 John Hiwell, who declared himself a former inspector of music in the American army, advertised that he would give a concert for his benefit and teach all instruments if he got enough scholars. He met with enough success to remain in Savannah eight months and perhaps longer. Music teachers sometimes also set up in Augusta when they did not get sufficient encouragement in Savannah. Dancing schools were popular. In the fall of 1785, Mr. Godwin, the actor, advertised a dancing school with morning, afternoon and evening sessions. The next March he announced that he was giving up the stage but would continue to teach dancing. Charles Francis Chevalier advertised a school where he taught dancing and fencing in Savannah in 1783 and in Augusta three years later. Besides these and other teachers who located in Savannah, there were visiting artists (mainly musicians and portrait painters) who stopped in Savannah to display their talents.[139]

After independence Georgia enacted a state constitution in 1777. Education was mentioned in this constitution, but little or no machinery was included to activate an educational system. The nearest reference to implementation was a clause saying "as the Legislature shall hereafter point out." The most outstanding piece of legislation pertaining to education was perhaps the Act of 1785, which created the State University. The authors of this act envisioned the university as the seat of all educational enterprises in the state with general supervision of all instructional activities in the state. As pointed out earlier in this chapter, this elaborate dream never came into existence.

The General Assembly began chartering academies in the early 1780s. This movement peaked during the 1830s, when nearly 300 academies received charters. There is not enough evidence to show that all which were chartered succeeded as educational centers. However, many were very successful. After the Revolutionary War and in the early 1800s, movements to develop education throughout the state were influenced by leaders in the academies and schools established for the purpose of instructing children in "the early branches of an English education."

The schools established in the post-Revolutionary period were certainly varied. The most influential, of course, were the academies, but also developed in this and later periods were the old field schools, the poor schools, the manual labor schools and, in some instances, the municipal and specially chartered institutions.

Especially in the academies, the curricular offerings usually were of a classical nature and certainly were mostly preparation for college entrance. Supported by tuition and some small state charter grants, the trustees, the headmasters and the patrons usually determined the subjects to be taught. Consideration was in favor of college entrance. Some of the smaller schools could offer only a limited list of subjects, especially those schools which attempted little or no work beyond the elementary level. Those with very limited staff or facilities were usually confined to reading, writing, arithmetic, spelling and grammar.

A news article appearing in the *Savannah Georgian* in November 1841, states,

> Mr. Mallette respectfully informs his friends and the
> public generally, that he has taken charge of the Effing-
> ham Academy at Springfield. Persons wishing to send

their sons or daughters to this institution may rest assured that their instruction, both moral and intellectual, will be carefully attended to . . . Boys will be prepared for college in the shortest possible time.

> Board may be had in and about the village.
>
> Rates: Reading, writing, arithmetic $3.00 per qr.
>
> English Grammar, etc.,   5.00 per qr.
>
> Latin, Greek, etc.,   8.00 per qr.[140]

With more than 400 academies being chartered in the two decades from 1820 to 1840, it is likely that competition became very keen for students, and advertising sought to recruit students. Appearing in the Macon *Georgia Messenger* in December 1823, was this advertisement.

> Pleasant Mount Academy, open for reception of pupils, to be taught Orthography (Spelling), Reading, Writing, English Grammar, Arithmetic, Geography, Bookkeeping, Geometry, etc. Situated near junction of roads leading from Fort Hawkins and Stone Creek Meeting House to Marion, Twiggs County. The situation is high and pleasant, with a never failing spring of water. Good board can be had in respectable families in the immediate neighborhood on reasonable rates. Terms of tuition moderate.
>
> December 17, 1823   M. M. Johnson, Teacher [141]

With no specific direction from the preceding state constitutions and with less legislative guidance, the academies were very much at liberty to offer such courses as circumstances permitted. Prior to 1870 any legal structure for curricular offerings was missing. Even though some small state grants were sometimes available, state restrictions were vague.

The areas of instruction were perhaps as varied and great in number as were academies. Elementary grade offerings were more or less standard, with spelling, reading, writing, arithmetic, geography and English Grammar making up the courses. The upper grades listed logic, chemistry, philosophy, intellectual science, physics, Latin, Greek, French, astronomy, algebra, geometry, trigonometry, mechanical drawing, analytical geometry and calculus. In the female academies drawing, painting, fine needlework and music were offered for additional tuition.

All of these of course, were not required; in fact, a student could take one or all of them as it suited him or his purse. The struggling country youth eager to acquire education would take every course possible.[142] Some of the more sophisticated schools added one or more such subjects as engineering, architecture, geology, navigation, Italian, Spanish, accounting, German and *belles lettres*.[143]

Some unusual methods naturally appeared in schools with so many and diverse instructors. For instance, in the Female Academy at Sparta, Hancock County, considerable attention was given to method as it was described: "The plan of education in this Academy is somewhat peculiar, and differs in some important points from the system pursued in most Female Seminaries; it is the Rensselaer Plan." [144] The Rensselaer Plan gives special emphasis to the teaching of science and engineering. On his return to Georgia in 1815 from his service as Minister to France, William H. Crawford introduced in Georgia the plan of Pestalozzianism.[145] This was a system of instruction in which the sense perceptions are first trained and the other faculties are then developed in what is held to be the natural order. Many years later in some annual reports of the State Department of Education some of the school leaders were questioning the competence of teachers to pursue the Pestalozzian methods. Also introduced in the early academies was the plan of Lancasterianism, which was used in the Augusta Free School as early as 1821.[146] This was a method, or monitorial system, of instruction in which advanced pupils in a school teach pupils below them. Though not always identified by this name, the procedure was used extensively in the state, especially in the one-teacher and two-teacher schools.

An article in *Report of the* (U.S.) *Commissioner of Education* in 1894-95 urges the use of the Lancasterian system in the South. Following a considerable discourse on the subject the article concludes with the following statement.

> If the schools of the children of the South are supplied with all the modern means of obtaining an education; and if they have sanitary school buildings, equipped with apparatus to accommodate all pupils who ought to attend the school; if these buildings are supplied with first-class teachers with first-class salaries then the argument that

would be urged in favor of the monotorial (sic) schools would be futile. But if, on the contrary, there exists today in the South a large number of children who, for the lack of these provisions, are not being educated, and if for those children monotorial masters could be obtained, then there is certainly something in the monotorial system for the children of the South.[147]

Though many of the early teachers and headmasters of the academies were itinerant wanderers who possessed little professional inclinations, the academies did produce some stalwart leaders who helped in the survival of early education in the state. Those whom the literature identifies as having great impact on these pioneer efforts include the following.

Francis Meson, Meson Academy
Sereno Taylor, Sparta Female Academy
William McWhir, Sunbury Academy
William C. Wilkes, Eatonton Academy
Salem Towne, Powellton Academy
Carlisle Beman, Mt. Zion Academy (Hancock County)
Simpson Fouche, Washington Academy
Walter T. Knight, Jackson Academy
James Shannon, Sunbury Academy
Shaler Hillyer, Scottsborough Academy

The old field schools also had their place in early Georgia. They were usually private endeavors of parents in a community who lived close enough to each other to hold a school. The building was most often an abandoned tenant house or a roughly constructed building in an abandoned field. (The practice of wearing out the soil and moving to new ground was prevalent in those days, and the worn out or abandoned fields were the sites for the "old field schools.") The teachers often were drifters or wanderers who did not make the grade or could not qualify as instructors in an academy. The curriculum in these schools was mostly reading, writing, arithmetic and spelling, along with any other subject the teacher had the time and qualification to teach. Though usually of a lower quality in instruction, the old field school was an effort at reaching the rural students with rudimentary education.

The poor schools were initiated by the General Assembly, not because poverty was popular, but as an effort to reach more students than the academies were accommodating. A state grant was sent to the academies if they were chartered by the state; however, the academies were also charging tuition, which meant that many children were not given an opportunity to attend school. The Poor School Act of 1817 and subsequent years required the judges of the inferior courts to enumerate the parents who paid less than 51 cents per year in taxes so that their children could attend a school with the tuition paid by the state. The rate of tuition was five cents per day for each child in attendance. Shown below is a listing of students and days attended from the records in the office of the ordinary of Tattnall County. When some of the descendants of the pupils listed viewed these Tattnall County records in 1975, they could not understand how their ancestors could qualify for "poor school funds" when the families owned hundreds of acres of land, supposedly during the years indicated on the enumeration list.

Schooling under the poor school fund was limited to not more than three terms. These terms were usually three months. So the amount of free schooling was very meager and consisted mostly of the usual reading, writing, arithmetic and spelling. The plan failed for several reasons—not all children were reported who were eligible; not all reported eligible students took advantage of the plan; some parents did not wish to have the stigma "poor people" attached to their names; the maximum number of terms was limited to three, and many governmental officials, including some governors, were opposed to free public education.

The manual labor school movement originated in Georgia during the late 1820s and the early 1830s. A number of religious and educational leaders contended that the mind influenced the body and physical condition affected the mind; therefore, the body and mind should be educated together. Since manual labor would furnish natural exercise, equip students with practical knowledge, make education less expensive and work to break down class distinctions, they advocated using poor school funds to establish manual labor schools. Their plan called for each county to attach a workshop or farm to each county academy. The manual labor school idea spread, in large measure, due to the support of the major religious denominations and the financial relief expected from the student labors. The name was somewhat misleading, as it might be expected some type of vocational or manual arts would be taught. This was not the case; the students worked a given amount of time in the shop or on the farm each day, but the major portion of the instruction was similar to that in the academies, which emphasized a classical education for their students. In large measure the experiment was unsuccessful. The major denominations, Baptists, Methodists and Presbyterians, founded manual labor schools which eventually developed into Mercer University, Emory University and Oglethorpe University, respectively. The success of these three institutions can be attributed largely to the leadership of the schools then and in subsequent years. Mercer originated at Penfield in Greene County and later moved to Macon. Oglethorpe originated in Baldwin County and moved twice, first to downtown Atlanta and later to the northern outskirts of Atlanta.

The elite schools of the pre-Civil War era were those operating under special legislation. These schools could draw their share of state funds and also levy local taxes to supplement state funds. In order to enjoy such privileges each county or city needed a special act of the legislature authorizing in detail what local ordinances and regulations that particular county or city could enact for the operation of its schools. Most renowned of these early special districts were Glynn County, Chatham County, Bibb County and Richmond County. With the exception of Glynn County, these special systems began within the city and expanded to the county through later acts of the General Assembly. For a more detailed description of the origin of these four systems, see Appendix II. Columbus was another early city system operating under special law. A few of the academies received local supplements but were not covered under the special legislation.

These early special districts enjoyed longer school terms, better trained staffs, better housing and better equipment than perhaps any other schools in the state. Their course offerings included the classical, some vocational or industrial and basic subjects. They were not limited to the elementary branches of an English education and could offer such high school subjects as the local boards, staffs and patrons requested.

The depression of 1837 which affected the state school funds did have some impact on these special tax systems, but the results were not as devastating as those experienced by the poor schools, the manual labor schools and the old field schools.

Attempts were made by other counties and cities to initiate special districts, but they did not survive the trials presented by local taxation, indifference and economics. Many of the academies continued to operate under their original names when after the 1870s they became a part of the public school system. Some kept their names into the twentieth century. Later curricular studies and examinations caused them to change from the mostly classic education to a less restrictive program more nearly meeting the needs of all the children in their attendance areas.

The *Report of the (U. S.) Commissioner of Education* in 1894-95, in an article, "Early Education in Georgia," may have summarized well the conditions and conclusions pertaining to education in Georgia during the era. The article concludes with this summary.

This period in the pedagogy of that region passed not without leaving some salutary results. Any system, however crude, is better than no system. On the confines of existences so far different from each other, it was as indispensable as elsewhere to get some instruction, at least in elementary education. This was all that at first was sought. Neglect of it has been too long already amid the hardships of one long war and threatenings of another. To read, write, become familiar with elementary rules in numbers, and get some acquaintance with forms of polite speech, these must be gotten after a fashion of some sort from the only persons who came forward to undertake the task of imparting. Weaklings as these generally were, need of subsistence which they were incompetent to obtain out of other vocations, continuance of endeavors to enhance their fitness for this their only, with pressure from outside, begot in time a familiarity with its duties which, if not satisfactory, was tolerable. The very crudeness habitually breaking out in those old schoolhouses contrasted with those in which good sense, manners, and tastes were hereditary, served as a foil to make the latter more clearly recognized and more easily practiced. Super-added to this the habit of entire obedience to authority of however trifling dignity, but taught to be of equal force with that by which it was delegated, tended strongly to the development of generous manhood, of neighborly kindliness, of lifelong friendships, of good citizenship. In a community situate far from cultured circles, activities sometimes too ardent, even degrees of lawlessness, must exist. Among the systems tending to repress them among the young, old-field schools, despite their eccentricities, made their own contribution, and it was respectable. Then their glaring imperfections intensified the sense of need of better, and expedited their introduction.[148]

Education of the Deaf

Educating deaf citizens in Georgia was completely ignored for 100 years following the state's founding in 1733. The consensus during that time was that deaf people were incapable of learning even rudimentary mental skills; therefore, any effort spent to provide for their education would be wasted. The first historic evidence of any interest in education of deaf Georgians is a record of John J. Flournoy's petition to the state legislature on December 20, 1833, "praying the establishment of an institution for the deaf and dumb." [1] Flournoy, a deaf young man from Jackson County, was educated in the type of institution for which he was appealing. However, since provisions for educating Georgia's deaf were nonexistent, he had been forced to attend school outside the state. Flournoy sought to make the educational benefits he had received elsewhere available to the deaf citizens inside the state of Georgia.

A committee from the legislature referred his plea to Governor Wilson Lumpkin for further consideration. While investigating the matter, Governor Lumpkin grew vitally interested in the welfare of Georgia's deaf citizens and became increasingly aware of their state of educational neglect. He strongly recommended that the ensuing General Assembly seriously look into the feasibility of establishing an institution for educating the deaf element of Georgia's population.[2]

Shortly afterward, Lewis Weld from the American Asylum for the Deaf and Dumb in Hartford, Connecticut, visited Georgia with a class of pupils of the school who demonstrated their learning skills and abilities. This aroused a certain amount of interest in educating the deaf and, perhaps more than anything else, made the greatest impression on members of the legislature.

In 1834, after further research, the Senate Committee on Public Education advised the General Assembly that the number of deaf citizens was insufficient to warrant the founding of a separate institution for their education; as an alternative measure, the legislature appropriated $3,000 to send deaf students between the ages of 10 and 30 to the American Asylum for the Deaf and Dumb at Hartford to be educated there for four-year terms.

The act also empowered the governor to appoint someone to collect and accompany the deaf students to Hartford. Although the position was filled successively by three people, the Reverend Jesse H. Campbell is outstanding among those individuals because he is the one to whom deaf Georgians "are indebted more than to any other person for the location and endowment of an institution for their education." [3]

Only a few Georgians were taking advantage of the Hartford opportunity due to inadequate transportation for such a long distance and to parental reluctance to send children so far away for such an extended period of time. To alleviate this problem, the Reverend Campbell procured an amendment to the original act whereby deaf students could be educated within the state as well as at Hartford. The legislature appropriated funds for the undertaking.[4]

Campbell then corresponded with officials of several institutions regarding teaching deaf students. When a considerable amount of interest was exhibited by the Hearn Manual Labor School located at Cave Spring in Floyd County, Georgia,[5] he obtained an agreement from the officials that they would establish a department for instructing deaf students. O. P. Fannin, the assistant principal, resigned his position and traveled to Hartford to learn their method of teaching the deaf. He was instructed to bring back to Georgia those students who were attending school there and start a department for deaf pupils at the Hearn School.

After a year of training, Fannin returned with four students—Martin McDuffie, Elmira Pugh, Temperance Jordan and Thomas Mimms—and set up a classroom in a primitive log cabin behind the main building of the Hearn School on May 15, 1846. From this date in 1846 until 1972 the history of public education for the deaf in Georgia is totally encapsulated in the history of this one-room school at Cave Spring and its subsequent multi-unit campus known as the Georgia School for the Deaf.

A legislative bill passed in 1847 listed the school's first official title as the "Georgia Asylum for the Deaf and Dumb." [6] This same act established a board of five commissioners to govern the school. Since the student enrollment had increased from the original four to 12 by the end of the school year in 1847, the board's first action was to quickly appoint J. B. Edwards, a Hartford graduate, as assistant teacher to O. P. Fannin. Thus, Edwards became the first deaf teacher of the deaf in Georgia.[7]

Furthermore, the Act of 1847 endowed the school with annual appropriations for maintenance expenses and allocated funds to purchase land and erect school buildings. The school was to become residential following the completion of an adequate structure for housing students. Until this time, students boarded in private homes in the village of Cave Spring.

A two-story brick building considered large enough for the number of students anticipated for admission was completed and dedicated as Fannin Hall on July 1, 1849. On that date, the school began its first legitimate operation as the tenth institution of its kind in the United States.

The Act of 1847 also provided that   ,

> Indigent deaf and dumb persons, resident anywhere within the state, shall be received into the Asylum and School, and maintained and educated gratuitously, so far as the funds of the institution will admit . . . Provided, always, That no persons under ten, nor more than thirty years old shall be admitted, and no beneficiary allowed to remain more than four years.[8]

As a consequence, in 1850, less than one year after the building's dedication, more room was needed to house the students who wished to enter school. Within the year an eastward ell was added to Fannin Hall. During the ensuing years, several other extensions were made and a few additional buildings erected. The rapidly growing population of indigent students caused the legislature in 1851 to nearly double the annual appropriation of $4,500 to $8,000.[9]

Under Fannin's competent leadership the Asylum for the Deaf and Dumb flourished. When he retired in 1858, he left an admirable record as teacher, principal and superintendent. Not only did he benefit the deaf by his personal dedication to their cause, but he also motivated others to help them, through education, became useful, productive members of Georgia society. In the few years between Fannin's retirement and the advent of the Civil War, S. F. Dunlop and William D. Cook successively served as superintendent.

In 1862 the school closed for the duration of the Civil War. Gibbons proudly claims, "the Georgia School is the only school for the deaf in the United States to withstand the ravages of actual warfare." [10] However, in this case, the ravages were not very extensive. In spite of the fact that the buildings were in the hands of both sides at different times, they were not damaged much materially. This is attributed to the fact that the school served as a hospital during most of the war, and though the armies made away with all removables, the buildings and equipment were left basically intact.[11]

In 1866 the legislature appropriated funds and appointed a board of trustees to reopen the school. Wesley O. Connor, one of five teachers on the staff immediately before the outbreak of the war, returned at the request of the trustees and resumed operations in 1867. He faced the awesome task of converting the place from use as a hospital back into an institution for learning. His successful guidance enabled the school to grow strong again and expand further. Among the most important additions he made were those dealing with curriculum content. Records show that the only subjects taught during the early years of the school were simple language lessons and arithmetic.[12] Connor introduced other subjects that would help the deaf deal more effectively with the world outside once they left the school. He particularly possessed keen insight into the problems the students would face in adjusting to the labor market, and he advocated vocational training in many fields. His strong campaign for vocational education for the deaf resulted in a print shop, a shoemaker's shop, courses in gardening, agriculture, blacksmithing, drawing and painting, woodcarving, woodworking, carpentry, sewing and tailoring. By 1901 the print shop was such a huge success that it was printing the village newspaper, *"The Cave Spring Enterprise,"* as well as several other publications. Likewise, the shoemaking trade advanced to a point of proficiency that enabled it to furnish outlets in major cities of Georgia, Florida and Alabama.[13] Muse compliments Connor on his astute assessment of the need for a change in educational training.

> Since the closing years of the Industrial Revolution and the beginning of the machine age comprised the era, Mr. Connor's activities reveal foresight and comprehension of the need for a progressive type of education carrying over and on from the older liberal arts format of strict academic training only to the then growing idea of trade and vocational education.[14]

James O. Connor gave 60 years of service to educating deaf Georgians. Forty-three of them were spent as superintendent of the school at Cave Spring, making his the longest tenure on record.

In 1876 the general assembly passed an act which affected the school in two ways. The first was of only slight importance; it lowered the maximum age of admission from 30 years to 27 years. The second was of great significance; it provided for "the admission of colored deaf mutes to the benefits of the Deaf and Dumb Asylum of the State" and authorized the purchase of suitable property for erecting buildings in addition to appropriating money for the cause.[15] The black students did not share the same educational facilities as the whites but were set up in a separate building which was treated as an additional department of the school. It too was under the auspices of the superintendent and board of trustees.

Sometime during this period, the school's name was changed from the Georgia Asylum for the Deaf and Dumb to The Institution for the Education of the Deaf and Dumb in an effort to more clearly denote the school's intent and purpose. The name was later changed to The Georgia School for the Deaf.

When James Coffee Harris succeeded James O. Connor as superintendent in 1916, many problems faced his administration. According to Muse,

> His entire time in office was fraught with difficulties. He faced the trying years of World War I, the flu epidemic that followed, the tragic problems of the so called "roaring twenties" when intemperate speculation, soaring costs and ill-fated real estate bonanzas led eventually to the shocking stock market crash, destruction of the national economy, and the dismal depression of the thirties.[16]

Despite the hardships and scarcity of funds, Harris was able to bring about two major accomplishments for the school in his 21-year tenure. He erected a hospital building in 1931 and converted the shoemaker's shop into a shoe repair shop.

Prosperity for the institution returned during the Roosevelt and Truman years. In 1937, under the superintendency of Clayton Hollingsworth, a vast physical expansion took place. With federal WPA grants and state appropriations, Hollingsworth undertook the complete renovation of all existing buildings and erected four additional ones. He used the additional funds to introduce elective and extension courses and to develop new fields. He bought modern machinery and investigated new methods for learning trades.

Other superintendents, John L. Cagle, Alfred Davis, S. A. Newton and Fred L. Sparks, served during the 1940s, '50s and '60s to make the school that was once a one-room log cabin into the largest school for the deaf east of the Mississippi River. With nearly 600 pupils, it boasts the largest student body of any residential school for the deaf in the United States. By the 1960s, students at the Georgia School for the Deaf were attending school for a term of 12 years, as did students in other public schools. The educational curriculum had been departmentalized and categorized. Helen Muse explains,

> The primary department receives beginning students and upon entry each child is carefully examined and evaluated in an effort to ascertain degree of deafness, mental ability,

and other possible physical handicaps. The children are taught the rudiments of speech and those who have residual hearing are given auditory in addition to oral training. In the intermediate department, the oral program is continued except where a pronounced lack of ability to cope with speech and speechreading (lipreading) is evident. For the less fortunate children, the manual method of teaching is used. In the advanced department, or the high school, the need to prepare students for college and to impart all possible additional information to those not preparing for higher education makes it imperative to use whatever method best suits the situation.[17]

Both the elementary and high school departments were fully accredited by the Georgia Accrediting Commission. Continual efforts to improve standards and keep up with changes in modern education resulted in many graduates meeting requirements for entry into Gallaudet College. Others gained entrance to vocational schools, art schools and colleges of cosmetology.

The school curriculum was designed along the same lines as the curriculum in schools for hearing children throughout the state. The high school curriculum closely resembled that found in any other Georgia high school. It consisted of American and English literature; mathematics, algebra and geometry; Georgia history, American history, world history, civics, government and global geography; general science, biology, physiology, physical science, chemistry, geology, physics and astronomy. Physical education also played a big part in the school's curriculum.

In addition, the vocational department offered training in 12 general categories and numerous related fields. The categories were art, body and fender work, business practices, cosmetology, home economics, laundry and dry cleaning, masonry, power sewing, printing and offset, shoe repair, upholstery and woodworking. The Georgia School for the Deaf was the first in the country to receive federal assistance in vocational work under the Smith-Hughes and George-Dean Acts. It was also the first to become a participating member of the Georgia High School Association.

Control of the school has always been directly governmental, although it was moved from time to time to different departments within the framework of state jurisdiction. At first a board of commissioners governed. Then in 1866, after the Civil War, a board of trustees was appointed. This lasted until 1931 when the school, along with the state mental hospital, the soldiers' home and the tuberculosis sanatorium, was put under the administrative power of the Board of Control of Eleemosynary Institutions.[18]

When the board of control was abolished in 1937, governance of the school was given to the department of public welfare.[19] The final change came in 1943, when control of the institution was put into the hands of the Georgia Department of Education.[20]

In 1972 the department of education created the Atlanta Area School for the Deaf to expand the realm of education for the deaf in Georgia. Designed as a day school rather than a residential institution, it enabled hearing impaired children within the metropolitan Atlanta area to receive a comprehensive public school education without having to become residents of the Georgia School for the Deaf.

Preschool through middle school programs were set up using all forms of communication including auditory training, sign language, speech, speechreading, fingerspelling, gestures, reading and writing.

In addition, an infant training program was begun to help parents begin teaching hearing impaired children as soon as the handicap is discovered. This program trains parents to work in the home with their deaf children who range in age from birth to three years old. This, in turn, enables some of the children to later enter regular public school classes. Others are referred to agencies serving the deaf or continue at the Atlanta Area School for the Deaf.

Education of the Blind

The movement to educate the blind in Georgia began in 1851 when W. S. Fortescue founded the Georgia Academy for the Blind in Macon. A history of Macon, Georgia, published in 1950, relates the following account of the event.

> W. S. Fortescue, himself blind and highly cultured, came to Macon during the early part of the year from Philadelphia for the purpose of founding a school for the blind in Georgia. At a meeting called by Dr. James M. Green at

the Council Chamber . . . measures were adopted that laid the foundation for the establishment, in Macon, of the Academy for the Blind, State of Georgia. The Hon. E. A. Nisbet was named chairman of the group working on this project and A. R. Freeman acted as secretary. The committee raised funds for the immediate instruction of four blind students by Mr. Fortescue, and laid the groundwork which resulted in the state legislature chartering the institution and providing for its maintenance the following year.[1]

Fortescue was educated at the Pennsylvania Institution for the Blind of which Dr. Robley Dunglinson was a trustee. Dr. Dunglinson, who had been a tutor of Drs. James M. and H. K. Green of Macon at the time they had attended Jefferson Medical College,[2] advised Fortescue that the Greens could be of invaluable assistance in the establishment of an institution for educating the blind in Georgia. His advice was of great merit, for the Greens cordially received Fortescue and related his philanthropic purpose to many prominent citizens in positions to aid his cause. Dr. James Green also enlisted the help of the city's press. On April 5, 1851, an editorial published in the *Georgia Citizen* encouraged its readers to support the cause of the blind. An excerpt from the editorial reads,

We are happy to learn that an effort is now making for the commencement of an Institution for the education of the blind youth of our State, and that a meeting for the purpose of encouraging and sustaining this effort, will be held on Monday evening next, at half-past seven o'clock, at the Methodist Church. An address will be delivered on this occasion by Walter S. Fortescue, a graduate of the Pennsylvania Institution for the Blind, and more recently a graduate of the University of that State, at the close of which, preparatory measures for the establishment of an institution of this character will doubtless be taken by the citizens. When it is remembered that the Legislatures of more than two-thirds of the States have already made ample arrangements for the education of their blind, it is to us a matter of surprise that Georgia, occupying so prominent a position in the Union as she does, should have so long remained indifferent to the educational interests of this class of her youth. The period has now certainly come, if we would redeem our character, to unite our aid, sympathy and influence in the furtherance of so benevolent an object. Our citizens, it is hoped, will therefore come forward, on Monday evening, and give their warmest support to a cause, upon whose success are depending the welfare and happiness of the blind youth of our State.[3]

Other articles in *The Macon Telegraph* and *The Messenger* announced Fortescue's intent to the public, endorsed the cause and encouraged participation in the upcoming meeting on April 15.

By July 10, the committee had collected a total of $802.[4] On that same date, a board of seven trustees was appointed, with Nathan C. Munroe as president and Robert A. Smith as secretary. Other members included E. B. Weed, Col. J. B. Lamar, James M. Green, A. H. Chappell and E. Graves. W. S. Fortescue served as secretary *pro-tem.* In addition to electing officers, the trustees drew up the preamble and articles relating to the organization of the academy. They also gave Fortescue permission to begin immediate instruction of four sightless students— Mary Wimberly, Mary Fairner, Mary Wooten and Francis Hodges.[5] Support for Fortescue's school increased greatly when an assessment a few months later showed that the students not only had made substantial progress but also had advanced even further than sighted children their own ages.

In January 1952 the legislature enacted a bill to incorporate and endow the Georgia Academy for the Blind. The board of trustees was reorganized under the charter granted by electing the following officers: James M. Green, president; Nathan C. Munroe, treasurer; Robert A. Smith, secretary; W. S. Fortescue, principal of the academy; M. B. Clark, musical instructor; Hannah Guillan, literary instructor and Mrs. J. Griswold, matron.[6]

Governor Howell Cobb advocated the cause of the blind by proposing that one third of the revenue for state roads would be shared among the academy and two other charitable institutions. This proposal was meant to supplement the $5,000 annual appropriation allocated by the state legislature to defray expenses of the academy and to educate indigent blind pupils between the ages of 12 and 20.[7]

The original site of the academy was a building on the corner of Third and Mulberry Streets in Macon.[8] Due to lack of sufficient accommodations, the location changed in October 1852, to a building erected by the city for a hospital beyond the southwest portion of the town. Two years later, when this location proved to be unsatisfactory, the trustees used $10,000 to purchase the residence of the late Charles Cotton and two acres of land on which the house stood. This building served as the home of the academy for a number of years.

Several public demonstrations of the students' abilities took place during the next few years, many of them for the benefit of the legislature and other interested parties. The blind students progressed rapidly and so did state appropriations for the school building fund. In January 1858, Governor Joseph Brown accepted a bond in the amount of $75,000 from the trustees for the disbursement of the money appropriated by the legislature to erect a new school building. A large, four-story structure was completed and occupied by January 1860.[9]

Fortescue did not remain with the institution for a long period of time. The first annual report of the trustees, dated 1853, shows that he served as principal of the school for that year, but by 1854 he was no longer there. Henry Dutton succeeded Fortescue as principal of the academy.

During the Civil War and the years immediately following, Georgia was in a state of political upheaval, causing the academy to suffer the hardest years in its history. The new building constructed in 1860 was taken over by the Confederate Army in November of 1863 to be used as a hospital for wounded soldiers. The academy and all its students were moved to a site in Fort Valley, Georgia. Principal William D. Williams was almost exclusively in charge of the relocation. Because of the proximity of the location to other military hospitals in the area, he and his family were required to live on the site for the safety of the students.

Of course, the South lost the war. The minutes of the May 11, 1865, meeting of the board of trustees admitted,

> The fact being recognized that the entire support of the Institution derived from the State had been cut off by recent political changes, and also that the Academy building which had been in use as a military hospital under the

Confederate authorities had been occupied in that use
by the Federals: On motion, the President of the Board
and the Principal were appointed to confer immediately
with the medical officer of the Federal army in order to
ascertain whether they would be willing to pay rent for
the same. After a short absence the committee returned
and reported that they were unable to make any arrangements by which rent might be derived for the use of the
Academy, and therefore it was ordered that the Principal
should send the pupils home as soon as practicable and
close the school.[10]

However, when they received notice one week later that the
commanding officer would allow the commissary to furnish
the school with supplies, the trustees immediately rescinded
their order for closing the academy.

By the fall of 1865, the building in Macon had been abandoned by both the Confederate and Federal armies. Principal
Williams inspected the building, assessed the damage done
and decided that reoccupation was a feasible undertaking,
although not before the state of disrepair in which he found
the premises could be remedied. The school's books, supplies
and all other removables had been taken by the troops. The
building was in such bad shape that the local board of health
had condemned it as a public nuisance.[11] The roof was almost
totally decayed and presented a fire hazard in that condition.
In spite of all this, Williams felt that the building could be
made livable again. He cleaned it thoroughly and attended to
all minor repairs. The only imperative major repair need was
for a new roof. Williams estimated that one of good quality
would cost $2,500. The trustees gave him permission to borrow
up to $2,000 for recovering the roof and up to that same
amount for supplies, provisions and maintenance.

That the school for the first time incurred a debt seems
suspect when the records of the board of trustees showed over
$10,000 on hand. The 1865 annual report explained, "Of this
balance, $9,400 is an investment in Confederate securities . . .
which is now, of course, worthless. The remainder, $800.46 is
in Georgia State Treasury notes, now out of circulation, and
their value problematical." [12] Principal Williams and Miss
Guillan advanced their personal money for the support of the

school until the middle of 1866 when the debt to them had reached over $5,000. After the legislature convened and appropriations to the institution were restored, they were fully reimbursed.

The political uproar in Georgia in 1867 forestalled the meeting of the general assembly; consequently, no appropriations were made to the academy for the following year. Governor Jenkins attempted to remedy the situation by recruiting the assistance of the railroads.[13] He issued an executive order to the superintendent of the Western and Atlantic Railroad in December 1868, for a $2,750 advance in favor of the academy. Foreseeing the impending takeover of his administration, Governor Jenkins urged the trustees to make haste in carrying out his instructions.[14] The superintendent did not make the advance but turned the funds over to Military Governor T. H. Ruger, who had taken command of Georgia's government shortly after the order was issued.

The trustees sent Williams as a delegate to Ruger to plead the cause of the academy. Ruger claimed that there were no funds for the school in the state treasury; however, he issued assurances that allowed the school to operate on credit until appropriations could be generated. Funds in a sufficient amount to put the academy completely out of debt were restored by the end of 1869.

When Georgians regained control of the government in 1871, the school's biggest trial was over. With funds restored and the assurance of an annual allocation, the administration turned its attention to the problems of curriculum, enrollment and adequate housing facilities.

It is questionable whether or not the school could have survived the trying years of the war and immediately afterwards if it had not been for Principal Williams and the extraordinary literary instructor, Miss Hannah Guillan, who devoted a good part of her life to the Georgia Academy for the Blind. Miss Guillan was there from the beginning as one of the original members of its staff. Her loyalty to the school was unquestionable. It was never more clearly evident than during the traumatic Civil War period. She not only remained with the students through the hard times when they were moved from one place to another but also helped support the school with her personal money when needed funds were not available.

Miss Guillan, herself blind, gave her all to the cause of educating blind children. Fellow educators claimed her talents seemed intuitive and lauded her as an excellent teacher and a dynamo of organizing power. After her death on June 1, 1898, the board of trustees requested that a memorial to Miss Guillan be placed in the annual report to the governor. Part of that memorial states,

> Miss Hannah Guillan was born in England. In early life she lost both of her parents, and was sent to this country to some people living in the mountains of Pennsylvania. The people, thoughtless of the care and tenderness due the little orphan girl, endeavored to bring her up in menial work, and early put her to do the milking for the family. In doing this work she was exposed to the inclement climate, her eyes became affected by the intense cold, snows, sleet, and bleak winds, and she lost one eye, the sight of the other also being nearly destroyed. In this condition a traveling preacher found her. He had some knowledge of the Institution for the Blind in Philadelphia, and took her as soon as he could to Philadelphia, and placed her in the care of Mr. Friedlander, the superintendent of that then young institution. There she grew up and became highly educated. She was early given a place as subordinate teacher in that school, in which place she showed great talent and made a success. One of her schoolmates, Mr. N. S. Fortescue, founder of the Georgia Academy for the Blind, as soon as he had seen the Academy established by a charter of incorporation, knowing the aptitude of Miss Guillan for the instruction of the blind, sent for her to come to Georgia, and gave her the principal place of teaching in this institution. Here she was loved by the entire household, and her death on the first of June was a sad bereavement, lamented by all who knew her.[15]

When William D. Williams came to the Georgia Academy for the Blind in 1858, he had never instructed blind students. In spite of this deficiency, he was well equipped to carry out his administrative duties as principal of the institution. The Putnam County-born scholar attended the University of Georgia in 1848. Afterwards he taught school in Talbot County, at the Madison Female College in Madison and at Emory University in Oxford, Georgia. By 1858 he had 10 years' experience of educating Georgia students to his credit.

Williams looked upon administering the needs of the Georgia Academy for the Blind as his life's work. Under his leadership several changes came about and many improvements in the school took place. He strongly endorsed separation of the sexes in living areas and age-graded living quarters, and campaigned vigorously for new buildings with more space until this goal was realized. The age-graded curriculum was also put into effect during his administration, as were the services of a school physician and an oculist for the students.

With the help of Miss Guillan, he kept the school alive through its most trying years, often using his own money when other funds did not materialize. When he died in December 1898, the school lost a faithful servant of 40 years.

The academy did not grow very rapidly in enrollment during the first few years. The four students of 1851 had increased to only 15 by 1853 and 27 by 1861. The outbreak of the war stunted growth of the school in every way. Near the end of the 1860s, Williams reported,

> During the war and since its close very little has been done to increase the School. There have been insuperable difficulties in the way. Blindness, however, has in this time increased in the State. From the best sources of information to which I have had access, I estimate the number of blind and purblind youth in the State at from ninety to one hundred. Including the present number of pupils, and others known to me who will be sent in as soon as it shall be ascertained that maintenance is provided, we may rely upon having an average attendance of thirty during the next year. To pay the salaries of officers, and maintain the indigent and partly indigent (nearly the entire number), I respectfully recommend the Board to ask an appropriation of seven thousand dollars. This sum is the same as that granted in 1861, when the number of pupils was twenty-seven.[17]

By 1880 the population of blind children in Georgia was thought to have grown much larger. Census statistics for 1840 and 1850 listed the number of blind children in Georgia as

136 and 230, respectively. Williams believed both reports were erroneous. He ascertained from information reported to him by reliable sources that there was "in each county an average of one not returned in the state census. This number would be properly estimated as above three hundred." [18] The percentage of these children being served by the academy was not very high. During most of the Reconstruction period, the average number of students remained in the thirties. Afterwards a sharp increase in enrollment took place, so that by 1900 there were 113 students in attendance. This great surge in enrollment was occasioned by two events—the lowering of the minimum age of admission from 12 to six and the admission of black students into the academy.

Up to the close of the Civil War, census statistics showed only two black children of suitable age for admission into the academy. In 1878 State School Commissioner Gustavus Orr reported the number of blind black children between the ages of six and 20 to be 145, 10 more than the white population of 135. Williams felt that provisions should be made for educating sightless black children and in 1880 recommended that preparations be made for their admission to the academy. Up to this time, only two blacks had received the benefits that the academy offered. They were two young men who took day classes in the handicrafts department in order to be self-supporting.

Appropriations for educating black blind children raised the total funds of the Academy to $12,000 for salaries, maintenance, furnishings and buildings by 1881. In 1882 school buildings were constructed on a three-and-a-half acre lot at the northern limits of Madison Street, very remote from the building where the white students resided. The school opened in 1884 with only a few students in attendance. In 1885 the student population was 11 and by 1900 had reached 33.[19]

The curriculum was revised and augmented to fit the needs of the students. In 1858 the girls learned to crochet, sew and do fancy beadwork in order to be of service to the families into which they were received upon leaving school. In 1866 the board of trustees purchased equipment with which to start a handicrafts department for the male students. They received instruction in making brooms, brushes and mattresses, caning chairs, weaving rag carpets and making doormats. This department practically supported itself from sale of its goods during the lean years of the institution in the mid-to-late 1860s.

By 1900, the curriculum was divided into three separate departments. The common school consisted of eight grades which taught reading (with raised letters), writing, math, algebra, physiology, typewriting, geography, history, government, chemistry and plant and animal studies. The music department provided supervision in mastering the piano, violin, organ, flute, guitar and mandolin. It also provided instruction in music theory, writing and voice. The industrial department included the handicrafts of broom and brushmaking, mattress making and chair caning for the males, and sewing, knitting, crocheting and needlework for the females.[20]

The Georgia Academy for the Blind has been the responsibility of several different departments within the state government at various times. The board of trustees of the academy was abolished in 1931, and the school, along with the Georgia School for the Deaf, was put under the jurisdiction of the Board of Control of Eleemosynary Institutions, a new department which supervised many charitable institutions receiving state appropriations.[21] In 1937 the board of control was dissolved and the department of public welfare was put in administrative control of the academy.[22] This came to an end in 1943 when the Georgia Department of Education assumed responsibility for governing the school.[23]

Improvement was a result of this final change. The teaching staff was upgraded and the school gained access to supplies, equipment, materials and curriculum services not available before.

The academy experienced a great leap forward in buildings and facilities following the passage of a bill in 1951 which created a state school building authority for the blind. Under this law, the building authority was granted permission to "acquire, construct, operate, and maintain self-liquidating projects embracing buildings and facilities intended for use as school buildings, classrooms, laboratories, dormitories and housing accommodations and utilities and other facilities in connection therewith" supervised by the State Board of Education.[24] Revenue bonds paid the cost of the projects. As a consequence of these activities, the Georgia Academy for the

Blind soon took on the appearance of other public schools under the direction of the department of education.

Today, the school offers a 12-month program for grades kindergarten through 12. Orientation mobility, Braille training and other self-help skills are part of the school's curriculum, and housing, home life care, food and nursing are provided routinely. The school still operates two campuses, not for the purpose of segregation but to house the number of students enrolled.

CHAPTER I

FOOTNOTES

1. Sarah B. Gober Temple and Kenneth Coleman, eds., *Georgia Journeys*, (Athens: University of Georgia Press, 1961), p. 299.
2. *Ibid.*, p. 292.
3. Carl Mauelshagen, *Salzburg Lutheran Expulsion and Its Impact*, (New York: Vantage Press, 1962), pp. 151, 155.
4. George Fenwick Jones, ed., *Detailed Reports on the Salzburg Emigrants Who Settled in America . . . Edited by Samuel Urlsperger, (1734-1735)*, (Athens: University of Georgia Press, 1969), II, xii.
5. George Fenwick Jones, ed., *Henry Newman's Salzburger Letterbooks*, (Athens: University of Georgia Press, 1966), pp. 59-60.
6. James Ross McCain, *Georgia As a Proprietary Province*, (Boston: Richard G. Badger, 1917), pp. 42-43.
7. Allen D. Candler and Lucian Lamar Knight, eds., *The Colonial Records of the State of Georgia, 1904-1916*, I-XXIX (Atlanta: Franklin Turner Co.), pp. 177, 137. Volumes 27-39 in manuscript at the Georgia Department of Archives and History, Atlanta. (Hereinafter referred to as *CRG*.)
8. Jones, ed., *Henry Newman's Letterbooks*, pp. 61-62, 66, 68-69.
9. *Ibid.*, p. 16.
10. Mauelshagen, *Salzburg Lutheran Expulsion*, p. 151.
11. E. Merton Coulter and Albert B. Saye, *A List of the Early Settlers of Georgia*, (Athens: University of Georgia Press, 1949), p. 38.
12. *Detailed Reports on the Salzburgers*, I, 68.
13. *Ibid.*, p. 85.
14. *Ibid.*, II, 3.
15. *Ibid.*, pp. 46-47.
16. *Ibid.*, pp. 55, 69, 170.
17. *Ibid.*, pp. 32-33.
18. *Ibid.*, pp. 203-204.
19. *CRG*, GXII, pt. 2, 161-162.
20. McCain, *Georgia as a Proprietary Province*, p. 281.
21. P. A. Strobel, *The Salzburgers and Their Descendants*, (Athens: University of Georgia Press, 1963), p. 106.
22. Ira L. Brown, *The Georgia Colony*, (New York: Macmillan, 1970), p. 86.
23. *CRG*, XXI, 229.
24. Strobel, *The Salzburgers and Their Descendants*, p. 54. See a description of "Francke's Institutions" from Ellwood P. Cubberly, *The History of Education*, (Boston: Houghton Mifflin, 1948), pp. 418-420.
25. Robert L. McCaul, "*A Documentary History of Education in Colonial Georgia*," (unpublished doctoral dissertation, University of Chicago, Chicago, 1953), p. 32.

26. *Ibid.*, pp. 49-50; Coulter and Saye, eds., *List of Early Settlers of Georgia*, p. 13.
27. *CRG*, Burnside to Trustees, January 6, 1735, XX, 128; Coulter and Saye, eds. *A List of Early Settlers of Georgia*, p. 7.
28. *CRG*, p. 308.
29. Adelaide L. Fries, *The Moravians in Georgia 1735-1740*, (Baltimore: Genealogical Publishing Company, 1967), pp. 38, 48, 65. McCain, *Georgia as a Proprietary Province*, pp. 284-285. William Bacon Stevens, *A History of Georgia From Its Discovery by Europeans to the Adoption of the Present Constitution in MDCCXCVII*, (Philadelphia: E. H. Butler) I, 365.
30. Fries, *The Moravians in Georgia*, pp. 98-99.
31. *Ibid.*, pp. 152-153; *CRG*, Ingham to Phillips, September 15, 1736, p. 22.
32. Fries, *The Moravians in Georgia*, p. 168.
33. *Ibid.*, p. 229.
34. *The Journal of John Wesley*. Edited by Percy T. Parker. Chicago, 1951.
35. *CRG*, II, 251-252, 260.
36. *Ibid.*, XXI, 432.
37. *Ibid.*, p. 377.
38. *Ibid.*, I, 408.
39. John Gillies, *Memoirs of Rev. George Whitefield*, (Middletown: Hunt & Noyes, 1837), p. 31.
40. *CRG*, V, Board of Trade, Whitefield to Trustees, May 19, 1740, XXI, 257-258.
41. Cubberly, *The History of Education*, pp. 400-401.
42. *CRG*, I, 59.
43. *Ibid.*, II, 510.
44. *Ibid.*, I, 552.
45. *Ibid.*, XXVI, 257-258.
46. Collections of the Georgia Historical Society, VI, Habersham to Rev. Thomas Broughton, Secretary to the Society for Promoting Christian Knowledge, December 1, 1770, *Savannah Morning News Print*, Savannah, 1904, p. 101.
47. *CRG*, XVII, 136.
48. *Ibid.*, XXIX, pt. 1, 242-243.
49. McCaul, *A Documentary History of Education*, p. 27.
50. *Georgia Gazette*, June 16, 1763, Savannah; John Protress, as example.
51. Barratt Wilkins, "A View of Savannah on the Eve of Revolution," *The Georgia Historical Quarterly*, Savannah, 1970, LIV, 580. (Hereinafter referred to as *GHQ*.)
52. Kenneth Coleman, *The American Revolution in Georgia 1763-1789*, (Athens: University of Georgia Press, 1958), p. 177.
53. Georgia G. Smith, Jr., *The Story of Georgia and the Georgia People*, 1732-1860, (Atlanta: Franklin Printing and Publishing Co., 1900), pp. 108-109.
54. *Ibid.*, pp. 66-68.
55. Robert Watkins and George Watkins, *A Digest of the Laws of the State of Georgia From Its first Establishment as a British Province Down to the Year 1798, Inclusive, and the Principal Acts of 1799*, (Philadelphia: R. Aiken, 1800), p. 15.
56. George White, *Statistics of the State of Georgia*, (Savannah: W. Thorne Williams, 1849), p. 66.
57. Elbert W. G. Boogher, *Secondary Education in Georgia 1732-1858*, (Camden: I. F. Huntzinger, 1933), XIX, 38.
58. *CRG*, pt. 2, 133.
59. J. A. Cuthbert, *A Digest of All the Laws and Resolutions Now in Force in the State of Georgia on the Subject of Public Education*

   and Free Schools Prepared under a Resolution of the legislature,
   (Milledgeville: Polhill & Cuthbert Printers, 1832), p. 1.
60. Oliver H. Prince, *A Digest of the Laws of the State of Georgia . . .
   previous to the session of the General Assembly of Dec., 1837 . . .
   Compiled by the appointment, and under the authority of the General Asembly,* (Athens: published by the author, Second Edition,
   1837), p. 530.
61. *Ibid.,* p. 17.
62. Cubberly, *The History of Education,* pp. 44, 272.
63. H. Marbury and W. H. Crawford, *Digest of the Laws of the State
   of Georgia from its settlement as a British Province, in 1755, to
   the session of the General Assembly in 1800, inclusive. Compiled,
   arranged and digested from original records and under the special
   authority of the State,* (Savannah: Seymour Woolhopter & Stebbens, 1802), pp. 132-34.
64. Marbury and Crawford, *Digest,* p. 563.
65. Watkins and Watkins, *Digest,* p. 381.
66. Marbury and Crawford, *Digest,* pp. 598-599.
67. Augustin Smith Clayton, *A Compilation of the Laws of the State
   of Georgia, passed by the Legislature since the political year 1800
   to the year 1810, inclusive,* (Augusta: Adams & Duyckinck, 1812),
   pp. 149-159, 181.
68. Cuthbert, *Digest,* pp. 135-136.
69. *Ibid.,* p. 61.
70. Clayton, *A Compilation,* p. 666.
71. G. Cordle, *"An Ante-Bellum Academy of Richmond County 1783-
   1853",* (unpublished master's thesis, University of Georgia, Athens,
   1935).
72. Boogher, *Secondary Education in Georgia,* p. 84.
73. Prince, *Digest,* pp. 866-869.
74. E. Merton Coulter, "Ante-Bellum Academy Movement in Georgia,"
   GHQ, IV, December 1921, 15.
75. William H. Kilpatrick, "The Beginnings of the Public School System
   in Georgia," GHQ, III, September 1921, 5-6.
76. Charles William Dabney, *Universal Education in the South from
   the Beginning to 1900,* (Chapel Hill: University of North Carolina
   Press, 1936), p. 246.
77. *Ibid.,* p. 434.
78. Boogher, *Secondary Education in Georgia,* p. 85.
79. J. S. Stewart, "High School Development in Georgia Before the
   Civil War," *GHQ,* IV, July 1913.
80. Richard Malcolm Johnston, "Early Educational Life in Middle
   Georgia," *Report of the Commissioner of Education for the Year
   1894-95,* (Washington: Government Printing Office, 1896), II, pt. 2,
   1699.
81. B. M. Zettler, *War Stories and School Day Incidents,* (New York:
   Neale Publishing, 1912), p. 71.
82. White, *Statistics of the State of Georgia,* p. 71.
83. Adiel Sherwood, *A Gazetteer of Georgia,* (Atlanta: J. Richards,
   1860), p. 62.
84. *Western Herald, Auraria.* December 14 (3,5), 1833; *Southern
   Banner,* Athens, April 24 (1,5), 1834, as reported by E. Merton
   Coulter, *Auraria, The Story of a Georgia Gold Mining Town,*
   (Athens: University of Georgia Press, 1956), pp. 44-45.
85. Frank Lawrence Owsley, *The South: Old and New Frontiers,
   Selected Essays,* Harriett Chappell Owsley, ed., (Athens, University
   of Georgia Press, 1969), p. 47.
86. John Donald Wade, *Augustus Baldwin Longstreet—A Study of the
   Development of Culture in the South,* (Athens: University of
   Georgia Press, 1969), p. 17.

87. *Ibid.*, p.20.
88. Boogher, *Secondary Education in Georgia*, p. 170.
89. Zettler, War Stories and School Day Incidents, p. 26.
90. Johnston, "Early Educational Life in Middle Georgia," p. 863.
91. Boogher, *Secondary Education in Georgia*, p. 125.
92. Spencer B. King, Jr., *Georgia Voices, A Documentary History to 1872*, (Athens: University of Georgia Press, 1966), p. 207.
93. Smith, *The Story of Georgia People*, p. 183.
94. George White, *Historical Collections of Georgia*, (New York: Pudney & Russell Publishers, 1854), pp. 581-582.
95. E. Merton Coulter, *Old Petersburg and the Broad River Valley of Georgia, Their Rise and Decline*, (Athens: University of Georgia Press, 1965), p. 28.
96. Smith, *The Story of Georgia People*, p. 183; *Georgia Scenes Characters, Incidents, etc., in the First Half-Century of the Republic by a Georgia Native*, (New York: Harper and Brothers Publishers, 1840), pp. 97-98.
97. George G. Smith, *The History of Methodism in Georgia and Florida, from 1785 to 1865*, (Macon: J. W. Burke & Company, 1881), p. 205.
98. Prince, *Digest*, p. 18.
99. *Ibid.*
100. *Ibid.*
101. *Ibid.*, p. 19.
102. *Ibid.*, p. 20.
103. A. D. Mayo, *Report of the Commissioner of Education for the Year 1895-96*, I, pt. 1, (Washington: Government Printing Office, 1897), 298.
104. George R. Gilmer, *Sketches of Some of the First Settlers of Upper Georgia, of the Cherokees, and the Author*, (Baltimore: Genealogical Publishing Company, 1970), p. 345.
105. Dabney, *Universal Education in the South*, p. 250.
106. Mayo, "Common Schools in the South 1830-1860." *Report of the United States Commissioner of Education 1899-1900*, (Washington: Government Printing Office, 1901), I, 679.
107. Coulter, *Ante-Bellum Movement*, p. 29.
108. Prince, *Digest*, pp. 20-21.
109. Dawson, *Digest*, pp. 15-16.
110. Prince, *Digest*, pp. 26-27.
111. Dorothy Orr, *A History of Education in Georgia*, (Chapel Hill: University of North Carolina Press, 1950), pp. 89-95.
112. *Acts of the Legislature*, 1837, pp. 94-99.
113. *Acts of the Legislature*, 1840, pp. 61-65.
114. Smith, *The Story of Georgia*, pp. 466-67.
115. King, *Georgia Voices*, p. 213.
116. Johnston, *Early Educational Life in Middle Georgia*, 866-873; minutes of the proceedings of the Teacher's Society, convened at Milledgeville, December 17-19, 1832. Pamphlet reproduced from copy of the minutes in the Library of University of Georgia, Athens, pp. 11-15.
118. *Acts of the General Assembly*, 1834, Senate Resolution, pp. 279-280.
119. For a full discussion of the early efforts to reorganize a Teacher's Association, see Peggy S. Steelmon, *Growth and Development of the Georgia Education Association*, (unpublished doctoral dissertation, University of Georgia, Athens, 1966), pp. 14-47; Orr, *History of Education in Georgia*, pp. 104-129.
120. Orr, *History of Education in Georgia*, p. 100.
121. *Acts of the Legislature*, 1843.
122. Georgia General Assembly *Senate Journal*, 1847, p. 298.
123. Smith, *The Story of Georgia People*, pp. 488-489.
124. E. Merton Coulter, "A Georgia Educational Movement During the Eighteen Hundred Fifties." *GHQ*, March 1925, IX.

125. Orr, *History of Education in Georgia*, pp. 158-159.
126. Coulter, "Educational Movement," pp. 12-13.
127. *Ibid.*, p. 17.
128. *Ibid.*, p. 28.
129. *Ibid.*, p. 30.
130. *Acts of the General Assembly*, 1858, pp. 49-51.
131. C. Mildred Thompson, *Reconstruction in Georgia*, (Atlanta: Cherokee Publishing, 1971).
132. *Acts of the General Assembly*, 1866, pp. 58-65.
133. Orr, *A History of Education in Georgia*, p. 182.
134. Peggy Steelmon, *Growth and Development of the Georgia Education Association*, pp. 39-47.
135. George Ephraim Usher, *Development of the Georgia Education Association*, (unpublished master's thesis, Duke University, Durham, N. C. 1935).
136. Orr, *History of Education in Georgia*, pp. 181-196.
137. Steelmon, *Growth and Development of the Georgia Education Association*, pp. 48-49; J. S. Stewart, Speech to the Georgia Teachers Association, 1897. *Report of the State School Commissioner of Georgia to the General Assembly*, p. 93; Paul Ellison, "The Legal Growth of the Common School System of Georgia," *Georgia State School Items*, VIII (2), 1831, p. 14; Martin Calvin, Recent Progress of Public Education in the South, a paper read before the Georgia Teachers Association at Savannah, May 5, 1870 (pamphlet). *Report on the System of Public Schools for the State of Georgia*, adopted by the State Teachers Association, Macon, 1869 (pamphlet), Savannah Morning News Steam-Power Press, 1870; I. W. Avery, *The History of the State of Georgia from 1850-1881*, (New York: Brown & Derby, 1881), p. 375; *Acts of the General Assembly 1870*, pp. 49-61.
138. Coleman, *American Revolution in Georgia*, p. 14.
139. *Ibid.*, p. 234.
140. Boogher, *Secondary Education in Georgia*, p. 319.
141. Kathleen Jones Carswell, ed., *Collections of Twiggs County—Here and There*, 1973. Quote taken from the *Georgia Genealogical Magazine*, IV, October 1954, p. 873, as it appeared in the "Georgia Messenger," Macon, Georgia, December 23, 1923. The Collection of Mrs. Carswell has other advertisements and announcements of work in the academies in the 1820's and 1830's.
142. Owsley, *The South: Old and New Frontiers*, pp. 46-47.
143. Boogher, *Secondary Education in Georgia*, pp. 162-168.
144. *Ibid.*, p. 172.
145. *Ibid.*, p. 174.
146. *Ibid.*, p. 175.
147. B. G. Morrison, "The Bell and Lancaster System—What is in it for the Schools of the South," from the *Report of the U. S. Commissioner of Education for the Year 1894-95*, (Washington, D. C.: Government Printing Office, 1896). II, pt. 2, pp. 1153-1160.
148. Richard Malcolm Johnston, "Early Education in Georgia," from the *Report of the U. S. Commissioner of Education for the year 1894-95*, II, pt. 2, 1896, pp. 1699-1733.

FOOTNOTES ON EDUCATION OF THE DEAF

1. *Georgia Laws, 1833*, p. 363.
2. Nell A. Gibbons. "A Short History from the Life of the Georgia School for the Deaf, Centennial Celebration, 1848-1948," *The School Helper*, Georgia School for the Deaf Press, Cave Spring, Georgia, 1948.
3. *Ibid.*
4. *Ibid.*
5. *Georgia Laws, 1839*, pp. 130-132.

6. *Georgia Laws, 1847,* pp. 94-96.
7. Helen E. Muse, "The Georgia School for the Deaf at Cave Spring," *The Deaf American,* October, 1966, v. 19(2), pp. 3-4.
8. *Georgia Laws, 1847.*
9. *Georgia Laws, 1851,* pp. 80-81.
10. Gibbons.
11. Muse, p. 4.
12. Gibbons.
13. *Ibid.*
14. Muse, p. 4.
15. *Georgia Laws, 1876,* pp. 117-118.
16. Muse, pp. 4-5.
17. *Ibid.,* pp. 6-7.
18. *Georgia Laws, 1931,* pp. 15-20.
19. *Georgia Laws, 1937,* pp. 355-368.
20. *Georgia Laws, 1943,* pp. 230-232.

FOOTNOTES ON EDUCATION OF THE BLIND

1. Ida Young, Julius Gholson, and Clara Nell Hargrove, *The History of Macon, Georgia, 1823-1949,* Lyon, Marshall, and Brooks, Macon, pp. 151-152.
2. John G. Butler, *Origin and History of the Georgia Academy for the Blind, with Documents from the Beginning,* 1851, J. W. Burke, Macon, p. 5.
3. *Ibid.,* p. 5.
4. *Ibid.,* p. 9.
5. Young, Gholson and Hargrove, p. 152.
6. *Ibid.,* p. 15.
7. *Georgia Laws, 1852,* pp. 4-6.
8. Butler, p. 15.
9. *Ibid.*
10. *Ibid.,* p. 22.
11. Butler, p. 194.
12. *Fourteenth Annual Report of the Trustees of the Georgia Academy for the Blind to the Governor,* 1865, p. 188.
13. Thomas D. Clark and Albert D. Kirwan, *The South Since Appomattox, A Century of Regional Change,* Oxford University Press, New York, p. 269.
14. Butler, pp. 24-25.
15. *Forty-Seventh Annual Report of the Trustees of the Georgia Academy for the Blind to the Governor of Georgia 1897-98,* Press of Smith and Watson, Macon, pp. 16-17.
16. *Forty-Eighth Annual Report of the Trustees of the Georgia Academy for the Blind to the Governor of Georgia, 1899,* Press of Smith and Watson, Macon, 1899, pp. 35-36.
17. Butler, p. 195.
18. Butler, p. 39.
19. See annual reports for years cited.
20. *Forty-Eighth Annual Report of the Trustees of the Georgia Academy for the Blind to the Governor of Georgia 1898-99,* Press of Smith and Watson, Macon, pp. 14-16.
21. *Georgia Laws, 1931,* pp. 15-20.
22. *Georgia Laws, 1937,* pp. 355-368.
23. *Georgia Laws, 1943,* p. 230.
24. *Georgia Laws, 1951,* p. 637.

Illustrations

The collection of historic photographs which follows was contributed by Anthoney R. Dees, Karen E. Osvald and M. Susan Shepherd, Georgia Historical Society, Savannah; Robert M. Willingham and J. Larry Gulley, University of Georgia Library, Athens; Craig DuPriest and Yvonne Veasey, Muscogee County Schools, Columbus; Gail Miller, Georgia Department of Archives and History, Atlanta, the State Board of Education, Miss Lillian Eason, curriculum director, Tattnall County Schools; Probate Court Judge Bazemore of Tattnall County; B. Arnold; Morgan County and Bartow County school officials; Mrs. Kathleen Carswell; George E. Luce of Ft. Valley; and private citizens. The authors and editors also contributed photographs. Appreciation is extended to each of these individuals and groups for their efforts and contributions.

The photographs are arranged in chronological order. The historic documents reproduced here are translated literally to make them more easily read.

THE EDITORS

JOHN R. LEWIS
State School Commissioner
1870-1872

DR. GUSTAVUS JOHN ORR
State School Commissioner
1872-1887

JUDGE JAMES SCHLEY HOOK
State School Commissioner
1888-1891

CAPTAIN S. D. BRADWELL
State School Commissioner
1891-1895

GUSTAVUS RICHARD GLENN
State School Commissioner
1895-1903

WILLIAM B. MERRITT
State School Commissioner
1903-1907

DR. JERE M. POUND
State School Commissioner
1907-1910

DR. MARION L. BRITTAIN
State School Commissioner
1910-1911
State School Superintendent
1911-1922

DR. MARVIN M. PARKS
State Superintendent of Schools
1922-1923

NATHANIEL H. BALLARD
State School Superintendent
1923-1925

FORT ELMO LAND
State School Superintendent
1925-1927

DR. MELL R. DUGGAN
State School Superintendent
1927-1933

DR. M. D. COLLINS
State School Superintendent
1933-1958

DR. CLAUDE PURCELL
State School Superintendent
1958-1965

DR. JACK P. NIX
State School Superintendent
1966-1977

DR. CHARLES McDANIEL
State School Superintendent
1977-

(Handwritten ledger — Poor School Fund Accounts, Tattnall County, Georgia, 1843)

Georgia   Tattnall County

The Commissioners of the Poor School Funds
To J.A.J. Lane   Dr.

1843		$	cts.
April 24	To the Tuition of Matilda Brewton 64½ days over 5 years old and under 15 years old at 5 cents per day	3	22½
"	To the same of William Brewton 59½ days 5c. p.d.	2	97½
"	the same of James B. Brewton 65 da.	3	25
"	the same of James Brewton 63½ do.	3	17½
"	the same of James Watters 65 do.	3	25
"	the same of Bryan Brewton 65 do.	3	25
"	the same of Martha Brewton 61 do.	3	05
"	the same of Avery Watters 63 do.	3	15
"	the same of Ezekiel Brewton 64 do.	3	20
"	the same of James W. Brewton 61½ do.	3	0½
"	the same of Martin Brewton 63 do.	3	15
"	the same of John Sikes 21 do.	1	05
"	the same of Mary Brewton 49 do.	2	45
"	the same of Eliza Brewton 47 do.	2	35
	Sworn to before me this the 28 July 1843	$40	60

We the Trustees appointed to examine a school taught by
J.A.J. Lane in the 41st dist. G.M. have examined said school
and do report favorable of said institution as we believe said Lane
has done his duty as a Teacher to the above named children that
they have made as much improvement as could be expected and
we think said Teacher worthy of his pay for the tuition
of said children July 26th 1843

Trustees   Nathan Brewton
           Benj. F. Brewton
           Samuel Brewton

TRANSLATION
(Poor School Fund Accounts, Tattnall County, c. 1843)
Georgia   Tattnall County
The Commissioners of the Poor School Funds $ cts.
To J.A.J. Lane   Dr.

1843

April 24		To the tuition of Matilda Brewton 64 ½ days over 5 years old and under 15 years old at 5 cents per day		3	22 ½
"	"	To the same of William Brewton 59 ½ days at 5 c. p.d.		2	97 ½
"	"	" the same of James F. Brewton 65 da.		3	25
"	"	" the same of Jane Brewton 63 ½ da.		3	17 ½
"	"	" the same of James Walters 65 da.		3	25
"	"	" the same of Berryan Brewton 65 da.		3	25
"	"	" the same of Martha Brewton 61 da.		3	05
"	"	" the same of Nancy Walters 63 da.		3	15
"	"	" the same of Ezekiel Brewton 64 da.		3	20
"	"	" the same of James W. Brewton 61 ½ da.		3	07 ½
"	"	" the same of Martin Brewton 63 da.		3	15
"	"	" the same of John Sikes 21 da.		1	05
"	"	" the same of Morry Brewton 49 da.		2	45
"	"	" the same of Eliza Brewton 47 da.		2	35
				$40	60

Sworn to before me this the 28 July 1843

James P. Daniel J.P.

We the Trustees appointed to Examine a school taught by J.A.J. Lane in the 41 d. dest. G.M. have examined said school and do report favorable of said institution as we believe said Lane has done his duty as a Teacher to the above named Children that they have made as much improvement as could be expected and we think said teacher worthy of his pay for the tuition of said children July 26th 1843

Trustees   Nathan Brewton Jr.
Benj. Brewton
Samuel Brewton

Rec. of Benjamin Alexander clerk and treasurer of the Poor School Fund of Tattnall County forty dollars and 60 cents the full amount of the written account

Jno. H. Smith

Voucher No. 59

Examined approved and ordered to be paid by the board of commissioners this 13th of October 1843 the sum of forty dollars and 60 cents

J. A. Mattox
M. M. Mattox   Comm.
James Alexander

Early photograph of Georgia's State Capitol, first occupied June 15, 1889.

TRANSLATION

Articles of agreement made and entered into between Thos. C. Omary of the first part and we the undersigned of the second.

The said Thos. Omary agrees to teach an English School for the term of three months at the rate of one dollar 25 cts per student per month to commence on the first day of August and end on the 30 of October A.D. 1871 in Georgia.

The said Omary agrees to keep good order in school and use his best exertions to promote the advancement of each student committed to his care. For such service rendered we the undersigned agree to pay the said teacher one dollar 25 cts per scholar per month due at the expirati of said term. Given under our hand July 25th 1871

Organization of County Board

Madison, Morgan County, Ga. May 7 18—

In accordance with an act of the Legislature of the State of Georgia, approved October 13 1870 entitled an act "to Establish a System of public instruction" for each County of the State, the following Citizens, elected School Commissioners, assembled this day, — viz.

Leroy M. Willow — from City of Madison
R. R. Thurmond — " " dist — no. 276
I. F. Hanson — " " " 400
I. W. Martin — " " " 277
I. C. Few. Sr — " " " 397
P. Shows — " " " 284
P. Willow — " " " 396
W. D. Barker — " " " 285
D. C. Green — " " " 279
G. F. Ponder — " " " 280

they being a majority of School Commissioners elect, for the County of Morgan, proceeded to organize. After being qualified by the Ordinary in & for Said County, and thereby Commissioned — they elected Leroy M. Willow temporary President, and R. R. Thurmond, Secretary pro-tem.

On Motion of I. F. Hanson, it was Resolved that the election of permanent Officers, be by ballot, and, that a majority of those present, be necessary to an election. Upon ballot, Leroy M. Willow was made President of the Board.

W. D. Barker; C. B. Barrow; I. F. Patterson; I. F. Hanson, & C. H. Andrews, were Nominated for the office of Secretary of the Board.

The question arose, as to whether, other than one of the Commissioners Could act as Secretary, & was decided in the affirmative.

Upon the fifth Counting of ballots, C. H. Andrews, was elected Secretary.

The Sec. was requested to read the act, under Which this Board was organized.

The Sec. was directed to inform C. H. Andrews.

There being no further business, the Board adjourned, to meet on 1st Tuesday in August.

C. H. Andrews
Sec. &c.

TRANSLATION

Organization of County Board
Madison, Morgan County, Ga. July 7, 1871

In accordance with an act of the Legislature of the State of Georgia, approved October 13, 1870, entitled an act "to Establish a System of public instruction"—for each County of the State, the following Citizens, elected School Commissioners, assembled this day,—viz.

Leroy M. Willson— from City of Madison.
R. R. Thurmond— from city dist. no. 276.
I. F. Hanson—   ”   ”   ”   ”   400.
I. W. Martin—   ”   ”   ”   ”   277.
I. C. Few Sr.—   ”   ”   ”   ”   397.
P. Shouse—   ”   ”   ”   ”   284.
P. Wilson—   ”   ”   ”   ”   396.
W. D. Barker—   ”   ”   ”   ”   283.
D. G. Gunn—   ”   ”   ”   ”   279.
G. F. Ponder—   ”   ”   ”   ”   280.

They being a majority of School Commissioners elect for the County of Morgan, proceeded to organize. After being qualified by the Ordinary in and for Said County, and thereby Commissioned—they elected Leroy M. Willson temporary President, and R. R. Thurmond, Secretary pro-tem.

On motion of I. F. Hanson, it was—"Resolved that the election of permanent Officers be by ballot, and, that a majority of those present, be necessary to an election." Upon ballot, Leroy M. Willson was made President of the Board.

W. D. Barker: C. B. Barrow: I. F. Patterson: I. F. Hanson, and C. H. Andrews, were nominated for the office of Secretary of the Board.

The question arose, as to whether, other than one of the Commissioners could act as Secretary, & was decided in the affirmative.

Upon the fifth counting of ballots, C. H. Andrews, was elected Secretary.

The Sec. was requested to read the act, under which this Board was organized.

The Sec. was directed to inform C. H. Andrews.

There being no further business, the Board adjourned, to meet on 1st Tuesday in August.

C. H. Andrews
Sec. & c.

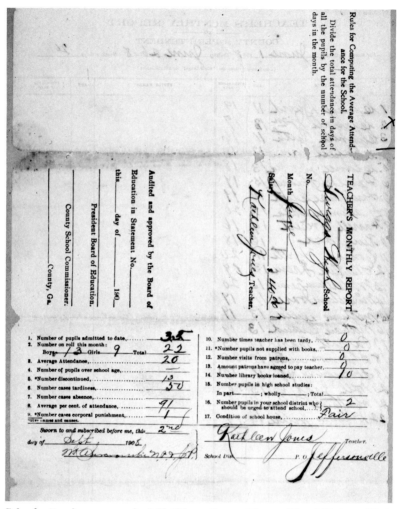

School attendance record of Kathleen Jones (Carswell) of Twiggs High School, June 1908. Furnished by Mrs. Kathleen Carswell.

Form 2

TEACHER'S MONTHLY REPORT
— to —
COUNTY SUPERINTENDENT

For month beginning _June 1_ 190_5_ Ending _June 6_ 190_5_ Number days _20_

[Keep Record of "Branches of Study Taught" for Annual Report.]

PUPILS' NAMES	AGE	ATTENDANCE IN DAYS	PUPILS' NAMES	AGE	ATTENDANCE IN DAYS
1 Califf David	11	19			
2 Carswell Jim	13	17			
3 Chapell Ruth	11	16			
4 Chapell Willie	12	16			
5 Clancy James	13	18			
6 Faulk Shedrick	15	19			
7 Gallemore Elijah	14	19			
8 Gallemore Lille	12	20			
9 Harrell Everett	14	16			
10 King Ira	16	18			
11 Conrad Myrtle	11	20			
12 Martin Irene	13	19			
13 McCallum Fanny	13	20			
14 McCallum Grace	11	19			
15 Mathews Della	13	19			
16 Mathews Claud	13	19			
17 Parrott Mary	14	13			
18 Shannon Sudie	13	20			
19 Solomon Boyce	11	15			
20 Hall Jackie	13	18			
21 Whitehead Di Rene	11	20			
22 Williams Willie	16	19			
		399			

Carswell document, reverse side showing listing of students.

CHEROKEE ALPHABET.

CHARACTERS SYSTEMATICALLY ARRANGED WITH THE SOUNDS.

Ꭰ a	Ꭱ e	Ꭲ i	Ꭳ o	Ꭴ u	Ꭵ v
Ꭶ ga Ꭷ ka	Ꭸ ge	Ꭹ gi	Ꭺ go	Ꭻ gu	Ꭼ gv
Ꭽ ha	Ꭾ he	Ꭿ hi	Ꮀ ho	Ꮁ hu	Ꮂ hv
Ꮃ la	Ꮄ le	Ꮅ li	Ꮆ lo	Ꮇ lu	Ꮈ lv
Ꮉ ma	Ꮊ me	Ꮋ mi	Ꮌ mo	Ꮍ mu	
Ꮎ na Ꮏ hna Ꮐ nah	Ꮑ ne	Ꮒ ni	Ꮓ no	Ꮔ nu	Ꮕ nv
Ꮖ qua	Ꮗ que	Ꮘ qui	Ꮙ quo	Ꮚ quu	Ꮛ quv
Ꮜ s Ꮝ sa	Ꮞ se	Ꮟ si	Ꮠ so	Ꮡ su	Ꮢ sv
Ꮣ da Ꮤ ta	Ꮥ de Ꮦ te	Ꮧ di Ꮨ ti	Ꮩ to	Ꮪ du	Ꮫ dv
Ꮬ dla Ꮭ tla	Ꮮ tle	Ꮯ tli	Ꮰ tlo	Ꮱ tlu	Ꮲ tlv
Ꮳ tsa	Ꮴ tse	Ꮵ tsi	Ꮶ tso	Ꮷ tsu	Ꮸ tsv
Ꮹ wa	Ꮺ we	Ꮻ wi	Ꮼ wo	Ꮽ wu	Ꮾ wv
Ꮿ ya	Ᏸ ye	Ᏹ yi	Ᏺ yo	Ᏻ yu	Ᏼ yv

SOUNDS REPRESENTED BY VOWELS.

a as *a* in *father*, or short as *a* in *rival*,
e as *a* in *hate*, or short as *e* in *met*,
i as *i* in *pique*, or short as *i* in *pin*,
o as *o* in *note*, but as approaching to *aw* in *law*,
u as *oo* in *moon*, or short as *u* in *pull*,
v as *u* in *but*, nasalized.

CONSONANT SOUNDS.

g is sounded hard, approaching to k; sometimes before e, i, o, u and v, its sound is k. d has a sound between the English d and t; sometimes, before o, u and v, its sound is t, when written before l and s the same analogy prevails.

All other letters as in English.

Sylables beginning with g, except ga, have sometimes the power of k; sylables written with tl, except tla, sometimes vary to dl.

Photo Courtesy the University of Georgia Library

The Cherokee alphabet as used by the Indian school children at New Echota, their settlement near Calhoun (Gordon County). c. 1830.

Two views of the Salzburger settlement at Ebenezer 25 miles north of Savannah, c. 1740. The Salzburgers were the first religious sect to establish schools in Georgia. Their schoolmaster, Christopher Ortman, became the first teacher in the colony on his arrival in 1734.

Photo Courtesy the University of Georgia Library

The entrance to the Bethesda Orphan house located near the Isle of Hope about 10 miles from Savannah. The school was named "Bethesda" or "House of Mercy" by George Whitefield when he laid the first brick in 1740. In addition to orphans, the school was open to all children of the province. James Habersham was the first school master at Bethesda.

Photo Courtesy Georgia Historical Society

An early engraving of Chatham Academy, Savannah, established February 1, 1788, by an act of the Georgia General Assembly then holding its sessions in Augusta. It had a board of trustees appointed by the state and opened on Jan. 5, 1813, with an enrollment of 219 pupils.

Photo Courtesy Georgia Department of Archives and History

The Valdosta Institute on Central Avenue, Valdosta, c. 1866. Samuel Varnedoe settled in Valdosta in 1865 and opened this impressive school soon after. It was one of the earliest schools offering formal education in South Georgia.

Photo Courtesy Muscogee County Schools

The old Freedmen's Bureau Building at Fifth Avenue and 16th Street, Columbus. Following the Civil War until the end of Reconstruction, the Freedmen's Bureau coordinated educational opportunities for former slaves.

Rockville School, Putnam County, built in 1889, consolidated in 1890 and graded in 1892, is said to have been the first consolidated rural school in Georgia, also the first Standard rural school and the first vocational rural school in the state. The first trustees were H. R. DeJarnette, chairman; W. M. Flanagan, K. D. Little, W. M. Gregory and H. D. Welch. The first teachers were J. R. Lin and Miss Mary Baugh.

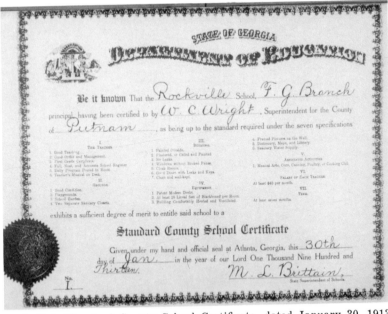

Rockville's Standard County School Certificate, dated January 30, 1913.

The wooden portion of Emanuel County Institute (pictured) was finished in 1897 and housed grades 1-11. Funds for the construction of this building were derived from a special district tax created by the General Assembly for the express purpose of constructing the Emanuel County Institute. Legislation permitting this special tax levy was enacted during the early 1890s. Much of the labor and materials was donated by people in the district.

One-room school house, c. 1890, located between Valdosta and Statenville in Lowndes County.

Black students are shown with their white teachers outside their coastal Georgia school, c. 1890.

The campus of Georgia Industrial College, Savannah, c. 1893. This historically important black educational institute later became Savannah State College. Many of the state's teachers continue to receive their training here.

LUCY COBB INSTITUTE, Athens, Ga.

A Boarding School for Girls. Lady Teachers. All Denominations Represented. Board, $15.00 a Month. No Secret Societies. Health Record Unsurpassed.

MISS M. RUTHERFORD, Principal.

Photo Courtesy the University of Georgia Library

A nineteenth century newspaper advertisement for Lucy Cobb Institute. Many of the young ladies of this "finishing school" went into the education profession.

Photo Courtesy Georgia Department of Archives and History

The main building at the Georgia Academy for the Blind, Macon, shown c. 1896. The building was begun in the early 1850s.

Superintendent William Clyde Woodall (front center) is shown with faculty of Columbus Public Schools, c. 1898.

St. Patrick's School, Savannah, in an undated photograph. Private, church-related schools such as this have historically provided education to a significant portion of the state's school age population.

A late nineteenth century photo of Chatham Academy, Savannah, as it appeared following extensive renovations. The school was one of the earliest chartered educational institutions in Georgia.

The main building of Andrew Female College, Cuthbert (Randolph County), c. 1900. The school trained many young women for the teaching profession.

Students and teachers are shown in this patriotic photograph of a Dodge County school house in Eastman, c. 1900.

Mill Creek School was the original school at Pooler in Chatham County. A one-room school, it was originally constructed around 1900. After it was abandoned for school use, the school became the city hall for the town of Pooler. It was later used as the Pooler City Jail, which accounts for the bars at the windows. After another jail was constructed, this building was converted to a general store. Its last use was as a paint and repair shop.

Miss Martha Berry and her teacher assistants are shown in a classroom of the Berry Schools. c. 1902. Located in Rome (Floyd County), the campus of approximately 100 buildings provided mountain boys and girls educational opportunities through a student work system which paid instead of cash for room, board and tuition. A four-year senior college was added in 1930.

Students and teachers pose in front of the Mt. Giliad rural school, Lumpkin County, c. 1903. The school house was located six miles east of Dahlonega on Highway 52.

Students of the Negro Industrial School on Fifth Avenue, Columbus, are shown with their instructor, Prof. G. F. Rivers, at far right, c. 1906. Another industrial high school for white students was built on Rose Hill, later becoming Jordan Vocational High School. It was said to be the only secondary vocational school in the world municipally operated and open to both sexes.

Pelham High School, Pelham, was built in 1906 at a cost of $17,000. The all brick, two-story structure was a show place for educational instruction in this southwest Georgia community for a number of years.

Students and teachers in front of Bird School, Bulloch County, c. 1910.

Live Oak Community School, Polk County, c. 1910, was located between Senay and Rockmart. It was a private school operated by Joe Dobb (1842-1911), shown standing at right with beard. Cost was $1 per month, per pupil.

These Chattooga County teachers and administrators are shown on steps of the Chattooga County Courthouse in Trion, c. 1914.

The Yahoola School in central Lumpkin County, c. 1915. The school took its name from the Yahoola River located nearby.

Students and teachers are shown in front of Clyattville School, Lowndes County, c. 1923.

Black elementary school students pose with their teacher in front of a Savannah school, c. 1925-1926.

Kindergarten students pose in their patriotic operetta costumes following the 1927 commencement exercises at Lucy Cobb Institute, Athens (Clarke County). Many of the institute's female students went on to teach in Georgia's public and private schools.

Georgia's first school bus built by Blue Bird Body Company, Fort Valley. Standing beside the bus is the builder, A. L. Luce, Sr. The bus was used to carry school children in Marshallville for 11 years.

Students in this Elbert County school are pictured receiving vaccinations. c. 1927-1928. Adults shown left to right are Lula Peek, home demonstration agent; Dr. B. B. Mattox, pediatrician; Mary Bradshaw, nurse; Nobie Fortson, nurse; and Dr. George Ward, practitioner.

Demonstration of farming equipment for students at Murray County High School, Chatsworth, c. 1933-1935. Such demonstrations were an important part of the curriculum for students taking agricultural programs in rural areas of the state.

Addition to a rural school building under construction by the Works Progress Administration (WPA), c. 1936.

Teacher and students in a kindergarten class, possibly DeKalb County, c. 1936.

Mr. and Mrs. Henry Ford tour a kindergarten class held on their 70,000 acre estate near Ways Station, later Richmond Hill. Between 1927 and 1947 the Detroit auto magnate and his wife assembled a 70,000 acre winter retreat in Bryan and Chatham counties. They privately financed a year-'round health and educational system for both black and white area children on this estate outside Savannah.

A school building goes up on the 70,000-acre Ford estate outside Savannah, c. 1935. Students like these, who received valuable vocational skill training erecting school buildings, often later received more academic training in the school when it was completed.

Interior of a school house on the Ford estate outside Savannah, c. 1935. Private philanthropy such as Ford's on both a small and large scale has often provided a boost to education efforts in the state.

Provisions of the Smith-Hughes Act greatly expanded vocational education opportunities. These Columbus area students are shown in an outdoor bricklaying class conducted under the direction of F. R. Lumpkin, principal, standing at left.

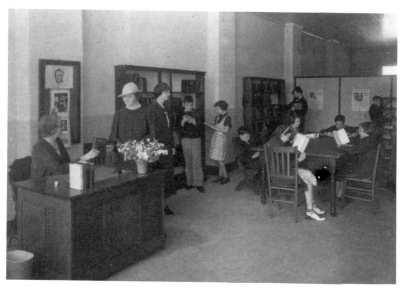

Interior showing a portion of a school library, possibly DeKalb County, c. 1936.

Members of a basket weaving class at Georgia State Women's College, Valdosta, in an undated photo. This women's school later became Valdosta State College, an important coeducational institution for teacher training in the state.

Interior of a classroom, possibly Hart County, c. 1930-1940. These well dressed students, all 4-H Club Members, dispel the myth that agricultural students always wore overalls.

An evening adult education class, c. 1936.

Fort Mountain School, Murray County, c. 1938. This one-room school house was still in use until about 1950, when students were transferred to Chatsworth Elementary School.

Mrs. Annie Bridges is shown at the wheel of this 1938 school bus. She is reputed to have been the first woman school bus driver in the state. Note absence of glass windows in the vehicle. Early County, June 14, 1938.

Students and parents march in Columbus in support of a local school bond election, c. 1940.

ROTC became an important aspect of Georgia's high school curriculum as World War II approached. These Savannah High School students are shown on the drilling field, c. 1940.

Students and teachers at the East Broad Street School, Savannah, c. 1943.

Students at Waters Avenue School, Savannah, are pictured during a school crossing demonstration, c. 1946.

School pageants such as this one were at one time a popular student activity in Georgia schools. Large ones were often held away from the school in municipal auditoriums to accommodate larger audiences.

Students at Alexander No. 3 School participating in May Day activities are shown grouped around the traditional May Pole. The school was located in North Highlands, a suburb of Macon.

The interior of a classroom at Mathews School, Barrow County. Mrs. Doris Sheats, standing at left, taught the importance of good breakfasts to her first and second grade students. Note breakfasts on desks, furnace at rear of classroom, bookcases made from apple crates and musical instruments on top shelf made from gourds and horseshoes.

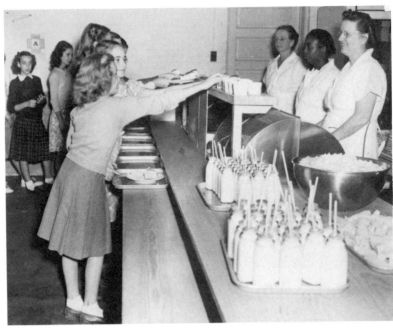

Columbus area students are shown passing through a food service line in an early lunchroom photo. Many such school lunch programs in Georgia schools were begun in the basements of existing school buildings.

Fair View Elementary School, Floyd County, replaced in the 1951-55 School Building program.

These four pages picture school buildings in Bartow County which were replaced by new buildings under the first State School Building Program from 1951 to 1955.

Pine Log, Stilesboro and Adairsville Elementary Schools were consolidated as Bartow Elementary School.

Pine Log

Stilesboro

Adairsville

Euharlee Elementary School

Cass Consolidated Elementary and High School

Peeples Valley and Smithville Elementary Schools, consolidated as Clover-leaf School.

Kingston Elementary School

Cartersville High School, in current use, built under the first State School Building Program.

An engraving of Gustavus John Orr, Georgia's second state school commissioner.

Sidney Lanier (1842-1881), Georgia's best-known poet. His popular poems, "The Marshes of Glynn" and "Song of the Chattahoochee," were often used by school children for rote memory exercises.

George Foster Peabody, a northern philanthropist and native Georgian. He established the Peabody Education Fund to further educational opportunities in the South and Southwest. He reportedly gave over $1 million to promote education in Georgia in his lifetime. He was later to serve as treasurer of the Democratic National Committee.

Joel Chandler Harris (1848-1908). Georgia journalist and author. His Uncle Remus tales of Br'er Rabbit and Br'er Fox are still read and loved by school children all over the world.

Offices of the Georgia Department of Education, including the office of the State Superintendent of Schools. State government administration building constructed in 1939 under the administration of Governor E. D. Rivers.

CHAPTER II

The Development of Public Education, 1868-1904

Public education in Georgia was the outgrowth of a movement which was well advanced at the beginning of the Civil War, although Georgia had been slower than many states to inaugurate public schools because of the predominance of agricultural traditions and the relative isolation of its people. Also, the state's leading religious denominations had placed little emphasis on an educated ministry; therefore, unlike in New England, little effective clerical influence was brought to bear on educational development. Georgians who were in political control before the war were largely products of private schools and, as conservative property owners, they were reluctant to support the idea of tax levies for education.[1]

The period of Reconstruction produced one new and highly significant element in the public school movement. This was the need to educate children of former slaves who were now citizens, a task which could be accomplished only at public expense. This, together with the fact that the state was impoverished and saddled with new economic and social problems, created difficulties in resumption of the pre-war public school movement.

Despite its earlier beginnings, it has been customary to date the Georgia system of public education from the Constitution of 1868. The convention which wrote this document assembled in Atlanta in December 1867. While often referred to as the Negro-Carpetbag Convention, its membership of 189 delegates comprised largely native white men who were collaborating with the reconstructionists. These native whites were called "scalawags" by conservatives who were largely banned from office, only 12 being members of the convention. Of the remaining white delegates, many had come to Georgia from other states, and four had been born in foreign countries. Only about 10 members were from northern states and were true carpetbaggers.[2] However, these men—called radicals by the Democrats—were aligned with the Republican Party, and they

69

provided the leadership of the convention. The political character of this convention was one of the principal reasons why the system of public education they inaugurated was slow to win acceptance by those who later were to control the destinies of the state.

Four months prior to this convention, 25 educators from various colleges and private schools met in Atlanta and organized the Georgia Teachers Association to promote better education in the state. Many of the leaders in the August 1867, action had previously been active in the short-lived Georgia Education Society, which had been created in 1823 by the Presbyterians.[3] (The association changed its name in 1900 to the Georgia Educational Association, and again in 1922 to the Georgia Education Association.)

Georgia was culturally, economically and socially devastated at the time the state's leading educators were organizing a teachers' association. Not only had the war destroyed its resources and freed its slaves, but a new generation of illiterates was growing up throughout the South. Funds appropriated for the schools were being used to pay other state expenses, the state was under military law and public confidence in the future of education was badly shaken.

The leadership in the Georgia Teachers Association sought the assistance of a noted philanthropist, George Peabody, in making a study of educational needs in the state. Dr. Barnos Sears of the Peabody Foundation attended several meetings of the association in the late 1860s. When George Peabody granted money in 1867 for a study of the state's educational needs, the Georgia Teachers Association formed a committee to work with the George Peabody Fund trustees to develop a state system of public schools.[4]

The Constitution of 1868 was developed shortly after the committee began its work. Article VI of this constitution, entitled Education, provided three sections to (1) establish a thorough system of general education to be free to all children of the state to be paid from taxation or otherwise, (2) provide for the appointment by the governor of a state school commissioner, and (3) authorize for education purposes all taxes levied on shows, malt and spirituous liquors, a poll tax and proceeds from the commutation of military services. The act stated further that if these funds were not sufficient, the legislature could tax property for schools.[5] All educational funds then belonging to the state were placed in the school budget except the endowment and debt due the University of Georgia. The constitution stated that the General Assembly at its first session after the adoption of that document "shall provide a thorough system of General Education to be forever free to all children of the State, the expense of which shall be provided for by taxation or otherwise." [6] Thus, the Constitution of 1868 provided a basis for enactment of substantial statutes pertaining to education.

No general school law was enacted when the legislature met in a called session on July 4, 1868, more than two months after the adoption of the constitution. It did appropriate $44,000 to those schools and colleges which had been authorized in 1866 to enroll maimed and indigent veterans of the Civil War. The sum was to be applied only to past due payments to these institutions, for they were notified to accept no additional veterans. One year later the veteran aid bill was repealed.[7]

As previously noted, a group of educational leaders known as the Georgia Teachers Association had formed a committee to frame a recommendation on the public school law to present to the legislature. This committee was composed of Gustavus J. Orr and Bernard Mallon of Atlanta; Martin V. Calvin, Augusta; David W. Lewis, Dahlonega; and J. M. Bonnell, Macon. Each member of this committee studied the problem independently and concluded with remarkably similar ideas, all of which embodied a combination of state and local support.[8]

Before the legislature officially assembled, federal military authorities purged some of the Democratic members, and radicals were seated in their place. Because of this situation, the committee decided not to submit the program to the legislature at this time; the members believed that even if the program were adopted under existing circumstances, it would be clothed in such disrepute as to be unacceptable to the general public. However, as the legislative session advanced, enactment of some kind of school law could be predicted, for Bullock and his followers were anxious to win Negro support by offering them free schools.[9]

The program the Georgia Teachers Association had approved was belatedly submitted to the education committee of the General Assembly of 1870, and the association proposed that it be redrafted into law. In retrospect, many believe the law's most glaring omission was the failure to grant to county boards of education definite authority to levy school taxes to supplement the state fund. Such a provision would have eliminated the necessity of maintaining private schools to fill the void above the level of primary education.[10]

The 1870 law did confer power on local boards to levy taxes for school houses and "school conveniences," but not for general purposes.[11] Some doubted the constitutional power of the General Assembly even to delegate such limited taxing powers to county and municipal authorities, excepting those local systems already in operation before 1868. (However, this power was sustained in a decision of the Georgia Supreme Court late in 1873.)

The First Legislation

The association's bill, containing the committee's recommendations, was enacted on October 13, 1870, becoming the first comprehensive school legislation under the new constitution—"An Act to Establish a System of Public Instruction."

On that same day Rufus Bullock carried out one provision of the act by appointing the first state school commissioner, John R. Lewis. He was a native of Pennsylvania and an erstwhile dentist who had risen to the rank of colonel in the Union army. Later he was an official of the Freedmen's Bureau in Georgia, where he came to the attention of radical politicians.[12]

His carpetbagger background was a liability both to his own effectiveness as a state official and to the cause of public education which he represented. People looked upon the common school system as "a badge of our subjection to another portion of the Union." [13] The superintendent was hampered further by having a staff consisting of only one clerk employed for 10 months.

At best, Lewis faced a difficult task in seeking to turn the educational tide from the old field school with its enforced and thorough mastery of such subjects as Latin and Greek and its rigid drill and discipline designed as a stepping-stone to higher learning and the professions. Laboring under secret opposition and open distrust, with neither sufficient state money nor local units having power to levy local taxes, he also had to contend with the problem of clarifying certain ambiguities in the 1870 school law so it could be administered effectively.[14] This law did not clearly distinguish between the duties and prerogatives of the county board of trustees and the local trustees, particularly in the employment and dismissal of teachers. The commissioner believed that counties should not be called school districts, but that this term should refer to local sub-districts. The secretary of the county boards, he stated, should be termed county superintendent, and board members should be called commissioners.

Lewis found that in many counties there were no records of boundaries of militia districts, which were the legal units from which rural board members were elected and which provided the logical definition of a school sub-district. Such county records as did exist were incomplete and unreliable, he found, with some showing the same numbers for different districts. So basic was this problem to effective organization that Lewis recommended an entirely new system of numbering militia districts in the state.[15] He also was plagued with apathetic local officials. In some counties, the lack of interest was so great that many who were elected to county boards refused to serve, thus making it impossible to obtain a quorum at meetings.[16]

The law of 1870 provided for a State Board of Education, but the board lacked authority to accomplish its mission. Provisions of the law of 1870 included (1) powers and duties of the State Board of Education, (2) method of selecting textbooks and reference books, (3) duties of State School Commissioner, (4) apportionment of school funds based on census of school-age youth, (5) method of appeals to State Board of Education, (6) establishment of county board of education and sub-districts, (7) appointments of county school commissioners and definition of their duties, (8) authorization of powers of county boards of education, (9) issuance and classification of teachers' licenses, (10) instruction of white and colored youth in separate schools, (11) enumeration of school youth annually, (12) exemption of school property from taxation, (13) designation of school term as three months, (14) forfeiture of state funds for noncompliance with minimum term, (15) establishment of ambulatory and manual labor schools and (16) sources of taxation for schools.[17]

The legislation provided for a State Board of Education composed of the governor, the attorney general, the comptroller general, the secretary of state, and a state school commissioner who was appointed by the governor with the consent of the Senate. The commissioner's term of office ran concurrently with that of the governor. He was the state board's chief executive officer and was charged with general supervision of the public schools. His annual salary was fixed at $2,500.

Each county was to consist of a single school district under a county board of education. The latter was composed of one member elected from each militia district, plus one from each city ward and incorporated town which might be located within the county. After the first election, which was to be held in January 1871, each board was to have an organizational meeting and choose a president and a secretary, with the latter to serve as the county school commissioner. The county school commissioner was required to visit each school at least once a year and to collect data on all schools and colleges in his county, including non-public institutions.

At this organizational meeting, the boards were required to lay out and define a number of school sub-districts, each of which was to contain no less than 30 people "between ages 6 and 21" and to establish a school in each of these units.[18] The county boards were given complete control over the administration of schools within the limits of the general school laws. They had the duties of taking the annual school census of the county and of allocating the county's share of the state fund for the various schools. Also, they had the power to employ and dismiss teachers; to examine applicants; to prepare and administer examinations to them; to issue licenses of first, second and third grades (good for one, two or three years according to grade) and to prescribe rules.

The Act of 1870 did not provide for state centralization of licenses; that responsibility was assigned at the county level. Section 32 of Public Law number 53 was as follows.

> It shall be the duty of the County Commissioners to hold public examinations of all applicants for license to teach within their respective counties, and before their respective county board of education at each regular time of meeting of said board at the county-site. . . . If, from the ratio of correct answer and other evidences disclosed by examination, the applicant is found to possess knowledge which is sufficient . . . to successfully teach in a common school of the State, orthography, reading, writing, arithmetic, English grammar, and geography, and to govern such a school, said commissioners shall give to said applicant a license of the first, second, or third grade, according to the ratio of the correct answers. [19]

The state school commissioner was empowered to determine the grades necessary for each grade certificate. Three certificate grades were issued, each for a different length of time— Grade one, three years; Grade two, two years; and Grade three, one year.

The grading and licensing of teachers for the common schools, begun in 1871, continued for many years in a loose and haphazard fashion. As noted, the examinations were made up by the county school commissioners, who also graded the papers and issued licenses. The average grade of 70 on the examination was considered the minimum for licensing, although no grade under 50 on any special branch was acceptable.[20] If a teacher's service was badly needed and there were no qualified applicants, the examination might be impromptu and informal and great latitude could be exercised in issuing a license. The lowest acceptable grade entitled a person to a one-year certificate. Certificates of two and of three years were also issued, the latter representing a grade in excess of 90 percent. However, no candidate could receive more than a one-year license unless he or she acquired a year's teaching experience. All candidates were required to furnish evidence of good moral character, a factor which often carried as much weight as professional competence.[21]

Neither did the Act of 1870 establish requirements for teachers. On the contrary, the law of 1870 stated no educational background was necessary for teachers to be employed. The examinations were to assess knowledge sufficient to teach orthography, reading, writing, arithmetic, English grammar and geography—subjects which were thought to be necessary elements of the common school's curriculum. Very few of the early teachers had more than a common school education themselves.

The law of 1870 gave county school superintendents the responsibility of organizing county teachers' institutes. Lewis, in *Circular Number One*, had stated that the county school superintendent "shall organize as soon as practicable a County Teachers' Institute for the mutual benefit of the teachers and the elevation of the standard of teaching and general improvement of the condition of the Common Schools of his county." [22] No funds were available for institutes, however.

Lack of significant educational qualifications was not limited to teachers. To illustrate, the 1870 law authorized the county school commissioner to be elected by the members of the county board of education. The county voters elected the members of the county board of education. The next year, in 1871, the law was amended to provide that the grand jury of a county would appoint five freeholders to serve as the county board of education. These five board members elected from their number a president and a secretary, and the secretary served as the county school commissioner.[23] Thus, no real educational qualifications were stated. Likewise, none were stated for the state school commissioner; he was appointed by the governor. It was several decades after the founding of the public school system in 1870 before any attempt was made to prescribe qualifications for this important position.

With reference to the county's top education leader, Carl G. Renfroe said,

> Since the creation of this office, it has been subject to political influence. In a remarkable way the county superintendency has escaped the controls that developed and shaped the standards for the classroom teacher's certificate, as well as those of other administrative personnel including even the superintendents of the independent systems.
>
> This condition has been perhaps the weakest link in the chain of events that has raised Georgia from a state whose

educational needs were supplied largely by a group of wandering non-de-scripts, lightly termed 'pedagogues' in spite of their general lack of formal training, to a state which can hold up its head . . . qualifications for the county superintendent have lagged behind those of the classroom teacher and only in 1960 did they surpass those required for a beginning teacher in the elementary school. [24]

On January 15, 1871, the State Board of Education approved the content of *Circular Number One,* which was prepared for State Commissioner Lewis to send to all county school superintendents. The circular described responsibilities concerning examinations, issuing licenses and record keeping.

County school superintendents were instructed to hold public examinations at each regular meeting of the county board of all applicants for license to teach in that county. Also, they could hold examinations at adjourned or special meetings of the county board. Commissioner Lewis instructed the county school superintendent always to invite one or more education persons to assist in these examinations.

County superintendents were responsible for writing examinations, administering examinations, grading the tests, determining the grade of license to be issued, issuing the license and keeping records on all their actions on licensure. Also, they were instructed to enter in a book the names of all applicants for examination, their race or color, age, residence, date of examination and grade of certificate issued.

The Act of 1870 provided also for revocation of county licenses by the county school superintendent. Revocation of certificates was to be for incompetency, immorality, cruelty or general neglect of the business of the school. The county school superintendent was required to visit teachers in the schools to determine competency.

Each county school superintendent was instructed to report annually to Commissioner Lewis on the names of all persons licensed, giving their color, age, residence and grade of certificate, plus the number examined to whom no license was granted and the names of persons whose licenses had been revoked. In addition to these annual reports, provision was made for more frequent reports, if needed.

Lewis reported in the *First Annual Report* that a total of 1,325 males and 438 females had sought licenses. One hundred and eight males were rejected and 26 females were rejected.

The number of county licenses issued was as follows:

Grade one   (license good for three years) .. 466
Grade two   (license good for two years) 291
Grade three (license good for one year) ... 863

Total ....1,620 [25]

Lewis' instructions for the examination of teachers were as follows.

INSTRUCTIONS FOR THE EXAMINATION OF TEACHERS

Every precaution should be taken to make the examinations fair and just, and to prevent any candidate receiving, through dishonest means, a certificate which he does not strictly deserve. To this end the following instructions will be observed:

1. Candidates will be notified, as soon as practicable after their application, of the place and time the examination will be held.

2. A new set of questions will be prepared, under the direction of the County School Commissioner, for each examination, and ten or more questions will be given in each study.

3. Examine all of the candidates at one time, and upon one subject at a time—all being provided with pen, ink and paper.

4. State the questions distinctly, and require the answers to be written before the next question is proposed; or all the questions on the branch under examination may be printed and distributed to the candidates; or they may be written on the blackboard where all may see them.

5. Do not propose, write or distribute the questions on the second study until all the questions of the first set have been answered and collected, and so on to the last.

6. Allow no candidate to leave the room or communicate with any other person while the examination in any one branch is in progress.

7. In addition to the written examination, each candidate should be required to answer orally such other questions as may be necessary to accurately determine the grade of certificate to which he is entitled.

8. Mark each answer on the scale of 10, according to its worth. Those entirely incorrect mark 0; those perfect mark 10, and to all others give an intermediate value, according to the merits of each. The sum of the marks thus given to ten answers in one branch will be the grade required in the scale of 100, or one-half the sum of the marks thus given to twenty answers and proportionately of any other number of answers.

9. The special average of each candidate in each branch, and his general average in all, will be thus determined.

10. No candidate will be granted a certificate whose special average in any one branch specified in the law is less than 50, or whose general average is less than 70.

11. No candidate will be granted a certificate for more than one year whose special average in any one branch is less than 70; whose general average is less than 90; or who has had less than one year's experience in teaching.

12. Certificates for three years will only be granted to experienced teachers, whose special average in each branch shall exceed 90.

13. All candidates will be required to furnish testimonials from School Trustees, or other responsible persons, as to their moral character and experience in teaching.

14. Candidates will be examined and granted such credit as they merit, in the following additional studies and special qualifications, if they desire and so state in their application, viz: United States History, Algebra, Geometry, Physiology, Natural Philosophy, Chemistry, Bookkeeping, Music, Drawing, Gymnastics, Elocution, School Law of Georgia, Theory and Practice of Teaching.

15. County School Commissioners will bear in mind, in preparing the questions, that the object of the examination is simply to ascertain if the candidate is qualified to successfuly teach a common school.

J. R. Lewis
State School Commissioner [26]

In addition to providing for a county school board, the school law of 1870 required voters in each sub-district to elect three local trustees with staggered terms of three years. It set forth their duty "to take control of its local interest and affairs," to employ teachers, to certify the amounts due them by the county board, and to report teachers to them for dismissal. They were required to visit the school twice during each term and to examine students for their progress and proficiency "in collaboration with a person competent to make such an examination." They also were charged with the duty of supplying fuel, leasing, constructing or repairing school houses, the cost for which was to be determined by the county board. Exempted from state and county tax levies were all houses and other property used for schools, including land not in excess of four acres.[27]

The 1870 law levied no local taxes on property for school revenue, relying on tax sources specifically embraced in the constitution. It did make provisions for endowments and gifts, and it added to the school fund one-half the net earnings of the state-owned Western and Atlantic Railroad.[28] Cities and towns could levy taxes for schools, but counties could not do so without special legislation. A few populous counties that enjoyed able leadership convinced the legislature that they could support their own schools and secured the legal authority to levy school taxes. Chatham, Bibb, Richmond and Glynn Counties provide outstanding examples of counties where this local option worked.

Lewis was a far abler man than his record in office implies. When he accepted the position he was unaware of the actual financial situation concerning funding of the public school system. He stated in a circular to newspapers his estimate that the school fund for the year would amount to $450,000 and that it would be available for distribution in the fall of 1871.[29] He estimated there were 400,000 children of school age, probably only half of whom would attend school. County boards might expect, therefore, to expend two dollars for each child who attended. Finally, he stated that teachers might be employed for $33.33 monthly for three months based on an average attendance of 40 to 60 pupils. He suggested that a local tax be levied to supplement the state fund or perhaps collected by subscription for use by patrons of white schools who wished to extend the length of the school term.[30]

The amount available for schools in 1871, however, was only $185,000. Of this amount, $10,000 was utilized for the payment of office expenses of the state school commissioner, leaving only $175,000 for the actual operation of the schools.[31] The discrepancy between Lewis' figures and what proved to be actually available was the result neither of poor accounting by Lewis nor of over optimism. Rather, it is a story of corruption and fraud which became part of almost every phase of Governor Bullock's administration.

The General Assembly, dominated by Bullock's followers, had enacted a law in July 1871, which bore the elusive title of "An Act to set apart and secure the School Fund." This law was enacted some three months before the passage of the first school law, and its intentions may have been part of a well conceived plan to defraud the state. The law enabled the governor to withdraw the school funds from the treasury and place in their stead seven percent state bonds which could be sold only to meet appropriations for school purposes. Instead of securing the school fund, as the law stated, the procedure made it possible for these funds to be stolen or diverted to other uses. The bonds placed in the treasury in place of the withdrawn funds were illegally issued by the governor. The state treasurer, Dr. N. L. Angier, was not required to sign the bonds as law and practice require in such cases; however, his signature was lithographed on each bond by the printer. Angier, an honest and conscientious public official, later stated that Bullock had tried unsuccessfully to sell the bonds in the national markets before pawning them off on the treasury and on the new department of education.[32] Thus the public school system began in utter chaos and failure.

In addition to the financial dilemma, counties were experiencing organizational difficulties. August 1871 was the official date for the beginning of the new system, and few counties managed to begin operations.[33] However, at the end of the year some counties still had not organized according to law. Records show that no school commissioner had been named for the counties of Camden, Dougherty, Lee and Towns. There was a total of 25 county board members and 208 district trustees yet to be named. Of the 1,291 sub-districts in 1871, all were militia districts except 162, of which incorporated towns accounted for 134 and city wards accounted for the remaining 28. School board elections had been held in only 959 of the sub-districts by the end of November.[34]

During 1871 a total of only 49,570 pupils enrolled in the public schools, of whom a mere 6,664 were blacks. County administrators had been told to assure teachers that their salaries would be paid despite appropriation to other purposes of nearly $330,000 of the school fund.[35] More than 1,100 teachers had been employed who, together with other innocent persons, were deceived and defrauded. In a few counties the salaries promised teachers were paid by patrons. In others the claims of teachers were discounted and bought up for trifling sums. Although about half the debt was paid in 1873, the state made no serious attempt to provide for full payment until 1874. Even then it was not until the following year—more than four years after the services of the teachers were rendered—that money became available. It was not until 1878 that all claimants were paid in the counties of Stewart, Chattahoochee, Randolph, Butts, Union, Gilmer and Whitfield.[36]

Since J. R. Lewis was state school commissioner for little more than a year, he had little time to work toward improving qualifications of teachers. Also, there were problems with legislative funds available to operate schools. Although identified with the carpetbag administration, Lewis had some keen insights into early educational needs.

In November 1871, a new General Assembly met which had a Democratic majority. Soon after this legislature assembled and demonstrated its violent opposition to the reconstructionists, Governor Bullock resigned and left the state. While State Commissioner Lewis attempted to hold on to his office despite public opposition to him, pressure for his resignation mounted. He followed Bullock into retirement early in January and departed for the North. He returned to Georgia a few years later, as did Bullock, and in 1890 he was appointed postmaster at Atlanta.[37]

The Orr Administration

Bullock's successor, Gov. James M. Smith, on January 16, 1872, appointed Dr. Gustavus James Orr as the second state school commissioner. Orr's appointment was peculiarly wise and appropriate. Educated in the old classical tradition, he became a professor of mathematics at Emory College in 1849. After the war he was president for a time of the Southern Masonic Female College at Covington. At the time of his appointment by Governor Smith, he held the chair of mathematics at Oglethorpe University.

Orr had not held a public office except that of superintendent at Oxford, yet when he had tried to vote in the election of 1867, under the "ironclad oath" which disqualified the old Southern political leadership, he was refused this privilege. Federal authorities based this refusal on the fact that he had served on the commission to run the boundary line between Georgia and Florida in the winter of 1859-60.[38]

The new commissioner was recognized as outstanding in education and had already served for 28 years in the field. He had been a leader in organizing the Georgia Teachers Association, had drafted early education legislation and was on the committee of the Georgia Teachers Association which essentially developed the School Law of 1870.

Orr was responsible for eliminating some of the flaws in the bill related to financing schools. In his report of January 1873, to the General Assembly, Orr began, "There were no public schools in operation under the general school laws of the State in the year 1872." [39]

Orr was very concerned about the education and instructional performance of teachers. However, he was unable to accomplish any significant change in the qualifications of teachers due to financial constraints. Orr believed that the principal support of the public school system should come from local taxes levied by voluntary action of the people. He advocated a relatively small state fund and a large, supplementary amount raised locally.[40]

Orr's background and his political credentials were exactly opposite those of his predecessor. Despite his complete identification with the old conservative leaderships, Orr was an ardent advocate of the public school system which he was called upon to administer. His greatest problem was to win for this system the support and approval of the people. In pursuing this objective, he became one of the earliest advocates on record of the revisionist school of Reconstruction history. Departing radically from the prevailing temper of his class, he maintained that the Constitution of 1868, while forced on the people and not voluntarily adopted, had many peculiarly wise features. The convention which framed that document, he maintained, "was a remarkable body." Among its leaders, he claimed, "were men of wisdom, virtue, patriotism and conservative outlook," and to these the state owed a debt not yet realized. The law of July 1870, which resulted in diverting school funds to other uses, he admitted was "reprehensible in its immediate intent and purpose," but it did provide that bonds be issued to secure money thus diverted. He did not believe that future governors would be dishonest enough to issue spurious bonds as Bullock had done, and he obtained Governor Smith's promise that legal bonds would be issued in their place.[41]

Orr's task was even more formidable than Lewis' had been. Recognizing an inherited debt of some $300,000, he was determined to avoid the errors of his predecessor. He forthwith notified school officials in the counties not to organize schools for the year 1872 but to encourage the use of whatever private schools that were available to them. He then set himself to the task of unsnarling the acute financial situation and of obtaining passage of a more adequate school law.[42]

While the Bullock administration had attempted to make great political gain out of the radicals' zeal for free education benefiting the Negro, Orr displayed a genuine personal concern for fair and equitable treatment of black children. This was one of the more far-reaching and progressive qualities of his character and his leadership.[43]

However, Orr was not the only leader shaping post-Civil War education in Georgia. Included as key figures in the state's development in education were Martin Calvin, principal, Houghton Institute, Augusta; Bernard Mallon, superintendent of Atlanta City Schools; John Bonnell, president of Wesleyan College; David Lewis, president of North Georgia College; H. H. Tucker, president of Mercer University; Leroy Broun, University of Georgia; and Alexander Means, president of Oxford College.[44]

The origin of the common school in Reconstruction politics made it highly suspect. It was often called a Yankee school by conservative white men who had regained control over the state's affairs. Many were wondering if the Negro child should be taught at all and, if so, they believed that his subjects should be confined to vocational and manual skills to the exclusion of literary subjects.[45] Under the Freedmen's Bureau, which had lasted five years following the war, the federal government had spent approximately $6 million in staffing some 2500 Negro schools in the South and introducing to 150,000 black children the rudiments of traditional education. Imbued with a passion for northern idealism, bureau officials ignored local culture and traditions in their attempt to remake the South into the Yankee mold. This caused aloofness and some hatred on the part of the old ruling order whose representatives were once again in power. Yet their cooperation was essential for the implementation of the common school law.[46]

Obviously, no education official in Georgia ever faced a more difficult problem of public relations than Gustavus J. Orr. The emancipation of the slaves had almost doubled the number of children to be educated. At the same time, the state's ability to provide for their needs was much less than half of what it had been before the war when 45 percent of its taxable property was in slaves. This situation led to a common assertion that only those taxes paid directly by Negro citizens should be used for the support of their schools. If adopted, such a policy would have virtually eliminated the black child from the common schools. Orr countered this argument by stating his belief that Negro citizens already were paying indirectly nearly all of what the state was contributing to the education of their children. The sources of school revenue, he claimed, were selected in such a manner as to place all taxes which Negroes paid into the school fund. In order to determine the amount of direct taxes paid by Negro citizens, the legislature enacted a law in February 1874, requiring county officials to make separate tax returns for Negroes and whites and to require the comptroller general to exhibit them separately in his reports.[47]

While Orr was always careful not to antagonize the public or to offend members of the legislature, he took the position that the Negro child had a moral as well as the legal right to free education along with white children. "The white and colored races are so dissolubly linked together," he wrote, "that they are destined . . . to be common occupants of our territory. . . . It is certainly (to) the highest interest of both races that reasonable means be used for their elevation and improvement." He believed that guidance and intelligent leadership on the part of responsible white men were needed to make the situation tolerable. "I am in favor of affording them a fair field for self-development, that they may have the opportunity of exhibiting to the world . . . what they can accomplish," he concluded.[48]

The poor quality of teachers also was a continuing problem for Orr. In his *Annual Report of 1875* to the legislature, the commissioner wrote,

> . . . A considerable number of these (white teachers), however, it must be admitted, are incompetent for the work they have undertaken. Nevertheless, in view of the smallness of our state school fund, and the general condition of the people, I cannot recommend the expenditure of money at present for their improvement, either by the establishment of the Teacher's Institutes, or normal schools, or in colleges of the state. We must, for the present, trust for our supply to such young men and young ladies coming out annually from the University, and from our colleges and high schools, as may voluntarily adopt the teacher's profession.
>
> . . . The number of colored men and women capable of teaching is very small—so small as to interfere seriously in many places with the chance of establishing colored schools. . . . If we mean seriously to seek the elevation of the colored race, we must take steps which will at least

gradually insure a supply of teachers from their own ranks.[49]

Orr recommended in this same report establishing and supporting a school for thoroughly preparing colored youth for becoming teachers in the colored schools of the state. However, it was to be after the term of several other state school commissioners before this recommendation came to pass.

Throughout Orr's tenure in office of nearly 16 years, he never relinquished his firm conviction that the black child should have his full share of educational opportunities. While he adhered strictly to the doctrine of separate schools, he believed that it was wise to employ white teachers to instruct Negro children, and a few such schools were established.[50]

Orr's successors in office throughout the remainder of the century all showed a genuine interest in upgrading Negro schools and particularly in improving the quality of their instruction. However, Negro schools taught by white teachers never gained popular acceptance. "If the colored children . . . could have had white teachers or teachers . . . capable of instructing them properly, their condition today would be altogether different," wrote State Commissioner Gustavus R. Glenn in 1899.[51]

An effort to provide more competent Negro teachers was attempted in 1874, when the General Assembly appropriated $8,000 annually to Atlanta University. In return, this institution agreed to admit free of tuition as many black students as there were members of the lower house of the legislature.[52] Since Atlanta University was a sectarian institution and in no way responsible to state authority, Orr stated his belief that the appropriation was unconstitutional. He asked that this money be devoted to a normal school for Negroes, which he believed would prepare four times as many teachers. Atlanta University was committed to the ancient classics, mathematics and science; therefore, Orr did not believe that the attainments of its students could be turned to practical account in the common school systems. What teachers needed most, he said, was thorough instruction in the elements of an English education. He expressed a fear that students from this Negro university who went into rural areas to teach might cause serious trouble and bring public sentiment to bear against the operation of Negro schools. He mentioned "certain social usages which are repugnant to the feelings and tastes of our people." While refraining from condemning the custom of Atlanta University's white teachers and Negro students participating freely in all aspects of social life at that institution, he cited this practice as an example of what he believed it was necessary to avoid.[53]

In another facet of education, Orr was progressive in promoting vocational education. When he became commissioner, the struggle for the establishment of vocational education in the schools of Georgia was continuing after authorization of Manual Labor Schools. Vocational courses were offered primarily in privately supported academies or denominational schools, and leaders who developed these beginning programs of vocational education were interested in educating pupils for everyday living or fitting youth for honorable service to mankind.

A quotation from the *Third Report of the State School Commissioner* submitted to the General Assembly of the State of Georgia in 1874 reveals Orr's interest in vocational education and his effort to provide programs of vocational education.

> In 1870 the Commissioner of Education at Washington prepared a circular containing a number of questions, one object of which was to ascertain the opinion of experienced men upon the productiveness of labor. Three thousand copies of this circular were sent out, North, South, East, and West to men employing large numbers of laborers in agricultural, mining and other various branches of manufactures. The results of the investigation, as a whole, furnished proof as decisive as testimony can well make it, that the educated laborer is a much more efficient producer than the ignorant one . . .
>
> Our State cannot afford to stand still while others are moving forward in the march of progress inaugurated by the great educational awakening now prevailing almost everywhere both at home and abroad.[54]

From a financial view, the future of public education was cloudy. The legislature, in 1871 and again in the 1872-73 session, failed to enact a general local tax law, although by exceedingly small margins.[55] Undaunted, friends of the law proposed a new local tax bill in 1874. It would limit the local tax to 10 cents on each $100 of assessed property. Despite these conservative features, the bill was again rejected. Now the only feasible method by which a county could supplement its public school fund appeared to be through subscription and tuition fees.[56] Thus the matter remained until the Constitution of 1877 was ratified.

The major portion of the schools' state funds during the 1870s came from rental paid by the state-owned Western and Atlantic Railroad. In 1878, the legislature added the liquor tax revenues to the state school fund. For the most part, the funds appropriated for school purposes were handled in an irresponsible manner, and many communities were unable to open their schools.[57]

When Georgia adopted a new state constitution in 1877, it limited public education to the elementary levels. The common schools could teach only basic courses such as reading, writing, arithmetic, grammar and spelling. Rental monies from the Western and Atlantic Railroad portion of the public school support plan specifically were prohibited from use for teaching courses beyond the elementary level. Most secondary schools in the state were privately or municipally owned, and the new laws protected the owners in their monopoly of secondary education.[58]

Private schools were permitted to collect from the public fund after complying with all the procedures required by law. Throughout the remainder of the century, public and private schools were barely distinguishable in many sections of the state. All who drew public funds were required, among other things, to make a full report of their pupils, showing the average daily attendance upon which the teacher's public stipend was based. Provisions were made for ambulatory schools where there were three contiguous districts, each having a low population density. Since the law anticipated a six-months term, a school was to be maintained in each district for two months annually. Also, the law clearly provided that Negro children should have the same facilities as white children, but they should be taught in separate schools.[59]

Training and Licensing of Teachers

In 1882 Orr reported on the qualifications of Georgia's teachers. He wrote,

> The 243,000 children who were in our schools last year were taught by 6,128 teachers. Three hundred and seventy-one of these teachers were teachers in cities and counties under local laws. A few hundred of them were college graduates. I think it might be safely assumed that five thousand of these teachers were persons of limited education. . . . The Constitution says there shall be a 'thorough system of common schools, and there cannot be a thorough system without thoroughly prepared teachers, and these, in turn, cannot be had without the Normal School.[61]

Another statement which stressed the importance of the normal school was as follows.

> Of two teachers, having the same gifts, and of like attainments, one of whom has received, in addition, professional training, and the other has not, the former will do twofold more efficient work. This is conceded all over the world where Normal School instruction has been tested.[62]

The specialized training of teachers for their role in the classroom goes back to eighteenth century New England, the seedbed of public education in America. Called normal schools, there were only 12 in the entire country before the Civil War, but numerous colleges had inaugurated special courses for teachers.[63] Georgia's first attempt to establish a normal school occurred in 1879, when both houses of the legislature agreed to an annual appropriation of $6,000 if the Peabody Normal College were removed to Georgia from Nashville. However, no agreement was reached with the Peabody trustees on the new location.[64]

Although Orr believed in professional preparation and worked with the legislature in the 1880s to establish both institutes and normal schools, he believed it took little more than a common school education to have the knowledge necessary to teach in the common school. This fact is borne out by the following statement of Orr's.

Really, it is necessary for one to spend so much time and money in preparing himself to teach in which nothing more is taught than 'the elementary branches of an English education.' Are not the means expended disproportionate to the end? A person who teaches a common school ought to be taught in branches, to a certain extent, beyond the curriculum of such a school. Is it by no means necessary, however, for him to pass entirely through a college curriculum.[65]

In 1886 Orr stated,

Twelve or eighteen months bestowed upon one previously well taught in a country school would fit him very well for entering upon his life-work as a country school teacher. The instruction given in such a normal school should be, in the main, professional.[66]

Even though the legislature failed to supply funds for three institutes as Orr had requested in 1880, he applied to the General Agent of the Peabody Fund for means to conduct three institutes for teachers and received a grant of $2,000. With this sum he conducted three institutes in 1882, one in south Georgia, at Americus; one in middle Georgia, at Milledgeville; and one in north Georgia, at Toccoa. The three institutes were held simultaneously during the whole of the month of August. James H. Smart, former Indiana school superintendent and a professor with wide experience in conducting institutes, was selected as general superintendent. A total of 252 teachers attended (154 white and 98 black). Thirty county school superintendents also attended, and Commissioner Orr provided several days of instruction in the duties of their office.[67]

These institutes were the first successful efforts to improve the qualifications of teachers on a broad basis and to improve the work of the county superintendents.

What did these institutes for teachers try to do? Brief excerpts from the programs of these institutes follow.[68]

Institute at Americus

Director: W. H. Baker, Superintendent, Savannah
Associates: John M. Gannon, Savannah
John Neely, Americus
B. T. Hunter, Albany

... Daily instruction was given in arithmetic, English grammar, geography, reading and spelling. The instruction was not entirely of a technical and theoretical character, but it was the endeavor of each instructor to give it that direction which would make the same available in the practical work of the school room . . .

In the colored class, the work was of a very elementary character. These teachers, however, addressed themselves with great zeal to the performance of the duties required . . .

At the close of the session a written examination was had on each subject and the results of the same placed upon the certificate given to each teacher.

Dr. A. J. Battle and Professor J. E. Willett of Mercer University and Honorable J. H. Smart gave lectures during the institute.

Institute at Milledgeville

Director: B. M. Zettler, Superintendent
Associates: Benjamin Neely, Superintendent, Augusta
Rev. J. T. McLaughlin, Talbotton
Professor W. Bonnell, Covington

... Such questions as the following were propounded and discussed.

1. How can regular attendance be secured?
2. How can good lessons be secured?
3. Ought prizes to be offered in school?
4. How long ought geography be studied in a daily session?
5. When should English be taken up?
6. How can reading be taught when each child in the class has a different reading book?
7. Should pupils be kept after school?
8. What is the best form of report to send to parents?

Each of the subjects was also taught, with arithmetic assigned to Neely, reading and spelling assigned to McLaughlin, English grammar and composition assigned to Bonnell, and geography and penmanship assigned to Zettler.

Honorable J. H. Smart and Rev. Mr. Stoney of Milledgeville delivered lectures in the evening.

Institute at Toccoa

Director: H. C. Mitchell, Superintendent
Associates: Professor S. P. Sanford, Mercer University
Miss Laura Haygood, Toccoa Girls' High School
Mrs. T. C. Mallon, Atlanta

. . . This institute also included a series of scientific lectures by prominent educators and public men during the evenings. Among the lecturers were Dr. H. H. Tucker, Judge Bleckley, Professor White of Athens, Dr. C. W. Lane of Athens, Col. Samuel Barnett, Professor Rufus Smith, Col. David W. Lewis, and Dr. J. H. Smart.

In addition to the three institutes, a few teachers benefitted from scholarships awarded by the Peabody Fund to attend the State Normal School at Nashville and at Atlanta University.

Although anticipating additional financial support from the Peabody Fund, Orr went back to the General Assembly in 1882, asking for authority to use annually, for institutes under the State Board of Education, $2,500 of the school fund, as much of it as might be necessary. The assembly failed to appropriate the funds requested in 1882; however, he continued to request funds for institutes and normal schools each time the General Assembly was in session. His only source for funds to improve the qualifications of teachers continued to be those from private sources.[69] However, the impact was being felt from the early institutes and one in Atlanta in August 1886, attended by almost 600 people and sponsored by the Peabody Fund.[70]

Commissioner Orr wrote letters and instructions to county superintendents regularly. He felt it important to have meetings with the superintendents, as indicated in his discussion with them in the 1882 institutes. To facilitate conduct of a full meeting with all superintendents, Orr succeeded in having the following resolution passed by the State Board.

> Resolved. That, in the opinion of this board, the County Boards of Education may encourage County School Commissioners to attend the Summer Peabody Institutes for the purpose of meeting with the State School Commissioner that he may examine into their mode of administering the school law, counsel with them, and instruct them in their official duties.
>
> Resolved. That in our opinion, the several County Boards may allow the County School Commissioners their regular per diem, for three or four days, for the purpose expressed in the foregoing resolution.[71]

This marked the first attempt to assemble all county superintendents for an in-service meeting.

Orr's term of office brought a significant change in licensure procedures. Throughout his service as state school commissioner, 1872-1887, the Act of 1870 governed licensure procedures. Beginning in January 1882, teachers evidencing the highest degree of scholarship received a first grade license which continued in force for three years. A license of the second grade was good for two years, and a third grade license expired after one year. A fourth grade license was issued for those who qualified in only a portion of the subjects covered on the license examination; it was good only for six months, and the holders were permitted to teach "in some particular sub-district in which children . . . made but little advancement."[72]

Orr had been concerned about the fact that each county school superintendent wrote his own examinations. He felt there should be the same quality of examination for all teachers over the state and that teachers should receive a state license which would qualify a person to teach in any county in the state. During Commissioner Orr's last year in office, a new school bill was passed. It was known as the Denny Law of 1887.[73]

Several sections of the Denny Act dealt with aspects of licensure. First, the procedure for selecting the county school commissioner changed. Until the Denny Act, the county school commissioners elected one of their members to be the county school superintendent. This new law required that a county board of five members be selected by the grand jury, except in those counties where other methods had been provided for in special legislation. In turn, the county board was required to select a commissioner of education who should be "ex-officio county superintendent of public schools" for a four-year term. The applicant might not be a member of the board, but he was required to be a citizen of the county. Before his election, the applicant was to be examined either by the president of the county board or someone appointed by him. The Denny Act required the applicants for county school commissioner to pass an examination on the subjects taught in the common schools, upon the science and theory of common school teaching and government and upon such other subjects as the state school commissioner should deem proper.[74] The examination was prepared by the state school commissioner. Passing the examination satisfactorily, having good moral character and business qualifications and giving bond with good security were necessary for his election by the county board of education.

The Denny Act continued the procedure of having the county school commissioner examine all applicants for license to teach. The date, or dates, for the examination were set by the state school commissioner; the examination was held throughout the state on the same day. The state school commissioner was required to prepare for and supply to the county school commissioners the questions for examinations and the printed instructions as to grading applicants; also the county school commissioners graded the applicants according to instructions furnished them by the state school commissioner. Each applicant submitted in writing with his examination paper satisfactory evidence of good moral character. This procedure was an attempt to equalize to a greater degree the qualifications of teachers. The county board of education granted the appropriate license; first, second, and third grade licenses continued to be the grades.

Another new practice made possible by the act was that licenses also could be issued by the state school commissioner. He issued a state license which was both permanent and valid in any county of the state and which only he could revoke. The county school commissioner sent the state commissioner for his review the examination papers of those who seemed to have exhibited unusual merit. The state commissioner issued licenses to those whose papers in his opinion were of unusual merit.[75]

While licenses were being issued for teaching in the elementary schools, examinations were required on orthography, reading, writing, English grammar, geography, arithmetic and the science and practice of teaching in common schools; all of these were required subjects taught in the common schools.[76]

This revised code of 1887 attempted to make teachers' examinations uniform throughout the state by requiring that questions be made up in the state school commissioner's office and mailed out to the counties where examinations were held on fixed days.[77] However, the county commissioners continued to read and grade the papers. Except for those on arithmetic, all questions were largely subjective. The fourth grade license was eliminated, but provisions later were made for granting special emergency licenses.[78] A permit issued in one county was valid in any county after endorsement by the county's school commissioner. A permanent state license was also authorized. Any examinee's paper on which the grade was 95 or above might be sent to the state school commissioner together with other credentials, and that officer might issue a non-expiring state license. Such a license was issued only to those with at least five years of teaching experience.[79]

Administrative Beginnings

While the Constitution of 1868 prescribed a three-month school, it was a decade before this became a full reality. In rural districts in particular, the school term was considerably shorter than it was in the towns and cities, and holidays were unknown. The short term had liabilities on the teacher as well as on the pupil, the most significant of which was its failure to provide sufficient employment to justify devotion to the job. Therefore, it became customary in many communities to convert the school into a private facility on occasions, assessing tuition charges to cover the last few weeks of the term. A law designed to encourage this procedure was passed in 1881 creating long term schools. Under the general supervision of the county board, formal contracts could be made between the teacher and the patrons for tuition payments to carry the school beyond the limit fixed by the public contract.[80] Private elementary schools could easily obtain the benefits of the public fund. However, their teachers were required to be licensed by the state and to make certain reports to county school officials.[81]

By 1888 the public fund still barely provided for a term of three months. It was estimated that a statewide, four-months school could be provided for $840,000 plus an administrative cost of $28,000.[82] After 1890 the state fund was gradually increased, and with it came an increase in the average length of the school term. In 1897 it was slightly in excess of six months. By the end of the century the full nine-months term existed only in the larger communities having independent systems.[83]

The school term was fixed by the board in each county, and there was the widest variation in the dates on which sessions began and ended. In most instances the term embraced the period from July to September, at which time there was little farm work which children could perform. In Pierce County schools were permitted to run at any time between January 1 and December 15, thus making it possible for the same teacher to operate each of two schools, and sometimes three, in the same calendar year. The opening of one school might be delayed awaiting the availability of a teacher from another. Some schools began late in July in order to employ vacationing college students, a practice made less difficult in 1895 when the school year was made to coincide with the calendar year.[84]

Many ministers supplemented their income by teaching, and occasionally schools were suspended during August revivals. On these occasions, pupils might be marched to church to sit through long, midday sermons delivered by their teacher playing the role of revivalist. Rural physicians also frequently taught school while waiting for professional calls. Both of these professional groups had an unusually large representation among teachers. Of the 137 county school commissioners in 1892, approximately 12 percent were members of these two professions, and they were about equal in number.[85] It is significant to note that members of the medical profession owed their superior status to the specialized training which was usually required of them, and not to the above average incomes which they were to enjoy a century later.

While it is difficult to discover discrimination against black children in the highest echelons of public school administration during this period, its existence on the local level was quite apparent. Since nearly all teacher contracts were negotiated, county boards could employ Negro teachers at half the salary offered to white instructors, and women of both races commanded less pay than their male counterparts. Negroes tended to hold licenses of a low grade; this, also, was a factor in their lower salary scale. As late as 1901, only 12 percent of Negro teachers held a first grade license as compared to 88 percent of white teachers. At the end of the century, the average monthly salary of Negro teachers was less than $25. The range was $65 for a white male in Burke County to $10 for a Negro woman holding a third grade license in Berrien County.[86]

Of the 137 counties at the end of the century, only 16 appeared not to discriminate on salary payments to Negro teachers. These were Banks, Carroll, Catoosa, Cherokee, Lumpkin, Milton, Murray, Oconee, Paulding, Towns, and Union in the northern part of the state, and Appling, Charlton, Clay, Laurens, and Ware in the southern part. Towns and Union Counties each employed only one black instructor, and these two teachers held third grade licenses. Ware County paid all of its teachers $22.98 per month regardless of race, sex or license classification. Oconee County's salary schedule was unique in that it prescribed more for Negro teachers than for white teachers, probably because of the scarcity of competent Negro teachers. Burke, Clayton, Calhoun and Newton Counties paid Negroes holding a first grade license less than half the salary paid to whites holding a license of the same classification.

A typical salary schedule in 1900 was that of Baldwin County, which prescribed for white teachers a monthly salary of $35, $25 and $20 for holders of first, second, and third grade license, respectively. Negro teachers holding these licenses received $24, $20 and $18, respectively. This was for a term of 120 days of six months, making a total annual salary range of $210 to $108. The lowest salary schedule in 1900 was that of

Clayton County, where blacks holding a license of any grade were paid only $10 per month.[87] This amounted to 50 cents per day and was less than the amount that could be earned picking cotton.

While salary discrimination based on race appears to have existed in a majority of the counties, another principal reason for low salaries paid to black teachers was their low license classification. Few Negroes at this time could pass the examination for a teacher's license, and most of those who were able to do so received a license of the third grade. Many Negroes employed as teachers could barely read and write. J. B. Bond, the school commissioner of McIntosh County, found in 1899 that only one Negro applicant out of 15 was capable of passing a satisfactory examination for any kind of license. He advocated giving them a less rigid examination than that administered to white applicants.[88]

It is significant to note that Orr in his annual reports never provided statistical tables which emphasized the low qualification of Negro teachers. While all reports gave separate statistics for schools of the two races, it was not until the 1890s that significant comparisons could be drawn concerning white and black teachers. At the end of the century, 70 percent of black teachers held a license of only the third grade (21 held no license at all), while only 21 percent of the white teachers were in this category. Conversely, approximately half of all white teachers held a first grade license, compared to less than 14 percent of the black teachers. At this time, 41 percent of white teachers were men, while only 32.7 percent of all Negro teachers were male. There was a preponderance of men engaged in teaching in nearly all the counties of North Georgia. This situation was completely reversed in Middle and South Georgia, where women teachers predominated, although exceptions occurred in the counties of Bullock, Berrien, Clinch, Coffee, Echols and Emanuel.[89]

Some of Orr's reluctance to reveal the extremely low quality of Negro teachers and their schools undoubtedly stemmed from his desire to win public support for the system and to obtain for it adequate legislative funding. By an act approved in February 1873, the public school fund was to include all revenue from poll taxes, the taxes on shows and liquor, one-half the W. & A. rentals, "and such other money as now by law belongs to the school fund," plus other sums which the legislature might raise by direct tax or other methods. Revenues distributed by Commissioner Orr through 1876 totaled approximately $1.25 million dollars distributed as follows: on the school debt of 1871, $174,000; on the school fund for 1873, $250,000; for 1874, $265,000; and for 1875, $291,000, which was the approximate amount in the budget estimate for 1876. The average was slightly over $250,000 annually.[90]

Of the amount spent on the common schools for 1875, the largest amount was derived from the W. & A. rentals, amounting to $150,000. Slightly over $140,000 was received from poll taxes, which were retained in the counties where they were collected and turned over to local commissioners after certain deductions by local tax authorities.[91] The income from the tax on shows and exhibitions was negligible.

By 1883 a tax on liquor dealers had been added for schools, plus revenue was available from the net hire of convicts and net fees from fertilizer inspection as well as dividends on stock which the state held in the Georgia Railroad Company. The poll tax netted the largest single sum, $178,112.65. The rentals on the W. & A. Railroad remained at $150,000. Ranking third was revenue from fertilizer inspection fees, which amounted to $56,212.52. The liquor tax yielded $51,554.14 and the net hire of convicts added $18,173.24. Railroad stock dividends and the tax on shows each yielded less than $10,000. The total amount of the state fund for 1883 was $460,334.16, which was 90 cents per capita for the school population for that year.[92] In 1887, with the same sources of revenue, the total figure had increased to $489,000.

On the uppermost rungs of the educational ladder were less than a half dozen local tax systems already in existence when the Constitution of 1868 went into effect and which were left unchanged by that event. Savannah had enjoyed a long tradition of free schools, extending from its earliest colonial history. The nucleus of its modern system was a donation by Peter Massie in 1842. In 1854 Savannah teachers were placed on the city payroll and in December 1866, the system was extended to the entire county of Chatham. Throughout the Reconstruction era, however, the Chatham County school board operated schools only for white children, because the Freedmen's Bureau and certain philanthropic agencies that supported schools for Negro children were reluctant to relinquish their operations. In 1870 Chatham County had 3,600 white children enrolled in its public system, while approximately 1,300 were enrolled in private and parochial schools.[93]

Macon's public school system was established in 1859, but it did not begin to prosper until near the end of the Civil War, when it received a gift of $50,000 from Elam Alexander. The system was extended to Bibb County in 1872 through a program of countywide taxation.[94] A public school system was authorized for Columbus in December 1866. In the following year, the school opened in a church building on Second Avenue. However, this system was not merged with that of Muscogee County until 1950.[95]

The common school system of Richmond County might be said to have had its origin as early as 1821, when the Augusta Free School was founded, although it was not until 1872 that schools of Augusta and Richmond County were united under one board, thus creating Georgia's third countywide system under local taxation.[96] In the following year, the schools of Brunswick and those of Glynn County were transferred by legislative act to the county board of education. Atlanta, in January 1872, formally opened its city school system; the city provided local tax support for its schools and voted bonds for the construction of three school buildings.[97]

By 1875 Griffin had joined the list of local school systems. At that time a total of $142,727.63 was raised by school taxes in the seven systems operating under local laws, a sum almost half that of the state fund, which for 1876 was only $291,319. In the local tax schools, 15,715 pupils were enrolled, of whom 42 percent were blacks; in the common schools of the state, the enrollment was 179,405, of whom 32 percent were blacks.[98] The per capita expenditure for pupils in local systems was slightly above $9 annually, while in the common schools it was $1.62. All of the independent local systems had one or more high schools each except Richmond County, which relied upon private schools for higher instruction.[99] No high schools could be supported by the state fund, and parents living in rural areas and towns had to rely on numerous private schools for intermediate instruction of their children.[100]

In every measurable way, the local tax systems far outranked the common school system for which only the state was responsible. In the independent local systems, 70 of the 128 individual schools were graded, and all operated for nine months each year except those of Chatham County. Where the state fund was the sole source for educational funds, the allocation remained for many years insufficient for the operation of a school term of even three months.[101]

When the 1877 "Home Rule Constitution" replaced the Reconstruction document of 1868, the towns of West Point and Americus were in the process of joining the list of independent school systems. Special legislation in 1877 enabled West Point to organize a system somewhat typical of those created for other incorporated communities which organized local tax systems in the 30 years following. The municipality was empowered to levy a school tax on real and personal property not to exceed 75 cents on each $100 of property assessment. In addition, it might use license fees collected from liquor dealers, billiard table operators and sporting devices, and special taxes on shows, auctioneers, traders, insurance and sewing machine agents and salesmen.[102]

These independent local tax systems not only enjoyed local tax support, but they were entitled to draw their *pro rata* of the common school fund based on certain minimum requirements which they could meet without difficulty. Since common school fund allocations were geared to average daily attendance—which was considerably higher in the towns than in rural communities—they drew a relatively high share of the common school fund.[103]

Reacting from the corruption and extravagance of the Bullock era, the Constitution of 1877 is notable for the parsimony it manifested, not only in educational expenditures but in all other forms of public spending. It specifically limited state expenditures for education to the elementary branches of an English education only, and it precluded the use of any state money for instruction on the intermediate or high school level. However, it did not place such restrictions on the use of local school taxes.[104] Like its predecessor, this constitution preserved

intact all local systems already in existence, and it did not prohibit the creation of new local systems to be funded through
local taxes. However, the creation of additional local systems
was made extremely difficult, and most communities found it
impossible to do so. The procedure required approval of two-
thirds of the voters, which could be sought only after favorable
recommendations of two successive grand juries (or the corporate authority of a municipality). Also the constitutional
provision was not self-performing; in each case, the local unit
had to be granted legislative authority.[105]

Public school leaders actively sought passage of a local
option law which would enable each county and municipality
at any time to avail itself of constitutional provisions without
resort to special legislation.[106] State school commissioners of
this period—notably Orr, Glenn and Merritt—complained bit-
terly that the constitutional provisions virtually denied people
the right of local taxation for schools. Orr pointed out the inconsistency of those who wrote the constitution in providing
state support to two universities (one of which was for black
youth) and then prohibiting the people from taxing themselves
to provide instruction for their children above the elementary
grades. Glenn stated that each county should be required to
levy a local tax equal to what was received from the state,
and that each county should function as an effective educational unit as did Chatham, Richmond, Glynn and Bibb.[107]
He emphasized the difficulty under existing laws of obtaining
favorable recommendations by two successive grand juries.
He cited the fact that jurors all were conservative property
owners, most of whom had already educated their own children. Also, when the required recommendations were obtained,
it was next to impossible to get a favorable two-thirds vote of
the people. He blamed the latter on the inaccessibility of poll-
ing places to rural voters, ignorance, indifference and prejudice. Many objected to a local levy because so much of the
money would be used for the education of black children whose
parents owned no taxable property. It also was pointed out that
all voters who were absent from the polls for providential or
other reasons, as well as those who had died or who had moved
from the community (but whose names were still on the voting

lists) were automatically counted with those who actually voted their disapproval.[108]

Indeed it was the requirement of a two-thirds approval by voters which offered the greatest obstacle to the program. Between 1887 and 1892 inclusive, legislative approval for holding such elections was accorded 37 municipalities and counties, out of which number only 24 municipalities were able to meet the two-thirds vote requirement. Countywide systems were more difficult to create than municipal systems. (Even as late as 1918, with more liberal laws under which to operate, only Rabun County in the entire North Georgia region had succeeded in voting a countywide school tax.[109]

While the Constitution of 1877 limited to the elementary branches the educational services which the state or the county might provide, there was no such limitation placed on what a municipality or a local district might do through a program of local taxation.[110] The McMichael Law, therefore, provided some impetus to the development of public high schools, although its main purpose seems to have been the strengthening of rural schools by lengthening of the school term, improving school houses and creating more graded schools as well as high schools.

The high school of this period was usually called an intermediate school, because it stood between the common school and the college. The terms high school and college often were used interchangeably, and there was no general agreement on just what type of curriculum should be designed for those who pursued their education beyond the common school program. Before the Civil War, all intermediate instruction had been under the aegis of the county academy, which was supported, except in a few rare instances, by private tuition fees. There were perhaps 100 county academies in Georgia in 1860.[111] Instead of diminishing with the advent of the public school program, the number of private intermediate schools increased sharply, although they seem to diminish in quality. In 1885, a total of 150 county academies operated, employing a total of 321 teachers and enrolling 10,493 pupils, nearly all of whom were white. The only institution for blacks was Jackson Academy at Forsyth, with approximately 100 pupils.[112]

It is evident that the Georgia Common School System (common to all children of all races) was far from achieving uniformity throughout the state. Many schools were supported solely from the state fund, while others had this fund supplemented by local taxes or tuition and sometimes by both. Other schools might be essentially private ones which transformed themselves into public schools in order to offer a longer term than they might have otherwise. Finally, the general school law was subject to numerous amendments recognizing special conditions in certain counties and granting special privileges to them. One of these occurred in 1872, when 47 counties were placed in a special category regarding school organization and administration. At State Commissioner Orr's insistence upon more complete unity, this provision was repealed after two years.[113]

In 1877 a law relieved the county school commissioners in seven counties of southeast Georgia (Ware, Echols, Lowndes, Berrien, Charlton, Dodge and Clinch) of the duty of visiting and inspecting their schools; it delegated this responsibility to a group of appointed "competent persons" in each subdistrict. Each of the seven commissioners also was to receive as their compensation a flat fee of two and a half percent of the county school fund disbursed by them.[114] Haralson County, for 13 years following 1872, enjoyed the benefit of a special law providing that school commissioners be elected from each militia district and their jurisdiction extended to give them control over all the county's finances, its roads, bridges and public buildings.[115] In 1877 the section on ambulatory schools was changed to permit three counties (Wayne, Miller and Pierce) to qualify for these schools with a minimum of only 10 students instead of 15 as the original law provided.[116]

Independent or local tax school systems were subjected to an even greater number of special laws than were the common schools. Each one had come into existence by a separate enabling act, and each one tended to differ from the others either in organizational structure or in the local tax base. Only a limited number of general laws applied to all of them equally, and typical of these was a law in 1881 authorizing city boards to require smallpox vaccinations of pupils as a prerequisite to school admission.[117]

The number of local tax systems was growing. By 1892, expansion from the nine systems in existence 15 years previously had resulted in the following additional municipal systems: Athens, Carrollton, Cartersville, Cedartown, Covington, Dalton, Dallas, Dawson, Eatonton, Fort Valley, Gainesville, Hawkinsville, Lumpkin, Marietta, Marshallville, Montezuma, Newnan, Perry, Richland, Rome, Sandersville, Tallapoosa, Toccoa and Waycross.[118] Many of these had been compelled to offer highly conservative tax programs to obtain voter approval. For example, Sandersville used license fees on barrooms together with interest and dividends from the city's previous investment in the Sandersville and Tennille Railroad.[119] Cartersville was able to succeed by including in the enabling act a provision for a second election. Carrollton was among those whose citizens voted twice on the issue, the second being a contest in 1890 to abolish the system after one year of operation.[120] Like many others, Rome failed on its initial attempt but succeeded with continued effort.[121] The enabling act for Athens in 1885 was unusual in its provisions; it included city bonds for school houses and simply gave blanket authority to the city council to levy taxes to supplement the state fund without naming either the tax source or the rate.[122]

No countywide local tax systems were created between 1877 and 1892. A law approved in September 1891 eliminated the requirement for any enabling act to create county systems, which now could be initiated by two successive grand jury recommendations after which the ordinary called an election. The tax was not to exceed 25 cents on each $100 property valuation, and the county school board was to fix the rate within this limit. The two-thirds voter approval was still required; however, the law provided for updating voting lists. If a county included an incorporated town already having a school system sustained by local taxation, the residents of that town were not permitted to vote in the countywide election on the issue of a school tax, nor was their taxable property to be included in the new school tax assessment.[123]

While an 1891 law eliminated the need for special legislation to inaugurate countywide systems, it did not apply to individual municipalities or to local sub-districts or militia districts.

From 1892 to the end of the century a total of 53 additional enabling laws was enacted for municipalities. By the end of the century there was a total of 50 local tax systems in Georgia, only four of which were countywide—Bibb, Richmond, Glynn and Chatham. All of these had been created before or immediately following the Civil War. Only in these counties had the school term reached nine months in length.[124]

One of the most outstanding advantages of local tax systems was their ability to construct adequate school houses and to equip them with teaching aids. Well designed masonry buildings were found in a few cities and towns where bond issues were available for financing construction.[125] On the other hand, only after 1887 did county school boards own the first school house in the state. Nor did they before have the means of acquiring either buildings or sites. Eight years later a mere 277 school buildings had been acquired out of a total of 7,253 which were operating under the common school system.[126] At this time each county had an average of 60 school houses, the total value of which was less than $2,000.[127] For the most part they were without toilets of any kind and a common receptacle held drinking water from a well or spring. It was estimated that less than 10 percent of the buildings in each county was suitable for the purposes for which they were used, even under the primitive standards of that day. This situation caused schools in many communities to close completely during the winter months. Long summer terms competed with the distractions of hot weather, religious revivals and farm work.

Commissioner Orr in 1880 estimated that a third of the parents of white children who attended school were as poor as the great bulk of the black population and that half of all rural children did not attend school when it conflicted with farm work.[128]

Providing and maintaining a school house was the responsibility of patrons or the people in the school district. In Banks County they were told simply to obtain a house "good enough to winter a cow," and the county board would establish a school there.[129] G. D. Griffith, the school commissioner of Haralson County, complained of the inadequacy of school houses for winter use. He described "forty or fifty children crowded in one shack" with sawmill slabs used for seats "from morning until night, five days in the week."[130] Lena Sewell Jackson taught in 1888 in one of these schools located eight miles from Bowdon on the old Columbus road. She described a log house 18 feet square without windows but having a door at each of two opposite sides. Puncheon seats were arranged in a circle around the room, which had only a dirt floor. A rough pine table and a teacher's stool stood near the door. A small hand bell to call the children in from play was the only additional equipment.[131] In most schools there was not even a bell. The end of recess was announced by the teacher rapping on the door with a stick. Often referred to as settlement schools, these rural schools were held in churches whenever they were available, but more often in abandoned tenant houses, hastily constructed shacks or dilapidated log huts.[132]

Because school houses were flimsy and transitory, schools in many places were needlessly multiplied and sites were changed from year to year. In Putnam County in 1885 there was a school at almost every crossroad, and each structure was small and almost untenable. Four years later the county was redistricted and new school houses were located. They found that better houses caused the people to demand better teachers and more effective school organization. By the end of the century Putnam County had pioneered in introducing the graded system into all of its schools.[133]

The movement for better school houses began about 1895, when many newspapers, notably the *Atlanta Constitution* and the *Augusta Chronicle,* joined in the campaign. Each year thereafter about $100,000 was spent for buildings. This was accomplished by various methods, but the greatest contributions were made by school patrons. In Jasper County the local communities furnished the rough framing and the labor while the county board provided dressed lumber, shingles, doors and windows. The board made these resources available when several teachers failed to obtain licenses and no schools were opened in some districts. In Gwinnett County nine new school houses were constructed in 1900, only two of which received funding from the county board.[134] In these two instances, money from teachers' salaries was used. There was some question whether the law permitted this use of the state fund, but it was generally conceded that it could be diverted to such uses under special conditions.[135]

The Hook Administration

Commissioner Orr, who initiated a wide variety of education improvements in Georgia, died in 1887. He was succeeded by James S. Hook, a lawyer from Sandersville in Washington County. He had served in the General Assembly and as a member of the 1865 Constitutional Convention. Prior to his appointment as state school commissioner he was a judge of the Georgia Middle Circuit Court.[136]

Following Orr's example, Commissioner Hook continued to press the General Assembly for funds to be used for teacher institutes. Some of the county school commissioners held institutes paid for by local funds, and Hook used this fact to impress the General Assembly with the need for funds. His statement was, "I feel that in making this appeal to you, I am backed up by the unanimous voice of all the teachers, as well as all the school boards and County School Commissioners throughout the State. I have been much gratified by a movement among school officials and teachers, by which they seek to hold in some of the counties, 'County Normal Institutes,' taking the only day they have to spare for the purpose—Saturday. While this is highly commendable, I would ask, would it not be better to meet this most evident want by such legislation as would at proper time and places, allow opportunities for regularly organized normal instruction, by the appointment and support of the State, and let these earnest and devoted teachers thus anxious to fully fit themselves for their duties, take Saturdays for wholesome rest and recreation." [137] Commissioner Hook was certainly overly optimistic when he added, ". . . if we can have normal instruction provided for teachers in Georgia, then will all the educational wants of the State be supplied." [138]

Commissioner Hook had to continue without state funds for three more years, relying on Peabody funds for state institutes for white and Negro teachers. In 1889 an institute was held at Piedmont Chatauqua grounds; in 1890 an institute was held in Augusta for Negro teachers. Lawton B. Evans, superintendent in Augusta, conducted both of these institutes. At the institute at the Piedmont Chatauqua grounds, the teachers drew up a resolution which Commissioner Hook presented to the General Assembly.[139]

Resolved, That the following committee, to-wit: Honorable James S. Hook, Major W. F. Slaton and Professor W. H. Woodall, be appointed to urge upon the next General Assembly the provision by law for County Institute Instruction—the plan preferred by this body being the appointment of four State Instructors, who shall reserve ample salaries from the State Treasurer, and shall be under the control of the State School Commissioner.

It shall be the duty of these conductors to give their whole time to work, obtaining in the various counties such local voluntary assistance as may be available.

This was a forward look in 1890; however, it was about 20 years before this request came to fruition.

In 1891 there were Peabody Institutes at Lithia Springs, Milledgeville and Waycross, each for 10 days. A total of 319 white teachers and 147 Negro teachers attended these three institutes. In 1892 Peabody Institutes were held in Athens, Savannah and Americus. A total of 471 white teachers and 295 Negro teachers attended these three institutes, with Negro teachers and white teachers attending separate classes. In 1892 there were 4,920 white teachers and 2,500 Negro teachers.[140] Thus the institutes, carried on for a period of 10 years through the financing of the Peabody Fund, reached at the most 10 percent of the teachers for a period of 10 days to a full month. Each year a very few other teachers were attending the Normal School in Nashville, Tennessee.[141]

Finally, in 1891, legislation came for both institutes and the first state normal school. The first institutes were financed in 1892; the normal school in 1895. The state commissioner wanted an institute for a month. The School Bill of 1891 made the required time a week. Bill Number 643 was an Act to amend Section 12 of the Common School Laws of Georgia approved October 27, 1887. This bill, approved October 13, 1891, included the following items (not complete).[142]

The State School Commissioner shall organize and establish in each county in Georgia a Teacher's County

Institute for the assembling and instruction of the common school teachers of each county in the State.

The annual institute shall be of one week's duration in the period of June, July, and August, unless the State Commissioner deems another month better.

The State Commissioner may combine several counties for one institute.

The State Commissioner is to prepare a program of exercises, with a syllabus of each subject named in each program, for each day's session.

All teachers, white and colored, holding teacher's licenses shall be required to attend (separate for white and Negro teachers) and the teacher will pay a penalty if he does not attend—unless providentially hindered.

Twenty-five dollars will be paid to the County Superintendent to pay for an expert's services to do the teaching in the institute and to pay his expenses for the week.

The County School Superintendent may not teach in the institute. He is to administer it.

Thus, beginning in 1892, teachers were required to attend a county institute for one week during the summer. In addition, they were required to attend Saturday institutes once each month during the public school term; these were conducted by the county superintendent for all teachers in the county. Fines were assessed for absence; they were collected by the county school superintendent and used to purchase books for a teachers' library in the county. Held at county seats, Saturday institutes proved unsatisfactory because they imposed an expense on teachers which they could ill afford; they were discontinued after a short trial.[143]

Summer institutes of one month, located at various geographic centers throughout the state, continued to be conducted, as were county institutes.

These institutes were required of all teachers to continue teaching. The state superintendent began planning the dates for the examination for licenses at the close of the institutes. The normal programs which began at Savannah, Milledgeville, Athens and Dahlonega in the colleges located there during the period 1877 to 1892 were available but not required. The qualifications for teachers were essentially the same in 1892 as in 1870.[144]

At five regional institutes held for Negro teachers in 1895, more than 40 percent of all Negro teachers was in attendance.[145] An insight into the type of discussions which took place at these gatherings is revealed in a discussion of "the teaching of American history to Southern children" in which the following questions were raised:

> How would you deal with secession and the Civil War? How would you counteract the false impression liable to be made upon children by the prejudiced accounts . . . found in nearly all histories by Northern writers? Why are textbooks in history almost necessarily dull to children and how may teachers overcome this unavoidable defect? How much memorizing of dates should be required? [146]

While teachers' institutes continued well into the twentieth century, they received less emphasis after the development of institutions having specialized programs in teacher training.[147]

State School Commissioner James S. Hook was the one to carry out the law's provisions. Commissioner Orr said the purpose of the Act of 1887, making possible for the first time a state license to teach, was to elevate the grades of teaching capacity. In Commissioner Hook's first year as commissioner, 1888, he had the county school commissioners send to him more than 100 of the examination papers of candidates seeking permanent state licenses. In most cases, Commissioner Hook felt the papers warranted the issuance of the state license. He issued 96 permanent licenses in 1888, including several to black teachers.[148]

The system of a dual process of issuing licenses, county and state, continued from 1888 to 1924, although changes in the types of certificates issued and in qualifications for these types changed several times during this period. (Until 1924, however, the county school superintendent remained the chief "certifying agent" with broad powers. The state licenses issued by the state school superintendent were considered to have more merit but were fewer in number.)

The Act of 1887 enabled a county board of education, through the county school commissioner, to hold examinations in special cases at its discretion and for a successful applicant to be licensed temporarily. The license would be good only until the next regular appointed examination and only within the limits of the county wherein it was granted.[149] This was the beginning of issuing temporary licenses, a practice which continued to the 1970s.

Finally, on October 27, 1887, it was mandated by legislation that all persons, white and black, teaching in Georgia, or having licenses entitling them to teach in the state, must attend all sessions of institutes held in the county of their residence and perform all duties required at the institute unless providentially hindered. Monthly Saturday institutes in each county were also required. These requirements went into operation fully in 1892.[150]

The fact that the three classes of county licenses reflected grades made on the tests and set by the state school commissioner served as a stimulus for self-improvement. And, in reality, the state certificate offered another level.[151]

Gustavus R. Glenn was appointed state school commissioner by Gov. William Atkinson in December 1894. He had served as a school principal in Columbus and later as President of Columbus Female College. Nine years prior to his term as state school commissioner, he was professor of physics at Wesleyan Female College in Macon. After leaving the commissioner's office in 1904, he became president of North Georgia Agricultural College at Dahlonega, where he served until 1922.[152]

In Commissioner Glenn's instructions to the county superintendents, he said, "In grading papers, use as heretofore 100 as the maximum. To secure a first grade license (which was valid for three years) the average of the candidate must be 90 or above; to secure a license of the second grade (valid for two years) the candidate must make 80 or above; to secure a license of the third grade, the candidate must have an average of 70 or above. To find the average in any branch, give the applicant on each question for so much of 100 as the answer warrants, then sum these credits and divide by the number of questions under that branch; the quotient will be the average of that branch. The general average will be the sum of all branches divided by the number of branches.

"The County School Commissioner must use the greatest discretion in the recommendation of candidates for permanent license. There must be the most satisfactory evidence furnished along with the application that the candidate has professional character won by experience in the schoolroom, and his experience must cover a considerable number of years." [153]

In 1887 the law was changed to require the county board of education to select from the citizens of its county a county commissioner of education who "shall pass an examination furnished by the State School Commissioner and administered by the President of the County Board." [154] The board was required to elect an applicant who stood the examination satisfactorily and who possessed good moral character and business qualifications. (Thus, from 1887 to 1911, the state school commissioner, to a large extent, determined the type of knowledge the county commissioner of education should have.)

Perhaps a much more important change occurred two years later when a portion of the state fund was raised by direct taxation. The general tax act of 1888 authorized assessment for common school purposes on the taxable property of the state of one-half mill for 1889 and one mill for 1890. The latter produced $330,000. In addition, the school fund was augmented through a provision that the schools should receive all taxes from assessed property in the state in excess of $360 million. This yielded $50,575 in the last half of the year beginning in July 1889, and $140,606 for the full year of 1890. [155]

By 1893 the amount of the school fund raised by direct taxation had increased to $699,560. [156] The appropriations law of the previous year had allocated $600,000 for the common schools and, in addition, "whatever funds may be in the treasury" at the time of making the appointment. Also, it provided that if the returns of taxable property for 1893 and 1894 proved to be greater than $475 million, then the sums arising from the general tax levy in excess of this amount would become an additional appropriation to the common schools. The 1893 tax returns amounted to $505 million, producing an additional $85,560. [157] The revenue from other fixed sources such as W. & A. rentals, poll tax, convict hire, railroad stock, inspection fees and taxes on liquor and on shows brought the total amount for 1893 to $1,021,512. This was the first time the educational fund exceeded $1 million.

Although revenues fell slightly in 1894, the general trend for the remainder of the period was upward.[158] In 1898 it was slightly in excess of $1.5 million. By 1905 the direct levy alone produced $1 million. The poll tax was second with $273,650. The W. & A. rentals were producing $210,000 annually, and the liquor tax brought in $182,784. Fertilizer and oil inspection fees together accounted for $33,943. Revenue from the hire of convicts had disappeared with a decision to liquidate the vicious lease systems, but additional miscellaneous revenue added approximately $11,000, which made a total of $1,711,844.[159]

The apportionment sheet for 1904 shows that sums apportioned to counties ranged from $43,793.91 for Chatham down to $1,867.13 for Echols. Apportionment to 58 local systems ranged from $50,992.41 for Atlanta to $146.77 for Roberta in Crawford county.[160]

When the state fund was approaching the $1 million mark in 1892, it was pointed out that 34 counties failed to collect in state taxes an amount equal to the school allotment which they received from the state. Those 34 counties occupied the lower rungs of the educational ladder. These communities were quickly stigmatized with the appellation of "pauper counties," but this was discouraged by school leaders who were quick to explain the underlying social philosophy of public education. Most of the deficit counties were in North Georgia where the Negro population was exceedingly small, and in the central Georgia section where the Negro population was exceedingly large. Gilmer county in North Georgia received the largest overpayment ($2,056.32), while those receiving overpayment of $1,000 and above were Burke, Columbia, Fannin, Oglethorpe, Taliaferro and Union.[161]

After 1890, when William J. Northen began the first of his two terms as governor, considerable encouragement was given to the development of institutions with specialized programs in teacher training.[162] An erstwhile school teacher in Hancock county, Northen had been backed for the governorship by the Farmers Alliance and the incipient Populist organization in Georgia, which advocated better educational advantages for rural children.

Following his recommendation, the legislature created at Athens the Georgia Normal School but failed to appropriate money either for buildings or for operation. The University of Georgia donated Rock College, one mile northwest of Athens, together with the annual income from the Gilmer Fund which produced slightly over $1,000 annually. The Peabody Fund supplied another $800. In addition, funds from five institutes in counties in the vicinity of Athens provided an additional $125, bringing the total to slightly less than $2,000. This sum financed the school's initial session during the summer of 1892. A similar amount was obtained for the 1893 summer session, when Athens and Clarke county donated nearly $1,000 for the purpose. Lawton B. Evans of Augusta was appointed temporary president, and a faculty of seven was chosen. A total of 116 students enrolled for the 1893 course, which continued for six weeks, the cost being $18 to $30 each.[163]

Rock College was an old three-story building which provided all the space used by the school, its two upper stories sparsely equipped as a dormitory. All drinking water came from a common well.[164] The school received an appropriation of $10,000 for 1895, and its first regular term opened in that year at a cost to each student of only $75 for a term of eight months. Samuel D. Bradwell became its first permanent president in 1895. He previously served as state school commissioner under Governor Northen's appointment, that office not yet having become elective by popular vote.[165]

The normal school lacked most of the qualities and facilities which it should have possessed. Its teachers, like those in the common schools, were overworked, insufficiently prepared and poorly paid. The majority of its students were received from and returned after graduation to the county schools. This produced low entrance requirements and low standards. Of the 446 students registered in 1903-04, only 129 came with diplomas from reputable preparatory schools. Two hundred had taught before enrolling.[166]

More fortunate than the Georgia Normal School in the matter of public support were the Georgia Normal and Industrial College, established at Milledgeville in 1889 for women exclusively, and the Georgia Industrial College established at

Savannah in 1891 for Negroes. Both of these schools received state funding from the beginning, and both had large normal departments. At Milledgeville the registration for normal students in 1894 was 158, which was a little over half of the total. College preparatory classes were a necessary part of the program of these institutions during their early years of operation.[167]

The Peabody Fund

Adding considerable impetus to the upgrading of teachers during this period was the Peabody Fund for the promotion of "intellectual, moral and industrial education" among the youth of southern and southwestern states. The policy set forth by the trustees was to make no allocations to colleges nor to private and sectarian schools; their philosophy was that the state had full responsibility for providing education to its youth. Without exhibiting overtones of racial bias, the fund was used greatly to benefit the Negro.[168]

From 1868 to 1900 the Peabody Trustees spent a total of more than $177,000 in Georgia. Annual expenditures varied from $13,750 in 1873 to only $1,200 in 1888. In one year, 1875, the Griffin system received $2,000, Columbus, $900, and from $800 to $300 went to each of several other schools, some of which were militia districts. Conditions of such gifts were that people in the local community were required to pay in the form of taxes or gifts two or three times as much as they received.[169]

The fund was used generously for scholarships to normal colleges and for teacher training. Dr. J. L. M. Curry, a native Georgian who was a former congressman and minister to Spain, succeeded Barnas Sears in 1881 as the general agent for the fund. The fund was closed out two years following Curry's death in 1903. At that time, $1,500,000 was given as an endowment to Peabody Normal College in Nashville and $250,000 was given to the Slater Fund, begun in 1882, for industrial education of Negroes. Both the Peabody and the Slater funds were instrumental in raising the grade level of black teachers.[170]

Examinations, licensing and teacher qualifications continued to be problems during the nineteenth century's final years. One problem erupted in 1894 when fraud was discovered in connection with the teachers' examination; someone acquired advance copies of the questions and either sold or otherwise distributed them. County officials were asked to annul the examination where they had reasons to suspect fraud and to grant no licenses to those who might be responsible. The altering or forging of licenses was made a penal offense in 1900.[171]

State Commissioner G. R. Glenn reported in 1897 that at least two books on school management and methods were required as preparation for the general examinations; he specified the two books.[172]

Several attempts were made to permit a license to be issued without examination for those who had completed certain specified normal institutes. State Commissioner S. D. Bradwell, in his annual report of July 1893, recommended empowering the state school commissioner to grant permanent licenses to Georgia graduates of the Peabody Normal College at Nashville and to graduates of Georgia Normal and Industrial College at Milledgeville and the State Normal College at Athens.[173]

The president of Georgia State Industrial College at Savannah in 1895 stated a major purpose of that new institution was to furnish (Negro) teachers for the public schools. A two-year course of study was prescribed in this area.[174]

The president of North Georgia Agricultural College, reporting in 1897 to Commissioner Glenn, stated that, "By an act of the General Assembly of Georgia, approved February 23, 1877, the faculty is authorized to grant certificates or licenses to students intending to teach." [175] These licenses were granted in conformity with state laws and enabled the recipients to be employed as teachers in the primary common schools of the state without examination by or license from any board of education or county school commissioner. They were issued usually at commencement, and only upon special examinations held to test the qualifications of the applicants.

In 1898, a first grade license to teach was awarded on the basis of college credits without further examination, marking the first time examinations were not required.[176] The idea of granting licenses solely on the basis of work completed in normal schools lived a brief span of one year, after which examinations again were required. The idea of granting licenses solely on the basis of college credit got fresh support from the state commissioner in 1911, but it was 1924 before this concept was completely accepted.[177]

State School Commissioners Orr, Hook and Bradwell expressed concerns about examinations used for issuing certificates. The examinations did furnish a degree of standardization of material that teachers were expected to know. However, as long as the county school commissioners graded the papers, no real uniformity of licenses would be obtained.[178]

While the law of 1887 defined the county school commissioner as ex-officio county superintendent of public schools, the term did not become official for the county's principal school executive until the early part of the new century.[179] This position never had been one of great prestige, and it was not even moderately remunerative. Several attempts were made to abolish the office during the 1870s, principally on grounds of economy —despite the fact that the commissioner's stipend was limited to $3 per diem for each day actually employed in the discharge of school duties; many counties paid only $1 per day until well in the 1890s.[180] It was not until 1893 that a law was enacted to provide the school official with office space in the court house, and this was to be done only if space was available after all other county officers had been accommodated. A fixed salary for county school commissioners was not authorized until 1896, and this law applied only to counties of 60,000 population and above.[181]

The average annual compensation for county school commissioners in 1892 was less than $340 each, which represented the total administrative cost of the district schools and amounted to approximately four percent of the county's fund. On the other hand, the median salary of school superintendents in the 26 independent systems was approximately $1,500. The highest salary paid to any school official in the state was $4,200, which was the stipend received by the superintendent of the Chatham County schools. The city of Marshallville paid only $45 annually, while Toccoa paid $810 and Dalton paid $900. All 26 of the independent systems received a total of $591,039.65 in school funds, of which 72 percent was derived from local taxes.[182]

In contrast to high salaries paid administrators of the independent systems such as those in Atlanta, Macon and Savannah, the salary of the state school commissioner had never exceeded $2,500. His office clerk received $1,200 annually. Commissioner Orr, who died in office, literally was worked to death. His last report to the legislators included a plea for additional office help, stating that he was compelled to devote time largely to routine clerical duties which confined him to a desk from seven to nine hours each day. Members of his family performed many days of free labor in his office. Records show he carried on an extensive correspondence, including letters to school officials in 137 counties, to numerous teachers and to school authorities in other states and foreign countries. The law required him to perform a broad spectrum of administrative functions including personal visits to the various counties, yet the school law was extremely conservative in providing travel expenses. He was able to secure reduced rates and free passes from a few railroads and on one or two occasions the Peabody Fund came to his rescue in providing hotel expenses and an office clerk during his absence.[183]

Salaries paid to common school teachers during this period were on the scale of low-paid farm labor, and academic achievement was gauged by the scale of bare literacy. Thirty dollars per month was considered to be the standard salary of teachers as late as 1887, when it was assumed that one could operate a school of 45 pupils and expect an average attendance of 30, thus giving the teacher one dollar per month per pupil.[184] Throughout the 1890s the average annual pay of teachers in the common school system (which often was now called the country system) was less than $130 for a term which had not yet reached five months in length. In contrast, this average was slightly above $450 in the independent systems. While the city child was supported by an annual expenditure of $12.91, the rural child's support was only $2.89. Only a part of this differential was a result of the nine months school term, which nearly all of the independent systems had inaugurated by the end of the century.[185]

State Commissioner Hook sought to overcome this differential partly by advocating a five month school term staggered to enable a person to teach two separate terms during the year and thereby earn his or her total livelihood from teaching. This, he said, would eliminate "those half-handed teachers that just teach . . . to help out a crop," and it would do much toward upgrading the profession.[186]

As meager as they were, salaries were long delayed in their payment. Holders of teachers' vouchers waited many weary months, and too often they were forced to resort to money-lenders to whom they traded their paper at a discount of 10 to 25 percent. "I consider it . . . little short of outrage for teachers who have to wait on the state for money due . . . from six to twelve months," wrote H. P. Bernard of Clarke County in 1890.[187] State Commissioner Glenn called the usurious rates of some money sharks "brazenly illegal . . . and shamefully iniquitous." He reported the case of a teacher having a claim against the state of $60, which was bought for $48. This, he pointed out, "was 60 percent interest for work done in August to be paid in December." This situation was "a damnable sin and an unblushing shame," he stated. As a result of his protests, many counties made arrangements to discount the paper at the regular rate of eight percent.[188]

The tardy arrival of paychecks was partly a result of the original school law which stipulated that the school fund be disbursed only after teachers and county boards had made their reports on attendance, which meant that no money could be released until long after the schools had closed. This delay was often increased further by the slowness of tax collections and by priorities given to other agencies and departments, sometimes causing a delay of 10 to 15 months.[189] An effort to relieve this situation somewhat was made in 1894, when county ordinaries were authorized to approve the accounts of the county boards so that teachers might be paid quarterly, thus reducing the maximum waiting period to three months.[190] In 1898 a law provided for monthly payments; however, this law was inoperative except for a brief period after its enactment, because the state seldom had sufficient funds at the end of the month.[191] In 1901 State Commissioner Glenn still was protesting the fact that teachers were having to wait at least six months for salary payments. He pointed out that the laborers who cleaned the streets in Atlanta not only received higher wages than county school teachers, but they received them at the end of each week. Also, the street cleaner enjoyed 300 days of employment each year while the teacher had only 100. He stated that eight-ninths of Georgia's 65,000 school children reported in the school census of 1898 were in rural schools, and their teachers received less than $130 annually, with even this small amount grudgingly and tardily paid. He called this "an unspeakable, burning shame." [192]

Despite inadequate compensation and other obstacles to professional status, the Georgia Teachers Association met annually during the 1890s and displayed a rare concept of professional ethics and responsibilities. At their thirty-first annual meeting, held at Cumberland Island in July 1895, they formulated a code of ethics which included a decorous and dignified attitude toward other members of their profession. They would not criticize another teacher's scholarship, his character or his classroom methods. They would not disparage any educational institution or apply for a position until it became vacant They would live up to the letter of their contracts and would not underbid each other in their negotiation. They agreed not to receive expelled pupils from other schools except under certain stated conditions. At a meeting in Warm Springs the following year, they endorsed a resolution to undertake the creation of a strong sentiment "against the injurious habit of cigarette smoking among youths, that this nefarious practice may be stopped." [193]

It should be noted that the Georgia Teachers Association comprised largely school administrators and teachers serving in the independent city systems. Throughout the rural countryside, teachers on the whole lacked "book-learning," and they were not seriously concerned with professional ethics. Often, they were just barely literate. A case of chronic rheumatism, the loss of an arm or a leg in the Civil War, or any other ailment unfitting one for manual labor might be a person's only qualification as a teacher. Also, the religious or the political leaning of a candidate often determined both his appointment and his success in the community.[194]

Like tenant farmers, teachers tended to change their locations frequently. In one county, only five out of a total of 35 teachers returned to their schools for a second year. One boy stated that he had three different teachers during his last three terms in school, and "each one had carried him as far as South America in his geography." [195] Contributing to the itinerant character of public school teaching was the fact that many college students taught school during the summer months, after which they returned to their studies. One official declared that the public school was "making a greater number of preachers, lawyers and doctors than professional teachers" by giving them part-time employment needed to finance their professional study. [196]

The real competence of teachers in this period is impossible to judge with exactness, but all available data indicate that it was exceedingly low. School commissioners found it difficult during the early years of the system to gather the necessary statistics because the teachers were unfamiliar with simple record-keeping and making reports. Some were unable to figure average daily attendance upon which their stipend was based, and some of those who did so were found to be padding the figures to increase their remuneration. Commissioner John R. Lewis in 1871 urged that teachers be employed at a fixed salary based on "their intelligence, education and competency" and the size and grade of the school. "The comparatively ignorant and incompetent teacher will descend to use unworthy means to fill up his school," he said, "while the better teacher . . . has empty benches and a miserably inadequate salary." [197]

A citizen of the Villa Rica community in 1886 noted the widespread opening of public schools following the "laying-by season" when crops were cultivated. "It is marvelous the number of school teachers developed by the Public Fund," he wrote. "Nearly every little empty house throughout the country contains a dozen or two of children and a Professor." Many of the latter he claimed were sitting in as teachers to make enough money to splice out the crop or to buy a mule. "It makes no difference who teaches the children, just so it is cheap," he concluded. [198]

As already noted, one purpose of the Denny Law of 1887 was the improvement of the system of grading and licensing teachers. The requirement that examination questions be made out by the state school commissioner caused consternation in some counties where there was a great paucity of qualified teachers. For Franklin and Rabun Counties, special legislation provided that county boards might pay teachers at uniform rates based only on average attendance and not on the grade of license held.[199] To discourage pupils from absenting themselves for trivial causes and thus reducing the teacher's stipend, Clarke County instituted a rule to expel chronic absentees who could not show legitimate reasons for their absence. Clayton County officials found unsatisfactory the plan of using the daily attendance as a basis for salary. In addition to encouraging teachers to falsify reports, they found that this practice promoted lax discipline in the schools.[200]

While some teachers were known to neglect discipline in order to have a full school, many communities measured a teacher's success solely by his or her ability as a disciplinarian. How to manage an unruly boy short of corporal punishment was a frequent question on teachers' examinations. However, the general public considered punishment by flogging to be the simplest and most effective procedure. One method used to administer such punishment was called "the horse and rider" which had the offender placed on the back of another boy to make his posterior more vulnerable to blows from a hickory rod. The "circus way" involved group punishment, in which the culprits were marched clockwise in a circle and whipped as they passed by.[201] If a teacher were overzealous in having his pupils exhibit signs of progress in learning, he did not hesitate to use the threat of flogging to achieve these ends; a pupil's slow progress might endanger a schoolmaster's reputation if not his chance for re-employment. It is a tragic commentary on the schools of this period to note the widespread use of corporal punishment as a remedy for poor performance on a class recitation.

A pupil's performance and his or her progress in mastering certain rudiments of learning were exhibited in the public examination of pupils, a custom which the teacher was required to follow in many rural communities. These were held at the end of the school term in July, and usually were followed by an exhibition of the entire school. Ample opportunity for patrons to pass judgment on the teacher's talents and competence were provided by such occasions.

At the public examination held at Linton in Hancock County, the pupils were examined not only by their teacher but by parents and visitors as well; the ordeal lasted a full day. In the evening about 700 people assembled to hear the exhibition at which 20 boys declaimed and as many girls read compositions. Judges awarded prizes to those adjudged to be worthy of this recognition.[202]

In July 1884 a large audience assembled at Reese's Academy in Carrollton to witness the exhibition of Mrs. Thomas Bogg Slade's school. People jammed the little auditorium; disorder prevailed. Not surprisingly an observer characterized it as "an unappreciative and boisterous house," for the program lasted until midnight. It featured dialogues, recitations, tableaux, operettas and calisthenics, as well as songs and other types of musical performances.[203] Despite its amateur character, such entertainment provided many communities with a pleasing social evening at a period when such opportunities were rare.

State Commissioner Gustavus R. Glenn in 1896 asked Atlanta architects Bruce and Morgan to prepare plans for rural school houses with one to three rooms.[204] These plans were made available to county boards, which were encouraged to promote the building of more attractive and functional buildings. During 1900-05, an average of more than 200 new buildings was constructed annually, although as yet county school boards had no specific authority to do so. There were 237 new school houses built in rural areas in 1903 alone, averaging in value only a little over $400 each; 14 new buildings constructed in towns under local tax systems averaged more than $7,000 each in value. Almost everywhere in rural Georgia school buildings were no better than poor quality homes, dilapidated church buildings and ramshackle farms. However, some progress was occurring.

In addition to encouraging better school houses, county boards were giving some attention for the first time to improving school grounds and planting them with flowers, shrubs and trees.[205] Stimulating appreciation by pupils of the natural beauty of trees as well as their economic value was the apparent intent of a law in 1890 requiring schools to observe Arbor Day on the first Friday in December. This first special observance day for school children specified the day as one for "practical tree planting on school, church and other public lots, lawns, as well as on the public highway."

Other school observances and holidays were fixed by individual boards and varied widely in number and in importance with which they were to be observed. At the end of the century, Atlanta schools were celebrating not only Arbor Day, but also Thanksgiving Day and the birthdays of Lee and Washington as well. Thomasville added Memorial Day to this list. Rome added Decoration Day. Dublin's school holidays included Memorial Day and May Day in addition to four others. Clarke County's schools adjourned on all legal holidays. And in 1909, Georgia Day observances were set by legislative act.[206]

Early Vocational Education

At the same time Commissioner Glenn was pushing for better physical facilities in rural areas, he was promoting what could be described as vocational education. In a lengthy report to the General Assembly in 1897, he urged the enactment of legislation to provide more industrial education. Commissioner Glenn's speech covered the following needs for public education.

1. The course of study in the public schools of the state needs broadening. Industrial features should be added to our public school course.

2. The teachers should be paid monthly instead of quarterly.

3. Additional legislation is needed in regard to the conduct of industrial studies. Provision should be made for securing for this work the very best talent in the state.

4. Compulsory grading of country schools on some scheme such as that proposed by the State Teachers' Association.

5. Legislation requiring longer contracts with teachers. We adopt books for five years; why not adopt teachers for five years?

6. The appointment of a commission whose duty it shall be to ascertain what industrial course of study can be added to the schools of the state, commission to be appointed by the Governor.[207]

Also, the plea Glenn made to members of the Georgia legislature in his *Annual Report of 1889* reveals his interest in having the state provide vocational training. Some of his statements follow.

> In my judgment the time has come to add new features to our system of public education in Georgia. The radical defect in our system is that it educates our boys and girls to desire a way of escaping manual labor when there ought to be embodied in the system a training that will prepare the children to engage in some form or other of manual toil. The skilled manual labor that will have to be applied in the development of our industrial resources ought to be trained here at home. We should not be driven to the necessity of importing the kind of labor that Georgia will want on her farms, in her manufactories, in her foundries, in her machine shops and elsewhere. The potential citizens of the future will be the citizens whose hands have been trained to do things that the world wants done and that the world is willing to pay for. This training, so necessary to our present situation, must be provided for our children here at home while they are at school.

> I need not urge further upon the Legislature the necessity for insisting upon industrial education for our children at the present moment. Every member of the body knows that the future of Georgia depends largely upon the character of the industrial development that may be carried on in the State for years to come—

> I believe the time is here when every girl in the State of Georgia whether rich or poor, white or black, should be compelled to learn at school how to prepare, economically, a wholesome appetizing meal.[208]

Between 1895 and 1905, there appeared in Georgia several educational programs which tended to put into practice the philosophy of Orr and Glenn. In 1895 or 1896, at Rockville Academy in Putnam County under the leadership of F. G. Branch, "domestic science" for girls was introduced into the curriculum. Miss Frankie Williams was the teacher. Reports show that practical laboratory facilities were provided for teaching the girls how to prepare and serve meals. At Columbus in 1898, under the guidance of Superintendent Carlton B.

Gibson, cooking, sewing and handicrafts were taught in the elementary school of the cotton mill section.

As an outgrowth of this program in 1906, home economics was included in the offerings of the Industrial High School of Columbus. The Augusta school system introduced its first course in home economics around 1900 under Superintendent Lawton B. Evans. "It was started as a cottage plan for girls in the mill area. Afterwards it was expanded into the 'Domestic Science' department in the John Milledge School . . ." [209]

In 1904 home economics was introduced in the Macon Schools where Jere M. Pound was superintendent. The first teacher was Miss Mary Pearce. The work was elective and open to girls of the seventh grade and the high school grades. [210]

While there were many who wished to see industrial education a required part of all common schools, it had been authorized only in those schools supported by local taxation. [211] Courses of this nature were undertaken only in certain specialized schools, most of which were called "Model Schools." One of the earliest of these was established in 1902 at Danielsville by the Georgia Federation of Women's Clubs, which matched the sum of $700 raised locally by patrons. This sum of $1,400 enabled them to employ four teachers for five months and to purchase a cooking stove, utensils and materials for what they called a domestic science department. Also, equipment was acquired for boys' shops. A garden was operated by the school, and both boys and girls were engaged in such handicrafts as making baskets, hats and mats out of straw, corn shucks, grass and hickory splits. There were similar schools at Baldwin, Rome, Atlanta, Temple, Cass Station and Rabun Gap.

The Rabun Industrial School was founded in 1904 by Andrew J. Ritchie, who put his own meager savings into the school and raised money by subscription throughout the county. Each pupil worked an hour and a half each day at the shop, workroom or kitchen or on the school farm. [212] At Cass Station in Bartow County, each pupil was given one lesson each week in cooking, drawing, woodwork or basketry. This school's unusual equipment included a microscope, maps, a globe, organ and a school library. As yet no school funds could be spent for library books. [213]

The State Department of Education's *Annual Report of 1904* states,

> Hancock County was the first County in Georgia where serious efforts were made toward the systematic instruction of manual training into the course of study of an entire county system of rural schools. Local funds, supplemented by funds from the General Education Board of New York, were used to construct a building and purchase equipment. The building, located on grounds of the Sparta High School, consisted of three large rooms and areas for storage. It was equipped with tables, benches, tools, models, blackboards, and everything necessary to first class manual training shops.[214]

In 1903 two events took place that had a great deal to do with the future development of vocational education in Georgia. First, the year marked the passage of an act of the Georgia Legislature which made mandatory the teaching of agriculture "in the common public schools of Georgia." [215] Second, in 1903, Dr. Joseph S. Stewart made a speech at the annual meeting of the Georgia school commissioners in which he recommended that "a public high school be established in each county of the state and that agriculture, business, and manual training be offered along with other courses of English, mathematics, history, Latin, Greek, geography, and physics." [216]

Agriculture seems to have been introduced at the high school level in Georgia during the same year. According to that year's *Annual Report,*

> In 1903, Ira W. Williams, a graduate of the Agriculture College of the University of Georgia, organized an agricultural course for boys in the Temple High School of Carroll County. This is doubtless the first high school course in agriculture ever developed in Georgia. The school was termed "The Agricultural School of Carroll County." It is mentioned in a special bulletin of the University of Georgia, which was published in August, 1903. The Honorable Hoke Smith, then a prominent lawyer of Atlanta, encouraged Mr. Williams in his attempt to teach agriculture by placing one of his farms at the disposal of the school without charge for its use. Mr. Smith also

provided teams, equipment, and finances for operating
this farm on a practical basis . . .

The Honorable Hoke Smith also sponsored an agricultural school at Euharlee in Bartow County. This institution was located a distance of some 20 miles from the
Temple High School. The date when the teaching of agriculture was begun in the Euharlee School is not now available, but it is definitely known that Mr. J. Phil Campbell
was principal of that school in 1904 and taught agriculture. At any rate, it is safe to conclude that Ira Williams
and J. Phil Campbell were the first teachers of agriculture
in the high schools of Georgia.[217]

The Temple Model School in Carroll County was begun in
1902, when a group of enterprising citizens raised money to
supplement the state fund, receiving sizable gifts from people
in Atlanta and elsewhere. "We believe that education should
touch the life and work of the people . . . with those things
which touch his life as a farmer," read the 1904 prospectus
of the school.[218]

As noted, Williams functioned as superintendent and
Campbell was the principal and Williams' assistant. (It might
be noted that Campbell later became a prominent figure in the
agricultural program of the New Deal.) Included among the
teachers was Madam Dell Antonia, a music teacher from
Austria. The school had only 10 grades, but the high school
curriculum included Latin, Greek, geology, physics, botany,
and trigonometry, carefully arranged so that the college preparatory pupil could complete four years of Latin and two of
Greek. Non-preparatory students entered the terminal program, studying such subjects as drawing, manual training,
agriculture and engineering, while girls studied domestic
science. Elementary students engaged in such activities as
nature study, clay modeling and paper-cutting, as well as in
the traditional subjects.

Like many other model schools, the Temple School endured
only for a brief period. Not only did the community lack the
resources to meet its financial commitments, but also its con-
servatism often clashed with the progressive ideas of Ira Williams and his staff. At the end of the 1907 term, it resumed
a more orthodox pattern but remained one of the better village

schools of the state. One reason for the demise of the Temple experiment was the establishment in 1906 of the congressional district agricultural schools, one of which was at Carrollton a few miles south of Temple. It is significant to note that Ira Williams' counsel was solicited in the organization of these schools, and he taught in one of them briefly before becoming state entomologist.[219]

First Transportation Efforts

One of the unusual features of the Temple Model School was its success in consolidating small neighboring districts and the transportation of children to school in covered wagons. Ira Williams had begun this experiment in 1903 when he was principal at Sand Hill a few miles southeast of Temple. At Sand Hill he had combined the features of consolidation and a model school. The trustees rented a farm on which there was a house that could be used for the primary school. Profits from this farm met the cost of renting and feeding the mules. Only one wagon was used to transport children three or four miles from another district.[220]

School consolidation was attempted in Georgia as early as 1894, but a great drawback to this experiment was dependence on patrons to provide larger school houses. This they were reluctant to do when the school was to be removed from its traditional location and placed in the center of the area to be served.[221]

From 1898 to 1905 some 10 or 12 counties attempted some degree of consolidation and experimented with public transportation. These included Carroll, Clarke, Henry, Muscogee, Newton, Randolph, Walton and Washington Counties. During this period, 73 small schools were discontinued and 46 consolidated schools were established. In some instances county boards made contracts with the teacher, giving him or her the money allocated to all of the schools which were to be combined, and the teacher arranged transportation and secured needed subscriptions. In other instances wagons and teams were owned by county boards.

The cost of converting a two-horse farm wagon into a covered bus with seats along the sides (and in some instances provided with heaters) was $25. The cost of operating each wagon was $26.75 per month or $1.31 per pupil transported. In many instances older school boys drove the teams. Only in Newton County was there a very firm and detailed contract with drivers. Although consolidation and free transportation were provided by law in 18 states in 1900, transportation did not receive legislative sanction in Georgia until the passage of the Barrett-Rogers Act of 1919.[222]

In the 1890s, the Grange and Farmers' Alliance developed a serious interest in promoting public education and found an ally in the Georgia Teachers Association. Together, these groups inaugurated a campaign to increase the state support of all education.[223] As a result, in 1903, the legislature passed a tax measure which represented a very significant achievement in the long struggle to liberalize procedures for enacting local school tax laws. A former teacher, Edward H. McMichael of Marion County, introduced a bill calling for a constitutional amendment that would extend to counties and to local school districts the privilege of enacting school tax laws.[224] Though limited to a tax of one mill, the McMichael Bill was the first legislation to authorize local taxation throughout the state for school purposes.

A committee composed of Chancellor Walter B. Hill of the University of Georgia, Warren A. Candler, Hoke Smith, William J. Northen, William B. Merritt and M. L. Duggan organized school rallies throughout the state, issued literature and invoked the aid of the press. The General Education Board provided money for the campaign, which was climaxed by a statewide rally on Thanksgiving Day, 1903. The amendment was ratified in the following year.[225]

This amendment was implemented by a law of August 23, 1905, which provided that an election on a local tax law could be called after a petition from 25 percent of the voters, although passage still required two-thirds approval. The tax levy was limited to 50 cents on each $100 of property assessment. Citizens in any sub-district of a county might follow the same procedure in securing tax support for rural schools, and such units were permitted a tax rate of 75 cents. Municipalities already having a public school tax were not to be included in the procedure unless they wished to abolish their own system and become part of the county system.

Provision was made for the election of three trustees in each sub-district to be commissioned by the county board of education. The three-man local board had the power to build and equip school houses, fix tuition for non-resident pupils and issue fifas against delinquent tax-payers; however, it could not employ and dismiss teachers.[226] Since some counties never had created sub-districts for school purposes and were using unrealistic militia districts as school units, the law specifically required the immediate creation of new school districts. These were to be clearly defined by roads, streams, lot and district land lines. Each was to be not less than 16 square miles unless local topography such as mountains and streams placed a prohibition on this rule. By consent of a municipality its school district might include adjacent rural territory.[227]

Unfortunately the discretions permitted in laying out school districts provided a wide loophole for discrimination against certain rural areas. Often the more affluent areas, particularly those containing corporate property which was easy to tax, were gerrymandered in such a way as to create sub-districts containing the bulk of the county's taxable resources, leaving other areas without an adequate tax base. Thus, the richer parts of a county were often gerrymandered into separate school districts, leaving poorer sections with meager tax resources.

Also, cities and towns found it advantageous to withdraw from the county system and to inaugurate independent systems which had a more lucrative tax base than they would have enjoyed as part of a rural county.[228] However, the law did bring about a general increase of local tax levies resulting in better schools and longer terms in some areas. By the end of 1905 there were three additional countywide systems in operation—Fulton, Hancock and Monroe—and there were 128 subdistricts and municipalities now under local tax laws. These embraced a total of 565 schools.[229]

Although Georgia had provided limited state support for its elementary schools and colleges during the closing part of the nineteenth century, the academies and high schools supported privately in the urban centers offered the only secondary school program in the state. Numerous attempts had been made to get the General Assembly to pass legislation permitting local communities to support high schools, but these had been defeated.

Members of the Georgia Teachers Association at each annual meeting urged some type of legislative support for free public high schools to be paid from state funds. Dr. Joseph Stewart, who was a past president of the association, subsequently became the first state high school supervisor, working with the University of Georgia. With the leaders of the Georgia Teachers Association, he delivered papers and speeches urging legislation on the high school issue.[230] Through the years, the association kept the issue alive, even soliciting the support of businessmen.[231] The association and the state school commissioner continued to pursue this cause rather diligently.[232]

In 1894 Commissioner Glenn strongly urged the legislature to establish the county unit system as the basis for public education. He gave as examples Bibb, Richmond, Chatham and Glynn Counties as being models in the nation. He also made a broad report on the status of the Bibb County system which, he stated, proved the need for local taxes and a county high school to serve all of the county's elementary attendance areas.[233]

At the same time efforts were underway to improve the instructional progress by facilitating acquisition of textbooks. Despite the relatively low prices of textbooks late in the nineteenth century, many pupils were unable to acquire them, and there was no way to coerce them into doing so. Originally, the books were selected by county boards of education and by local boards in the independent systems. Book publishers were charged with conspiring to keep competition at a minimum, and local book dealers were criticized for high charges. In some counties they were shown to be making more than a 40 percent profit on sales to pupils. One patron called this situation "the unholy robbery of the poor." [234]

The first state law which attempted any regulation of this problem came in 1881, when board members having any interest in a textbook publishing company were disqualified from holding this office.[235] It was not until 1897 that the countywide adoption system was amended to prevent frequent and unnecessary changes by county boards, thus permitting greater resale of used books.[236] In 1903 the legislature enacted a state-wide uniformity law in an attempt both to obtain reduced prices and to unify the work of the schools. The State School-book Commission (originally consisting of the members of the State Board of Education) was empowered to procure a uniform series of textbooks for the common schools and to negotiate bids and contracts. Publishers whose books were adopted were required to keep a central depository in the state and to maintain agencies for book distribution in each county.[237]

The first adoptions under the new law went into effect on January 1, 1904, and were to continue until the end of 1908. Books adopted included Wheeler's *Primer*, Bacon's *Primary and Intermediate Arithmetic*, Branson's *Speller*, three books of Edna Henry Lee's *Readers*, Buehler's *Modern English Grammar*, Hyde's *English Lessons*, Reed and Kellog's *Graded Lessons in English*, Fry's *Geography*, Roudenbush's *Writing System*, Evans' *History of Georgia*, Field's *History of the United States*, Swinton's *Word Book*, Hutchinson's *Lessons in Physiology and Hygiene*, Conn's *Elementary Physiology*, Peteman's *Civil Government* and Hunnicutt's *Agriculture for the Common Schools*.[238]

While the state adoption law did not apply to local tax systems and to private schools, these might avail themselves of its benefits in securing lower priced books for their pupils. Most of the private schools in the 1890s were doing some kind of high school work for which no state adoptions had been made.

Early High Schools

Private high schools by 1900 had diminished in number, but the number of public high schools had more than doubled. State Commissioner Glenn listed 90 in his annual report for that year. Only a small number of these were found in the rural districts, and they apparently were of low quality. One outstanding exception was the Mount Zion Seminary in Carroll County. It was organized in 1880 under a joint stock plan conceived by James Mitchell, a minister of the Methodist Episcopal Church, who had come to Georgia from Indiana. Members of the little community not only bought shares of stock, but they also donated labor and materials for construction. Substantial support also came from the church's conference fund for education, and the school's primary department shared in the state fund. As the century closed the enrollment at Mount Zion had reached 200 pupils, of whom 160 were in high school courses. Two dormitories were filled to capacity, and many pupils were boarding in private homes. Mitchell and a number of his relatives came to Mount Zion to teach and to direct the school. They brought to this isolated community an unusual degree of learning, charm and graciousness. So dominant was the influence of these leaders that they are said to have changed the speech patterns of their pupils. For many years it was claimed that a Mount Zion graduate could be spotted by his midwestern accent.[239]

While Mount Zion was an unusually effective and successful rural high school, it was perhaps no better than a majority of the private high schools located in the larger towns and cities. This group of schools had an average term of nine months. They averaged four instructors and enrolled 123 pupils.[240]

Public high schools suffered in comparison to these schools, particularly those outside cities and larger towns. Generally they were conducted as an appendage to the elementary school and financed largely by the state fund. When patrons had to supplement the contract of a teacher in the common school, making the school partly public and partly private, endless confusion resulted from conflict among the school board, the patrons and the teacher. Some teachers who had advanced pupils in their classes were accused of spending a disproportionate part of the day on these to the neglect of elementary students for whom the state fund was designated. Often, there was only one teacher for all high school subjects.[241]

The curriculum at the high school level almost without exception varied widely and was of a nondescript character. Seventy-nine percent of all high school students was enrolled in Latin, 65 percent in algebra. Rhetoric was third with 42 percent of total course registrations, while physical geography had 30 percent and geometry 25 percent. Less than 20 percent was in physics, chemistry, trigonometry, geology, astronomy, Greek, French and German. The program did not prepare students for anything in particular. At the end of the century, only about one-half of one percent of the state's population was enrolled in high school as compared to 16 percent enrolled in the common schools.[242]

A principal reason for this disparity was the relatively small number of high schools. There was a gap of at least three years between the amount of instruction in the common school system and that offered in the public colleges. The gap was inadequately filled by fragmentary high schools, by preparatory departments of colleges, by college admissions under certain conditions and by admission to professional study (law, medicine, dentistry) of those who had not completed high school. Many youth with rare intellect and ambition who might have succeeded well in college thus became dropouts at the end of their seventh or eighth year in public school. This tragedy fell heaviest on blacks and on rural youth of both races.[243]

No single group of educators deplored this situation more than did college administrators and their faculties. It not only greatly limited college enrollments, but it also hampered curriculum development and undermined academic standards. Joseph S. Stewart, president of North Georgia Agricultural College at Dahlonega, stated in 1897 that there were almost as many standards of scholarship as there were colleges conferring degrees. "A college may be any school from the University of Georgia . . . down through all the stages of a village school with all the classes from abc to calculus taught by one wise head," he wrote.[244] He stated that an A.B. graduate from one college might be unable to enter the freshman class of another.[245]

At that time a high school committee of the Georgia Teachers Association came to an agreement with representatives from the University of Georgia, Emory, Mercer and Wesleyan concerning college entrance requirements to begin the following year. In addition to algebra, quadratics, geometry, rhetoric, English grammar and work in literature and composition, the curriculum was to include four years of Latin and two of Greek.[246] These standards followed closely the prescription for entrance requirements set by the Association of Colleges and Preparatory Schools of the Southern States, a group organized in Atlanta in 1894. Thus for the first time it was possible to define freshman college work and to identify creditable high school preparation as well.[247]

In 1903 Stewart was brought to the University of Georgia as state agent in charge of high school accreditation. He recommended an accrediting system which was adopted in the following year. High schools were required to have at least two teachers, one of whom might be the principal of the school. Teachers were permitted no more than 10 recitations of 30 minutes each per day, and students were allowed a maximum of five prepared lessons per day. Thirteen units of acceptable high school subjects were required for college admission, although conditions were permitted in three of these. While these requirements were to seem low to future generations, they proved to be exceedingly high for that period. The University of Georgia made the rules governing accrediting and issued all blank forms to private as well as to public schools.

Only 11 four-year high schools were accredited during the first year, in 1904-05. Seven of these were public high schools, all in the larger cities and towns. In addition, 39 three-year public high schools were accredited, making a total of 50 on the first list. These 50 schools had a total registration of 3,500 pupils and employed 150 teachers. Stewart's plan was so successful that it came to be adopted in other southern states.[248]

Stewart was given the title of Professor of Secondary Education at the University of Georgia. He traveled over the state encouraging the establishment of high schools through local support and urging the unification of these schools with the elementary schools below and the colleges above. He called the high school the people's college and said he hoped to see at least one in every county where cooperative boarding would make them accessible to every rural boy and girl. Stewart's first objective was to establish accredited schools mainly for college preparation. Later he would work for the addition of courses in agriculture, home economics and industrial training to prepare students for life.[249]

In another area of education—the school library—progress was very slow during the period between 1870 and 1937. The earliest reference to a public school library is in Bowden's *Two Hundred Years of Education* in connection with the free school in the settlement of Irene. The three-room school house was completed in 1736 and had a library with it.[250] In addition, the academies which developed in the late 1700s generally had library collections as part of their equipment.[251]

As public schools developed, there was at least some concern for providing reading materials. State School Commissioner Glenn in his annual report for 1895 said, "I am able to report that considerable interest has been manifested during the last year in the matter of providing suitable books for the children to read and creating permanent libraries for teachers." [252] A report in 1897 from a committee appointed to prepare a course of study for the common schools of Georgia contained the following statement, "The course is based upon the cooperation of the library with every school, thus supplying material for individual research, collateral reading and study, and affording the teacher an opportunity to cultivate a love of good books and a habit of reading." [253]

That annual report also included an announcement of the "Georgia Reading Circle for Teachers and Young People Founded in 1894 by the Georgia Teachers' Association" and a copy of the Georgia Reading Circle card developed by W. R. Power, county school commissioner of Cobb County.[254] This was, no doubt, the forerunner of the highly successful summer vacation reading clubs sponsored by the Library Commission, which later became the Public Library Services Division of the Georgia Department of Education.

Commissioner Glenn, in the annual report for 1900, describes the reference and circulating library located in the office of the school commissioner of Newton County. The books were boxed and circulated to the schools for six weeks to two months, then returned to the commissioner's office and a new group supplied. Records of 1899 indicate that 27 white schools took advantage of these grouped libraries, which numbered 38. No mention is made of participation by black schools.[255] This annual report included statistics showing a total of 267 libraries in the state valued at $19,340.77.[256] The majority of these likely were travelling libraries or classroom collections and not centralized school libraries as exist today.

CHAPTER II

FOOTNOTES

1. William H. Kilpatrick, "The Beginnings of the Public School System in Georgia," *Georgia Historical Quarterly*, V (September 1921), p. 19; See also Dorothy Orr, *A History of Education in Georgia*, (Chapel Hill: University of North Carolina Press, 1950), p. 187. (Hereinafter referred to as *Education in Georgia*.)
2. Gustavus J. Orr, *Fifth Annual Report* of the State School Commissioner of Georgia to the General Assembly of the State of Georgia at its Session in January 1876, pp. 19-22.
3. Haywood S. Bowden, *The Building of the Empire State*, (Savannah: Braid and Hutton, 1925), pp. 40-44.
4. George Ephriam Usher, *Development of the Georgia Education Association*, (unpublished master's thesis, Duke University, Durham, 1935), p. 3.
5. Francis Newton Thorpe, ed., *The Federal and State Constitutions, Colonial Charters, and Other Organic Laws, etc.*, p. 838.
6. *Journal of the Proceedings of the Constitutional Convention of the People of Georgia . . . 1868*, p. 542.
7. *Georgia Laws*, Special Session, July 4—October 6, 1868, p. 12; 1869, p. 22.
8. *Proceedings of Georgia Teachers Association*, 1869, p. 8.
9. Georgia Department of Education *Annual Report*, 1876, pp. 21-23.
10. Georgia Department of Education *Annual Report*, 1870-71, p. 16.
11. *Ibid.*, p. 9.
12. Orr, *Education in Georgia*, pp. 399-400; *Atlanta Constitution*, February 10, 1900.
13. Georgia Department of Education *Annual Report*, 1877, p. 5.
14. Georgia Department of Education *Annual Report*, 1895, p. 146.
15. Georgia Department of Education *Annual Report*, 1870-71, p. 17
16. *Ibid.*, p. 7.
17. *Georgia Laws*, 1870, pp. 49-66.
18. Georgia Department of Education *Annual Report*, 1870-71, p. 5.
19. *Georgia Laws*, 1870, Public Law No. 53, p. 54.
20. Georgia Department of Education *Annual Report*, 1905, p. 58.
21. Georgia Department of Education *Annual Report*, 1870-71, pp. 32-33.
22. State Board of Education, *Minutes*, January 18, 1871, p. 11.
23. *Georgia Laws*, 1871-72, p. 279.
24. Carl G. Renfroe, *The Growth and Development of Teacher Education in Georgia*, (unpublished doctoral dissertation, University of Georgia, Athens, 1964), p. 166.
25. *First Annual Report of the State School Commissioner*, p. 71.
26. *Ibid.*, Appendix, p. 33.
27. *Georgia Laws*, 1870, pp. 49-61; 1872, p. 490.
28. *Ibid.*
29. Georgia Department of Education *Annual Report*, 1870-71, pp. 5-6.
30. *Ibid.*, p. 35; *Federal Union*, August 9, 1871.
31. Georgia Department of Education *Annual Report*, 1872, pp. 28.
32. *Ibid.*, p. 24.
33. Georgia Department of Education *Annual Report*, 1876, pp. 22-28.
34. Georgia Department of Education *Annual Report*, 1870-71, pp. 5-6.
35. Georgia Department of Education *Annual Report*, 1872, pp. 23-28.
36. Georgia Department of Education *Annual Report*, 1897, pp. 95-96; Georgia Department of Education *Annual Report*, 1872, pp. 25-28; 1874, pp. 1-7; 1875, p. 11; *Georgia Laws*, 1874, pp. 30-33; 1877, pp. 344, 347-348.
37. Orr, *Education in Georgia*, pp. 204-206, 406, 399-400; *Atlanta Constitution*, February 10, 1900.

38. Georgia Department of Education *Annual Report*, 1876, p. 20.
39. *Annual Report* of the State School Commissioner to the General Assembly of the State of Georgia for the year 1872, p. 5.
40. Georgia Department of Education *Annual Report*, 1870-71, p. 19; Georgia Department of Education *Annual Report*, 1872, pp. 14-15; Georgia Department of Education *Annual Report*, 1874, p. 23.
41. Georgia Department of Education *Annual Report*, 1872, pp. 28-29; Georgia Department of Education *Annual Report*, 1876, pp. 19-22.
42. *Ibid.*, 1872, pp. 25-28; 1875, pp. 12-13; 1876, pp. 23-28.
43. *Federal Union*, November 15, 1871.
44. Georgia Teachers' Association, *Proceedings*, 1871, p. 20.
45. Adolph E. Meyer, *An Educational History of the American People*, (New York, 1957), pp. 122, 212, 219, 421.
46. *Ibid.*, pp. 212-213.
47. *Georgia Laws*, 1874, p. 109; Georgia Department of Education *Annual Report*, 1883-84, p. 32.
48. Georgia Department of Education *Annual Report*, 1876, pp. 86-94.
49. *Report* of the State School Commissioner to the General Assembly of the State of Georgia 1875, pp. 23-24.
50. *Union and Recorder*, August 6, 1873.
51. Georgia Department of Education *Annual Report*, 1899, p. 67.
52. *Georgia Laws*, 1874, pp. 32-33; Georgia Department of Education *Annual Report*, 1874, p. 30.
53. Georgia Department of Education *Annual Report*, 1876, pp. 10-12.
54. Georgia Department of Education *Annual Report*, 1874, pp. 15-17.
55. Georgia Department of Education *Annual Report*, 1873, p. 1; Georgia Department of Education *Annual Report*, 1874, pp. 23, 29.
56. *Ibid.*, 1874, p. 29, 1876, p. 23.
57. Jim B. Pearson and Edgar Fuller, eds. *Education in the States: Historical Development and Outlook*, (Washington: National Education Association, 1969), p. 260.
58. *Ibid.*, p. 260.
59. *Georgia Laws*, 1870, pp. 57, 49-61; 1872, p. 490.
60. *Report* of the State School Commissioner to the General Assembly of the State of Georgia, 1883, p. 40.
61. *Ibid.*, p. 41.
62. *Ibid.*, p. 42.
63. Harry Gehman Good, *A History of American Education* (New York, 1962), pp. 158, 163, 213.
64. Georgia Department of Education *Annual Report*, 1879-80, pp. 36-40.
65. *Ibid.*, 1883, p. 41.
66. *Report* of the State School Commissioner to the General Assembly of the State of Georgia, 1886, p. 16.
67. *Report* of the State School Commissioner to the General Assembly of the State of Georgia, 1882, pp. 43-44.
68. *Ibid.*, pp. 45-52.
69. *Report* of the State School Commissioner of Georgia to the General Assembly for 1893, p. 11.
70. Georgia Department of Education *Annual Report*, 1885-86, p. 26.
71. State Board of Education, *Minutes*, January 26, 1884, p. 69.
72. *Georgia Laws*, 1880-81, p. 97.
73. *Georgia Laws*, 1887, pp. 68-83.
74. *Georgia Laws*, 1886-87, pp. 11, 68-86; Georgia Department of Education *Annual Report*, 1887-88, pp. 27-34.
75. *Georgia Laws*, 1887, pp. 74-77.
76. *Ibid.*, pp. 74-77.
77. *Georgia* Laws, 1887, p. 76.
78. *Georgia Laws*, 1890-91, pp. 118-123.

79. Georgia Department of Education *Annual Report*, 1903, pp. 52-53; Georgia Department of Education *Annual Report*, 1876, p. 2-3; 1898, p. 78; 1899, p. 59.
80. Georgia Department of Education *Annual Report*, 1876, pp. 23-28.
81. "Important Decisions by Captain Bradwell," (manuscript in private possession); *Georgia Laws*, 1882, pp. 86-87.
82. Georgia Department of Education *Annual Report*, 1885-86, p. 7; Georgia Department of Education *Annual Report*, 1887-88, p. 19.
83. Georgia Department of Education *Annual Report*, 1905, p. 58; Georgia Department of Education *Annual Report*, 1897, p. 249.
84. M. L. Brittain, *Georgia School Laws and Decisions*, (Atlanta, 1911), p. 26; Georgia Department of Education *Annual Report*, 1889-90, p. 66.
85. *Carroll Free Press*, July 7, 1893; Georgia Department of Education *Annual Report*, 1892, pp. 49-112.
86. Orr, *Education in Georgia*, p. 317.
87. Georgia Department of Education *Annual Report*, 1899, Table 1, "Statistics of the Common School," p. cclxvii.
88. *Ibid.*, p. 100.
89. Georgia Department of Education *Annual Report*, 1903, pp. 242-245.
90. Georgia Department of Education *Annual Report*, 1877, p. 7; *Georgia Laws*, 1873, pp. 62-63.
91. Georgia Department of Education *Annual Report*, 1876, pp. 6-7.
92. Georgia Department of Education *Annual Report*, 1880-81, p. 98; 1883-84, p. 4.
93. Georgia Department of Education *Annual Report*, 1894, p. 93.
94. Orr, *Education in Georgia*, p. 176.
95. *Ibid.*, p. 208.
96. *Ibid.*, p. 177.
97. *Ibid.*, pp. 177-178.
98. Georgia Department of Education *Annual Report*, 1876, p. 9.
99. *Ibid.*, 1876, appendix, xv; 1877, pp. 7-8, p. 38; 1879-80, p. 5.
100. *Ibid.*, 1876, p. 8.
101. *Ibid.*, 1876, appendix, xv.
102. *Ibid.*, 1876, p. 38; *Georgia Laws*, 1877, p. 192.
103. *Georgia Laws*, pp. 192-193.
104. Albert B. Saye, *A Constitutional History of Georgia, 1832-1945*, (Athens, University of Georgia Press, 1948), pp. 279-309.
105. Georgia Department of Education *Annual Report*, 1903, pp. 49-50.
106. Georgia Department of Education *Annual Report*, 1889-90, p. 12.
107. Georgia Department of Education *Annual Report*, 1878, p. 11; Georgia Department of Education *Annual Report*, 1894, pp. 13-14.
108. Georgia Department of Education *Annual Report*, 1900, p. 18; Georgia Department of Education *Annual Report*, 1903, p. 32.
109. Georgia Department of Education *Annual Report*, 1892, p. 156; M. L. Duggan, *Educational Survey of Tift County, Georgia*, (Bulletin 23), State Department of Education, 1918, p. 2; *Georgia Laws*, 1877, pp. 345-348; 1878-79, pp. 287-290; 1881, p. 429; 1888, p. 323.
110. Georgia Department of Education *Annual Report*, 1879-80, p. 23.
111. Georgia Department of Education *Annual Report*, 1885-86, pp. 8-9.
112. Georgia Department of Education *Annual Report*, 1879-80, p. 77.
113. Georgia Department of Education *Annual Report*, 1873, p. 490; 1874, p. 397.
114. *Georgia Laws*, 1877, pp. 348-349.
115. *Georgia Laws*, 1884-85, p. 598.
116. *Georgia Laws*, 1877, p. 350.
117. *Georgia Laws*, 1880-81, p. 98.
118. Georgia Department of Education *Annual Report*, 1892, p. 156.
119. *Georgia Laws*, 1880-81, p. 429.
120. *Georgia Laws*, 1878-79, pp. 287-290; 1881, p. 454; 1888, p. 323.

121. *Carroll Free Press*, September 13 and 20, 1889; *Rome Public Schools, Eighth Annual Report, 1901-02*, (Rome, 1902), p. 15.
122. *Georgia Laws*, 1884-85, p. 603.
123. *Georgia Laws*, 1890-91, v. 1, p. 124.
124. Georgia Department of Education *Annual Report*, 1900, appendix, p. ccccxlvii.
125. *Georgia Laws*, 1887-88, p. 340; 1898, p. 340.
126. *Georgia Laws*, 1886-87, 11, 68 *et passim;* Georgia Department of Education *Annual Report*, 1883-84, pp. 26-27.
127. Georgia Department of Education *Annual Report*, 1895, p. 25.
128. Georgia Department of Eduction *Annual Report*, 1894, pp. 7-8; Georgia Department of Education *Annual Report*, 1880, p. 9.
129. Georgia Department of Education *Annual Report*, 1890, p. 89.
130. Georgia Department of Education *Annual Report*, 1889-90, pp. 45-79.
131. Lena Sewell Jackson, "Memories," *Carroll Free Press*, March 1, 1928.
132. Georgia Department of Education *Annual Report*, 1905, p. 58.
133. Georgia Department of Education *Annual Report*, 1902, p. 70; Georgia Department of Education *Annual Report*, 1897, p. 229.
134. Georgia Department of Education *Annual Report*, 1899, p. 23; Georgia Department of Education *Annual Report*, 1900, pp. 88-89.
135. *Ibid.*, 1900, p. 87.
136. Orr, *History of Education in Georgia*, p. 394.
137. *Report* of the State School Commissioner to the General Assembly of the State of Georgia, 1888, pp. 35-36.
138. State Board of Education *Minutes*, January 26, 1884, p. 69.
139. *Report* of the State School Commissioner to the General Assembly of the State of Georgia, 1888, p. 36.
140. *Report* of the State School Commissioner to the General Assembly of the State of Georgia, 1890.
141. *Report* of the State School Commissioner to the General Assembly of the State of Georgia, 1892, p. 11.
142. *Georgia Laws*, 1890-91, pp. 120-123.
143. *Georgia Laws*, 1890-91, p. 120; Georgia Department of Education *Annual Report*, 1892, pp. 25-28.
144. Review of State School Commissioners' *Annual Reports* to the General Assembly from 1870 to 1892 reveals no changes in teachers' qualifications for the period.
145. Georgia Department of Education *Annual Report*, 1895, p. 58; Georgia Department of Education *Annual Report*, 1892, pp. 17-18; 1893; p. 10.
146. Georgia Department of Education *Annual Report*, 1894, p. 111.
147. Georgia Department of Education *Annual Report*, 1900, p. 23.
148. *Report* of the State School Commissioner to the General Assembly, November, 1888, pp. 34-49.
149. *Georgia Laws*, 1890-91, p. 119.
150. *Georgia Laws*, 1892, p. 87.
151. *Georgia Laws*, 1887, p. 76.
152. Orr, *Education in Georgia*, pp. 393-94.
153. *Report* of the State School Commissioner to the General Assembly of the State of Georgia, 1895, p. 126.
154. *Georgia Laws*, 1887, pp. 74-75.
155. Georgia Department of Education *Annual Report*, 1887-88, pp. 5-8; Georgia Department of Education *Annual Report*, 1889-90, pp. 7-8; *Georgia Laws*, 1889, pp. 19-20.
156. Georgia Department of Education *Annual Report*, 1892, p. 4.
157. Georgia Department of Education *Annual Report*, 1893, p. 5; *Georgia Laws*, 1892, pp. 13-14.
158. Georgia Department of Education *Annual Report*, 1901, p. 41.

159. Georgia Department of Education *Annual Report*, 1905, p. 254.
160. Georgia Department of Education *Annual Report*, 1903, pp. 215-216.
161. Georgia Department of Education *Annual Report*, 1891-92, p. 13; Georgia Department of Education *Annual Report*, 1892, p. 23.
162. Georgia Department of Education *Annual Report*, 1900, p. 23.
163. Georgia Department of Education *Annual Report*, 1892, pp. 117-18; *Journal of the Proceedings of the Constitutional Convention of the People of Georgia . . . 1867 . . . 1868*, (Augusta, 1868), p. 452; James C. Bonner, *The Gubernatorial Career of William J. Northen*, (unpublished master's thesis, Athens: University of Georgia, 1936), pp. 33-36.
164. Georgia Department of Education *Annual Report*, 1892, p. 119; Georgia Department of Education *Annual Report*, 1894, p. 93.
165. Georgia Department of Education *Annual Report*, 1894, pp. 11-12, p. 93.
166. "Report of the State Norman School, March 28, 1904," Georgia Department of Education *Annual Report*, 1903, p. 99.
167. Georgia Department of Education *Annual Report*, 1894, p. 73.
168. Meyer, *An Educational History of the American People*, 213ff.; Georgia Department of Education *Annual Report*, 1877, p. 23.
169. Georgia Department of Education *Annual Report*, 1897, pp. 95-96; 1899, p. 29; Georgia Department of Education *Annual Report*, 1876, p. 14.
170. Georgia Department of Education *Annual Report*, 1879-80, pp. 25-26; Georgia Department of Education *Annual Report*, 1902, p. 138; Georgia Department of Education *Annual Report*, 1900, p. 24; Meyer, *An Educational History of the American People*, 213 *et passim*.
171. Georgia Department of Education *Annual Report*, 1894, pp. 135-136; *Georgia Laws* 1900, p. 69.
172. *Ibid.*, November, 1888, pp. 24, 34 and 49. (Recommended books changed from year to year; in 1895, and other years, Page's *Theory and Practice of Teaching* and White's *School Management* were recommended; Georgia Department of Education *Annual Report*, 1895, p. 120.
173. Georgia Department of Education *Annual Report*, 1894, p. 20.
174. Georgia Department of Education *Annual Report*, 1895, pp. 261-262.
175. *Report* of State School Commissioner to the General Assembly of the State of Georgia for 1895, p. 194.
176. Renfroe, *The Growth and Development of Teacher Certification in Georgia*, p. 114.
177. Georgia Department of Education *Annual Report*, 1924, pp. 13, 58-59.
178. Summary of those portions of Georgia Department of Education *Annual Reports* of State School Commissioners Orr, Hook and Bradwell, pertaining to examinations for teachers, 1872-1893.
179. Georgia Department of Education *Annual Report*, 1902, pp. 126-127.
180. Georgia Department of Education *Annual Report*, 1895, p. 21; 1876, pp. 23-32; Georgia Department of Education *Annual Report*, 1891, p. 6; *Georgia Laws*, 1887, p. 77.
181. *Georgia Laws*, 1893, p. 63; 1896, p. 71.
182. *Georgia Laws*, 1886-87, II. 68 *et passim*; Georgia Department of Education *Annual Report*, 1892, p. 27, pp. 78-79.
183. Georgia Department of Education *Annual Report*, 1878, p. 5; Georgia Department of Education *Annual Report*, 1887-88, pp. 48-50.
184. Georgia Department of Education *Annual Report*, 1887-88, p. 8.

185. Georgia Department of Education *Annual Report*, 1894, p. 20; 1897, pp. 23-25; 1900, p. 13.
186. Georgia Department of Education *Annual Report*, 1899, p. 9.
187. Georgia Department of Education *Annual Report*, 1892, pp. 41-42; Georgia Department of Education *Annual Report*, 1883-84, p. 3.
188. Georgia Department of Education *Annual Report*, 1889-90, pp. 45-79; Georgia Department of Education *Annual Report*, 1900, p. 13; Georgia Department of Education *Annual Report*, 1874, p. 24.
189. Georgia Department of Education *Annual Report*, 1875, p. 14; Georgia Department of Education *Annual Report*, 1895, pp. 41-42.
190. Georgia Department of Education *Annual Report*, 1895, p. 179; 1897, p. 21.
191. Georgia Department of Education *Annual Report*, 1899, p. 85; *Georgia Laws*, 1898, p. 70.
192. Georgia Department of Education *Annual Report*, 1900, p. 13; 1901, p. 13.
193. Georgia Department of Education *Annual Report*, 1895, pp. 82-85; p. 179.
194. Georgia Department of Education *Annual Report*, 1896, p. 103; Georgia Department of Education *Annual Report*, 1905, p. 58.
195. Georgia Department of Education *Annual Report*, 1897, pp. 23-25.
196. *Ibid.*, p. 249.
197. James C. Bonner, *The Educational History of Carroll County*, (Milledgeville, 1868), p. 15; Georgia Department of Education *Annual Report*, 1876, p. 8; Georgia Department of Education *Annual Report*, 1870-71, p. 11.
198. *Carroll Free Press*, February 2, 1933.
199. *Georgia Laws*, 1884-85, p. 598; 1882-83, p. 647; Georgia Department of Education *Annual Report*, 1887-88, pp. 34-35.
200. Georgia Department of Education *Annual Report*, 1876, p. 73; Georgia Department of Education *Annual Report*, 1897, pp. 214-215.
201. John Cook, "The History and Development of the Chattooga County School System," (unpublished manuscript, n.d.), p. 91.
202. *The Federal Union*, July 10, 1872.
203. *Carroll County Free Press*, July 4, 1884.
204. Georgia Department of Education *Annual Report*, 1896, p. 16.
205. Georgia Department of Education *Annual Report*, 1903, p. 23; 1905, pp. 9-10.
206. *First Annual Report of the Public Schools of Thomasville, Georgia, 1901-02*, (Thomasville, 1902), pp. 9-10; *Rome Public Schools, Eighth Annual Report, 1901-02* (Rome, 1902), p. 15; William T. Garrett, *Dublin Public Schools*, (Dublin, 1916), p. 1; John L. Hopkins. *The Code of the State of Georgia Adopted August 15, 1910*, (Atlanta, 1911), p. 219; Georgia Department of Education *Annual Report*, 1902, pp. 172-175.
207. *Twenty-Sixth Annual Report from Department of Education to the General Assembly of the State of Georgia*, 1897, pp. 10-31.
208. Georgia Department of Education *Annual Report*, 1889, pp. 10-18.
209. Standards Committee, Georgia Home Economics Association, *History of Home Economics in Georgia*, 1933, p. 20.
210. *Ibid.*, p. 21.
211. *Georgia Laws*, 1884-85, p. 72.
212. Georgia Department of Education *Annual Report*, 1902, p. 281; 1905, pp. 147-148.
213. *Ibid.*, 1902, p. 21; 1905, p. 237; *Georgia Laws*, 1901, p. 52.
214. Georgia Department of Education *Annual Report*, 1904, pp. 173-178.
215. *Statutes of Georgia Passed by the General Assembly of 1903*, p. 64.
216. Georgia Department of Education *Annual Report*, 1903, pp. 44-45.
217. Wheeler, *Two Hundred Years*, pp. 22-23.

218. *The Model School,* (Temple, Georgia, ca. 1904), p. 6.
219. *Ibid.,* pp. 5, 17, 27; Paul Cobb to James C. Bonner, August 20, 1965, in private possession; James C. Bonner and Lucien E. Roberts, eds., *Studies in Georgia History and Government,* (Athens, 1940), pp. 172-190.
220. Georgia Department of Education *Annual Report,* 1902, pp. 11, 279.
221. Georgia Department of Education *Annual Report,* 1894, pp. 16-17.
222. Wheeler, *Two Hundred Years of Agricultural Education in Georgia,* p. 255; Georgia Department of Education *Annual Report,* 1905, pp. 131-132; Georgia Department of Education *Annual Report,* 1899, p. 12; 1900, p. 43.
223. Pearson and Fuller, eds., op cit., p. 260.
224. Georgia Department of Education *Annual Report,* 1902, p. 19.
225. Georgia Department of Education *Annual Report,* 1903, p. 27, p. 33, pp. 53-54; Orr, *Education in Georgia,* p. 177; *Georgia Laws,* 1903, pp. 23-24.
226. *Georgia Laws,* 1906, pp. 61-72.
227. Georgia Department of Education *Annual Report,* 1897, p. 225; *Georgia Laws,* 1905, pp. 425-429.
228. Orr, *Education in Georgia,* p. 262.
229. Georgia Department of Education *Annual Report,* 1905, p. 268.
230. *Program of the 1896 Georgia Teachers' Association Annual Meeting.* (Notation made by Joseph S. Stewart), p. 4.
231. T. J. Woofter, "Report of Committee on Betterment of Education in Georgia," *Proceedings and Addresses of the Forty-Second Annual Meeting of the Georgia Educational Association,* (Valdosta, Georgia: Times Publishing Co., 1908), p. 41.
232. Peggy S. Steelmon, *Growth and Development of the Georgia Education Association,* (Unpublished doctoral dissertation, Athens: University of Georgia, 1966), pp. 95-103.
233. Georgia Department of Education *Annual Report,* 1894, pp. 13-20.
234. Georgia Department of Education *Annual Report,* 1894, p. 10.
235. *Georgia Laws,* 1880-81, p. 97.
236. *Georgia Laws,* 1887, p. 80.
237. *Georgia Laws,* 1903, p. 53, p. 64; Georgia Department of Education *Annual Report,* 1903, pp. 15-19.
238. Georgia Department of Education *Annual Report,* 1903, pp. 34-35.
239. Mary Edward Mitchell, *Memories of James Mitchell,* n.p., n.d., p. 16 *et passim;* Mt. Zion Seminary Association, *Minutes,* Carroll County Georgia, 1878-1895; *Carroll Free Press,* January 3, 1890, August 11, 1893, April 12, 1895, and January 1, 1932; *Mount Zion Methodist Centennial, 1875-1965,* (Carrollton, Georgia, 1965).
240. Georgia Department of Education *Annual Report,* 1900, "Statistics of Public Schools," (Statistical Table No. 3), appendix, p. ccccxxiv *et passim.*
241. Georgia Depaartment of Education *Annual Report,* 1897, pp. 248-49.
242. Georgia Department of Education *Annual Report,* 1903, pp. 39-46.
243. Georgia Department of Education *Annual Report,* 1902, p. 7.
244. Dabney, *Universal Education in the South,* (Chapel Hill, 1936), II, p. 416.
245. Georgia Department of Education *Annual Report,* 1896, p. 101.
246. Georgia Department of Education *Annual Report,* pp. 97, 101.
247. *Ibid.,* 1895, p. 215.
248. Georgia Department of Education *Annual Report,* 1903, pp. 14-16, 33, 39-46; Dabney, *Universal Education in the South,* II, p. 411.
249. Georgia Department of Education *Annual Report,* 1899, p. 12; Dabney, *Universal Education in the South,* II, p. 410.
250. Haygood S. Bowden, *Two Hundred Years of Education,* (Richmond: Dietz Printing Company, 1932), p. 27.

251. Grace Hightower, *Growth of Libraries in the Public Schools of Georgia*, (Nashville: Peabody Library School, 1965), p. 7.
252. Georgia Department of Education *Annual Report*, 1895, (Atlanta: Franklin Printing and Publishing Co., 1896), p. 27.
253. Georgia Department of Education *Annual Report*, 1897, (Atlanta: Franklin Printing and Publishing Co., 1898), p. 102.
254. *Ibid.*, pp. 207-08.
255. Georgia Department of Education *Annual Report*, 1900, (Atlanta: Franklin Printing and Publishing Co., 1901), pp. 50-52).
256. *Ibid.*, "Statistics of Public Schools," (Table I), p. ccccxii.

CHAPTER III

Building on the Framework, 1905-1937

To understand early twentieth century advances in education, one must reflect on the accomplishments of Georgians during the final years of the preceding century. By 1900 the framework of Georgia's public school system had been established. Capable and dedicated people had nursed it through the formative years. Hundreds of devoted teachers had expended themselves in the cause of education. Despite limited funds and restrictions of a legal and constitutional order, small but solid beginnings had been made. There was a growing anticipation that vigorous changes would soon improve Georgia's education. Wallace Buttrick, secretary to the General Education Board, shortly after his election in 1903, traveled through the southern states to determine firsthand the hindrances to universal education. Hindrances he found in plenty, but he also noted an attitude which gave much promise.

> A great change in sentiment and conviction was taking place in recent years and universal education at public expense had become a political catchword, but any careful observer of conditions at the South will quickly see that the old aristocratic ideal of society still mightily regards the program of Free Schools for all the People.' [1]

The reason most often advanced for the slow and ineffective development of education in Georgia during its formative years was the lack of adequate financial support. The causes were to be found in the inadequacy of the State School Fund and the obstacles which stood in the way of increasing it through local taxation. The Constitution of 1877, which determined the taxing power of the state for nearly half a century, attempted to regulate the support and management of schools and provided for a school fund to be distributed to the counties on the basis of school-age children in the population.[2] The fund consisted of fees, rentals of state-owned

148

property, fines, income from the investments of the state, a poll tax of $1 each on male citizens of voting age and, for a limited period, one-half of the income from the lease of convicts. These funds were relatively stable in amounts and bore little relationship to the state's wealth or income. The size of the fund barely kept pace with the increase in population and provided little more for the support of a child's education than was provided for that of his father at the beginning of the public school system.

Although the Constitution of 1877 provided elementary school education through the equal distribution of the State School Fund, based on numbers of school-age children, almost insurmountable restrictions were placed on supplementing the state fund from local taxes. Without the payment of tuition, the income was barely enough to support a free school for more than 100 days. School buildings were of the poorest quality, and the few teachers who could be recruited were poorly paid. Often their academic training was little beyond that of the children they taught. Such were the schools attended by over three-fourths of the children of Georgia.

The section of the constitution which imposed difficulty in the levy of local taxes for education made the following provision.

SECTION 4. Authority may be granted to counties upon the recommendation of two grand juries, and to municipal corporations on recommendation of the corporate authority, to establish and maintain public schools in their respective limits by local taxation *but no such local laws shall take effect until the same shall have been submitted to a vote of the qualified voters in each county or municipal corporation and approved by a two-thirds vote of persons qualified to vote at such election and the General Assembly may prescribe who shall vote on such question.*[3]

This provision imposed such difficulty that it discouraged all efforts to proceed by that method to secure a local tax for schools. It is reported that only one school district, Glynn County in 1886, was able to meet the conditions and levy a tax for local school support.[4] During the period under consideration a large number of municipalities applied for charters.

Those having a population of 2,000 or more were privileged to establish an independent school system and to provide for its support and administration.[5]

In a study of the legal development of the common schools of the state, Paul Ellison comments,

> . . . cities, towns and villages began to have special legislation passed. Much of this was in self defense. The state appropriations were insufficient to maintain the type of schools that the public demanded, and as the various legislatures refused to pass any laws permitting the people to vote for a district or countywide tax, the towns had their authority written into their charters, both city and school.[6]

In these independent tax units educational opportunities were noticeably better—teachers were better qualified, were paid higher salaries for longer terms and remained for longer periods in the same school. The schools were housed in better buildings which were better equipped for school work.

Despite limited funds and legal and constitutional restrictions, a great deal of progress had been made toward a system of schools. The vision of its ultimate development at this time was only dimly seen in Georgia, but improvement was vigorously sought and friends of public education were increasing.

In order that rural people might tax themselves for better schools, it would be necessary to remove the constitutional limitations. To overcome such an obstacle, a campaign would have to be organized to include people from all walks of life, and such an effort was initiated in the annual meeting of county school commissioners at Dublin in May 1904.

> The convention approved unanimously the proposed amendment which the General Assembly enacted last year in regard to a modification of present law in regard to local taxation in counties and school districts. The endorsement was in form of a resolution presented by James T. Smith of Laurens which was adopted:
> *Whereas,* At the general election in October, 1904, the question of the ratification of the local taxation amendment for school purposes is to be submitted for a vote of the people of the State; and

Whereas, In our opinion the ratification of said amendment would be of incalculable advantage to the cause of education in our State; therefore be it

Resolved, That every County School Commissioner in Georgia and every Board of Education in the State be requested to use every legitimate and just means in their power to inform the masses in their respective counties in reference to the ratification of said amendment and to urge the people to go to the polls and vote for the ratification of the same.[7]

M. L. Duggan, county school commissioner of Hancock and secretary of the commissioners' association, "offered a resolution to petition the next General Assembly of Georgia to amend the law so as to allow the districts or counties to vote on the amendment immediately after its passage, should it pass." [8]

At the June 20, 1904, meeting of the Georgia Education Association, the convention was addressed by M. L. Brittain, commissioner of Fulton County Schools, and W. B. Merritt, state school commissioner, on the subject of ratification of the constitutional amendment.[9] The Educational Campaign Committee sponsored a meeting of business executives at which Governor Joseph M. Terrell was one of the speakers. He said,

This amendment will be submitted to the people at the next general election in October, 1904. We believe that the people can be trusted; most of all they can be trusted not to tax themselves too heavily. The amendment in effect, merely restores to the people the right of local taxation.[10]

Growing out of this conference a committee was appointed to prepare and publish an address, engage in speaking and use any available measure to focus popular sentiment. The committee consisted of Walter B. Hill, chancellor of the university; Commissioner Merritt; Duggan; Warren A. Chandler; Hoke Smith and W. J. Northen.[11] The conference held in Atlanta subscribed to the following declaration.

1. We appeal to the people to adopt the constitutional amendment restoring for themselves the right of sup-

plementary local taxation to be exercised in those communities that desire it in accordance with the democratic principle of home rule.

2. We declare ourselves in favor of advancement in our educational system; better training and payment of teachers, expert school supervision; longer terms; the consolidation (where practicable) of weak and scattered schools into strong and more efficient organizations; and the improvement of schoolhouses and grounds.

3. Realizing the strong devotion of the women of the State to the welfare of the children, we appeal to them to organize school improvement societies in every county and locality.

4. We invoke the aid of the great agencies, the pulpit and press; we recommend that the friends of the school hold educational rallies in all the counties of the State, and we invite the co-operation of all good citizens in this effort for the intellectual, industrial, and moral elevation of the citizenship of the future.[12]

The initial bill was introduced in the General Assembly by Senator E. H. McMichael from Marion County. It provided for a constitutional change simplifying the manner of establishing local tax districts for schools. The sponsor, E. H. McMichael, a native of Schley County, was born February 4, 1870. His father, Dr. James R. McMichael, was a leading physician of that area and was prominent in public life. Senator McMichael was married to Mary Stewart of Tazwell, Georgia. McMichael's political record began with his election to the office of county surveyor of Marion County before he had reached the age of 21. He attended Emory College and returned to Marion County to engage in teaching and farming. His race for and election to the State Senate was reported as one of the exciting campaigns of that period in which his reputation as an eloquent and aggressive campaigner became known. In the legislature he was a member of the Education Committee.[13]

After a summer of vigorous lobbying activity throughout Georgia, on October 5, 1904, the voters of the state ratified the constitutional amendment as follows.

Authority may be granted to counties, militia districts, and to municipal corporations upon the recommendation of the corporate authority, to establish and maintain public schools in their respective limits by local taxation; but no such laws shall take effect until the same have been submitted *to a vote of the qualified voters in each county, militia district, school district or municipal corporation and approved by two-thirds majority of the persons voting* at such election, and the General Assembly may prescribe who shall vote on such questions.[14]

No time was lost in making legislative capital of the constitutional change. The enabling legislation for this amendment, approved on August 23, 1905, empowered the board of education in each county to divide their territory into districts of approximately 16 square miles, following as far as possible the lines of natural division such as streams, public roads, land-lot lines, militia district or county lines. The board was allowed freedom to exercise judgment so as not to create undue hardships in reaching the schools or school sites. The specific instructions applied to mountains, unbridged streams or unsafe roads; however, the efforts to minimize nature's hazards and hardships came close to making the law ineffective. The permitted flexibility became the pretext for making districts too small in size to be effective. Some districts were created in deliberate attempts to build small districts around important corporate establishments so that a low tax would assure much income for the support of schools while the poorer sections of the county faced insurmountable financial problems.

The maximum rate of tax that could be levied on property of the district was one half of one percent, or five mills. On petition of one-fourth of the voters of the district, an election was called and the people voted for or against local school tax. At the same time three trustees were to be elected for the district. The requirement for a successful election was a two-thirds majority of the votes cast.[15]

The success of the measures to secure local taxation, by first amending the constitution and then passing the enabling act, must be credited to the combined efforts of an extensive grassroots organization of enthusiastic supporters. No small part

of the victory was the placing of public education at the forefront of government affairs. From this major effort to publicize and gain support for education, a lesson of great value
was learned.

School districts were organized and new school buildings
were erected throughout the state. The term of instruction
also increased. In his report for 1904, Commissioner Merritt
said,

> This question of supremest concern is solved by local
> taxation. . . The sentiment in favor of local taxation has
> grown in the last two years, and is growing rapidly, as
> shown by the fact that eight counties and one hundred
> and eighty districts have adopted it. The State Educa-
> tional Campaign Committee is helping this movement
> greatly by sending speakers and literature to those coun-
> ties enough interested in the question to agitate the
> subject.[16]

Commissioner Merritt's statement described the continued
effort to acquaint the people with the provisions of the law
and the conduct of local campaigns to secure its passage.
Wherever interest was visible, help was available to explain
the law's provisions and to show its benefits to the district
school. Proponents of free education for all the children seriously considered their personal roles in its support.

Although Commissioner Merritt supported the amendment
and bill for local tax districts and worked for their establishment, he believed the county to be the more effective tax unit.
In his report of 1904, he expressed this view. He thought the
county should, wherever possible, be the unit or area for local
taxation for schools. Four counties, Bibb, Chatham, Glynn and
Richmond, had school systems which were considered the very
best by school officials. Merritt gave their excellence as his
reasons why an entire county should form one school system.

1. As the State school fund is distributed to the counties
   according to their school population, and a majority of
   the counties receive of school funds a larger amount than
   they pay in school taxes, it is just and proper that each
   county should provide a school system that could train

for citizenship the children of every district in the county.

2. If the entire county should adopt local taxation for schools by separate districts, these districts, in some features, would remain apart from each other.

3. The placing of rural and urban schools into one system will make them mutually helpful.

4. The larger work will always demand an efficient superintendent.

5. Good schools throughout the county will hold on the farms the men who make valuable both rural and urban property.

6. The county is the civil district; and all parts of the county should be as much concerned in the establishing and maintaining of a good school in every district of the county as they are in building bridges, and opening public roads and keeping these roads in good condition.[17]

Commissioner Merritt willingly gave his cooperation to the plan of local district taxes. He hoped that by extending district organization to the logical end, county units would form automatically for educational purposes. He was right; the early reports on adoption of the local tax measure gave some indication that the district tax units would indeed merge into county unit systems. Merritt reported for 1905 that,

Progressive school communities and counties have turned to the recent local taxation law as a means of securing longer terms for the schools and a satisfactory school system. Within the last year many school districts and four counties, namely Fulton, Hancock, Monroe and Randolph have voted for local taxation for schools.[18]

In 1906 some unforeseen benefits from local taxation were being reported. Commissioner Merritt said,

It has been most gratifying to note that in the rural districts when the school term has been lengthened by local taxation, the attendance for the entire long term has been much better than it was for the short term. This seems an indication of an underlying principle that parents appreciate better advantages when they have had some part in bringing about this condition by contributing toward the support of schools.[19]

Commissioner Merritt stated that no law passed in recent years affecting the educational system of the state had "provoked wider discussion, created more annoyance or done more good . . . the discussion and annoyance are the price we have had to pay for its very substantial benefits." [20] For 1906, he reported 15 counties were supplementing funds received from the state through local taxes, and 332 local systems were doing the same thing. The amount of money raised by local taxation was $750,578. When added to other forms of income, it created a sum of $3,011,768, the largest amount available for schools to date.[21]

The report for 1908 stated,

> The people are learning that education is not only a State, but a community problem and in local taxation lies the only hope of all men, and particularly of men whose means are limited, that their children have adequate educational advantages. The per capita expenditure per school-age child in 1907 was $2.43, for 1908, it was $2.85, and for the current year, the expenditure for education is $3.05. It is expected that the school fund will go to $4,000,000 in 1909.[22]

Seldom does a piece of legislation as comprehensive as the McMichael Bill, which required modification of the constitution before passage, come to life full grown and perfect. As might be expected, several amendments would be necessary before its defects could be cured. One reason for "annoyance and discussion" of the McMichael Bill may have derived from the fact that Georgia's whole program of school support had been keyed to a State School Fund which was available without effort. Now, a new source of revenue was within reach but only through some effort to secure it.[23]

While Georgians were making monumental changes in financial support for their educational system, parallel changes were occurring in such areas as the creation of public high school, the advent of a vocational education program, entrance requirements for institutes of higher education, school library facilities and teacher preparation.

The High School Emerges

Among the most important trends was the emergence, albeit late and then slow, of the public high school. In 1905, Commissioner Merritt urged the legislature to provide public high schools. He emphasized that nearly all high schools were in towns and cities, with country children having no opportunities above the elementary grades; he stated further that a public school system without a high school was sadly incomplete. Merritt projected the argument that insufficient state funds existed for five months of elementary schools; therefore, high schools necessarily would have to be financed with local taxation. He also made a plea for equal educational opportunities for all children in the state.[24]

Public high schools were planned in the countywide systems of Chatham, Richmond, Bibb and Glynn Counties and in the systems of towns and cities supported by local taxation under terms of the municipal charters. Private and semi-private institutions, also operating under charter, had functioned for several years. For the colleges not having their own attached academies, these private academies and preparatory schools served mainly to prepare students for college.

The Constitution of 1877 had provided only for education in the elementary branches of an English education and for gifts to support the university. No provision had been made, either from the State School Fund or from local taxes, for the aid of secondary schools. The constitution appeared to spell out in detail a prohibition of aid to public high schools and, despite efforts to circumvent the constitutional provision, it remained as a barrier to public aid for high schools.

Because of these legal and financial restrictions, the high schools of Georgia at the turn of the century were operating under a serious handicap; thus they usually were limited to private academies and independent city systems supported in whole or part by taxes and tuition. (It is said, but not documented, that Georgia was the last state officially to recognize the high school as a part of the public education system.) In

1903, there were hardly a dozen high schools in the state offering a program which articulated even closely with that of the better colleges. Great diversity existed in the length of the programs, their organization and content and the quality of instruction and facilities. The ambitious titles by which many of them were known bore little resemblance to the scope, content and quality of their offerings.

Most of the colleges maintained preparatory departments to overcome the deficiencies of entering students. Those which did not were limited in the number of applicants that could be admitted; as a result, enrollments were severely restricted. The University of Georgia was among the colleges which had no preparatory department and which had to compete with other colleges in recruiting a freshman class from a pool of fewer than 600 graduates.[25]

One might conclude from the review of obstacles to the development of high schools in Georgia that little was accomplished until state aid was made available for their support. Such, however, was not the case. If Georgia seemed short on legislative initiative and liberal financial support for high schools, the state was not short of leadership; under this leadership, much progress was made before any constitutional restrictions were removed.

Chancellor Walter B. Hill of the state university noted that in several of the midwestern states there was an arrangement between the high schools and the state universities whereby the high schools were encouraged to attain a certain level of competence through inspection and accreditation by the state university; the plan allowed graduates of such schools to be admitted to the colleges without the necessity of entrance examinations. Chancellor Hill desired such an arrangement between the University of Georgia and the high schools of the state. He was hopeful that the university would be joined by other colleges of the state in the event such an arrangement might be worked out.[26]

Many of the western states like Minnesota and Wisconsin, had such systems of accredited schools which seemed to work well. For instance, Minnesota had given in 1894 just $400 to each high school which came up to its required standard for an accredited high school in its course of study, equipment, and teachers. The effect on the school was favorable, as it brought in boarding students from the surrounding territory and enabled thousands to extend their students beyond the elementary school and enter the University.[27]

In 1903 Chancellor Hill recommended that Joseph Spencer Stewart, then president of the North Georgia Agricultural College, serve as high school agent to promote good relationships between the high schools and the university and to develop a system of accrediting similar to those of the midwestern states. The university trustees approved the appointment of Stewart to this new position, a part of his salary being paid for two years by George Foster Peabody, whose generosity to the university had been demonstrated on other occasions. Although Chancellor Hill did not live to see the consequences of this decision, it proved to be a fortunate one for the university, for the high schools of Georgia and for the advancement of secondary education throughout the country.[28]

Stewart was born September 23, 1863, in Oxford, Georgia, where he remained until the completion of his college education and graduation from Emory College in 1883. He was employed successively as principal of Cherokee Institute, Cave Spring; as president for two years of the Harwood Seminary in Marietta; as organizer and superintendent of the Marietta public schools; and as president of the North Georgia Agricultural College, beginning in 1897.[29]

He entered upon his new field of work as high school agent in 1903 at the age of 40; for the remainder of his life, his time and efforts were devoted to the upbuilding of high schools in Georgia. Whether serving as high school agent, professor of secondary education on the university faculty, directing the programs of the district high school associations as director of the university summer school or serving on the accrediting commission of the Southern Association, his major concern was the advancement of secondary education in Georgia.

Stewart traveled widely over the state in 1903-1904, visiting the high schools and learning as much as possible about the level and quality of their work. In his meetings with groups around the state, in his addresses and in articles prepared for educational publications, Stewart emphasized the organic relationship between the units of the education system and the peculiar role of the high school in its relation to the elementary school below and to the college and university above. He attempted to strengthen relations between the Georgia high schools and the university and to find points of common interest, especially in the area of college preparation. As a consequence of this study, he recommended to the university faculty a plan for accrediting the high schools of Georgia according to predetermined standards and specifications.

> The University of Georgia was the first of the southern states to appoint a special professor for the purpose of organizing accredited high schools and to adopt an accredited system with unit values given to high school subjects.[30]

He proposed the adoption of a system of accreditation similar to that of the midwestern states. It was approved in 1904, and a handbook of the rules was published including the forms requesting inspection.[31]

The handbook of regulations for accrediting high schools in Georgia was reprinted in the University of Georgia *Catalog* of 1903-1904. Although stated at some length, the preliminary announcement contained the basic principles on which the authority and plan of accreditation rested. It was addressed to boards of education, superintendents and principals of schools.

> The Charter of the University, granted in 1785, states that the authorities shall consult and advise not only upon the affairs of the University, but also to remedy the defects and advance the interests of literature throughout the State in general. They shall recommend what kind of schools and academies shall be instituted and shall visit these schools and examine into their order and performance.
>
> The authorities of the University recognize the fact that the university is designed to be the apex of the public school system of education, and that in order to secure the highest and best results, there should be hearty cooperation between the parts of the system.

Acting with the approval of the Board of Trustees, the University offers to establish such relations with high schools and academies as will be to their mutual aid and to the bringing into some kind of system the school interests of the State.

A State Agent has been appointed by the Board of Trustees to examine the work and equipment of such high schools and academies as desire to be accredited by the University. As a preliminary step in this work, the authorities of such schools are invited to forward to the Agent the information called for on special blank forms. Many of the states have such a system of accredited schools. Eighty per cent of the students in the leading Western colleges enter thus on certificate. It is the almost universal verdict of colleges and high schools that the system has worked to the advantage of the schools and colleges and has proved of special advantage to the cause of education in the State.[32]

The plan of accreditation concerned two types of high schools—those which fully met admission requirements and whose graduates were admitted on certificate alone, and those which did only part of the preparatory work but were doing it with satisfaction. Students from these schools were to be certified on the subjects which met admission requirements. Students from the first type of school would be admitted unconditionally, while students from the second type would be admitted without condition on the subjects approved for admission.

The regulations applied to high schools, academies, seminaries or other schools meeting the following conditions.

Students may upon a vote of the University Committee of Accredited Schools, after examination by the Agent, be accredited as making full preparation for one or more of the University courses.

1. The course of study must not be less than three years of 36 weeks each in length, following an elementary course of not less than seven years in length.
2. There must be at least two teachers in the high school, one of which may be superintendent. Graduates of the

universities or colleges of recognized standing are preferred.

3. Schools seeking considerable credit in science must
demonstrate their ability to do successful laboratory
work.

4. Schools seeking considerable credit in History and
English must give evidence of special library equipment
for these branches.

5. The school must give satisfactory instruction in the
following subjects:
English, 6 units; Mathematics, 6 units; History, 4
units; Latin, 6 units; Physical Science, 4 units; Greek
or other optional studies, 4 units.
A unit is defined as one-half year's work in each subject, with five periods a week, of not less than 30 minutes of time devoted to actual teaching

For admission to the Freshman class, not less than 26
units and not more than 8 units may be presented in one
subject.[33]

The University of Georgia Bulletin of 1904-1905 stated the
admission requirements in Carnegie units, and a total of 13
was required for admission. It elaborated upon the work of
the high school agent, defining the procedure of admission
upon certificate and giving a list of 54 high schools applying
for accreditation after inspection.[34]

Only seven four-year public high schools and four private
four-year high schools were accredited in 1904-1905. There
were 39 three-year public high schools accredited the same
year, making a total of 50 high schools announced in the first
list.[35]

Growth of Vocational Education

The public education system in Georgia historically lacked a
continuous plan of progression from primary grades through
college. Although the University of Georgia had been state
supported since its founding in the late 1700s, no funds were
allocated to high schools. When a statewide public education
system was created in 1870, the constitution specified that
state support would be limited to the basic elements of an
English elementary education. State school commissioners and

other professional educators strongly encouraged legislative action permitting state funding of secondary schools. Public high schools operated only through municipalities and special districts which had secured special legislation. The rural areas, with few public high schools or private academies, suffered a tremendous void in their education systems beyond the elementary grades. The greatest inconsistency was lack of state support for students of high school age, even though great efforts were made to expand and improve the University of Georgia.

The University of Georgia functioned as the focal point for agricultural development, a top state priority. Economic growth depended on training students in agriculture. An agriculturally oriented General Assembly strongly favored agricultural schools whose graduates would affect the state's economic growth.

In 1902, as newly elected Governor, Joseph M. Terrell recommended to the General Assembly the creation of an agricultural school in each of the eleven congressional districts of the state. In his recommendation, Governor Terrell said in part,

> Georgia is pre-eminently an agricultural state, and while we are fostering other interests, we should be specially active to encourage that business in which the whole state is most vitally concerned. If here we lag behind, the whole state suffers, and if in this we can forge to the front, all the people will be directly benefited . . . Nothing could be more helpful to this great interest than the establishment and maintenance of an agricultural school in each Congressional District of the State. Such schools would furnish an opportunity for the intelligent teaching and training annually of several thousand of young men and women engaged in agriculture and kindred pursuits . . .
>
> The experiment has been tried elsewhere with great success, and insomuch as no constitution objection could be insisted upon should they be made branches of the university, I urge the General Assembly to enact such legislation as will permit the establishment and maintenance of these schools . . .[36]

Although the legislation was not enacted immediately, the bill creating the district schools finally passed four years later, in August 1906.

Passage of the Perry Bill in 1906 to establish the 12 District Agricultural and Mechanical Schools resulted in the placement of a type of high school within reach of many rural youth. These schools were supported by fertilizer inspection fees collected through the State Department of Agriculture. The A. & M. schools provided living facilities for students living outside commuting distances.[37] The school locations follow.

1st District Statesboro	2nd District Tifton
3rd District Americus	4th District Carrollton
5th District Monroe	6th District Barnesville
7th District Powder Springs	8th District Madison
9th District Clarkesville	10th District Sparta
11th District Douglas	12th District Cochran

The district schools offered high school work in agriculture and home economics. Dormitories and dining halls were constructed as integral parts of the campus. Records show that approximately 85 percent of the students lived on the campus of these institutions.

The A. & M. schools were in operation for a period of about 25 years.[38] An evaluation of them was made later by Irvine S. Ingram, principal of the Carrollton A. & M. School, as a thesis study. His conclusions in part were as follows.

The schools appeared at a given time and in response to a specific situation. They ran their period of activity through a quarter of a century, made their contribution, and passed away . . .

It seems obvious, then, that the district agricultural and mechanical schools were but a passing phase of an enduring attempt to meet a profound and basic problem in the social and economic life of a state made up largely of rural people; that during the period of their activity, they succeeded in developing among them a consciousness of their need for a more direct and immediate approach to their problems; and too, a feeling of want or

need for those additional learnings which are traditionally regarded as cultural. That they contributed in no
small degree to a more rapid development of the secondary schools seems obvious. It is not too much to contend
further that they were undoubtedly instrumental in lending to secondary education a distinctly practical or vocational emphasis which found its way eventually into the
curricula of the high schools as they arose all over the
State.[39]

The early demise of A. & M. schools was basically caused
by the following reasons. In 1912 a state constitutional amendment permitted state support for public high schools. Two
Georgians in the U. S. Congress, Hoke S. Smith and Dudley
M. Hughes, authorized the first Vocational Education Act in
1917, which heavily supported the teaching of agriculture and
home economics in the public high schools. In 1919, a state
constitutional amendment authorized county boards of education to issue schoolhouse bonds. Also in 1919, high school
consolidation was given a boost through the Barrett-Rogers
Act, which granted annual subsidies to consolidated standard
high schools. In 1924 the State Department of Education initiated the issuance of teachers' certificates based on college
training. The administrations of some A. & M. schools detected a need for more teacher training institutions and felt
that their schools furnished fertile ground for such an en-
endeavor. Guy H. Wells, a leading educator of the time, said,
"If there is no longer a need to grow cotton and corn, there
is certainly a need to grow more teachers."

In 1931 Governor Richard B. Russell Jr. proposed the reorganization of several phases of state government. The General Assembly approved a plan creating the University System State Board of Regents. The district A. & M. schools, as
well as all state supported colleges, were placed under the
newly created Board of Regents. Some of the A. & M. schools
had, before 1931, converted to some junior and senior college
work. In the transfer to the Board of Regents the Georgia
Laws listed as A. & M. schools those at Carrollton, Sparta,
Clarkesville, Powder Springs and Madison.[40] The remaining
seven schools were approved for college work. Later the school
at Carrollton was approved for college work and is now West

Georgia College. Powder Springs and Madison have been phased out, and on their sites the local county boards are operating high schools. Sparta and Monroe were later abandoned, and Clarkesville is North Georgia Technical and Vocational School. Other schools that started out as district A. & M. schools were in 1976 strong units in the University System of Georgia, as follows.

Statesboro ....Georgia Southern College
Tifton ....Abraham Baldwin Agricultural College
Americus ....Georgia Southwestern College
Douglas ....South Georgia College
Barnesville ....Gordon Junior College
Cochran ....Middle Georgia College

Though never a part of the public school system of the state, the agricultural and mechanical schools could be labeled as forerunners of either the area vocational technical schools or the university junior college plan.

Although W. B. Merritt was state school commissioner at the time the Perry Bill was passed in 1906, he resigned less than a year later. Governor Hoke Smith named Jere M. Pound as Merritt's successor. Pound had served as head of the Normal Department of the Georgia Normal and Industrial College; president of Gordon Institute, Barnesville; superintendent of Bibb County Schools, and superintendent of East Florida Seminary. His knowledge of school affairs was extensive. Commissioner Pound felt under some constraint to set forth a brief statement of his views and philosophy of education as these related to the Georgia system of public education.

I believe in a thoroughly articulated system of schools from the University and colleges all the way down through primary schools of the lowest grade . . . To these and other ends State-aided high, or secondary, schools in every county are absolutely fundamental and necessary.[41]

Commenting on the significance of the A. & M. schools and their anticipated role in Georgia education, Commissioner Pound said,

The future of these schools and their fate depends upon your wisdom. We have classical schools, the technological schools, normal schools, schools of medicine, schools of law, schools of science; but these constitute the only recognition we have ever given in an educational way to a business in which three-fourths of our children will engage.[42]

Even as the A. & M. schools were being established, curricular change was occurring in some of the local high schools, with particular attention being given to the evidence that "a distinctly practical or vocational emphasis" was finding its way into their curricula.

In his *Annual Report* to the General Assembly of Georgia in 1906, Commissioner Merritt made these statements.

With the establishment of our eleven agricultural schools, and the magnificent secondary school in Columbus, where every child, both white and colored, is given an opportunity to secure training which fits him to become a bread winner; with the introduction into most of our city schools and many of our rural schools manual training and domestic science, our minds naturally dwell just now on this work.[43]

In the Columbus Industrial School, established in 1906, vocational offerings were provided for both boys and girls. Several courses in mechanical arts and machine work were offered for boys, while girls had available courses in home economics, industrial sewing and secretarial work.

In addition to the A. & M. schools and the Columbus school, several other schools or systems provided instruction in home economics for the first time in 1906. These included Martha Berry High School, North Avenue Presbyterian School, Washington Seminary, Albany, Atlanta, Americus, Rome, Fulton County, Waycross and Griffin. Home economics was first taught in the Savannah schools in 1908.[44]

Concern over examinations used in issuing teaching licenses continued as a major issue, even while educators and the public discussed other issues. During his tenure as commissioner, W. B. Merritt had made the grading system for the issuance of the license a little more complex, but the same general principles remained. The grades of the licenses were determined by scores made on the examinations.

Commissioner Pound, in his report of December 31, 1909, pointed up problems with examinations for issuing licenses. He said, "No two men, reading the papers submitted in an examination and acting independently of each other, will agree in their grading. One hundred forty-two Boards will have one hundred forty-two standards." And he said it was impossible for the papers to be graded by the state school commissioner who wrote the questions.[45]

During his three years as state school commissioner (1907-10), Pound worked toward increasing the number of normal schools. He also worked to improve the status of the teacher institutes; he felt the institutes had come "to be regarded by the teachers not as an 'innocuous' but a really 'nocuous desuetude.'" [46] It cost the teachers a month's salary to attend a week-long institute.

Pound also pointed up problems in issuing licenses based on examination. He recommended a higher rank certificate for those who passed a creditable examination in the high school grades.

One of the greatest accomplishments in the decade of 1900 and during Jere Pound's administration was a bill of September 16, 1909, which required the county school commissioner also to pass an examination before being appointed.

Although little was accomplished in raising the qualifications of teachers during Pound's term of office, before he resigned effective July 1, 1910, Pound cited several needs which were to be accomplished by his successor, M. L. Brittain, 1910-1922.

Meanwhile, the position of county school commissioner had been growing in stature for several years, with communities realizing in the early 1900s the importance of the job and the need for it to be held by a person knowledgeable in the field of education. In his report for 1907, Commissioner Merritt noted,

. . . the fact that 133 commissioners were elected at approximately the same time did not mitigate the problem as all of them must undergo some degree of adjustment to the requirement of the office and until this was accomplished the state commissioner would have to deal with many problems arising from their lack of experience.[47]

County school commissioners were not only making their voices heard in the progressive movements in education, but their service had merited them substantial salary increases. These were far from adequate but appeared to bring them a step closer to full-time service. Among those who were active in this group during the period 1900 to 1915 were many of the leaders in Georgia education in later years.[48] The importance of the work of county school commissioners was emphasized by Pound in the 1907 annual report, which was his first as state school commissioner.

> I believe that the county school commissioner stands at the strategic spot of the entire educational system and is a central and controlling figure in all educational movements; that, therefore, he should be a man possessing all the qualities of successful leadership—frankness, courage, enthusiasm, insight, etc. and that the law should allow him, if he is not a trained educator, to have in his office as an assistant and advisor, some one who is, and who can give his entire time to the supervisory function of the office.[49]

Another change during this period concerned the impact of accredited high schools on the admission policy of institutions of higher education. As previously noted, 50 high schools were included in the first list announced in 1905.

Included in his report for 1906, Commissioner Merritt reported a total of 82 Georgia high schools had received accredited status.[50] Schools continued to be accredited in terms of the subjects in which quality work was done, and this varied from four subjects in a small high school with two teachers to ten subjects in one of the largest high schools with six teachers. A large percentage of the high schools was being organized on the departmental plan.

Chancellor David C. Barrow, in reporting for the university and its branches in 1907, gave the enrollment of the university as 435 students and stated that this record attendance had not been achieved at the expense of other colleges, since their enrollments likewise had shown an increase. He noted that graduates of a large number of accredited high schools were accepted on certificate by the university and by other colleges which were willing to accept the certificates of accredited high schools.[61]

The subtle effect of accreditation vs. examination was to destroy largely the uncertainty in the minds of young people as to the future attainment of an educational goal, because accreditation provided a procedure by which they could attain the goal simply by graduating with credit from the local accredited high school.

In spite of the accomplishments of Stewart as high school agent and the accrediting procedures which he helped to establish, together with the ground-swell of interest in high schools, the benefits of high school still were no closer to boys and girls living in the rural counties where no high schools existed.

The state school commissioner, in an address before the Georgia School Commissioners' Association in April 1907, spoke on county high schools.

> The need of county high schools is a pressing one. Last year thirty-eight pupils in Jones county went out of the county to obtain the necessary training for college. The establishment of a high school in each county is not only a necessity, it is an economic measure, and will bring back financial return. The constitution of this State should be so amended as to allow State aid to be extended to such schools.[52]

The Business Men's Conference, held in Atlanta May 24, 1907, to consider educational needs from the point of view of the layman, regarded the need for public high schools as paramount.

> We believe that we should have a system of State aided secondary schools. High schools are included in all of our city systems, and our urban school population is thus enabled, at public expense, to pass from the grammar schools through the high schools, on to our agricultural, normal, technological and professional colleges, whereas our rural population is forced to stop with the meager and unsatisfying instruction in the 'elementary

branches of an English education only,' or reach our state aided higher institutions only through self-denying efforts of devoted parents.[53]

The impact of the pressure for public high schools climaxed in 1910. At that time, a constitutional amendment was introduced by Rep. Ogden Persons of Monroe County seeking to remove restrictions on the taxing power of the county.[54] An amendment sponsored by Dr. A. S. Stovall of Elbert County and ratified in 1912 struck the restricting phrase from the constitution's educational section, thereby making high school a part of the public school system.[55] By these amendments, the high school became a part of the public school system for the first time since 1877 and began to serve to unite the elementary schools with the university. County and local school districts now could levy taxes for public schools including the high school.

School Library Service Expands

Certainly, the first decade of the twentieth century was a vibrant period in Georgia's educational growth. This growth included an expanded interest in school library service. The statistics in the *Annual Report* for 1910 indicated there were 1,036 libraries with a total of 166,392 volumes valued at $158,-742.50.[56] Some of the libraries were supplied from sources other than the local county school commissioner's office. In 1908, Mrs. Eugene B. Heard reported that during the 11 years of their existence, the traveling libraries operated by the Seaboard Air Line Railway through the generosity of Andrew Carnegie had reached 125 rural schools in Georgia.[57]

The ten-year period between 1910 and 1920 showed a steady growth in the number of school libraries. Statistics for 1920 indicated that there were 1,880 libraries in the white schools with a total of 33,152 volumes valued at $313,610.78. The Negro schools reported 98 libraries with a total of 13,1458 volumes valued at $8,097.00.[58] These libraries must have been largely classroom collections or a central collection of a few shelves of books, since the average would come to approximately 177 volumes per white school library and 137 volumes per Negro school library. Undoubtedly some of the school libraries had much more extensive holdings, so the number of books in many schools reporting libraries must have been exceedingly meager.

The slow growth of school libraries and book collections was due not so much to a lack of interest on the part of state and local school administrators and personnel as to the lack of funds to establish libraries and improve book collections.

Back in 1902, Commissioner Merritt recommended to the General Assembly that it authorize county boards of education to apply not more than one percent of the county school funds of each county to assist in securing school libraries.[59] Stewart, while he was president of the North Georgia Agricultural College, also made an eloquent plea on behalf of the establishment of school libraries. During the annual convention of the County School Commissioners of Georgia in Macon in 1903, he referred to a bill that had passed the Senate and was pending in the House; it authorized county boards of education to appropriate from school funds annually an amount not to exceed $10 to be used for school libraries by each school that would match this amount.[60] The bill was endorsed by the convention, but it did not pass.

While school libraries and vocational education were being expanded along with many other facets of the school program in Georgia, change also was occurring in relationships between and among individual schools. In the fall of 1907, under authority of the Georgia Education Association, the Congressional District High School Associations were formed. Stewart, then serving as high school agent, was requested to appoint committees from each of the congressional districts. He chose from each of the 11 districts a committee of five. From the beginning, these committees were selected from the high school principals. The initial committees were as follows.

First District: B. F. Pickett, Savannah; E. A. Brinson, Statesboro; E. L. Ray, Vidalia; J. R. York, Swainsboro; W. N. Newson, Claxton.

Second District: S. R. DeJarnette, Albany; T. H. Wilkinson, Pelham; O. A. Taxton, Norman Park; J. A. Caldwell, Bainbridge; Homer Hamby, Cuthbert.

Third District: A. G. Miller, Americus; J. M. Richardson, Montezuma; F. E. Land, Cordele; T. G. Polhill, Hawkinsville; E. L. Brauner, Richland.

Fourth District: C. L. Smith, LaGrange; C. K. Henderson, Jr., Newnan; C. B. Gibson, Columbus; H. B. Adams, Carrollton; A. W. Strozier, Buena Vista.

Fifth District: W. F. Dykes, Atlanta; J. C. Woodward, College Park; J. C. Upshaw, Monroe; W. B. Griffin, Stone Mountain; W. E. Dendy, Douglasville.

Sixth District: R. J. Coats, Macon; J. D. Smith, Barnesville; W. T. Garrett, Griffin; F. F. Rowe, Thomasville; M. C. Allen, Forsyth.

Seventh District: W. T. Dumas, Marietta; H. L. Sewell, Cartersville; J. C. Harris, Rome; William Ransom, LaFayette; J. E. Purks, Cedartown; A. L. Brewer, Tallapoosa.

Eighth District: Wilber Colvin; Elberton; E. B. Mell, Athens; J. H. Purks, Greensboro; W. C. Wright, Eatonton; J. P. Cash, Hartwell.

Ninth District: J. W. Marion, Cornelia; E. J. Robeson, Gainesville; W. F. Brown, Commerce; H. M. Ivey, Jefferson; A. L. Archer, Toccoa.

Tenth District: T. H. Garrett, Augusta; John Gibson, Sandersville; H. P. Carreker, Warrenton; J. H. Smoot, Sparta; A. F. Ware, Wadley.

Eleventh District: E. A. Pound, Waycross; R. S. Daniel, Valdosta; K. T. Alfriend, Dublin; N. H. Ballard, Brunswick; R. J. Strozier, McRae.[61]

A basic constitution was furnished each committee in order to "obtain some unity of plan." The major purpose, as stated in the constitution, was as follows.

> . . . to promote the cause of education through the establishment and adequate maintenance and equipment of public high schools in every county as a necessity in any modern system of education, a right of every boy and girl, rural and urban, and an efficient means of linking the elementary public schools with the colleges and universities and of improving the scholarship of the rank and file of public school teachers, and the intelligence and efficiency of the entire citizenship of the state.[62]

Membership included teachers and officers in the above mentioned high schools, board members and the county school commissioners of the counties in the district. Provision was made for an annual conference to be held in each district on the same date and for representation at the Georgia Education Association and the high school conference held during the state summer school.

The wide ranging influence of this organization did much to consolidate and unify high school interests throughout the state as well as to establish a competitive effort to excel. Within the organization, every high school and its principal, teachers, board members, pupils and parents had a distinct role.

The efforts and interests of high school students were stimulated through contests in literary and athletic activities at the county, district and state levels. Through these contests, interest of the school community was enlisted; altogether, it became an organization of far-reaching influence. Specific rules for governing contests were stated in the bylaws. In time, the provisions of this part of the constitution assumed great detail as they related to the intricacies of regulation and adjudication of the many kinds of contests which developed.[63]

In spite of the keen competition among students in literary and athletic events, meetings of this organization tended to be concerned with common problems and interests and were, therefore, a unifying influence rather than a divisive one.

In his report of 1908, Stewart noted some additions to the constitution and general organization. State officers consisted of president, a position held by Stewart each year until his death in 1934; vice-president and secretary-treasurer. An executive committee was named to consist of the state officers and the president or one member from each of the district associations. One of the functions of this committee was the arrangement of the conference program, copies of which were sent to each member of the organization. One of the policies of the executive committee was to make the rules so clear and explicit that there could be no occasion for ill will to arise through misunderstandings.

At the conclusion of his report for the school year 1908, Stewart said,

Great interest was manifested in the District meetings last year. Large crowds were in attendance in seven of the Districts. One of the most valuable features is the conference of High School teachers. This should not be omitted. We must create more high school sentiment by giving more knowledge of the work of the high school.[64]

As a stimulus to competition, winners in all the district contests could compete in the state meet, which offered a still higher goal, a more compelling challenge. The state meet was held in Athens during the high school conference, usually the second week in July. Coinciding with the literary and athletic meets was the annual high school conference for teachers and principals, who participated in a carefully prepared program including problems and matters of most concern. The faculty of the university and specialists from other states also participated in these work conferences. The conference program for 1909 dealt with the following areas of high school interest.

Function of the high school

History of high schools in Georgia

Material equipment—buildings, grounds, library, laboratories, etc.

Organization and management—departmental plan—program of studies

The program of studies—curricula

The accredited system

The high school teacher—scholarship, training, personality, sex

The high school pupil—co-education, separate classes, adolescent growth

Methods of government, class exercise, social activities

What the high school does for the community—how the community can help

Vocational training in the high school

Manual training

Moral and social aspects of high school development

Causes for elimination of pupils—drop outs

Plans for unifying the work of the high schools of a county

High School Association—suggested amendments to constitution, bylaws [65]

Other facilities of the university were made available to the high school students and their sponsors who had come to parcipate in the various contests. Winning schools and individuals were given recognition. The winning school received a coveted loving cup to keep for one year, and each individual first place winner received special notice in a widely circulated report of the events. Stuart, in his report of 1909, commented on the great interest the contests appeared to arouse over the state.

> With the contests in each district culminating in the State meet at the State University during the Summer School, and the district and state conference of high school teachers, the associations are arousing an interest in the high school unprecedented in the history of the State. Thousands of boys and girls entered the preliminary contests. The annual contests are attended by thousands. The occasion is made a holiday, entertainment is furnished by the town to the hundreds of visiting pupils and teachers. Marked improvement is seen in the standard of the contests.[66]

The names of winning contestants and their records, particularly in track events, were given, and the high school conference undoubtedly devoted some time each summer to refining the handbook and making explicit the instructions to officials and judges of the contests.

The conference of 1911 gave special emphasis to high school subjects, a topic on which study was continued in the conference of 1912. A committee was appointed in advance to study each selected topic, and a member of the university or other college faculty was assigned to most. As an example, the conference committee for ancient language had as members Jere A. Pound, chairman; O. H. Langford, Prof. W. D. Hooper, J. E. Ricketson, Prof. Peppler, Emory; Miss Stanford.

Both districts and the state attempted to enhance the exchange of ideas and the exhibition of skills among the schools, but significant differences in resources and school capabilities clearly were visible, reminders of the distinction between the county systems and their city counterparts. In a few instances, independent county systems existed because local laws to create them were enacted prior to the State Constitution of 1877. Complete county unit systems included Chatham (1866), Bibb (1859), Richmond (1872) and Glynn (1873).

In his report of 1909, Commissioner Jere M. Pound noted the character of these systems.

> Bibb, Chatham, Richmond, and Glynn are among the very best of our school systems. They likewise contain some of our best city schools. We have no better schools than those of Macon, Augusta, Savannah, and Brunswick. These cities are a part of the county system, but town and country alike are completely satisfied.[67]

Throughout their early history, these county systems had strong, capable leadership, chosen with care by elected boards and sought wherever competent people could be found and retained as long as they rendered acceptable service.

In these four counties, the restrictions and limitations of the Constitution of 1877 did not apply. In their history an unbroken period of development extended backward to a time before the public education system existed. In the period since their formation, these systems had been evaluated frequently and usually with favorable comment.

Five aspects of their superiority have been cited as examples of good school management. These include (1) their operation by a single administrative organization, the county board and superintendent; (2) support by a tax applied uniformly throughout the county; (3) equal training and compensation of teachers; (4) improved school buildings throughout the county and (5) the operation of the school for nine months each year. The people participated by electing members of the school board and authorizing the board to select the superintendent for an indefinite term on the basis of professional qualifications and general character.

C. B. Chapman, superintendent of Bibb County schools, in reporting to the state commissioner in 1907, stated,

> The schools of the city and county are operated under the management of a single board of education, and under the supervision of one superintendent. The same grade teacher is employed in county and city schools, the course

of study is the same, and a pupil may be transferred from any one school into another within the county.[68]

A measure of community belief in the soundness of an educational system is the willingness of men of means to make substantial contributions to its welfare. A gift of $5,000 from Peter Massie helped to remove the stigma of "poor" from children attending the Savannah schools. Similar support was manifested by Elam Alexander in a gift of $50,000 in 1864 to help the Bibb County system in its time of need.[69]

The school systems of Bibb, Chatham, Richmond and Glynn were recognized as existing independent systems in 1872 when the school laws of Georgia were formulated, and they were protected in this right by the framers of the Constitution of 1877. Although their fiscal autonomy has diminished somewhat through modern educational practices, their fundamental rights have been preserved and their integrity respected.

According to the provisions of the McMichael amendment and subsequent bill of 1905, districts and counties could levy taxes for the better support of their schools. The voters of an entire county could establish a countywide tax district by the simple procedure of casting their vote, or the county could become a special tax county by creating special tax districts until all the districts of the county had voted. The motive which had accomplished the constitutional change and had established the legal basis also caused a large number of districts to move as one toward local tax districts. The number increased rapidly from year to year; 15 in 1906, 19 in 1908, 27 in 1912, 40 in 1916 and 67 in 1920.

In 1907 Commissioner Merritt said in his annual report,

> In addition to Chatham, Bibb, Richmond and Glynn . . . there are now fifteen counties supplementing the funds received from the State by local taxes; and there are 331 districts and 105 local systems doing the same thing. The amount of money raised by local taxation during the year, as reported to us, is $750,587 and this added to other incomes available for school purposes raises the amount of the school fund to the magnificent sum of $3,011,768.

The number of new schoolhouses built during the year was 298, as against 243 for the preceding year; and the value of school property has been raised from $5,295,970 to $5,822,172.[70]

As previously noted, certain defects became apparent as a result of the operation of the McMichael law; some districts in a county were unwilling to levy a local tax and continued to depend on the state fund exclusively. Coupled with efforts in some areas to create districts composed almost totally of the more affluent, even greater inequities in school support were produced.

Jere M. Pound, in his report for 1909, noted the conditions arising from this fact.

> The lack of a local tax provides the basis for discrimination among teachers. The best qualified go where the salaries are best leaving the less well qualified for the non-tax districts and the lowest possible salaries . . .
>
> On the whole, it is an open question whether the Legislature was wise in making districts partly autonomous under certain conditions. Very many believe the county alone could have been made the unit for the purposes of both taxation and administration. The only hope which one gets from the present status is that, ultimately, conditions will become so unequal and intolerable as to force an adoption by Legislature of some system of local taxation that will include the entire county.[71]

In the same report, he said,

> Every session of the Legislature is called upon to grant more or less of such charters and the grants are made as a matter of course and of courtesy to the local member asking for them. There are now 70 of such chartered towns drawing their public school money through this Department. About 80 others received their funds from the county school commissioners. The last Legislature alone granted at least ten, and succeeding sessions will be called upon to charter an increasing number.[72]

Commissioner Pound, in 1909 discussing the tendency of rural teachers to seek teaching places in the city, said,

This condition, however, is not the fault, particularly of the towns, though they are not entirely without blame for being too thoughtless of their country cousins. In their desire for better educational facilities, they have impatiently drawn a line around themselves, cut aloof from the more slowly moving county systems, and gone deep into their pockets for money with which to build beautiful school houses and secure trained and competent teachers.[73]

The Constitution requires that there should be a thorough system of public schools as nearly uniform as possible. The Constitution has never been obeyed in this particular a single day. On the contrary, our schools are as nearly lacking in uniformity as it is possible to make them, and we seem to take pains to keep as near the limit of such possibilities as we can. We have not one system but hundreds of systems. All our general school laws have so many exceptions as practically to make them feeble and inert where they touch the larger and stronger communities. . . . The Constitution is right in its demand for uniformity. Its provisions ought to be realized. There may be cases, perhaps, which would justify some towns in withdrawing from their county systems, but there cannot be many. In fact, as I see it, there are none at all . . . It is true that at times the cities experience advantages by cutting themselves aloof. But these advantages are temporary, and in the long run, they must prove positively hurtful. The city lives upon the country . . . The city feeds upon the country's produce. It also draws constantly the best blood and brain from the country . . . But the population of cities themselves must be constantly replenished from the country as from a reservoir. As the reservoir deteriorates in quality, how shall it fare with the towns and cities . . . Any man of wide vision must clearly perceive that, first and last and all the time, the interests of city man, or urban child and rural child, are one and the same.[74]

There should then be no aloofness, no separation in educational opportunities or facilities. The school machinery should be as much alike as possible and both classes should contribute, as they are able, to keep that machinery in perfect condition, the more prosperous class not complaining that it has the greater burden to carry, but thanking God rather that it has been chosen by good fortune to carry it.

To this end, I suggest that the education committees of the General Assembly inspect more rigidly all requests of municipalities for charter privileges to operate local school systems and that when it is deemed wise to grant these privileges, they be made absolutely uniform.[75]

The address continues, heaping argument upon argument for a plan of school organization that would minimize the vast differences in educational opportunity between children on opposite sides of a city's boundary line. As the fortunes of legislation veered from city to county, charters for town and city frequently were abolished, only to be reinstated when the tides of support reigned again in favor of the city. No way has been found to legislate righteousness and compassion and voluntary sharing by the affluent with the impoverished, but this inequality stands in the way of each attempt to establish educational equality. Even the wisest and most beneficent laws are subject to manipulation of the unscrupulous.

It appears unlikely that equalization of educational opportunity will come about voluntarily within the scope of present administrative practice. The long established procedures and built-in prejudices do not lend themselves to internal modification.

Already experiments are being made with larger and more flexible units which have a two-fold purpose: to equalize educational opportunity within a much larger unit, even larger than the county, and to minimize costs by eliminating duplication of administrative personnel and replacing them with more expert service better adapted to the large area concept. Georgia, with an abundance of small counties and numerous independent systems, would be an ideal setting for such planning. Were it possible to conceive the elimination of all barriers and regard the state as the area of equalization, it would be feasible to achieve equalization of educational costs; however, this would probably cause the loss of local incentive, that aspect of equalization which enables each community to make the best possible investment in the education of its children.

A review of school board meeting minutes from 1895 to the 1920s of two rural counties—Pulaski and Screven—indicates some tremendous struggles to obtain properly trained teachers with the amount of funds available. The examination and licensing of teachers consumed a large portion of the county commissioner's time. An allotment sheet from State School Commissioner Merritt in December 1903 to Pulaski County showed that the county's share of state funds for 1904 was $13,389.94. He also called attention to a recently enacted law that permitted the use of funds derived from the hire of convicts for schools. The state commissioner also commented on other facts, including (1) examination of the county school commissioner, (2) expiration date of the county school commissioner's term and (3) handling the sale of state approved textbooks.[76]

The matter of handling textbooks posed serious problems for county and state officials. Many laws were passed governing the adoption of textbooks. The General Assembly appointed a committee in 1913 to investigate the high prices of textbooks,[77] and in 1914, the General Assembly appropriated funds to finance the work of the investigating committee.[78]

The Screven County Board of Education minutes reflect monthly salaries of teachers from $15 to $25 in 1898.[79] The minutes of October 5, 1897, show two important resolutions:[80] (1) "Resolved, that our representative in the legislature be requested to oppose all efforts to repeal the laws increasing the school fund" and (2) "Resolved it is the opinion of this Board that $4,000 added to the school fund of the state by the last legislature should be used to increase the compensation of teachers and to increase the public school term to six months instead of five." [81]

Following the enactment of the McMichael Bill, the Screven County Board of Education, on August 9, 1906, initiated a campaign to call an election on local taxes for operational purposes.[82] On September 18, 1906, the board invited State School Commissioner Merritt to speak at a public mass meeting on the need for local taxation.[83] A committee appointed by the board subsequently came up with a plan to divide the county into 42 separate districts and attendance areas.[84] This fragmentation, and others similar, evoked a statement years later from State School Superintendent Brittain to the effect that sub-tax districts enabled boards of education to fence off wealthy sections of a county, thereby providing unequal support for children of a county.[85]

As would be expected, acquisition of more financial resources for local school systems promptly led to increased demands for better qualified administrative personnel. In the past, stiff requirements had not existed. For example, in 1896, a professional committee headed by Lawton B. Evans emphasized the necessity for establishing some qualifications to be required of the county school commissioner. The committee stated,

> If it is desirable to insist upon a certain degree of qualifications for a school teacher in the humblest district in the state, and this proposition has passed the realm of discussion, it would seem that there is no question that the superior officer clothed by statute with extended powers as a School Commissioner ought to be a person possessing some fixed qualifications for the performance of the duties of his office.[86]

It was generally conceded that examinations for these posts were less comprehensive than those given to teachers. On the examination given in February 1904, for example, only 25 questions were asked. Four each were on school law, arithmetic, grammar and history; and nine were on all other topics combined. The history tests required the date, author and provision of the "Omnibus Bill," a brief account of William H. Crawford's services to the state and the nation, the naming of four Civil War battles in which General John B. Gordon participated, and the steps required for a foreigner to become a naturalized citizen of the United States. Satisfactory answers were required to 75 percent of the questions.[87]

In 1908 Commissioner Pound enforced his view that the county commissioner is "at the strategic center of all school operations." He continued,

... It is but a trite statement that these men ought to be the best procurable. By 'best' is not meant merely the morally best. Their morals, of course, should be above reproach and unimpeachable. But they ought to be trained men—not only men who know but men who know how to do, to lead, to bring things to pass; and in every county there ought to be such a man giving his entire time and thought to work of organizing schools, ordering the courses of study, training and directing teachers, conducting institutes, holding conferences and developing in the system latent possibilities for good.[88]

The above observations may have been expressed as foreboding of what actually happened in 1909 when, by act of the legislature, the office of county school commissioner was made elective by popular vote. This manner of selecting the local school administrator by popular election and placing over him a board appointed through another authority would plague local school operations in Georgia for many years to come. Instead of giving an elected board the authority to choose the best executive available regardless of where he might live, as was true in the city school systems, the county schools were inevitably to be directed by one of their number able to secure a majority of votes, with little regard for his professional abilities.[89]

Provisions of the law stated that the county school commissioners "shall be elected by the electors of their respective counties, who are entitled to vote for members of the General Assembly, at the general election held for such members next preceding the expiration of the county school commissioner's present term of office, and every four years thereafter." Their qualifications were to be ascertained through an examination held and graded by the county board. To qualify as a candidate a minimum grade of 85 percent on the examination was required.[90] Because the law was not explicit, confusion arose at many points, requiring interpretations both by the state board and state commissioner. Problems were experienced as to defining the nature of the qualifying examination, the critical grade necessary for approved candidacy, completion of the examination before the date necessary to get a name on the party primary ticket and what to do in case of failure to qualify. Other problems had to do with the eligibility of voters living in an independent city system and what effect, if any, the place of residence of the candidate might have on his qualification.

Deploring the action of the legislature in making the office of county superintendent a political one, Commissioner Pound expressed the view held by many educators.

> To the minds of most thinking teachers, a better plan would be to choose the Board by popular election, to restore to it this right which alone makes it respectable and efficient, to untie its hands and let it seek for trained supervisors wherever they may be found; and no improvement worth while is possible without them.[91]

Commissioner Pound began to feel the first effects from the early administration of the law. It was expected that he would prepare the qualifying examination, send it to the county boards who would in turn administer the examination, grade the examination papers and notify the aspirant of his qualification or failure. Of this procedure he said,

> It is to be presumed too, since an examination is required in which an average of 85 per cent must be made, that a uniform standard of competency and scholarship was sought. If so, the machinery for securing it is absurdly imperfect and ineffective. No two men, reading the papers submitted in an examination and acting independently of each other, will agree in their grading. One hundred forty-two boards will have one hundred forty-two standards.[92]

After the passage of the law to elect the county commissioners by popular election, a number of the county commissioners resigned leaving in each case several months of an unfinished term. Among these was M. L. Brittain, commissioner of Fulton County. He was appointed to fill the unexpired term of Commissioner Pound, who resigned his state position in May 1909.

During this same year, Stewart presented his first annual summary of freshman grades recorded at Georgia colleges. Prepared under his supervision, these were obtained from records supplied by the colleges at the end of the first quarter or semester. For each student, the summary contained his initials, his high school, college attended, how admitted, the grade on college work and any subjects failed.

This report was valuable to the college, to the high school and to the boys and girls whose records were involved. The repetition of this report from year to year had a stimulating effect, particularly on the high school. It served as something of a measure of excellence for the college in determining future admission policies and for the student who could match high school records with the college standards.[93]

Through the agency of a committee appointed by the Southern Association of Colleges and Secondary Schools in 1911, there developed the High School Accrediting Commission. The commission, which was approved in 1912, was composed of three representatives from each state in the association. Preliminary work involved the preparation of a uniform admission blank of high school transcript, the forms necessary for a full description of the high school applying for admission, a statement of proposed standards by which the high school would be judged and a list of the schools already accredited by each state. The meeting of 1912 devoted much time to the committee's report and ended by adopting the report with modifications. The Commission on High School Accreditation was chosen and began to function in 1912. Georgia could note with pride the contribution which it made in these procedures. The motion to create the commission was made by Joseph Stewart, and he was a member of the committee appointed to present a preliminary plan of operation. After its adoption, he was chairman of the commission for four years.

In 1912 Georgia reported 74 accredited high schools, of which 45 were fully accredited four-year schools.[94] By 1915, 19 of the Georgia high schools had won Southern Association approval,[95] and in 1916 the number had increased to 36.[96] Over the years since the beginning of the work of this commission, one of the coveted ambitions of the high school has been to win membership in the Southern Association; to retain membership from year to year was a measure of excellence to be cherished.[97]

The White Bill of 1911 provided for a state certificate for high school teachers. Up to this date, licensed teachers holding elementary certificates taught in the high schools. By a regulation of 1915, high school teachers were required to hold state certificates in the subject areas in which they taught. These laws began to have their effect in strengthening instruction in the high school, but several years were required to secure full enforcement. Those who taught in the private secondary schools were not required to have valid state certificates, their qualifications being determined by the conditions of their employment.[98]

From the beginning of his work in 1903, Stewart prepared an annual report which was incorporated in the *Report of the State Superintendent to the Chief Executive and General Assembly*. This report contained comments and items of information about the high schools of Georgia, a listing and classification of accredited high schools, and information about the District High School Associations. The high school conference, held for a week during the university summer school, became the professional agency for high school teachers and principals and served until superseded by the appropriate branch of the Georgia Education Association. This conference was made to coincide with the state meet for district contest winners.

There was in the early years no satisfactory publication for high school personnel. In his report for 1913 Stewart wrote,

> We approached the High School teachers on the proposition of establishing a High School Quarterly as a medium for the profession. They promptly backed it with over 600 paid subscriptions. It is now extending its circulation to other states.[99]

Joseph Stewart became the editor of the *High School Quarterly* with the first issue and continued to edit the quarterly until the month of his death in March 1934. The quarterly was a dignified publication under the editorship of Stewart and contributed significantly to the professional growth of Georgia's high school principals and teachers. *High School Quarterly* was widely read and contributions were received from throughout the country. From the first, it was more than a local journal.

As previously described, Stewart was active in several facets of education in Georgia. In addition to his efforts with school accreditation and classification, he continued to work with the district associations. He was engaged as professor of secondary education, University of Georgia; State High School Inspector; president of the State and Congressional High School Associations; editor of the *High School Quarterly;* chairman of the High School Commission of the Southern Association of Colleges and Preparatory Schools; and director of the Summer School, University of Georgia. He wrote extensively and spoke frequently.

Reporting on activities of the district association for 1913, Stewart called attention to school exhibits which were arranged in some of the districts and counties. He encouraged these as part of the program in each district, the collection of choice pieces of student work including notebooks, examination papers, drawings, sewing, cookery, shopwork, pictures of school buildings, well arranged classrooms, playground arrangement, gardens; in fact, everything that pertained to the life of the school should be exhibited, he said. Two days were usually given to the district meetings. A recommended plan was to begin the meetings on Sunday with attendance at places of worship in the town serving as host to the conference. Sunday talks focused on inspirational themes. Then, Monday would be spent in group and departmental discussions relating to the work of the schools and the projected plan for the summer conference.

The high school conference was attended by a large number of principals and teachers. In order to secure better representation, Stewart recommended that the expenses of the representative from each high school be borne by the local school board.

In 1913 state contests were held at the University of Georgia during the first week in July. These were reported as the most successful from the standpoint of attendance and wide participation of any contest previously held. In his report, Stewart noted,

The 1913 high school contests enlisted the largest number of students in the several contests and brought together the largest crowds in the six years since the State was organized. Fully three thousand high school students took part in the preliminary and final contests. There are few high schools of any standing that are not now members of one of the associations. The associations have developed track athletics throughout the state, have revived declamation training, improved the piano instruction, cultivated essay writing, improved the spelling, organized State-wide debates, and created a loyal school spirit that is a pleasure to experience. It is remarkable how in many towns the annual meets have enlisted the interest of the business men of the community in the high school. They encourage the students while training and accompany them to the district meets.[100]

In 1914 the high school contests increased in appeal and influence. Representation from the schools at the district meets generally was large, in one case going over 2,000. The effect of these contests on the county schools was also reflected in a large number of county meets. All 12 of the district associations held meetings.

Much interest in the contests and other activities began to reach down into the elementary school. To stimulate general interest in physical development and skill, Stewart set up a standard of attainment within reach of sixth and seventh grade boys and girls and induced the *Atlanta Constitution* to offer bronze medals for all who met the standard. Silver pins were given to students of the high school who met substantially high requirements.[101]

One of the subtle effects of this program, extending from the most remote village school to the university, was to promote a degree of intercommunication among high school pupils that left no child in an isolated and backward situation. Each was encouraged to measure self-worth regardless of circumstance and to reach for the highest goal attainable. Backwardness ceased to be regarded as the inevitable badge of poverty; instead it was something to be overcome through personal effort in an environment enriched with many opportunities to discover and develop an identity. The boy who, from running a measured course along the cotton rows, developed the skill and endurance to run the 100-yard dash in 11 seconds or less knew a resource by which he could barter for many things once believed unattainable.

In 1915 all the district associations held meetings. Debating had come to the fore; more than 100 debates were held on the subject, "Resolved that Capital Punishment Should be Abolished in Georgia." Large audiences attended and supported the teams with enthusiasm. It was not always easy for the town followers to agree with the decisions of the judges. Tensions ran high and generally good sportsmanship prevailed, though on occasion the officials did leave the scene of action a bit hurriedly.

As usual, the state participants were listed and the winner especially designated. In addition to points for the school, substantial prizes were offered in some of the events. Although these were usually in the form of books or other usable items, prizes other than points were discouraged.

The Athletic Cup was a handsome prize given by the *Atlanta Constitution*. The State Literary Cup was given by Dr. S. V. Sanford of the University of Georgia faculty. These were rewards of merit in the state meet. Lesser prizes were offered in the district contests.

In 1916 the tenth district won the Literary Cup, the fourth district won the Athletic Cup. Savannah won the individual literary cup, and Newnan won the individual athletic cup. Stewart was pleased when the schools over the state were represented. Regarding the contests of 1916, he said,

> Almost every one of the accredited schools sent representatives to the District Meets. Each school is limited to fifteen representatives. These places are won in local contests in each school. It will thus be seen that several thousand boys and girls in the accredited schools are stimulated to extra effort in one or more of the many events. Physical training is gradually finding its place in the high school. The high school conferences and school exhibits held in connection with the Meets were organized in 1905 and have become a definite part of the high school development of the State. The plan is gradually working

down into the lower schools. Several counties now hold
county contests with favorable results.[102]

Commissioner Brittain came into the office on July 1, 1910,
at a time when problems surrounding the change to elected
county commissioners were at their peak. Ordinarily a mild
mannered man, he denounced the practice with all the vigor
of a well stored vocabulary. He regarded this step as a
calamity for the rural schools, where he believed there was
greatest need for expert supervision. His mature judgments
were vehement in denouncing the legislation which "dragged
the head of the county schools into politics, thus denying the
country child the right to get the best county school superintendent possible from any source whatever."
He said,

> I suppose it is unwise and even useless at this time to
> ask for legislation correcting this law by reason of the
> fact that those elected will not assume their new duties
> until 1912 but at least we should have the change of
> name. Georgia should have State and County Superin-
> tendents and let the very title show the character of the
> work desired from the incumbent.[103]

And like his predecessor, Commissioner Pound, Brittain
recommended the election of the county board by popular
vote and appointment of the county superintendent by the
board. He recommended a salary of $1,200 and the require-
ment that it be a full-time position. He hoped such a plan
might be enacted at the expiration of the term of office of
those who had just been elected. He voiced another plan
which seemed remote at the time.

> It would be far better if the educational boards and of-
> ficials of the city and county were enlarged and united
> and the children of both given the same close supervision
> and education. The multiplication of boards and ma-
> chinery causes needless friction and unjustice to all. The
> consolidation would allow even the weaker counties of
> the state to have an expert educator as superintendent.[104]

The law was amended in 1911 to provide alternatives in
years of training and experience required for the examina-

tion, and for those taking the examination, only a "satisfactory" grade was required. The law was amended again in 1912 to make the terms uniform and concurrent beginning in 1913 and terminating in 1917.[105]

Commissioner Brittain also was vocal on the subject of teacher examinations and licensing practices. He said,

> The present method of examinations and licensing of teachers was perhaps adequate 30 years ago and met conditions in existence when the public school system in Georgia was founded. Today, this is by no means the case. Such legislation as we have had upon the subject has tended to weaken and destroy the original plan. The specially chartered systems have secured exemption from the State examinations and licenses. The larger cities were benefitted in some cases because they were enabled to give tests better suited to individual needs—particularly with regard to high school instruction. In many instances, however, this freedom from the general law has led to laxity which has caused harm to our work. Numbers of the smaller local systems have taken advantage of the law and for years have required neither examinations, normal work, nor license. Scores of schools have employed teachers without proper qualifications or the requisite ability to secure even a license of low grade.[106]

The year 1911 marked a significant change in the certification process. From 1870 to 1911 changes in certification standards and processes were made by enactment of the legislature. The school law of 1911 gave authority to the State Board of Education for providing rules and regulations for supervision of all schools in the state. From 1911 until the present, the State Board of Education has had the authority to set certification regulations. (The Board adopted new regulations for certificate types and grades in 1912.)

Other significant results of the 1911 session of the General Assembly included several changes in existing school laws, such as, (1) to change the office of State School Commissioner to State School Superintendent, (2) to provide for the employment of three state school supervisors and a state school auditor, (3) to recover any school funds in the event of mis-application of funds, (4) to change the position of county school commissioner to county school superintendent and to set his compensation, qualifications, elections, powers and duties, (5) to consolidate schools and provide for the transportation of pupils living more than three miles from the newly consolidated school.[107]

Also, the 1911 session approved a constitutional amendment which was similar to a bill defeated by the previous legislature. This was a measure to delete the phrase ". . . in the elements of an English education only" from the Georgia constitution, and it was defeated in 1910 by only 14 votes.[108] This phrase was the portion that restricted the use of state school funds for instruction in the elements of an English education only and mitigated against the establishment of public high schools. As voted, a similar bill in the form of a constitutional amendment was introduced and passed in 1911.[109] It was ratified by the voters and was activated in 1912; thus, Georgia became the last state in the union to approve free public high schools as a part of the state school plan. (As early as 1910, there had been 63 accredited four-year high schools and 107 accredited three-year high schools, with these numbers including private, parochial and district A. & M. schools. Some high schools had as few as two teachers.) [110]

The School Law of 1911 changed the title of "commissioner" to that of "superintendent." Also, the law emphasized supervision of county normals and institutes and supervision of all schools in the county through visitations to the schools. In his visitations the superintendent was to see what advancement was being made by pupils and to advise teachers and assist in the advancement of education.

Along with greater emphasis on assisting in the advancement of education as one of the superintendent's responsibilities came some required qualifications.

1. At least three years practical experience in teaching, one year of which shall have been in the schools of Georgia, and

2. Hold a first grade license, or in lieu thereof shall have a diploma from a reputable College or Normal School, or

3. Five years experience in actual supervision of schools, or

4. Stand an approved examination before the State Board.[111]

The superintendent had to be a resident of the county and be a person of good moral character, never convicted of any crime involving moral turpitude.

The same law also specified for the first time qualifications of the state school superintendent. He was required to "be a man of good moral character, of high educational standing, have had at least three years practical experience as a teacher, or in lieu thereof shall have a diploma from a reputable College or Normal School or shall have had five years experience in the actual supervision of schools and be at least thirty years of age." [112]

Public school laws were revised in 1911. The revision gave authority to the State Board of Education to determine the regulations which governed teacher education and certification. As a result of this new authorization and pressure from educators in the state, a classification system was set up. Licenses were still to be issued by examinations developed by the State Superintendent of Schools. Licenses were issued for the following.

1. Primary teachers (first four classes)
2. General elementary
3. High school and supervisory

Special subject certificates were issued in domestic science and art, vocal music, manual training, physical education, drawing, kindergarten, commercial branches and stenography. Each of these required special preparation before passing an examination for the certificate.

All teachers were required to pass examinations on Georgia history. Teachers holding certificates from other states had to present evidence of moral character and pass an examination on Georgia history. For the first time, recognition was given for special college study in subject areas and for completion of an approved normal school.

By this time normal schools were extensions of study in high schools. When South Georgia State Normal College opened in 1913 in Valdosta, the program extended "about two or three years above schools of the rank of our best accredited high schools." [113] Other normal schools in the state had advanced to a level beyond high school also. Since few high schools were available to the public, the normal schools were often four-year programs; two years were devoted to work on the high school level and two to a combination of general education and professional education. Usually the programs included manual arts and domestic science also.

The school law of 1911 made provision for the State Superintendent of Schools to employ three state school supervisors. The duties of these supervisors were "to act as instructors of institutes, to give state normal instruction and training as the state superintendent may direct in each county, to grade the papers of applicants for professional certificates or state licenses, and to aid generally in supervising, systemizing and improving the schools of the State under the direction of the State Superintendent of Schools." [114]

Following the approval of free public high schools and the appointment of the state school supervisors, the State Department of Education planned additional penetration into the school districts. There were more teachers' institutes, the adoption and application of minimum school standards and visits to encourage the passage of local school tax referendums. One of the supervisors, M. L. Duggan, stated in his report to Brittain in 1913 that school surveys were becoming fashionable. [115]

As noted, a major purpose for employing state supervisors was to help upgrade the institutes still required for every county. It was possible to combine teachers from several counties for one institute. Since few elementary schools had more than five months of school, there was time throughout the year to hold institutes. Commissioner—now Superintendent—Brittain employed the first three supervisors. In his report of December 1913 to the General Assembly, he named the first supervisors who had been at work for at least a year.

1. Celeste S. Parrish, Supervisor for North Georgia
2. M. L. Duggan, Supervisor for Middle Georgia (identified previously)
3. F. E. Land, Supervisor for South Georgia

These three supervisors paid by state funds worked largely with white schools and teachers. The General Education Board supplied funds for employing a supervisor to work with Negro schools and teachers, and George D. Godard became the first special supervisor for Negro teachers. Almost immediately he was able, through the General Education Fund, to employ the first Negro state industrial worker, Clara Scott from Arabi, Georgia. The Slater Fund and the General Education Board financed institutes for the Negro teachers; no state funds at this time were used for institutes for the Negro teachers.

Dr. George D. Godard reported as follows on institutes held for Negro teachers in 1915.

These institutes have been so directed as to bring to the attention of the teachers and the people the pressing need of industrial work in the schools. About half the time of the teachers was employed in actual handwork of various types, such as basketry, chair-caning, shuck-mat making, horse collars, woodwork, plain sewing and simple cooking. A portion of the time was devoted to a discussion of sanitation, farming and general betterment of the homes of the colored people. The literary work of the institutes was confined to the teaching of simple methods of instruction in reading, writing, arithmetic and geography.[116]

In each of these institutes the larger part of one day was devoted to a county mass-meeting for farmers, their wives and children, teachers and all classes of workers. At these meetings the need for better homes, better schools, better farming, better churches and greater respect for law and order were insisted upon. Usually the County Superintendent, members of county boards of education and city boards of education and other white people were present and participated in the discussions. Summer schools for colored teachers were conducted during the summer of 1915, at Fort Valley, Quitman, Valdosta, Queensland, and Statesboro. About 250 colored teachers had four weeks training in these schools, for the rural school work.[117]

The reports of all three state supervisors for white teachers indicated they helped the schools to meet the necessary requirements of standard schools as well as to hold annual institutes. They also secured services of college staff, combined counties for institutes and increased the length of institutes. Superintendent Brittain stated in 1915,

The work done by the supervisors demonstrates more clearly every year the wisdom of having these trained instructors to aid the teachers in place of the old-fashioned institutes with the so-called experts in charge.[118]

Among college staff members who aided the state supervisors early in teaching in these state administered institutes were the following.

Eurie Belle Boston, Georgia Normal and Industrial College
Jessie Burton, State College of Agriculture
Professor Firor, State College of Agriculture
Lula Edwards, State Illiteracy Commission
Elizabeth Moore
Professor D. L. Earnest, State Normal School of Athens
Caro Lane, Georgia Normal and Industrial College
Dr. Dorothy Bocker, State Board of Health
Lurline Parker, Georgia Normal and Industrial College
Susan Matthews, State College of Agriculture
Susan Myrick, Georgia Normal and Industrial College
Julia Bethune, Georgia Normal and Industrial College

In 1918 the General Education Board provided funds for Duggan and Godard to attend Harvard Summer School to prepare them more completely for working in the rural areas, where the need for supervision was great. Of a total of 8,359 schools, 4,867 were one-room schools. J. O. Martin joined the state supervisory staff to replace M. L. Duggan, who became Supervisor for Rural Education in 1914. Celeste Parrish died in 1918 and was replaced by I. S. Smith.

In addition to the annual institutes, all of the state supervisors worked to develop summer schools. The university
summer school was authorized by the General Assembly in
1904 chiefly as a school for teachers. Summer school for
teachers was held at Georgia Normal and Industrial College
for the first time in 1916; it lasted three weeks. The faculty
of the college gave their services without a regular salary,
and Milledgeville citizens provided funds to bring in distinguished educators and lecturers to aid in the work. A
chautaqua course of evening lectures was held during the
same period. There were also musical attractions and varied
forms of entertainment.[119] Summer schools also were held at
State Normal School. In 1917, in addition to the institutes,
George Godard held five summer schools of four weeks duration for Negro teachers: Fort Valley High and Industrial
School, Valdosta Colored High School, Monroe County Training School at Forsyth, Industrial School at Sandersville and
Statesboro High and Industrial School.[120] No state funds
were used to support these summer schools. The General
Education Board also sent 14 Negro teachers to Hampton
Institute, Virginia, in 1917, for a course of four weeks in
industrial features of education.

County training schools for Negroes were organized to aid
Negro teachers in upgrading their common school education
background. Among the first training schools were those in
Ben Hill County, Adel, Bullock County, Sandersville, Monroe
County and Tift County. These programs went through the
ninth and tenth grades [121] and were provided by the Slater
Fund. The state provided funds for developing the Georgia
Normal and Agricultural School for Negroes in Albany,
Georgia, in 1917, where the early work was of a high school
level.

Parallel to the new work of the state supervisors was the
old problem of teacher certification. The use of examinations
for the issuance of certificates continued, and Superintendent
Brittain expressed concerns about the licensing of teachers.
He was concerned that teachers in private schools hold a
license. In 1916 he said, "The state law requires an examination and license of every public school teacher. This is just
and right . . . (It is just as true that) no teacher should prac-

tice upon the minds and bodies of the little boys and girls in the community without authority and certification. The public has the same right to expect this protection in the case of private and denominational schools as it has of those under public authority and I recommend the passage of a bill requiring such instructors to obtain certificates in accordance with the regulations of the State Board before teaching in any of the primary or elementary schools of the state." [122]

Brittain in the same year recommended a State Board of Examiners to grade papers according to the same standard instead of having 152 different county superintendents each with different standards.

Through the collection of common data on teachers by Stewart as high school agent, some uniformity was now in existence in Georgia. Information on each teacher in the accredited high schools of Georgia was collected by him and published in the annual report from time to time. In the one for 1916, the following information was given.

1. Office held	5. Subjects taught
2. School	6. Years of experience
3. College attended	7. Number of recitations per
4. Degree received	day

The facts contained in this report of nearly 30 pages impressed the high school inspector. He was encouraged by the progress made by high school teachers to obtain the best teacher training possible. As teachers' salaries were increased, opportunities became more abundant to complete college and to return as often as possible for summer study.[123]

The Smith-Hughes Act and Vocational Education

Vocational education has been alluded to in previous portions of this chapter; however, a broad review of this growing facet of Georgia education in the early 1900s has not occurred. Vocational education—with that specific identification—arrived with passage of the Smith-Hughes Act of 1917, the first national act to provide any appropriation of federal funds for vocational education. This act provided for a continuing appropriation for vocational education in agriculture, trades and industry and home economics. Funds were appropriated for salaries of teachers, for teacher training and for the administration of the program on a national level. In the words of I. A. Dickerson,

> The Act provided for a Federal Board for Vocational Education and a State Board. Each state was required to prepare a state plan for vocational education and to agree (1) that the federally aided program of vocational education would be under public supervision and control, (2) that the controlling purpose would be to fit for useful employment, (3) that the vocational education would be of less than college grade and designed to meet the needs of persons over 14 years of age who had entered upon or who were preparing to enter the occupation for which they were receiving training, and (4) that the state or local community or both would provide the necessary plant and equipment.[124]

The bill passed Congress on February 23, 1917, to provide federal aid to high schools for industrial, agricultural and home economics education. The grant to Georgia was made up according to rural population, urban population and total population in relation to the rural, urban and total population of the nation. The initial sum allotted to Georgia was $42,000, and because of the constitutional limitation on state support for high schools, the federal grant was matched by receipts from the rental of the state-owned railroad. Due to the limitations of this fund and the fact that many of the high schools could not meet the necessary standards for receiving the aid, a portion of the grant reverted to the federal treasury.[125] Provisions were included in the act for training teachers for these subjects and supervisors for the teachers in service. Training programs were carried on at the University of Georgia, the Negro colleges at Albany and Savannah, and later a program of home economics education was established at the Georgia State College for Women at Milledgeville.

Immediately following passage of this act by Congress, the Georgia legislature passed a bill providing for a State Vocational Board and giving it $15,000 to take advantage of the federal appropriation together with whatever help could be secured from local sources. The appointed board consisted of

D. C. Barrow, Chancellor, University of Georgia, Athens; M. L. Brittain, State Superintendent of Schools, Atlanta; Dudley M. Hughes, Danville; J. Randolph Anderson, Savannah; Sam Tate, Tate; B. H. Hardy, Barnesville; and Ross Copeland, Augusta.[126]

While several important events in the development of vocational education occurred during the 1905-37 span to enable the provision of realistic programs in Georgia, the Smith-Hughes Act was the most important. It should be noted that changes in Georgia schools during this period included increases in the number of accredited high schools, in the enrollment in those schools and in the percentage of graduates going to college. The number of high schools increased from 12 in 1905 to 417 in 1930, and the number of students enrolled in these schools increased from 420 in 1905 to 86,398 in 1937.[127]

A significant change in reasons for attending high school occurred during this period as more students enrolled. In 1905, 91.1 percent of the graduates of accredited schools went to college; in 1930, 23 percent were going to college.[128] These data doubtless had much to do with the provision of vocational education for graduates who were not going to college for professional training.

In the beginning, relatively few schools and systems in the state were ready to initiate innovative programs of vocational education. At the end of the first year under the provisions of the Smith-Hughes Act, Georgia had qualified for $27,357-.80.[129] Local boards of education were not familiar with the purpose of the Smith-Hughes Act, and while many boards desired federal aid, they were not anxious to subscribe to the rules and regulations of the act. In addition, it was very difficult to secure qualified teachers, particularly due to World War I.

The second year's work brought about a better understanding of the law, especially its aim. A sufficient number of applications were received to utilize the entire amount of federal funds available for vocational education purposes, but because teachers were unavailable, only four new schools could be added to the list of those providing vocational education.[130]

The availability of federal and state funds and the encouragement received from members of the State Board for Vocational Education were incentives to local officials, and vocational programs were provided in many areas of the state beginning in 1917 and 1918. The District A. & M. schools served as a nucleus for beginning programs; by July 1918, eight of the schools met the qualifications for vocational funding. By January 1, 1919, all of the 12 schools were involved in the new undertaking. These 12 A. & M. schools (named in the order of their district number) were located at or near the following towns: Statesboro, Tifton, Americus, Carrollton, Monroe, Barnesville, Powder Springs, Madison, Clarkesville, Sparta, Douglas and Cochran.[131]

Another indication of the growth of vocational programs in Georgia high schools was revealed in *The Forty-Fifth Annual School Report of Georgia* made by Superintendent Brittain in 1917. The report listed the amount of funds used by local school officials for purchasing equipment for commercial subjects, domestic science and manual training in their respective schools. The report covered a two-year period and showed the amount of money spent for vocationally oriented programs.

FUNDS SPENT FOR EQUIPMENT
BY LOCAL SCHOOLS

Year	Subject Area		
	Commercial subjects	Domestic science	Manual training
1916	$19,462	$20,110	$52,554
1917	26,573	29,516	54,874

Funds were used to purchase commercial equipment in 23 schools, domestic science equipment in 36 schools and manual training equipment in 20 schools.[132]

As a parallel to these developments in local secondary schools, colleges were modifying their programs to help prepare instructors for vocational schools. Colleges with programs in home economics were broadening the scope of their offerings in this area to meet the changing needs in the home and in the schools. This influenced to a great degree the subject matter taught in the schools.[133] In 1907, the College of

Agriculture, University of Georgia, received $25,000 in federal funds to provide courses for the special preparation of instructors to teach the elements of agriculture and the mechanic arts. The money was received through the Nelson Fund.[134]

The Georgia State Board for Vocational Education, which was created by the General Assembly soon after passage of the federal law, held its first meeting in 1917 soon after its members were appointed. At its first meeting, the board appointed J. S. Stewart, professor of secondary education and high school inspector for the university, as general supervisor of vocational education.[135]

Individuals serving on the administrative staff of vocational education in the early years were M. L. Brittain, executive officer and state director; Robert D. Maltby, state supervisor of agricultural education; L. M. Sheffer, assistant state supervisor of agricultural education and itinerant teacher trainer; J. F. Cannon, state supervisor of trade and industrial education; Katherine Dozier, assistant state supervisor of trade and industrial education; Mary E. Cresswell, state supervisor of home economics education; and Epsie Campbell, assistant state supervisor of home economics education.[136]

The aims and objectives of the various groups in vocational education were quite different from those of the academic programs found in the public schools of 1917. Also, the methods used in teaching individuals how to participate successfully in the occupations for which training was to be provided had to be quite different. Leaders in the field of vocational education and the members in Congress realized that teachers who were to work in vocational education should be specifically trained for the particular field in which they were to work: agriculture, home economics, or trades and industries. One of the first responsibilities of the new State Board for Vocational Education was that of selecting state institutions of higher education for training teachers in these three areas. In 1918, four state institutions were approved to provide training for prospective teachers of both races in agriculture, home

In some instances some major modifications had to be made in these institutions to meet the state's needs for teachers. economics and trades and industries.[137]

For example, in 1917-18 none of the state institutions was offering a four-year degree course in home economics. In 1918, the State College of Agriculture at the University of Georgia, then offering a two-year program, established a four-year degree program and began that year by offering junior class work.[138]

INSTITUTIONS APPROVED FOR TEACHER TRAINING
1918

Institution and Location	Training to be provided	Race for which provided
Albany Normal School, Albany	Agriculture and Home Economics	Negro
Georgia School of Technology, Atlanta	Trades and Industries	White
Georgia State College of Agriculture, University of Georgia, Athens	Agriculture and Home Economics	White
Georgia State Industrial College, Savannah	Home Economics and Trades and Industries	Negro

After the institutions for teacher training had been designated, the individuals to head and carry on the programs had to be selected. The achievements of such individuals as John T. Wheeler, professor of agricultural education at the Georgia State College of Agriculture, and T. H. Quigley, professor of trade and industrial education at the Georgia School of Technology, indicate clearly that wise choices were made. These were strongly motivated, resourceful, creative people, able to get things done.

For example, when John T. Wheeler took over his responsibilities, he realized the need for observation centers where prospective teachers, as students, could study local school situations and observe competent and successful teachers as they carried on various aspects of their professional activities. Arrangements for such a center for both agriculture and home economics were made at the Winterville High School in

Clarke County. Funds for a special building for these programs were provided jointly by the Georgia State College of Agriculture, the Winterville School and private subscription. The building, which still stands, contained classrooms, laboratories and a farm mechanics shop.

Later, other centers near the university were developed for observation purposes in agriculture and home economics— Bogart, Watkinsville and the Demonstration School (a county high school on the university campus). During the years 1936-39, the Bogart and Watkinsville centers were supplied with complete vocational buildings, including farm shops and community canning units. The Demonstration School on the university campus included classrooms, a shop and a community canning unit.

The administration of these observation centers was not directly under the control of the Department of Agricultural Education of the university. The policy was to aid the schools financially and professionally so that they might become outstanding departments under conditions of normal administrative control.[139]

The course of study for students of agriculture was part of the approved course adopted by the state board. During the first year the students were required to study farm crops and farm crop production. Each vocational pupil was required to do at least six months of practical farm work in connection with his instruction in school. The practice given in connection with the first year's course consisted of crop projects in all schools and farm practice and farm crops in the District A. & M. schools. Farm shop work was required, through which boys were taught about the common wood working tools and their use in general carpentry work around the farm.

The pupil's second year consisted of the study of livestock and was based upon the fundamental principles of animal production, feeding, breeding, types, etc. The project work dealt with general care of farm animals, while the shop work was a continuation of the first year.

The third year consisted largely of horticulture study dealing with both fruit and garden. In the year's course, the student was given a more complete knowledge of soil types, their chemical composition and a knowledge of fertilizers. His supervised practice work dealt primarily with those crops common to orchard and garden. Each student was expected to become familiar with methods of propagation such as grafting and budding.

The fourth year was an attempt to bring together all the various problems of the farm in the three lines of husbandry studied during the three previous years. The students actually were provided training in farm management. Supervised practice work dealt with farm management problems, farm accounting and rural engineering. Mechanical work for the last two years included working with iron, operation and maintenance of farm machinery and problems in terracing, drainage, etc. Students who took four years of agriculture with the supplementary practices were familiar with the major problems and the science of production on the farm.

Home economics was taught in three kinds of schools or classes—evening schools or classes, part-time home economics schools or classes or day schools or classes.

The offerings for evening class members consisted of plain sewing for 10 evenings, garment making for 15 evenings, bread making for 10 evenings and instruction in home nursing for 20 evenings.

Instruction in cooking included kitchen care, hygiene, food nutrients, menu making, table settings, cooking methods and the preparation and cooking of various foods.

Day school home economics courses were divided into four years. First year students were taught elementary garment making and food study and cooking. Students in the second year were taught housekeeping and laundering, planning and serving meals and elementary dressmaking. When students reached the third year of home economics they were taught clothing design, house planning and furnishing, advanced cookery, planning and serving meals, home management and how to plan household accounts.

In the fourth year instruction in textile, millinery and dressmaking was scheduled, as well as elementary dietetics, care and feeding of children, cooking for invalids and home management.

Trade and industrial education courses were taught in evening industrial schools for white and black, part-time schools or classes for white and black, unit trade-day schools or classes for white and black, and in general industrial day schools or classes in towns and cities of less than 25,000 population.

The course of study in trade and industrial education was broad and covered various areas of industry. The three-year course in textiles included carding, spinning, weaving and knitting, designing, textile calculations, dyeing and industrial chemistry.

The course for mechanics included training on lathe, milling machine, shaper, drill press, grinder, bench work, shop organization, shop arithmetic, mechanical drawing and shop sketching.

An example of courses offered for first-year trade and industrial education included cabinet making, upholstery, mat work and related mathematics. Second year, or advanced, students were taught cabinet making, upholstery, mat work and shop mathematics and drafting.

In schools providing trade and industrial education for Negroes, the course offerings included wheelwrighting, wagon repair, blacksmithing, carpentry, masonry and cement construction for boys and dressmaking for girls. All courses were not offered in every school or center, however. All courses offered met the requirements specified by the State Vocational Board in Bulletin No. 4 published in 1918.[140]

The Smith-Hughes Fund was regarded as an aid "to the ninety percent of boys and girls who must take up the work of life without the chance for college education." Coming at this time, it provided an enormous boost both in the actual service rendered and in the acceleration of the progress of high schools in the state.

There was an additional element of pride in accepting these federal vocational grants, since they were secured through the leadership of two of Georgia's own national representatives, Sen. Hoke Smith and Rep. Dudley Hughes.

At the end of the first year of operation, Superintendent Brittain commented,

> The Georgia State Vocational work for the year became still better known to our people and its management received the commendation of the Federal authorities at

Washington. Like practically all funds granted from the
U. S. Treasury, there are many safeguards and techni-
calities connected with the appropriation. In many re-
spects, however, this is advantageous by reason of the
fact that it forbids careless, slovenly work and requires
strict attention to details. It is the clearest light in dark
places to show educational efficiency—or its lack—that
we have had besides affording the best methods yet found
for teaching the leading vocations in agriculture, trades
and home economics.[141]

The first local high schools offering vocational agriculture
were Baldwin, Banks County, with C. S. Hubbard as teacher;
Wrens, Jefferson County, with J. K. Callahan as teacher; and
Dawsonville, Dawson County, with M. E. Free as teacher.

Other high schools establishing programs of vocational
agriculture before June 30, 1918, were Baxley, Appling
County; Chipley, Harris County; Clayton, Rabun County;
Stone Mountain, DeKalb County; Franklin, Heard County;
Hopeful, Mitchell County; and Rutland, Bibb County.[142]

In 1918 Stewart, as high school inspector, approved the first
schools to receive aid in home economics programs. The first
white schools were Fitzgerald, Quitman, Sandersville, Jefferson, Rome and Commercial High in Atlanta. The Negro
schools were located in Americus and Columbus.[143]

The *Forty-Eighth Annual School Report* for the year ending
June 30, 1919, reveals that trade and industrial courses were
offered for white and colored students in Columbus and for
colored students at Georgia State Industrial College, Savannah, and in Macon. It assumed that these schools and/or systems were the first to qualify for vocational funds for trade
and industrial education.

In spite of the difficulties, records show that programs in
vocational education were being established in new centers in
1918-19. Vocational agriculture was offered in 21 white and
four colored schools. Trade and industrial training was offered in five white and five colored centers. Home economics
was made available for white students in eight schools and for
colored students in two schools.[144]

The development of stronger high schools also received a
significant boost in 1918 from the Barrett-Rogers Act, which

provided for state funds to be expended throughout Georgia in an effort to promote consolidation of the weaker high schools and to transfer high school instruction from the elementary schools. "A sum of $1,000 was offered to the counties without a standard A-grade high school to consolidate their high school work at the best and most accessible place and give the instruction there free to the boys and girls of the county." [145] Also, grants of $500 to elementary schools were provided where consolidations had been carried out in accordance with the provisions of the bill. The restricting phrase remained, however, as a barrier to participation in the State School Fund, although its powers to retard public high school development largely were broken.

In his annual report of 1919, Superintendent M. L. Brittain recorded the series of legislative acts which had retarded the development of high schools in Georgia.

> By means of these several acts of the Legislature the restrictions put upon the high schools by the Constitution of 1877 have been practically removed, and provision is now made for ample support of both elementary and secondary schools in every county of the State, especially since section 109 of the new *School Code* passed this year requires that one-half of the total revenue of the State must be set aside hereafter for the maintenance of the public schools of the State.[146]

The amount of the state subsidy through the Barrett-Rogers Act was small in comparison with the total amounts received. In a large number of cases, the funds were both a financial and a moral stimulus to provide adequate opportunities for high school pupils. In 1920, there were 63 applications for Barrett-Rogers aid pending.[147]

Elders-Carswell

The same legislature (1919) passed the Elders-Carswell Bill, which made available additional local funds which for the first time could be spent on high schools. It required each county to levy a tax of five mills and permitted sub-districts to levy an additional tax.[148]

Herschel Elders, a veteran of several terms in the General Assembly and a vigorous attorney practicing in Tattnall County, was one of the men most aware of the needs of Georgia schools. In 1919, he was chairman of the Senate Education Committee and the administration floor leader for Governor Hugh Dorsey. With his thorough, firsthand knowledge of school needs—and perhaps prompted by editorials in the Tattnall Journal—Elders sponsored an education reform bill.

In the lower house, George Carswell of Wilkinson County took the lead in writing the new education proposals. Carswell had served several years on the Wilkinson County Board of Education and was personally acquainted with the rural schools' struggle to survive.[149] He had served several terms in both the lower and upper houses of the General Assembly, and during the 1919 session he was the administration's floor leader in the House.

Elders and Carswell together prepared a bill that they introduced the first day of the assembly's 1919 session.[160] The state's leading educators and legislators, who favored stronger education bills, had been frustrated in their efforts to secure the adoption of a new school code. They faced in this session the usual opposition against a new tax. Nevertheless, they had high hopes that the Elders-Carswell Bill would alleviate many school problems, so they gave them their support. The state school superintendent, M. L. Brittain, speaking before the General Assembly in favor of this new school code, made the following speech.

The importance of this legislation is seen in view of the fact that there has never been a school code in the state. In consequence, there are dozens of laws interfering with each other. Some of them partially overlap laws passed years ago; others nullify some parts of the law and leave in force others, and again legislation has passed occasionally which left other conflicting laws on the subject still in force. Such, for instance, is the case with the State Board of Education. The regular state code of general laws prepared in 1914 shows in one place the professional State Board of Education provided by the laws of 1911 and in another the old *ex-officio* board which served prior to that time.

Besides correcting old troubles and making a code which superintendents, boards and parents may definitely and clearly understand, the new school code makes needed suggestions and recommendations as required by law. For instance, the recommendation is made for the employment of an attendance officer to secure the attendance of pupils from eight to 14 years. There has never been proper enforcement of compulsory laws without an official. This legislation is further strengthened by the recommendation of six months instead of four months attendance, requiring completion of the seventh instead of the fourth grade.

The suggestion is made that appropriations to the public schools shall be made on a definite scale of $3\frac{1}{2}$ mills and providing that it shall never be less than $3,500,000 per annum. This gives stability and certainty instead of leaving it to the uncertainty of legislation passing yearly. The right to establish junior high schools of vocational or other character is given to boards of education where there are sufficient local funds to provide same.

The construction of public school buildings no matter how small must be approved by the county and city school authorities.

Changes in the laws are also made so that the state law will not conflict with the use of the Smith-Hughes funds for vocational education. This is needed because there is not provision for part-time and evening schools at present.

There are many other helpful suggestions in this new code besides the elimination of laws which are no longer in force and impossible enforcement under present circumstances.

The code is the result of careful preparation by the committee. For the good of the schools and those interested in education, it is hoped that it will pass without delay.[151]

The county school superintendents had worked diligently for years to secure the type of legislation proposed in the new school code. On July 17, 1919, at a meeting held at the University of Georgia, they agreed to send the legislature the following resolutions.

RESOLVED: That we fully endorse and urge the speedy passage of the Elders-Carswell Bill, providing for state-wide local taxation for public schools.

That we especially urge the importance of the adoption by passing legislation of a school code, which will give to us and the general public the school laws of the state in such logical order as will make them clear and definite, instead of the present confused and confusing shape.

That we ask the strengthening of the compulsory attendance laws in order that we may properly enforce the same.

That we would welcome and encourage legislation to facilitate the consolidation of schools.

That the salary of the State School Superintendent be increased.

That the number of School Supervisors be increased—there is too few.[152]

People throughout the state were studying the bill and voicing their opinions. While the legislature still was considering the measure, 100 Negroes appeared before the State Board of Education to request consideration of the following items: larger salaries for Negro teachers, longer school terms, better school buildings, help in securing a normal school for training Negro teachers, more district agricultural schools for Negroes, a more equitable share for Negroes of federal funds coming to Georgia, a Negro to be assistant state supervisor of Negro schools and appropriations for training Negro teachers in summer schools.[153]

These requests had a definite influence in the passage of the Elders-Carswell Bill, the most far-reaching laws for education enacted in Georgia up to this time. The laws, which passed overwhelmingly, provided for levying local taxes to maintain and operate schools and for issuing schoolhouse bonds, defined the duties of local boards of education and placed some budgetary responsibilities on state and local officials. The new laws also set up grants to school systems that consolidated their small schools, permitted districts to provide transportation and placed the licensing of teachers in the hands of the state board.[154]

In addition to codifying all existing school laws, the 1919 session of the General Assembly approved several major pieces of additional legislation to strengthen the public school program. One act required, beginning January 1, 1922, that one-half of all state revenue from all sources of taxation be used in the support of the common schools.[155] A constitutional amendment providing local tax levies without an election, but on the recommendation of the board of education, was approved.[156]

Also, as previously noted, the Barrett-Rogers Act provided $500 and $1,000 grants to elementary and high schools, respectively,[157] and this consolidation bill provided a real shot in the arm for improvement of rural schools during the 1920s. Of the 184 sections in the 1919 Code, 37 sections were devoted to legislation attempting to provide safeguards for textbook selection, sale and distribution.

While the 1919 acts corrected many educational problems, they still lacked several provisions necessary for a good school system. The maximum of five mills the laws allowed the counties to levy pointed up dramatically the inequality existing in the state's 160 counties. Nevertheless, both the compulsory countywide tax and the optional local or county tax yielded revenue which stimulated high school growth.

These measures and the stimulus they gave to high school expansion made necessary the services of a high school supervisor. This was met by a grant from the General Education Board, and E. A. Pound, who for 17 years had served the schools of Waycross, was appointed to the new position. Until this time, the entire load of responsibility in promoting the growth of standard high schools had been the work of Joseph S. Stewart. Pound became a member of the Department of Education and was responsible to the state school superintendent. His knowledge of school problems and his services in the area of consolidation and other high school improvements were of immense value. He had the tact and discretion not to detract from the great work of Stewart, and for the few years he filled this position, the two men worked amiably at the common task. (Pound remained in the position of high school supervisor until 1924, when he accepted the new state department position as director of certification.)

The legislation of 1919, including the provisions of the Elders-Carswell bill amending the constitution and providing for both compulsory and optional taxes in the counties, and the Barrett-Rogers bill which made liberal state grants for consolidation of elementary and high schools in the rural areas, eliminated most of the objections to preceding laws and indeed made the county the unit of tax support and administration for Georgia schools. The county unit had finally attained acceptance. Section 142 of the School Code approved in 1919 stated,

> While it is the purpose and spirit of this article to encourage individual action and local self-help upon the part of the school districts, it is expressly understood that the general school laws of this State as administered by the County Board of Education shall be observed.[158]

EARLY GROWTH OF LOCAL TAX COUNTIES

Year	No. County Systems
1905	7
1910	18
1915	37
1920	67

While their numbers during the first two-plus decades of the twentieth century did not match the county systems in terms of percentages of growth, independent city school systems were firmly on the education scene.

INDEPENDENT CITY SCHOOL SYSTEMS OF GEORGIA
1903-1938

Year	No. County Systems
1903	87
1908	65
1913	79
1918	76
1922	81
1928	105
1933	84
1937	71 [159]

Without question, these school systems operated independently of the county board and dealt in all school matters directly with the State Department of Education. Also, there was no question of authority or extent of privilege in relation to school administration. The charter made clear the nature of this relationship and was the basis of legal interpretation when differences of opinion arose.

What was not clear was the status of the semi-independent systems, which reported school data to and received their pro rata share of state funds from county school authorities. They presented a problem in their relationship to the county. Through a test case involving Washington (Georgia) and Wilkes County, the Supreme Court held that "the city of Washington is entirely independent of the system of public schools in the county of Wilkes and people residing in Washington cannot legally participate in an election of the County School Superintendent" by furnishing a candidate or voting for the superintendent. This condition was deplored as another step toward reducing further the pool of talent from which the county could draw in filling places of school leadership.

One provision of the new school code which was objectionable to Superintendent Brittain was the result of this court ruling which prohibited citizens living in a municipal system within the county from voting for the county school superintendent. Regarding this ruling, Brittain said,

> Experience shows that while apparently logical, it works a hardship in many cases. The amendment is unsatisfactory, because it interferes with the right expressly granted in the Constitution to all citizens to vote for county officers.[160]

He further noted to the legislature,

> I must . . . call attention to two of your acts of (1919) which were not beneficial. One was the amendment to Section 147 of the School Code which prevents the voters of city and town systems from taking part in the election of county superintendent. Experience shows that while logical, it works a hardship in many cases. The majority of those who took part in the election of these officers

during the last six months agree with this opinion. Further, this amendment which was made to the code is, I think, unsatisfactory, because it interferes with the right expressly granted in the constitution to all citizens to vote for their county officers. The other unwise legislation was the failure to change the method of electing the county school superintendent.[161]

He had used stronger words two years earlier in his annual report (1917) to the General Assembly. At that time, Superintendent Brittain made a most vigorous denunciation of the law providing for the popular election of the county superintendent.

In 1909 the legislature passed a law requiring county superintendents of schools to be elected by the people. It was a cheap piece of demagogic legislation and while its additions to the number of candidates undoubtedly pleased ward heelers and other mildewed men who infest political campaigns, it was reactionary and hurtful to the educational interests of the state. It was just as sensible as to elect the manager of a factory or the cashier of a bank by popular vote. Its injurious effects have already been felt. This law should be changed, and the boards of education should get the best superintendents possible from anywhere—in or out of the state, and make women also eligible to this position. They are already found in this work in many states and make the very best of school officials. We should give the county children the same chance as those in the town for an expert supervisor rather than a successful hand-shaker or campaigner.[162]

At this time, more than half of the independent systems were of the type whose legal status prevented citizens of the district from voting or being employed by county systems. To the extent that they contained a monopoly of the people qualified to supervise and administer schools, the county administrative body had to be composed of persons with inferior qualifications. The county grand jury was under similar restrictions in the selection of county school board members. These persons must be drawn from outside the corporate limits of the independent city systems. In some cases it was necessary for the qualified candidates for office to establish rural residence in order to comply with the practice, as the county outside the town or city might contain no person meeting even the minimum qualifications.

In 1919 Superintendent Brittain commended the General Assembly for the most constructive legislation that had ever been enacted in one year—The Elders-Carswell amendment providing for countywide tax levies, the Barrett-Rogers bill encouraging consolidation and subsidizing the construction of school buildings and the final passage of a bill to provide a State School Code. Having done so, he again expressed his disappointment that one of the laws most harmful to education yet remained on the statute books.

> Members of the General Assembly will recall the effort made last year to elect members of county boards of education by the people and let these boards have the power and right to appoint as superintendent the best man that could be secured either from within or without the county. It failed and so this year we have had, from the mountains to the sea, elections by the people for county superintendents of schools . . . The unrest and ill feeling engendered by these campaigns for county superintendents of schools throughout the State this year has almost nullified much of the advance which could have been expected otherwise on account of the new laws passed last summer. In many instances the county superintendents have frequently confessed that they were afraid to do anything until after the election, with such important matters as consolidating rural schools, enforcing the compulsory attendance law or prompting the adult illiteracy work . . . Those who were defeated in the primaries in the spring can hardly be expected to feel enthusiastic about pressing any movement for better schools among the voters who defeated them on account of this very issue . . . I have placed this situation before you as plainly as I could for your consideration at this meeting of the General Assembly. It is certainly worth your attention, for the election of county superintendents by the people is the greatest influence for evil in the Georgia system of education. It looks like a fair proposition for the people

to elect this official, but it is just as unbusinesslike and foolish as to select a bank cashier or a railroad engineer by popular vote.[163]

Rural Supervisor J. O. Martin, in completing his report to Superintendent Brittain in 1919, expressed concern for the lack of supervision in the county schools—an aspect of the superintendent's work which Martin rated above all else. In his search for an answer, he made a statewide study of the income received by county superintendents and how they spent their time. To each of them he addressed three questions: "What is your present salary? Do you devote all of your time to your work? If not, what salary, including travel expense, would enable you to do so?"

The response to 142 inquiries is summed up as follows.

Answer to the first question shows that half of the number receive less than $1,400 and that sixteen receive the minimum of $600 per year. Answers to the second question show that 35 devote their entire time to their school work, while the remaining one hundred seventeen do not. Of this number 22 are lawyers, 38 are farmers, 9 are preachers, 8 are merchants, 3 are real estate dealers, 2 are bank cashiers, one a dentist, five are doctors, three are bookkeepers, two are editors, three are cotton dealers, three are automobile dealers, two are garage men, three are teachers, one is a soft drink bottler, one is a piano tuner and the others are men of all work.

Answers to the third question range from $7,700 down to $1,000 with the median at $2,000. Hence the remedy seems apparent. Pay the superintendents a living wage so that they can devote all of their time to their work, and since $2,000 is the median salary asked, why not make this the minimum salary paid to any?

To add strength to this, the Legislature should allow county boards of education to elect the Superintendents subject to the approval or disapproval by the state board of education and their territory of selection should be as wide as the opportunity and taken from either sex.[164]

In order to provide for the newly elected superintendents some assistance in understanding the duties and services as

well as the opportunities of their jobs, former county superintendent M. L. Duggan (later a member of the State Department of Education) was designated to provide an orientation.
In his report for 1919, he described this work.

> This is the year for the elections by popular vote for a
> four-year term of every county school superintendent in
> the state except four . . . Arrangements have been made
> for me to give a course at the University Summer School
> to newly elected County Superintendents and others in
> Georgia school laws and in county school administration
> and supervision. It is earnestly desired that this will be
> a large class . . . with the increased financial ability of
> the rural districts, we may confidently look for greater
> progress in rural education in the near future than any
> of us have heretofore witnessed. The outlook is entirely
> hopeful, with the single exception of the political handi-
> cap imposed upon county administration and super-
> vision.[165]

An unforeseen detriment to county-city mergers in a unified program of education was the effect which an unprofes-
sional county superintendent might have when placed over
city principals of proven academic and supervisory ability.
In his report of 1919 Superintendent Brittain noted one such
failure and intimated others.

He cited other cases in which success of educational effort,
dependent on full support of the county superintendent, often
failed because the superintendent was fearful of the effect
which his enthusiastic support might have upon his political
status. This was noted particularly in relation to the failure
of superintendents to support the illiteracy campaign which
coincided with election year.[166]

State High School Supervisor E. A. Pound reports an effort
of a more constructive nature among the department of education and elected superintendents and their county boards
through a series of meetings.

> One of the most helpful innovations during the past year
> was the calling of eighteen regional conferences by the
> State Superintendents. They were held in January and
> were attended by 138 of the 160 county superintendents,

by many members of boards of education in the different counties, by the State Superintendent, whenever possible, and by all of (State Department) Supervisors.

These conferences afforded an opportunity for the supervisors to confer with the county superintendents with reference to their local problems, to explain the new school laws and to develop the ideals and standards that should obtain educationally in the state. On the other hand, the county superintendents had the opportunity of developing their plans for the next four years and of discussing with the supervisors the development of a unified system of schools in their various counties.[167]

In 1921 Superintendent Brittain reported that, throughout the state, people hoped a law would be passed which would enable cities, towns and counties to work together under the county unit plan. Good laws setting aside undesirable practices and providing more adequately for education in Georgia had been passed by cooperative legislatures when there was evidence of a real demand. A carefully framed bill, believed to be a reflection of general feeling, was readied by Senator E. W. Childs for the legislative session of 1922. Its title was

An Act to establish Boards of Education under the county-unit plan, whenever this is decided by vote of electors, prescribe their qualifications, duties, to provide for the appointment of the County Superintendent's Treasurers of School funds, and for other purposes.[168]

Because of its permissive character, observers thought the bill would pass handily. It was reported that 40 or 50 systems in the state were ready to adopt the terms of the act. In this post-war year, many cities were contemplating better facilities which only expensive bond issues could provide, and if county and city were united in one common effort, it would mean a more comprehensive plan to make the facilities available throughout the county. At this time, towns and cities were proceeding to organize their own educational needs; yet, in so doing, they made more difficult the possibility of forming county-unit systems.

The effect of the bill's failure is now history. Whatever may have been its merits in uniting city and county under responsible leadership, the bill was defeated by those who stood to benefit most from its passage. The towns and cities continued to withdraw themselves into systems in which they could travel toward educational goals at a more rapid pace under charters granted from the state. E. P. Cubberly, using Georgia as an example of widespread use of this system, said, "Almost every city of any size in the State had at some time been granted a special educational charter." [169]

The term "Independent School System" has more general usage in Georgia than in any other state. *The Dictionary of Education*, Carter V. Good, Ed., defines "city school district" as,

A geographical area, generally co-terminous with a legally established municipality, of which the population may be relatively high in number and density and which has been designated as a local, often by State Authority, to be governed by a local school board in terms of powers and duties delegated by the State.[170]

COMPARISON OF REVENUE FROM THE STATE SCHOOL FUND AND LOCAL TAXATION
1907-1921

(See footnote for description of column "Total School Fund") [171]

Year	Receipts from Local Tax	Receipts from State School Fund	Total School Fund
1907	750,578	2,016,758	3,011,678
1908	1,010,679	2,163,207	3,786,831
1909	1,261,471	2,203,128	4,229,255
1910	1,307,137	2,237,852	4,606,411
1911	1,566,655	2,320,913	5,282,652
1912	1,891,860	2,375,510	5,365,855
1913	1,836,815	2,591,730	5,584,334
1914	2,076,347	2,429,942	5,765,040
1915	2,387,729	2,608,487	6,406,071
1916	2,583,163	2,724,330	6,554,269
1917	2,941,424	2,698,941	6,907,711
1918	3,373,194	3,025,364	7,610,268
1919	4,295,941	3,480,885	9,270,135
1920	5,963,205	3,688,827	11,948,307
1921	6,686,408	4,296,190	14,567,334

This financial comparison shows income from local taxes and its effect on the total school fund. After 1920, substantial income was derived from the countywide mandatory tax resulting from the Elders-Carswell amendment and bill. Had the schools remained dependent on the state school fund alone, they would have had about one-fourth of the revenue they received in 1920.

The levying of local taxes under provisions of the Mc-Michael Bill had some unforeseen effects upon the support of schools in Georgia. While the organization of the county into school districts and provisions for the election of trustees were mandatory, the levying of a tax to apply on the support of the district school was optional. The particular rate of taxation also was optional, so long as it did not exceed five mills. A two-thirds majority of those voting was necessary to pass the tax law.

After laying out the school districts and electing trustees, the districts could choose to do nothing further. A very large majority of the districts at first chose to do nothing about levying a tax and even failed to replace members on the district board who were lost by resignation or otherwise. They would hold an election for a local tax only to have it defeated by those who opposed any tax to help educate other people's children, or they might vote a maximum tax on property of low evaluation and still have insufficient means to operate the schools in a satisfactory way. In contrast, the wealthy districts could vote a minimum tax and have sufficient revenue for good schools by the standards that existed at that time. In the end, each of these experiences was multiplied in great number throughout the state, causing wider variations in educational opportunity than had existed before. The major immediate value of the McMichael law, however, was the assurance that school improvement for a large portion of the population lay within the grasp of people composing the school districts in rural communities.

In reviewing the steps of progress toward full acceptance of the idea of tax support for public education, Superintendent N. H. Ballard said,

> The Constitution (1877) had hardly been adopted before bill after bill had been introduced in the Legislature modi-

fying it and giving to the districts and counties the right of taxation for schools . . . It always met bitter opposition in the Legislature and its opponents were successful in defeating it until 1905 when the McMichael Bill was passed that made it, for the first time, possible for districts to organize, to vote local tax for school purposes and, under restrictions non prohibitory. This marked the beginning of Georgia's progress; from that date its growth has been phenomenal.

There are districts in Georgia whose sacrifices are indeed heroic, far away from railroads, without any corporate property to tax, with their little farms . . . yet are taxing themselves more than twenty mills that they might give their children better opportunities.[172]

Also, in spite of the financial abuses carried out in many counties under provisions of the McMichael Bill, such as creation of a school district to encompass only the wealthy part of a county, the McMichael legislation facilitated the levying of an education tax by each district of a county. A logical next step was to make the tax uniform for the county, thereby establishing a countywide school system. This was accomplished in part in 1916 when the legislature passed permissive legislation for county unit systems maintained by local taxes.

Whenever the citizens of any county wish to supplement the public school fund received from the State by levying a tax upon the property of the county, it shall be the duty of the ordinary to order an election not earlier than 20 days nor later than 60 days, after receiving a petition of one-fourth of the qualified voters of the county unless it shall exceed 5,000 in which event the Ordinary shall order the election after receiving a petition of one-tenth of the voters . . . This is not to replace any right of taxation now possessed by the county.[173]

This law placed within the hands of people a means by which they could have some of the benefits of the county unit system. The law, however, was permissive, and in a large number of counties which attempted to secure the benefits of the measure, it was killed by districts representing concentrated wealth who stood to suffer a comparative loss in revenue by merging into the larger tax unit. A uniform tax over the county—expended for the education of children wherever they are, whether in city or country—is not often the ambition of a county with towns and concentrations of corporate property.

While supporting the county unit system, Superintendent Brittain pointed out the need for continuing some aspect of the district plans. He recommended that they be retained in order to escape the rigidity which complete uniformity might produce.

> Our county unit plan is universally recognized by those familiar with educational work and progress as far superior to that by the district. A serious trouble, however, is being increasingly felt. It happens in many counties that some districts desire a longer term than others. Even in some of the large urban counties there will frequently be found a district or two wishing a shorter term . . . In most of the counties there are two or three districts that desire a term of nine months where the rest of the county wishes seven. It is requested that the McMichael law be modified so that a larger tax may be levied in any district or districts desiring this without separation from the rest of the county.[174]

In a similar vein and in an earlier period, Commissioner Pound had voiced one of the fears which might evolve from the adoption of the county as the tax unit for schools.

> It is very desirable, I think, that the county should be the favored unit of our common school system; and many towns are willing to give up their independent systems for this purpose, but they are not willing to have the Legislature abolish their rights to support local schools first and hazard an election throughout the county afterwards. In the event the election should issue adversely, such towns would become dependent upon the county board for all educational facilities and would be able to tax themselves neither as a part of a county system nor alone in spite of their willingness to do so, for better schools.[175]

This concern was visible in the last years of that decade when the legislature approved a bill (The Elders-Carswell

Bill) that permitted a sub-district tax in addition to the required countywide tax.

Thus, before many years had passed, legal measures more liberal than the McMichael Bill were approved, adding their collective weight to the growing public consciousness of educational needs. In face of these developments, the law of permissive taxation for local school support in many places became a detriment to equalization.

From the comparison tabulation of revenue from the State School Fund and Local Taxation (page 221), it may be seen that local district and municipal taxes increased to the point that they represented a large part of the total income. The extent to which white and Negro children shared in the benefits from the fund is not directly known. Dorothy Orr, in her *History of Education in Georgia,* states,

> The fund for the common school was not divided on the basis of race but was apportioned by the State to the counties upon the basis of the entire school population . . . The state school fund was divided between the races by the County Board of Education and supplemented by such local taxes as the county decided to vote. The appropriations for the Negro schools were almost entirely dependent upon the local sentiment of the white school board.[176]

Until the passage of the compulsory attendance law in 1916, a large majority of those not in attendance were the Negro children. And, if they were not in school, no provision was made for their instruction. By default, they received a minor share of the revenue derived from this source.[177]

Superintendent Brittain's report for 1923 announced the election of county superintendents the following year and gave the new criteria for qualification.

> Before any person can be a candidate, or especially before his name can appear upon the ticket for a general election, he must have a certificate of qualification from the State Board of Education.
>
> The law prescribes the following ways:
> 1. Have at least three years practical experience in teaching and hold a first grade license, or

2. Have a diploma from a literary college or normal school, or

3. Have five years experience in the actual supervision of schools—superintendent of a county or independent system of schools, or

4. Stand an approved examination before the State Board of Education as to his qualifications.[178]

In an attempt to write into the law requirements which would safeguard the office against incompetent or designing candidates, frequent amendments were made. It was the function of the department of education to certify the educational qualifications. Requirements as to residency, sound moral character and conformity to election practices were imposed by the county authorities. Finally, the candidate must win a plurality vote.[179] The basic law made no reference to character and did not directly specify that the candidate be a citizen of the county. Later attempts to legislate on matters which developed as areas of difficulty tended to confuse rather than clarify. As previously noted, the court ruled that it would be improper for a board member of the county schools to reside in the independent district or to move into a district having already a board member and retain the office. However, there appears to be no such restriction upon the county school superintendent. Having met the requirement as citizen of the county, there was no apparent restriction relative to his residence in the county.[180]

Superintendent Brittain never relented in his opinion that the political choice of county superintendent by popular vote brought to the office people of mediocre ability, particularly weak in the art of supervision. His parting remarks, contained in the annual report for 1924, said,

As is superintendent, so is the school. Wherever you find a good superintendent you will be very apt to find a splendid school system. Indeed, a good superintendent can correct many of the errors of poor and untrained teachers and obtain splendid results, whereas if there is no supervision, even a school with good teachers may secure poor results.

Our present method of electing county school superintendents is not conducive to obtaining the best results. Too
often whole counties had not a man in them such as would
make an acceptable county school superintendent. I am
sure that the best results and equal opportunity for Georgia's children can never be obtained until the present
method is changed and the county school superintendent
is elected by the board of education from anywhere they
may get the best man.[181]

During these years, the state school supervisors spent considerable time conducting school surveys. During the years
of 1923 and 1924, surveys were conducted in every county in
the state. However, many counties had been surveyed prior
to 1923. The earlier surveys described the conditions in every
school in the county. In most surveys, the condition of the
building was brought out with emphasis. Other factors included were local tax support, qualifications and salaries of
teachers and instructional supplies. A summary of the survey
of Rabun County Schools in November 1914, by State School
Supervisor M. L. Duggan described the "Standard School
Concept" in conducting surveys.[182]

The following minimum standard of efficiency for rural
schools sent to the various counties by the State School
Superintendent has been largely used as the basis of
measurement in the survey.

Educational results and good teaching generally are not
often secured in a shiftless-looking building in which
neither patrons, nor teachers take any pride. Indefinite-
ness has been removed at this point through the standard
school. In the larger towns and cities pressure of public
sentiment and the comment of visitors will sooner or later
force good educational conditions—and they are improving constantly. Rural communities need to be shown and
inspired by educational leaders and we have sent diplomas to more than one hundred county schools where the
superintendents were certified to the fact that they have
measured up to the standard in every particular. Fulton,
Newton and Hancock have received half of these, and

there are a number of localities in the State where the feeling is that no rural community in the county is able to bring its school up to these very reasonable requirements. I cannot help but think that this is a mistaken view and that some standard schools could be secured in every county in Georgia and that these would serve to inspire the others to progress. Superintendents have written that the use of this efficiency test has developed more progress in the past twelve months than for years previous in the way of improvement. The plan is of no value, however, where it is not used or applied and I earnestly hope we will have the effort at least of every superintendent in the State to have his county represented on this roll of honor. The list will be published in the next Annual Report. The standard is not unreasonably high and no more than the Georgia parent has the right to expect. Copies should be posted in every county school room in the State and can be secured for this purpose at any time on application to the State Department of Education. To be entitled to a diploma, a school should measure up to the standard in the following particulars:

I.

THE TEACHER.

1. Good Teaching.
2. Good Order and Management.
3. First Grade Certificate.
4. Full, Neat, and Accurate School Register.
5. Daily Program Posted in Room.
6. Teacher's Manual on Desk.

II.

GROUNDS.

1. Good Condition.
2. Playgrounds.
3. School Garden.
4. Two Separate Sanitary Closets.

III.

BUILDING.

1. Painted Outside.
2. Plastered, or Ceiled and Painted.
3. No Leaks.
4. Windows Without Broken Panes.
5. Cloak Rooms.
6. Good Doors with Locks and Keys.
7. Clean and well-kept.

IV.

EQUIPMENT.

1. Patent Modern Desks.
2. At least 20 lineal feet of Blackboard per Room.
3. Building Comfortably Heated and Ventilated.
4. Framed Pictures on the Wall.
5. Dictionary, Maps, and Library.
6. Sanitary Water Supply.

V.

ASSOCIATED ACTIVITIES

1. Manual Arts, Corn, Canning, Poultry, or Cooking Clubs.

VI.

SALARY OF TEACHER.

1. At least $40 per month.

VII.

TERM.

1. At least seven months.

In the Rabun County survey, Brittain and Duggan commended highly the Rabun County System for being the first mountain county to vote a local tax. The report also stated, "Excepting the solution of the problem of maintenance by adoption of *local taxation* probably the next great item of progress is apparent in the good school houses, as is strikingly shown in photographs which were made for and are herein given as an important part of this survey." [183]

By 1916, the survey plan had evolved to include more data on financial support and extracurricular activities such as clubs. The survey of Wayne County schools in 1916 included the following conclusions.

> The first school I visited pays the teacher eighteen dollars per month, and the patrons add four more dollars to this man's salary. The county school commissioner supports his family, pays rent, keeps his horse and buggy, and received four dollars per month for his services. However, his school work seems to be all that can interest him, so he will finally succeed.

Present conditions fully verify this prophecy.

> The first rural school supervisor for Georgia (Prof. R. H. Powell, now President South Georgia State Normal School) devoted a considerable portion of his first year's work to Wayne County. This was in 1910. The work was fundamental in its nature, such as creating and stimulating sentiment for better school conditions, waging a campaign for better financial support of the schools (local taxation), planning consolidations, better school hours, etc., etc.
>
> As a result of these efforts and previous work by the county superintendent the county voted "for local taxation" in 1910.
>
> In 1910 the total school fund was $9,789.80.
>
>   Showing an increase in five years of nearly 300%. (*sic*)
> In 1910 the length of the school year was 80 days.
> In 1915 the length of the school year was 110 days.
>   Showing an increase in five years of 37%.
> In 1915 the monthly salaries of teachers averaged $51.20.
>   Showing an increase in five years of 35%.
> In 1910 total value of school property in county was $17,775.
> In 1915 total value of school property in county was $54,036.

Showing an increase in five years of over 300%.

There are many educational agencies actively at work in the county in 1916 that there were not even thought of in 1910, such as the Farm Demonstration and Home Economics Work under trained agents, and a wide-spread and more vital interest in public schools generally.

The photographs of some of the present public school buildings in the county and the old ones replaced by them . . . give striking indications of progress accomplished in the past few years.

The great dissatisfaction at present conditions and increasing demand for still greater progress manifested throughout the county are probably the best evidences of what is to be.

The success of the Agricultural and Home Economics workers is particularly gratifying. There has been bitter prejudice against this work in the county, but the number of members of the corn, canning, and pig clubs, distributed through nearly all the schools of the county, give evidence of the progress in the public sentiment and fully justifies the wisdom and persistence of the school officials.

THE NEGRO SCHOOLS.

There are eighteen Negro schools in the county, Negro population being small. These have made very little progress, as their photographs given herein will show. They are without equipment, with one exception, having nothing more than very poor blackboards. Annual salaries for the Negro teachers vary from $110.00 to $175.00.

SUGGESTIONS FOR THE FUTURE.

1. The educational interests of the children of the county demand better schools and longer terms than the present school funds will pay for.

The rate of tax levied against the property for the benefit of the children is only twenty-five cents on the hundred. For the sake of the children, the property can stand a higher rate. Some counties are raising more money locally for their schools than they receive from the state;

and every county ought to. Nearly half of the property of Wayne County as returned for taxation is owned by railroads and other corporations; and therefore little over half of any school tax levied is borne by the people whose children get the benefit. Under these circumstances, the people will stand for a higher school tax. A more liberal maintenance is at the bottom of the solution of nearly all of our educational problems.

2. There are too many schools in the county. By observing their location with reference to each as given in the Bulletin, it will be seen that the school districts are generally below the minimum size contemplated by law (16 square miles). A consolidation of many of the small schools into larger ones will admit of more teachers to each school, thus greatly increasing their efficiency. At every one-teacher school there are, necessarily, more lessons per day than any one teacher can well teach. The children are the sufferers. The administration should take the lead in this important matter, but cannot succeed without the co-operation of the patrons concerned. It will also involve some seeking sacrifices on the part of patrons, but the gains in increased efficiency will more than justify any apparent loss.[184]

A larger staff of supervisors was employed by the State Department of Education in the early 1920s, and these supervisors concentrated in their surveys on needs and organization. It is evident that the 1919 school consolidation bill (Barrett-Rogers Act) had an impact on the school program, as the number of schools was decreased from 8,441 in 1919[185] to 7,130[186] in 1924. The state school supervisors made surveys of all of the 160 county school systems in the state and the independent systems within the counties during the years of 1923 and 1924, and a recap of the findings, by schools, was reported in the State School Superintendent's *Annual Report*.[187] Each school received a grade or rating in this report on size, number of teachers, grades taught, classification and salaries of teachers and conditions of buildings, grounds and equipment. Much was said about disparities in tax support and wealth available for tax purposes.

These surveys provided a basis for many studies on the problem of equalizing educational support within the state.

One of the most important of several studies concerning this inequality of education was conducted by Gordon G. Singleton of Columbia University's Teachers College.[188] In 1925, he analyzed the tax support programs in Georgia and concluded that, despite a permissive five mill tax levy, property in various counties was not assessed uniformly. For example, teachers' average salaries in the 160 counties, comprising about 80 percent of the state's total educational cost, ranged from $292 to $1,418 annually. To provide a minimum program, he advocated an equalization plan that would require the following.

> That every county levy a uniform tax to provide its contribution to the minimum offering on equalized valuation; that the amount of this tax rate be determined by the tax rate it would be necessary for the wealthiest county in the state to levy in order to provide the minimum educational offering the state agrees to equalize; that the state supply the difference between the amount thus raised by each county and the total amount necessary to finance the minimum offering; and that the state set up administrative conditions for participation in the state fund which will provide adequate information for the accurate determination of the state's financial responsibility and insure economical expenditure of all funds necessary to provide the minimum offering the state assumes to equalize. These elements . . . are accepted as the elements of the proposed plan of school support for Georgia.[189]

On the basis of Singleton's recommendation, an equalization bill was presented to the legislature. The Georgia Education Association, the State Superintendent and Governor Clifford Walker all backed it vigorously. There was no apparent organized opposition to the bill. The Equalization Act finally passed in March 1926; it earmarked certain gasoline taxes to equalize educational opportunities in the poor districts and gave the state board responsibility to develop a formula by which these funds would be distributed.[190]

Singleton's study and the resulting Equalization Act of 1926 were of singular importance to Georgia's educational improvements. They were successive steps in the search to fund adequately the state's educational system. During the same time span, the 1920s, a continuing problem was being struggled with again—certification.

State Superintendent M. M. Parks, in his annual report of 1922, made a statement which implied the great importance of state certification. He reported, "During the past year, the State Board of Education made slight changes in the system of certification of teachers, arranging for somewhat stricter standards in the issuing of licenses and certificates. A clear-cut distinction has been made also between the *License* and the *Certificate*."

> The county license can be secured by examination under the County School Superintendent. The State Superintendent furnished the examinations to be given on specified dates. The state professional certificates can be secured through the State Board of Education.[191]

N. H. Ballard had run for the office of state superintendent in 1923, using a new system of certification as the chief plank in his platform. After his selection to a two-year term, this new system was introduced. The State Board of Education finally realized that as long as there were 161 county superintendents issuing licenses on the basis of examinations, there would be as many standards. In February 1924 they adopted the new plans which were aimed at a greater degree of uniformity.[192]

The major change in the process was that all certificates would be issued by the state. Also, there were changes in classification and standards. The following statement was issued by Superintendent Ballard in the February 1924 issue of *Georgia State School Items.*

> Certificates to teach hereafter will be issued by the State Superintendent of Schools under authority of the State Board of Education. The County School Superintendent may issue special temporary certificates, good until the next State Examination.[193]

Some of the certificates issued by the state superintendent of schools were still to be issued by examination. At this time.

however, recognition was given finally to proficiency gained from completion of programs in approved schools and colleges. Persons completing programs in approved schools and colleges were certified without examination. This was the first time on a statewide basis this procedure had been accepted.[194]

As noted previously, E. A. Pound had been made a high school supervisor by Dr. M. L. Brittain in 1920. With the 1924 plan for issuance of all certificates by the state, Pound became the first director of certification. He began this responsibility late in June 1924, and after October 1, Rebecca Hearn was made his assistant. Pound continued with the dual role of high school supervisor and director of certification through 1930. Hearn was his assistant through 1926. The State Superintendent's *Annual Report* to the General Assembly in 1928 listed Janie Hearn as Pound's assistant.

When the details of the new plan of certification (1924) were released by the State Board of Education, they produced an immediate, adverse reaction from many teachers. A storm of protest arose at the spring meeting of the Georgia Education Association. This body appointed a special committee composed of R. H. Powell and E. H. Scott, registrar at Georgia State College for Women. This committee met with the state board in May 1924 to convey the objections of the teachers. The state board then appointed a committee, composed of Rufus W. Weaver, president of Mercer University; E. A. Pound, director of certification; and F. E. Land to work with the teachers' representatives.[195]

The committee appointed by the State Board of Education reported that teachers holding a county license felt it was unfair to be made to take a state examination to renew the certificates and be issued a state certificate. Many teachers were in process of renewing their certificate by attending summer school or other ways possible under county license procedures.[196]

Superintendent Ballard gave his own interpretation of the controversy. He stated that the objections of teachers appeared to stem from these factors.

1. The natural reluctance to apply for a new certificate when one is already in hand.

2. The speed of enactment.

3. The new terminology used for many certificates.

4. The belief by the teachers that graduates from certain normal schools should be awarded professional certificates without any successful experience by the applicant.[197]

To meet the objection as to speed, the State Board granted a year's extension of the old county certificates. Meanwhile, some teachers who had sought employment in other states found to their chagrin that their old certificates were not acceptable and hurried calls came to the state department for the new state certificates. News of the greater acceptance by other states of the new type certificate spread quickly over Georgia and increased the demand for new forms.[198]

When Pound assumed the office of director of certification in late June, he secured office space in the Commercial High School through the courtesy of the Atlanta school authorities. The legislature was in session and there was no room in the State Department of Education. He and a committee of 20 persons began work and continued unremittingly through December 1924.

As soon as the legislature adjourned, the committee was assigned the Senate Chamber, and for several months every desk in the chamber was filled with applications and credit blanks, so great was the task assigned.

The adoption of a plan of certification was an absolute necessity for the following reasons.

1. Old and well prepared teachers found it trying and irksome to respond to the law which required that they stand examinations at certain intervals, thereby necessitating a loss of time to them, although they had proven themselves well qualified in every way.

2. Teachers going to other states found that, with the adoption of plans of certification by other states, the old county licenses issued by this State were not acceptable to those states, and they immediately began to ask that they be granted a state certificate.

3. To both of the above classes of teachers the plan has proven acceptable, and to the younger teachers it has

been stimulating as all such teachers realize that with such a plan they have a real objective—and that objective is the desire to perfect themselves in all that appertains to teaching in such a way as will be recognized by this and other states.

4. Under the old plan there was very little inspiration to the average teacher. Under the new plan hundreds who were issued provisional certificates are preparing to attend summer and normal schools in order the better to prepare themselves for the work which they are to do.[199]

As a consequence of the measures providing freedom from constitutional restriction and greatly increased financial support, Georgia high schools entered into a period of very rapid growth. In 1924 J. S. Stewart was able to report,

All but 15 counties of the 160 now have accredited schools. How was it done? The people and Board of Education and City Councils asked for a bond issue for high school building, and then everybody went to work to put it over. Over $15,000,000 have been spent in Georgia for modern school buildings by the towns and cities.[200]

In July 1924, the Georgia Public School Officials' Association met in Athens. The statewide survey of schools had been completed, and special addresses were being made to publicize the problems which derived from this study. A major address was made by Rufus W. Weaver, president of Mercer University and a relative newcomer to the state. He was, however, not a stranger to Georgia public schools, having served on the state board and on the Illiteracy Commission. President Weaver reviewed the high points of Georgia's educational history. He noted the laws and provisions which had a significant effect on education and singled out several problem areas for special emphasis. The first was the subsidizing of private and denominational schools for giving instruction in the elementary grades. He denounced this practice, since it placed educational funds in the hands of those whom it was not possible to supervise. Another problem which drew a particularly sharp tongue was the "method by which the county Board of Education was chosen." He said,

No other American state has ever before or since adopted
the curious method of selecting its county board of education by a grand jury, a body of men whose names are
drawn out of a box by the judge of the superior court.
The selection of men to whom we entrust the most important function of the state as it affects the future by a
procedure which may have some Biblical support, namely,
by lot, has created in recent days a situation against
which our Revolutionary ancesters took up arms against
mother country. The county board has the right to im-
pose taxation and thus we have in Georgia 'taxation
without representation.' [201]

In the same address he expressed his views regarding the
method by which the office of county superintendent was filled.

In many counties the schools are controlled by men selected of their political influence rather than for their
educational fitness. . . While it is my conviction that any
law which may be enacted now relative to the election of
county superintendents by a county board of education
which in turn has been elected by the people, should not
be made effective until your term of office has expired.
I do believe every one of you should lend his influence to
the abolition of this undemocratic and utterly foolish
method of selecting the county board of education by the
grand jury, a species of belated paternalism; and that
you personally should favor the selection as the superintendent of the county schools the best trained and most
experienced men who can be secured to fill that position
and that you shall take this view because you are high-
minded, unselfish men, placing above all personal interest, the welfare of the children of your county.[202]

M. L. Duggan, acting in the capacity of secretary of the
Georgia Public School Officials' Association, noted that Superintendent T. T. Benton of Jackson County and Superintendent-
elect Mrs. McArthur Jones of Early, in their respective addresses, said county school superintendents should be elected
by vote of the people whom they serve.[203]

It is unfortunate that more of the attitude of the superintendents who served under this law is not available. All of the

foregoing statements have expressed views held by those in opposition to this plan. There appears to have been the general belief that the choice of county superintendent by popular vote did bring the management of schools closer to the people. That this right of popular engagement could have been more effectively accomplished by popular election of the county board, the real authority in local school management, was apparently obscured by the fact that the superintendent had become the symbol of that authority.

Dr. Ralph E. Wager, department of education, Emory University, assisted in a summary and report of educational problems revealed through the statewide survey of 1923-24; it was made in the name of the State Education Council. Wager cited the procedure in filling the office of county school superintendent as a problem area which should be remedied, calling attention to the need for close and expert supervision which could not be assured through the manner in which the county superintendent was chosen. The probability of securing adequate supervision through the method of popular election, he thought, would be accidental. He noted that the character of the politician's appeal often bore no relation to any of the desirable characteristics expected in this officer. Among the requisites of a county superintendent was the ability to organize and stimulate groups of teachers in the study of their tasks. "He should be able to guide them in their thinking and provide useful suggestions with respect to their methods. . . He should be able to demonstrate effectively the theories and practices which he advocates." Such leadership, Wager thought, "cannot be had so long as the position under question is open only to those of the county who seek it through an appeal to the public franchise." [204]

It was noted by Wager that according to the laws in effect in 1925, the annual compensation of the county school superintendent was $450 per year plus $150 for expenses for travel within the county and to maintain his office. To remedy this and other defects resulting from inadequate support, it was recommended that the superintendent cease to perform merely clerical services, that a salary of $2,500 with $1,000 for expenses be provided, that the office become appointive and that the appointing board have the liberty to find the most competent person for the position without restriction. Also, it was recommended that such a person, when installed in office, devote his time largely to improvement of instruction through close supervision and educational planning at a high level.

Wager believed there should be a close, functional relationship between the department of education and the county organization, saying, "In order to do these things, it is essential that the county administrator be intelligent, aggressive and progressive, that he be in sympathy with plans and purposes of the State Department. . ." [205]

At a meeting of county school officials in April 1925, a number of resolutions were drawn up looking toward the advancement of education in the state. One of the resolutions of this group proposed, "A bill to permit any county and city desiring to adopt a county unit plan as set forth in a general law." [206]

In recognition of the ambiguity of the proposal, it was pointed out that abolition of any independent district would automatically make a county unit, but to have a local option permitting counties to have the superintendent elected by the board of education would be in conflict with the constitution which "requires all county officials to be uniform."

Another resolution requested the appointment of a commission to study the Georgia school system and that of other states and present to the General Assembly a body of laws which, if enacted, would result in a more effective system of common schools.

A statement of general principles was drawn up by the committee, most of whom were county superintendents. One of the specific recommendations was, "That the county Board should be elected by the people and given the right of taxation."

The committee concurred in the view that, "The county superintendent should be an educator, trained in supervision, selected by the county boards and these boards should be free to obtain the best superintendent that they are able to get without any restriction." [207]

By 1925, concern was apparently shifting from the cause of an undesirable condition to a means of remedying the defect. In his report of 1926-1927, F. E. Land, state superintendent, expressed the need for county unit school systems throughout the state with all schools of both town and county under one board of education. The board, he believed, should be authorized to select a well qualified superintendent from anywhere in the state or nation. He believed the office to be a professional one and "should not be thrown into politics every four years." Provision should be made for competent supervision, he thought.

Under a proper system of expert supervision, the taxpayer's dollars can be made to buy from one to ten dollars more in education than they are getting under the present conditions.[208]

Another way of securing the needed services of qualified supervisors was noted in the 1926 report of M. L. Duggan. The rural school agent said,

Without constant professional supervision, we can never accomplish satisfactory results in our county schools any more than in any other large business enterprise. Nowhere else is expert supervision denied except in our rural schools. . . It is well nigh bankrupting them educationally when judged by the result. I must regard professional supervision as the one great need of our county school system of Georgia. No county superintendent can in addition to his administrative duties give more than a very general supervision to his schools.[209]

In the report of Supervisor I. S. Smith in 1928, the need for supervision is further emphasized. He said,

Most of my counties are large and have a considerable number of teachers. With the many duties of the County Superintendent it is impossible for them to do close and effective supervision of the class work in the various schools of the county.

I do not believe in our entire public school system there exists a greater need than a county supervisor for the primary and elementary grades. The Legislature could not make an appropriation that would pay more in return to the state than one to meet the various counties on a fifty-fifty basis for the procuring of a well trained supervisor.[210]

On the whole, the county superintendents were regarded as deficient in the expertise necessary for effective supervision. It was found that the newly elected superintendents were inept in the process of business and administration. State School Auditor Tom Wisdon pointed out in his report of 1928,

> With our system of electing school superintendents every four years there is necessarily each time a larger turnover. New superintendents who came into office without particular training in business administration in school affairs cause some confusion. This is particularly noticeable when outgoing superintendents fail to make out and leave a complete record of the financial standing at the time they leave office.[211]

Probably no law on the statute books has been challenged so vigorously, so often and by so many people at different levels of education as the procedure of choosing a county board of education by a group who themselves were chosen by lot (the grand jury), and the election of the county superintendent by popular vote in the same manner as other county political officers. This procedure has survived through the years with little effort on the part of the incumbents to defend their position or to claim the superiority of the process. On the other hand, they have withstood constant, vigorous and sometime violent denunciation by exponents of "correct educational practice." For over 100 years the people have had no voice in choosing a board which has a large latitude of power within the county, and for over 50 years they have had one who is virtually secretary to this body elected by popular ballot.

In his report for 1924 Superintendent N. H. Ballard probably stated the most potent reason why the practice has persisted.

> For many years there has existed a strong sentiment in favor of the appointment of county superintendents of schools by boards of education rather than through the election by the people. This has been expressed in numerous reports from the Georgia Education Association, as well as from the Association of County Superintendents and School Officials.

However, I doubt if this is the proper time to present it to the Legislature, for if it should be passed and made a law, it could do grave injustice to many persons who have been nominated as county superintendents for the next four years and who are certainly entitled to serve out their terms of office. Again the schools cannot be removed too far from the people.[212]

People had a part in the phantom of power believed to reside in the office of the county superintendent, and they were willing to accept this instead of the greater role of choosing the board members, a choice which is a part of the ancient lineage from "lot" to "grand jury."

Superintendent Ballard, not a vigorous opponent of the manner of choosing the county board and county superintendent, nevertheless pointed out some of the inconsistencies involved.

Since the school superintendent represents the professional side and is the Executive of the Board, and the real power is in the Board itself, not only to make rules and regulations for the government of the schools, but now the power has recently been conferred upon them to levy a tax for from one to five mills for school purposes. It is fundamental in our government that the people should have the right to name those having taxing power. Indeed the minute this power is given to any board there immediately follows a demand for election by the people, and the result has been that in more than forty states of the Union the people elect the boards of education. The argument presented by many is that the election of the Board by the people would not elect as good men as the present system, but that the best men would not offer, has proved untrue in other states of the Union, where boards are elected. Nor even so, in this State, for there is one county in Georgia that has for all time elected its board members by the people and the personnel of the board is of the highest.[213]

The counties whose school organizations were established before the Constitution of 1877 had freedom to exercise local authority in setting up the plan of administration for their schools. These systems elected the county boards, and the board in turn selected the superintendent. (This plan has continued over the years to the present time.)

In the year 1919 there were new developments which affected the level of education of teachers. A law passed in 1918 made it possible to codify school laws. Then, in 1919, the codification, known as the Elders-Carswell Bills, was passed by the General Assembly. This legislation also provided for the establishment of high schools.

> The Board of Education of any county or municipality shall have the right to establish one or more high schools or junior high schools as in their opinion may be necessary and may be possible through local taxation.[214]

Free tuition to all between the ages of six and 18 years was a provision of the same bill. In the same year, 1919, the Barrett-Rogers Bill on consolidation provided for $1,000 to be paid by the state to aid in the payment of the salaries of the principal and at least one assistant high school teacher. In 1919 only one payment of $1,000 could be made to a county, and none to the counties in which were located the District Agricultural and Mechanical schools.[215] These A. & M. schools provided for high school level work. In 1920, the bill was revised to permit payment for more than one high school in a county if there were funds available after all other counties in the state had had the opportunity for this aid.

Immediately after high schools were established, M. L. Brittain took advantage of these schools to raise the level of education of teachers. As there were few high schools free of tuition up to 1919, most of the teachers came from common schools. They were educated through the required annual institutes, and only 45 percent of the teachers had any kind of special training. The average preparation of teachers in the county schools was less than the completion of a four-year high school course. Some, of course, were graduates of normal schools which provided high school and normal school work. In 1920 only 685 persons graduated from the three state normal schools, together with all the denominational schools offering normal courses. Compulsory school attendance in 1919 increased the demand for numbers of teachers, also increasing the shortage of teachers.

In 1920 Brittain wrote a letter to county superintendents.[216]

> The shortage of teachers and the inability of the normal schools and other high institutes to supply the demand, forces upon the State Department of Education the duty of arranging a plan for teacher-training in the High Schools beginning with the school year, September, 1920.

The teacher training was limited to accredited high schools. Brittain's idea was to give every teacher a course in a standard high school and some professional training. To do so was a step forward in 1920. The first such high school programs began in the fall of 1920. The requirements for approval were as follows.[217]

THE PLAN

1. High Schools desiring to qualify for such classes must make application on official blanks for recognition.

2. The high school must be a four-year school, duly accredited. Teachers of this course must be approved.

3. It must have a library (including at least thirty reference books on teaching) ; a laboratory, home economics and physical training.

4. Provision must be made for practice teaching and observation.

5. There will be a uniform course for these classes, given during the fourth year of the High School to occupy not less than one-fifth of the time, with extra work on nine Saturdays. Pupils should be at least seventeen years of age. One unit's credit will be allowed this course toward graduation.

6. The work of these classes will be supervised by the State Department. The professional work should be taught by one of the High School teachers, but in practice teaching, the instructor should be assisted by the Principal of the elementary school.

7. The final papers in the Teacher-Training Courses should be corrected by the Teacher and sent to the State Department with the final record of the pupil in all studies of the High School completed for graduation.

8. On the pupil's completing the High School and the Teacher-Training Course, the State Department will issue a provisional license to teach in the public schools of the State, good for two years. This license may be renewed either by the completion of three courses at the State Summer School or one term's work at Normal School or College, or the regular examination upon the Reading Course. City Training School pupils, through state inspection and examination, may secure this provisional license.

THE COURSE OF STUDY FOR TEACHER-TRAINING CLASS

FOURTH YEAR—FIRST QUARTER: SEPTEMBER, OCTOBER, NOVEMBER: THEORY

A study of "The Science and Art of Teaching," LaRue, The American Book Company.

There should be frequent observation tests in the school grades to illustrate the test, and the principles should be applied constantly during the second and third quarters' work.

SECOND QUARTER: DECEMBER, JANUARY, FEBRUARY: PRACTICE.

A Study of the State Manual, with observations and practice teaching of the various subjects with groups and whole grades.

THIRD QUARTER: MARCH, APRIL, MAY: REVIEW COURSE.

A review with intensive study of advanced Arithmetic, Grammar, Geography, and American History and Civics. There should be a review of the year's Teaching-Training Course in this last month. Students will be given administrative duties in supervising children; practice in making out reports, schedules, programs, lesson outlines; in presiding over meetings and assisting grade teachers.

The first high school to be approved was the Augusta Training School, where Lawton B. Evans was county superintendent. Twenty-one pupils, all girls, took the course. E. A. Pound in 1921 reported that there were 17 high schools given teacher training courses in 1920-21, graduating 177 teachers. During the year 1921-22, 35 schools gave such courses with an average enrollment of 345 pupils.[218] In 1922-23, there were 47 teacher training high schools.

As high schools became the expected level for teachers of the elementary schools, the curriculum of the elementary schools broadened and examination questions were more advanced.[219]

ILLUSTRATIVE QUESTIONS

For High school and Supervisory Certificates

1. Who were Aristotle, Constantine, Alario, Cicero, Justinian, Mary Queen of Scots, Xenophon?
2. Compare the French Revolution with the American Revolution as to causes and results.
3. Give an account of the Norman Conquest of England and its results upon English civilization.

General Elementary—English Grammar

3. Analyze the following:
   I found a brilliant jewel, of the size of an ostrich egg, which was placed upon a small stool and diffused light like that of a candle.
4. Parse each word in the sentence just given.

History and Civics

1. Give a lesson plan for teaching the settlement of the original thirteen colonies.
2. State some historical fact in connection with each of the following: Hamilton, Webster, Clay, Calhoun, Penn, Franklin, Dewey, Jefferson.

Senator Kea introduced a bill to the legislature in 1920 to provide physical education and training in the common, grade, state normal and all other public schools of Georgia. The bill was approved in August 1920,[220] with one part requiring normal schools to prepare teachers to teach physical education and training. Superintendent Brittain sent a letter on September 9, 1920, to all county school superintendents informing them of their responsibilities resulting from the bill.

J. O. Martin and Dr. Ralph E. Wager of Emory University made a study of the preparation of teachers in Georgia in

1920-21. They found that 87 percent of Georgia teachers were women; that one-third of the teachers quit the profession each year; that colleges were supplying an inadequate number of teachers each year; that only 45 percent of all Georgia teachers—elementary and secondary—had college, normal school or summer school training; that colleges had inadequate facilities and staff to accept more than one-half the high school graduates applying for admission to normal schools and colleges; that the cry and need for trained teachers was great.[221]

Resulting from the School Laws of 1919 and from better opportunities in the colleges—though still inadequate—certification changes were made. Life certificates were instituted for three years of successful teaching experience and the master's degree from an approved university with one year course in professional education. Requirements for certificates for vocational teachers were advanced beyond those for other teachers. White agriculture teachers were required to have a degree with four years of college preparation. The Negro agriculture teachers were required to have two years of college preparation and practical farm experience. All home economics teachers were required to hold a degree.[222]

J. O. Martin's study in 1921 showed that a majority of the untrained teachers were teaching in the primary grades. The study's results distressed Dr. M. M. Parks, who succeeded M. L. Brittain as state school superintendent in 1922. In his report to the General Assembly, Parks said,

> From improved lower school will come a larger number of scholars for the higher schools. . .
> Strong teachers must be held in the elementary school and especially in the Primary grades. Such a plan will reduce illiteracy; it will help attendance; it will give the child a good foundation, than which nothing is more important in education. But the strong teachers are often drawn away from our rural schools and from the Primary schools by better salaries in higher grades and in cities and in neighboring states. We need more money and more leaders in the Primary and Elementary schools. Here is our biggest education problem.[223]

As ways of solving the problem of teacher preparation, Parks suggested using the 12 District Agricultural and Mechanical Schools in the summers to give teachers already in service an opportunity to get professional training. He also suggested a four-quarter school plan.

Parks raised requirements for obtaining the professional certificate. He was sure that schools would improve if the level of education were raised and the teachers were professionally prepared. He used the certificates as a way of encouraging a higher degree of education.[224]

THE LICENSE BY EXAMINATION

Hereafter, in order to obtain a first grade License to teach, the applicant must pass an examination under the County School Superintendent, making an average of 90 per cent and in addition, the applicant must have had four years of high school work or four years of experience.

THE CERTIFICATE BY COLLEGE WORK

The Professional Normal Certificate is issued by the State Board with a minimum of two years of college or Normal School work above the high school. The Professional College Certificate is issued by the State Board after the applicant has completed four years of standard college work. The Life Certificate is issued by the State Board after the applicant has taken the Master's or Doctor's degree with three years of experience in teaching, or after the applicant has taken the Bachelor's degree in a standard four-year college with ten years experience in teaching.

THE PURPOSE OF THE STATE BOARD

The object of the Board of Education has been to raise the standard of certification so that Georgia Certificates would more easily get recognition in various states of the Union. The object of the State Board in raising some of the qualifications for the first grade License was to encourage more recognition by License and by salary to the experienced and trained teacher, the ultimate purpose being to encourage the professional training of teachers so that schools could have an increasing number of efficient teachers.

THE PROVISIONAL HIGH SCHOOL LICENSE

The regulations for the provisional high school license were left unchanged by the present Board of Education, though it is desirable that the standard for this license be raised soon.

Parks served only a short time as state school superintendent, being succeeded by N. H. Ballard. Ballard also expressed concern about the preparation of teachers for young children. He made use of Martin's and Wager's study. The conclusions and recommendations of Martin were heartily endorsed by Superintendent Ballard in 1924, as follows.[225]

. . . The following deductions can be made:

1. Too many of the teachers of the entire state are lacking in scholarship.
2. That these teachers who are lacking in scholarship are teaching the majority of the children.
3. That the untrained teachers are teaching a majority of the primary children.
4. That the untrained teachers are teaching the one and two-teacher schools and are teaching the primary grades in the three and four-teacher schools.
5. That the untrained teachers remain in the service the shortest length of time.
6. That the untrained teacher remains in one position the shortest length of time.
7. That the untrained teacher remains in the county the shortest length of time.
8. That 882 additional teachers are needed in the state. (This estimate is based on the standard of 35 children per room.)
9. That the largest enrollment is found in the first grade.
10. That the greatest mortality is found between the first and second grades.
11. That one-half of the children do not go beyond the fourth grade.

12. That only 1.8% of the total number of children are in the eleventh grade.

13. That the first, fourth, seventh, and eighth grades are the pivotal points for retardation and morality, and that in these grades more attention should be paid to the training of teachers who are employed to teach them.

14. That the greatest amount of retardation is found in those counties whose terms are shortest, salaries lower, and teachers lacking in scholarship and professional training.

15. That the counties of Bibb, Chatham, Fulton, Muscogee and Richmond, which have, on the whole, superior advantages, lead in positive conditions.

RECOMMENDATIONS

On the basis of this investigation we make at least the following recommendations:

1. That the State build, equip, and maintain a sufficient normal school and university capacity to train an adequate number of teachers.

2. That the State make a more definite and extensive effort to train the teachers who are now in service.

3. That a fund be created with which to equalize a length of term and salaries of teachers based upon educational qualification in all counties of the state; for equalization of county school superintendents' salaries; and for the employment of an adequate number of supervisors; to promote consolidation through a building fund.

These things should be done in order to equalize educational opportunity for all the children of all the people of all the communities of all the counties of Georgia.

Because of these strong recommendations based on facts, the General Assembly of 1923 set aside $20,000 from the General School Fund to be used in conducting summer institutes for teachers. J. O. Martin organized and conducted all of these, held in 13 regional institutes at the 12 district A. & M. schools and at Ellijay during the month of July 1924. Thirteen hundred teachers attended at only $20 expense to the teacher. Three hours credit was allowed for satisfactory work done toward professionalizing elementary certificates. These came to be known as summer schools.

The majority of teachers who attended these institutes never had completed the high school grades. They were given the fundamentals in textbook subject matter. Institutes were held in the same places for a month in 1925. Also, having those with limited scholarship in the state summer schools enabled the colleges to organize their curricula to meet the requirements of students who sought college training and degrees.[226] F. E. Land, succeeding N. H. Ballard as state superintendent, continued the summer programs. By 1928 M. L. Duggan, then state superintendent, reported on summer schools.

> With the increased number of trained teachers and the constantly increasing opportunities for teacher-training through college extension class and otherwise there is decreasing need for the continuation of the summer schools operated by the State Department of Education. The demand is, however, greater and will continue longer in some sections of the State than others.
>
> I would recommend that the allotment from the school fund be continued as heretofore, but that the State Board of Education be authorized to use it either in teacher-training in summer schools or extension work as they deem for the best interests of the cause.[227]

The summer school program conducted by the State Department of Education for which academic credit was given continued under the direction of J. O. Martin through the summer of 1932. At that time, Superintendent Duggan reported,

> The summer schools for teachers under the State Department of Education authorized for a number of years past at an annual expense to the state school fund of $20,000.00 may well be discontinued. They have served a good purpose and have justified their cost, but now have an over supply of teachers which is being added to rapidly by the several teacher training colleges. These colleges are

also offering ample facilities for summer school opportunities.[228]

During this period of time, several philanthropic organizations and associations had continued to aid in the education
of the Negro teacher. Dr. Walter B. Hill succeeded George
Goddard in 1920 as special state supervisor for Negro Education. Lydia B. Thornton, a graduate of Tuskegee, worked
with Hill. Hill remained in this position until July 1930,
when he was succeeded by Dr. J. C. Dixon. Both Hill and
Dixon made progress in providing equal opportunities for
Negro teachers. The progress they achieved was due in a
large degree to the wise use of foundation eleemosynary funds.
The Peabody Fund provided scholarships to colleges and funds
for early institutes. The General Education Board provided
supervisory staff for the State Department of Education and
funds for institutes and other teacher education projects in
schools and colleges. The John F. Slater Fund aided in the
development of schools for Negroes in rural or small town
areas. Training schools in counties all over the state helped
to raise the educational level of teachers. In the early thirties,
the Slater Fund was used to help move high schools toward
accreditation status.

The Anna T. Jeanes Foundation provided funds to pay part
of the salary of a Negro woman variously referred to as a
"Jeanes supervisor," "Jeanes teacher" or "visiting teacher"
for as many counties as could be interested in the work. The
need for these supervisors was great. Even in 1932, only 2,320
of 5,606 Negro teachers had state teachers' certificates, while
at the same time no white teacher could have been employed
by a superintendent without a state certificate. A survey made
in 1931-32 revealed that many Negro teachers were teaching
seven grades while their own training, in some instances, did
not reach that level. The majority of these teachers was holding second and third grade county licenses. The Jeanes supervisors assisted the superintendent and attendance officer with
the ever-present problems of enrollment and attendance,
helped with the cleaning and caring for Negro school buildings, worked with school authorities and trustees to preserve
public school property, recognized the deficiency in training
and cultural attainment of the average Negro teacher and

rendered real assistance through technical subject supervision, through inauguration of health programs, through the enlistment of public interest in education and in many other ways.[229]

Also, the Julius Rosenwald Fund contributed toward supplying vocational education staff for Negroes, toward building adequate school buildings and later in other teacher education projects. In 1930-31, the Rosenwald Fund contributed $44,-798.78 towards the various phases of Negro education in Georgia.[230]

The state had supplied funds for normal schools at Savannah and at Albany, plus an A. & M. school in Forsyth for Negro youth. State funds were used to help pay the salaries of Jeanes supervisors and for summer schools at Albany and Savannah. These funds, however, were incomparable to funds spent for educating and upgrading white teachers.

Dr. J. C. Dixon reported in 1932,[231]

An increased interest in and a more liberal attitude toward the education of Negro children is evident in Georgia . . .

He added:

1. We get what we pay for.
2. The white race and the Negro race together inhabit this state of ours, and the destinies of those two preponderant races now living in Georgia are so closely inwoven that they cannot be considered separately.
3. It is impossible for either race, when two races are living under the same political and other types of control, to progress at a maximum speed without carrying the other one along with it. It is economically, politically, and otherwise unsound, if not impossible, for two ethnic groups to coexist at different levels.
4. Progress in a democracy is to some extent directly related to and dependent on education.
5. If, as we claim, education is a public function, a function of the state, we cannot simply offer to a child the quality and amount of public education he can pay for or purchase.

6. Except as racial differences affect the cost of realizing and maintaining a standard of living, equal work should receive equal pay.

7. The more backward, retarded, and underprivileged the child the better the teacher needed.

8. Lack of an adequate education constitutes an economic loss, intensifies the possibility of maladjustment to the social group, and increases the number of social pariahs and governmental wards.

9. It is certainly more reasonable, more logical, and more humane (and possibly cheaper) to spend public money to train people into good citizenship than it is to spend it to operate penal and corrective institutions for them when they are not so trained.

Recognition of the reasonableness and validity of these constitutes a prerequisite to the development of an adequate program of education for Georgia's Negro children. The problem, then, for some time to come, is partly a matter of technical education effort.

In 1932 Robert L. Cousins began working with Dixon; when Dixon left the State Department of Education to become the director of the Southern Education Foundation in 1936, Cousins became the director of Negro education, where he remained until 1961. Helen Whiting, who began work in 1932 as a state consultant and supervisor for Negro education, continued her efforts with Cousins. L. M. Lester served as a supervisor of Negro education from 1936 to 1941 when Cousins was the director. These people all contributed greatly to the advancement of the qualifications of Negro teachers in the State of Georgia as well as to Negro education in general.

M. D. Collins Administration

Upon assuming office as state school superintendent in January 1933, Dr. M. D. Collins hit the ground running. Among his first official acts was to cut his own salary. He said that he and other staff members would not accept any increase in salary until the salaries of rural school teachers could be improved. His five immediate predecessors in office, Brittain,

Parks, Ballard, Land and Duggan, had echoed the theory of equalization. Collins had studied the reports of these men and other authorities on school finance. He concluded that flat grants on a census basis were unfair; he also saw the discrepancies in the local sub-tax districts, especially as applied to rural districts compared to urban districts.

Collins had served previously as superintendent of Campbell County Schools. He felt strongly that the children in Campbell County did not have the resources for school support that Fulton County provided. He advocated and supported a plan to merge Campbell County with Fulton County; this merger was accomplished.

Prior to the enactment of the McMichael Bill in 1903, the funds for school support were derived largely from state flat grants on a per capita basis. Local taxes, as permitted in the McMichael Act, supplemented state funds. However, these supplements tended to illustrate the unequal resources in sub-tax districts as well as from county to county; and while the 1926 equalization act gave some relief, it did not eliminate the problem. Collins was convinced that if educational opportunities in the entire state were to be equalized it would require a greater portion of state funds rather than local sources alone. His problem was to convince the voters to elect an education-minded legislature. He sought the aid of the Georgia Education Association and other business and professional leaders. The Georgia Education Association approved two resolutions in 1932 on this topic. They were presented by Boyce Grier and Ralph Newton, superintendents of Athens and Waycross City Systems, respectively, and read as follows.

> Money continues to be the most immediate need of Georgia's common schools. We cannot view with complacency the shortened term, low and unpaid salaries, and curtailed services of the schools.
>
> We urge again a complete reform of the present antiquated tax system of Georgia as basic to the proper financial support. Not only for schools but for all other legitimate activities of the State, and we put ourselves on record as strongly favoring a sales tax or some other ready means of supplying our deficiencies in revenue.[232]

The following language in the report of the GEA Educational Campaign Committee, whose chairman was B. M. Grier, expressed views parallel with the Resolution Committee.

> The collapse of local support under the strain of an economic depression weighs very heavily as an argument for State support. In many communities bank failures, tax delinquencies, credit shortages, and personal losses have made school support wholly impossible. Local administrative units cannot handle these forces of economic chaos. The fluctuations of income, due to economic maladjustment, can more nearly be eliminated through shifting the tax load to the broader unit of the state.[233]

Despite progress under these important school laws, college professors, school superintendents, public school teachers, the Georgia Education Association, the American Legion and the Georgia Laymen's Educational Convention continued to work on plans to improve the state's educational structure. Many interested business and professional leaders in these groups held a Georgia Educational Convention in Macon in April 1934. They proposed that the legislature adopt laws to ensure a state-supported, minimum nine-month school term; the proper minimum preparation of teachers, a state minimum salary schedule for teachers and a sound taxation program for the schools.

When the General Assembly convened in 1935, it was faced with conflicting information. Governor Eugene Talmadge, in his State of the State address, indicated that he anticipated a substantial reduction in revenue and directed all department heads to reduce their budget requests by 20 percent.[234] However, the state auditor's report showed a greater balance in the treasury than at any other time in the state's history.[235] Less than two months later, the Governor again cautioned legislators to go slow in spending the money, warning, "Heads of the common school system, the university system and the elementary system agreed they could operate on funds recommended by the budget committee. To increase funds would encourage extravagance and affect other departments." [236]

Although the Depression forced all government officials to proceed with caution in projecting their future needs, the

1935 session—famous as the "no appropriation session"—
did pass a series of education bills sponsored by House Speaker
E. D. Rivers and embodying the provisions of the resolutions
drafted at the Macon convention the previous year. The Governor vetoed the first bill, stating, "This bill appropriates no
funds for free textbooks. It would put an idle gesture on the
statute books."[237] Of a bill designed to let the state superintendent fix the salary schedule for teachers (which could be
supplemented by local pay if money was available), the Governor stated his opposition to a uniform school law. "It proposes to change the law. The superintendent of schools would
draw a warrant on the treasury and disburse instead of the
governor drawing the warrant." [238]

At this time (1935), there were 64 independent city systems in Georgia. The research study of J. R. Burgess, superintendent of the Pitts Consolidated School, dealt with various
aspects of the school boards of these city systems. The average
board was one of five members, but the number varied from
three to nine. About one-fourth of the boards had *ex officio*
members, a tendency which appeared to be on the decrease.
About half of the boards were elected by the people; the remainder were appointed by the city council. Burgess learned
that the appointed board was coming into disfavor, particularly when the board thus named chose the superintendent.
A majority of the board members served for terms of two or
three years. There were 23 different qualifications for members of the city boards. Qualifications found in five cities were
—resident of the city for a specified time, a qualified voter,
citizen of the city, 21 years of age and a free-holder.[239]

The city systems exhibited greater uniformity in the selection of the superintendent. In nearly all cases the superintendent was selected by the city board, to whom this function was
usually delegated by charter and by-laws. In a large number
of cases, superintendents were obtained through a process of
friendly pirating. Men whose success had been demonstrated
in other cities were induced to accept new positions in larger
places until they reached the peak of usefulness. Except in the
larger cities, superintendents were, as a rule, chosen from
the ranks of superintendents within the state. Often strong
attachments were formed between the superintendent and the

city in which he worked, and he remained in office during a large portion of his useful life.

The number of men and women who have served the city schools of Georgia with effectiveness and distinction is almost endless. They usually have been at the forefront of progress, and they have been the leaders and exponents of every movement undertaken to roll back the walls of ignorance and complacency surrounding the schools and people of Georgia, not only in the service of their own system schools but also in the larger educational movements of the state. This situation is not confined to Georgia, according to the *Cyclopedia of Education,* edited by Paul Monroe.

> It is in the cities we find the supervision of instruction best developed and the work of the school supervision placed on the best professional basis. This is largely due to the fact that almost from the first the cities have been free to develop their school systems as they have seen fit, and also to freely go into the markets of the whole country and get the best persons available for the superintendents of their schools, entirely free from such restrictions as local residence, party nomination and elections and a fixed salary schedule which for so long have hampered the county's superintendency in its development along professional lines. There are, of course superintendents and cities afflicted with local and personal politics, but in general the city superintendent is the educational leader of his city and a leader in the sense that the county superintendent is not. The best educational thinking by the practical school men of America today is done by our City Superintendents and almost all of the important educational advances of the past 25 years have been made by our city schools.[240]

Among the points of superiority claimed for the independent city schools, the following are found in the literature descriptive of educational progress in Georgia.

1. The bonding capacity of the city is sufficient to provide better buildings and facilities.
2. The longer term and increased salaries can attract better teachers.

3. City schools can be operated more economically—at less administrative cost per pupil.
4. Only limited amount of busing is required as compared with county consolidated schools.
5. New and experimental procedures can be tested and funded.
6. Extensive, expert supervision becomes available in city schools.
7. Many of the modern teaching facilities and pupil services were initiated in the city schools.
8. In the larger cities an administrative staff of specialists is possible.
9. Effective counseling and adaptation of school opportunities to pupil needs are more often available in the city school system.[241]

In reviewing the merits of the city school system, not all judgments are on the favorable side. In spite of the superior advantages and facilities of the schools of an independent system, there is much negative comment relating to them or to the conditions of society which enable them to thrive while the neighboring communities are impoverished. This is not in criticism of the cities, which are only using their material resources to create better opportunities for their children; instead it is directed at their tendency to shut out the county children having needs that cannot be supplied within the limits of the county economy.

Curriculum

Enactment of the 1905 McMichael Tax Act promised to bring better opportunities for school-age children of the state, especially those in the rural areas. After years of urging authorization to supplement state school funds with local taxes, local officials felt encouraged by the tax, even though state funds were still not authorized for high schools until 1912. Prior to the 1905 Act very few high schools offered programs preparing students for college.

In 1909, the General Assembly revised some of the school laws giving the State Board of Education special authority to establish a course of study and to adopt appropriate textbooks.[242] This act also changed the name of the State School Commissioner to State School Superintendent, who was now authorized to appoint three State School Supervisors. The supervisors' duties included grading applications for professional certificates and improving the schools according to the state school superintendent's directions. With February 12 designated as Georgia Day, the schools conducted annual programs related to Georgia history and the lives of distinguished Georgians.[243]

In a letter to superintendents in 1912, Brittain listed the high school courses approved by the State Board of Education. In English, the board approved grammar and literature, rhetoric, composition and the classics. In mathematics, the board approved algebra, geometry, trigonometry and surveying. The sciences included physics, chemistry, biology and general science. History, civics and government made up the list of social studies. Electives included agriculture, manual arts, domestic science and some commercial work.[244]

A teachers' manual prepared by the State Department of Education in 1911 and published in 1912 opens with this preface by the new state school superintendent, Dr. M. L. Brittain:

> For the last few years there has been a constantly increasing demand for a new manual of methods. The one we have had is good in many particulars, but no matter how excellent a work of this kind may be, it wrongs the teachers of a state to force them to study it continuously for many years. My predecessor, Honorable J. M. Pound, felt this truth and two years ago asked several of us to aid in the preparation of a new text. Circumstances prevented the accomplishment of the task at that time, however, and so for months past I have been securing manuscripts from well-known educators who have contributed the best part of this volume. The state is under obligations to them for this service. As will be seen by a reference to the writers there is not an unpractical theorist among them. They have demonstrated by efficient and notable service their ability to 'practice as well as preach' that which is accepted as best in a modern education. In addition to the topics treated in the old manual we have

added history of education, special day programs, the chief features of the state school laws, and other material, endeavoring to make the work an indispensable handbook for Georgia teachers.

Manuals were subsequently published in 1916 and 1921. Because of the laws permitting the operation of high schools and other recent legislation, especially the Acts of 1919 and 1920, the manual of 1921 devoted more attention to high school subjects, courses, and operations than to other phases of school work. A special section interpreted the new law on teaching physical education in all schools.[245] From 1918 through 1928 high schools grew rapidly. The Barrett-Rogers Consolidation Bill decreased the number of high schools after about 1924, but enrollment continued to grow in high schools as well as agricultural and mechanical schools, vocational education and vocational rehabilitation. All forms of education developed during this period.

Standards for Schools, as prescribed by the State Department of Education, applied to the following topics: 1. The Teacher; II. The Grounds; III. The Buildings; IV Equipment; V. Associated Activities; VI. Salary of Teacher and VII. Term. In his correspondence to county superintendents in 1912, Superintendent Brittain states,

> Upon compliance with every point under each of the seven heads, the State Department of Education will send a certificate which can be framed and will designate the institution as a standard county school . . . The requirements urged in order to bring the schools up to a creditable standard are reasonable and some counties can meet them now in almost every particular throughout their systems. These are comparatively few, however, and the wide variation is easy to be seen since many others have no schools with the equipment outlined and will have difficulty in securing it. Show teachers and patrons the real model school or mark at which we are to aim and attainment will follow, however, as certainly in rural as well as in urban education.[246]

Quoting in the High School Quarterly, Dr. Joseph Stewart tells of his joint concern with Superintendent Brittain regarding the needed requirements for seventh grade graduation, as follows.

Supt. M. L. Brittain has sent out to the Georgia schools the following standards of what a pupil completing the common schools ought to know. It is hoped that teachers will test their students by these standards:

WHAT AN EIGHTH GRADE PUPIL OUGHT TO KNOW

1. How to speak and read the English language with fair accuracy.
2. How to write with fair legibility, in particular, ordinary business letters.
3. How to use the principles of arithmetic in ordinary business transactions.
4. How to spell at least the words used in ordinary business transactions.
5. Enough geography to appreciate current events, and to know something of the nations of the world.
6. The leading facts of American history; to feel a patriotic pride in the deeds of our fathers and to give reasons for opinions as to men and measures.
7. The value of physiology and hygiene—what it means to have a healthful body and hygienic surroundings.
8. To know something of the plants, birds, trees and agricultural life of the vicinity.
9. The civic virtues—to be honest, trustworthy, obedient, truthful and polite.

These are minimum essentials and represent the tools of an education. Can we ask for less for seven years instruction? [247]

Physical education became a required course for public schools in the early 1920s. Charlton County Schools' physical education program, under the direction of Norman Zarfos in 1921, offered activities for students at each grade level. The local representative in the General Assembly, L. E. Mallard, became interested in the physical education program on the state level as a result of Mr. Zarfos' work.[248] However, Dr.

Stewart, reporting in the High School Quarterly in 1921, attributes the introduction of the physical education bill to Senator Kea.[249] The prescribed course in physical education was enacted in 1920.[250]

The General Assembly passed a series of bills from 1919 through 1943 dealing with adult illiteracy. In 1919, an act empowered the State Board of Education to collect data and procure surveys of all communities to learn the extent of adult illiteracy in Georgia. The State Board of Education received funds for the education of illiterate adults.[251] This act was further clarified by an amendment in 1931.[252] The county commissioners and ordinaries were authorized to establish schools for adult illiterates in 1920.[253] The Act of 1920 specified that school operating costs would be paid from local taxes levied by the commissioners or the ordinaries. In 1943, an act provided that county boards of education could establish schools to educate illiterate adults in those counties where neither the county commissioners nor the ordinaries had made such provisions.[254] The act stated that such education would be in the elementary branches of an English education, that any funds made available for such purposes may be so used and that these county boards of education would cooperate with any state or federal agency or authority in promoting adult education and reducing adult illiteracy within their respective counties.

Adult education in Georgia received two great boosts in the 1960s. Federal programs were provided through Title II-B of the Economic Opportunity Act of 1964[255] and the Adult Education Act in 1966.[256] The state has been supplementing federal programs continuously. Title III of the ESEA in 1969 further increased services in this area.[257] From a meager beginning in 1919 Georgia's program has grown to be a most effective resource in education of adults.

As Georgia's high school inspector, Stewart kept in touch constantly with the school leaders in all areas of education. In addition to school visits, he edited the *High School Quarterly* which reported activities, findings, editorials and information from the State Department of Education and the University of Georgia. Some of his editorials were very strong as well as convincing. Typical are some of the following.

1. In Volume II, January 1914, No. 2, page 66, he has a scorching editorial on the harm being done by high school football and strongly urges school leaders to replace the sport with less dangerous games.

2. In Volume III, January 1914, No. 2, page 80, he deplores the lack of supervision in the schools and insists that Georgia needs more and better trained supervisors for its schools.

3. In Volume V, October 1916, No. 1, page 1, he urges a review of required courses for high school students and says that there should be a better basis than tradition for deciding on required courses. He says all students do not necessarily need four years of history, or science, or mathematics, or Latin, but that present needs such as home efficiency, vocational efficiency, health, and intellectual efficiency should be taken into consideration.

4. In Volume V, January 1917, No. 2, page 119, he reports on a study in the Southern States on the length of the school day, school lunches, and physical education and recommends that schools give more consideration to these topics.

5. In Volume VI, January 1918, No. 2, page 73, he says, "How much longer, Mr. Superintendent, will you permit the one room rural teacher to try to teach high school subjects at the bidding of some prominent patron, to the neglect of the many for whom this school is organized? It is as futile as it is illegal. The high school work must be consolidated in definite centers in the county, if results are to be secured for either the elementary or the high school pupils."

6. In Volume VI, January 1918, No. 4, page 206, he reports on a Committee of the NEA Study of the Teaching of Music in the high schools. He supports the committee's recommendation that music be offered in the high schools on an equal basis with other subjects and credit be given towards graduation on such studies.

7. In Volume VIII, July 1920, No. 4, page 218, he commends results of the newly created Georgia Illiteracy Commission. He cites figures indicating that 31,500 adults have

enrolled in these classes using more than 50,000 textbooks. He urges the continuation of this work.

8. In Volume IX, January 1921, No. 2, page 126, he commends the innovation of physical education in the public schools and describes how the State School Supervisors can aid the teachers in implementing the programs
   in the schools.

9. In Volume X, October 1921, No. 1, page 83, he prints an
   article by H. R. Mahler of Thomasville City Schools on
   the topic "The Use of Leisure." Dr. Stewart then follows
   the article with suggestions for using athletics, walking,
   reading, music, fine arts, drama as valuable ways to improve leisure activities. He suggests that the school
   should be making an effort to include these areas in the
   curriculum, and even says that the high school should be
   sponsor for the social evening.

The District High School Association, another innovation
by Stewart, stimulated the growth of literary studies and
contests on district and later statewide levels. Stewart recognized the school's potential impact on a changing society.

In his annual report to the General Assembly for the year
1922, State School Superintendent Marvin M. Parks made
three significant statements about public school instruction
and curriculum. Though several statements contradicted popular educational attitudes, they were effective and thought-
provoking for the era. On page nine of the report, he says,

A Top-Heavy System of Leadership

For many years the state work has been top-heavy—top-
heavy in administration, in organization, in expenditures,
in propaganda, and in educational objectives; at the same
time, the primary and county schools have suffered for
lack of a sufficient number of leaders.

Unfortunately, our system of salaries and promotions,
and organization draws many leaders away from elementary fields, where leaders are most needed, and found.
It is startling to note how few pupils have reached the
higher classes in schools and colleges.

Theory and propaganda will not do. We must have better
results. Only 1 percent of the children of school age are

in college; it is our business to see that more attention is given to the remaining 99 percent. We have sadly neglected the elementary schools. Because the majority of our lower schools have been defective, literally hundreds of thousands of children have dropped out of school with dwarfed and stunted lives. We have blundered. It is time to reform.[258]

The above criticism has been familiar through the years and certainly the claim is a valid point. In a slightly more optimistic mood, Parks comments,

Course of Study

It is a real pleasure to record the great growth in Georgia high schools, but the mere fact of existence of a school should not content us. It is not a question of how many schools we have, but of what kind of schools are they? In other words, are all of our high schools meeting the real objective of a high school? Are they teaching the child to use facts as well as to learn facts? Are they teaching them to use information as well as to become informed? Are they really developing the latent ability in the child, or are they merely continuing to track the textbooks, thereby throttling any inspiration a child may have?

The old and the traditional yet have some hold upon our high schools. Too many high school teachers yet seem to believe that there is something sacred in some of the high school studies and that every child should take them. The child should not be fitted to the curriculum but the curriculum to the child. The best interests of the child should more often be taken into consideration. It is true that in the small high schools many courses of study cannot and should not be given. We ought not to attempt the impossible. It is no longer necessary that this or that subject be given for the entire four years, and yet there are many who seem to entertain the idea that their schools cannot become accredited unless they give certain subjects for the entire time. It is only necessary to read the rules and regulations of the Accrediting Board or the regulations set forth in the State Manual in order to eliminate such an idea. Not more than nine units are specified by the high school regulations and so the other six may be selected with reference to the best interest of the child and the welfare of the community. Every school has then the right of so developing its course of study as will minister to the essential needs of every community, if not of the individual.

Many of the high schools are rapidly adapting their curricula and are meeting the real requirements of the high schools by limiting their work to the fundamental elements: English language and literature; those studies that make contributions to physical welfare; those that deal with materials of common need; and those that make real contributions towards good citizenship and social efficiency. These schools are placing emphasis upon English, the social sciences, civics, physical education, and general science. Some electives should be offered but they cannot be offered in many schools until we learn to economize both time and money by a different arrangement in offering studies.[259]

He addressed the elementary curriculum in this 1922 report.

State Examination Questions for the Seventh Grade, March 1923

Each spring many superintendents and teachers ask for test questions for those pupils who have completed the general elementary work. The list enclosed is suggestive merely and intended for those only who desire this help. Besides the grading in regular studies prescribed it would be beneficial to show progress made in declamation and debate. It is advisable also to include under deportment such civic virtues as obedience, industry, honesty, truthfulness and courtesy. Composition, penmanship and spelling marks are to be made up from the entire paper. Require answers to be made with pen and ink. If a pupil has not studied one of the subjects belonging to this grade and cannot answer a question, the mark for this should be zero. An average of 75 percent entitles a pupil to a Seventh Grade Certificate.[260]

Each of Superintendent Parks' reports indicates a growing state level concern for curriculum improvement at all grade levels. When the high school movement began attracting considerable interest, concern developed that this new emphasis may detract from elementary school needs. Especially important was the growth in interest in the rural schools which had not received great attention in the past. Though not typical of all rural school systems in the state, an historical sketch of the schools in Charlton County described some remarkable developments for rural schools, including a plan of school supervision begun in 1924, development of long-term objectives by teachers and board members and budgeting and auditing procedures in the mid-1920s. A week of pre-planning and a week of post-planning was inaugurated when the county board started paying the teachers on a twelve-month basis in 1930, an innovative plan instituted prior to the state-level plan for either program. In 1931, the county provided free textbooks to all elementary students. School libraries, started in 1925, continued to grow for use by students as well as teachers. Charlton County pioneered school food services, starting in 1936. Without any outside help, the service rapidly spread throughout the county.[261] In an interview with former Charlton County School Superintendent John Harris on September 9, 1975, the 102-year-old man vividly recalled his weekly elementary schools story telling sessions. At first he told and retold children's classics, but then he made up stories about Bobby Squirrel and other local animals which the children seemed to enjoy even more. Now, when Harris meets his former students in various parts of the state, they still recall the famous Bobby Squirrel stories. Another unprecedented move was Superintendent Harris' decision to build a dormitory for the rural students wishing to attend Folkston High School. During the 1975 interview he pointed out where the old dormitory had stood and served for many years until pupil transportation was provided for the high school students of the county.

Superintendent Harris was very careful to present all known facts and data to the Board of Education and to the public. He periodically published documents similar to that reprinted here.

AN ANNUAL SURVEY REPORT OF THE
CHARLTON COUNTY SCHOOL SYSTEM
FOR THE YEAR ENDING JUNE 1930

Containing

History of the School System   Purposes of this Report
Powers of the Board   Duties of Local Trustees
Duties of the Treasurer   Duties of Principals
Duties of the Superintendent

Tabulation Showing Cost per Pupil in Each Unit
Tabulation Showing Cost of Transportation
Annual Financial Statement of County and Districts
Scholarship Accomplishments in Fundamental Subjects

1. Average Grade Standings in All Units
2. Comparative Standing-Process Chart
3. Pupils Reaching U. S. Standards
4. Tabulation of Age-Grade Retardation

Attendance in White and Negro Schools for Year
Causes of Absences of Pupils for the Year
Standard Scoring of Buildings and Grounds
Teacher Salary Scale   Report of Health Service
Requests for Suggestions   Efficiency Rating
            Conclusions and Recommendations

Prepared by John Harris, Superintendent
Charlton County Schools
Folkston, Georgia

On the state level, manuals were issued as needed and were distributed to all Georgia school systems. In 1926 a 59-page Safety Education manual was published. In 1929 a bulletin on elementary accreditation was published which read in part,

> The State Department of Education accredits elementary schools meeting minimum standards. Applications or information should be requested of the State Department of Education . . . High Schools are accredited only by the Association of Colleges and High Schools through their accrediting commission, Dr. J. S. Stewart, Chairman, Athens, Georgia, to whom requests for information should be addressed.

The bulletin contained the list of elementary school standards and a list of the approved schools for 1929. Schools then were accredited as Class A, B and C.[262]

Volume IX of Georgia School Items of 1932, No. 6, entitled "A Course of Study in English in the High Schools," included a course outline, a reading list prepared by Dr. R. E. Park at the University of Georgia 1931 summer school and a course of study for elementary schools.

Consolidation into larger units significantly increased instructional opportunities. Local boards of education were authorized to contract with each other for the care and education of their pupils. In November 1927, the Troup County Board of Education contracted with the City of LaGrange for the education of its high school students residing outside the City of LaGrange.[263] Other consolidations and contracts, taking place in the 1920s, secured better program offerings for their students. Fiscal economy was rarely considered when arranging consolidations and contracts.

When Dr. M. D. Collins became State School Superintendent in 1933, leaders throughout the state planned to reexamine the aims of education, the scope of the curriculum and procedures for reaching the largest group of Georgia teachers and parents. Collins began the Georgia Program for the Improvement of Instruction in November 1933, just ten months after he assumed office. Cooperating with the State Department of Education in this vast study were the colleges of the University of Georgia System, many private and denominational colleges and the Georgia Education Association. Superintendents, principals and teachers in 119 counties participated in the early studies dealing with the stated objectives.

1. To improve the quality of teaching.
2. To provide the state with public school curricula more nearly in harmony with present needs.
3. To offer state citizens a fuller realization of the school's function in developing human and material resources.

Local study groups were formed in many school systems, where resource personnel from the colleges assisted with all phases of the study. Of course, there developed in many areas some opposition to the so-called drastic changes suggested by many of the groups. A great deal of the professional literature used in the studies came under fire as being un-American in concept and in theory.

Local leaders and consultants prepared many guides and materials to be used by teachers when implementing the suggested procedures, which will be discussed in the next chapter. The Georgia Program for the Improvement of Instruction was planned as a permanent group whose continuous effort would meet teachers' needs by developing current materials to be used in the classrooms. Techniques in the problem-solving approach to learning were emphasized throughout the several years of study.

The 1937 Seven Months School Law added momentum to the Georgia Program for the Improvement of Instruction. Prior to the 1937 legislation, there were many counties where local school districts operated four, five or six months school terms. An editorial in the *Bulloch Times and Statesboro News* in 1931 deplored the fact that some schools in Bulloch County closed at the end of a five-month term.[264] Another editorial in the same paper stated that the legislative task of consolidating the counties had reached the stage at which maps were being published reducing the number of counties from 161 to 24. The editor announced plans to continue his breathing as it would not do to hold his breath until consolidation of counties was accomplished.[265]

At one time Georgia had 161 counties, but in the 1930s Campbell and Milton counties merged with Fulton County, thereby reducing the number to 159.

Vocational Rehabilitation

Vocational rehabilitation programs provide handicapped people with vocational skills qualifying them for paid employment. In their earliest years these programs trained those persons who had been injured in industry, providing little or no concern for persons with congenital disabilities.

Early public efforts at rehabilitation of the latter group were strongly opposed due to expense, efforts to keep the handicapped out of public view and even the attitude that those born with handicaps had been visited by evil gods in their displeasure.

Before the adoption of the first federal act in 1920, only six states, California, Oregon, Massachusetts, Minnesota, New Jersey and Pennsylvania, permitted training of the handicapped from state funds.[266]

Perhaps the greatest impetus for a federal vocational rehabilitation act was the need for rehabilitating war injured veterans. As early as 1917 the American Red Cross had initiated a program for disabled soldiers and sailors.[267] In 1915, Goodwill Industries formed a self-help program [268] through which disabled persons earned wages by repairing and reclaiming old clothing and furniture.[269] In Atlanta, Georgia, the Scottish Rite had established a hospital for the treatment of handicapped children. The American Red Cross, Goodwill Industries and the Scottish Rite Councils reflected Americans' changing attitudes toward rehabilitation. Although opposition still existed, it was becoming more apparent that the governmental sector must and would become involved in training the handicapped.

The Federal Board of Vocational Education, created by the Smith-Hughes Vocational Education Act in 1917, administered vocational rehabilitation. The Smith-Sears Bill created the Veterans Rehabilitation Act in 1918, and in 1920 the Civilian Vocational Rehabilitation Bill by Georgia Senator Hoke Smith and Ohio Representative Fess permitted the states and the federal government to become partners in vocational rehabilitation training programs. The Smith-Fess law, whose funding provisions had to be renewed about every three years, eventually was assured permanence with inclusion into the 1935 Social Security Act.[270] The 1920 act restricted programs to vocational training only, with no federal funds for restoration, hospitalization, medical treatment, appliances or surgery. In 1943 these inadequacies were corrected through the Barden-LaFollette Act.[271]

On December 1, 1920, Georgia officially became a partner with the federal government in successful vocational rehabilitation.[272] Through 1974, 198,608 persons had been rehabilitated in Georgia through this program. (See Appendix III.)

Appropriations of federal funds for the first three years were $500,000, $750,000 and $1 million, respectively. Funds were apportioned to each state according to its relationship to the national population.[273]

One measure of the program's success is the many instances in Georgia of clients paying more taxes in the first year after the completion of their programs than was paid for the total cost of their rehabilitation. But more important is the positive effect on the individuals, their families, communities and the increased general productivity and efficiency of their efforts. Georgia's program was boosted in 1927 with the creation of the Georgia Warm Springs Foundation by Franklin D. Roosevelt.

The U. S. Congress in 1943 enacted P. L. 113,[274] which made services available to the mentally and emotionally ill. That year alone the number of rehabilitations increased five times over the preceding year, from 413 to 2,109.

By 1949 Georgia's program had been broadened to include such services as placement, equipment, counseling and guidance, training, maintenance, prosthetic appliances, physical restoration and medical examination. That year alone there were over 13,000 cases on the rolls, with 3,075 cases completed.

The next major expansion came about in 1954 through Public Law 565,[275] which liberalized the appropriation authority and adjusted the allotment method to increase the matching ratios from federal funds. Research, demonstration and traineeships became part of the rapidly expanding program.

Revolutionary in design and concept and as expansive as almost all previous legislation, Public Law 89-333, which President Johnson signed on November 8, 1965, improved the program by making available funds for new rehabilitation facilities, grants to speed improvements of workshops for the handicapped and other adjustments in allotment procedures including a uniform share of 75 percent of program cost, the elimination of economic need as a requirement for eligibility, study of architectural barriers and federal funding for statewide planning for rehabilitation needs and services.[276]

Georgia has supplied three presidents of the National Rehabilitation Association, Paul Barrett, Dr. A. P. Jarrell and

John S. Prickett, Jr., each of whom directed the program in Georgia. Each appeared numerous times before congressional committees in Washington, D. C., and had tremendous influence on subsequent legislation and appropriations.

CHAPTER III

FOOTNOTES

1. Charles William Dabney, *Universal Education in the South*, (Chapel Hill: University of North Carolina Press, 1936), II P. 128.
2. Report of a Constitutional Convention, Constitution of 1877, pp. 621-623.
3. *Ibid.*, p. 621.
4. Georgia Department of Education *Annual Report*, 1924, p. 21.
5. *Georgia Laws*, 1872, p. 62.
6. Georgia Department of Education, *Georgia State School Items*, February 1931, VIII (2), p. 27.
7. Georgia Department of Education *Annual Report*, 1903, p. 22.
8. *Ibid.*, p. 23.
9. *Ibid.*, p. 48.
10. *Ibid.*, p. 32.
11. Dorothy Orr, *History of Education in Georgia* (Chapel Hill, University of North Carolina Press, 1950), p. 261.
12. Georgia Department of Education *Annual Report*, 1903, p. 33.
13. Nomes W. Loyles, ed., *Georgia's Public Men.* (Atlanta: Byrd Printing Co., 1903), p. 72.
14. Constitutional Amendment, ratified October 5, 1904.
15. *Georgia Laws*, 1905, pp. 425-429.
16. Georgia Department of Education *Annual Report*, 1906, p. 244.
17. Georgia Department of Education *Annual Report*, 1904, pp. 19-20.
18. Georgia Department of Education *Annual Report*, 1908, p. 71.
19. Georgia Department of Education *Annual Report*, 1906, p. 12.
20. Georgia Department of Education *Annual Report*, 1907, p. 10.
21. *Ibid.*, p. 8.
22. Georgia Department of Education *Annual Report*, 1908, p. 12.
23. Georgia Department of Education *Annual Report*, 1907, p. 10.
24. Georgia Department of Education *Annual Report*, 1897, pp. 10-31.
25. Georgia Department of Education *Annual Report*, 1911, p. 244.
26. Dabney, *Universal Education in the South*, II, p. 410-411.
27. *Ibid.*, p. 410.
28. Georgia Department of Education *Annual Report*, 1905, p. 12.
29. J. W. Reed, "Life of Joseph S. Stewart," *High School Quarterly*, XXII, 22.
30. Dabney, *Universal Education in the South*, p. 412.
31. University of Georgia *Bulletin*, 1903-1904, p. 83.
32. *Ibid.*, p. 83.
33. *Ibid.*, p.84.
34. *Ibid.*, 1904-1905, pp. 17-24.
35. Dabney, *Universal Education in the South*, p. 412.
36. Georgia General Assembly *House Journal*, October 22, 1904, pp. 429-450.
37. Georgia Department of Education *Annual Report*, 1906, p. 72.
38. John T. Wheeler, *Two Hundred Years of Agricultural Education in Georgia* (Danville, Ill.: The Interstate Co., 1948), p. 3.
39. *Ibid.*, pp. 69-70.
40. *Georgia Laws*, 1931, pp. 20-21.

41. Georgia Department of Education *Annual Report*, 1907, p. 33.
42. *Ibid.*, p. 19.
43. Georgia Department of Education *Annual Report*, 1906, pp. 14-16.
44. Georgia Home Economics Association, Report of the Standards Committee, *History of Home Economics in Georgia*, 1933, p. 22.
45. Report of State School Commission to the General Assembly, December 31, 1909.
46. Georgia Department of Education *Annual Report*, 1907, pp. 26-77.
47. *Ibid.*, p. 24.
48. *Ibid.*, p. 14, 131.
49. *Ibid.*, p. 32.
50. Georgia Department of Education *Annual Report*, 1906, p. 202.
51. *Ibid.*, p. 198.
52. *Ibid.*, p. 245.
53. *Ibid.*, p. 271.
54. *Georgia Laws*, 1910, p. 45.
55. *Georgia Laws*, 1912, pp. 176-179.
56. Georgia Department of Education *Annual Report*, 1911, p. 447.
57. Georgia Department of Education *Annual Report*, 1908, p. 428.
58. Georgia Department of Education *Annual Report*, 1930, p. 485.
59. Georgia Department of Education *Annual Report*, 1903, p. 21.
60. *Ibid.*, pp. 75-76.
61. Georgia Department of Education *Annual Report*, 1907, p. 218.
62. *Ibid.*, pp. 219-220.
63. Georgia Department of Education *Annual Report*, 1908, pp. 220-221.
64. *Ibid.*, p. 220.
65. Georgia Department of Education *Annual Report*, 1909, pp. 299-300.
66. Georgia Department of Education *Annual Report*, 1911, p. 264.
67. Georgia Department of Education *Annual Report*, 1909, p. 13.
68. Georgia Department of Education *Annual Report*, 1907, p. 64.
69. Orr, *History of Education*, p. 176.
70. Georgia Department of Education *Annual Report*, 1907, p. 9.
71. *Ibid.*, 1909, p. 11.
72. *Ibid.*
73. *Ibid.*
74. *Ibid.*, p. 21.
75. *Ibid.*, p. 14
76. Pulaski County Board of Education, *Minutes*, Meeting of December 19, 1903.
77. *Georgia Laws*, 1913, pp. 1303-04.
78. *Georgia Laws*. 1914, pp. 1237-38.
79. Screven County Board of Education, *Minutes*, Meetings of December 1896 to March 1929.
80. *Ibid.*
81. *Ibid.*, p. 7.
82. *Ibid.*, p. 58.
83. *Ibid.*, p. 59.
84. *Ibid.*, pp. 58-59 and 364-89.
85. Georgia Department of Education *Annual Report*, 1910, pp. 26-27.
86. Georgia Department of Education *Annual Report*, 1896, pp. 98-99.
87. Georgia Department of Education *Annual Report*, 1903, pp. 62-63.
88. Georgia Department of Education *Annual Report*, 1908, p. 23.
89. Georgia Department of Education *Annual Report*, 1909, pp. 15-17.
90. *Georgia Laws*, 1909, p. 154.
91. Georgia Department of Education *Annual Report*, 1909, p. 23.
92. *Ibid.*, p. 19.
93. *High School Quaterly*, XIII, October, 1923.
94. Georgia Department of Education *Annual Report*, 1912, p. 240.

95. Georgia Department of Education *Annual Report*, 1914, p. 256.
96. Georgia Department of Education Annual Report, 1915, p. 243.
97. Guy Snavely, "A Short History of the Southern Association," *Southern Association's Quarterly*, IX, 1938, pp. 423-459.
98. *High School Quarterly*, XIII, (October 1923), 40.
99. Georgia Department of Education *Annual Report*, 1913, p. 286.
100. *Ibid.*, pp. 295-296.
101. Georgia Department of Education *Annual Report*, 1914, pp. 271-276.
102. Georgia Department of Education *Annual Report*, 1915, pp. 248-250.
103. Georgia Department of Education *Annual Report*, 1910, p. 13.
104. *Ibid.*, p. 14.
105. *Georgia Laws*, 1912, p. 180.
106. *Report* of School Commission to the General Assembly, December 31, 1910, p. 17.
107. *Georgia Laws*, 1911, pp. 96-108.
108. Georgia Department of Education *Annual Report*, 1911, pp. 23-24.
109. *Georgia Laws*, 1911, pp. 46-48.
110. Georgia Department of Education *Annual Report*, 1910, pp. 198-202.
111. *Georgia Laws*, 1911, p. 102.
112. *Ibid.*, pp. 98-99.
113. Georgia Department of Education *Annual Report*, 1912, p. 176.
114. *Georgia Laws*, 1911, pp. 99-100.
115. Georgia Department of Education *Annual Report*, 1913, p. 49.
116. Georgia Department of Education *Annual Report*, 1915, p. 38.
117. *Ibid.*, pp. 38-39.
118. *Ibd.*, p. 18.
119. Georgia Department of Education *Annual Report*, 1916, p. 187.
120. Georgia Department of Education *Annual Report*, 1917, p. 38.
121. Georgia Department of Education *Annual Report*, 1918, p. 46.
122. *Georgia Laws*, 1911, p. 96.
123. Georgia Department of Education *Annual Report*, 1916, p. 254.
124. I. A. Dickerson, *A Study of Vocational and Technical Education in Georgia* . . ., 1969, pp. 13-14.
125. Dabney, *Universal Education in the South*, p. 205.
126. Georgia Department of Education *Annual Report*, 1918, pp. 20-21.
127. J. Harold Saxon, "The Accredited High Schools of Georgia," University of Georgia *Bulletin*, 1938, XXXIX, 5.
128. Wheeler, *Two Hundred Years*, p. 67.
129. Georgia Department of Education *Annual Report*, 1918, pp. 20-21.
130. M. L. Brittain, "The Administration of the Smith-Hughes Vocational Act in Georgia, For the Second Year, July 1, 1918 to July 1, 1919, 9," p. 91.
131. Wheeler, *Two Hundred Years*, p. 69.
132. Georgia Department of Education *Annual Report*, 1916, pp. 236-239.
133. Georgia Home Economics Association, *History of Home Economics*, 1933, p. 22.
134. Wheeler, *Two Hundred Years*, p. 87.
135. *Ibid.*, pp. 326-38.
136. Brittain, "The Administration of the Smith-Hughes Vocational Act in Georgia, For the Second Year," p. 3.
137. M. L. Brittain, "Georgia State Plan for Vocational Education under the Smith-Hughes Law, 1918, 4," pp. 34-47.
138. Brittain, "The Administration of the Smith-Hughes Vocational Act in Georgia, For the Second Year," p. 48.
139. Wheeler, *Two Hundred Years*, pp. 309-310.
140. Brittain, "State Plan, 1918" 4. pp. 7-47, and "Administration, 1919" 9, pp. 10-11.
141. Georgia Department of Education *Annual Report*, 1919, p. 21.
142. Wheeler, *Two Hundred Years*, pp. 222-224.

143. Georgia Home Economics Association, *History of Home Economics,* 1933, p. 24.
144. Georgia Department of Education *Annual Report,* 1919, pp. 22-26.
145. *Georgia Laws,* 1919, pp. 287-288.
146. Georgia Department of Education *Annual Report,* 1919, p. 256.
147. Georgia Department of Education *Annual Report,* 1920, p. 21.
148. *Georgia Laws,* 1919, pp. 66-68.
149. Victor Davidson, *The History of Wilkinson County,* (J. W. Burke: Macon, Ga., 1930), p. 479.
150. *Atlanta Constitution,* (June 27, 1919), 9.
151. *Ibid.,* (July 3, 1919), 9.
152. *Ibid.,* (July 18, 1919), 6.
153. *Ibid.,* (July 3, 1919), 9.
154. *Georgia Laws,* 1919, pp. 282-331.
155. *Ibid.,* p. 288.
156. *Ibid.,* p. 66-68.
157. *Ibid.,* p. 286-288.
158. *Georgia School Code,* 1919, p. 49.
159. Data for this table obtained from Georgia Department of Education Annual Reports for years cited in table.
160. Georgia Department of Education *Annual Report,* 1919, p. 56.
161. *Ibid.,* p. 18.
162. Georgia Department of Education *Annual Report,* 1917, p. 5.
163. Georgia Department of Education *Annual Report,* 1919, pp. 19-20.
164. *Ibid.,* pp. 38-39.
165. *Ibid.,* p. 19.
166. Georgia Department of Education *Annual Report,* 1920, p. 40.
167. *Ibid.,* 1921, p. 98.
168. *Ibid.,* p. 18.
169. E. P. Cubberly, *Public School Administration,* (Boston: Houghton Mifflin, 1922), p. 85.
170. Carter V. Good, ed., *The Dictionary of Education,* (New York: McGraw-Hill, 1959), p. 181.
171. Data for this table obtained from Annual Reports of the Georgia Department of Education. Column headed "Total School Fund" also includes federal funds, grants from philanthropic agencies and tuition. The primary purpose of this table is to compare the annual increases in local and state funds for the period.
172. *Georgia State School Items,* July 1, 1925, II, (10), 20.
173. *Georgia Laws,* 1916, pp. 37-38.
174. Georgia Department of Education *Annual Report,* 1916, p. 15.
175. *Ibid.,* 1907, p. 11.
176. Orr, *History of Education,* p. 315.
177. Georgia Department of Education *Annual Report,* 1922, p. 18.
178. *Georgia State School Items,* November 5, 1923, p. 3.
179. *Ibid.,* December 15, 1923, p. 6.
180. *Ibid.,* January 15, 1923, p. 6.
181. *Ibid.,* July 1, 1924, p. 4.
182. M. L. Brittain, ed., *Survey of Rabun County Schools,* 1914, p. 48.
183. *Ibid.,* p. 6.
184. M. L. Brittain, ed., *Survey of Wayne County Schools,* 1916, pp. 6-8.
185. Georgia Department of Education *Annual Report,* 1919, p. 480.
186. Georgia Department of Education *Annual Report,* 1924, p. 271.
187. Georgia Department of Education *Annual Report,* 1923-24, p. 1.
188. Gordon G. Singleton, "State Responsibility for the Support of Education in Georgia," Contribution to Education No. 181 (New York: Columbia University Teachers College, 1925), p. 20.
189. *Ibid.,* pp. 40-41.
190. *Georgia Laws,* 1926, Extraordinary Session, pp. 39-40.

191. Georgia Department of Education *Annual Report*, 1916, p. 13.
192. Georgia Department of Education *Annual Report*, 1922, p. 38.
193. Carl G. Renfroe, *"The Growth and Development of Teacher Certification in Georgia"* (unpublished doctoral dissertation, University of Georgia, 1964), p. 72.
194. *Georgia State School Items*, February 1, 1924, 1.
195. Renfroe, *Growth*, 1964, p. 74.
196. *Ibid.*, p. 75.
197. *Ibid.*
198. Georgia Department of Education *Annual Report*, 1924, pp. 56-57.
199. Jamie Hearn, *History of Certification in Georgia*, 1944, p. 8.
200. *High School Quarterly*, 13, October, 1923, p. 7.
201. *Georgia State School Items*, July 1, 1924, p. 4.
202. *Ibid.*, p. 5.
203. *Ibid.*, p. 4.
204. *Georgia State School Items*, February, 1925, pp. 69-70.
205. *Ibid.*, p. 83.
206. *Ibid.*, April, 1925, p. 2.
207. *Ibid.*, pp. 6-7.
208. *Ibid.*, December 15, 1925, p. 10.
209. Georgia Department of Education *Biennial Report*, 1925-26, p. 7.
210. Georgia Department of Education *Biennial Report*, 1927-28, p. 51.
211. *Ibid.*, p. 52.
212. *Georgia State School Items*, June 1, 1924, p. 14.
213. *Ibid.*, July 1, 1924, p. 14.
214. *Georgia Laws*, 1919, pp. 330-331.
215. *Ibid.*, p. 287.
216. Georgia Department of Education *Annual Report*, 1920, p. 117.
217. *Ibid.*, pp. 118-119.
218. Georgia Department of Education *Annual Report*, 1921, p. 91.
219. Georgia Department of Education *Annual Report*, 1920, pp. 126-127.
220. *Georgia Laws*, 1920, pp. 232-34.
221. Georgia Department of Education *Annual Report*, 1921, pp. 44-49.
222. *Ibid.*, pp. 530-531.
223. Georgia Department of Education *Annual Report*, 1922, pp. 12-13.
224. *Ibid.*, pp. 38-39.
225. Georgia Department of Education *Annual Report*, 1924, pp. 8-9.
226. *Ibid.*, pp. 29-30.
227. Georgia Department of Education *Annual Report*, 1928, p. 45.
228. *Ibid.*, pp. 29-30.
229. *Ibid.*, pp. 38-39.
230. *Ibid.*, p. 34.
231. *Ibid.*, pp. 27-38.
232. "Resolutions of the 1934 Representative Assembly of the Georgia Education Association," *Georgia Education Journal* 26, (May, 1934), p. 13.
233. *Ibid.*, p. 11.
234. *Atlanta Constitution*, January 11, 1935, p. 1.
235. *Atlanta Constitution*, January 12, 1935, p. 1.
236. *Atlanta Constitution*, March 4, 1935.
237. *Atlanta Constitution*, March 29, 1935.
238. *Ibid.*
239. J. R. Burgess, "Composition of Boards of Education of Independent City Districts of Georgia," *Georgia Education Journal*, March 1936, pp. 13-14.
240. Paul Monroe, ed., "City District Superintendents," *Cyclopedia of Education*, (New York: Macmillan, 1925), 5, p. 464.
241. Georgia Department of Education *Annual Report*, 1909, pp. 10-19.
242. *Georgia Laws*, 1909, p. 94.
243. *Ibid.*, p. 190.

244. Georgia Department of Education *Annual Report*, 1912, pp. 71-72.
245. *Georgia Laws*, 1920, pp. 232-233.
246. Georgia Department of Education *Annual Report*, 1912, pp. 91-92.
247. *High School Quarterly*, January, 1915, III (2), p. 81.
248. *Charlton County Historical Notes*, 1972, p. 24.
249. *High School Quarterly*, 1921, IX (2), 126.
250. *Georgia Laws*, 1920, pp. 232-233.
251. *Georgia Laws*, 1919, pp. 253-255.
252. *Georgia Laws*, 1931, pp. 7, 40.
253. *Georgia Laws*, 1920, p. 249.
254. *Georgia Laws*, 1943, p. 355.
255. U. S. Congress, Public Law 88-452, 1964.
256. U. S. Congress, Public Law 89-750, 1966.
257. U. S. Congress, Public Law 91-230, 1969.
258. Georgia Department of Education *Annual Report*, 1922, p. 9.
259. *Ibid.*, pp. 124-125.
260. *Ibid.*, p. 186.
261. *Charlton County Historical Notes*, pp. 22-29.
262. *Accredited Elementary Schools Bulletin*, 6, 1929.
263. Troup County Board of Education *Minutes*, November, 1927.
264. *Bulloch Times and Statesboro News*, 1931, 40 (49), p. 2.
265. *Bulloch Times and Statesboro News*, 1931, 40 (48), p. 4.
266. Edgar Fuller and Jim B. Pearson, eds., *Education in the States: Nationwide Development Since 1900*, National Education Association, Washington, D. C., 1969, p. 613.
267. Russell J. N. Dean, *New Life for Millions: Rehabilitation for America's Disabled* (New York: Hastings House, 1972), pp. 12-19.
268. *Ibid.*, pp. 8, 65.
269. Document of Goodwill Industries of America, Inc., *Goodwill's Story*, 9200 Wisconsin Ave., Washington, D. C., 1972.
270. C. Esco Obermann, *A History of Vocational Rehabilitation in America* (Minneapolis: T. S. Denison, 1968), p. 338.
271. *Ibid.*, pp. 175-177.
272. *Georgia Laws*, 1920, pp. 279-281.
273. Fuller and Pearson, eds., *op. cit.*, p. 615.
274. Obermann, *History of Vocational Rehabilitation*, pp. 286-287.
275. *Ibid.*, pp. 316-323.
276. *Ibid.*, pp. 323-324.

CHAPTER IV

Years of Struggle, Recovery and War, 1937-1948

In his report for 1935-1936, Superintendent M. D. Collins recommended equalizing educational opportunity for all the children through a system more adequately supported by state funds. Areas needing special attention included better trained teachers, increased length of the school term, better school buildings, teaching aids and textbooks.[1]

Among the legislative measures of 1935 was a proposed constitutional amendment placing a limit of 15 mills on the amount of property taxes that could be levied by the state. Much of the support for education was provided by property tax, and in some cases at a rate considerably above 15 mills.[2] Having lost the prospect of the seven months equalization program, which they had hoped could be supported by a retail sales tax, school people began to urge the defeat of the tax limitation amendment. Georgia schools stood to lose much revenue if the amendment was approved.[3]

The campaign for a better school program was resumed with much of the vigorous organization and leadership reminiscent of previous years. President J. Harold Saxon urged all members of the Georgia Education Association to register and vote.[4] The candidates for office—from the governor down to local representatives—were requested to declare their stand on support for schools and educational reforms. Their statements were given public notice.

Under the direction of the new state Steering Committee appointed in Macon on January 17, 1936, and consisting of Malcolm Bryan, B. M. Grier, Jere A. Wells, J. E. Purks, Mark Smith, A. G. Cleveland and Miss Annie Kelley, the proposed legislation began to take shape. Aided by legal counsel, it was organized in three separate bills—(1) a state supported school of seven months, (2) a state lay board of education and (3) free textbooks.[5]

Governor E. D. Rivers fully endorsed and supported the proposed legislation. The Steering Committee and other education leaders, at the invitation of President Saxon, met at the Henry Grady Hotel on January 14, 1937, to review the bills. The group gave its collective endorsement and the bills were introduced in the legislature on January 15.

House Bill No. 123, introduced by J. M. Simmons of Decatur County, provided for seven months state supported schools; House Bill No. 125, introduced by John Parker of Colquitt County, provided for the election of a state lay board of education and House Bill No. 141, introduced by Scott W. Davis of Floyd County, made provision for free textbooks.[6]

The General Assembly passed the education package—this time known both as The Seven Months School Law and the Equalization of Educational Opportunities Law. It was signed by Governor Rivers. The new law required all schools to have a seven-month term with provisions for local units to pay supplements. The state agreed to pay a given number of teachers in each system from state funds, based on a formula involving the average daily attendance of pupils and the pupil-density ratio.[7] Eighteen sections of the act dealt with specific provisions for equalizing financial support to counties and cities. The law also provided for free textbooks for all students, state support for pupil transportation services, minimum courses of study and revision of the curriculum.[8]

In his article prepared for the September 1937, issue of *Georgia Education Journal* entitled "What the Legislature Did for Georgia Schools," Superintendent Collins outlined the Seven Months School Law, noting that the state board was to become the authority for administering the law. The plan of equalization was based on the teacher unit with differentials for elementary and high school and for areas of varying population density. The state board was required to classify and certify teachers and to fix an annual minimum salary schedule. The law authorized local units to operate schools longer than seven months and to pay higher salaries than the minimum scale.[9]

Local units were required to file copies of their budgets shortly after the beginning of the fiscal year, to agree to follow the budget in expenditures and to give an account of local receipts and all expenditures.

An element of flexibility within the provisions assured their continued usefulness though economic circumstances might vary. The following salary schedule was announced for 1937-1938.[10]

White teachers holding

County licenses ....$35-40 per month
Elementary certificates .... 50-60 per month
Normal and Junior College
certificates .... 60-70 per month
Certificates based on three years of
college .... 65-75 per month
College certificates .... 75-80 per month

Regulations published by the state board for administering the Seven Months School Law indicate an enthusiastic attempt to follow the law in detail, except when an isolated change seemed preferable.

Just one year after the Seven Months School Law was implemented, a 1938-39 study described the law's effectiveness in salary equalization, with the following quote.

The purpose of the state salary schedule was to place all schools on an equalized minimum basis of operation. This applies to one-teacher schools as well as to the city systems. This is the first time that a state has made a guarantee of any given length of school term. The minimum salary schedule affected mostly the salaries of teachers in the smaller schools. The minimum salary is no more than the amounts usually paid in most of the larger schools.

The introduction of the state salary schedule has probably caused the improvement of the qualifications of the teachers throughout the state by rewarding this additional training with salary increments. This improvement in qualifications is gradual and will continue to be slow, due to the length of time required for a teacher to add one or more years of college training by attending summer sessions and extension courses. However, the position of the teachers in smaller schools, as well as in some of the larger ones, has been improved. It remains to be seen whether or not the recommendations of the state department of education will cause boards of education to select teachers on a basis of training and merit.[11]

The legislative provision of 1937, known as the Free Textbook Law, directed the state board to provide textbooks for use in the elementary and high schools and to make them available to children without cost.[12] The state board was instructed to provide multiple listings of books for use in the various grades and to authorize county and independent system superintendents to exercise a choice among the listed books. Initial book selections were made by professional committees selected according to subject or grade level.[13] As a result of their work, a complete listing was made of all textbooks recommended for use in the school. A Division of Textbooks and Libraries was established in the Department of Education to administer the program and to distribute text and library books and various teaching aids.[14]

State financing of textbook purchases originated even before the free textbook bill was presented to the legislature. The legalized sale of beer and wine, a 1935 legislative issue, provided a source of revenue specially designated to provide free textbooks to children attending the common schools.[15] When the textbook act was passed in 1937, revenue from the sale of wine also was allocated to the purchase of the books.[16]

The slavish use of textbooks had been a major educational problem in previous years. Free textbook distribution solved this problem by providing teachers greater freedom in selecting appropriate texts from the multiple listings.[17] A "budget plan," adopted in 1939, offered teachers even greater freedom. Under this plan, money allocated to the textbook program was distributed among the school systems on a per pupil basis. Superintendents could then requisition books according to the need within the range of their budgets.[18]

The Georgia system of free textbooks attracted favorable consideration throughout the country.[19]

To further assist school personnel in effectively using free textbooks, the Division of Publications of the Department of Education produced a *Guide to Use of the State Adopted Textbooks*. This bulletin was published in sufficient quantity for every teacher to have a copy.

A third legislative enactment of 1937 created a state board of education comprising lay members. This bill replaced the previous board (made up of professional school leaders and ex-officio members) with a non-professional board of 11 members. Its composition included the governor as chief executive; the state school superintendent as executive secretary and one member from each of the congressional districts, appointed by the governor.

The board's scope of duties was increased to include some matters over which the legislature formerly had jurisdiction. The new board would serve in areas of administration, finance, and certification of teachers; it would exercise authority in matters of curriculum, provide for the distribution of free textbooks and administer library services; it would serve as supervisory agent for the Department of Education, act as state board for vocational education and serve as an appellate court for disagreements arising in the school districts.

The provisions of the act became effective July 1, 1937. The new board was appointed by Governor E. D. Rivers and included the following members.[20]

E. D. Rivers, Chairman
First District, Dr. R. J. Kennedy
Second District, Mrs. A. B. Conger
Third District, Mrs. Frank David
Fourth District, Judge Alvin H. Freeman
Fifth District, Walter H. Rich
Sixth District, H. C. Williams
Seventh District, Mrs. Elizabeth McWaters
Eighth District, S. I. Watson
Ninth District, W. W. McCay
Tenth District, W. C. Clary, Jr.
M. D. Collins, Executive Secretary

Two of the above were appointed for two-year terms, four for four-year terms and six for six-year terms.[21] Notably, three women were appointed members of the board. By law, appointees were required to be citizens of Georgia for five years and to be unaffiliated with and unrelated to anyone affiliated with textbook publication. Board meetings were held quarterly.

The state school superintendent, as executive secretary, was expected to furnish technical information as the board might demand. Compensation of board members was set at $7.00 per day plus travel expenses at the state approved mileage rate. Regarding this legislation, Superintendent Collins said,

We are proud of the accomplishments thus far attained and we feel that the laws which were enacted have given us a basis for a much improved school system.[22]

The effects of this legislation prompted Superintendent Collins to say in 1937 that the schools of Georgia had improved a marked degree during the biennium. Increased appropriations had enabled all of the schools to operate for a term of seven months. Substantial increases in salary schedules enabled schools to secure better prepared teachers. Free textbooks provided each child access to books and materials of a quality and quantity never known before in Georgia education.[23]

Along with the improvements of an extended school term, textbooks and the state board's composition, the year 1937 marked a significant development in vocational education. The George-Dean Act, passed on July 1, 1937, contributed directly to a rapid expansion of vocational education throughout Georgia.[24] During the pre-war years the state of Georgia set national records for two consecutive years by establishing more new departments of vocational home economics than any other state in America.[25]

The George-Dean Act most significantly provided funds for training in distributive occupations. Distributive education, therefore, was identified as a member of the vocational education family for the first time.[26] In its early years, training in distributive occupations was conducted only for part-time evening class groups. Classes were conducted either in schools equipped for the purpose or in business establishments.[27]

The Free Textbook Law of 1937 offered the first viable opportunity for state aid to school libraries, and it was a major opportunity. There had been growing concern on the part of educational leaders and organizations such as the Georgia Library Association that school library services be expanded and improved. Collins, as state superintendent, asked the Law Department for an opinion on whether or not textbook funds could be used to purchase school library books. Attorney General M. J. Yeomans, in reply to this request, ruled that, ". . . If the course of study prescribed by the State Board of Education should be liberal and in line with present day demands and tendencies to give liberal opportunities to all children of the state then the word 'textbooks' would include any book which the State Board should designate as an aid to education . . ." [28] This opened the door for the State Board of Education to assume a leadership role in the area of school libraries.

The biennial report of the State Department of Education for 1937-38 describes the first steps. "The Library Division, a part of the Textbook Division, was established to meet the increasing requests on the part of teachers and school officials for a program which would insure to all the schools of Georgia adequate school library facilities and central direction in school library activities. The State Board of Education in the summer of 1937 authorized the State Superintendent of Schools to appoint a Supervisor of School Libraries (Miss Sarah Jones) and in the spring of 1938 set aside funds ($50,-000.00) to aid the elementary schools in the purchase of library books. This money was prorated (on a per pupil basis) to each county and independent school system in the state and was to be matched on a fifty-fifty basis. Thirty-four systems have taken up their entire allotment, and 158 systems have used a part of their allotment. Approximately 350,000 library books have been thus far purchased by the schools of Georgia this year."

All books purchased with state aid are selected by the individual schools or systems from the Georgia Elementary Library List which was compiled by reading and library specialists. It was possible, with the State Department of Education acting as purchasing agent for the schools of the state, to secure as high as a 40 percent reduction in the prices of books.

A complete set of all titles included in the list was placed in each of the teacher-training institutions in Georgia in order that they might be examined and used by teachers in preparing their programs of classroom instruction.[29]

The year 1937 also marked a significant event in the continuing effort to improve the level of academic education for Georgia's teachers. In the 1937 adopted system of certification, the State Board of Education approved a salary scale based on level of education and number of years' teaching experience. Prior to 1937 the salary schedule made a difference in pay only through the bachelor's degree and did not increase with a master's degree.

The law authorizing the state board to act on certification was updated as follows.

> Section 3. The State Board of Education shall provide rules and regulations for the supervision of all public schools of this state; they shall provide a course for all common and high schools receiving State aid and may in their discretion, approve additional courses of study set up by the local units of administration; provide for curriculum revisions and for the classification and certification of teachers.[30]

The Seven Months School Law had an impact on the supply of well qualified teachers. Economics always has had its influence on well qualified people entering teaching as a life profession. L. M. Lester said,

> Up until 1937, because of employment conditions in industry and business, it had been possible to induce well prepared people to enter teaching as a last resort, despite the fact that they were the lowest paid of all salaried workers and rated along with farm labor and domestic service in being specifically excluded from the terms of the Social Security Act. After 1937 the state guarantee of seven months salary and a schedule based on amount of training were followed by a rapid upgrading of the profession.[31]

Special certificates for non-classroom teachers, initiated by law in 1937, provided administrative and supervisory certificates for school superintendents and supervisors, respectively. These were the first certificates to indicate particular types of work, other than that of classroom teachers. Until 1943, this special preparation was included as part of a bachelor's degree program.[32]

Although the Jeanes Project had provided a financial support for supervisors of Negro schools for almost three decades, there were no supervisors in the white schools to aid teachers. The forerunner for a program of white supervisors was initiated in 1935 by the Board of Regents at South Georgia Teachers College in Statesboro.[33] Jane Franseth of Michigan, the demonstration supervisor, served three counties in southeast Georgia for two years. Then, in 1936-37, she served in Bulloch County.[34] This expert supervision was the prelude to preparing white supervisors for Georgia schools. Like that for Jeanes supervisors, the program began with special emphasis on improving rural education.

During 1937-38, the state's first program to prepare white supervisors was instituted at South Georgia Teachers College under the administration of President Marvin S. Pittman. He had acquired expertise in rural supervision in Michigan before coming to Georgia.

In the spring of 1937, Pittman mounted an extensive letter campaign to superintendents in Georgia to locate applicants for Rosenwald Fund scholarships, designed to prepare them for rural supervisor posts in elementary schools.[35] Pittman described the admission qualifications in his letter. "Select men and women of superior ability, personality, leadership, and educational interest. They must have taught at least four years, must be interested in the promotion of better rural life in Georgia, and must not be over forty years old." [36]

In a later letter to the applicants, Pittman said, "It is understood that you must be not less than 23 years old and not more than forty, that you must have completed the equivalent of a two-year normal diploma course, that you are eligible for junior standing, and that you have taught for at least four years." [37]

Franseth wrote to those who were accepted in the program, "It is expected that you will attend throughout the regular sessions, 1937-38 and 1938-39, and that you will have earned your degree (bachelor's) by June, 1939." [38]

In the two-year program leading to a bachelor's degree at Georgia State Teachers College, Kate Houx directed the program of studies on campus. Franseth, as supervisor of elementary schools in Bulloch County, supervised the work of these students as they engaged in internships in the county schools. Some of the students completed their degrees in 1938, others in 1939.

These first supervisors were called "helping teachers" or "supervising teachers." In 1938 the State Board of Education took its first action, stating "Regulations Governing Employment of Supervising Teachers" as follows.

- All beginning supervising teachers must hold Supervisor's Certificates. Those already in service as supervising teachers holding certificates based upon four years of college work will be given until September 1940 to qualify.
- No supervising teachers may be employed for a teaching unit of less than thirty teachers.
- The entire time of the supervising teacher must be devoted to supervisor duties.
- Payment of the supervising teacher may be as follows.
  a. The supervising teacher may be listed in the quota of teachers allotted to the local system and may receive salary as such.
  b. The state will allow a sum not to exceed $400.00, plus $200.00 for each approved colored supervisor which must be matched by an equal sum of the local system.
- Two or more systems may cooperate in employing a supervising teacher.[39]

By 1938 the complex of agencies now involved in teacher education and certification demonstrated a need for some plan of coordination. The increasing pre-service requirements for teachers, the in-service agencies and their regulation and the institutional adjustments affecting college training programs were all involved. The Department of Education felt it must find a way to utilize them effectively in an enlarged program of teacher education.

An early step toward coordination was taken in the fall of 1938 when the State Board of Education authorized the appointment of an advisory committee on teacher education and curriculum development.[40]

The first meeting of the Advisory Committee on Teacher Education was held in Atlanta during October 28-29. The committee included members of each of the white colleges engaged in teacher education, representatives of white public school teachers, members of the Department of Education and the executive secretary of the Georgia Education Association. It was agreed that the committee would meet at least three times each year, would engage in local study through college groups and form committees to study more comprehensive problems. The members agreed to publicize the programs of teacher education in the weekly papers. According to an announcement, the study of teacher education would encourage representation of all groups involved in the planning of the teacher education program for Georgia.[41]

Variations among the teacher training institutions indicated the need for an inclusive study of all professional content courses. This became the area of one study group. Subcommittees analyzed individual courses such as educational psychology, introduction to education, child psychology, educational measurements and others.[42]

In addition to the educational legislation fostered during Governor Rivers' first term, other programs known as the little "New Deal" provided additional services in health, welfare, improved highways, a state office building, State Highway Patrol and homestead and household tax exemption limited to $2,300.[43] The increase in educational costs alone amounted to $4 million.

Financial Crisis

Unfortunately, the legislature which made these benefits available failed to make adequate provision to finance them.[44] Governor Rivers' second term, 1939-1940, was largely concerned with financing legislation already on the statute books. By use of a number of devices, none of which produced new revenue, it was possible to keep the services operative during the first two-year term.[45]

Anticipating a shortage of revenue to meet certain fixed obligations, a Stabilization Fund was established to operate from January 1, 1938, to January 1940. Into this fund went 10 percent of all revenue, and from it the most distressing needs were met.[46] Future rentals on the state-owned railroad were sold for ready cash, and there was much borrowing and lending, especially of surplus highway funds held to match federal subsidies.

The revenue received in 1937-1938 had not paid in full the school appropriation for that year, and schools opened in the fall of 1938 with the prospect of an even greater deficit in the coming year. If the budgets, based on the approved salary schedule, were paid according to regulations of the state board, a considerable deficit would result. A resolution of the Legislative Committee of the Georgia Education Association in September 1938, recommended that the organization use its influence "toward bringing about a thoroughgoing revision of the state's tax structure so that all the state's agencies may be financed and that the cost of financing them may be equitably distributed among the citizens of the state." [47]

It was evident that with reduced income from property taxes due to the homestead and household exemptions, new sources of revenue must be found. This was pointed out in an editorial of the *Georgia Education Journal,* October 1938.[48]

Before the General Assembly met in January 1939, a crisis for Georgia's public schools loomed large on the horizon. It was with the definite understanding of legislative relief that school people held on, even beyond their resources.

In spite of impending disaster, the regular session of the 1939 General Assembly ended without any effective plan to fully finance the laws then in operation. In the legislature, divisive elements were at work to thwart any constructive plan to secure permanent relief. The people generally were pleased with the new services and wished to see them continued. Some credited the predicament to waste, inefficiency, unnecessary services and excess personnel and were reluctant to tax themselves further until these allegations had been disproved.

A resolution, introduced in the House on January 24, 1939, requested the appointment of a committee from members of the House "to make an investigation of the several state departments, the cost of operating the same and the number of employed, and the salaries paid in the interest of economy in state government." [49]

The committee consisted of Wilmer D. Lanier, chairman; James V. Carmichael, vice chairman; Joseph Blackshear; T. G. Connell and Cleveland Rees. A room in the state capitol was set aside for the committee's use and hours arranged for meetings and hearings. The committee agreed not to receive confidential information but required the name and address of each person giving testimony and an agreement to appear before the committee if requested to do so. The committee generally held open meetings but could declare itself in executive session when it chose to do so.[50] It had the power to subpoena testimony and the use of public records. When the full committee was not holding hearings and deliberations, the secretary was on duty to take testimony. People from all over the state were invited to make reports to the committee, but at their own expense.[51]

The Committee on Economy and Efficiency in Government began alloting costs in each of the departments of government.[52] Some people hoped that sufficient funds might be obtained in this way to meet the most pressing obligations. Others regarded the economy effort as a distraction from the real need for providing new sources of revenue.

Close investigation revealed that the general fund receipts for schools in 1937-1938 were 74 percent of appropriations, leaving a deficit of 26 percent or $2,406,560. For 1938-1939, the estimated revenue would be only $5,268,277, or just 56 percent of the appropriation.[53] Having been notified by the state auditor that funds would be available for only four months of the school year 1939-1940, education groups in the state petitioned that these be the first four months of the school year.[54]

Since education represented one of the major costs of government, this department received very careful scrutiny and apparently occupied much of the committee's time.[55] On February 3, the committee reported on excess personnel and waste in the Department of Education with recommendations for the elimination of programs and personnel. Among the chief targets were the program of Information and Publications including a director and seven staff members; the library program and one employee; the audio-visual program, plus the director and two-member staff; the Forum, its director and a staff of three assistants and the adult education staff. The Finance and Textbook division included a salary reduction of $1,000 for the head of the division. Though the committee apparently reached its decisions without consultation with the Department of Education, the recommendations it made were regarded as final. Consequently, the state board put them into effect at once.[56]

While the committee's hearings were taking place, the Georgia Education Association authorized a fact-finding committee of its own. This committee was authorized to investigate alleged waste and extravagance in the Department of Education, to find an answer to reasons for the closing of schools and to learn whether or not funds could be diverted to the education department to meet the crisis confronting the public schools. The committee, consisting of Jere A. Wells, chairman; R. L. Ramsey; Mark Smith; W. L. Walker; Dr. E. G. Kirby; N. P. Malcom; J. Scott Davis; W. P. Lunsford and Woods Hammond, reported its findings in the *Georgia Education Journal*, May 1939.[57]

The article was reproduced as a fact-finding bulletin at the expense of the Georgia Education Association and mailed extensively over the state. The investigation covered generally the same areas explored by the Economy Committee. Arranged in the form of questions and answers, the article treated 104 questions raised by school people. It reported that elimination of the personnel and services in the Department of Education recommended by the Economy Commission would save $45,000. An additional $223,000 could be saved with discontinuation of new books for the library program and textbooks for the adult illiteracy classes. The article noted, however, that the entire savings proposed would be less than the amount required to operate the state public schools for one day.[58]

One week later, on February 10, a second report to the State Board called attention to the vast number of bulletins reporting statewide curriculum revision and instructional improvement programs. It recommended that these be discontinued. In complying with this request, the extensive program of curriculum improvement which had been in progress for a number of years suddenly was halted.[59]

A later recommendation of the Economy Committee, noted in the minutes of the State Board of Education, requested that the district supervisors discontinue all activities for 30 days in order to thoroughly ascertain the economics which could be affected through consolidation, elimination of teachers, reduction in cost of transportation and other areas and to render a report to the State Board of Education.[60] The forced consolidations and reduced services recommended by this committee brought such a clamor of protest from the people that ultimately few changes were made.

In its report to the legislature, the Economy Committee listed savings in the administration of public schools under the following. "Savings in administration of State Department of Education by reduction in salaries and personnel general funds, $33,091; savings in textbook fund allocations, $237,380; savings under Seven Months School Law for 1939-1940 pursuant to the economies recommended by this committee, general funds, $310,390; savings as a result of reduction in amount to Bibb, Chatham and Richmond Counties under Seven Months School Law general funds, $259,293; savings in administration of textbook allocated funds, $3,479. The total reported savings, General Fund, $602,674; Allocated Funds $240,859, amounted to a grand total of $843,533.47." [61] Assuming all to be legitimate and applicable, this figure was sufficient to operate the public schools for less than 12 days.

The legislature, during the first several weeks of its session in 1939, produced nothing to support schools other than the savings which resulted from curtailment of some services. Then, on the request of the governor and state superintendent of schools, a joint study of the school conditions of the state was authorized.[62] The committee, consisting of the governor, state superintendent of schools, the state treasurer and two senators, investigated the situation. Their report revealed, in effect, that many school systems had reached the end of their resources and were faced with a premature closing.

As a consequence of this report, it was recommended that "The state borrow such funds as the banks would lend against the anticipated revenue allocated to the school system." [63]

However, since there was no appropriation to pay the interest on such a loan, it would be necessary for the General Assembly to pass legislation for a special appropriation for this purpose. Members of the joint committee pledged themselves to work for the passage of the measure. The committee stated that in the event the measure should pass, it would enable the state to borrow for schools approximately $2,181,000, an insufficient sum. The legislature did not obtain the loan.[64]

It was noted in a house resolution of March 13, 1939, that many schools were closing and that students unable to complete the full term would not graduate, thus jeopardizing their chances of entering college in the fall. Help was sought from the Department of Education to remove this hardship from the path of the students.[65]

A survey of the county school systems, conducted in mid-March by the Georgia Education Association, indicated that of the 159 counties in the state, at least 107 were facing one of three alternatives, (1) to close the schools, (2) to keep schools in operation and ask teachers to work without salaries or (3) to raise as much money as possible locally and ask the teachers to continue work at greatly reduced salaries.[66]

A resolution by the Georgia Education Association representative assembly of March 25 urged the General Assembly to reconvene immediately and provide the funds it was pledged to raise to "redeem its promise to the teachers of the State." [67]

In an article dated February 2, 1939, the Bulloch County teachers reported resolutions from this unit, one of which stated,

> 4. That it is ridiculous and deliberately misleading to say that these three minimum essentials; (seven months school, expanded health program, public welfare provisions) can be realized by economy measures. Economy measures could not at the most, provide over five per cent of the revenue.[68]

An editorial from a mid-Georgia county weekly paper of March 20, 1939, stated,

> . . . The needs of Georgia must be met, we must decide what these needs are and then provide for them. This is

a time for thinking and not a time to wave the red flag of prejudice and demagoguery. The people ought to see that the efforts of one faction to pass the buck to the other are no good. The trouble is more fundamental. The school teachers, the old people, the blind, the insane, the health services, all of them suffer while a crisis continues. The solution is not reached by a legislature that votes appropriations and then nullifies them by not passing a tax program to pay the appropriation.[69]

During these months, activity designed to provide teacher relief and to meet other obligations was too little and too late. The end of the school year was near, and little could be gained from a special session of a legislature that had not acted on significant legislation for education during its regular session.

Many of the teachers continued to work without pay or with greatly reduced salaries. In some cases reemployment was made contingent upon teachers working to the end of the year on whatever terms the boards could make. Fortunately, in most cases, the agreements were reached cooperatively. A large number of school systems were unable to continue school for the minimum number of days required. By a strict interpretation of accreditation requirements, these systems lost the professional rating of their schools. It was difficult, and sometimes impossible, for their graduates to be admitted to college without conditions.[70] Ironically, promises and studied procrastination on the part of the legislature kept teachers on the job long enough to prevent a majority of the high schools from being discredited.[71]

The Economy Committee continued its work and presented a final report June 3, 1939.[72]

In spite of large and ominous problems confronting education in Georgia late in the 1930s, some advancements were being realized. Audio-visual materials were introduced as teaching aids in the late 1930s by Walter S. Bell, who had been utilizing records, films and other audio-visual materials as teaching aids in the Atlanta City Schools. A central bureau of these teaching aids had been established and made available to teachers throughout the system.

In October 1937 the first in a series of southeastern conferences on audio-visual education was held at the Biltmore

Hotel in Atlanta. It was organized by J. C. Wardlaw of the University Extension Division, who was assisted by Bell; L. L. Perry of the State Department of Education; Lamdin Kay of radio station WSB and others.[73] This widely attended conference was hailed as the most significant of any conducted in Georgia within a decade. Outstanding speakers from throughout the country were present for the three-day meeting. Educators enthusiastically expressed desire to use these media in the schools as teaching aids. Wardlaw was in the process of adding teaching films, both silent and sound, on a rental basis to the Extension Division Program.

The Curriculum Development Program, interested in effective devices to improve and enrich teaching, approved of audio-visual teaching aids. When the school laws of 1937 made provision for free text and library books, a broad interpretation included other forms of instructional materials such as films, slides and recordings.

In October 1937 the State Department of Education, under the direction of L. L. Perry, planned to acquire audio-visual materials—mainly recordings, filmstrips and sound films—for school distribution. Superintendent Collins stated in his biennial report in 1937-1938 that the division, "for the past year and a half has laid the foundation for the organization of an audio-visual program in the state schools involving the promotion and development of the proper use of modern teaching aids including the radio and motion pictures."

A progress report and a proposed program were submitted to the State Board of Education in April 1938, and in November the board approved operation of the program on a limited basis. People from over the state with an interest in audio-visual teaching aids were invited to review critically several hundred educational films chosen in relation to the seven persistent problems of education developed in the *Guide to Curriculum Organization*.[74] According to the proposal, prints of approved films would be supplied without cost to schools having satisfactory facilities for their use.[75]

Although authorized by the Board of Education and promoted by the Department of Education, the new division had hardly begun its program when all activity was halted by legislative action. As previously noted, the Economy and Efficiency Committee, in an effort to secure funds for the operation of public schools, made severe reductions in 1939. With the abolishment of the entire Division of Information and Publications,[76] the $30,000 Audio-Visual Education Program was dropped.[77]

Despite these cutbacks, this period in the history of Georgia education marked the first significant inroad for state aid for school libraries. With passage of the Free Textbook Law, education leaders and organizations like the Georgia Library Association expressed the need to expand and improve school library service. Until this time no state aid existed for purchase of school library books. Most elementary schools had no libraries, and many high schools were limited to collections made available by local parent-teacher organizations and community book drives.[78]

The state's program of curriculum improvement stressed using books both as resource material and for personal enjoyment. Increased requests from teachers and school officials caused the state school superintendent to investigate the possibilities of using part of the textbook fund for purchase of library books.[79] The earliest funds—$50,000 in 1937-38—were used for elementary school library book budgets.[80]

For the second year of state aid (1938-1939), the amount was increased to $100,000; and the following year the State Board of Education made $150,000 available for the purchase of both elementary and high school library books and visual-aid materials. Shortly thereafter, on recommendation of the Economy Committee of the state legislature, the board withdrew these funds.[81] State aid for school libraries was halted, but only temporarily, because its popularity was undeniable.

Failure of the legislature in 1939 to provide financial relief for teachers ended prospects for assistance from this branch of state government until the 1941 session. Therefore, in the face of reduced revenues, city and county boards negotiated contracts with teachers in terms of prospective income, spreading the deficit more evenly throughout the year. In the meantime, the Georgia Education Association mounted a carefully planned publicity campaign. In May 1940, it published a "Statement of Policy" including a plan for adequate school support with the following specifications.

- Make payments when they are due.
- Finance salary schedule adopted in 1937 for the Seven Months School.
- Provide adequate revenue to operate the University System.
- Appropriate necessary revenue to put the equalization law into operation.
- Finance the Free Textbook Law.
- Appropriate money to match in full Federal programs including vocational education and vocational rehabilitation.
- Provide funds for proper operation of the State Department of Education. Retain the laws relating to education that were passed in 1937.[82]

A questionnaire was sent to each legislative candidate running in the state primary requesting a statement on his stand on the proposed education program. Replies were to be published in a special issue of the *Georgia Education Journal*.[83] Teachers registered to vote and personally tried to secure the support of their local representatives.

Governor Eugene Talmadge returned to the capitol January 14, 1941, amid the fanfare of six bands and confronted by the microphones of three radio stations. His first serious remarks dealt with taxes and his pledge not to increase taxes. In short, pointed statements he proceeded to sum up the state of the state. He said Georgia was approximately $32 million in debt including $3,910,000 to the school system. He pledged to pay teachers their back salaries by March 1.[84]

J. I. Allman, president of the Georgia Education Association, was able to report in February that checks for unpaid salaries of 1938-39 would be in the mail on March 1.[85] After a lapse of only 10 months, the popular school library program was reactivated.[86] The matching basis was changed to two-thirds state funds and one-third local funds, and allotments were made to local systems on a per teacher basis.[87] This change in the basis of allotment gave a small advantage to rural schools.

Beginning with an allocation of $50,000 for half of the school year 1938, state aid continued with $150,000 annually from 1939-1940 to 1949-1950, when the amount was doubled.

Additional funds were later received from national sources to purchase books and materials in strategic areas. In 1940, State Board of Education member Mrs. A. B. Conger moved successfully for the board to set aside a sum not to exceed 10 percent of the school's textbook allotment for library books on a non-matching basis.[88]

Growth of Libraries and Librarians

Dr. W. L. Downs, state high school supervisor, wrote in his 1932 annual report, "The school library is ninety percent librarian. Much progress has been made in school libraries throughout the state. This has been due to the large number of teacher librarians who have had six to twenty-four hours of Library Science. The school library is no longer thought of as a collection of books stored away in a room which is opened once or twice a week. A large per cent of the school libraries is really functioning as a vital force in the program of the school." [89]

Because of the demonstrated need for school librarians, by 1937 Georgia institutions began providing library science programs of six to 12 semester hours. Standards for training school librarians adopted by the Southern Association of Colleges and High Schools in 1927 and requirements set by the University of Georgia Accrediting System in 1932 formed the basis for these library science programs.[90]

By 1937 the State Board of Education had approved requirements for the certification of school librarians. These requirements provided that a teacher librarian have 12 semester hours in library science in addition to meeting the professional requirements for teachers. The courses were to include the organization and administration of the library, reading guidance and reference. Certification as a professional librarian required 30 semester hours in library science.[91] The courses offered at the undergraduate level (12 semester hours) varied greatly in quality and in terminology, resulting in the accumulation of credits without following a planned program of library study.

The Southern Association, in 1933, had begun the accreditation of library science departments in member institutions.[92]

This action, together with conferences within the state designed to secure agreement on terminology and course content, helped strengthen existing programs and alleviate confusion in meeting certification requirements.

The regulation concerning library certification was changed in 1940 to read, "Graduation from a professional library school accredited under the American Library Association." [93] Fortunately, Georgia had two such schools—Atlanta University School of Library Service and the Emory University Library, later to become the Division of Librarianship. The University of Georgia now offers a planned program for school librarians at the graduate level.

Many programs of in-service education have been implemented in Georgia. Some have been designed for meeting specific problems, some have been in the nature of sharing information and others have been concerned with evaluation and goal setting for school library service.

The earliest record of in-service programs for school librarians was a 1941 series of clinics sponsored by the Library Division of the State Department of Education, the University of Georgia and the school systems in which they were held. Clinics gave small groups of librarians an opportunity to see and evaluate a good high school library program and to discuss school library problems.[94]

Renewal of the audio-visual program within the State Department of Education came 10 months after its termination by the legislative Economy and Efficiency Committee in 1939. A professional committee similar to the State Textbook Committee was approved by the state board to serve as a reviewing board for the selection of educational films and other teaching aids. The first committee consisted of G. L. Hutchenson, K. B. Edwards, J. L. Dendy, W. B. Pirkle and H. Grady Loudermilk. The announcement stated that an approved list "of audio-visual materials had been compiled and these materials were available throughout the state library program on the same basis as literary materials." [95]

Despite the salary crisis at the close of the 1930s, Georgia continued its search to improve teacher education programs and to raise the qualifications of teachers. Shortly after adopting the state guarantee of the seven month school term and a new salary schedule in 1938, Georgia raised the minimum preparation for beginning teachers to two years. Shortly thereafter, however, World War II erupted and its impact on the quantity and qualifications of teachers lasted for many years. Some people believe that without the intervention of World War II, Georgia would have moved at that time to a minimum preparation of four years.[96]

Ominous clouds of war did not preclude Georgia educators from a forward movement. Their efforts resulted in noteworthy innovations early in the 1940s. On January 23, 1940, a subcommittee of the Georgia Advisory Committee on Teacher Education asked to join New York and Michigan as a third unit in a three-year program on teacher education sponsored by the National Commission on Teacher Education of the American Council on Education. The fact that Georgia already operated statewide agencies for coordinating teacher training probably had much to do with program acceptance.[97]

Those on the Georgia subcommittee requesting the funds were

> M. E. Thompson, director of Teacher Education, Certification and Curriculum; J. L. Yaden, superintendent, Moultrie Public Schools; Walter D. Cocking, dean, College of Education, University of Georgia; Sterling G. Brankley, professor of education, Emory University and Harry A. Little, head of Department of Education, Georgia State College for Women.[98]

An excerpt from the request stated,

> "The state of Georgia offers good opportunities for a state-wide program of teacher education. As stated above, there are no legal restrictions on teacher education or certification but this program is being developed on a co-operative state-wide basis." [99]

Georgia received $36,000 for the study. The state paid the salary of an executive secretary, a project secretary and travel. The funds were used for meetings for school leaders, civic leaders, college staff and State Department of Education staff to develop cooperatively a plan for teacher education in Georgia. J. H. Cook, one of the state school supervisors, was transferred to Teacher Training, Curriculum and Certification Division in 1941 to be the executive secretary of this study.

The study basically became the work of the two councils— The Georgia Council on Teacher Education for whites and the Georgia Committee on Cooperation in Teacher Education for Negroes. Purposes were to clarify the goals of education and to unify the teacher preparation and school programs.

The first National Clinic on Teacher Education was held in Georgia in November 1946. Sponsored by the National Council on Cooperation in Teacher Education, the clinic was attended by representatives from 34 states. Its chief value to Georgia was in modifying points of view and creating greater understanding of the state's educational problems.[100]

The program had been in operation slightly over a year when Georgia's Governor, Eugene Talmadge, brought about the dismissal of key people in two of the participating state institutions. Consequently, the commission froze the budget and program until further directions could be determined.[101]

After a period of four months, on advice of a state subcommittee, the commission decided to proceed with some of the projected activities. The program was ultimately resumed under a full-time coordinator late in the summer of 1941.[102] The first phase, which began in January 1940, emphasized preservice aspects of teacher education. Coordinators from the commission began working with the subcommittees of the state organization in a thorough analysis and appraisal of the professional content of the teacher preparation curricula, with a coordinator serving each subcommittee.

The second phase of the program was more concerned with in-service programs and methods of upgrading the teaching profession. With wartime demands taking a large number of the young teachers and principals out of the classroom, good in-service programs were needed to retrain former teachers.

Until the expiration of the program in 1943, the Teacher Education Commission developed techniques and methods which were continued under local momentum. The commission judged the three-year program a success for having developed more effective school leadership in the state.[103]

The position of Georgia's Advisory Committee on Teacher Education was strengthened at every point by its association with the national group. The capable, dedicated members of the Georgia program left their imprint on every phase of the teacher education program.

Upgrading the Profession

The impact of the Advisory Committee on Teacher Education was broad. It established a similar organization for Negro teacher education, the College Council, which consisted of a series of annual meetings set up by the state supervisor of Negro schools. Until 1943, it had no fixed membership but recruited anew for each meeting. The College Council meetings were held three times a year and were in session one or two days at each meeting. Plans for the year and matters of statewide concern were reviewed in a fall conference. The winter meeting was used to plan summer programs and the arrangement of summer school schedules.[104]

Influenced by the cooperative studies carried on in the Advisory Committee on Teacher Education, the College Council, in its spring conference at Savannah in 1942, was enlarged to include teachers, principals and supervisors. They addressed themselves to the question "How can teacher educating faculties, staff members of the Department of Education, supervisors, principals and classroom teachers produce the kind of teachers that youth need?"

The conference was regarded as a major achievement. At later meetings both school and college people were involved in similar discussions. The fall meeting of 1943 established the College Council with permanent status and a planning commission for postwar needs. A representative from each of the nine colleges, together with the state supervisor and state director of teacher education, constituted a permanent planning committee for this group.[105]

Georgia's Advisory Committee on Teacher Education changed its name in 1943, becoming the Advisory Council on Teacher Education. The council was generally referred to as "The Teacher Education Council." Its work was organized in three areas—pre-service, in-service and standards—with each division in charge of a statewide committee. It remained a voluntary group composed of representatives from colleges, public schools and the Department of Education. Later, the Georgia Education Association assumed the work of the Standards Committee, one phase of which was ably directed for a number of years by H. S. Shearouse under the designation Teacher Education and Professional Standards—or simply T.E.P.S.

The T.E.P.S. workshop was among the best known of the in-service modes of teacher education. Its flexible organization and adaptable method made it a popular device for both campus and off-campus groups.

The workshop coordinator was assisted by specialists or consultants. The group analyzed problems and made some effort to solve them. Other related activities such as art, recreation, health and local projects sometimes were carried on under the direction of the workshop. The workshop was organized in timetable form with each block of time having a specific objective. The last period pulled together experiences and evaluated the workshop's basic and subsidiary accomplishments. Most workshops directed and staffed by qualified people carried a college credit proportional to the time spent. However, except when expressly organized at the graduate level, credit earned in the workshop was applicable only toward undergraduate degrees. There was usually no formal examination and, in most instances, no attempt at qualitative grading since most of the work involved group participation rather than strictly individualized effort. J. H. Cook, coordinator of teacher education for the State Department of Education, was associated with the early development of the workshop as an instructional device for teachers.

During World War II the general workshop provided a refresher experience as well as a preview of modern school techniques for those who were returning to the classroom after years of absence. For several years, it was an all-purpose experience adapted to the needs of those filling emergency posts.

A review of certification requirements for this period would indicate that the constant goal had been to raise or upgrade basic academic and professional requirements. During the war years, and for many years afterwards, there was a tendency for former graduates who had left the classroom to rear a family to return to college in order to meet the new minimum qualifications for teaching. Those whose professional training had prepared them for schools of a former day were permitted to substitute planned workshop credit for some current professional courses. This applied particularly to directed observation and practice teaching for those who had a year or more of previous teaching experience. Many of these people, now with grown children, found teaching in the modern school to be an exciting experience. Many not only met the basic requirements for teachers but also completed degree programs and special programs requiring graduate work.

During the three-year program, Georgia worked with the national commission planning a conference and working on a clinic which served to diagnose problem areas and isolate needs. Both were of shorter duration, more intensive and oriented to fewer problems than the workshop.[106]

A national clinic on teacher education with 160 representatives from 34 states was held November 3-8, 1946, using Georgia as the object of diagnosis. The clinic was held under the auspices of the State Department of Education with assistance from colleges. L. D. Haskew, coordinator for programs of teacher education at Emory and Agnes Scott, was state director.[107]

The national clinic held in Georgia was far-reaching in its influence, both as a study of one state's program of teacher education and as a device for investigating educational practices. Through wide representation and publicity, many people came to know the problems of teacher education in Georgia and the agencies being used in their solution.[108]

When the directors of the Rosenwald Foundation began putting investments in Georgia to help teachers, principals and supervisors, they selected people to participate in carefully designed college programs leading to undergraduate degrees. In 1939, the directors felt they should support leadership programs at the graduate level. Dr. Walter Cocking, dean of the College of Education at the University of Georgia, negotiated for a contract with the Rosenwald Board whereby, for a two-year period, selected personnel were to be provided scholarships of $400 for one year of graduate study in supervision and related areas.

Dr. Floyd Jordan, the first director of the graduate program during 1939-1940, was assisted by Dr. Rachael Sutton and Kate Houx, who had moved from South Georgia Teachers College in Statesboro to the University of Georgia when the program was transferred to the university.

Due to political interference from Governor Eugene Talmadge in opposition to use of Rosenwald Funds, the program was discontinued for two years. In 1943, however, it began again. Jane Franseth, who had been associated with the program in south Georgia, was called to the University of Georgia to direct the program.

In the summer of 1948, Dr. Johnnye Cox, a member of the first class of supervisors at South Georgia Teachers College, became the director of the program at the University of Georgia. She remained with the program through June 1971. Beginning in 1943, the Georgia Council on Teacher Education sponsored the program at the University of Georgia. The council appointed a committee to advise in selecting teachers admitted to the program. The committee also provided advice on the content and sequence of experiences in the program.

Dr. Mildred English, at Georgia State College for Women in Milledgeville, and Katie Downs, at West Georgia College in Carrollton, both contributed experiences to the supervisors in training. These supervisors studied and observed at Sand Hill School, a model school for West Georgia College which had received national recognition for its accomplishments as a community school. This unique program required a year-long on-the-job internship supervised by a staff member from the University of Georgia. The internship consisted of many visits with a university professor and a planned sequence of seminars throughout the year.

Likewise, the Georgia Committee on Cooperation in Teacher Education for Negroes sponsored the program for Jeanes supervisors. A 1944 report from the State Department of Education to the General Assembly said,

> During the 1943-1944 school term, a cooperative program for the training of Jeanes Supervising Teachers was in-

augurated. This project was carried on under the direction of a committee selected from the Georgia Committee on Cooperation in Teacher Education. Six applicants were selected who were between the ages of 25 and 40 years, who had completed a minimum of three years teaching, mainly in rural elementary schools, who manifested an unusual interest in education, and who possessed qualities of leadership which seemed essential for supervision.

The Julius Rosenwald Fund bore the expense for room and board for the six trainees. The state, through the Board of Regents, paid for the tuition of five of the trainees who registered from within the state. Atlanta University provided the facilities, the major part of the instructional staff, and the tuition for the sixth trainee who registered from outside the state. The General Education Board helped to finance conferences, field trips, and part of the expense incident to apprentice supervision. Colleges within and without the state contributed the time of instructors for planning and supervising the work of the trainees. State and federal agencies interested in health and education contributed time and personnel. The Jeanes Supervising Teachers in six counties where apprentice training was done gave unstintingly of their time to the project.

The first semester was devoted mainly to a background training at the University which included a core program in supervision, a problem seminar, selected group work based upon the needs of the students and visits to nearby schools. During the second semester the program included an extended observation period of seventeen centers in the southeast and field work under joint supervision of the University staff and cooperating Jeanes Supervising Teachers. The last four weeks of the second semester were spent in a final summary period on the campus of the University.

The year of training for supervision earned for the students the professional supervisor's certificate. The work was then evaluated by Atlanta University and the students were permitted to finish their residential work for

the master's degree in one single summer session beyond
the academic year of training. The six trainees were given
contracts as Jeanes Supervising Teachers. The cooperative training program is being continued during 1944-45
with ten persons being trained.[109]

State Department of Education and University of Georgia
personnel maintained close contact with the Georgia instructional supervisors, with the Georgia Jeanes Program and with
those in leadership roles with the Jeanes Program.

In 1943 the State Board of Education provided provisional
and professional certification for supervisors which was the
same format as that for superintendents. The professional
four-year teacher's certificate and a minimum of three years'
teaching experience as well as nine graduate courses of special preparation for supervision were required for admission
to the program. In 1948, the master's degree was required.[110]

As would be expected, changes in certification and qualification requirements accompanied changes in the state's teacher
education program. Graduate programs were first recognized
in 1943 when the State Board of Education authorized certification of master teachers, superintendents, principals and
supervisors. Similar programs were approved for visiting
teachers in 1945 and school counselors in 1948. Programs for
these certificates were worked out cooperatively by the Department of Education and the University of Georgia Division of Research and Field Studies and were first offered at
the University of Georgia. The principal's certificate became
mandatory in 1947 for all principals of schools having five or
more teachers.[111]

In 1941 and 1942, limitations were placed on the amount of
credit that could be earned during the school year and calendar year and on the total credit toward a four-year professional certificate that could be earned through correspondence
or extension.[112] Modifications were made in certification procedure to compensate for the wartime scarcity of teachers.
These, however, were classified as emergency measures and
carried a terminal clause.

It should be noted that in 1940, practice teaching or an approved equivalent became a requirement for the professional
certificate.[113]

Local school systems and the various divisions of the State Department of Education were not the only components of the education landscape being scrutinized by educational and political leaders in Georgia. The State Board of Education was also under study by several groups.

Action to establish a constitutional State Board of Education was precipitated by a series of events over a period of many years. To understand the change that in 1943 culminated in legislation creating a constitutional body, it is necessary to review quickly the history of the board as a part of the state's decision-making process.

The State Board of Education

The Georgia State Board of Education, provided for in the Act of 1870, was an ex-officio board with limited responsibilities. It was composed of the attorney general, secretary of state, comptroller general, the State School Commissioner and the governor.[114] There was no fixed term of office. In 1911 the law was altered to provide a state board composed of the governor, the state school superintendent and four appointees, three of whom were to be engaged in school work and familiar with educational practices in rural schools.[115] This change grew out of a proposed school code recommended by Superintendent M. L. Brittain in 1910. Brittain believed that the school board should include representatives of the teaching profession, and boards of this pattern continued until the series of educational reforms in 1937 changed the board's form, size and function.[116]

The new law provided for a lay board of 11 members, one from each congressional district together with the governor.[117] The state school superintendent was made executive secretary of the board. The term of office was established at six years. People employed in school work or engaged in the publishing business were ineligible for appointment.

It may be observed that in each different composition of the board, the governor had been a member. His influence, both in his appointive power and his actual presence on the board, obviously had undue weight on educational decisions. Late in the 1930s, the State Board of Education had fallen heir to a number of statewide functions, making it a very influential body. Among the newer services over which the state board now had control were textbook programs, school and public libraries, teacher certification, transportation of school children, establishment of minimum salary schedules, adoption and enforcement of school building standards and the school lunch program. Altogether, the board's functions had grown to comprehensive scope.[118]

Theoretically, the powers of the board, circumscribed with legislative controls, left little opportunity for irregularities. Often, however, only a thin line separated the policy-making process from the execution of policies. The change in 1937 from a semi-professional to a lay board and the increase in membership from six to 11 gave the governor the responsibility of appointing the entire board. It also provided him with the opportunity to establish a powerful agency for central control and manipulation of important educational functions. Thus a governor with complete subservience from the board possessed vast potential for the control of public education.[119]

From the minutes of the State Board of Education in 1939-1942, there were apparent tendencies for the board to extend itself into areas previously assumed to lie outside its scope of action. Examples were the establishment of standards and accreditation of provisional schools,[120] textbook evaluation and selection,[121] administrative control of the eleemosynary institutions and the dismissal and arbitrary transfer of state department employees.[122] Although apparently not vicious in intent, such direct board action circumvented the authority delegated to the Department of Education and created a degree of confusion and distrust.

Under a system in which the governor could, by advantageous appointment, surround himself with a particularly favorable board, he was in position to manipulate the authority lodged within this body and turn it to personal advantage. Foreseeing this possibility, a plan to prevent the immediate misuse of appointive power was written into the platform of candidate Ellis Arnall in his successful race for governor in 1942.

Following the practice of many other states, a constitutional board was proposed that eliminated the governor from membership. The act providing for such a board was approved early in the legislative session and was passed with little opposition on February 4, 1943.[123] The constitutional amendment was ratified at the general election.

By this act, the old board was abolished and a new board created. It provided for qualifications, term of office, tenure, filling of vacancies, powers and duties of the new State Board of Education and the revision of the laws relative to the State Board of Education.[124] As noted, the governor was not eligible to serve on the State Board of Education. Although the powers and duties of the board remained unchanged, establishment of a constitutional board had certain advantages. It placed the operation of the state school system beyond the power of the governor, and it required a constitutional amendment with a popular referendum to change the board's policies.

The War Years

After Pearl Harbor, it became evident that the United States was to be involved in a long war that would engage every segment of the population and commit all national resources. At the request of the federal government, the State Department of Education initiated an extensive vocational training program for war production workers on July 1, 1940. This program was divided into two parts—(1) Vocational Training for War Production Workers and (2) Rural War Production Training. It was funded wholly by the federal government and approximately $1 million in training equipment was placed in vocational shops in the state under its provisions.[125]

A request by the War Manpower Commission to mobilize the schools in a useful war effort led to the establishment of a Wartime Education Commission, appointed by State School Superintendent M. D. Collins early in the summer of 1942. School people at all levels and representatives of related groups formed the commission. L. M. Lester from the Department of Education was named executive secretary. At three meetings held in the summer of 1942, an early decision was made to learn the abilities of young men approaching draft age and to train them to serve where the need appeared greatest.[126] An executive committee outlined the scope of effort directed at various age groups, while subcommittees conducted special studies for each age group. These studies were scheduled for discussion in the fall regional meetings of the Georgia Education Association.

Continuing funds under the George-Dean Act, with provisions from the Vocational Training for War Production Workers Program, facilitated vocational education's important contribution to an all-out war effort. The Rural War Production Training Program was conducted in schools offering vocational agriculture instruction. In this program, out-of-state rural youth were given training in the following courses.

- Operation, care and repair of tractors, trucks and automobiles;
- Metal work, including simple welds, tempering, drilling and shaping and machinery repair;
- Woodworking; and
- Elementary electricity, including operation, care and repair of electrical equipment and wiring for light and power.[127]

These courses provided rural youth with basic training in the operation and maintenance of farm equipment and a general knowledge of tools. The equipment for this training program, costing approximately $300,000 in federal funds, became the property of the State Board of Education. It was used not only to train people in war-essential operations, but also for instructing regularly enrolled high school boys and farmers enrolled in adult classes.[128]

With the war effort occupying all facets of American life, a meeting was called on August 28-31, 1942, in Washington, D. C., by the U. S. commissioner of education. It was attended by school people from over the nation, together with representatives of the military services and others related to the war effort. Georgia had a delegation of eight representatives, including some members of the Georgia Wartime Education Commission. Following the Washington meeting, a handbook was published to provide guidelines under which the schools could contribute more specifically to the war effort. Copies were sent to officers of local GEA units.[129]

There was a tendency, after the Washington meeting, to merge the work of the Georgia Wartime Commission into a national effort. From that date, the High School Victory Corps occupied the center of attention. This was a national voluntary organization designed to mobilize high school students for more effective preparation for participation in wartime service.[130]

Dr. O. C. Aderhold, professor of vocational education, University of Georgia, became state director of the program.[131] In December 1942, he announced the purposes of the organization and gave an outline of its major objectives.[132] As the victory program was getting underway in the state, the Board of Education approved $200,000 to be added to the textbook fund for full compliance with the requirements on physical fitness, war training courses and anticipated needs in science, mathematics and pre-flight aeronautics.[133]

Every student enrolled in high school could join the general membership division. Students in the last two years of high school were eligible for membership in one of five special divisions—land service, air service, sea service, production service and community service. For those enrolled in the first three groups, the high school reorganized its program to provide basic pre-induction training, both physical and technical.[134] The widespread locations of the battlefronts indicated the need of preliminary training for specialized service in the navy and air corps rather than for trench warfare. These services called for advanced courses in mathematics and science.

The alarming number of draftees turned down because of physical deficiencies placed a high premium upon "physical fitness" as one of the major areas to be emphasized in the Victory Corps Program. In order to acquire greatest gain in the shortest order, the Victory Corps Manual on Physical Fitness was recommended. Students were motivated toward good health, stamina and physical skills attuned to wartime demands.[135]

Writing for the *Georgia Education Journal* in January 1943, Aderhold gave a more detailed account of the Georgia organization, officially launched November 1, 1942. He noted that the details had been worked out by 50 leading Georgia educators and published as Bulletin No. 1 by the Department of Education. By January 1943, the program had been carried to every high school in the state through efforts of a group of volunteer workers known as "minutemen." The major concerns in Georgia were the development of strong, healthy, vigorous young people who could participate effectively in the war effort through preflight training in aviation, and production skills for use in wartime industry and other aspects of needed service. Schools were urged to study the wartime educational programs and make curriculum changes to obtain the maximum results.[136]

An early statewide effort was made in the area of physical fitness. In January 1943, 14 physical fitness institutes were held in strategic locations over the state. These were two-day meetings attended by school superintendents, principals and physical education directors. On the first day, the scope and work of the Victory Corps were fully presented. The second day's program included a discussion and demonstration of the physical fitness program with the *Victory Corps Manual* serving as a guide.[137] The launching of the Victory Corps was listed among the leading educational events of 1942.[138]

Schools effectively integrated wartime curriculum changes into their guidance programs by using tests and inventories. Student aptitudes were isolated and specialized training provided. Use of mass instruction techniques simulating those of the armed forces was encouraged where possible. Adequate facilities were a great asset in most aspects of the program.

State Director Aderhold reported a remarkable range of achievements at the end of one year of Victory Corps operation. He said,

> "The degree to which the high schools of Georgia reorganized their educational activities is not only astounding but the enthusiasm with which both teachers and pupils participated has been a source of gratification to those who have worked at the program throughout the year." [139]

The Victory Corps program was established in 508 Georgia high schools. More than 80 percent of all schools was involved. Victory Corps participants included 63,000 in the physical fitness program, 62,000 in guidance and more than 60,000 in wartime citizenship. Preflight aeronautics was taught in 106 high schools, up from eight schools the previous year. Schools in 31 counties adjusted their terms to permit students to participate in the peak-season farm program and over 100,000 part-time farm workers were drawn from the school-age population.[140]

The first phase of the Victory Corps program throughout the nation ended in the early days of 1944. Thereafter, both elementary and secondary schools would be certified as victory schools. In the new program, more emphasis was given to pupil participation and planning with whole faculty cooperation. The requirements for recommendation as a victory school were more definite and stringent.

The new statewide staff, composed of 61 representatives from victory schools, helped organize potential victory schools and recommended their membership to the Executive Committee of the Wartime Education Commission. Through this medium, the transition from a national to a state program was made, thereby preserving the more permanent aspects of school planning. For those schools remaining in the Victory Corps, requirements increased. Comprehensive selective service records were required for each student. Specialized victory schools were given surplus war materials to use for more advanced training. The screening examinations conducted in the high schools and the guidance service in the specialized programs became the state director's top priority.[141]

The director's enthusiasm for the Victory Corps program was evident when he said, "for the first time the (school) program became meaningful to many students because the objectives were definite and the student could see practical applications of his learning to the problems of living in a wartime world." [142]

As World War II ended, the amount of surplus property increased. In 1946, Georgia became an agency for distributing surplus property to eligible recipients, with the state school superintendent directing the State Agency for Surplus Property.

The eighty-first Congress in 1949 enacted Public Law 152 authorizing the state agency to receive federal surplus properties and distribute them to eligible health and educational institutions and civil defense units. This law also authorized the transfer of surplus real estate to eligible state and local agencies.

Georgia continued to operate under the executive order plan until 1964, when Senate Bill 180, Section 53, authorized the State Board of Education to establish and operate a State Agency for Surplus Property, its purpose being to receive and distribute surplus properties pursuant to the federal act.

The State Agency for Surplus Property is responsible for acquiring, storing and distributing federal surplus property. Eligible recipients include approved or accredited tax-supported or nonprofit schools, school systems, colleges or universities, schools for the mentally retarded, schools for the physically handicapped, educational radio and TV stations, hospitals, clinics, health centers, public libraries and civil defense units. The agency currently serves all of the state public school systems and their individual schools, the University System and all affiliated colleges, 85 private elementary and secondary schools, 69 private colleges, 70 schools for the mentally retarded and physically handicapped, 30 public libraries, eight educational TV stations, 159 hospitals, 140 health centers and 216 civil defense units. Recipients are served by three distribution centers located in Atlanta, Americus and Swainsboro.

Because this agency operates without federal or state funds, it charges a small service fee for operating expenses. These charges are based on the original cost of property to the federal government, its condition when acquired, costs of acquiring and storing and the desirability of the property. The agency accepts no cash transaction; remittance is made by business check only. All funds are deposited in the State Department of Education's central accounting office, and all expenditures are paid from this account. Adequate fiscal and property accounting records are maintained by the agency with corresponding fiscal records maintained by central accounting. The acquisition cost of property, service charges assessed and number of transactions during FY 74 were as follows.

Type of Institution	Acquisition Costs of Property	Service Charges	No. Transactions
Education	$6,909,879	$346,692	4,869
Health	$2,104,204	$ 47,168	704
Civil Defense	$2,604,798	$131,644	1,220
Total	$11,618,881	$525,504	6,793

Operating expenses totaled $489,106.

Surplus materials provide a great boon to Georgia schools. Teachers have easy access to teaching aids that they would otherwise be unable to purchase. Surplus vehicles, tractors and bulldozers have saved schools and school systems many thousands of dollars. Metal for use in vocational shops and for building purposes has contributed to operational savings for the schools. Availability of surplus materials has made it possible for health institutions and civil defense units to acquire useful and needed items at nominal expense.

On July 1, 1978, by act of the legislature, administration of the surplus property agency was transferred to the State Department of Administrative Services. School systems continue to receive a large proportion of its benefits, however.

Although the war effort mobilized a sizable number of new programs in Georgia, it terminated others. One such casualty was the national school lunch program started in 1935 under sponsorship of the WPA. This program had a threefold purpose—to employ women in the community, to help farmers dispose of surplus produce and to provide meals for undernourished school children. The U. S. Department of Agriculture furnished surplus food and the WPA provided compensation to lunchroom workers. Local communities were required to furnish space, equipment and other facilities, most of which was supplied by the Surplus Commodity Corporation, local PTAs, civic clubs, private gifts, boards of education, boards of commissioners and city councils. Under this program nearly 1,000 Georgia schools organized school lunch service.[143]

In Bryan County the board of commissioners supplemented the funds for every child served a noon meal in the county. Another generous individual, H. W. Caldwell, who owned a chain of ice manufacturing plants, gave free ice and refrigeration facilities to the schools in each of the counties served by his plants. Now children could bring milk from home and keep it properly refrigerated until lunch time. About 12,000 students were provided this service in the county schools of Tattnall, Bryan, Meriwether, Evans, Troup, Bulloch and Toombs counties. Most of the milk was brought to school in screw-top, pint liquor bottles. Their brand names helped in the storage and identification of each student's bottle, but also formed a colorful, changing display of milk containers each day. (In these same counties Caldwell also supplemented local funds up to 50 percent to purchase school library and reading materials and sewing machines for the homemaking departments.)

At the Riceboro School in Liberty County, a 12-month school garden was maintained by the community and the students. This project produced food for the entire school lunch program for Riceboro students. In its early stages the garden labor posed one problem. The school had purchased a mule with which to tend the garden, but plowing a mule was considered demeaning by the school boys. After a serious budget study it was found that the mule could be traded in on a riding garden tractor. The boys then stood in line to ride the tractor. Cultivating the garden became a status symbol. The school boasted of serving watermelons until Christmas and fresh vegetables all year long.

The school lunch program had gained such a degree of popular interest that when the WPA program was abolished in 1943, the U. S. secretary of agriculture announced a plan for reimbursing schools for local food purchases. The State Department of Education then agreed to continue the hot lunch program as an integral part of the school program. The latter did not come easily. Three attorneys general ruled that no tax funds could be used to support a lunch program, even though federal operations flowed through the State Board of Education for this purpose. More complete details of these rulings may be found in the official reports of Attorneys General M. J. Youmans in November 1937, Ellis Arnall in April 1939 and T. Grady Head in August 1943.

In February 1943 state board members C. W. Parker, Jack Traver and Roy McGinty formed a committee to work with Superintendent Collins, State Auditor B. E. Thrasher and the U. S. Department of Agriculture in setting up the program for Georgia. The State Board of Education developed and administered the state school lunch program, which was carried out under the supervision of the Department of Education.[144] The board authorized Superintendent Collins to sign agreements between the Food Distribution Administration and the state in connection with the use of surplus agricultural commodities.[145] At the April 1943 meeting of the Board of Education, Lucille Watson was appointed state supervisor of lunchrooms.[146] A year later, Superintendent Collins reported that more than 1,200 schools in 149 counties had lunchrooms in operation.[147] Over 28 million meals were served that year, of which nearly four million were free.

Mrs. Watson and her assistants interpreted the school lunch program in speeches to schools and lay groups. They prepared and distributed literature on the lunch program, encouraged expansion of the service and gave direct personal assistance where needed.[148] The Georgia program in 1944-1945 was almost a $5 million undertaking, of which $2,429,107 resulted from the sale of lunches, $2,100,204 from federal aid and the remainder from local sources.[149]

The temporary nature of the agreements between the U. S. Department of Agriculture and the states for federal reimbursement of money spent for food supplies made many people uneasy. Termination of these agreements might end all free lunches for needy children. Representatives from Congress and organizations interested in the welfare of children argued for the continuation of a lunch program under federal aid, contending it an essential factor in the development of state plans and future congressional programs.

A bill was introduced in Congress by Georgia Senator Richard B. Russell for the continued support through federal aid of a nationwide program of school lunches. The National School Lunch Act, designed to safeguard the health and well-being of the nation's children and to encourage the domestic consumption of nutritious agricultural commodities and other food, became law on June 4, 1946. Because of his sponsorship and special efforts, Senator Russell was known as "the father of the school lunch program." [150]

Georgia's first Minimum Foundation Program for Education Act, passed by the General Assembly in 1949 and implemented in 1951, prescribed the state's responsibility for administering the food service program. Implementation of the MFPE Act facilitated an ambitious state school building program. School food service facilities were constructed in all new buildings and added to many existing buildings.

In 1952, the Georgia General Assembly authorized school food service workers to be covered under the Social Security Act, thereby making them eligible for a retirement plan.

Constitutional amendments based on 1958 congressional resolutions, H.R. 165-519b and H.R. 164-519a, providing tax funds to support school food services, were rejected by voters in 1958. A new MFPE law, Senate Bill 180 of the 1964 session, prescribed that school lunch would be a part of the total Georgia school program. The 1965 session appropriated funds to supplement the salaries of school food service managers who had taken training-in-depth courses offered by the State Department of Education. The question was raised again by the state auditor about the legality of using tax funds to support certain phases of the lunch program. In December 1966, Attorney General Arthur Bolton ruled that tax funds could not be used for operating a food service program.

The Georgia School Food Service Association immediately filed a friendly suit to determine the validity of the attorney general's ruling. The case was first heard before Judge Lilly in Colquitt County Superior Court in September 1967, then at the State Supreme Court on November 13, 1967. The majority opinion issued on January 2, 1968, stated in part ". . . the mere fact that the school lunch program may render pupils more efficient does not make it for 'educational purposes'; and further if school funds can be expended for feeding lunches to pupils why also would not the providing of proper clothing, suitable dwellings, proper medical attention or breakfast and dinner for pupils be 'for educational purposes'? The answer is obvious. There would be no limit to the purposes for which state taxes could be expended."

While the feeding of children is a worthy and beneficial undertaking and may well embrace the opportunities for a better learning situation, we are forced to the conclusion that eating is not education. Thus, the expenditure of funds derived from taxation over the whole state in support of school lunch program is not an expenditure "for educational purposes" within the meaning of Art. VII, Section 11 Par. 1 of the Georgia Constitution.[151]

In the 1968 session of the General Assembly a resolution was passed calling for another constitutional amendment which would include "II. For school lunch purposes." as one of the purposes for which taxes may be used. Seventy-nine percent of the voters approved this amendment in the next general election, and it now became legal for tax funds to be used for school lunch purposes. The 1969 General Assembly approved enabling legislation and also appropriated $1.7 million to help pay school food service labor costs. Subsequent sessions of the legislature have increased the appropriation; for fiscal year 1975, the total state appropriation for school lunch purposes was $8,364,446.

Many schools in Georgia had determined a crying need for a breakfast program and served needy children on any basis they could manage—mostly with local funds and aid from civic groups. The U. S. Congress, in 1966, passed a Child Nutrition Act authorizing a school breakfast program on a two-year pilot basis, extended the act in 1968 for three years and in 1971 in P. L. 92-93 extended it again. The breakfast program has become an integral part of school food service after a meager beginning in the 1950s.

Another Georgia Senator, Herman Talmadge, sponsored the Reform School Lunch Act in 1970, which made available more funds for the needy children program and nutrition education and training program and set national standards for free and reduced price lunches. This act focused on food services as part of a total educational program. In 1971 Senator Talmadge sponsored P. L. 92-153, which again increased funds for needy children. Subsequent legislation has authorized increased rates of reimbursement. By the end of FY 74, the reimbursement rate increased to 10½ cents per meal. The average rate for free meals had been 45 cents since 1973. Senator Talmadge's legislation included an escalator feature which encouraged greater local participation in the number of meals served.

Although distribution of United States Department of Agriculture foods in Georgia has never been a function of the School Food Service Unit, U.S.D.A. foods (formerly surplus commodities) have provided the greatest financial asset to the school lunch program. Since the program's inception in 1935, food distribution in Georgia has been a service of the State Department of Education. A majority of the foods distributed in Georgia has gone to the schools to be used in the lunch program, although in recent years the distribution of U.S.D.A. foods has been extended to include such other agencies as state institutions, the Needy Family Program, nonprofit and tax-exempt charity agencies, summer camps, disaster relief and Title VII of Older American Act Nutrition for the Elderly Program. From 1970 to 1975, over $70 million in U.S.D.A. foods went to the schools, representing about 60 percent of the total U.S.D.A. foods distributed in Georgia. The most valuable items included beef, turkey, milk and cheese, as well as numerous grain and vegetable products.

In 1967 the State Board of Education adopted as standard requirement that "The school system shall have a School Food Service Program which is nutritionally adequate, educationally effective and financially sound." The board firmly regards school food service as an essential part of the total education program which should be used as a learning laboratory. Governors, the legislature and the public in general have supported the State Board of Education in developing a strong school food service program.

The school lunch program was only one post-war issue. To deal with other problems, the Georgia Education Association initiated a survey of public education in Georgia as a preliminary step to developing plans for the state. The survey was endorsed by the Department of Education.[152]

A comprehensive planning board organized the Agricultural and Industrial Development Board, with panels in several broad areas. Each panel was made up of three or more appointed members who, in turn, selected a director. The Education Panel consisted of Superintendent Collins, chairman; Mrs. Frank C. David and Wilson Williams. O. C. Aderhold was named director of the panel activities. Aderhold had become a well-known leader in Georgia education as a teacher of vocational agriculture, as a principal and superintendent of public schools and as associate professor of vocational education at the University of Georgia.[153] As previously noted, he had been the director for Georgia's successful high school Victory Corps Program.

The early organization of the Education Panel was reminiscent of the Victory Corps Program. Some of the techniques and methods of the Education Panel were apparently derived from experience with the Victory Corps. In its first year, the Education Panel engaged in several assigned projects including a study of school buildings in Georgia, pupil transportation, problems of administrative organization, teacher supply and demand and a survey of the Georgia School for the Deaf.[154]

The panel also concentrated on developing local leadership for educational advancement in the postwar period. Work was conducted intensively by the field staff in twelve "spot" counties during the first year. To the extent possible, the panel staff was recruited in accordance with the type of work to be done. Several were obtained from colleges where enrollments had declined due to military service of the students. Among those participating in the specialized studies were W. A. Stumpf, L. O. Rogers, R. D. Pulliam, Claude Purcell, John T. Wheeler, Sam Clemons, W. O. Hampton, J. I. Allman and representatives of various state officers.

The field staff was composed of Paul Carroll, Charles Hudgins, Ralph Tolbert, Nell Wynn, Johnnye Cox and T. E. Smith, with initial assistance from Dr. Paul Morrow of the university faculty. This staff directed the program of school-community services during the first year.[155] In preparation for the year of intensive work in the "spot" counties, the group devoted a portion of the summer of 1944 to the preparation of A School Leader's Manual.

The field staff for the second year, including J. D. Messer, Pendleton Mitchell, James L. Dickerson and some members of the previous year's staff, revised and printed *The School Leader's Manual* as a working tool in the development of local leadership. The groups assisted representatives of the local communities to recognize the needs of their schools, to bring these needs into focus, to suggest ways of meeting them and to work toward the means, facilities and leadership for putting them into operation. A secondary value was the establishment of identities between the varied groups and the community school.

Dr. J. Greene from the university faculty, Dr. W. O. Hampton from North Georgia College, W. A. Stumpf from the University of Chicago, Joe A. Williams, who had recently left the U. S. Navy, and T. E. Smith from Georgia Southwestern College assembled, organized and interpreted the data being considered for specialized studies. Several future projects of statewide import were beginning to emerge.[156] Aderhold made a progress report to the State Board of Education at its meeting on July 13, 1944.

Then, on February 15, 1946, he reported to the state board on the panel's Teacher Supply and Demand Study. He said that over one-half of the white and more than two-thirds of the Negro teachers in Georgia did not have four years of college training. He also reported that more than 1,100 additional teachers were needed to fill vacancies existing at the time of the study. The state needed 4,864 white and 1,106 Negro teachers to take care of increases in enrollment expected during 1950-1951. The Education Panel issued a revised school leader's manual in 1947. It was written as a guide for superintendents, principals, teachers and leading lay citizens to use in planning more adequate educational opportunities for all the people of Georgia.[157]

From its inception in March 1944 until January 1946, the Education Panel operated as a unit of the Agricultural and Industrial Development Board and was more closely related to the executive branch of government. On January 1, 1946, the Educational Panel was transferred to the State Board of Education and made a division of the Department of Education. In this relationship, the panel staff was related more directly to the public schools, and their services became available to local school systems.[158] In the summer of 1945, Aderhold was made dean of the College of Education, University of Georgia, replacing Dean Edwin D. Pusey, who retired.

In its last year, the Education Panel conducted a number of significant studies including educational opportunities for veterans, the needs of vocational education in the state and the beginning of an extensive study related to the organization and financing of education in Georgia.[159]

The committee submitted its report, "A Survey of Public Education of Less Than College Grade in Georgia," to the legislature in January 1947. Superintendent Collins coordinated the efforts of all lay and professional groups to lobby for the enactment of the Georgia Minimum Foundation Act it recommended. The proposal passed two years later but was not put into action until 1951 because the state lacked the necessary funds.[160] Although the panel also studied textbook and library needs, school lunch programs, curricular and instructional needs and teacher qualifications and supply, probably its most valuable effort was its exhaustive analysis of public education on which the state's Minimum Foundation Program for Education was based.

On recommendation of a joint committee of the State Board of Education and State Board of Regents in April 1947, the panel changed its name to The Bureau of Research and Field Service and became a permanent adjunct of the University of Georgia College of Education.[161] It continued as the approved agency for conducting and reporting research for the Department of Education and was responsible for assembling and reporting a number of valuable studies.

Teacher Retirement

While World War II had kept Georgia's attention riveted to current affairs, one back-burner issue, teacher retirement, received occasional notice for several years before becoming a major issue in the 1940s.

One of the first to recognize the significance of such a program was Superintendent Mark Smith. In 1935, he stated that 22 states already had statewide teacher retirement programs and 17 others, some of which were in the South, had permissive laws providing for retirement pensions. He attacked the critics of teacher retirement who argued that it would be excessive and unwise of the state to assist one group in this manner. He believed that the quality of service rendered by teachers warranted help, while the low pay which they received made it impossible for them to establish private annuities.[162]

No immediate effort was made to follow up Smith's proposal. In 1935, Georgia was beginning to emerge from a depression which had reduced greatly the small salaries teachers were promised. However, with the return of moderate prosperity, interest in teacher retirement was renewed. A bill providing for a constitutional amendment permitting the state, counties and municipalities to establish retirement programs was being readied for legislative action in December 1938. A letter signed jointly by B. M. Grier, president of the Georgia Education Association, and Ralph Ramsey, secretary, was sent to local superintendents urging them to bring the bill favorably to the attention of their senators and representatives. Since the bill was permissive in nature and would require no additional revenue unless local systems should desire to set up retirement programs for their teachers, many believed it would pass.[163] During the 1939 legislative session the constitutional amendment did pass providing for establishment of retirement systems in counties of specified population and for raising and administering the retirement fund.[164]

The credit for organizing and planning this successful legislation belongs almost completely to the Georgia Education Association. From its inception as a practical possibility until final implementation, it was under the watchcare and direction of the GEA. The *Georgia Education Journal* of February 1943 included an editorial by Secretary Ramsey briefly describing the steps and procedures leading to the successful enactment of a teacher retirement law in Georgia. No one was more competent than Ramsey to speak on this subject, since he had been closely identified with the project from the time it was launched as a major step toward acquiring security for Georgia teachers.[165]

Although the need had been recognized in previous years, no steps had been taken to write teacher retirement legislation until 1941, when the Georgia Education Association authorized the following committee to develop a workable plan.

Superintendent Paul Munro, Columbus, Georgia
Superintendent Willis A. Sutton, Atlanta, Georgia
Superintendent W. E. Knox, Gray, Georgia
Dr. L. D. Haskew, Emory University
Mrs. R. A. Long, president, Georgia Congress of Parents and Teachers
Knox Walker, supervisor, Fulton County Schools, and president of GEA
Marvin T. Shields, state school supervisor, Lafayette, Georgia
Dr. John I. Allman, assistant state school superintendent
Superintendent S. C. Copeland, Richmond County Schools, Augusta, Georgia

At meetings conducted throughout the state, committee members exchanged ideas with Georgia educators. They analyzed the practical needs of retired Georgia teachers and determined the costs of an actuarially sound program.[166] For a full year they carefully researched the most effective teacher retirement systems in the nation, seeking counsel from representatives of other state retirement programs. The profession as a whole enthusiastically participated in the project. Educators across the state sought support from local political candidates and later made voluntary contributions of approximately $1.00 per member to retain the George B. Buck firm of New York as consulting actuary.[167]

Concerned that poor testing might damage their retirement system, the committee tested every feature of the proposed program to insure actuarial soundness and economic feasibility.[168] At its meeting in November 1942, the Georgia Association of School Administrators passed resolutions giving it full endorsement.[169]

Both the retirement plan and a retirement bill, prepared by Buck, were given extended study by the committee and reviewed further by the state's legal department, the attorney for the retirement program and the constitutional amendment.[170] In order to put the program into effect, a constitutional amendment was drawn incorporating the phraseology necessary for official action.

The main features of the retirement plan were presented by the committee chairperson, Paul Munro, in the *Georgia Edu-*

cation Journal of December 1942, in order that teachers might become familiar with it. The article probed 40 questions dealing with retirement.[171]

Although several legislative leaders, including Governor-elect Ellis Arnall, had urged the passage and full financing of a strong teachers' retirement law, it became increasingly incumbent on the committee and the actuary to draft legislation which would appeal to all. Finally, the best portions of several plans were included in the bill presented to the General Assembly in 1943. The most attractive features included such benefits as

- The "money double" plan whereby a percentage of the employee's salary is contributed by employers and employees and matched by the state. At the time of retirement, the sum is paid as a monthly annuity for life. Only teachers who serve until minimum retirement age are eligible for the matching pension.
- A prior service plan whereby the state includes in the pension the value of members' service prior to the date the retirement system began operations. The state provides funds to finance the prior service section over a period of years, paying to the retirement system a percentage of salaries in addition to the cost of the current membership service.
- Disability retirement to provide for members who cannot remain in service to age 60 because of incapacitation.
- Provision for a constitutional amendment to permit the voters to approve the use of tax funds for teacher retirement purposes.
- Creation of a Board of Trustees to administer the system.
- Five different plans of retirement.
- A provision to freeze membership for teachers who leave the profession before reaching retirement age.

The bill passed the legislature without a dissenting vote.[172]

The timeliness of this legislation was one of the reasons for its prompt and successful passage. Governor Arnall had made teacher retirement a campaign pledge. It had been fully publicized by the *Georgia Education Journal* and other media.

It was carefully designed, had been endorsed by educational leaders and supported by the general public. Its passage was hailed as the greatest single step advancing the teaching profession in the last half century.[173]

Due to wartime travel restrictions, no effort was made to hold a full session of the Georgia Education Association in 1943. President Haskew, in his address to the Representative Assembly, thanked the membership for voluntary contributions from teachers, amounting to over $4,000, and their support in other ways.

By invitation, Governor Arnall attended the meeting of the State Board of Education on April 23. He told the board that he was anxious for the people to ratify the constitutional amendments including authorization for setting up teacher retirement in the state.[174] At the legislative session of 1943, money was set aside to establish the retirement organization, but none was appropriated to finance the program.

An article in the *Georgia Education Journal*, November 1943, announced that Ralph Ramsey, the *Journal's* former editor, would relinquish his post as secretary of the Georgia Education Association to assume responsibility for directing the establishment and operation of the Georgia State Teacher Retirement System.[175]

A full text of the retirement bill was carried in the October 1943 *Journal*. In summary, the term teacher, as broadly defined in the act, included a wide range of people above the clerical or technical level engaged in public school work for not less than half-time service. Persons classified as teachers were to become members unless exempted on request before January 1, 1944. Membership was mandatory for all teachers beginning service after this date. A member in service might retire at age 60. Retirement at age 70 was compulsory, while age 65 was generally regarded as the age of official retirement. Permanently disabled persons could retire on full compensation with a service record of 10 years or more.

The program was administered by a board of seven members composed of the state auditor, ex-officio; the state insurance commissioner, ex officio; the secretary of the Georgia Education Association, ex-officio; three members chosen by the Representative Assembly of the Georgia Education Association including a school administrator or principal; an employee of the State Board of Regents of the University System; a classroom teacher not an employee of the Board of Regents and a seventh member to be a citizen of the state, not a member of the Retirement System, experienced in investment of money, elected by the remaining six trustees.[176]

The University System, then considering a retirement system of its own, did not immediately request to be included in the Georgia Retirement Program but did enter a few years later.[177]

With adequate revenue, it was expected that the program could go into operation by January 1945.[178] On February 8, 1945, checks were issued to Aline Clayton, Inez Hendricks and E. T. Booth, the first beneficiaries of the Georgia Teacher Retirement Program. Present to witness and participate in the act were Governor Arnall, Secretary Ramsey and the Retirement Board.[179] (R. L. Ramsey served as executive secretary and director of the retirement program until November 30, 1945.)

During the next 30 years in 12 sessions of the General Assembly, the plan or law was amended 31 times to increase retirement benefits. Some of the major improvements up to 1975 include the following.

- A minimum of $9.00 per month is guaranteed for each year's creditable service. For example, a teacher with 40 years creditable service receives a minimum retirement payment of $360 per month, regardless of salary.
- Members with at least 30 years of creditable service may retire regardless of age.
- The multiplier in the formula has changed to an amount over "1.75 percent but not more than 2 percent." For fiscal year 1976, the multiplier was set by legislative action and appropriations at 1.76 percent. This results in calculations of benefits as follows. 1.76 times the number of years service times average monthly salary for five highest years equals monthly retirement payment. For example, earnings of a teacher with 35 years of creditable service who averaged $900 per month for the highest five years would be calculated as follows. 1.76 x 35 x $900 = $554 per month.

- The maximum salary on which benefits are computed has been removed.
- Teaching service may be transferred to Georgia from other states.
- Former members may renew membership after having withdrawn funds.
- Cost of living increments have become available to retirees.
- Increased benefits have been established to the estate or beneficiary of a member if death occurs prior to retirement.
- Credit for military service has been liberalized.
- Leave of absence policies have become more generous.
- Retirement benefits from the Georgia Teachers Retirement System have been exempted from state income taxes.[180]

The system is financed through funds from three sources.

- Member contributions, with teachers paying 6 percent of their gross salaries each month.
- Employer contributions, with the state and local boards of education paying 8.936 percent of the teachers' salaries.
- Income from the Retirement System's investments, subject to the same limitations imposed by law upon domestic life insurance companies.

In the first 30 years of its operation the Retirement System has employed only four executive secretary-treasurers.

Ralph Ramsey   from 1943 to 1945
J. L. Yaden   from 1945 to 1957
G. E. Pittman   from 1957 to 1969
Wesley Rucker   from 1969 to present

As of January 1, 1975, the Teachers Retirement System was paying monthly benefits to 11,200 retired members and beneficiaries. The monthly benefit payroll at that time was about $4 million. The goals and objectives envisioned by the Teacher Retirement Committee in 1942 continue toward achievement.

The Georgia Education Association, in addition to its teacher retirement efforts, was busy in other areas during the

1940s. The association assisted a number of lay groups (the Georgia Congress of Parents and Teachers, the Lions Club, the Georgia Federation of Women's Clubs and the Georgia Farm Bureau) in writing legislation to increase the standards for public education and to provide additional state support. In particular, every farm bureau chapter campaigned in its home county for a three percent sales tax, arguing that this was the only way to finance a minimum program for education throughout the state.

A New Constitution

The General Assembly had discussed for some time the need for an entirely new state constitution. The Constitution of 1877 seemed a confusing patchwork, having been amended about 300 times.

The Georgia Press Association teamed up with the Georgia Education Association, the Parent-Teacher Association and the Georgia Association of School Administrators to strengthen legal structure of public education. The State Department of Education gave valuable consultative services to a Constitution Revision Committee through Superintendent Collins, Assistant State School Superintendent John I. Allman and Administration Director Claude Purcell. The legislature approved the committee's report with minor changes, providing voters the opportunity to vote on a new constitution in a statewide referendum in 1945.[181]

Major changes affecting education made by the new constitution included a group of provisions relating to the executive, to taxation and local government. Most of the changes relating to the executive were made to prevent potential abuses.[182] Regarded among the most important changes was the elimination of the poll tax, a source of income traditionally applied to the state school fund, though it no longer provided a significant source of revenue.

Potential for upgrading public education was provided in the new constitution through the following measures.

- A lay state board of education was provided with seven year terms and with no ex-officio members.

- All local sub-tax districts were abolished. This action eliminated 1,257 local tax districts at one time and made the county and independent city boards of education the administering agencies in the several political subdivisions. This action led to the eventual consolidation of some 6,000 small, sub-standard schools.

- The method of voting on local district school bonds was amended to provide that an election would be carried if a majority of those voting approved the issue.

- Provision was made for classification, certification and compensation of county school superintendents.

- The 1945 Constitution authorized a 12-grade state supported public school system, an increase from the previous support of grades one through 11 only.

- The local school tax limit for counties was raised from five mills to 15 mills. (The five-mill maximum had been in effect for 26 years, since the passage of the Elders-Carswell Act of 1919.)

- Georgia's 1945 Constitution gave the right to vote to citizens age 18 or older. Even though this is not a direct educational issue, it gave status to the thrust later to provide a state-supported, 12-grade school system.[183] (Georgia was the first state in the Union to give the vote to 18-year old citizens.)

The most important change affecting education involved local government. The county, exclusive of independent systems, became the unit of support and management of schools, thereby abolishing 1,257 local subdistricts and eliminating much duplication and waste. The fiscal authority of the county could levy a tax for the support and maintenance of education within specified limits. Counties were permitted to enter into contractual relations with each other in matters relating to school services.

The tenure in office of county school board members was changed from four to five years with terms arranged so that the office of one member became vacant each year.[184] Independent city systems were permitted to continue operating under city charters, but no additional school districts of this character were to be established in the future.

Many people were unhappy with the constitution, though it was admittedly an improvement over the old one. The commission was accused of skirting gingerly around certain controversial matters rather than dealing with them in a forthright manner. In justifying their action, the commission indicated they feared the document would fail to pass if it were written to satisfy the liberals.[185]

School administrators had long advocated change. Over the years, resolutions had been passed by the Georgia Education Association and the Georgia Association of School Administrators urging changes in the manner of choosing state school board members, the Board of Regents and county school boards. The mode of electing state and county school superintendents likewise had come under frequent and sometimes vigorous criticism by school officials. These all remained unchanged. No change was made in the rate of local taxation for county schools or in the maximum bonded indebtedness. No provision was made directly or indirectly for the liquidation of bonded indebtedness of the local school districts which were abolished.[186]

Almost immediately, people interested in progressive legislation for education renewed their efforts to secure the desired reforms. In his series of articles appearing in the *Georgia Education Journal* during November and December 1945, H. S. Shearouse resumed the longstanding criticism of the method of choosing the county superintendent. Shearouse pointed out that elimination of local sub-districts and the prohibition of any new city school districts now made the county board the major tax authority for education. Legally, the county school superintendent was now the executive officer of the board of education, the sole authority for administering the total school program for the county. Great responsibility was conferred by the constitution on this office; yet it was still elective. Thus a significant problem remained unchanged— that of securing people of professional distinction under existing requirements and provisions for election. With the increased importance of this office under the new constitution, there was greater reason for these posts to be filled by administrators of unquestioned professional ability wherever such persons could be found. Shearouse supported his claim by comparing the technical responsibilities of the office with the minimum requirements necessary to qualify a candidate for election.

He recommended that professional qualifications be set up legally and that the minimum be not less than a master's degree from a recognized institution, with a major in school administration and not less than five years of public school experience as teacher and principal. He felt the first of these, which required only legislative enactment, should be approved at once. Removing the office from politics and making it appointive in strict conformity with the legal requirements would necessitate a constitutional amendment, he noted. Steps toward this objective were recommended.[187]

In a subsequent article, Shearouse focused on removing the county superintendency from a political setting. He cited numerous examples to show that county schools had not always operated with the children's highest welfare in mind.

Shearouse pointed out the unfortunate relationship existing between a county board chosen by a grand jury and a county school superintendent elected by the voters. Wherever good relationships were established between board and superintendent, it became necessary for the board members to enter the political arena in order to sustain the superintendent in office. If, perchance, the election were lost, an awkward situation would arise between the board and the superintendent whom the members had opposed.

The likelihood of securing superintendents of desired professional competence was reduced by the provision that candidates for office must be county residents. An alternate plan would be to elect, by popular vote, a lay board which would hire a school executive who met the established professional requirements for office.[188] Such recommendations had been made repeatedly to both the legislature and the commission appointed in 1943 to revise the state constitution.

Having failed to obtain these reforms in school administration at the county level through the new constitution, other groups continued to seek legislation which would bring about the desired changes. The Survey of Public Education in Georgia, submitted in January 1947, recommended that "county boards of education be chosen by the people at non-partisan elections held separately from the general elections." [189] It recommended also that the constitution be amended to permit county boards to choose the county superintendent and that the qualifications for this office be given equal professional status with the city superintendents.[190] Further, it recommended that county boards of education be encouraged to contract more freely with each other and with the independent systems for joint use of services, personnel and facilities.[191]

Resolutions by the Georgia Education Association in 1947 provided for a constitutional change permitting the selection of the county superintendent by the county board.[192] However, none of these proposals were ever implemented.

A new constitution was not the only major new entry on Georgia's educational scene in 1945. The year also brought passage of a compulsory attendance law. To deal with the persistent problems of delinquency and non-attendance, the Georgia Association of School Administrators at its November 1942 meeting passed a resolution favoring "a new attendance law that will more fully cope with the problems of school attendance." It was transmitted to the Legislative Committee of the Georgia Education Association.[193] A year later the request was repeated with more specific indications for reform. The administrators pledged themselves to work for "a compulsory school law which shall provide that the children from seven to sixteen years of age shall be required to attend school for a period each year concurrent with the school term." [194]

At the 1944 annual meeting of the Georgia Education Association, a resolution was passed recommending that the next legislature amend the compulsory school law to incorporate these provisions. A further clause in the resolution probably offered a clue to the ineffectiveness of the previous law, "that the amended law be so plain that judges cannot misconstrue its content when called on to enforce it." The resolution was strengthened further by advocating an adequate number of attendance officers, provided at the expense of the state board, to make enforcement possible.[195] In conforming with the resolution, a committee was appointed to phrase an attendance law for presentation at the next General Assembly. It was composed of Dr. Kenneth Williams, chairman; S. F. Burke; Raymond Duncan; Claude Purcell and Gerald Y. Smith.

In January 1945, the main points of the proposed attendance law were published. Variations from the previous attendance law included the following.

- The ages for required attendance were to be from seven to 16.
- The annual period of attendance was extended to include the entire school session.
- The law was to be administered by a visiting teacher whose duty it would be to discover the cause of non-attendance and work with parents and pupils to secure voluntary attendance.
- The penalty for non-compliance on the part of the parent would be a fine of $100 and/or 30 days of imprisonment.
- The penalty for non-compliance on part of the pupil would be set forth following proof of delinquency.[196]

A bill encompassing these provisions was passed at the legislative session in 1945 and was approved on March 8.[197]

Having repealed previous laws relating to compulsory attendance and established a new law with specific requirements, it was hoped that a fresh beginning could be made to deal with long standing problems in the area of school attendance. Probably the most significant, and certainly the most beneficial, aspect of the law was the provision for visiting teachers contained in Section 4 as follows.

". . . To facilitate the enforcement of this Act, each county and Independent School System Board of Education shall have authority to employ at least one competent and qualified full-time visiting teacher, whose duty it shall be to act as attendance officer to enforce the compulsory school attendance laws of the State, and to discharge such other duties as are usually performed by, or delegated to, visiting teachers." [198]

The county or independent system board was empowered to fix the salary of visiting teachers and to prescribe rules and regulations relative to the performances of their duties.

To assist in carrying out the purposes of the compulsory attendance law and to lend strength to the office, a group of educators including Mary Brooks, J. E. Owen, C. L. Purcell,

W. E. Pafford, Inez Wallace, Dr. Johnnye Cox, C. J. Cheves,
L. M. Lester, Elizabeth Donovan, I. V. Chandler and Kanka-
kee Anderson, went before the State Board of Education on
June 1, 1945, with resolutions calling for a definition of the
office of visiting teacher, a program for training visiting
teachers and compensation from the state above teacher allotments. Embodied in the petition was a strong plea for the
recognition of a professional office clothed with dignity and
authority. The board gave its unanimous approval and authorized the Department of Education to carry out the requests of the committee as noted in the resolutions.[199]

Visiting Teacher Services

When this law passed providing for the visiting teacher as
an agent in compulsory school attendance, Georgia became the
fourth state in the nation to provide this service, though the
office was not well known and the function of the visiting
teacher ill-defined.

As had become somewhat a custom in the work of the Department of Education, one member was usually designated
to have major responsibility in the planning and organization
of each new area of service. Claude Purcell was chosen to head
the new program of the visiting teacher. Purcell, from the
start, had been one of the leaders in the effort to adopt the
visiting teacher approach in dealing with attendance problems. Under his energetic and patient leadership, the program
was initiated smoothly and experienced orderly, professional
growth during its first decade in Georgia.

In October 1945 Purcell restated the law in simple terms
for the rank and file of teachers and administrators. He called
attention to the fact that "the enforcement of the attendance
law is the responsibility of the entire teaching and administrative force," coordinated by the visiting teacher in each county
and independent district. From the beginning, he regarded
this as a professional service and worked to develop high
quality visiting teachers.[200]

Following the committee report and its adoption by the
State Board of Education, Purcell assisted the board in establishing and carrying out its policies by clarifying and giv-

ing specific statements for the provision of adequate records, a listing of bona fide excuses for absence from school, the provisions for enforcement of the law when other methods had failed and, perhaps most important for visiting teachers, the steps to be taken to gain professional recognition and status through adequate training.

At the time the program began in the fall of 1946, no one in the state fully met the professional qualifications necessary for certification.[201] Positions at first were filled by experienced classroom teachers. Under the law, a school system could employ a person in the capacity of a visiting teacher if it could continue at its own expense to employ an attendance officer. Fortunately for the program, the great majority of the school systems readily adopted the visiting teacher program. To provide some basis for specialized training, Purcell was instrumental in securing a six-week workshop at the University of Georgia in the summer of 1946. Consultant services helped the new visiting teachers understand the specific nature of their work. This annual summer workshop, which later became a prerequisite for beginning visiting teachers, hastened the requirement of specialized graduate work for full certification.

The initial objective, to admit all children into school as rapidly as possible, immediately increased enrollment and improved attendance records. Though the objective was accomplished, it became evident that many children attending regularly were not using the school effectively. Consequently the visiting teacher's responsibilities expanded to maximize school children's educational opportunities.

At the 1946 GEA district meetings, the visiting teachers organized and elected chairpersons and secretaries from each congressional district. At these initial meetings, Purcell helped develop the statewide organization. Each chairperson's primary function was to interpret visiting teacher services to teachers, principals and the general public in that district. These meetings were well attended and did much to develop statewide uniformity. In planning for future meetings, the visiting teachers continued to develop ways to improve their work.[202]

After passage and implementation of the compulsory attendance law of 1945, making 16 the cut-off age for compulsory school attendance, it became necessary to rewrite the child labor laws to raise the minimum age for entering the labor force. The 1946 General Assembly repealed the law of 1933 regulating the labor of children and enacted a new law which would embrace and support the provisions of the school attendance law.[203]

The new child labor law, approved in January 1946, became operative July 1.[204] Major provisions of the law regulated employment of minors under age 18. Although children under 16 are employable under certain conditions, the provisions specified the time, place and nature of employment. Children under 16 were ineligible for night work, hazardous occupations or work during school hours. Children under 16 were limited to four hours work per day on school days, including on-the-job training provided by the distributive and related education programs.

Although the law made no sweeping changes from previous laws, its strength is evident in the provision for regulation and enforcement.[205] Every employed person under 18 years of age must file a certificate of employment. The school superintendent, the employer and the applying minor each sign the certificate. The child must have the promise of employment from the person, business or agency in which employment is sought. The permit is granted by the school superintendent and the applicant must provide personal data required by the form. The completed certificate includes the name, address, age and social security number of the applicant; name and address of parent or guardian; the job title or description; hours of employment and employer's name and address.[206] If the job is described as hazardous or occurring between 9 p.m. and 6 a.m., the true age of the applicant must be 16 or over. After age 18, the regulations provided for in this law are no longer applicable.[207]

Initially, after the law went into effect, the central enforcement agency was assisted by the supervisors who checked periodically with the issuing offices. Thus, cases of irregularity were detected promptly. The program operated with a high degree of effectiveness and employer cooperation. As visits from the supervisory branch became irregular, opportunities for evasion increased and the program lost some of its early vigilance. Also, as the labor market became more affected by transients, opportunities for employment of unregistered workers increased.

To make the law effective, daily vigilance was essential. The Office of Labor Commission needed sufficient supervisors to make necessary checks and follow-up investigations. Though the visiting teachers had access to records listing employed students within their districts, they had no official role in employment certification and were therefore unable to help make the law more effective.[208]

From its beginning, training for the visiting teacher position included a graduate program with a professional four-year college certificate as a prerequisite. The State Department of Education and the University of Georgia cooperatively developed a program for training and certifying visiting teachers. Local school administrators usually selected experienced classroom teachers to apply for the training program. The screening process was rigid; all who applied were not accepted.

At times, some economy-minded legislators have tried to reduce or eliminate the visiting teacher program, but educators have prevented their attempts. In fact, the school acts of 1964 provided special allotments for school systems to improve the services. The State Department of Education employed a full-time coordinator of the visiting teacher program in 1954 to assist the visiting teachers, the colleges and school administrators in promoting better services.

The work of the visiting teachers over the years has shown effective results. The 1964 issue of the National Education Association's *Rankings of the States* ranks Georgia fifth in the nation in the percentage of school age children in public schools. This was only eight years after Georgia had completed its transition from an eleventh grade school system to a twelfth grade system. The percentage of school age children in public schools peaked in 1964, however. Within the next three years the number of students in nonpublic schools increased from around 17,000 to above 50,000. In 1964, 95 percent of Georgia's school age population was in public schools; in 1967 only 89.1 percent of school age population was in public school. This exodus from the public schools did not reflect an ineffectiveness of the visiting teacher program, but instead has been attributed to the economic affluence of the 1960s and to the passage of the 1964 Civil Rights Act (Public Law 88-352) which stimulated the establishment of scores of private academies in the state.

By 1946, many schools had expanded their vocational education curricula. Now that students attended school until at least age 16, they offered courses designed to prepare them for "the outside world." This was especially true in rural areas, where studies in agriculture and home economics proved vital to postwar development of the state. Before examining the advancements of vocational education in this period, a review of the prewar years is appropriate.

Expansion of the agricultural curriculum in Georgia schools is reflected in the increase of vocational agriculture programs from 207 in 1937 to 485 in 1942. A comparable increase occurred in the number of teachers working in the program during this period.[209]

During the prewar years, O. C. Aderhold, then professor of agricultural education at the University of Georgia, made a concerted effort to improve instructional programs. Aderhold asked teachers to use problem-solving procedures in their teaching and to base their instructional programs on problems faced by students both in school and out of school. Home projects and farming operations were emphasized within the training program. Instructional programs in one school with certain farming situations and problems were often quite different from those in another school. Hence, more responsibility and initiative was placed upon teachers in formulating curricula for their classes.

That about 400 farm mechanics shops existed in Georgia schools proved that special emphasis was placed on farmers' specific needs.[210]

A food processing program was included in most vocational agriculture schools. During the biennium ending June 30, 1946, farm families processed 20,200,324 pints of fruits, meats and vegetables in community canning plants. Home economics teachers assisted agriculture teachers with canning operations.[211]

In addition to the regular vocational agriculture program, the Vocational Education Service, State Department of Education, was responsible for administering and supervising the Institutional On-Farm Training Program for Veterans. Federal funds made available by the Veterans Administration under provisions of the G.I. Bill of Rights financed the program, in which 12,463 veterans were enrolled by June 30, 1948.[212]

During the same period, homemaking education in Georgia increased in enrollment and number of programs offered. The quality of home projects carried on by in-school students and methods of teaching out-of-school students also improved markedly.

These developments were undoubtedly stimulated by cooperation with the nation's war effort.

Programs for in-school students emphasized production of food for rural families, consumer buying, home care of the sick, conservation of home, home equipment and furnishings and selection, care, construction and renovation of clothing.

Out-of-school groups learned nutrition, home gardening, "Food for Victory," processing foods for rural families, home care of the sick, home hygiene and food preservation.

During the late spring and early summer of 1942, a total of 137 home economics teachers enrolled in short unit courses (offered at the College of Agriculture at Athens and at the Abraham Baldwin Agricultural College at Tifton) to prepare themselves to supervise and manage school-community canning plants. Some homemaking teachers administered community canning plants after agriculture teachers were called to the armed services, while many others helped with the actual canning operation of the plants.[213]

During fiscal year 1945-1946 the Homemaking Service sponsored an experimental program in nutrition in eight selected elementary and high schools in Georgia. The University of Georgia and General Mills cooperated in the project, which resulted in a documentary educational film entitled "The School That Learned to Eat." The film, used for stimulating nutrition education programs, received international recognition.[214]

Among the most outstanding developments in the Homemaking Service during this period was the founding of the Georgia Association of Future Homemakers on August 6-11, 1945. This organization met the specific needs of homemaking students enrolled in secondary schools who had formerly belonged to the student division of the Georgia Home Economics Association.[215]

The New Homemakers of America, an organization for Negroes studying homemaking in junior and senior high schools, was organized in the mid-forties. Future Homemakers and New Homemakers merged in 1965, becoming Future Homemakers of America.[216]

The State Department of Education, Vocational Home Economics Service, in cooperation with the Department of Home Economics Education at the University of Georgia, published six bulletins dealing with curriculum problems and special in-service assistance to teachers.[217] A bulletin entitled "Planning the High School Homemaking Department" was prepared for architects, school officials and teachers. In fiscal year 1947-1948, the Homemaking Service published a research study entitled "Education for the Vocation of Homemaking in Georgia."[218] Federal funds for training in distributive occupations, made available through the George-Dean Act, incorporated distributive education as a significant part of the vocational program.[219] Prior to the George-Dean Act, training in distributive education and similar fields was conducted on a limited basis.[220]

The vocational distributive education program offered four types of training—(1) high school cooperative, (2) extension part-time, (3) evening and (4) college.

High school cooperative training was provided for high school students in junior and senior classes or on a post high school level. Students were required to be 16 years of age or older, regularly enrolled in school and employed in a distributive occupation such as merchandising, personnel administration or management. Schedules included two regular high school students in junior and senior classes or on a post high job activities and a minimum of 15 hours on-the-job work per week.

The state-certified coordinators placed students on the job and correlated the related study to job activities. They followed regular schedules of checking students by observing them on the job and securing periodic reports from employers. The coordinators also placed emphasis on the development of distribution clubs, a youth organization for students enrolled in the cooperative training programs. These clubs and others organized in later years were identified as Distributive Education Clubs of America (DECA). They promoted vocational understanding, civic consciousness, social intelligence, leadership development and satisfaction in a job well done.

During the first years, cooperative programs in distributive education were conducted in 19 schools in Augusta, Columbus, Fulton County, Macon and Savannah. In 1944-1945, enrollment in cooperative programs totaled 296, increasing to 426 the following year. Also enrolled were World War II veterans in distributive education programs.

The vocational division of the State Department of Education completed plans with the University of Georgia to activate a teacher training program for prospective teachers of distributive education.[221]

Trade and industrial education during this period consisted of training in-school groups in high school, part-time groups of out-of-school youth, evening class groups of adults and special groups in programs such as Vocational Training for War Production Workers and in programs to meet the needs of veterans under the G.I. Bill of Rights. Area and state vocational-technical schools were authorized to meet local demands for individual training in trade and industrial occupations.

Cooperative trade and industrial training was provided for some in-school students. The annual report of the Department of Education for 1940-1942 stated,

> "In the last two years probably the greatest growth in this type education has been in what has been known as the Diversified Cooperative Training Program. During the first year ending June 30, 1942, there were 56 such programs in operation in the high schools of the state with an enrollment of 909 trainees." [222]

For this cooperative endeavor between schools and local businesses, a coordinator helped high school youth find part-time work in the student's chosen occupation. The student and employer then developed a practical individualized training program. Part of the training was provided by the school and part by the employer.[223]

In 1946 the Georgia Federation of Diversified Cooperative Training (DCT) Club was organized. Through club activities, individual members developed leadership skills. The organization sought to foster high standards of workmanship, scholarship and ethics and to create an appreciation for the dignity of work. (In 1953, the name of the organization was changed to Vocational Industrial Clubs of America—VICA.)[224]

All day trade programs increased in popularity during the early 1940s. New courses were organized for high school students in auto mechanics, sheet metal and cosmetology in Macon; refrigeration and radio repair in Columbus and printing in Savannah. During the fiscal year ending June 30, 1944, enrollment reached 2,687, rising in the following year to 2,867.

In the biennium ending June 30, 1946, two new courses were added to the part-time trade extension program—(1) training for ground workers and linemen (for a group of Rural Electrification Administration Cooperatives) and (2) instruction in carburetion (for upgrading mechanics employed in the automotive field).[225]

The trade and industrial education personnel in Georgia developed 15 units of instructional materials for teacher use. Many other states in the nation used the training units developed in Georgia.[226]

The State Department of Education initiated the Vocational Training Program for War Production Workers on July 1, 1940. Georgia's trade community assumed much responsibility for training men and women to fill payroll jobs in war industries. In the two-year period ending June 30, 1942, more than 75,000 persons in Georgia received vocational training preparing them to further the nation's war effort. Courses they took included machine shop, machine tool operation, heat treating, ship sheet metal, aircraft sheet metal, sheet metal layout, pattern making, arc welding, gas welding, ship fitting, aircraft motors, radio repair, aircraft assembly, bombsight repair and mechanical drawing.[227]

In 1943 the Georgia legislature passed a significant enabling act which permitted the establishment of vocational and technical schools serving areas greater than a given school system. This basic legislation led to the establishment of two state-owned and operated vocational schools and later to the establishment of the area vocational-technical schools.[228]

R. E. Bodenhamer in 1968 wrote "A History of the Development of Area Vocational-Technical Schools in Georgia" as partial fulfillment of the requirements for a master's degree at the University of Georgia. A brief summary of his findings regarding the events immediately following the 1943 legislative act is given in the following paragraphs.

On July 23, 1943, Dr. M. D. Mobley, State Director of Vocational Education, and Mr. F. H. Rayfield, Chairman of the Vocational Education Advisory Committee for Metropolitan Atlanta appeared before the State Board of Education. They reported to the Board that there was a critical need for training of skilled workers in the Atlanta Area and requested the Board to support training for such skilled workers in the Atlanta Area. The State Board upon request of Dr. Mobley enacted a resolution requesting the State Superintendent of Schools and the State Director of Vocational Education to examine the need for training in the Atlanta Area and to make arrangements with the Atlanta and Fulton County School Systems to conduct such training as was possible within the limitations of funds available.

Two months later, on September 10, 1943, the State Board of Education directed Dr. Mobley to study the needs for vocational schools in the State and present to the Board a statewide plan for such schools. Dr. Mobley prepared a very detailed and thorough study as directed and reported back to the Board on October 8, 1943. The plan prepared by Dr. Mobley proposed that the State Board approve Area Trade Schools to be operated by local school systems with State support and State Trade Schools to be operated by the State. His plan suggested that possible locations for Area Schools include Dalton, Rome, Marietta, Atlanta, Macon, Columbus, Albany, Waycross, Brunswick and Savannah. He further made a firm proposal that State Schools be located at Milledgeville and Clarkesville immediately with others to be established later.

The State Board of Education approved Dr. Mobley's report. Local school systems were authorized to apply for designation as an Area School Center, but approval by the State Board did not necessarily obligate the State Board to provide any financial support other than that already being provided since additional funds were not then available. During the succeeding two years, fifteen Area Trade Schools were approved by the State Board, but due to lack of funds, these schools never came into being. The centers approved were Columbus, Macon, Marietta, Albany, Waycross, Augusta, Griffin, Dalton, Savannah, Rome, Atlanta, Fitzgerald, Brunswick, Athens and Moultrie.

The State Schools at Clarkesville and Milledgeville were also approved as recommended by Dr. Mobley. In connection with this it should be noted that the State Attorney General, in response to a request for an opinion from Dr. M. D. Collins, State Superintendent of Schools, had ruled that the State Board could not, under existing law, acquire land for the purpose of erecting and equipping buildings for State Trade Schools, but that the State Board could accept donations of land and facilities and operate such as a State Trade School. This opinion did not affect the Clarkesville and Milledgeville Schools since both of them were to be located on property donated to the State.

The State Board of Education allocated $100,000 from its general budget for fiscal year 1943-44 for the purpose of operating the school at Clarkesville. A lack of funds prevented budgeting for the school at Milledgeville.

The North Georgia Vocational School was established in facilities originally constructed for the Ninth District A & M School in the 1920s. The Ninth District A & M School closed in 1934 and in 1935 the National Youth Administration established at Clarkesville a training program which operated until 1943. The State Board of Education received the property as a donation in 1943.

The North Georgia Vocational School began classes in late 1943 as a residential vocational school. The purpose of the school was "to serve the State of Georgia and in particular the northern half of the State."

The first classes established were Auto Mechanics, Radio and Communications, Machine Shop, Welding, Cooking and Baking, Woodworking, and Laundry and Dry Cleaning. In the beginning, there were no set graduation dates. A student came to the school, and when he had accomplished his objective or finished the course, he was given a diploma and sent to a job.

During this time, the State Board of Education continued to debate the location of the State School to be located in South Georgia, and heard presentations from many communities who desired to be selected as the location of the school. Among those communities making particularly strong presentations were Thomasville, Waycross and Camilla. For some time however, no decision was made on a location.

Probably one of the greatest hindrances to a quick selection of a site for the South Georgia School was the condition of state finances. Governor Ellis Arnall, who met often with the State Board during those days, gave little encouragement as regards financing of the school. For this reason also, the school at Milledgeville never materialized.

In 1945, the General Assembly of Georgia enacted legislation which made it possible for the State Board to purchase land and carry out other acts necessary for the establishment and operation of vocational schools . . .

This Act, though providing the State Board with broad new powers, provided no funds, and no schools were immediately constructed.

The State Board of Education in the meantime had selected Camilla as the site for the South Georgia Vocational School. The site selected was a closed air base which was available for the purpose. The lack of money however, again stopped this project before it got started. An examination of the proposed facilities disclosed that approximately $600,000 in repairs to buildings would be

needed before operations could commence. This sum of
money was not available, and the school at Camilla died
before it was born.

In early 1946, a group of citizens from Americus appeared before the State Board and requested that a State
Vocational School be approved for Americus. They
pointed out that Graham Field was being deactivated and
would soon be available. After several months of discussion and after receiving assurances from the Governor
and Budget Commission that funds were available, the
State Board approved Americus as the location for the
South Georgia Vocational School at its regular meeting
on October 28, 1946. At that same meeting, it changed
the names of the two State Schools from North Georgia
Vocational School and South Georgia Vocational School
to North Georgia Trade and Technical School and South
Georgia Trade and Technical School respectively.[229]

AV Comes of Age

The 1940s brought increased activity in the use of audio-
visual aids. Even without a central organization and distribution service, teaching films were used considerably during
1940 and 1941. Many free films of high quality were offered
through government agencies, voluntary organizations and
commercial concerns.[230]

Through PTA and school-wide efforts, many schools began
to purchase motion picture and slide projectors, screens,
black-out curtains and other equipment. With the expansion
of REA practically all consolidated schools now had a source of
electrical power.

World War II brought a quick end to equipment accessibility. Schools that had purchased equipment before the
"freeze" were fortunate and could use the available films, but
there now were few projectors manufactured for school use.
Shortly after the close of the war, however, equipment became available through war surplus. Moreover, much had been
learned about the effective use of instructional films in the
armed services training programs. With the instructors returning to civilian life and the availability of equipment, a

need developed for a state level organization to select and distribute films.

Garland Bagley, formerly a member of the Department of Education, returned from military service in the fall of 1945 and was assigned to the Division of Textbooks and Libraries with chief responsibility in the area of audio-visual aids. In the following year, the idea of a state film library developed and was approved by the State Board of Education. The nucleus of the library included films and recordings previously purchased by the state, while new acquisitions were funded through an initial state grant.[231]

A Survey of Public Education of Less Than College Grade in Georgia, a report presented to the legislature in January 1947, recommended a reorganization of the Department of Education. Garland Bagley's position as director of multi-sensory aids and textbooks selection was organized under the jurisdiction of the director of curriculum development and supervision of instruction.[232]

The survey committee expressed with some force its belief in the importance of these materials as an aid to instruction.

No program for furnishing materials for schools is adequate without provision for such teaching aids as motion pictures, projectors, radios, record players and the like together with a wide selection of films and recordings.[233]

The department started with the largest collection of approved teaching films that could be secured and made them available to schools on the most attractive terms possible. During the 1947 school year more than 10,000 films were shipped to 350 schools throughout the state. The Department owned more than $100,000 worth of educational films and recordings. All were available to any public school that had equipment for using the materials and would insure their return to the film center. A sum of $75,000 was made available for the year 1948-1949, but the demand by users was so great that an additional $25,000 was needed.[234]

A professional audio-visual committee consisting of D. E. Nalley, Mrs. Hill A. White, Nell Still, Sarah Hightower and J. J. Jones reported to the state board at its meeting in June

1949. It made the following requests—(1) that $10,000 be set aside each year to assist counties and independent systems which would agree to match this amount for purchasing audio-visual materials. The allotments were to be limited to the first 10 systems making application each year and no system could receive the grant more than once; (2) that two or more regional libraries be set up, preferably one in the southeastern part of the state and one in the southwestern part from which films would be mailed to schools in these areas. The central library would serve the northern part of the state, and thus avoid third zone mailing rates; (3) that more adequate and fire-safe housing be provided in Atlanta for the state owned films located there; (4) that the insurance fee be increased to $10 per year per school; (5) that the department continue paying postage both ways on the materials; (6) that provision be made for in-service training in the selection and use of films and in the operation of equipment; (7) that a permanent professional committee be appointed to work with officials of the audio-visual department and aid in the selection of new audio-visual materials, revise the catalog, engage in the preparation of materials and assist in making the people of the state conscious of the benefits of the audio-visual program.[235]

The report of 1949-1950 stated that the division then had 10,000 prints of 1,600 titles and these were being distributed to 700 Georgia schools. There were 57,000 films booked and more than two million student showings. Also, 23 counties had matched the state fund to establish local film libraries. The basis of the grant had changed to provide $2,500 in state aid for $4,000 in local contributions extended over a four-year period, thus providing a total of $6,500 for the local film library. It was recommended that each county depository purchase some of the more frequently used films to relieve the regional libraries which were unable to meet the demand.[236] Regional libraries were located at Tifton, Collegeboro and Macon and the central library in Atlanta moved to a permanent location on Memorial Drive. The libraries together had 2,500 titles and served a total of 977 schools in 1950-1952. Twenty-eight additional county libraries were started during the biennium.[237]

The division was unique among the states in the fact that postage was paid both ways on materials sent out from the libraries. The only outlay by the school for film service was a $10 insurance fee paid annually by each participating school. The Georgia collection rapidly approached being the largest in the country. It was being expanded to include the regional book libraries to which films and other materials were mailed for periods up to 30 days, thus making them available to a number of schools in the library service area.[238]

Postwar changes in Georgia education obviously were not confined to curriculum. Certification and qualifications faced another wave of change. At the war's conclusion, Georgia was using the plan for issuing teacher certificates that it had initiated in 1924. During those intervening years, there had been many changes in standards, with higher standards being required progressively and the system of classification becoming more complex. However, the state continued to issue certificates by examination.

Georgia's dual plan of issuing certificates and county licenses based on records had many defects. Frequently, low standards were accepted for many certificates. The defects were eliminated through the slow process of gradual change, with examinations for state certificates finally being discontinued on September 1, 1941. County licenses continued to be issued on examinations until September 1, 1946.[239] Annie McMichael explained, "Although many state certificates were issued, it was necessary to continue the county license in a few systems until the 1949-1950 scholastic year because of the shortage of teachers." [240]

In 1947, the pre-service education committee of the Georgia Council on Teacher Education conceived a new teacher certification plan. With criteria agreed upon by all parties affected by certification, each teacher-preparing institution developed its own individual program without having to respond to state imposed regulation.

This new certification plan required each teacher education institution to design its own pre-service program based on criteria developed by the state councils. For full approval, these programs faced evaluation by a visiting committee appointed by the director of the Division of Teacher Education and Certification and approved by the State Board of Education. As a result of the study of the Georgia Council on Teacher Education, the new plan of certification was adopted by the State Board of Education in February 1948, effective September 1, 1950.

> Each training program must have been designed to prepare for a specific teaching field or school service. Responsibility for admitting the individual to training, guiding him through the program and for recommending him for the professional certificate will be with the Dean of the College of Education or the Director of the Division of Teacher Education in the institution offering the training. Upon receipt of a transcript of the student's record and an application which has been signed by administrative authorities of the college, the State Department of Education will issue the Professional Teacher's Certificate.[241]

Certification based on satisfactory completion of approved programs began with undergraduate teachers' programs and was later extended to master's, sixth year and doctoral levels. Instead of phasing out credit evaluations, as had been originally planned, shortages in teacher supply made it mandatory to continue a dual plan. (The dual plan has continued from 1948 to the present.)

The Georgia-approved program plan typified James B. Conant's philosophy that "each college or university should be permitted to develop in detail whatever program of teacher education it considers most desirable." A comparison of the two proposals led Dr. H. S. Shearouse to conclude,

> After a careful reading of Conant's book and with many years of close association with the Georgia program, I have the feeling that the spirit of the development of teacher education programs in this state corresponds very closely to the spirit of Conant's suggestions.[242]

While collecting data for writing his book, *The Education of American Teachers,* James B. Conant investigated Georgia's certification plan. When the book was published, Dr. H. Titus Singletary, Jr., associate superintendent for instructional services, represented the Georgia Department of Education at a meeting on teacher education and certification called by Conant at Northwestern University in January 1966. Georgia placed among the top ten states in its certification procedures.[243]

In February 1948 when a bachelor's degree became the minimum professional requirement for all secondary and elementary fields, fewer than 50 percent of all Georgia teachers had one. By 1952, 67 percent of the total number of teachers held bachelor's degrees. In 1954, it had risen to 77 percent, and by 1960, 88 percent held bachelor's degrees. Not only did all vocational home economics teachers hold degrees, but one third of them held master's degrees.

In 1954 almost 94 percent of the Negro teachers held bachelor's degrees while about 74 percent of the white teachers held bachelor's degrees. A larger percentage of white teachers than of Negro teachers held master's degrees at this time. Teachers with two and three years of college were issued provisional certificates while working toward the bachelor's degree.[244]

Setting standards that meet all needs can become a problem when attempting to upgrade teacher preparation programs. To avoid potential problems, the Georgia Council on Teacher Education developed qualitative rather than quantitative standards. The criteria related to staff load, facilities to support the programs offered, organization and administration, as well as content and instruction. The council's major achievements in the following years were criteria development for both certified teaching fields and newly established fields. The criteria were subject to State Board of Education approval.

Elementary education, science, social science, English, health and physical education received initial attention, while criteria for art education, music education, industrial arts, mathematics and business education were developed later. Fields in vocational education were evaluated by standards set up in the State Plan for Vocational Education, which had been approved by the United States Office of Education.[245]

Specific qualifications and state certification for local superintendents continued to be extremely limited. An educational commission, with M. L. Duggan, state superintendent, acting as chairman in 1929, reported as follows to Governor L. G. Hardeman.

> . . . All new applicants for this position (County Superintendent) after January 1, 1929, should be required to have a Professional Junior College or a Professional Normal Certificate or to be examined on equivalent work by the State Board of Education. In addition the candidate should have at least two years experience in active school work in teaching or administration.[246]

In 1935 the state board ruled that "the examination required for qualifications for County School Superintendent shall be the Junior College stand." [247]

In 1939 Joseph A. Williams found that all 69 superintendents of independent school systems held bachelor's degrees, while only 67.9 percent of the county school systems' superintendents held college degrees. Furthermore, 6.15 percent of the superintendents of the county systems had never attended college. Of the 81 superintendents of county school systems responding to a questionnaire, 11 had not had any previous educational experience, two had had no high school education, three had never attended college and one had not attended college since 1895.[248]

On April 23, 1943, the State Board of Education adopted a certification plan for recognizing special preparation as an administrator. The provisional certificate was issued on the following minimum qualifications.

- professional four-year teacher's certificate,
- three years successful experience as a teacher,
- nine semester hours on the graduate level of approved preparation for the work of superintendent.

The professional certificate required for the last item above,

> one year or three quarters of special preparation for the superintendent as approved by the Division of Teacher Education and Certification.[249]

An annual planning conference for superintendents was held each summer at the University of Georgia under the sponsorship of the Georgia Association of School Administrators, the College of Education of the University of Georgia and the State Department of Education.[250]

On February 20, 1948, the State Board of Education adopted a regulation requiring the completion of the master's degree and an approved program of training for the superintendent's professional certificate instead of a year of graduate study in the specialized field.[251]

Such regulations were permissive. The specifications of the 1911 law remained the minimum qualifications; however, the pay scale increased with provisional and professional certificates in administration. This additional salary encouraged many superintendents to prepare specifically for their positions of leadership, although the law did not prohibit a county board of education from supplementing the low income of a poorly qualified, uncertified county superintendent. Since 1948, the plan for preparing superintendents has remained basically the same.

School Accreditation

After the death of Joseph Stewart in 1934, members of the accrediting body organized the Georgia High School Accrediting Commission. A constitution was developed, and it provided for an organization of nine members—four members from the Georgia High School Association, four from the higher institutions to be designated by the Georgia College Association and a ninth member being the high school supervisor from the Department of Education.

In 1944, a constitutional change provided for the accreditation of elementary schools. Consequently, two members were added from the Department of Elementary Principals of the Georgia Education Association. With the addition of the chairman of the Georgia Committee of the Southern Association, the Georgia Accrediting Commission became a commission of 12 members.[252]

In 1947, the first accredited elementary schools were listed. In spite of various efforts, primarily by the Department of Education, there had been no strong citizen pressure for elementary schools to be maintained with optimum standards. There were no substantial penalties for failure to do so. With the accreditation of high schools made dependent upon accredited feeder schools, the accreditation of elementary schools became significant and the number increased rapidly.[253]

The 1940s produced a variety of educational changes, including many that directly affected teacher certification and qualifications. Twelve of the most significant developments were as follows.

- State teachers examinations were discontinued in September 1941, 70 years after they were first introduced.

- Certificates were established for leadership roles, supervisors, principals, superintendents, visiting teachers and counselors.

- The four-year college degree with a planned program for teachers became the minimum level requirement for the professional certificate in 1948.

- The Visiting Teacher Program was established in 1945 following a new compulsory School Attendance Law for ages seven to 16.

- Specialized subject matter for the elementary teacher to include study from English, science, social studies, health, music and art was established in 1947.

- A requirement for all teachers to study soil conservation was passed by the State Board of Education July 3, 1947.

- The issuance of life certificates was discontinued on February 20, 1948.

- Student teaching became a requirement for all teacher preparation programs in 1948.

- The salary scale was revised in 1944 establishing a salary differential between the teacher holding the bachelor's degree and the teacher holding the master's degree.

- High school teachers were required to have greater specialization in their teaching field areas. The teaching field was endorsed on the certificate. A broad "fields" approach was developed in all of the secondary fields and in art education, music education and health and physical education.

- In 1947 the school program was extended by the General Assembly to grade 12.

- The Minimum Program for Education Act was passed in 1949. This law resulted largely from the study of the Education Panel. It provided for a nine-month school term and permitted kindergartens.[254]

The twelfth grade became part of Georgia's educational scene late in the 1930s. Before that time, the number of years a student spent in school varied widely from place to place around the state.

In the early days of secondary education in Georgia, when local taxes and tuition were the primary support and the level and length of education varied widely, incoming college students were often required to enroll in preparatory classes before entering the freshman class.

When the constitution was amended to permit state support for high schools, the general pattern emerged for four year high school terms following seven year elementary school terms. This arrangement was governed more by the scarcity of money than by any theory which could be summoned to its support. However, it was claimed on the basis of comparisons that students having completed school under the 6-3-3 or 8-4 plan were not superior in the quality of college work to graduates from the 7-4 organization.[255] It was noted, however, that most of the state had or was planning a 12-grade public education program.

Some systems within the state were moving toward a span of 12 grades above the kindergarten. In 1938, Baldwin, Bibb, Chatham, Fulton, Glynn, Decatur and Thomas counties reported 2,658 students enrolled in the twelfth grade.[256] This was approximately one-sixth of their total eleventh grade enrollment. In each of these systems, the cost of the twelfth grade was borne by the local government.

The 7-4 pattern of organization continued on a statewide basis until 1947, when the 1937 law was amended to recognize the twelfth grade as part of the public school system. The twelfth grade was able to share in the free textbook program and to receive state funds.[257] In the meantime, all other states had adopted a minimum 12-year program of education supported by public funds.[258]

The stimulus for this law came from resolutions of the Georgia Association of School Administrators and the district meetings of the Georgia Education Association. A simultaneous effort was made to recognize kindergarten within the expanded school program. However, it was dropped to avoid delay in getting approval of the 12-year program.[259]

The bill providing for a seven-year elementary school and a five-year high school was approved by the legislature and signed into law on March 22, 1947. No money was appropriated at this session to finance the additional year. Except for those systems which had conducted 12-grade schools, most schools were not yet ready to implement the twelfth year. An effective transition to the expanded program would require several years of careful planning and professional guidance.

Superintendent Collins reported in September 1947 that a professional committee had reviewed textbooks suitable for the twelfth grade transition. He said the division of textbooks would honor requisitions although adoptions had not yet been made.[260]

A resolution presented to the State Board of Education by J. D. Cherry and L. M. Lester recommended that the board outline policies and regulations for the transition to a 12-grade public school system. The board approved the following policies. (1) To encourage all school systems to begin planning immediately for a 12-year program. (2) To permit each system to set the date for completion of the transition. (3) To permit each system to organize on the plan thought best suited to its needs and facilities, such as 8-4, 7-5, 6-6 or 6-3-3. (4) To make available sufficient personnel for consultative service to the systems desiring help. (5) To assume responsibility for the preparation of suitable guides outlining transitional procedures. (6) To provide a corresponding and equitable expansion for Negroes. (7) To set a date for the assumption of financial support of the expanded program.[261]

The state superintendent organized a study of transitional procedures [262] chaired by H. S. Shearouse.[263] A study guide was developed to help local study groups plan their local transitional programs.[264] Clinics held in each supervisory area during the spring of 1947 provided a forum by which superintendents and principals examined the new law and policies, and the state board learned reaction to certain transition policies. Fundamental agreements were reached, including the plan that local systems should adapt their programs from grades one through twelve to their present needs. Justification for the additional year of public school experience would be based on such an examination.

The executive committee, director and several other Department of Education personnel and representatives from teacher education institutions held a three-day meeting in August 1947 to prepare for consultant service.[265] Shearouse and his committee prepared criteria to test readiness for state aid. The criteria included four main provisions. (1) The school system must have gone through a period of transition for four years. (2) The system must have planned its program cooperatively with administrators, teachers, parents and the general public. (3) Six months before aid was expected, the system board must have presented a comprehensive developmental plan in writing to the Department of Education. (4) The system must have submitted a plan of program evaluation in writing to the State Department of Education before requesting financial support.[266]

The criteria were approved with minor modifications by the state board in December 1947. The state board recommended that all school systems should begin the transition for grades one, four and eight by September 1948.[267] The last provision was reinforced by a resolution from the Georgia Education Association in April 1948.

According to the indicated procedure, the transition would be completed within five years. For example, a school system initiating the program in the fall of 1948 should graduate its first 12-year class in 1953. During the period of transition, the State Department of Education sponsored local clinics and conferences for school personnel. In 1949, 16 curriculum conferences for principals were held over the state. In planning their transition procedures, they used the manual developed by the state department, a brochure of specific suggestions concerning the "Development of the Twelve-Year Program" prepared by a Program of Studies Committee composed of educational leaders throughout the state.[268]

More than 800 principals attended these conferences. Fifty-two consultants served in one or more of the meetings, besides those who were recruited from the teacher education institutions.

Superintendent Collins reported that about 60 percent of the systems not already operating on a 12-grade basis began the transition in 1948. Most of the remaining systems did so the following year. Six systems were further delayed by one or two years.[269] By 1953, all systems of the state had begun the transition. School systems entering the transition in 1947 graduated their first 12-year class in 1952; those entering transition in 1948 graduated their first class in 1953. By 1955, there were no 11-grade graduations.[270] Because many Georgia high schools had no graduating classes from 1951 to 1953, colleges keenly felt the transition's effect.

In his report for 1949-1950, Superintendent Collins noted the imminent need for state financing of the twelfth grade. He reminded local systems of an increasing need for buildings, transportation, teachers and textbooks to care for the increased enrollment. The increased birth rate of the war years had already begun to create a critical housing shortage. Soon the twelfth grade classes would increase the demand for space, especially in the urban centers where war surplus buildings and portable classrooms were being used as temporary housing for classrooms.[271]

School Buildings

Housing requirements for the twelfth grade added to Georgia's deficiencies in its school plant facilities. The physical inadequacies of Georgia's schools had been an issue since Superintendent Collins' mid-1940s action to determine their specific physical condition. In 1944, he employed L. O. Rogers to update information on the condition of school buildings.

Rogers visited as many schools as time and limited funds would permit, but with no funds to consolidate and upgrade schools, his many recommendations could not be effected. Before he could cover the state, the legislature created the Agricultural and Industrial Development Board, and Rogers was assigned to the Education Panel of that board with primary responsibility in the area of school buildings. The staff of the

State Department of Education was directed to assist in securing data for the Education Panel.[272]

After long and exhaustive work, the panel presented its findings on school building needs in January 1947. A digest of the summary of findings included the following.

- Deplorable schoolhouse conditions.
- There were too many schools, especially small ones.
- Negro schools were in worse condition than white schools.
- School systems did not have bonding capacity to construct the needed buildings.
- Very little planning had gone into schoolhouse construction.
- Most of the good facilities were in wealthier districts.
- The 1945 constitution eliminated local tax districts, thereby removing an area of inequality within a county. But the inequalities between counties and cities had not been removed.
- A large portion of state operating funds was being wasted for lack of housing facilities.
- County and city boards needed some incentive to aid in supplying more local funds for construction.
- Local comprehensive studies were needed in each county and city to determine possible consolidations and other school plant needs.
- The State Department of Education needed to furnish professionally trained personnel to assist local systems in planning for future needs.
- Legal provisions were needed for the state to underwrite financially the construction of needed schoolhouses.[273]

The 1947 session of the General Assembly accepted the panel's report seriously. While the specific statistical data were from 100 sample systems, a tabulation of the needs for the state as a whole was incomplete. Legislative leaders asked Collins to determine immediately the number of standard classrooms in the state. The state school supervisors completed a thorough statewide count of usable and non-usable classrooms. Results were startling. Not only were data from the 100 sample systems typical, but the statewide coverage further substantiated the need for a revolution in schoolhouse construction.

The 1949 Minimum Foundation Program for Education concentrated on a state capital outlay program. When the act was approved, the capital outlay phase included

- An annual allocation to each system of at least $200 per state-allotted teacher.
- Allotment of additional funds for exceptional needs.
- Allotments to be adjusted by local systems' bonding ability.
- Establishment by State Board of Education of minimum criteria to be met by local systems in order to qualify for participation in the capital outlay grants.
- Establishment by State Board of Education of priorities in the use of capital outlay funds.
- Provision for State Board of Education to conduct surveys of school plant needs in all local systems.[274]

Though funds were not appropriated for financing the 1949 act, a 1951 Sales Tax Act financed the entire foundation program. By this time, Collins and legislative leaders had determined that the minimum $200 per state-allotted teacher on an annual basis would inadequately fund long-range planning and construction. Georgia's constitution prohibited the issuance of state bonds. To ameliorate this desperate dilemma, the legislature created the State School Building Authority[275] and subsequently amended the foundation law to permit local boards of education and the State Board of Education to contract with the State School Building Authority.[276]

Immediately following the enactment of the 1951 amendment to the foundation law, the State Board of Education initiated school plant surveys in each school system in the state. These surveys determined the needs to construct buildings to remove students from overcrowded or sub-standard classrooms and consolidate small schools into more comprehensive programs.[277]

The State Board of Education received an appropriation from the General Assembly for allocations to the various school systems for capital outlay purposes. The 1951 session of the Georgia General Assembly created the State School

Building Authority, an agency whose bonds could pay the costs of school building construction.[278]

The State Board of Education developed a formula for the allocation of capital outlay funds to the various school systems; it was based on a space allotment per student at $7.50 per square foot plus 10 percent for architect's fees and contingencies, less one-half of the school system's bonding capacity. Allocation of funds was based on the number of students to be housed, the number of grades to be taught, the number of classrooms and other special facilities.

Under this program, the state, theoretically, had housed all students by the time projects under the 1955 bond series were completed. Therefore, the 1960 series included construction for increases in ADA since 1951. The annual allotments in 1960 were based on (1) $50 for each state-allotted teacher; and (2) $18 for each student increase in ADA since 1951. For a school system to receive funds for increased attendance, the system must have been bonded to one-half of its bonding capacity.[279]

Curriculum Development, 1937-1948

With the initiation of the Georgia Program for the Improvement of Instruction in 1933 by State School Superintendent M. D. Collins, the state embarked on one of its most extensive curriculum studies. Up to this time the few short term studies initiated had been given little direction from the state. This study, begun prior to the 1937 Seven Months School Law, had great impact on the direction the schools would take in the immediate future.

Collins, aware of the legal structure restricting the public school system, sought the state's best professional and legal advice. M. J. Rice has described the legal framework under which Georgia schools operate as follows.

> The four sources of Georgia School Law are the Constitution, the statutes, administrative regulations, and decisions of the Courts. Emanating from the sovereign, the Constitution of the State is fundamental and controlling; the statutes represent the legislative initiative; and administrative regulations combine a quasi-legislative

power with discretion of the executive. While the judiciary has no legislative initiative, Court decisions constitute the final and authoritative exposition of the law, irrespective of the source.[1]

Curriculum had been regarded traditionally as both the prescribed courses of study and content control through textbooks or other educational media and as the methodology of instruction. Sufficient data indicate that most early curricular research concentrated on the courses of study and textbooks and library materials. New concepts were evolving in Georgia regarding the scope and content of curricular offerings; the Georgia Program for the Improvement of Instruction focused on fundamental teaching techniques. In order to insure understanding of the program, great efforts were made to enroll teachers in cooperative curriculum study. The Georgia colleges responded generously to the request for help; summer schools offered many courses in curriculum, with special emphasis directed to the following.

- Fundamentals of Curriculum-making. For teachers, principals, supervisors and superintendents who expect to actively participate in the State Curriculum Program. Provides a comprehensive program of the public school's role in a democratic society.
- Planning of Curriculum Materials for Elementary or Secondary Grades. Classroom applications of the new curriculum principles. Prerequisite: Fundamentals of Curriculum-making.[2]

College instructors for these courses were drawn from the most progressive teachers' colleges and public school classrooms in America.[3] Library collections were expanded, sometimes with special curriculum laboratories. The State Department of Education offered credit for curriculum courses.[4] These early college courses in curriculum aided teachers in setting goals, formulating a common philosophy with administrators and patrons and creating a better understanding of Georgia's problems in order to more effectively meet the needs of Georgia's youth.

The Georgia Program for the Improvement of Instruction published a preliminary report in 1936 with specific recommendations for securing data on health, resources, citizenship, natural environment, social needs and spiritual values. The report recommended using education to acquire and transmit the social heritage and to conserve and improve human and material resources. This first major publication of the staff gave the school leaders a fundamental direction.

The early study group published its outstanding Bulletin No. I, "The Organization and Conduct of Teacher Study Groups," in September 1935. The bulletin, sometimes called "The Blue Book," was reprinted in 1936 and revised in 1937. In the foreword, Collins and Chancellor S. V. Sanford of the university system describe their philosophy regarding instruction.

> . . . After all is said and done, school finance, school organization, school administration and supervision exist for but one end—namely, to provide for boys and girls the most desirable situation possible for learning under teacher guidance, in the schoolrooms in Georgia. Nothing about school affairs is so important as the standard of work done by classroom teachers.
>
> This program for the improvement of instruction is essentially a teacher-training program. The teachers and administrators of Georgia should miss no opportunity to ally themselves heartily with this understanding. No sacrifice of time, energy or money is too great when the best education possible for the future citizens of Georgia is at stake.

The Blue Book suggested the following topics for the study courses.

Topic I. The Need for a Changed Education
Topic II. The New Meaning of the Curriculum
Topic III. A Democratic Educational Program
Topic IV. Individual Differences in Pupils
Topic V. The Effect of Mental Discipline on the Schools
Topic VI. College Entrance Requirements and the Public Schools
Topic VII. Education in Progressive Schools
Topic VIII. Psychological Foundation of Education
Topic IX. Learning in the Modern School

Topic X. The Place of Subject Matter in Education
Topic XI. Methods of Learning and Teaching
Topic XII. The Activity Program
Topic XIII. The Integrated School Program
Topic XIV. An Educational Program for Adults
Topic XV. Aims and Objectives in Education
Topic XVI. Curriculum Improvement
Topic XVII. The Learning Experience
Topic XVIII. Planning a Learning Experience
Topic XIX. Guidance in the Learning Experiences of Pupils
Topic XX. Evaluation in the Learning Experiences of Pupils

Each topic included an outline for study, suggested procedures and a full bibliography. The bulletin was recognized by Columbia University Teachers College as one of the outstanding curriculum publications of the country.[5]

Bulletin No. 2, entitled "Guide to Curriculum Improvement" or "Red Book," was published in 1937 and reprinted in 1942. Dealing extensively with such problems as philosophy, aims, scope and content of the curriculum, it also emphasized the relationship of the curriculum to the learner and to the community. Segregation of groups and race relations were issues addressed during this period when Georgia's constitution (Art. VIII, Section 1, Par. 1) still required separate schools. The section thoughtfully concluded with

... There are certain definite procedures for both white and colored schools that will make for this (bring to pass whatever wisdom suggests as right) and these should have a place in the curriculum of the schools. They should be worked out with great care for they involve controversial issues, but the problem is too vital to the well-being of all the people of Georgia and the school is too appropriate an agency for effective help in this matter for prejudice and short-sightedness to bar the way to a sensible course of action.[6]

Bulletin No. 2 related curriculum improvement to health, state history, standard of living, rural life, the democratic school and basic principles of education. This bulletin has been referred to for decades as a guide for curriculum study. Its bibliography continues to be a viable source for professional study.

The Journal of the Georgia Education Association published a monthly article, "Curriculum Page," edited by Dr. Mildred English from Georgia State College for Women, Milledgeville. The article reported the latest developments in the curriculum improvement program as well as news of local school systems' curriculum studies. The Journal reached almost all of the teachers in the state and was a source of enlightenment to those who were becoming more and more interested in the movement. The "Curriculum Page," appearing in the Journal from 1936 through 1939, carried such items as

- December, 1937, Vol. 30. No. 4. p. 35 announced the reprinting of the Blue Book with details on contents. Also had an article about a State Department of Education publication on problems of the modern curriculum to be used as a basis for study groups—a guide for uninstructed group leaders.

- October, 1937, Vol. 30. No. 2. p. 30 announced source materials of Scope Committee as follows
  A. Elizabeth Donovan, "Maintaining Physical, Mental, and Emotional Health."
  B. Paul Chapman, "Earning a Living."
  C. S. G. Brinkley, "Performing the Responsibilities of Citizenship."
  D. Paul Morrow, "Utilizing and Controlling the Natural Environment for Individual and Social Needs."
  E. T. E. Smith, "Source Materials of People and Commodities and Communicating with One Another."
  F. Mildred English, "Expressing Esthetic and Spiritual Impulses."
  G. L. M. Lester, "Utilizing Education as a Means of Acquiring and Transmitting the Social Heritage."
  This issue also announced that the fall district meetings of the GEA would be built around the Georgia Program for the Improvement of Instruction.

- January 1938, Vol. 30. No. 5. p. 16 announced four new publications of the State Department of Education on curriculum or related resources. Edited by Dr. Paul Morrow, they were

Georgia—Past and Present
Georgia Agriculture
Information on Natural Resources
Information on Industry and Commerce.

This issue of the Journal also announced a forthcoming bulletin on textbooks to be used as a guide to schools which maintain a traditional curriculum, as well as those schools in transition away from the traditional, and for schools which have departed altogether from traditional programs.

* May 1938, Vol. 30. No. 9. p. 34 carried announcements of curriculum courses to be offered in colleges during the summer of 1938 and included articles pertaining to textbooks and materials bureaus.

Another significant publication, entitled "A Teacher's Guide for Child, Adult, and Community Development in Negro Elementary Schools of Georgia," was developed by Negro educational leaders. Chapters included, "Guiding Principles of the Georgia Curriculum Program," "The Community as a Source of Materials of Instruction," "Life-Related Enterprise in Agreement with the Georgia Curriculum Program" and "Co-operative Supervision" ending with a full appendix and bibliography. A follow-up guide, Bulletin No. 4A entitled, "Guide to Life-Related Teaching in the Negro High Schools of Georgia," emphasized Negro high school curriculum. It provided self-study plans and an excellent bibliography.

Bulletin No. 3A, "A Practice Book for Observation and Teaching in Small Rural Schools," was edited by Mrs. Helen A. Whiting, state supervisor of colored elementary schools. Aimed at the pre-service teacher, it filled the gap between college theory and classroom practice by providing techniques for reading improvement and other school curriculum problems. Bulletin No. 3A became a useful daily guide for planning and developing life-related teaching under the direction of the state supervisors and the Jeanes supervising teachers.[7]

Georgia Program for the Improvement of Instruction issued other special interest publications relating to conservation, citizenship, parent participation, transportation, communications and occupational guidance. Though some educators disapproved of this shift from traditional instruction, the literature indicated that education in Georgia was becoming more alive for the students, whose interest in school work was showing an appreciable increase.

As studies in the field of curriculum development progressed, the State Board of Education in 1937 listed course work in curriculum and methods among the requirements for teaching certificates. Specifications for the courses stated in part

> This course should aim to develop the ability to organize and use specialized and integrated curricula, to meet the needs of (students to be taught—elementary or high school).
>
> Courses other than those given above should be offered only by institutions as are equipped for the purpose. Permission to give these additional courses for credit must be obtained from the State Department of Education.
>
> ... A professional certificate should include courses in the analysis, selection, adaptation, organization and development of instructional materials in integrated fields (on elementary or high school levels).
>
> Directed observation of the best teaching practice, and supervised teaching in typical (elementary or high school) situations.[8]

At its meeting on May 8, 1937, the State Board of Education appointed a committee to study the high school course work and make recommendations to the State Board of Education. This committee included

B. M. Grier, president of GEA

T. J. Dempsey, H. S. supervisor

J. C. Dixon, Rosenwald Foundation

Dr. Paul R. Morrow, University of Georgia

M. E. Thompson, director of study

H. T. McIntosh, chairman, Georgia Planning Commission

C. C. Center, president, Georgia Congress of PTA

Dr. Paul Chapman, University of Georgia

Ralph Ramsey, secretary of GEA

L. M. Lester, State Department of Education
W. E. Knox, superintendent, Jones County Schools
J. R. Greene, superintendent, Elberton City Schools
C. W. Peacock, superintendent, LaFayette City Schools
C. L. Purcell, superintendent, Habersham County Schools
W. E. Pafford, superintendent, Millen City Schools
Ralph Newton, superintendent, Waycross City Schools
Willis A. Sutton, superintendent, Atlanta City Schools
Ethel Adams, principal, Moultrie High School
Dorothy Haines, Richmond County Schools
E. V. Welchel, principal, Cook County High School [9]

These 20 educators served for several months in completing this study assigned by the State Board of Education.

The persons listed above comprised the major committee members. There were scores of subcommittee members at work throughout the state. Negro educational leaders assumed heavy responsibility for assistance in the Negro schools of the state. Among the Negroes in leadership roles were Helen A. Whiting, C. L. Harper, C. V. Troup, A. Z. Traylor, W. H. Dennis, R. W. Gadsden, Melvin Heard and Graham Jackson. They contributed to studies, seminars and the development of literature.

The 1939 Legislative Committee on Efficiency and Economy in Government recommended reducing the personnel who wrote and published the educational bulletins.[10] The State Board of Education complied with these recommendations and reduced its personnel accordingly.[11] Though the production of materials almost ceased, the implementation of curriculum seminars and study groups continued under the momentum generated by the state's leaders.

In January 1940, the curriculum committee submitted a report to the State Board of Education which reviewed public school activity and praised the recent studies of teachers and patrons. The report referred to the Free Textbook Law's impact on the school systems. One committee member's comment, "Georgia, undoubtedly, has one of the best programs for furnishing instructional materials to be found in the nation," reveals the curriculum committee's general feeling. The report recommended expanding commercial work, industrial arts, social science and language arts programs; providing better public school libraries and reducing the number of workbooks used by some school systems.[12] The next report, submitted in March 1940, stressed the need for a closer relationship between the curriculum committee and the textbook committee.[13]

Although the State Board of Education had reduced its publishing personnel in compliance with legislative recommendations, a Health Education Curriculum Bulletin was issued in May 1941. This guide encouraged using the many community agencies and resources in the local health programs.

In September 1942, another publication, "What the Schools Can Do to Help Win the War," provided a guide for the Victory Corps schools. Meetings were held throughout the state in 1942 for implementation of Victory Corps curricula. Schools were adjusting their programs to conform with the major areas suggested by the Victory Corps Plan—(1) land service, which called for preinduction training for all branches of the Army except the air; (2) air service; (3) sea service, which provided training for all branches of Navy except the air; (4) production service, which included preparation for war industries and agriculture and (5) community service, which consisted of preparation for medical nursing, teaching and business and civic services. Students who met qualifications for a particular service were awarded special insignia by the State Victory Corps Program. With more than 80 percent of the schools participating within the first year of operation, the state moved into nearly 100 percent cooperation before the end of the second year. The objectives of the program were (1) guidance of youth into critical services and occupations, (2) wartime citizenship training to insure better understanding of the war, (3) physical fitness, (4) voluntary military drill for boys, (5) competence in science and mathematics, (6) pre-flight training in aeronautics for those preparing for air service, (7) pre-induction training for critical occupations and (8) community service, including training for essential civilian activities.[14]

The *Georgia Education Journal* regularly published articles on developing local Victory Corps programs. Early emphasis on high school level activities included elementary schools which had become actively involved in the war effort. The Victory Corps program was not merely attached to the regular curriculum, it *was* the curriculum.

The Victory School Program revealed several new truths to all school people. (1) Educators on all levels can work cooperatively for a common goal. (2) Students can contribute to the curriculum planning procedure. (3) Education needs to include children under age six. (4) Teacher education needs more functional programs. (5) Education should be functional as well as theoretical.[15]

After the war the curriculum movement received a boost from the Southern Association of Colleges and Secondary Schools, which required all member schools to conduct self-studies of their entire school programs. Member schools were required to conduct studies every five years, while schools applying for new membership were required to conduct self-studies as well as studies by a committee. All schools used evaluative criteria established by the National Study of Secondary School Evaluation. In order to qualify, schools described their own philosophy of education, aims and objectives, and then evaluated their entire program in terms of these aims, objectives and philosophy. For many years, only schools with great local financial support could afford to meet Southern Association accreditation standards and membership fees. With school consolidation and better facilities, more schools qualified for membership.

In January 1947 the State Board of Education appointed a committee of school superintendents and principals to work on legislation for implementing a 12-grade school system.[16] Later that year the General Assembly approved the twelfth grade as part of the public school system.[17] While some of the larger and wealthier school systems had operated 12-grade schools for several years at local expense, most systems had been limited to 11 grades for their entire existence.

For the latter school systems, the State Board of Education enacted regulations requiring them to undergo a four year study in order to make reasonable and effective transition from 11 grades to 12 grades. The State Board of Education assumed responsibility for furnishing guides and consultants to the school systems for making the required studies.[18]

H. S. Shearouse was appointed director of the transition study. Personnel of the department organized ten seminars, four hours each, to thoroughly study transitional procedures. During the seminars the staff developed a study guide for the local school systems, entitled, "Study Guide for the Transition to a Twelve-Year Program."

In May 1947 a series of local clinics acquainted superintendents, principals, visiting teachers and instructional supervisors with legislation and possible transitional procedures. A fundamental agreement was reached that local systems should study their present programs and, in the light of their local needs, develop programs locally for grades one through 12.

The executive committee and director, together with staff of the Department of Education and selected personnel of the teacher training institutions, met for three days in August 1947, to prepare themselves as consultants to local systems. About 100 people attended this conference.

The executive committee and director prepared criteria for state aid for 12 grades of public education. These criteria were presented to several school groups which included the annual convention of the Georgia Association of School Administrators in October 1947.

On December 4 and 5, 1947, Shearouse presented "Criteria for Qualifying for State Aid for the Twelve-year Program" to the State Board of Education. The adopted criteria follow.

* A system (County or Independent) receiving aid for the twelfth grade, shall offer a twelve-year program of education for all the children in the system. The system shall have gone through a period of transition of not less than four years with the exception of those systems which had 12 years prior to September 1947. The State Board of Education recommends that the transition begin in grades one, four and eight, and it expects all systems that have not started the transition period to begin it in all schools by September 1948.

* A system (County or Independent) shall plan its program (grades one through 12) cooperatively, with all people concerned having an opportunity to share in the

planning. (As administrators, teachers, lay people and students.)

- Six months before aid is expected, the board of education (County or Independent) shall adopt a comprehensive developmental program of education for the system, and the superintendent shall submit this comprehensive plan of its program (grades one through 12) in writing to the State Department of Education.
- A system shall plan for a program of evaluation and submit the plan in writing to the State Department of Education before asking for aid. (A system should show progress in the areas which will be set up by a Statewide Professional Committee on Program of Studies.) [19]

Approximately 60 percent of the 11-grade school systems entered the 12-grade study in the 1947-48 school term. The representative assembly of the Georgia Education Association passed the following resolution encouraging all systems to enter the program at the earliest convenience. "Whereas, the General Assembly of 1947 passed a permissive bill providing for the twelfth grade as part of the public school program, and Whereas, many school systems have initiated the twelfth grade program; Therefore, Be it Resolved That the 81st Session of the Georgia Education Association ask that all school systems move into a 12-year program as soon as possible." [20]

The transition plan considered to have the greatest merit used the eighth grade as the transition grade and planned a new program for grades one through 12. Because all grades would be examined, and each would undergo some alteration to make a complete program of 12 grades, beginning with the eighth grade, the first graduation for a 12-year class would occur the fifth year after the program was initiated.

By the mid-1950s all schools had completed their transition study and had graduated a 12-year class. Those systems which had implemented their studies in fall 1947 were able to hold a 12-year graduation in the spring of 1952.

The transition had provided a great impetus for school leaders to review and re-examine their schools both philosophically and physically. The extra grade promoted a need for schoolhouse construction. In that regard, the curricular changes and facility changes complemented each other.

CHAPTER IV

1937-1949

1. Georgia Department of Education *Annual Report*, 1935-36, p. 4.
2. "The 15-Mill Tax Amendment," *Georgia Education Journal* (October 1936), p. 7.
3. "Taxes," *Georgia Education Journal* (September 1935), p. 22.
4. J. Harold Saxon, "President's Message," *Georgia Education Journal* (September 1935), p. 11.
5. Peggy Steelmon, "Growth and Development of the Georgia Education Association" (unpublished doctoral dissertation, University of Georgia, Athens, 1966), p. 148.
6. "Our Legislative Program," *Georgia Education Journal* (February 1937), p. 6.
7. *Georgia Laws*, 1937, pp. 882-892.
8. *Ibid.*, pp. 896-901.
9. M. D. Collins, "What the Legislature Did for Georgia Schools," *Georgia Education Journal* (September 1937), p. 14.
10. Georgia Board of Education, *Regulations for Administering the Seven Months School Law*, 1937, p. 2.
11. Oscar Hardy Joiner, "A Comparison of Local and Non-Local Teachers as to Their Training and Salaries, (unpublished master's thesis, Duke University, Durham, North Carolina, 1939), pp. 59-61.
12. *Georgia Laws*, 1937, p. 896.
13. Georgia Department of Education *Annual Report*, 1937-38, p. 26.
14. *Ibid.*, p. 17.
15. *Georgia Laws*, 1935, p. 78.
16. *Georgia Laws*, 1937, sec. 10.
17. *A Survey of Public Education of Less Than College Grade in Georgia*, University of Georgia, 1947, p. 181.
18. *Ibid.*, pp. 181-82.
19. *Ibid.*, p. 182.
20. Georgia Department of Education *Annual Report*, 1937-38, p. 11.
21. "Our Legislative Program," *Georgia Education Journal* (February, 1937, p. 6.
22. Collins, "What the Legislature Did for Georgia Schools," p. 14.
23. Georgia Department of Education *Annual Report*, 1937-38, p. 1.
24. I. A. Dickerson, "A Study of Vocational and Technical Education in Georgia" (paper presented to G. L. O'Kelley, Jr., of the faculty of the Department of Vocational Education, University of Georgia, Athens, in fulfillment of the requirement for Education 973, 1969), p. 15.
25. Georgia Department of Education *Annual Report*, 1938, p. 23.
26. Dickerson, p. 15.
27. Georgia Department of Education *Annual Report*, 1940, p. 37.
28. Letter, Attorney General M. J. Yeomans to Dr. M. D. Collins, state superintendent of schools, June 21, 1937, Georgia Archives.
29. Georgia Department of Education *Annual Report*, 1938, p. 18.
30. *Georgia Laws*, 1937, pp. 864-869.
31. Georgia Department of Education *Annual Report*, 1938, p. 27.
32. Carl G. Renfroe, "The Growth and Development of Teacher Certification in Georgia" (unpublished doctoral dissertation, University Georgia, Athens, 1964), p. 184.
33. *Annual Report* from the Regents of the University of Georgia, 1935, p. 49.
34. *Ibid.*
35. Letter, Marvin S. Pittman to Georgia school superintendents, spring 1937.

36. *Ibid.*
37. Letter, Marvin S. Pittman to applicants for scholarship to prepare for rural supervision, spring 1937.
38. Letter, Jane Franseth to recipients of scholarship to prepare for rural supervision, June 10, 1937.
39. Georgia Board of Education, *Minutes* (June 15, 1938), p. 11.
40. *Georgia Education Journal* (November 1938), p. 36.
41. *Georgia Education Journal* (December 1938), p. 30.
42. *Ibid.*
43. James C. Bonner, *The Georgia Story*, p. 426.
44. "The Light Must Not Fail," *Georgia Education Journal* (February 1939), p. 9.
45. Bonner, p. 427.
46. *Georgia Laws*, 1938, Stabilization Fund.
47. "Resolutions of the Georgia Education Association," *Georgia Education Journal* (September 1938), p. 26.
48. "From the Editor's Desk," *Georgia Education Journal* (October 1938), p. 7.
49. Georgia General Assembly, *Senate Journal* (January 24, 1939), p. 81.
50. Georgia General Assembly, *House Journal* (January 24, 1939), p. 177.
51. *Ibid.*, p. 178.
52. *Ibid.*, p. 177.
53. "The ABC of the School Situation in Georgia," *Georgia Education Journal* (May 1939), p. 10.
54. Georgia Board of Education, *Minutes* (August 23, 1939).
55. Georgia Board of Education, *Minutes* (February 13, 1939).
56. "Resolutions of the G.E.A. Representative Assembly," *Georgia Education Journal* (March 1939), p. 23.
57. "The ABC of the School Situation in Georgia," *Georgia Education Journal* (May 1939), pp. 8-11, 28.
58. *Ibid.*, p. 10.
59. Georgia Board of Education, *Minutes* (February 13, 1939).
60. Georgia Board of Education, *Minutes* (April 4-5, 1939).
61. Economy and Efficiency Committee, *Report*, p. 12.
62. Georgia General Assembly, *Senate Journal*, 1939, p. 208.
63. *Ibid.*
64. *Ibid.*
65. Georgia General Assembly, *House Journal* (March 13, 1939), p. 1282.
66. "Editorial," *Georgia Education Journal* (April 1939), p. 7.
67. "Resolutions of the Representative Assembly, Georgia Education Association," *Georgia Education Journal* (May 1939), p. 13.
68. "Resolutions by Bulloch Teachers," *Georiga Education Journal* (March 1939), p. 36.
69. *Milledgeville Union Recorder* (March 20, 1939), p. 3.
70. "The Accredited High Schools of Georgia," University of Georgia, *Bulletin*, (October 1939), p. 7.
71. "The Accredited High Schools of Georgia," University of Georgia, *Bulletin*, (1940-41), p. 9.
72. *Georgia Laws*, 1939, H. R. No. 9 and 206. Bound copy of report is in Georgia law library, dated June 3, 1939. Chapter two of report shows recommended appropriations for each of the several departments of state government including education. Chapter three covers economies recommended by the committee.
73. "Audio-Visual Conference," *Georgia Education Journal* (November 1937), p. 7.
74. Georgia Department of Education *Annual Report*, 1937-38, p. 22.
75. Advertisement for General Extension, *Georgia Education Journal* (November 1937), p. 3.

76. Economy and Efficiency Committee, *Report*, February 3, 1939.
77. Georgia Board of Education, *Minutes* (February 13, 1938).
78. Sara Jones, *School Libraries*, unpublished manuscript, Georgia Department of Education (Atlanta, 1972), pp. 1-4.
79. *Ibid.*, p. 5.
80. Georgia Department of Education *Annual Report*, 1937-38, p. 18.
81. Grace Hightower, *Growth of Libraries in the Public Schools of Georgia*, (unpublished doctoral dissertation, Peabody Library School, Nashville, 1965 , p. 23.
82. "Statement of Policy," *Georgia Education Journal* (April 1940), p. 7.
83. "Here They Stand," *Georgia Education Journal* (August 1940), p. 8.
84. Georgia General Assembly, *Senate Journal*, 1941.
85. J. I. Allman, "President's Message," *Georgia Education Journal* (February 1941), p. 8.
86. Jones, p. 6.
87. Hightower, p. 25.
88. Georgia Board of Education, *Minutes* (July 1, 1940).
89. Georgia Department of Education *Annual Report*, 1932, p. 68.
90. Hightower, p. 58.
91. *Ibid.,* p. 61.
92. *Ibid.*, p. 58.
93. *Ibid.*, p. 61.
94. *Report* of School Library Clinics, 1941. Files of the Library Services Unit, Georgia Department of Education.
95. *Georgia Education Journal* (February 1942), pp. 25-26.
96. Georgia Department of Education *Annual Report*, 1941-42, p. 27.
97. Georgia Department of Education *Annual Report*, 1939-40, p. 22.
98. Georgia Board of Education, *Minutes* (March 19, 1940).
99. *Ibid.*, p. 42.
100. Oscar H. Joiner, *Education in the States: Historical Development and Outlook*, 1969, p. 264.
101. Charles E. Proll, *State Programs for the Improvement of Teacher Education*, American Council on Education (Washington, D. C., 1946), p. 329.
102. *Ibid.*, p. 330.
103. *Ibid.*, p. 375.
104. *Ibid.*, p. 332.
105. *Ibid.*, p. 335.
106. *Ibid.*, p. 346.
107. L. D. Haskew, *The Educational Clinic*, American Council on Education (Washington, D. C., 1949), pp. 1-7.
108. H. S. Shearouse, *Historical Statement of the Teacher Standards Movement in Georgia* (unpublished manuscript, Georgia Department of Education, Atlanta), p. 3.
109. Georgia Department of Education *Annual Report*, 1944, pp. 64-65.
110. Georgia Board of Education, *Minutes* (April 23, 1943), p. 12.
111. Georgia Department of Education, *Short History of Certification*, 1958-60, p. 1.
112. Janie Hearn, *History of Certification in Georgia* (unpublished manuscript, 1944), p. 10.
113. Shearouse, p. 2.
114. *Georgia Laws*, 1870, State Board of Education.
115. *Georgia Laws*, 1911, p. 95.
116. Georgia Department of Education *Annual Report*, 1910, p. 18.
117. *Georgia Laws*, 1937, H. B. 125.
118. *Georgia Laws*, 1937, pp. 882-901.
119. *Ibid.*
120. Georgia Board of Education, *Minutes* (January 15, 1941).
121. *Ibid.*, September 18, 1940.
122. *Ibid.*, June 13, 1941.

123. *Georgia Laws*, 1943, p. 55.
124. *Ibid.*, p. 635.
125. Georgia Department of Education *Annual Report*, 1942, pp. 38-46.
126. "Georgia Wartime Education Commission," *Georgia Education Journal* (September 1942), p. 7.
127. Georgia Department of Education *Annual Report*, 1941-1942, p. 40.
128. *Ibid.*
129. O. C. Aderhold, "Pass the Ammunition," *Georgia Education Journal* (December 1942), p. 21.
130. *Bulletin I*, (Victory Corps Series), U. S. Office of Education, Washington, D. C., 1942.
131. Georgia Board of Education, *Minutes* (November 12, 1942).
132. Aderhold, p. 21.
133. Georgia Board of Education, *Minutes* (November 12, 1942).
134. Aderhold, "Pass the Ammunition," p. 21.
135. Thomas E. McDonough, "Physical Fitness War Time Program for High School Victory Corps," *Georgia Education Journal* (February 1943), p. 20.
136. O. C. Aderhold, "Georgia High Schools Organize Victory Corps," *Georgia Education Journal* (June 1943), p. 8.
137. *Ibid.*
138. "Outstanding Educational Events of 1942," *Georgia Education Journal* (February 1943), p. 25.
139. O. C. Aderhold, "Georgia Victory School Program," *Georgia Education Journal* (January 1944), p. 15.
140. *Ibid.*
141. *Ibid.*
142. *Ibid.*
143. Education Panel, *Survey of Education*, 1947, p. 187.
144. *Ibid.*
145. Georgia Board of Education, *Minutes* (February 23, 1943).
146. *Ibid.*, (April 23, 1943).
147. *Ibid.*, (January 28, 1944).
148. Education Panel, p. 190.
149. *Ibid.*
150. Flanagan, *School Food Services*, 1969, p. 566.
151. *Georgia Reports of Cases Decided in Supreme Court of the State of Georgia*, v. 224, pp. 10-11.
152. *Ibid.*
153. "Personalities," *Georgia Education Journal* (January 1946), p. 5.
154. Education Panel, *School Leader's Manual*, Georgia Department of Education (Atlanta, Georgia, 1945), p. iii.
155. *Ibid.*, p. iv.
156. *Ibid.*, pp. 3-19.
157. *Ibid.*, p. iv.
158. *Ibid.*
159. *Ibid.*, p. iii.
160. *Georgia Laws*, 1951, pp. 626-627.
161. "Education Panel," *Georgia Education Journal* (May 1947), p. 23.
162. Mark Smith, "Retirement System for Georgia Teachers," *Georgia Education Journal* (December 1935), p. 8.
163. J. H. Greene, "Plans for Teacher Retirement," *Georgia Education Journal* (December 1938), p. 16.
164. *Georgia Laws*, 1939, p. 372.
165. Ralph Ramsey, "Teacher Retirement," *Georgia Education Journal* (February 1943), pp. 7-8.
166. *Ibid.*
167. L. D. Askew, "Immediate Steps Necessary," *Georgia Education Journal* (May 1942), p. 20.
168. Ramsey, pp. 7-8.

169. *Georgia Education Journal* (December 1942), p. 36.
170. Ramsey, p. 7.
171. "Questions and Answers," *Georgia Education Journal* (December 1942), p. 14.
172. *Georgia Education Journal* (May 1943), p. 25.
173. *Georgia Education Journal* (February 1943), pp. 7-8.
174. Georgia Board of Education, *Minutes* (April 23, 1943).
175. *Georgia Education Journal* (November 1943), p. 15.
176. *Georgia Education Journal* (October 1943), pp. 16-21.
177. "Georgia Teacher Retirement Law," *Georgia Education Journal* (October 1943), p. 16.
178. *Georgia Education Journal* (December 1942), p. 14.
179. "Facts About Teacher Retirement," *Georgia Education Journal* (November 1943), p. 28.
180. Georgia *Civil Code*, secs. 32-2901-32-2932.
181. The author assisted in these campaigns with individuals and groups enumerated in the text, with the advice and direction of State School Superintendent M. D. Collins and the staff of the Georgia Department of Education.
182. Cullen B. Goswell and C. David Anderson, *Government and Administration of Georgia* (New York: Thomas Y. Crowell), pp. 26-27.
183. *Ibid.*, p. 28.
184. State of Georgia, *Constitution of 1945* Article VIII.
185. "Education in the New Constitution," *Georgia Education Journal* (May 1945), p. 28.
186. *Ibid.*, p. 30.
187. *Ibid.*, p. 28.
188. H. S. Shearouse, "Need to Professionalize the County School Superintendent," *Georgia Education Journal* (November 1945), p. 22.
189. *Ibid.*, p. 32.
190. Education Panel, *A Survey of Public Education*, p. 28.
191. *Ibid.*
192. *Ibid.*, p. 29.
193. "Resolutions," *Georgia Education Journal* (May 1947), pp. 23-25.
194. *Georgia Education Journal* (December 1942), p. 34.
195. *Georgia Education Journal* (December 1943), p. 20.
196. *Georgia Education Journal* (May 1944), p. 16.
197. *Georgia Education Journal* (January 1945), p. 5.
198. *Georgia Laws*, 1945, p. 343.
199. *Georgia Laws*, 1945, p. 344.
200. Georgia Board of Education, *Minutes* (June 1, 1945).
201. Claude Purcell, "The Compulsory Attendance Law," *Georgia Education Journal* (October 1945), p. 10.
202. Georgia Department of Education *Annual Report*, 1949-50, p. 21.
203. "Headlines and Highlights of District Meetings," *Georgia Education Journal* (December 1946), p. 16.
204. *Georgia Laws*, 1946, p. 67.
205. *Ibid.*, p. 72.
206. *Ibid.*, p. 70.
207. Copy of current employment form.
208. Report on current practice from office of superintendent, Baldwin County Schools.
209. *Georgia Laws*, 1945, pp. 343-346; and *State Board of Education Policies*, July 1945, (published January 1, 1957, pp. 9-16) outline many duties of visiting teachers, but abstain from any reference to employment roles.
210. Georgia Department of Education *Annual Report*, 1942, pp. 38-46.
211. John T. Wheeler, *Two Hundred Years of Agricultural Education in Georgia* (Danville, Illinois, 1948), p. 306.
212. Georgia Department of Education *Annual Report*, 1946, p. 26.

213. Georgia Department of Education *Annual Report*, 1948, p. 32.
214. Georgia Department of Education *Annual Report*, 1948, pp. 32, 36-37.
215. Georgia Department of Education *Annual Report*, 1946, p. 29.
216. Janet McGarity Barber, *The History and Development of the Georgia Association of Future Homemakers of America, 1944-45* (unpublished master's thesis, University of Georgia, Athens, 1966), p. 15.
217. *Chapter Guides, Facts and Figures*, National Office of Future Homemakers of America (Washington, D. C., 1974), p. 5.
218. Georgia Department of Education *Annual Report*, 1946, p. 29.
219. Georgia Department of Education *Annual Report*, 1948, pp. 36-37.
220. Dickerson, *A Study of Vocational and Technical Education in Georgia*, p. 15.
221. Georgia Department of Education *Annual Report*, 1940, p. 37.
222. Georgia Department of Education *Annual Report*, 1946, pp. 30-31.
223. Georgia Department of Education *Annual Report*, 1942.
224. *Ibid.*, pp. 38-46.
225. Statements of Mark Davis, personal interview.
226. Georgia Department of Education *Annual Report*, 1946, pp. 30-34.
227. Georgia Department of Education *Annual Report*, 1948, p. 46.
228. Georgia Department of Education *Annual Report*, 1942, pp. 38-46.
229. Georgia Department of Education *Annual Report*, 1946, p. 45.
230. R. E. Bodenhamer, *A History of the Development of Area Vocational-Technical Schools in Georgia*, (educational paper submitted in partial fulfillment in the requirement for EVO 965, 1968, Athens), pp. 7-12.
231. *Georgia Education Journal* (February 1942), p. 26.
232. Georgia Department of Education *Annual Report*, 1949-1950.
233. Education Panel, *A Survey of Public Education of Less Than College Grade in Georgia*, p. 413.
234. *Ibid.*, p. 186.
235. Georgia Department of Education *Annual Report*, 1947-48.
236. Georgia Board of Education, *Minutes* (June 28-29, 1949).
237. Georgia Department of Education *Annual Report*, 1949-50, p. 58.
238. Georgia Department of Education *Annual Report*, 1951-52, p. 53.
239. *Ibid.*, p. 54.
240. Annie Hixon McMichael, *Supplement to History of Certification*, 1961, p. 11.
241. Georgia Board of Education, *Minutes* (February 20, 1948).
242. Carl G. Renfroe, *The Growth and Development of Teacher Certification in Georgia* (unpublished doctoral dissertation, University of Georgia, Athens, 1964), p. 146.
243. *Ibid.*, p. 146. (This quote from Dr. Renfroe's dissertation was part of an article by Dr. H. S. Shearouse, "The Preparation of a Teacher," *The Atlanta Journal*, November 16, 1963, p. 2.)
244. Dr. Conant's staff interviewed Dr. Mary Ellen Perkins of the Georgia Department of Education in 1961-62 while compiling data for *The Education of American Teachers*, McGraw-Hill, New York, 1963. Comments in this paragraph are from Dr. Perkins' experiences in assisting in this publication. See Conant's preface, pp. v-ix.
245. Georgia Board of Education, *Minutes* (February 20, 1948, pp. 182-186).
246. Georgia Board of Education, *Minutes* (April 3, 1947, p. 102).
247. Georgia Board of Education, *Minutes* (May 13, 1929).
248. Georgia Board of Education, *Minutes* (October 15, 1935).
249. Renfroe, *Growth and Development*, pp. 173-74.
250. Georgia Board of Education, *Minutes* (April 23, 1943), p. 12.
251. Georgia Department of Education *Annual Report*, 1944, p. 28.
252. Georgia Board of Education, *Minutes* (February 20, 1948), p. 187.
253. Georgia Department of Education *Annual Report*, 1933-34, p. 4.

254. "The Georgia Accrediting Commission and its Role in the Accreditation of Elementary Schools," *Bulletin*, Georgia Association of Elementary School Principals, 1975, v. 12, pp. 4-9.
255. The 12 developments cited in this section are reflected in action of the Georgia Board of Education through the official minutes and/or acts of the Georgia General Assembly as shown below.
    1. Georgia Board of Education, *Minutes* (September 18, 1940), p. 102.
    2. Georgia Board of Education, *Minutes* (January 28, 1944), p. 171.
    3. Georgia Board of Education, *Minutes* (February 20, 1948), pp. 182-186.
    4. Georgia Board of Education, *Minutes* (June 1 and 2, 1945), p. 74.
    5. Georgia Board of Education, *Minutes* (April 3, 1947), p. 102.
    6. Georgia Board of Education, *Minutes* (July 3, 1947), p. 114.
    7. Georgia Board of Education, *Minutes* (February 20, 1948), p. 185.
    8. Georgia Board of Education, *Minutes* (February 20, 1948), p. 182-186.
    9. Georgia Board of Education, *Minutes* (July 13, 1944), pp. 215-217.
    10. Georgia Board of Education, *Minutes* (February 20, 1948), pp. 82-86.
    11. *Georgia Laws*, 1947, pp. 668-669.
    12. *Georgia Laws*, 1949, pp. 1406-1419.
256. Georgia Department of Education *Annual Report*, 1928, p. 59.
257. Georgia Department of Education *Annual Report*, 1937-38, p. 83.
258. *Georgia Laws*, 1947, p. 668.
259. Georgia Department of Education *Annual Report*, 1949-50, p. 9.
260. "Headlines and Highlights of District Meetings," *Georgia Education Journal* (December 1946), p. 12.
261. M. D. Collins, "Message from the Superintendent," *Georgia Education Journal* (September 1947), p. 11.
262. Georgia Board of Education, *Minutes* (April and July, 1947).
263. Georgia Department of Education *Annual Report*, 1949-1950, p. 31.
264. *Ibid.*
265. "Study Guide for the Transition to a Twelve Year Program," Georgia Department of Education, Atlanta, spring 1947, p. 26.
266. Georgia Department of Education *Annual Report*, 1949-1950, p. 32.
267. *Ibid.*
268. Georgia Board of Education, *Minutes* (December 1947).
269. "Specific Suggestions Concerning the Development of the 12-Year Program," Georgia Department of Education, 1947, p. 5.
270. Georgia Department of Education *Annual Report*, 1952-54.
271. *Report*, State School Superintendent, 1955-56, p. 237.
272. Georgia Department of Education *Annual Report*, 1949-50, pp. 44-46.
273. O. C. Aderhold, ed., *A Survey of Public Education of Less Than College Grade in Georgia* (a report to the General Assembly by its Special Committee on Education, Atlanta, 1947), p. v.
274. *Ibid.*, pp. 135-148.
275. *Georgia Laws*, 1949, pp. 1406-1412.
276. *Georgia Laws*, 1951, pp. 241-60.
277. *Georgia Laws*, 1951, pp. 677-678, pp. 753-754.
278. Georgia Board of Education, *Minutes* (May 16, 1951), pp. 9-10.
279. *Georgia Laws*, 1951, p. 249.
280. Georgia Board of Education, *Minutes* (September 19, 1960), pp. 3-4, and Exhibit "B" of official minutes, September 19, 1960.

CURRICULUM FOOTNOTES, 1937-1948

1. Marion Jennings Rice, *Georgia School Law: A Case Study Based on the Decisions of the Georgia Supreme Court and Court of Appeals*, (unpublished doctoral dissertation, University of Georgia, Athens, 1960), p. 8.

2. L. M. Lester, "Curriculum Revision in Georgia Summer Schools." *Georgia Education Journal*, Vol. 27, No. 8, Macon, Georgia. April 1935, pp. 28-29.

3. *Ibid.*, p. 28.

4. *Ibid.*, pp. 28-29.

5. "Curriculum Page." *Georgia Education Journal.* Vol. 30. No. 7. Atlanta, Ga., March 1938. p. 22.

6. *Guide to Curriculum Improvement, Bulletin No. 2.*, Georgia Program for the Improvement of Instruction. Published by the Georgia State Department of Education. Atlanta. Reprint January 1942. p. 26.

7. *A Practice Book for Observation and Teaching in Small Rural Schools. Bulletin No. 3A.* Georgia Program for the Improvement of Instruction. Published by Division of Negro Education, State Department of Education. Atlanta. November, 1938. p. 7.

8. *Certification of Teachers, 1937.* Bulletin of the State Department of Education, 1937. pp. 8-11.

9. Georgia Board of Education *Minutes.* May 8, 1937.

10. Georgia Board of Education *Minutes.* February 13, 1939.

11. *Ibid.*

12. Georgia Board of Education *Minutes.* January 16, 1940.

13. Georgia Board of Education *Minutes.* March 19, 1940.

14. *Pass the Ammunition.* Editorial, Georgia Education Journal. Atlanta, Vol. 36. No. 5. December, 1942. p. 21.

15. O. C. Aderhold, *Georgia Victory School Program.* Georgia Education Journal, Atlanta, Vol. 37. No. 5. January, 1944. pp. 15-7.

16. Georgia Board of Education *Minutes.* January 10, 1947.

17. *Acts of 1947. Georgia Laws.* pp. 668-9.

18. Georgia Board of Education *Minutes.* April 3, 1947.

19. Georgia Board of Education *Minutes.* December 4 and 5, 1947.

20. Report of Representative Assembly, *Georgia Education Journal,* Atlanta, Vol. 41. No. 7. March 1948, p. 16.

Chapter V

Foundations for the Future, 1949-1963

The Constitution of 1945 outlined the following significant improvements in Georgia's public school system.

- a lay state board of education,
- an 85 percent reduction in the number of school tax districts,
- a simplification of procedures for voting school bonds,
- the professionalization of the office of county school superintendent,
- the authority to extend the public school system from 11 to 12 grades,
- an increase in the maximum tax rate for schools from five to 15 mills,
- extension to citizens of age 18 the right to vote.

Workshops conducted by the Georgia Education Association and the State Department of Education in 1946 revealed that Georgians were ready to upgrade education. The workshops, held in each of the state's 10 congressional districts, examined school needs perceived by educators and the public. Discussion focused on instruction, teacher certification, guidance, the arts, transportation, buildings and citizenship. Recommended legislation, including tax revision and a state-supported kindergarten, was reported in the December *Georgia Education Journal* by Dr. J. I. Allman.[1] In its 1946 session, the legislature authorized a special committee to study Georgia's educational needs.[2] The study proposed (1) to make a complete and exhaustive investigation of Georgia common school operation, (2) to determine the cause of problems, (3) to propose solutions and (4) to make a complete report to the General Assembly which would guide its deliberations on improving the state's educational facilities.

Representing the executive and legislative branches of state government on the committee were Governor Ellis Arnall; Senate President Frank Gross; House Speaker Roy Harris;

Senators James L. Gillis Jr. and W. M. Holsenback; and House members Albert Swint, A. N. Darden and Max G. Hicks. Many prominent Georgians served on the committee to gather data for the study. Dr. O. C. Aderhold of the University of Georgia headed the group, assisted by Dr. Joe A. Williams, Dr. Johnnye Cox, Dr. W. A. Stumpf, L. O. Rogers, Dr. James L. Dickerson, J. D. Messer and others from the University of Georgia; Dr. Roe L. Johns from the University of Florida and Dr. Francis G. Cornell from the United States Office of Education. Major roles were carried by Dr. J. I. Allman, Dr. Claude Purcell, Pendleton Mitchell and W. E. Pafford. Working behind the scenes but ever present with materials, counsel and advice was State Auditor B. E. Thrasher.

In addition to thoroughly analyzing the state's financial structure and needs, the panel also studied school building needs, textbook and library needs, teacher qualifications and supply, pupil transportation, curricular and instructional needs, school food services, state and local education organization and administration. Many lay citizens assisted the educators in gathering, organizing and evaluating information for the study. During the one-year period over 20,000 citizens participated in the study. The committee submitted its report, "A Survey of Public Education of Less Than College Grade in Georgia," to the General Assembly in January 1947. The thorough study used pertinent data to support over 100 recommendations for improving public education in the state. Superintendent Collins coordinated the efforts of all lay and professional groups to urge the enactment of laws implementing the committee's recommendations. Legislation entitled "The Georgia Minimum Foundation Program for Education Act" (MFPE), passed in 1949,[3] included most of the report's major recommendations. Because implementation required a minimum of $47 million, almost $25 million more than the previous year's expenditures, the program remained inactive until 1951. By that date, however, the estimated cost had increased considerably, forcing the General Assembly to amend the 1949 act by delaying implementation until $70 million was appropriated and approved by the state budget bureau for one year's operation.[4] In the meantime, forces were at work trying to get a revised plan adopted to finance MFPE.

The MFPE Act revolutionized Georgia educational law by increasing the minimum school term to nine months, liberalizing the teacher allotment plan and improving standards for pupil transportation calculations and equipment. The act strengthened federally subsidized programs. A new plan of determining school systems' required local support was developed, using an economic index to determine ability to pay. Each district's required local amount was based on gross retail sales, state income taxes paid, taxable property, public utilities, motor tag taxes paid and effective buying power. The economic index of tax-paying ability measured the state's total ability as 100 percent, with each county's index representing a percentage of this total ability. The property tax factor was soon deleted from the index to encourage systems to re-evaluate their property without being penalized for improving their resources. The MFPE economic index, recommended by the study committee, was based on the doctoral dissertation of J. A. Williams, member of the panel.

Equalizing educational opportunities among the school systems of the state was the major incentive in passing the 1949 MFPE Act. According to public sentiment, broadening the state tax base would permit more citizens equal participation in educational support. A state sales tax was considered the most logical measure for extending the tax base fairly. Superintendent Collins again called on his lay and professional forces to carry the message.

The Georgia Farm Bureau Federation had long advocated a state sales tax for securing additional funds. The Lions Clubs, the Georgia Federation of Women's Clubs, the American Legion, the Georgia Teachers and Education Association, the Georgia Education Association and the Georgia League of Women Voters also pioneered the sales tax proposal. A statewide straw ballot in 1950 indicated much more campaigning was necessary, and all interested groups intensified their efforts. By the time the General Assembly convened in 1951, sufficient support had been gathered to pass the sales tax bill.[5]

The first MFPE became effective July 1, 1951.[6] Many amendments were subsequently added to strengthen the act. Even though professional educators and legislative leaders were trying desperately to present a full and complete program, some opposition to these efforts existed.

One group contended that 60 school systems would receive less money under the MFPE formula than they were currently receiving. Purcell corrected that misconception by distributing work sheets detailing each school system's revenue. While the greatest increases were earmarked specifically for teachers' salaries, transportation, capital outlay and textbooks, a set of unmarked funds allocated to local boards for general purpose spending provided another bone of contention.[7] In 1953 the General Assembly resolved that the educational factions who contended that the administration of funds under MFPE was wasteful[8] should file written recommendations with the State Board of Education suggesting where the funds might be more economically administered. The Governor was requested to make available to the State Board of Education any funds so saved. The resulting data represented sound and efficient use of state funds.

From the time the 1946 resolution was passed authorizing the study until the actual implementation of the MFPE in fiscal year 1951-52, state appropriations for public schools gradually increased from about $22 million to $86 million.

1945-46	....$21,968,000	1949-50	....$50,100,000
1946-47	 31,656,681	1950-51	 50,300,000
1947-48	 37,250,000	1951-52	 86,863,804
1948-49	 41,508,000		

Most of the 1946-47 increase augmented teacher salaries when the payment schedule increased from a 10-month to 12-month period, with no reduction in the monthly rate. The major portion of the 1949-50 increase again paid teacher salaries. The greatest increase, 1951-52, funded the Minimum Foundation Program implementation. Pupil transportation, capital outlay, instructional materials and teacher salaries were increased by this act. For the first time, the minimum state salaries for white and black teachers were equalized. Also for the first time, pupil transportation became available to all eligible students. Though the potential for transportation had existed before this time, some school systems were unable to finance it.

Development of Pupil Transportation Services

Pupil transportation services and school district consolidation have been parallel concerns throughout the history of American education. In Georgia and in other states, the earliest schools were established by parents. A few families, living near enough to make a school possible, voted themselves a school by whatever plan was authorized by existing laws. After the establishment of the state school system in 1870, parents and school boards became more concerned about the type of school their children were attending and began to look at some consolidations of small one- and two-teacher schools.

Early records indicate that student transportation began in the 1890s. The Bibb County budget records show a "stable and transportation" account which had increased from $48 annually in 1895 to $82 in 1908.[9] Early records in Twiggs County show the employment of a mule team to transport students who lived beyond a safe walking distance.[10]

In 1901, State School Commissioner Glenn reported a meeting of county school commissioners dealing with consolidation of rural schools and the transportation of children. Commissioner Glenn's report reprints the entire paper of Putnam County School Commissioner M. B. Dennis. Introducing his seven-page speech with the statement, "Consolidation is the order of the day," he goes on to present vividly the advantages of consolidation, reorganization and transportation. He emphasized the need for graded schools with better trained teachers in better facilities. Transportation was crucial in providing equal educational opportunities for rural children as well as those who resided in towns and cities. He said that, to his knowledge, transportation was being provided in the counties of Washington, Greene, Muscogee, Fulton, Twiggs and possibly others.[11] Following Dennis' speech, Jefferson County School Commissioner H. E. Smith gave the following account of his experiences in school consolidation and pupil transportation.

Last year we had four schools in our district. One had an enrollment of 25 scholars, and an average of 22, at a cost of $150. There were two others in five miles. In the first we had 16 pupils enrolled, and an average attendance of 7-10, at a cost of $150. The other had no weather-boarding, and the window lights were broken out. It was 20 by 16 feet, and had an enrollment of 12 pupils, and an average attendance of six and a very small fraction, at a cost of $125, or about 20 cents a day. In the fourth district, the people came together before the board of education, and asked for a school for their district. They claimed they had 24 pupils, but we never could find but 22. The board of education helped them build the house and furnish it.

It was afterwards decided that we should drive the wagon in the community. We bought a two-horse wagon at a cost of $85 and a set of harness at a cost of about $15. And the 22 pupils that we found came in this wagon to this central school, five miles. I should say that there are over 83 pupils in the school this year. The tuition is something over 7½ cents. The result has been that for five months we run the school at a cost of 7½ cents a day for 420 days. We then agreed to run it three months at a cost of $25.00 a month.

The average attendance of the other school was about 50 percent; now, up to the present time, it is 68 percent. Then the cost of running the four schools was 20 cents, 19½ cents and 12½ cents, making an average cost of 17½ cents. The cost now is 12½ cents for the pupil and 7½ for the teacher.

We had some difficulty in getting somebody to furnish the horse. They said you furnish the wagon, and now you furnish the horse. We told them, no, sir, that we would give it out by contract to any man who would bring the children for five cents a day. We had to change one of these wagons three times. The two-horse wagon is successfully run now by a widow lady, who keeps a horse to plow her garden and go visiting. When we asked her to let her children go to the school, she said, "No, sir, they might fall out and break their necks." She was so well pleased with the wagon that when the man who had been running it quit, she said, "I'll run it." She is very much pleased with the job and says she will never give it up.

The children come in better shape than those who live in 300 yards of the school, and they go back with no wet feet, and don't have to come to school in the weather and stay in all day with their wet clothes on. They come to school making melody in their hearts; they come singing; and they go home singing and making melody in their hearts. They like to go to school, and the attendance is 30 to 35 percent better than it was before we got the wagons.

We have two wagons: a one-horse wagon and a two-horse wagon. They are covered, and have seats in them. And we get better results now there is only one school, than we did when we had four schools.

. . . Transportation is a success. We transport our children for about a dollar a month, and carry them three or four miles. We have increased attendance, and our children come regularly to schools, and are thereby benefited.[12]

In 1905, Randolph County School Commissioner E. W. Childs published an elaborate report on the activities of the county schools, emphasizing a plan for consolidation of small schools and the construction of better buildings. He presented sound and logical advantages of consolidations.[13]

The thirty-fourth annual report of the State Department of Education in 1905 describes new buildings resulting from school consolidations in Newton County.[14] This report is illustrated with a chain of five wagons drawn by three yoke oxen transporting 100 Flint Hill School students to the Newton County oratorical contest.[15]

The thirty-fifth annual report of the State Department of Education in 1906 carries an item about the requests for schoolhouse building plans as a result of the need for newer and larger buildings. A subsequent publication was issued by the department to assist in this request.[16] The thirty-sixth annual report in 1907 describes the consolidation of two "weak" schools, Kent and Ogeechee, into one "handsome" building in Jenkins County. The County School Commissioner states

. . . This is the place where I was warned that a school could not run for more than two months in the year. It was pitiful to see the houses in which those bright children had to go to school. Now there is a splendid house 23x45 feet sitting in the pine grove with its spire rivaling some of the surrounding saplings in height. The building is complete. It is tastily painted and the windows have good roller shades. Hat hooks have been supplied, good furniture has been put in, blackboards have been provided and a good, earnest Christian teacher is in charge . . .[17]

The above citations indicate that the educational leadership of the age foresaw the need for graded schools. The Barrett-Rogers Act of 1919, also known as the School Consolidation Bill, offered financial incentives of $500 to $1,000, respectively, to elementary and high schools resulting from consolidations. These grants were made annually to the schools meeting certain standards. Also in 1919, the legislature authorized county boards of education to transport students.[18] In the five-year period, 1919 to 1924, the number of public schools in the state had been reduced by 1,383. These consolidations increased the need for transporting students to school. As mentioned earlier, the first transportation was by wagons drawn by mules, horses or oxen. Later the motorized bus was put into service. With no minimum standards for the construction of this equipment, the usual bus was a wooden body mounted behind the cab of a long frame truck. The structure was made of tongue and groove pine flooring mounted on a bed of 4 x 8 inch oak sills. Flexible canvas rolled on a long pole provided the sides to keep out wind and rain. Later, sheet metal replaced the pine flooring and glass windows replaced the canvas rolls. In 1935 a bill was introduced in the legislature to set minimum standards for school buses, but the only part of the bill to pass was that the words *school bus* must appear in six-inch letters on the front and rear of each bus. A picture of an early bus with its load of students is carried in the annual report of the State Department of Education to the state legislature for the year 1924. The picture shows 15 children riding the bus driven by a 16-year-old girl student, Wilda Reid, attending the Cuthbert School in Randolph County.

Prior to 1926, school transportation service was considered a local, district or county responsibility. The state assumed no responsibility until that year, when a half-cent-per-gallon tax on gasoline was authorized and allocated to local school systems as an equalization fund to be used for any legitimate education purpose including school transportation service. However, the state still had no legal authority to prescribe minimum standards for buses, regulate the operation of school buses or require liability insurance.

With the adoption of the Seven Months School Law in 1937, provisions were made for the State Department of Education to provide financial assistance to county boards of education through an equalization fund based on the type of equipment, number of students transported, the number of miles traveled and road conditions over which the pupils were transported.[19]

At the beginning of World War II, the United States Office of Defense Transportation assumed considerable responsibility in rationing transportation resources in the nation. Guidelines mandated that key personnel in each state be responsible for all areas having influence and direction of pupil personnel services. In 1942, State School Superintendent M. D. Collins appointed Claude Purcell to the position of assistant director of administrative services with major responsibility in the area of pupil transportation. Though Purcell did not serve full time in transportation, he was the first state director of pupil transportation services, dividing his time with other administrative duties such as attendance, visiting teacher services and teacher retirement.

The first major study of school transportation service was a part of the responsibility of the Special Committee on Education authorized by House Resolution 166-712A and approved January 31, 1946.

The report of the special committee states, "The transportation program that has grown to such magnitude within a quarter of a century has done so without much conscious planning or serious consideration and with little or no regard for a long-range program." Also, the report states, "The transportation program has grown to such an extent that it can no longer be considered a local function of the schools."

The most significant recommendation of the committee was that the "State of Georgia should develop a state owned and operated school transportation system such as is now in operation in North Carolina." [20] It suggested that legislation to establish a state system of school transportation should include the following.

- Take over the title to all buses now owned by counties and purchase bodies and chassis from private owners.
- Assume the full control and cost of transportation.
- Purchase all equipment and supplies centrally on the basis of competitive bids.
- Establish a statewide system of repair and maintenance.
- Establish a uniform salary schedule for drivers.
- Establish a program of education and certification for bus drivers.
- Establish school bus routes and schedules annually.
- Establish rules and regulations for the school transportation system relative to the duties and responsibilities of local school people.
- Establish minimum standards for the construction of school buses.
- Make any other rules or regulations necessary for the efficient operation of a state owned and state operated transportation system not in conflict with the state law.

"Until," the report stated, "it is possible to inaugurate a state owned and operated system of school transportation, it is recommended that legislation be enacted placing regulatory power over transportation in the hands of the State Board of Education." Thus empowered, the State Board of Education could (1) regulate school bus routes, (2) set up safe driving regulations and school bus driver qualifications, (3) establish minimum standards for construction of school buses and (4) establish a minimum salary schedule for school bus drivers.[21]

A state owned and operated system of pupil transportation had never been established in Georgia. However, the 1947 General Assembly authorized the State Board of Education to have regulatory power over school transportation service.[22]

School transportation service was included in the minimum foundation law in 1949, but it was not until 1951-52 that the minimum foundation law was financed.

Since the early 1950s, the State Board of Education and the State Department of Education have been exercising positive leadership in the area of school transportation service. About this time considerable emphasis was placed on school consolidation through the impetus of a $200 million school building program. As some 4,299 schools were consolidated, more and more pupils rode school buses.

Georgia Annotated Code Section 32-427 permits county boards of education to contract for school transportation service. So, the Georgia program developed under three ownership arrangements—county owned and operated buses, privately owned and operated buses and jointly owned and operated buses. Historically, the two contract types of ownership have been more expensive to operate and administer, while the county ownership arrangement is cheaper, more flexible and easily lends itself to routing adjustments.

The State Board of Education calculated allotments to systems on the basis of the cheaper method of operating county owned and operated buses. Naturally, this produced a decided tendency to use that system. In addition, school consolidation and the school building program began to have their impact on the number of buses operated.

With a well organized bus routing pattern, plus emphasis on the use of larger capacity bus bodies, there was an average annual increase of only 19 buses from 1959-60 through 1965-66. During that period, 528 buses were added to the total fleet while 409 unneeded buses were removed, making a net increase of 119 buses in the six-year period. This was accomplished in spite of an increase of 69,809 pupils transported and amounted to an annual saving of $1,402,730.

The survey approach to organizing local programs of transportation has proved to be a major contributor toward economical operation of local transportation programs. Under this plan, personnel with special organizing abilities were added to the State Department of Education staff. They helped conduct local studies making recommendations for the travel course of each bus needed; assigning buses to routes; designating loading stops, bus capacity needed and ownership of buses; providing for a retirement program for buses, attendance areas and shop standards; equalizing service among buses and analyzing budgets and expenditures.

The use of larger buses also reduced the number of units in service. Savings from more businesslike operations permitted boards of education to operate from 1961 through 1966 at no annual increase in state funds even though an increase of 69,809 pupils occurred in that five-year period.

Concurrent with the other 1947 acts dealing with pupil transportation was an amendment to the 1919 law which had prohibited boards of education from making contracts or debts beyond a current fiscal year.[23] The 1947 amendment added, "Provided county boards of education shall have the authority to contract for the transportation of pupils for a period not to exceed four years." [24] This section aided county boards of education as they sought to upgrade equipment or contract with private owners. As local boards began public ownership, the quality of transportation equipment improved greatly.

When the new MFPE Act of 1964 was passed by the General Assembly of Georgia, it contained many of the provisions the State Department of Education had already found successful. It provided uniform standards in areas of school transportation service and empowered the State Board of Education to develop a formula using standard costs to establish uniform standard financial allowances. As better business practices were implemented and refinements were made in standard costs, more uniformity of standard allowances as well as uniform practices became possible.

Pursuant to the authority and power granted to the State Board of Education by the 1964 MFPE Act (32-618), the State Board of Education approved recommendations for an operation policy statement for school transportation service on March 18, 1964. This policy statement became the criteria for operating local programs and administering the service at the state level.

After an 18-month study, on March 17, 1965,[25] the State Board of Education approved uniform standard purchase specifications for chassis and bodies as well as purchase procedures. Specifications continue to be reviewed and approved annually in order to take advantage of research in bus construction and experience in the operation of the new buses produced by the specifications. The purchase procedures require competitive bidding at the local level.

School bus drivers are required to pass the approved medical examination each year within 30 days of the opening of the school term and as often thereafter as is deemed necessary by the employing county board of education. Prospective drivers also must pass this examination. As often as practical, drivers take the test provided by a mobile testing laboratory.

No new driver who has reached his or her 59th birthday can be employed. The retirement age is 65. Bus drivers participate in social security and retirement benefits and in a sick leave program.

Annual workshops for bus mechanics are held. Likewise, a workshop is operated for local supervisors of school transportation service. These efforts have greatly enhanced the work performance of mechanics and supervision of local programs.

Not until 1954 did the State Department of Education employ a full-time staff consultant in the area of pupil transportation service. Later, some secretarial staff was added. During 1975 there were six full-time professional employees in this unit.

The State Board of Education has constantly upgraded bus specifications and requirements, and some modifications have been made in Georgia's program as a result of the National Highway Traffic Safety Administration Act which included school transportation services. Although many Georgia specifications exceeded those imposed by federal requirements, some additional changes have been made since the 1972 implementation of the act. For example, standards for small buses have been clarified. Federal P. L. 93-643 was amended in January 1975 to provide funds for the training of school bus drivers, a service Georgia had been offering to local boards of education for approximately 20 years.

The 1919 transportation laws authorized county boards of education to provide these services to students. None of the subsequent laws had ever authorized city boards of education to participate in state funds for such services until 1974. At that time, the General Assembly amended existing laws to include city boards of education as eligible systems. During the 1975-76 school year only 14 of the 29 independent city systems elected to participate in the use of state funds for transportation services. Atlanta, Georgia's largest independent system, did not elect to request state funds for transportation purposes. The Valdosta independent city system was the largest city system participating in state funds for FY 76. Of the nearly one million students enrolled in Georgia's public schools in 1975-76, approximately 653,000 were transported by bus.[26]

In the 1954 *Brown v. Topeka* case, the United States Supreme Court ruled that segregation of schools by race was unconstitutional. Controversy ensued among politicians, school people and the lay public, who debated whether the public school system of the state could be converted to a system of private schools. The General Assembly met in a special session in November and December of 1953. By resolution, the Georgia Commission on Education was created at this session.[27] Many of the state's constitutional officers, including the state school superintendent, were on this commission, and many other leaders throughout the state were appointed to serve. Under the resolution, the commission was charged to review present school laws and formulate a plan "whereby the state may by taxation continue to provide an adequate education for all of its citizens consistent with provisions of the U. S. and State Constitutions . . .". The section of the Georgia Constitution which said "separate schools shall be provided for the white and colored races" (Code 2-6401) was referred to in the resolution. The commission was instructed to receive as much information as feasible from individuals in the state.

On December 10, 1953, a constitutional amendment was approved by the General Assembly which provided educational grants to citizens from state and local funds.[28] If passed in the 1954 general election, this amendment would authorize the General Assembly to legalize granting tax funds to citizens for private school tuitions. The constitutional amendment was known as the "private school" amendment.

Under the sponsorship of the Georgia Commission on Education, hearings were conducted throughout the state on the amendment and related issues. As expected, opinions were divided and very strong feelings were expressed in each session.

State School Superintendent Collins contended that the proposed amendment would not meet any constitutional test and should not pass. He was joined in this position by J. Harold Saxon, executive secretary of the Georgia Education Association. Not all of the Georgia Education Association leadership agreed with Saxon's efforts. Some of the past presidents of the GEA gave tacit, if not always direct, approval of the "grants" plan, mostly for personal reasons.

Collins led the crusade to uphold the public school system [29] and was opposed by some of the strongest political leaders in the state. During 1954, the superintendent of a large metropolitan Atlanta school system announced his plan to run against Collins in the forthcoming election.[30] There were also rumors of impeachment,[31] yet Collins continued his earnest efforts to maintain the public school system.[32]

The "private school" issue dominated the 1954 general elections. Marvin Griffin and Ernest Vandiver were elected governor and lieutenant governor, respectively, on "private school" platforms, with Collins being re-elected without opposition. The "private school" amendment finally passed by a vote of 210,188 to 181,148.[33]

Concurrent with the political and "private school" campaigns and continuing through 1955 and 1956 was an effort on the part of the Georgia Education Association, the State Department of Education and the University System of Georgia to adopt an Adequate Program for Education in Georgia (APEG). This program attempted to update MFPE by improving teacher allotment, increasing maintenance and operation funds, increasing teacher salaries, improving transportation facilities, strengthening the curriculum, providing more teachers and instruction in the area of special education and expanding services and facilities at the University of

Georgia. The estimated increase in state funds for the first year of operation was about $37 million. A modest effort by a legislative committee failed to establish a plan for increasing taxes to supply the needed state funds. So entangled was APEG with other current issues that the upcoming sessions of the General Assembly did not give favorable consideration to APEG's passage.

After 25 years in the office, Collins retired as state school superintendent in 1958. He was succeeded by Dr. Claude L. Purcell, who had been in the State Department of Education for 16 years. His work had been mostly in the fields of administration and finance. Upon assuming his new position, Purcell immediately reviewed the study of a need for more local funds for education as well as more state support. He felt, as did many legislators, that more local financial support was needed before any major increases in state funds could be justified. Georgia, which had consistently ranked low in local support for education, was classified forty-sixth in the nation in 1958.[34] With the assistance of key legislators and local school superintendents, Purcell encouraged the General Assembly to again consider a revision of local tax structure. A constitutional amendment adopted in 1960 increased the maximum local tax rate from 15 mills to 20 mills for the maintenance and operation of local schools. Through this amendment, the millage rate continued to be determined by each county board of education.[35]

From 1958 through the early 1960s, the State Revenue Commission's property tax division conducted property tax studies based on sales assessment ratios. The division director, C. G. Campbell, had detected earlier that real estate was selling for sums several times the assessment for tax purposes. With encouragement from the State Department of Education and the County Commissioners' Association, Campbell made a study in every county in the state prior to 1963. (A digest of the study is filed in the office of the associate state school superintendent for school administrative services.) The studies showed the average assessment of real estate for tax purposes in the entire state was approximately 16 percent of the market value. The distribution by counties of assessment percentages was as follows.

Sales-assessment ratio percentage	Number of Counties
Under 10 percent	11
10 percent to 19 percent	81
20 percent to 29 percent	55
30 percent and above	12
Total	159

Such low assessments indicate that many home and farm owners were not paying any taxes at all for the operation of schools and other county government services. For example, (1) A home or farm valued at $20,000 and assessed at 10 percent of its value would be listed on the tax books at $2,000; a live-in owner would be entitled to $2,000 for homestead exemptions, thereby deleting all valuations for tax purposes. (2) In counties where the assessment was only seven or eight percent of market value, a live-in owner of a $25,000 home or farm would pay no taxes for school and county operations. (3) In the average county where the assessments were 16 percent of the market value, the live-in home or farm owner would pay no school or county taxes unless the value was above $12,500. The homestead exemption did not apply to school and county bond tax digests. In some low assessment counties there were no taxes for operations paid in the entire county on any residence in which the owner lived.

This study by Campbell and his staff not only revealed to county officials the need for re-evaluation of property for tax purposes, but it provided the impetus for a 1964 breakthrough in educational financing. Depressed assessments for tax purposes had long been prevalent in the state and were not sudden sins committed only in the 1950s. Beginning in 1960, county commissioners throughout the state introduced the use of professional tax appraisal firms into the process of re-evaluating property. The long and tedious task required almost 10 years to cover the state. Opposition to re-evaluation stemmed from several groups, especially in counties where low assessments had been the custom. Discontent emerged among those who were forced to pay property taxes for the first time. The State Board of Education, realizing county officials were reluctant to re-evaluate property in view of penalty grants, stated in a policy that minimum capital outlay bonding requirements for local systems would be based on a percentage of school systems' 1960 bonding capacity.[36] Remaining in effect five years, this policy gave school systems time to re-evaluate their property without penalty in capital outlay grants.[37]

Another section of the 1949 act related directly to the development of state supported school buildings. Although this service originated with Georgia's beginnings, its legal status as full state responsibility was clearly defined in the act.

Development of State Supported School Buildings

While some school systems trace their school building development from the little red schoolhouse to modern times, in Georgia the little red schoolhouse represents an advanced stage of schoolhouse construction. Descriptions of early school facilities, especially in unincorporated areas, depict crude and often unsafe structures. Elrod's history of Jackson County describes a "fort" school as a room added to a fort which had been constructed to protect the early settlers from the Indians.[38] These schools were common along the early frontiers. In Georgia and other states, parent groups initiated the earliest schools. A few families, living close enough to make a school possible under existing laws, were permitted to vote themselves a school district. Schools were erected on sites convenient to the most children, often on private property. The owner selected land unsuitable for cultivation, thus the name "old field school" was born. Agrarian communities constructed the "brush arbor" schools by standing poles upright in the ground and laying other poles across the top and then covering them with brush and tree limbs. "Brush arbor" schools were in session only during the summer months after completing crop planting, "laying by" and other labor.[39] Charlton County's earliest buildings were of the log and box-type construction.[40] Boones Creek School was built with no floor in the center so that a fire could be built on the ground in the winter. Incidentally, the record shows that this building burned.[41] In a history of Laurens County, Hart notes the development of early education. "Struggling with the hardships of frontier life and the vicissitudes of the ten-year Oconee Indian Wars, the people along the Oconee River had no time for establishing schools, but by the time Laurens County was created (1807) parents were becoming anxious for educational advantages for their children. Little groups of settlers began to build small log huts and employ teachers." [42]

During these early years, provisions permitting the construction of schoolhouses with tax funds were usually included when towns, cities and other special areas applied for municipal charters. Only rarely, however, did counties and rural areas enact special legislation permitting local taxes for schoolhouse construction.

Prior to 1870, public schools outside of municipal, academy and special districts were established under the Poor School Act, the Manual Labor School Act or the Old Field School Plan. Most of these schools flourished for a while but collapsed even before the Civil War. Some schools, however, did become active and vital elements of their growing communities.

Public education in the state became almost nonexistent during the Civil War. Sherman's march through Georgia left a wasteland from Chattanooga, Tennessee, to Atlanta and from there to Milledgeville and Savannah. The military and foraging forces cut a swath more than 60 miles wide through the state. Sherman's instructions to his officers gave tacit, if not implicit, license to take what the army could use and destroy the rest.[43]

Following the war, Georgia was educationally, economically and culturally devastated. The military troops had plundered and confiscated property and had disrupted nearly all the educational progress developed prior to 1860. In 1866, with the help of the George Peabody Foundation, school leaders began a two-year study that was to be adopted into law and which became the first statewide school system.

With the help of the new laws, the families and parents again united to establish new community schools. Municipalities and special districts revitalized their schools. The growth in the number of public schools is reflected in the respective annual reports of the State Department of Education.[44]

Year	Number of public schools in operation in Georgia
1895	7,253
1898	7,931
1911	7,968
1915	8,363
1917	8,513
1919	8,441
1924	7,130

The number peaked in Georgia in 1917 with 8,513, the year the number of schools nationwide peaked at 195,400. As school consolidation progressed after 1917, the national trend followed a similar, but less accelerated, trend than Georgia's.

As early as the 1890s, local boards of education were studying the shortcomings of small schools where one or two teachers taught all students in all grades. In 1898, Jefferson County School Commissioner H. E. Smith sent a lengthy report to State School Commissioner G. R. Glenn including the following local board policy on central schools.

> While small schools are indispensable in sparsely settled communities, the policy of our Board of Education is to build up strong schools in various parts of the county, in order that better teachers might be employed, better grading and classification secured, and that every bright, ambitious boy and girl should be in reach of a first-class school without boarding away from home. This is our aim.[45]

The public school leaders expressed concern for better schoolhouses, better school programs and more involved parents.

In response to an 1884 questionnaire sent by Gustavus R. Glenn to all county superintendents, Glenn learned of the appalling building conditions. Almost 90 percent of the county school buildings could not be heated and therefore operated only during the summer months. His survey showed 7,668 schools in the common school system. There were 285 schools in the city or independent systems, of which 39 were high schools. At that time, there were 33 independent systems.[46] The number of schools had been reduced to the figure shown in the preceding chart because of consolidation, for which he advocated state funds.[47]

State School Commissioner William B. Merritt pointed out in his report in 1905 the urgent need for school consolidation. He cited as advantages better schoolhouses, better teachers, more teachers per school and increased enthusiasm, pride and community effort.[48] He revealed in his 1906 report that 265 new school buildings were constructed in 1905, and again he urged state funds for schoolhouse construction.

With the wave of schoolhouse construction moving across the state in the early 1900s, there was a dire need for public funds to aid in properly providing facilities, as demonstrated by the following Screven County Board of Education order on August 1, 1905.

Ordered, that one hundred and fifty dollars be appropriated to the Zeigler school on condition that the patrons furnish a like sum in addition to the amount already invested in this school building, provided that the desks now in use in said school be given to the Board of Education to be used at their discretion and that the deed to the schoolhouse, school furniture and grounds be deeded to the Board of Education.

Ordered, that one hundred and fifty dollars be appropriated for the purpose of erecting and furnishing a suitable school building at Blue Springs provided the patrons furnish an equal sum, erect the building, ceil it with matched and dressed ceiling and tight flooring, furnish it with sashes, blinds and heating arrangements sufficient to make it comfortable in cold weather and that said building be built on land deeded to the Board of Education said deed to be approved by the Board before the money is paid.

On the above stated conditions one hundred and twenty-five dollars was appropriated to the Middleground School and fifty dollars to the Cameron School.

Whenever school buildings are not comfortable and well furnished the trustees of such schools are requested to report such conditions to the Board of Education in order that steps may be taken to improve this condition.

Ordered, that whenever the patrons build neat and comfortable schoolhouses of proper size with overhead and walls well ceiled with matching and dressed ceiling with good and tight floors and well fitting sashes and sufficient heating arrangements to make the rooms comfortable in cold weather, the Board of Education will pay half the cost of the seats and desks provided the patrons furnish to the Board the other half the cost and provided the location of such buildings is approved by the Board and that approved titles to said property be made to said Board of Education.[49]

Dr. M. L. Brittain became state school commissioner in 1910. He had formerly served as commissioner of Fulton County Schools. His ideas about schoolhouse construction, while not revolutionary, departed from accepted convention. In the foreword of a 1911 bulletin he published on school architecture, he wrote that building an attractive schoolhouse costs little more than building an ugly one. He employed an architect to design buildings of one, two and three-room sizes, and recommended that school boards employ architects to construct buildings of four rooms or larger. Drawings reprinted in his 1911 report to the General Assembly show colonial, mission and bungalow architectural designs.

Brittain strongly urged the county unit plan of school organization. In his 1910 report, he questioned the 1903 McMichael bill, which permitted sub-tax districts to fence off wealthy sections of a county. He and his successors recognized this bill, which was ratified by the voters in October 1904, as perpetuating unequal educational opportunities within a county. Brittain, as did his predecessors, listed Bibb, Chatham, Glynn and Richmond Counties as models of administrative organization. [50] Later, Richmond County teacher Elizabeth Holt became part-time consultant in schoolhouse planning.

Dr. M. L. Duggan, a former superintendent in Hancock County, became one of the rural school supervisors under Brittain's administration. He made the following report to Brittain in 1913.

A thorough and candid survey of schools and school systems in each town and county of the State would doubtless reveal facts and conditions which would lead the people to remedy defects and provide better educational facilities everywhere more surely and more speedily than would many arguments and much speech-making. It is well that "school surveys" are becoming fashionable. It is a very sensible fashion. "People do not permanently differ about facts which are open to the scrutiny of all." [51]

Duggan emphasized two pertinent points in the above report—the need for surveys and the fact that surveys were being accepted by the public. In his survey of Carroll County schools in 1918, he compared the per pupil cost of buildings in the southern states with the nation as a whole. Georgia ranked forty-fifth in the nation and next to last in the southern states in per pupil expenditure for school buildings. He also showed that Carroll County schools were worth about $7.50 per pupil, while the city of Carrollton paid about $75 per student for buildings within the city. He recommended at least $25 per student for buildings, stating that for a building 25 years old, the annual expenditure would be only $1.00 per child.

For the purpose of classifying schools as "standard schools," the State Department of Education developed criteria for adequate facilities and programs. A vigorous system of conducting surveys was begun around 1910 and was intensified through 1924. These surveys clearly determined the need for better school buildings. In 1917, there were 8,513 public schools in operation in the state,[52] with the general building quality showing little improvement. The 1912 session of the General Assembly approved Act No. 537, which permitted certain types of school districts to vote bonds for schoolhouse construction. There were restrictions in this bill that made the voting of bonds extremely difficult.[53]

Two acts of 1919 cleared the way for schoolhouse improvements. One simplified the procedure for issuing school bonds, while the other, the Barrett-Rogers Act, authorized an extra allotment of $1,000 and $500 in maintenance and operation funds to consolidated high and elementary schools, respectively.

The sub-tax school districts were established by county boards of education. District trustees elected by the voters of the district administered each sub-tax district and determined local bond tax elections. Except in independent or county unit systems, funds for Negro schools were excluded from the local tax district bond issues. Facilities for Negro children were almost non-existent in the common school system. Even in Glynn County, the best building for Negro children resulted from the efforts of D. G. Risley, a former Union army officer, who solicited funds up north for the construction of a Negro school.[54] In many other districts, outstanding Negro leaders canvassed various parts of the nation to solicit funds, gifts and endowments for buildings. Some of these local Negro leaders secured charters from the local courts incorporating a body so that the donors could receive income tax deductions and other credits for their donations. William James, a Negro teacher and local leader in Statesboro, secured a charter for Statesboro High and Industrial School (later named William James School). In 1922 the Rosenwald Fund made a contribution to this school.[55] Other Negroes in the state who followed this or a similar procedure for securing gifts were T. J. Elder in Sandersville, J. D. Dickerson in Vidalia, Paul J. Blackwell in Elberton, N. F. Williams in Swainsboro, W. M. Hubbard in Forsyth, A. S. Staley in Americus and Asbury Speight in Ft. Gaines.

The Rosenwald Foundation gave numerous grants for the construction of Negro facilities. Most of the buildings were of frame construction, but some were brick veneer on frame. Practically all buildings were shaped like the letters "L," "H," "E," "U," and those without auditoriums were "I" shaped. Most had six classrooms or more. This wave of construction led to the consolidation of many Negro schools in the state. In the 1920s and 1930s Dr. Curtis Dixon and Dr. R. L. Cousins from the Department of Education surveyed Georgia's Negro schools to help local boards best utilize the Rosenwald grants. By 1942, the number of Negro schools had consolidated from 3,528 in 1922 to 3,205, while the average attendance of Negro students had increased from 188,512 to 205,601.[56]

Because the Rosenwald building funds provided no money for small rural schools, the Jeanes supervisors, in addition to assisting teachers with improved instruction, felt obligated to procure improved housing for children and teachers. Often with limited assistance from local boards of education, the Jeanes supervisors worked through every community resource to convert any available housing to educational use. Lodge halls, churches, abandoned barracks buildings and abandoned farm homes and buildings were all considered potential school buildings. They often conducted drives and campaigns within the community to raise funds for schoolhouse construction. The funds raised by the Jeanes supervisors and Negro teachers provided well planned and attractive buildings which became the pride of the rural communities. (Interesting stories are related in *Jeanes Supervision in Georgia Schools—A Guiding Light in Education,* published by the Georgia Association of Jeanes Curriculum Directors in cooperation with the Southern Education Foundation, Inc., 1975.)

In spite of Brittain's numerous efforts to provide state assistance in school plant planning, the State Board of Education had assumed little responsibility in this area. After Brittain resigned in 1922 to become president of the Georgia Institute of Technology, his unexpired term was completed by Marvin Parks. N. H. Ballard and Fort E. Land served one two-year term each. Dr. M. L. Duggan became Georgia's twelfth chief state school officer in 1927.

The state first stepped into the area of school plant services with the 1919 laws authorizing the sale of schoolhouse bonds. Surveys and studies indicated a crucial need for local bonds to subsidize school facility construction. By the end of World War I, buildings were in dismal condition, especially in rural areas. Many educators, particularly Negroes, called for assistance to provide better buildings.

The Council of Chief State School Officers and the State Agents for Negro Education in the South met in Gulfport, Mississippi, in January 1925, to ask for help from the General Education Board and the Julius Rosenwald Fund to establish divisions of schoolhouse planning in the various states under trained directors. The General Education Board agreed to consider any state's application for funds to set up a division over a five-year period. Participants agreed to send carefully selected state directors to Peabody College for at least one year of graduate work in school plant problems. Both the

General Education Board and the Julius Rosenwald Fund provided scholarships for this training.

Before becoming state school superintendent, Duggan had been rural school agent in the State Department of Education. He had initiated the school survey plan and was well aware of the tremendous need for state aid in school house planning. He tapped James L. Graham for the General Education Board Scholarship at Peabody College to study school building problems. Graham had completed his A. B. degree at Emory and had worked three summers on his M. A. at Columbia University in New York when Duggan offered him $1,800 for one year's study at Peabody College. He had taught and coached at Fort Valley and had been school superintendent at Blakely and Millen. Graham spent the entire school year of 1928-29 at Peabody under the tutelage of Drs. Fletcher Dresslar, Doak Campbell, Bruce Payne and other experts in schoolhouse planning. Returning to Georgia in 1929, he became supervisor of schoolhouse planning and construction. He served in this position until November 1933, when he accepted a similar position in the Florida State Department of Education. In Georgia he designed and then developed a school plant services division to give consultative services to architects, school boards and superintendents through the state.[57] James Stripling, an architect, assisted him in the Georgia office, which was financed for five years by a grant from the General Education Board. For a short period, W. W. Simmons of McRae succeeded Graham in this office.

In 1935 J. M. Prance became head of the Georgia division of school plant services. Although he was not an architect, his many years as president of the Americus Agricultural and Mechanical School provided him with valuable practical experience in school building needs. For the 17 years that Prance was in this position, all support funds came from state sources with no assistance from the General Education Board. The small staff provided valuable services, especially to small school systems. Working primarily with architects, school boards and superintendents, the division assisted in surveys, preparing plans for small buildings and renovations for libraries, laboratories and lunchrooms. They assisted in site development and made drawings for construction of drinking fountains, incinerators, tables, book shelves, outdoor toilets, bus sheds and other equipment.

Dr. M. D. Collins, formerly superintendent in Campbell County, became state school superintendent in 1933. Campbell County had merged with Fulton County just prior to 1933. Collins continued the campaign to upgrade the condition of educational facilities, especially in rural areas. He felt that the local superintendents' annual reports failed to reflect the actual conditions of buildings and their proximity to other schools of similar grade levels. In 1944 he employed L. O. Rogers, a former superintendent of schools in Colquitt County, to thoroughly study school building conditions and make detailed and concrete recommendations. Rogers visited as many schools as time would permit. He made scores of recommendations on plausible consolidations, but with no funds to consolidate and upgrade schools, his recommendations were ineffective. Before he could cover the state, the legislature had created the Agricultural and Industrial Development Board, and Rogers was assigned to the education panel of that board with primary responsibility in the area of school buildings. The staff of the State Department of Education was directed to assist in securing data for the education panel.[58] After long and exhaustive work, the panel presented its findings on school building needs in January 1947. A digest of the summary of findings drew these conclusions.

- Schoolhouse conditions are deplorable.
- There are too many schools, especially small ones.
- Negro schools were in worse condition than white schools.
- School systems did not have bonding capacity to construct the needed buildings.
- Very little planning had gone into schoolhouse construction.
- Most of the good facilities were in wealthier districts.
- The 1945 constitution eliminated local tax districts, thereby removing an area of inequality within a county. However, the inequalities between counties and cities had not been removed.
- A large portion of state operating funds was being wasted for lack of housing facilities.

- County and city boards needed some incentive to aid in supplying more local funds for construction.

- Local comprehensive studies should be conducted in each county and city to determine possible consolidations and other school plant needs.

- The State Department of Education should furnish professionally trained personnel to assist local systems in planning for future needs.

- There should be legal provisions for the state to financially underwrite the construction of needed schoolhouses.[59]

The 1947 session of the General Assembly considered the panel's report. While the specific statistical data were from 100 sample systems, the needs for the state as a whole were incomplete. Legislative leaders asked Collins to determine immediately the number of "standard classrooms" within the state. The state school supervisors, through W. E. Pafford, completed a thorough statewide count of usable and non-usable classrooms. Results were startling. Not only were data from the 100 sample systems typical, but the statewide coverage further substantiated the need for a revolution in schoolhouse construction.

Enacting a state capital outlay program became the main concern when the 1949 Minimum Foundation Program for Education was being drafted. When the act was approved, the capital outlay phase provided

- an annual allocation to each system of at least $200 per state allotted teacher,

- allotment of additional funds for exceptional needs,

- allotments to be adjusted by local systems' bonding ability,

- establishment by State Board of Education of minimum criteria to be met by local systems in order to qualify for participation in the capital outlay grants,

- State Board of Education establishment of priorities in the use of capital outlay funds,

- provision for State Board of Education to conduct surveys of school plant needs in all local systems.[60]

Although funds were never appropriated for financing the 1949 act, a Sales Tax Act, passed in 1951, financed the foundation program. By this time, Collins and legislative leaders had determined that the minimum annual $200 per state allotted teacher would not go far enough in long-range planning and construction. Georgia's constitution prohibited the issuance of state bonds. To ameliorate this desperate dilemma, a constitutional amendment created the State School Building Authority [61] and subsequently amended the foundation law to permit local school boards of education and the State Board of Education to contract with the State School Building Authority.[62]

Immediately following the enactment of the 1951 amendment to the foundation law, the State Board of Education initiated school plant surveys in each school system in the state. These surveys determined the needs to construct buildings to remove students from overcrowded and/or sub-standard classrooms and to consolidate small schools into more comprehensive programs.

The General Assembly appropriated funds to the various school systems for capital outlay purposes and created the State School Building Authority (subsequently, the Georgia Education Authority—Schools), a public corporation which was an instrument of the State of Georgia. This agency, among other things, issued revenue bonds to cover costs of school building construction.[63]

The State Board of Education immediately established priorities for the expenditure of state capital outlay funds. Construction of approved classrooms and sanitary facilities ranked first, followed by libraries, laboratories, cafeterias, offices, clinics, mechanical systems (heating, plumbing, lighting and water in existing facilities) and equipment. Construction of gymnasiums and auditoriums was permitted on a dollar-for-dollar matching basis only after all other needs were met. Funds were unavailable for site acquisition and development, which were considered local responsibilities. When all construction needs had been met, local boards of education were permitted to use state funds to retire local schoolhouse bonds. Limited appropriations and a rigid formula for distribution restricted the use of state capital funds to the highest priorities. The division of school plant services was enlarged by employing full-time architects and directors. The State Board of Education, in cooperation with the state fire marshall's office, developed excellent specifications for all facilities to be constructed under the state program. (State Board of Education capital outlay policies (updated through May 1975) are shown in Appendix IV.)

The State Board of Education developed a formula for allocating capital outlay funds to the various school systems, based on a space allotment per student at $7.50 per square foot plus 10 percent for achitect's fees and contingencies, less one-half of the school system's bonding capacity. The number of students on which the funds were allocated was based on a comprehensive building program presented to the State Board of Education in the form of an application. This application, among other things, described each project by giving the number of students to be housed, as well as the number of grades, classrooms and other special facilities found at the project.

The state had housed all students under this program by the time the 1955 bond series projects were completed. Therefore, the 1960 series included construction for increases in ADA since 1951. The annual allotments in 1960 were based on these rates.

- $50 for each state allotted teacher, and
- $18 for each student increase in ADA since 1951.

For a school system to receive funds for increased attendance, the system must have been bonded to one-half its bonding capacity.

The 1962 General Assembly passed H. B. 1214,[64] which authorized the State Board of Education to allot funds for the consolidation of two or more small schools. The State Board of Education adopted policies for the implementation of H. B. 1214. At this time, the square footage allotment was increased to $10 plus 10 percent for architect's fees and contingencies.

With the enactment of Senate Bill 180 (1964 General Assembly), funds were appropriated for another building program. The State Board of Education, on July 8, 1964, amended its plan for allotment of capital outlay funds.

The first part provided for the growth in school population since 1960. Capital outlay funds were allocated by the state to systems with a growth in school population, provided that the school system was bonded to 75 percent of its 1960 capacity.

The second part provided capital outlay funds for new buildings when small schools were to be consolidated. School systems making application under this formula had to be bonded to 50 percent of their capacity.

The building program in the early and mid-1950s reduced the number of schools in Georgia to 2,480 by 1956. Of this number, only 1,058 were identified as Negro schools.[65] The number just 14 years earlier was 3,205. The allotments for the construction of these buildings were made during the "separate but equal" era in the nation's history. Subsequent federal court rulings have resulted in more consolidations and mergers. Even though school construction has continued annually, in 1968 there were only 1,915 public schools in operation.[66]

Georgia's school building program has been largely instrumental in the moving of the state's educational program from a frontier type to a contemporary one of which Georgians can be proud. A recap is shown in the following tables.[67]

SCHOOL BUILDINGS AS OF JUNE 30, 1968
(in 1,915 schools or school plants)

BUILDINGS (publicly owned)	*Number*
Available beginning of year	4,382
Abandoned during year	31
Completed during year	89
Available end of year	4,440

TYPE OF PUBLIC BUILDINGS	
Fire-resistive	2,941
Semi-fire resistive	729
Combustible	503
Mixed construction	267
Total	4,440

PUBLIC BUILDINGS BY DATE OF CONSTRUCTION

	Number
Constructed before 1921	179
Constructed 1921-1930	307
Constructed 1931-1940	568
Constructed 1941-1950	535
Constructed 1951-1960	1,720
Constructed since 1960	1,131
Total	4,440

INSTRUCTION ROOMS (publicly owned)

Available beginning of year	43,439
Abandoned during year	173
Completed during year	944
Available end of year	44,210

INSTRUCTION ROOMS (publicly owned)

Standard in use	42,355
Standard not in use	555
Sub-standard in use	1,116
Sub-standard not in use	184
Total	44,210

During the school year 1969-70, consolidation resulted in 102 fewer high schools and 84 fewer elementary schools than had operated the preceding year, thereby eliminating more substandard classrooms.

A report made by the National Education Association in 1964 showed that Georgia was seventh in the nation in the percentage of classrooms constructed since 1920.[68] A similar report in 1969 showed that Georgia ranked eleventh in the national increase of high school graduates from 1963 to 1968.[69] Another NEA report in 1965 showed that Georgia was fourth in the nation in the percentage of school-age population in public schools.[70] These national reports are further indications of the contribution of the school building program to the progress of public education in the state.

State appropriations for capital outlay grants to local school systems continued through the late 1960s and 1970s. (A listing of grants by years is shown in Appendix V.) Substantially all of the grants to school systems were financed through the Georgia Education Authority (Schools). In 1973 a constitutional amendment permitted the state to issue general obligation bonds. At the same time, the Georgia State Financing and Investment Commission was created to handle new allocations. The annual appropriation for FY 1973-74 was from federal revenue sharing funds and was processed through the Georgia State Financing and Investment Commission. Allocations to local systems for FY 1974-75 were made from general obligation bonds. (Appendices VI and VII show short histories of local bond elections for building costs.)

Georgia's constitution permits two or more local boards of education to contract with each other for educational purposes (Code 2-7202). For some years several systems had experienced decreasing enrollments, thereby restricting staff and curricular offerings. Superintendents in three rural counties, L. K. Moss of Marion County, A. T. Miller of Schley County and R. H. McDuffie of Webster County, were concerned about the paradox in which society demanded more of high school graduates at a time when they were being forced to curtail or halt educational expansion within their systems. These men conferred with each other, their local boards of education and State Department of Education staff and decided to study the feasibility of one comprehensive high school to serve the three counties. In September 1971 the State Department of Education conducted a survey of resources and potentials in Marion, Schley and Webster Counties.

The survey group recommended the construction of a new tri-county comprehensive high school to serve approximately 1,000 to 1,100 students in the three counties. The reports made to the citizens of the three counties outlined the potential curricular offerings in a school of the size recommended. With the favorable citizen response, the three boards of education consummated a 25-year contract for the development and operation of a tri-county comprehensive high school.

The Marion County Board of Education provided a 57-acre site in the Dranesville area, which was as equidistant from the centers of population in the three counties as was practical. The Marion County Board of Education submitted an application to the State Board of Education for capital outlay funds based on a proposed average daily attendance of approximately 1,000 students. Following the approval by the State Board of Education, the Marion County Board of Education employed an architect to draw plans and specifications for the new facility. The three superintendents, the three boards, the architect and State Department of Education staff studied plans and visited new facilities in many areas in order to design the most functional and economical plant possible. Construction funds came from six sources including state, federal and vocational monies. Over $2,605,000 went into construction and equipment.

The building, completed in 1975, consisted of 106,000 square feet including four vocational shops, departments for business education, homemaking, paramedical education, distributive education, music, physical education, language arts, math, social studies, science, driver training, library media, administration and school food service. The school has its own water, sewer and climate control systems.

Tri-County Comprehensive High School opened in August 1975 with 1,150 students registered in 190 classes under 51 professional personnel. Academic courses were offered on varying levels in order to meet individual needs of students, and a broad program of extracurricular activities has been developed.

The school, located in Marion County, is operated by the Marion County superintendent and board of education. The superintendent and board members of Webster and Schley Counties meet with the Marion County Board of Education when it is discussing Tri-County High School business. Operational costs of the high school are prorated among the counties on the basis of average daily attendance.

Other comprehensive high schools which opened for the 1975 school term are Lithia Springs in Douglas County, Newton County High School, Hawkinsville in Pulaski County and city high schools in Valdosta and Dalton. Some new elementary schools innovative in design and program are Russell School in Houston County, Trickum School in Gwinnett County, Woodridge School in DeKalb County and Cochran (City) Elementary School.

A report appeared in a Columbus newspaper on May 22, 1976, noting that the Clay County Board of Education had voted unanimously to join Randolph and Quitman Counties in a new comprehensive high school.[71] This action followed a vote in Clay County approving the proposal 320-125. Subsequent action depends on a long-term contract among the three participating school system boards of education and the State Board of Education, state funding provided by the General Assembly and federal and vocational funds. The new high school for the three counties has a potential enrollment of 1,350 students, a size sufficient to provide staff and facilities for an efficiently operated comprehensive high school.

Georgia's school building program has been unique since its inception. Such major factors as authority type financing, state-local partnership in cost sharing, and state participation only in survey recommended projects, have attracted widespread attention. Inquiries have been received from numerous states and foreign countries. A request for information came from the national minister of education in Belgium dated May 14, 1976. Delegations have come from South Carolina, Kentucky, Indiana, Illinois, Oklahoma, Hawaii, the Philippines, Australia and other places to study the state's capital outlay program.

The state school superintendents and their staffs, the State Board of Education, the Georgia Education Authority and the Georgia State Financing and Investment Commission have consistently attempted to improve the capital outlay program with each new legislative amendment and policy. A piece of legislation enacted in 1974, however, was regarded by some educators as having dubious validity.[72] The act authorized the State Board of Education to use state capital outlay funds for facilities to serve planned communities eligible for state development assistance. As part of the Planned Growth and Development Act of 1974, it provided state funds for local boards of education to purchase or lease facilities built by community developers. The lease arrangement was designed as a lease-purchase plan. Major opposition from educators was based on the state constitutional policy prohibiting local boards of education from contracting for periods in excess of one year.[73] Assuming the passage of a constitutional amendment to permit long-term lease-purchase plans with state funds, the act provides no assurance of annual appropriations by the legislature to pay developers throughout the life of the agreement. Also, a three-way contract, state-local board-land developer agreement, would involve vesting title to the property in the State School Building Authority or its successor, the Georgia State Financing and Investment Commission, which may require additional constitutional amendments and enabling legislation. Additional legislation may be required to set aside annual growth funds for the life of a lease agreement, thereby binding the state to a contract with the developers. The highest risks would be assumed by the state. Since there is no provision to insure payments on the lease agreement for a period of facility nonuse by local boards, placing on the State Board of Education the responsibility to judge whether or not a school is needed could lead to excessive entanglements with more parties than current laws permit.[74]

Should all of the conditional factors enumerated above be met legally, economic or other circumstances could result in the community development project's becoming a disappointment to its backers. The state would have expended capital outlay funds for facilities that could have been utilized more efficiently elsewhere. By July 1976 no developers or local boards of education had applied for funds under this act.

The 1954 private school constitutional amendment generated a mass of legislation, none of which came to full fruition because of a lack of funding by the General Assembly. Six of the first eight bills introduced in the Georgia Senate in 1956 dealt with grants for students wishing to attend private schools. Senate Bill No. 1 authorized the governor to close public schools in any system by executive order and to make grants to students in schools which were closed.[75] Senate Bill No. 2 made it a misdemeanor to trespass on public property closed by executive order.[76] Authority to lease public school property for use as a private school under certain conditions was provided in Senate Bill No. 3.[77] As many buildings in use at the time were new facilities under lease by contract with the State School Building Authority, Senate Bill No. 4 was enacted to permit the sub-leasing of State School Building Authority buildings for private educational purposes.[78] Senate Bill No. 6 retained teacher benefits provided by the Georgia Teachers Retirement System by opening the retirement system to teachers in private, non-sectarian schools.[79] Senate Bill No. 8 required private schools to meet fire safety standards prescribed by the state fire marshal.[80]

General Assembly House Bill No. 3, in the 1957 session, authorized the governor to suspend operation of the compulsory attendance law under certain circumstances.[81] Two years later, in 1959, six more laws were passed intended to facilitate the move to private schools. Senate Bill No. 1 authorized the governor to close public schools if conditions resulting from the transfer of one or more pupils to such schools were likely to result in or cause violence or public disorder in the community.[82] Also included in this bill was a plan for transferring students after a school had been closed. Senate Bill No. 2 related similar conditions to the University System of Georgia.[83] House Resolution No. 59 required the State Department of Education to prepare as quickly as possible a complete outline of grades and courses taught in the public schools of the state saying, "Such information will be of utmost value in assisting and solving the most pressing and grave problems ever to be presented to public education in this state." The resolution stated further, ". . . this outline should be so composed as to offer a teaching guide around which to build private schools in Georgia. . . ." [84] Under this resolution the State Department of Education was to receive no additional funds for the preparation of this outline or material, but was to finance this project under existing appropriations. Though not directly educational in nature, a bill was passed giving taxpayers credit for contributions to educational corporations, foundations and trusts where no part of its net income inured to the benefit of any private shareholder or individual.[85] Senate Bill No. 4 of the 1959 session authorized the governor to assign legal counsel to defend public officials in the state in suits brought against them when administering the duties of their offices.[86] Legislation in this session also provided for the payment of teacher salaries in public schools closed on executive order of the governor.[87] Senate Bill No. 8 abolished the Georgia Commission on Education.[88]

By resolution enacted in 1960 (Ga. Laws 1960, p. 1187), the General Assembly created the General Assembly Committee on Schools, which held public hearings on the question of maintaining public schools in Georgia in light of the pending Atlanta case, *Calhoun v. Board of Education of Atlanta*, 188 F. Supp. 401 (D. C. Ga. 1959) and the Atlanta pupil placement plan to become effective in 1961 (5 Race Rel. L. R. 65). The committee, popularly referred to as the Sibley Committee, organized and held public hearings and submitted its report in May 1960 (5 Race Rel. L. R. 509). A majority of the committee recommended changes in the state's school laws, among which was a constitutional amendment guaranteeing freedom of association, implementation of the tuition-grants amendment to the constitution adopted in 1954, modification of existing compulsory school closing laws and enactment of a local-option closing statute.

Shortly before the beginning of the 1961 General Assembly, a federal district court ordered the admission of two Negroes to the University of Georgia (*Holmes, et al., v. Danner*, 191 F. Supp. 394, D. C. Ga. 1961) and on January 12, 1961, the Court declared unconstitutional the state laws requiring the cut-off of funds from the university upon desegragation (5 Race Rel. L. R. 1093).

Governor Vandiver thereupon proposed three bills and a constitutional amendment which implemented the recommendations of the General Assembly Committee on Schools. The act repealed all state laws requiring segregation in the public schools and the closure of schools upon desegregation (Ga. Laws, 1961, p. 35). For the first time since 1951, the appropriations act adopted in 1961 (Ga. Laws, 1961, p. 356) deleted the provisions requiring the cut-off of funds to local school systems and the university system.

One of the early acts of the 1961 session specified the manner in which public schools could be suspended, as well as reopened, by public elections within a district. This bill also included a provision for suspending the compulsory attendance law.[89] Another act clarified the section of previous legislation relating to grants to students to attend private schools.[90] House Resolution No. 225 required the attorney general to study pupil placement admission requirements in public educational institutions and furnish information and recommendations to the several boards of education in the state.[91] Also introduced in the 1961 session was a constitutional amendment,[92] later ratified in the general election, stating, "Freedom from compulsory association at all levels of public education shall be preserved inviolate. The General Assembly shall by taxation provide for an adequate education for the citizens of Georgia." (2-7503)

In the following year, portions of the 1961 laws (pp. 35-38) were amended by striking sections 1-6 and substituting other sections in an attempt to clarify the meaning of "grants to students" to attend private schools.[93] In 1963, another amendment to the 1961 law (pp. 35-38) inserted a revised formula for determining grants to students to attend private schools.[94]

Lack of funding prevented the "grants for education" laws from being fully implemented. In the absence of action to fulfill these recent statutes, their constitutionality has not been challenged in the courts. Therefore, they still stand on the law books (1976).

In 1956, the Georgia House of Representatives became interested in lowering Georgia Accrediting Commission attendance requirements. Through H. R. No. 136, p. 128, the House requested that only 60 pupils in ADA be the minimum rather than the then 100 pupils.

From 1958 through 1963, legislation other than for "grants" included a provision which authorized the State Board of Education to provide training to severely mentally retarded children through contracts, grants or tuition to private schools, other states or other political sub-divisions.[95] Also in this session, Social Security coverage was extended to school bus drivers.[96] Approved in the 1959 session and ratified by the voters was a constitutional amendment which permitted the use of state funds for scholarships for prospective teachers in Georgia (Art. VII, Sec. 1, Par. 11). Subsequent appropriations have strengthened the state's teacher training programs.

Educational television made its debut in Georgia in the late 1950s. A federal grant, contingent on local matching funds, initiated educational television in the state. Seeing the great potential of ETV, Griffin, Purcell and Shearouse drafted a plan for reaching the far corners of the state with this new medium. Griffin pledged enough money from his emergency funds to encumber the federal grant. In September 1960 the Georgia Department of Education began broadcasting regular in-school telecourses over WGTV-TV, the University of Georgia owned and operated station, which was then the only state-owned educational television outlet. The university's station was constructed with grants from the Kellogg Foundation.[97]

In February 1961 the Federal Communications Commission awarded the State Board of Education a construction permit to erect its first station, WXGA-TV, near Waycross. It began service in December 1961. Contracts for two more stations were awarded soon afterwards, and in 1963 WVAN-TV near Pembroke and WJSP-TV near Warm Springs began telecasting.

State support and authorization for the State Board of Education to own and operate television stations were prescribed by the General Assembly in 1963. Broad in concept, the act gave the State Board of Education power to develop and transmit programs, construct stations, employ technical personnel and contract with other agencies for the production of educational television programs. An accompanying act authorized the State Board of Education to receive federal funds and other grants for educational television purposes at all levels of education.[98] Since 1963, stations have been erected by the state near Cochran, Pelham, Dawson, Wrens and Chatsworth. A station owned by Atlanta operates with the Georgia ETV Network. The Atlanta station was built with local funds and matching funds supplied by the Ford Foundation. In some mountainous areas of the state translators have been constructed to amplify ETV reception to the schools.

The possibility of a pilot television program, discussed by the State Board of Education at its August and October 1956, meetings, ultimately resulted in an agreement with the Fulton County Board of Education to establish a project at Conley

Hills Elementary School. The Fulton County Board of Education supplied the building and the students while the State Board of Education assumed responsibility for programming and purchasing equipment. Operation began in 1958 with amazing success.

As ETV grew in use and application, it became more apparent that all of the state's facilities should be contained in one building. The major portion of the staff and equipment had been housed at the Protestant Radio and Television Center on Clifton Road near Emory University, although two other locations were used in the metropolitan area for some services by 1960. The City of Atlanta offered a site adjacent to the Atlanta Area Technical School for a new facility. After much discussion and debate, the latter site was selected in 1964 and construction was begun.

Programming is made available to all of Georgia by the State Department of Education, which produces daytime viewing, and the University of Georgia and National Educational Television, which share nighttime broadcasting rights.[99] (A more complete story of ETV development can be found in *A History of the Development of Educational Television Services Division of the Georgia Department of Education from 1952 to 1969,* an unpublished M. A. thesis by Barbara Jean Brown at Pennsylvania State University in 1969.)

Operation Bootstrap was conceived by Dr. Claude Purcell as a means of providing school superintendents an opportunity to maintain their professional competence while on the job and simultaneously earn college credit for intensive work in specific fields. Dr. Doyne Smith, who in the 1950s was director of field studies and professor of school administration at the University of Georgia, joined Purcell in this endeavor. Seminars, held at the state FFA-FHA Camp three or four times annually, taught curriculum, school laws, finance, proposed legislation, school plant construction and educational innovations. Nationally known consultants, including college professors, U. S. Office of Education staff, representatives from other state departments of education, officials in national professional organizations, editors and government officers have participated in this unique project. A special feature of all sessions is the question and answer period in which a panel of superintendents has the opportunity to quiz the consultants. The department, the university and the superintendents have concluded that one of the project's best features is the conferences' comfortable, distraction-free location where sessions are held continuously.

The Bootstrap work sessions, devoted entirely to self-improvement, do not replace the regular meetings of the Association of School Superintendents. In its beginning, 60 percent of the participants participated in Bootstrap for college credit. As more and more superintendents earned advanced certification, the number seeking college credit decreased. Although credit has become a minor incentive for participation, Operation Bootstrap continues as a significant influence on school administration.

Inmates under age 16, incarcerated in Georgia correctional institutions, received no education until 1962, when legislation authorized establishing schools within the institutions.[100]

Area school districts were not established until the approval of a constitutional amendment in 1962 (2-7201, Par. 1). Although two related provisions had existed for years, neither had provided for area school districts. Under the Georgia constitution (2-7202, Par. 11) local boards of education could contract with each other for the care, transportation and education of their pupils, and under sections 32-2218 through 32-2223, authorization was provided to establish state area vocational and industrial schools.[101] Neither of the two latter citations provided the conditions essential to establishing area school districts; therefore, the constitution was amended to permit two or more school systems to merge by referendum of voters in the affected districts. The act creating the merged area school district provided for automatically abolishing the former districts and established methods of electing area board members and area superintendents.

Vocational education experienced drastic changes during the 1950s and 1960s. Prior to the enactment of the MFPE, vocational education in Georgia was restricted mostly to agriculture and home economics. Some innovative administrators, however, had ventured into the areas of business training, shop, industrial arts, diversified occupations and mechanical drawing. In 1952, there were one or more vocational subjects offered in every county in the state except one. By 1952, there were 70 fewer schools offering vocational agriculture than in 1942. School consolidations, farm mechanization and a dwindling farm population had affected the need for agriculture departments. Post-World War II economics had re-emphasized the status of the forestry and pulp industries. Industry helped the agricultural education service of the State Department of Education develop instructional programs, which included the best scientific techniques for teaching forestry culture. Farm programs for young and adult farmers emerged in the 1950s.

Comprehensive high schools and a lower farm population pointed to the need to expand vocational education's scope. As early as 1898, State School Commissioner Gustavus R. Glenn in his annual report realized that industrial education was greatly needed in Georgia.[102] Business and office training were introduced into the vocational education program in the mid-1950s. Distributive education also made its debut as a member of the vocational family in this era. Local high school programs acquired new interest and strength by affiliating with national vocational youth organizations such as Future Homemakers of America for home economics students, Future Business Leaders of America for business and office students, Future Farmers of America for agriculture students, Distributive Education Clubs of America for distributive education students and Vocational Industrial Clubs of America for trade and industrial students.

Constant efforts to upgrade the public school curriculum resulted in the development of special education services for thousands of Georgia children during the 1949-1963 period. All data are not available on school systems that had programs prior to 1949, although many systems did provide training to exceptional children. Atlanta had a class for the deaf in 1910, and 19 schools in the Atlanta system held special education classes in 1920. Columbus, Augusta and Morgan and Clinch Counties reported classes in the 1930s.[103] Speech correction classes were reported in the 1940s.[104] From 1944 to 1946, Louise Davison, president of the Georgia Speech Association, held clinics and demonstrated speech therapy to teachers and administrators at Georgia Education Association regional and state meetings. This was undoubtedly the first statewide attention to special education, even though the University of Georgia had offered courses in speech correction for several years.

In 1945 Georgia enacted its first special education legislation, giving authority to the State Board of Education and local school systems to establish and maintain special courses, classes or schools for speech correction and rehabilitation of children with defective hearing or speech. Although the law existed, it was never funded. In 1946, Emory University sponsored a summer conference for public school teachers and others interested in speech correction. With assistance from the Junior League of Atlanta, in 1948 Emory University initiated a graduate program in speech pathology and audiology.

Other statewide interest in special education emerged through the work of the Cerebral Palsy Society of Georgia. Working with many agencies, including the Easter Seal Society, this group led in both moral and financial support to secure proper legislation for a statewide program for children with special needs.

The Georgia School for the Deaf and the Academy for the Blind conducted the most intense special education programs, though limited to children with visual and hearing problems. There existed, therefore, a great void in the special education concept as to the special needs of other children.

Additional popular concern came from the educational panel, chaired by Dr. O. C. Aderhold, whose report, *A Survey of Public Education of Less Than College Grade in Georgia*, gave high priority to establishing a legal framework for educating exceptional children. Most of the panel's recommendations were enacted into law in Georgia's first Minimum Foundation Program. This act included local programs for adults, pre-school children and exceptional children at state and local expense.[105] The 1951 session of the General Assembly authorized through the appropriations bill the establishment of educational facilities for palsied children in cooperation with and funded by local boards of education.[106]

Implementation problems existed in spite of the legislation and funds to start the program in July 1951. Improperly trained staff and inadequate facilities posed the greatest problems. The estimated number of children in Georgia needing special education, using figures of the U. S. Office of Education as shown in the 1952 State Department of Education annual report, totaled at least 100,697.[107] Slowly, as funds became available, a staff was employed by the State Department of Education to develop local programs. Small school systems faced great difficulty because of the small number of students in each category of exceptionality. Classroom space was another problem, especially before the state school building program was completed. Too often, the special education classes were housed in sub-standard rooms which had been abandoned for regular classroom use. The University of Georgia, and soon other schools, offered courses to teachers who would work in various areas of special education. The allocation of teaching units was based primarily on a school system's ability to provide a teacher and a classroom.

The growth and effectiveness of the special education program in the early years could not have been achieved without the help of interested superintendents, principals, instructional supervisors, visiting teachers and local coordinators. Training and certification of special education teachers often became projects of civic groups and private individuals. Many communities developed strong programs for all children. Though limited in descriptive details of the growth of the program, the table below shows the years in which services were inaugurated.

Year	Services Added
1951-52	Speech impaired, multi-handicapped, hospital bound
1952-53	Educable mentally retarded, hearing impaired
1954-55	Brain injured
1955-56	Visually impaired
1959-60	Behavior disorders, psychological testing
1961-62	Trainable mentally retarded
1969-70	Specific learning disabilities, gifted
1974-75	Inter-related handicapped

By 1975 over 120,000 children were being served in 160 school systems by 5,000 persons trained in special education.

The State Department of Education provides trained consultants to school systems in each area of exceptionality.

Another curriculum change during the 1950s concerned a state course of study for the public schools. In November 1950 a small committee from the board was named, and later a committee of school superintendents and state staff composed a study group to work on a course of study. The latter group worked for several months and was composed of Chairman Mark Smith, superintendent, Bibb County; Zade Kinimer, superintendent, Harris County; and A. H. Gnann, superintendent, Burke County. State Department of Education staff included L. M. Lester, H. S. Shearouse and T. A. Carmichael. Questions posed by board members for committee scrutiny included, (1) Is the twelfth grade worthwhile? (2) Do extracurricular activities in the schools overbalance basic education? (3) Is a mandatory curriculum needed? and (4) Are accreditation requirements high enough to demand strict adherence for students' graduation?

With the help of 40 professional educators in the state, in March 1954 the committee presented its report to the State Board of Education. The board adopted the committee's curriculum framework and subsequently conducted workshops throughout the state for teachers, administrators, instructional supervisors and visiting teachers.[108] Critiques indicated favorable uses by teachers, administrators and other curriculum planners. Instructional improvements were soon noted in several areas, especially in mathematics, science, health and vocational education.

The new high school graduation requirements, amended by the State Board of Education in July 1957, became effective with the 1961 graduating class. The transition began with the 1958-59 school year when all high schools in the state were required to offer one additional unit in English, mathematics, physics and chemistry and two additional units in a foreign language. The final graduation requirements included three credits in English, three in social studies, including one in U. S. history and government, one in biology, one in mathematics, one in mathematics or science and nine electives. Thus, the requirements for all high school graduates became nine required units and nine elective units. Parents or guardians were required to approve the courses selected by the students. The course of study offered by each high school had to be approved by the State Department of Education and had to follow the preceding requirements.[109]

In accordance with the graduation requirements amendment in October 1957, the State Board of Education approved a program of in-service curriculum development.[110] The education committee of the Georgia Senate met with the State Board of Education in February 1958 to discuss a bill increasing mathematics and science in the high school curriculum. The board ruled, however, that schools could substitute other courses if staff were unequipped to conduct classes in the required courses.[111] The State Board of Education had previously approved about $214,000 to conduct summer workshops improving skills in teaching science.[112] In the April and May meetings of the State Board of Education, Shearouse and Carmichael reported increased enrollment and increased comprehension among high school students studying natural sciences.[113] Also in April, workshops were approved for teachers in the middle grades, emphasizing work on materials covered in all subjects and special learning techniques for students in grades seven, eight and nine.

Purcell presented a policy amending high school graduation requirements in July 1958. All qualifying students were required to complete two courses in algebra, one course in chemistry and one course in physics. The State Board of Education approved the amended policy and specified that the physical education requirements apply to elementary schools only.[114]

The 1949 Minimum Foundation Law provided an extended two-month summer program for 15 percent of the state-allotted teaching personnel.[115] This section was funded only on an experimental basis in a few pilot systems during the 1952-53 school year. Funds were reduced for the 1953-54 school year, and later ceased altogether. Its purpose, to provide enrichment and recreational activities to certain eligible students, was already funded by other State Board of Education programs.[116]

A grant of $25,000 from Governor Griffin had been approved for a governor's conference on education to stimulate interest in nuclear energy and to improve school programs in mathematics and science.[117] The National Defense Education Act and state funds supported nuclear energy studies in Georgia. Dr. Doak Campbell, president emeritus of Florida State University, was employed by the Nuclear Energy Commission to conduct the study and was given space and staff by Purcell.

In November 1960 Purcell reported on the non-graded primary project, offering criteria for selecting schools to receive operating grants. The board approved $2,000 for each center selected. There would be two such centers in each congressional district in the state.[118] The following month, the board approved a plan to select 10 school systems to develop experimental programs for academically talented children. The board approved $4,000 for each system selected, with one in each congressional district.[118] Also approved in this meeting were standards for implementing the special education unit for trainable mentally retarded children.

A sixth-year program of teacher training was authorized by the State Board of Education in November 1959.[120] Recently improved course content created a need for higher quality instructional training. The professional staff of the State Department of Education, working with the Georgia Council on Teacher Education, presented criteria for a sixth-year college certificate. It was assumed that a higher certificate would be identified in the state minimum salary schedule. The criteria approved by the State Board of Education included (1) the teacher must hold a fifth-year certificate in the field in which sixth-year certification is sought and (2) a teacher must earn at least 45 hours of approved courses beyond the fifth-year level.

The program provided that the individual planning the sixth-year program should consider her/his previous study and performance on the diagnostic examination. Within the student's graduate program, there was to be a formal provision for the development of research competence. Courses studied in the sixth year were to apply strictly to the field of specialization and were to include in-field content materials, nature and psychology of learning and problems of the school.[121]

Earning the six-year certificate improved the holder's qualifications. By 1962, 420 six-year certificates had been issued, the number increasing to 2,787 by 1972. Experience in this area has been gratifying.

By 1967 the State Board of Education had approved criteria for a seventh-year doctoral certificate. Certification for the sixth and seventh years could not be issued on an accumulation of credits picked up from random courses, but had to be planned for in-field specialties.

Administrators also upgraded professional competence at this time. The Southern Association of Colleges and Schools adopted a non-retroactive standard requiring all administrators of member schools and school systems to hold advanced degrees in administrative and supervisory functions, effective in the 1958-59 school term.[122] The Georgia Accrediting Commission adopted a similar standard effective in the 1960-61 school term.[123] The General Assembly in 1963 had amended the qualifications for county school superintendents by requiring, among other things, ". . . he shall have earned or held a five-year degree from an accredited college or university, or shall have not less than a four-year degree earned and held from an accredited college or university and shall have registered for courses leading toward obtaining the requirements for a five-year certificate, and shall not have less than three years of actual teaching or education administration experience . . ." [124]

Though leadership qualifications and requirements for superintendents had received little attention for 70 years, the 1960s brought rapid advances. Colleges and universities in Georgia and neighboring states cooperated with professional groups, Operation Bootstrap and other agencies in promoting improved competence among educational leaders. The Georgia Association of School Superintendents adopted a resolution in 1961 urging continued efforts by all agencies for upgrading the profession.[125]

Similar manifestations were noticeable in other leadership positions. During the improvement of instruction movement of the 1950s and 60s, the instructional supervisors became the directors of curriculum, their competence and services continuing to focus on instructional responsibilities.

The process of line-item budgeting and appropriations had considerable impact on services and support in the field of education.[126] The state budget had historically been directed by the governor and the state auditor.[127] Together with agency heads, they allocated appropriated funds to the various services within each agency. Shifting agency funds prior to line-item budgeting was easily accomplished by mutual agreement of the governor, auditor and agency head. In the early 1960s, the General Assembly became more concerned about fiscal responsibility and felt that the legislative branch of the government should have more power in determining the amount of funds going into each service within an agency.

The line-item budgeting process appropriated funds for a given service within an agency with no more to be spent for that service than the amount appropriated. Unused funds in one area of education could not be used for increased costs in another area.

After some years this restriction was eased when a legislative fiscal affairs committee, auditor and governor were given authority to assign certain transfers for good and sufficient reasons. The agency head was required to submit a detailed and substantially documented request for annual appropriations.

Though justification for budget requests posed no insurmountable problems, forecasting unforeseen events was impossible. Still the agency head was accountable. A typical problem occurred in the 1966-67 school year, a non-election year for county school superintendents. The 37 superintendent changes during that school year had been entirely unanticipated. Because 35 superintendents held higher certificates than their predecessors had, more state money was required to pay their salaries. In addition, the number of deaths, transfers, retirements and resignations among superintendents that year exceeded the normal turnover.

When defending the budget request before the joint appropriations committee of the Georgia House and Senate, the state school superintendent faces and must be prepared to answer the committee's diverse questions, of which examples follow.

- How many more school buses operated last year than the preceding year?
- How many mentally retarded children were enrolled in special classes last year?
- What was the average teacher's salary in a given county last year?
- How much would statewide kindergarten cost?
- What is the cost per square foot for school construction?
- What was the increase in school superintendent's salaries last year?
- How many schools use educational television?
- How many county school systems supplement bus drivers' salaries?
- How many schools employ assistant principals?
- Who selects the textbooks used in the schools of county "A"?

CHAPTER V

1. *Georgia Education Journal*, Reports of Meetings held October 25-November 14, XXXX, No. 4, December 1946, 13-16.
2. *Georgia Laws*, 1946, H. R. 166-713A, Act Number 83.
3. *Georgia Laws*, 1949, pp. 1406-22.
4. *Georgia Laws*, 1951, pp. 626-27.
5. *Ibid.*, pp. 360-387.
6. *Ibid.*, pp. 129-130, 417-444.
7. *The Atlanta Journal* and *The Atlanta Constitution*, Sunday, May 27, 1951, p. 9B.
8. *Georgia Laws*, 1953, pp. 435-36.
9. *Report of Bibb County Board of Education and Orphanage*, 1908.
10. Lanette O'Neal Faulk and Billy Walker Jones, *History of Twiggs County, Georgia*, (Jeffersonville, Georgia: Major General John Twiggs Chapter, Daughters of the American Revolution), p. 119.
11. Georgia Department of Education *Annual Report*, 1901, pp. 98-105.
12. *Ibid.*, pp. 105-106.
13. E. W. Childs, *Annual Report of Randolph County Public Schools*, (Cuthbert, Georgia: The Leader Print, 1905), pp. 6-10.
14. Georgia Department of Education *Annual Report*, 1905, pp. 88-89.
15. *Ibid.*, p. 88.
16. Georgia Department of Education *Annual Report*, 1906, p. 31.
17. Georgia Department of Education *Annual Report*, 1907, pp. 104-105.
18. *Georgia Laws*, 1919.
19. *Georgia Laws*, 1937, pp. 882-886.
20. O. C. Aderhold, ed., *A Survey of Public Education of Less Than College Grade in Georgia*, General Assembly of Georgia Special Committee on Education, (Atlanta, Georgia, 1947), p. 163.
21. *Ibid.*, pp. 163-64.
22. *Georgia Laws*, 1947, pp. 1461-1463.
23. *Georgia Laws*, 1919, pp. 288-329.
24. *Georgia Laws*, 1947, p. 1142.
25. State Board of Education, *Minutes* (March 17, 1965).
26. Georgia Department of Education records, 1975.
27. *Georgia Laws*, 1953, pp. 64-67.
28. *Ibid.*, pp. 241-242.
29. *The Atlanta Journal*, October 22, 1954, LXXII (205), p. 19.
30. *The Atlanta Journal* and *The Atlanta Constitution*, Sunday, May 9, 1954, IV, (53), 68.
31. *The Atlanta Journal*, November 1, 1954, LXXII, (213), 1.
32. *The Atlanta Constitution*, September 29, 1954, LXXXVII (89), 1.
33. *The Atlanta Journal* and *The Atlanta Constitution*, Sunday, November 14, 1954, V (26), 8C.
34. National Education Association, *Rankings of the States*, (Research Report, 1959-R4), Washington, D. C., 1959, p. 21.
35. *Georgia Laws*, 1960, I, p. 1444.
36. Georgia Board of Education, *Minutes* (July 8, 1964).
37. Georgia Board of Education, *Minutes* (May 21, 1969).
38. Frary Elrod, *Historical Notes on Jackson County, Georgia*, (Jefferson, Georgia, 1967), p. 138.
39. *Ibid.*
40. John Harris, *Charlton County, Georgia Historical Notes*. (Jesup, Georgia: Jesup Sentinel Press, 1972), p. 23.
41. Ibid., p. 48.
42. Bertha Sheppard Hart, *The Official History of Laurens County, Georgia, 1807-1941*. Atlanta: Cherokee Publishing Co., 1972), p. 181.
43. Mills Lane, ed., *"War Is Hell," William T. Sherman's Personal Narrative of His March Through Georgia*. (Savannah, Georgia: The Beehive Press, 1974), pp. 145, 156-157, 164, 170, 172-173.

44. Georgia Department of Education Annual Reports for the years cited.
45. Georgia Department of Education *Annual Report*, 1898, p. 230.
46. Georgia Department of Education *Annual Report*, 1894, p. 20.
47. *Ibid.*, p. 17.
48. Georgia Department of Education, *Annual Report*, 1904, pp. 85-86.
49. Screven County Board of Education, *Minutes* (August 1, 1905), pp. 47-49.
50. Georgia Department of Education *Annual Report*, 1910, pp. 25-27.
51. Georgia Department of Education *Annual Report*, 1913, p. 49.
52. *Ibid.*, p. 573.
53. *Georgia Laws*, 1912, pp. 176-177.
54. John Evans Burgess, *Development and Present Status of Public Education in Glynn County, Georgia*, (unpublished master's thesis, Duke University, Durham, North Carolina, 1939), pp. 44-45.
55. Leodel Coleman, ed., *Statesboro-A Century of Progress 1866-1966*, (Statesboro, Georgia: Bulloch Herald Publishing Co., 1969), pp. 266-270.
56. Georgia Department of Education *Annual Report*, 1942, p. 270.
57. Fannie Blitch Graham, "Those Were the Days," The Peabody *Reflector*, Georgia Peabody College for Teachers, Nashville, Tenn. 1972. Winter 1972. XLV (1), 8-12.
58. Aderhold, ed., *A Survey of Public Education*, p. v.
59. *Ibid.*, pp. 135-48.
60. *Georgia Laws*, 1949, pp. 1406-1412.
61. *Georgia Laws*, 1951, pp. 241-260.
62. *Ibid.*, pp. 677-678 and 753-754.
63. *Ibid.*, p. 249.
64. *Georgia Laws*, 1962, p. 140.
65. *Eighty-fourth and Eighty-fifth Annual Reports of the State Department of Education to the General Assembly of the State of Georgia—1954-55 and 1955-56*, p. 342.
66. *Ninety-sixth and Ninety-seventh Annual Reports of the Georgia Department of Education to the General Assembly of the State of Georgia 1966-67 and 1967-68*, p. 320.
67. *Ibid.*, pp. 320-332.
68. National Education Association, *Rankings of the States* (Research Report), 1964, p. 17.
69. National Education Association, *Rankings of the States* (Research Report), 1969, p. 29.
70. National Education Association, *Rankings of the States* (Research Report), 1965, p. 16.
71. *The Columbus Enquirer and Ledger*, Columbus, Georgia, Saturday, May 22, 1976, p. B-6.
72. *Georgia Laws*, 1974, pp. 1215-1219.
73. *Georgia Constitution*, Part 1, Art. VIII, Sect. VII.
74. Letter from State School Superintendent Jack P. Nix to Representative John Carlisle, Georgia House of Representatives, November 6, 1973.
75. *Georgia Laws*, 1956, pp. 7-9.
76. *Ibid.*, pp. 9-10.
77. *Ibid.*, pp. 10-11.
78. *Ibid.*, pp. 11-12.
79. *Ibid.*, pp. 13-14.
80. *Ibid.*, pp. 15-16.
81. *Georgia Laws*, 1957, pp. 168-169.
82. *Georgia Laws*, 1959, pp. 15-17.
83. *Ibid.*, p. 18.

84. *Ibid.*, pp. 78-79.
85. *Ibid.*, pp. 7-8.
86. *Ibid.*, pp. 18-19.
87. *Ibid.*, pp. 350-51.
88. *Ibid.*, p. 21.
89. *Georgia Laws*, 1961, pp. 31-35.
90. *Ibid.*, pp. 35-38.
91. *Ibid.*, pp. 261-262.
92. *Ibid.*, pp. 595-596.
93. *Georgia Laws*, 1962, pp. 552-558.
94. *Georgia Laws*, 1963, pp. 514-520.
95. *Georgia Laws*, 1958, pp. 206-207.
96. *Ibid.*, pp. 198-200.
97. *Georgia Laws*, 1963, pp. 431-432.
98. *Ibid.*
99. Georgia Department of Education *Annual Report*, 1968, pp. 101-106.
100. *Georgia Laws*, 1962, pp. 652-653.
101. *Georgia Laws*, 1945, pp. 229-232.
102. Georgia Department of Education *Annual Report*, 1898, pp. 10-12.
103. Mamie Joe Jones, *History for Program of Exceptional Children*, State Department of Education, 1951-170, (unpublished), p. 1.
104. *Ibid.*
105. *Georgia Laws*, 1949, pp. 1406-11.
106. *Georgia Laws*, 1951, pp. 422-23.
107. Georgia Department of Education *Annual Report*, 1952, p. 29.
108. Georgia Board of Education, *Minutes* (March 18-19, 1954).
109. Georgia Board of Education, *Minutes* (July 8-9, 1957).
110. Georgia Board of Education, *Minutes* (October 24, 1957).
111. Georgia Board of Education, *Minutes* (February 10, 1958).
112. Georgia Board of Education, *Minutes* (January 24, 1958).
113. Georgia Board of Education, *Minutes* (April 24, 1958; May 12, 1958).
114. Georgia Board of Education, *Minutes* (July 14, 1958).
115. *Georgia Laws*, 1949, pp. 1406, 1411.
116. Georgia Board of Education, *Minutes* (May 27-28, 1952).
117. Georgia Board of Education, *Minutes* (October 15-16, 1958).
118. Georgia Board of Education, *Minutes* (November 21, 1960).
119. Georgia Board of Education, *Minutes* (December 19, 1960).
120. Georgia Board of Education, *Minutes* (November 16-17, 1959).
121. Georgia Board of Education, *Minutes* (December 14-15, 1959).
122. Carl G. Renfroe, *The Growth and Development of Teacher Certification in Georgia* (unpublished doctoral dissertation, University of Georgia, 1964), p. 177.
123. *Ibid.*
124. *Georgia Laws*, 1963, p. 356.
125. Renfroe, *Teacher Certification*, p. 178.
126. *Georgia Laws*, 1962, pp. 17-37.
127. *Georgia Laws*, 1943, p. 298.

CHAPTER VI

Progress to the Present, 1964-1976

Throughout Georgia's history educational legislation was written to meet future needs. Ever since Governor George Gilmer's 1837 announcement of plans to correct the defects within public education,[1] this pledge has acquired a familiar ring in the speeches and reports of succeeding governors and state school commissioners. With succeeding pieces of legislation to improve education, politicians had thought or said in many cases, "Well, this should do for years to come." But economics, society, education, culture, civil rights, customs and competition have demanded an advancement from the existing states of affairs. Not only in the field of education, but in other government services as well, the public has usually secured its demands, if it is willing to pay for the improvements requested.

In 1941, commenting on the Barrett-Rogers Consolidation Act of 1919, one of its authors, Z. B. "Zeb" Rogers, said, "We thought with that bill we would have afforded the means whereby the state could develop the kind of high schools that we need. Modern times require more than we had anticipated." [2] One of the authors of another 1919 Act, the Elders-Carswell Bill, asked in 1943 for a set of McGuffey's Readers. Though they were out of print, Elders claimed they were the only materials needed in the public schools to teach reading. He wanted a set for his personal use.[3] The interviewer and Elders concurred in the opinion that the Elders-Carswell Bill was the most revolutionary educational legislation prior to 1919, but improvements were certainly appropriate at the time (1943).

When the Seven Months School Law was passed in 1937, many teachers, administrators, legislators, board members and Governor E. D. Rivers felt that its framework would require no further major changes in the law. Actually many amendments subsequently were added to the Seven Months School Law. By the mid-1940s educators recognized the need for another study to supersede this law's advances. This study resulted in the Educational Panel, headed by Dr. O. C. Ader-

441

hold. Consultant to the panel, State Auditor B. E. Thrasher, remarked that the recommendations of the panel could be implemented by laws already on the books, if the legislature would just appropriate adequate funds to authorize the additional services. Further study indicated, however, that many features, such as a drastic need for more local support, would mandate additional legislation. This, the first Minimum Foundation Law of 1949-51, was certainly another major breakthrough in educational legislation.

Although Georgia had made phenomenal progress in several phases of education between 1920 and 1960, educators acknowledged voids in the existing educational structure. Politicians and would-be politicians, looking for platform planks, often compared Georgia's educational defects with those in other states, but few critics admitted Georgia's continual ranking near the bottom in financial support for education. As Georgia increased its appropriations for education, other states were increasing their appropriations more rapidly than Georgia. In 1961, Georgia ranked forty-sixth among the states in financial support for education.[4]

In his gubernatorial campaign in 1962, Carl Sanders advocated another major revision in Georgia's education system. While recognizing the validity of the 1949 MFPE law, he detected a great need for expansion of services and further improvement in education. Upon taking office in 1963, Governor Sanders asked the General Assembly to authorize another, more comprehensive study of all phases of public education, even beyond high school. He envisioned meeting future educational needs and pledged full support of legislation necessary to accomplish recommendations. The governor learned of one revenue source from preliminary data supplied by the Property Tax Unit of the State Revenue Department. These data consisted of the sales-assessment ratio studies described in the preceding chapter. Governor Sanders tapped the experience of Augusta banker Douglas S. Barnard as executive secretary to establish a financially efficient administration.

Complying with Governor Sanders' request, the General Assembly authorized, through resolution in 1963, the Governor's Commission to Improve Education.[5] The commission consisted of 15 members of the General Assembly, including freshman Senator Jimmy Carter from Plains and 15 leading business, professional and civic leaders, including Dr. James S. Peters, chairman of the State Board of Education; Hazel Lewis, president of the Georgia Education Association; Dr. Horace Tate, executive secretary of the Georgia Teachers and Education Association; Dr. James L. Miller from the Southern Regional Education Board, who served as director of the commission; Dr. Woodrow Breland from George State College and Thomas W. Mahler from the University of Georgia, who served as associate director of the commission. Serving as consultants to the commission were Dr. John Ivey from Michigan State University, Dr. John Henry Fischer from Columbia University and Dr. John Dale Russell, educational consultant.

The commission, operating under a severe time limitation, submitted its report, *Educating Georgia's People—Investment in the Future,* to the General Assembly in January 1964. The report covered goals and made recommendations concerning educational planning, elementary and secondary schools, education beyond high school, educational television and educational finance.

Because of his background in educational legislation and law, Governor Sanders requested former Assistant Attorney General Donald E. Payton to draft the necessary legislation to implement the commission's recommendations. Purcell assigned office space and secretarial assistance to Payton for a period of more than three months. Payton worked full time on the bill, constantly consulting the commission, the governor, Purcell and Dr. Allen C. Smith, assistant state school superintendent.

As a preface to some recommendations in its report, the commission stated in part,[6]

> Georgia's educational accomplishments during recent years are recognized and applauded by the Commission. Georgia's present and prospective educational needs grow out of the rapidly changing demands of the space age rather than out of past negligence. (p. 17).

> Georgia needs an education program which is:

> 1. Of high quality.
> 2. Efficiently and effectively operated.
> 3. Relevant to the needs of individual students and of the state.

4. Comprehensive enough to meet the varied needs of students, of the state, and of the nation. (p. 17).

The full achievement of these goals will take a number of years. Many actions can be initiated immediately which will put Georgia on the road toward their accomplishment. A program to improve education cannot be achieved by any one Commission, one session of the legislature, one Governor's administration. (p. 67).

Improvement of quality and enrichment of programs will require further outlays which will bring the total to a rate about three times as great as present expenditures. The Commission recommends that every effort be exerted to at least triple financial support for education in the next 10 to 12 years, recognizing this is an investment which will be amply repaid in social and economic betterment and personal enrichment of the lives of Georgians. (p. 64).

The state (from state and local sources combined) will need to increase its proportionate effort in relation to income by approximately one-third to provide the necessary financial support for a quality program more comparable to national levels. (p. 64).

Most of the recommendations proposed by the commission were adopted into law. Three specific types of recommendations either were not included in the original draft of the bill or were deleted by the legislature. These recommendations which did not survive include the following.

1. Organization and Administration

Early in its deliberations, the commission became convinced that educational improvement in Georgia would necessitate certain revisions in the constitution and statutes. In order to identify state responsibility for public schools, the commission recommended that

"The state Constitution should establish and identify the State Public School System, free and equal to all citizens, to be supported by public funds as provided by law."

Functions of the office of superintendent were clarified by the following recommendations.

In Article VIII, Section III, Paragraph I, the following wording was suggested as a substitute: "There shall be a State Superintendent of Schools who shall be the administrative officer of the State Department of Education and the executive officer of the State Board of Education."

The above revision would have removed the existing constitutional requirement that the state superintendent be elected, with qualifications and salary set by law.

The commission gave more specific attention to the selection of the State Board of Education members and the state superintendent of schools. Representing each congressional district, the State Board of Education's 10 members were appointed by the governor and approved by the Senate for seven-year, staggered terms. The state superintendent was elected by the citizenry for a four-year term at the same time as the governor. The commission recommended that

> The Constitution should be revised to provide that the State Superintendent of Schools be appointed by the State Board of Education.

and that

> The members of the State Board of Education should be selected in the following manner: as vacancies on the present board occur, the local school board members in each congressional district shall caucus and nominate three candidates for the affected district; the Governor shall then make the appointment from said three candidates in each district.

In order to further insure representation of various groups of people on the Georgia Board of Education, it was recommended that "Five additional members from the state at large should be appointed by the Governor to the State Board of Education."

It was thought by the commission that many Georgia school laws dealing with minor details might be better determined by school boards and administrative personnel rather than by statutory provisions. Furthermore, laws often were contradictory, overlapping and ineffective. Therefore, the commission recommended that

The Georgia School Laws should be revised and recodified to remove archaic and confused provisions and to support the new constitutional provisions and recommendations of this Commission. Specifically, the Commission recommends that a complete recodification of Georgia's educational laws be undertaken.

When considering local school organization and administration, the commission concluded that strong administrative leadership operates effectively when directed by a policy-making board responsive to the public; therefore, it recommended "In Article VIII, Section VI, Paragraph I, of the Constitution of Georgia, the following language should be substituted: 'The local school superintendent be the administrative officer of the local school system and executive officer of the local board of education.' "

The above revision would also have removed the constitutional requirement that local superintendents be elected, with their qualifications and salaries set by law, and it would have specified functions of the superintendent.

2. State/Local Support of Education

A recommendation that would have removed the homestead exemption for school purposes stated, "It is recommended that the Constitution and statutes of Georgia be revised so that no property will be exempt from ad valorem taxes for school purposes."

Another recommendation would have allowed systems to provide greater support for their schools by altogether removing the millage limitation for school purposes only. "Tax limitation for the support of public education shall not apply to the provision of the Constitution establishing the State Public School System."

For the many districts having difficulty financing needed plant facilities, the commission recommended that "The present constitutional limit for local bonds be raised from 7% to 10% of the assessed value of the unit."

3. Teachers

The commission made several recommendations related to teachers' salaries, qualifications and teacher-pupil ratio. The following recommendation has been discussed at many subsequent legislative sessions, but by 1975 had not been enacted into a law.

The Commission is impressed by many of the arguments in favor of merit pay for teachers, and it also is impressed by the problems (which may or may not be insurmountable) which are entailed in the development of such a plan. The Commission hopes that continued study and experimentation will be carried on at the state and local levels concerning this question.

Merit pay continues to be a debatable topic among legislators and educators. Proposals pertaining to teachers that were enacted into law are discussed later in this chapter.

Major recommendations ultimately adopted into law were activated as rapidly as funds were appropriated. They included the following.

1. Planning

Planning must take place at all levels and involve consideration of both broad and detailed problems. To meet this need,

Both the State Board of Education and the Board of Regents of the University System should take immediate action to accomplish whatever changes are necessary in policy, organization, and staffing to enable the respective boards and their ranking staff officers to devote considerable time and attention to long-range planning and to provide for them the types of information which will be necessary in planning.

Each should establish a unit within its organizational structure with specific responsibilities of this nature, and these units should be staffed with personnel of high competence.

This section specifically recommended research at both the State Board of Education and Board of Regents levels. It also recommended establishing a continuing agency with representatives from the two boards, the General Assembly and the general public to study educational needs and make recommendations for meeting them.

From this recommendation the Georgia Educational Improvement Council was formed in 1964 (Act 984. S. B. 198). Other recommendations of this and subsequent sections can be found in S. B. 180 of the 1964 session. To strengthen the applied research and planning, the commission stressed the need to develop basic research in education at the universities.

2. The School Program

Recommendations in this section were implemented directly by the State Board of Education and required no additional legislation. The proposals executed by the State Board of Education are presented later in this chapter. Becoming law through S. B. 180 of 1964 were the following recommendations.[7]

The Minimum Foundation Program for Education should provide for all essential elements of a high quality program including a comprehensive curriculum, highly qualified teachers, sufficient well-qualified adminstrative leadership and supporting services, sufficient materials and equipment, and complete school plant facilities.

The Minimum Foundation Program for Education should be revised to add specific allocations for certain categories of essential personnel such as principals, librarians, and guidance personnel who presently are financed through the basic teacher allocation.

The present allocation practice increases the actual number of children per teacher above that provided by the foundation program, the commission said.

Because some school systems were not providing the expected minimum program at the time, the commission recommended that

Statutory authority should be given to the State Board of Education to establish and enforce minimum standards for schools and for school systems. Standards should be based upon such factors as program offerings, quality, and administrative efficiency; and these factors should be measured in a variety of ways, including but not restricted to school size and district size. The Board's enforcement authority should include but not be restricted to the right to withhold part or all of the state funds to which a district might otherwise be entitled.

Equal educational opportunities should be provided to all of the children and youth within each local school district. Practices of local school systems which are at variance with this principle should be changed.

The importance of preschool experience to later successes in school is addressed by the recommendation, "This Commission recommends that kindergartens be encouraged at the local level and endorses their use wherever practicable."

The commission made specific recommendations concerning several other aspects of the total school program. The following representational list presents typical items of current importance.

The proper school curriculum authority should conduct a re-examination of the curriculums in secondary schools to determine if changes and improvements can be made in them.

A statewide program should be developed for gifted high school students, possibly through correspondence courses or summer work in the colleges.

Special attention should be given to problems of grades 7, 8 and 9—with separate junior high schools a major consideration in districts large enough to make this practicable.

Greater emphasis should be placed upon the teaching of economic education and courses related to industrial management.

Local systems should be encouraged to provide driver education in a manner that will not interfere with the regular school program.

Special programs of instruction are necessary to develop the full potential of exceptional children—gifted, retarded, and handicapped. Continued and additional emphasis and support should be given by the State Department of Education to local systems to provide special programs for exceptional children.

The school lunch program should be considered as an essential part of the school program and should be adequately supported.

3. Larger School Units

Because small school units with an average daily attendance of fewer than 2,000 students were unable to provide the comprehensive programs outlined above, the commission proposed its only recommendation requiring a change in law. "Statutes and board regulations should be developed to encourage consolidation of small districts and provision of school services across local district boundaries."

The commission considered the implementation of this recommendation to be the single most important step in effecting immediate improvements in Georgia's educational program.

This recommendation led to the establishment of Shared Services Projects across system lines and subsequently to Cooperative Educational Service Agencies, (32-4001, 1972, pp. 550-551) and pupils attending school in adjacent school systems (32-650, 1964. pp. 3, 44.), but the clause referring to "consolidation of small districts" had not been enacted into law by 1975.

4. Teachers

The commission cited numerous data indicating a correlation between the quality of instruction and the number and quality of teachers. Georgia ranked forty-sixth in the nation in terms of number of pupils per teacher, and again ranked forty-sixth in the nation in per pupil support for education. Several recommendations concerning teachers' qualifications resulted in legislation.

> The legislature should reinstate and fully finance the excellent programs of scholarships for prospective teachers and grants-in-aid for study by in-service teachers. These programs have done much to improve the qualifications of Georgia's teachers and they should be continued. In general, these should be restricted to the content field in which the teacher is engaged or will be engaged immediately thereafter.

In the following recommendations the commission recognized the importance of teachers' salaries to attract and maintain competent people.

> The present teacher salary schedule in Georgia is not conducive to attracting or holding the best teachers. The

Commission specifically recommends that attention be given to the following.

1. The level of teacher salaries should be raised to make the profession of teaching in Georgia competitive with other professions and occupations and competitive with teaching in other states. Georgia's immediate objective should be to catch up as quickly as possible with her neighboring states of North Carolina and Florida, and we do not think it unreasonable for the Empire State of the South to aspire to equal or exceed the national average within a reasonable number of years.

2. The practice of increasing the teacher salary level in the Minimum Foundation Program on an across-the-board basis should be discontinued. The Commission is impressed with the "index" type of salary schedule which has been developed by the State Salary Committee and approved in principle by a number of educational organizations, and it recommends that this type of salary schedule be adopted and periodically adjusted to meet changing needs.

Improved teaching conditions will play an important part in attracting and holding capable teachers. Needed improvements range from a reduction in the excessively high number of children in many classes and provision of more adequate buildings, equipment, materials and teaching aids to the development of imaginative educational programs which will capture and hold the interest of teachers.

We recommend that a firm policy be established giving all principals the responsibility and authority to recommend the employment of teaching personnel to the superintendent who will in turn recommend such personnel to the Board of Education.

5. Educational Effectiveness

Though greater efficiency would effect some improvement in the present educational system, the commission recognized that substantial improvement could be achieved only with skilled personnel. "Experimentation with new teaching methods should be widely encouraged and financial support should be provided for it from state as well as local sources. Promising new ideas should be promoted vigorously by the State Department of Education."

This recommendation was, of course, integral to the research and planning functions discussed in other sections of the report. It created a built-in self-improvement arrangement at both state and local levels.

The extent to which modern technology can increase efficiency in teaching and learning was explored, leading to the recommendation that, "New teaching media such as television, programmed instruction, language laboratories, audio-visual film libraries, and similar specialized facilities should be utilized as widely as possible."

In order to insure the highest educational return from each tax dollar, the commission considered changing statutes and policies.

> The Commission recommends a policy of centralized purchasing of many major items of school equipment including, but not limited to, such items as buses, gasoline, oil, insurance, and others. Local systems should be given the option to accept state bids or use their own bids, provided the local bid is no higher than the state bid.

> Consideration should be given to the desirability of placing the transportation section of the Minimum Foundation Program on the basis of payments based upon a determination of the needs of an efficient system, rather than payments based upon reimbursement of actual expenses.

Local systems wishing to change selection procedures for school boards or superintendents were forced to tackle a cumbersome constitutional amendment and legislative process. The commission therefore recommended that

> The method of selecting local school boards and local superintendents should be a matter of local option. Appropriate constitutional and statutory changes should be made to simplify the procedures by which a local school system changes the method of selecting these officials. The Commission expresses its belief that appointment of local superintendents is the preferable system.

6. Vocational Programs

Better vocational education would provide training for the 80 percent of college-age Georgians not attending college. Anticipating a 31 percent decrease in employment in farm occupations and an increase in clerical, sales and artisan occupations of 44 percent within a 15-year period, as well as tremendous importance of technicians and skilled workers, the commission stated,

Vocational education programs in high schools, area schools, state schools, and for adults, should be continually adjusted to needs of students and to available employment opportunities.

The present trend in vocational education toward a greater emphasis upon trade and industrial programs and a proportionately smaller emphasis upon agricultural programs is in keeping with employment trends in the state and should be expected to continue.

Greater emphasis should be placed upon education for business and for the distributive and diversified occupations.

The possibility should be considered of developing cooperative programs between high schools and area vocational-technical schools under which high school credit might be given for course work taken in the vocational-technical school under the cooperative plan. However, whenever possible the vocational-technical education should be included in the comprehensive high school program.

The possibility of utilizing vocational agriculture teachers and home economics teachers to teach in other vocational fields or in science and other related subjects should be explored, since in many cases this would require only a limited amount of additional training and would provide teachers in needed fields.

7. Education Beyond the High School

Because Georgia ranked low in the percentage of college-age citizens attending college, the commission recommended that all efforts be made to increase the number of college-age Georgians pursuing higher education. Sources such as community colleges, graduate schools and adult education classes in the state's public schools and colleges were suggested avenues for broadening adult educational participation.

State-financed transportation to area vocational-technical schools was authorized and subsequently realized under the 1964 act. Emphasized throughout this section was the need for a close working relationship between the community colleges and the area vocational-technical schools, which also necessitated a close working relationship between the State Board of Regents and the State Board of Education.

8. Television

The commission evaluated the progress of ETV and recommended future programming improvements.

> Planning for educational television should be greatly expanded to include state network facilities, statewide curriculum planning project, expansion of adult and cultural programs for evening hours, and more effective use of broadcast and closed circuit television.

The State Board of Education and the State Board of Regents have continued to cooperate in programming, curriculum development, staff sharing and facility improvement throughout the state network. The state administration and General Assembly have been equally cooperative.

9. Finance

The commission spent considerable time studying educational costs to determine projections for the immediate future. The figures were astronomical. For years, Georgia had ranked low in national school costs. Before presenting any of its concrete recommendations, the commission stated, ". . . .since neither the nation nor Georgia will 'freeze' their educational systems, it is even reasonable to assume that in the normal course of events both Georgia and the nation will continue to up-grade their educational systems, with the net result that 10 years from now: (1) both Georgia and the nation will have better educational systems than they have now, and (2) Georgia's people will still be among the most poorly educated in the 50 states. The cost of this hold the line educational program by 1975 will be approximately double the present cost of Georgia's educational program." (By 1972, Georgia's rank in educational revenue receipts per student had dropped to 48th in the nation [8] in spite of increased appropriations in the state. Other states had increased proportionately more than Georgia.) Another statement prefacing the firm recommendation was, "The Commission did not attempt to formulate specific financial recommendations concerning actions the 1964 session, or any other session of the General Assembly, should take, other than to stress the urgent need for action, the immense size of the task, and the consequent necessity for making a substantial beginning and for following up on this in future years." Thus, the recommendations which were translated into law at the 1964 session included some of the most valid mechanics for improving educational financing in the nation at that time.

10. State-Local Support of Education

The commission critically reviewed Georgia's Minimum Foundation Program for Education, particularly the provisions dealing with the share of financial support borne by the state and by local districts. Concurring with the Minimum Foundation Program's underlying purpose to guarantee equal opportunity for all children regardless of where they live, the report stated,

The Commission affirms its belief in the basic principals of equalization under which state funds are the factor which helps insure that no child in Georgia will be deprived of educational opportunities because the locality in which he lives is too poor to provide them.

The Minimum Foundation Program for Education should be based upon an equitable and understandable fair-share formula which includes both state and local contributions. At present the Commission believes that an 85%-15% statewide average for state and local contributions constitutes a fair sharing of the financial burden. However the Commission recommends that this be re-evaluated from time to time.

Adequate steps should be taken to insure that local districts actually raise and spend for the educational purpose, within the areas designated by MFPE, at least the

amount of money determined through the Minimum
Foundation Program formula to be the "fair" local share.
To accomplish this, adequate budgeting, reporting, and
auditing procedures (perhaps including pre-auditing)
should be instituted, such as those recommended by the
Commission on Efficiency and Improvement in Government.

In order to make sure that the procedures outlined above
would be carried out, the commission further recommended
that

> There is a need for an agency or commission to determine
> the ability of a local school unit of administration to sup-
> port itself and to review continuously the financial ability
> of each local unit of administration. The commission rec-
> ommends that an agency or commission, with legal au-
> thority to provide the services herein stated, be created
> at the next session of the Georgia General Assembly.

The commission realized that local authorities who attempted to contribute their fair share faced a variety of obstacles
including the lack of property revaluation in many counties,
millage limitations and the homestead exemption provision
of the constitution. The following recommendation intended
to remove these obstacles.

> Property revaluation for tax purposes should be en-
> couraged in all of the school districts which have not
> already undertaken action along these lines, and consider-
> tion should be given to methods whereby the present pro-
> gram of state assistance in such studies can be stepped
> up. State action should be taken to adjust upward the
> maximum millage limitations in counties which have low
> property assessment rates so that, until revaluation oc-
> curs, the tax return which can be secured is as high as
> though the property were assessed at the statewide aver-
> age.

Major recommendations referring to State Board of Education policies and regulations enacted into law included the
following.

1. Curriculum changes at all levels
2. Guidance and counseling at all levels
3. Extension of visiting teacher services
4. Instruction in lower grades and at remedial levels
5. Re-evaluation of extra-curricular activities
6. Extension of the school day
7. Larger elementary and high school units
8. Teacher certification standards and requirements
9. Re-evaluation and expansion of vocational programs
10. Cooperative programs with high and vocational-technical schools
11. Cooperative programs with State Board of Regents in Teacher training
   Educational Television
   Community Colleges
   Adult education for out-of-school age citizens
12. Re-organization of the State Department of Education

The final item was also included in the new law (Sec. 32-654). The State Board of Education assumed leadership in this area. Out-of-state consultants assisting in this project were Dr. Harold Alderfer, a former assistant state school superintendent in Pennsylvania; Rodman Porter from Texas and Dr. James Gibbs, administrative specialist with the U. S. Office of Education. Instructional services received special emphasis in the reorganization plan. After much study with the visiting consultants and a nationally reputed management firm, the State Board of Education authorized a plan placing offices of services within the areas of administration, instruction, rehabilitation and staff. The new law, requiring more internal accounting and services and an expansion of data processing, necessitated creating the Office of Staff Services.

The commission report highlighted the great void in the financial structure of the schools of the state, concluding with these statements.

The nub of the problem, the Commission found, lies in the extra effort that will be required to bring about real improvement. This extra effort includes an extra financial investment beyond the amount required simply to care for natural growth, and an extra amount of political and educational courage and leadership beyond that required simply to maintain the status quo and "keep up." The Commission is convinced that this extra effort is essential to the future well-being of Georgia.

Although the foundation act of 1949, financed by the Sales Tax Act of 1951, had many excellent characteristics, the 1964 Minimum Foundation Program was more far-reaching and offered many additional services. It provided a bona fide partnership between the state and each county and independent city school system in Georgia. Under this law, the minimum needs of each school system were calculated by formulas prescribed by law.

Each school system's required local support was determined through an adjusted tax digest. For example, a county with two percent of the total computed uniform digest for the state was expected to assume two percent of the total required local effort. The computed uniform digest replaced the economic index in the old foundation law as the basis for distributing the total required local effort among all school systems of the state.

The 1964 session, through another law, required the state auditor to be responsible for establishing the new computed digest using experts familiar with operations of this kind.[9] The steps in the development of such a digest for a county are as follows.

1. All valid sales of property in the county during a given year would be listed with the sale price of the property as indicated by tax stamps on the deed.
2. The sale price of each parcel of property would be compared with the value returned for tax purposes on the books of county tax receivers or collectors.
3. Based on these comparisons of sale price with values returned, the percent of valuation as compared with true value would be established. For example, if property valued on the tax records as $5,000 should be sold for $20,000, the percentage of true value returned for tax purposes would be valued at one-fourth of true value.
4. When the average percent of valuation as compared with true value was determined, the total digest for

the county, including the public utilities digest, can be adjusted for the purposes of this law to 100 percent or some other uniform percentage decided upon for the state as a whole.

5. The adjusted digests for all 159 counties would be added together to establish the computed uniform digest for the state as a whole.

6. The percent of the digest for each county would be computed by dividing the computed digest for the county by the total for the state.

7. The percent for each county would then be multiplied by the total required statewide local effort to determine that county's share of the required local effort.

The computed adjusted tax digest provided in Senate Bill 180 was to be used for one purpose only—to provide an objective formula for the distribution of required local effort among the 159 counties of the state. Each county would establish its own digest for collection of taxes as heretofore.

Counties with independent city systems shared the total required local effort between the county and independent city school systems, using a one-third increase factor on the independent city digest.

To determine the minimum needs of each school system, the law provided that the cost be calculated on the payment of the following 11 items.

1. Regular teachers' salaries
2. Salaries of professional leadership personnel
3. Cost of maintenance, operation and sick leave
4. Purchase of free textbooks
5. Purchase of consumable materials
6. Purchase of school library materials
7. Added cost of operating isolated schools
8. Pupil transportation
9. Travel expenses
10. Special education programs
11. Operating a statewide educational television network

The 1969 General Assembly removed as a foundation item the cost of operating the statewide television network.[10] Of the above-named, item five had not been activated as of 1971 inasmuch as no funds had been appropriated for consumable supplies. Appropriations for funding Section 32-628, which equalized contingency funds, were discontinued in 1966. Legislators in counties ineligible for these funds maneuvered the deletion of equalization funds.

After the minimum costs for each system were determined, the required local support was subtracted from the minimum costs, and the state underwrote the balance, thereby providing a minimum program for each system.

Dr. Claude Purcell, who succeeded Dr. M. D. Collins in 1958, had long advocated several principles of educational finance that became a part of the 1964 act. Most outstanding were (1) state allotment of leadership personnel, (2) an index teacher salary schedule and (3) additional state allotments for geographically isolated schools. By receiving state funds for leadership personnel, local school systems could employ non-teaching professionals as principals, libararians, counselors, visiting teachers, curriculum consultants and administrators without damaging classroom allotments.

The 1964 foundation program also provided the following.

1. Assurance of state support for at least a minimum program for each school system in the state.
2. The assurance that state funds would not replace local responsibility.
3. The assurance of a reasonable equity for all taxpayers.
4. Provision for sound, efficient organization and administration.
5. At the local level, maximum opportunity for expansion beyond the minimum.
6. An equalization factor.
7. Provision for continuous and long-range planning.

The first three items refer primarily to school support. The state receives most of its revenue for school support from the state sales tax and the state income tax. The local, county and independent city school systems receive their support primarily from property taxes. This arrangement maintains a fairly delicate balance between the three major sources of revenue for school purposes.

The Georgia financial structure is regarded by many authorities as meeting criteria for foundation financing. The

National Educational Finance Project ranked the Georgia plan as eleventh in the nation in 1968-69 in the degree of equalization.[11] At the same time in 1967-68, Georgia ranked fourth in the nation in the percent of revenue from state sources allocated to public elementary and secondary schools.

The State Board of Education is responsible for developing policies, rules and regulations for implementing the many services specified by the legislature. Therefore, with the advice and consultation of the state superintendent, the state board organizes and trains the staff who perform the duties designated by law.

When the legislature enacted the 1964 foundation law, the state board followed Purcell's recommendation and assigned the George Peabody College Division of Surveys and Field Services the responsibility for studying the public schools in Georgia and developing suitable criteria. It also directed the Georgia Department of Education to establish and enforce minimum standards for operating all phases of public education in Georgia.

The Peabody report in 1965 attributed Georgia's educational progress to dissatisfaction with the status quo.[12] It contained sweeping recommendations for school district reorganization. Even though the state reduced the number of districts in 1945 from 1,454 to 197, the report stated that Georgia needed no more than 50 school districts, each with a minimum of 10,000 students. While these recommendations have not yet been implemented, their publication has had a dramatic effect on Georgians.

Jack P. Nix Administration

Dr. Jack P. Nix, who succeeded Dr. Claude Purcell in 1965, realized that the future of education in Georgia depends on long-range plans and goals. He recommended that the State Board of Education consider a plan for studying educational needs.

The state board initiated plans in 1968 for identifying future needs through the Georgia Assessment Project. This advisory commission of top-flight business and professional leaders studied the measurable impact of educational programs, determined relationships between costs and educational benefits and developed long-range planning.[13]

The commission's extensive and comprehensive report has been the state board's blueprint for future developments. The department's application of minimum standards in all schools provides excellent evidence of Georgia's increased quality of education. From its beginning, this movement has shown unusual potential. Most Georgians agree with former Governor Carl E. Sanders' speech of October 11, 1966, when he dedicated the state's fifth educational TV station. Governor Sanders said, "The single most important job of state and local government is the education of our children. Georgia can have splendid highways, ultra-modern physical and mental health services, unlimited natural resources and a stubborn determination to improve, yet unless our children receive the finest education obtainable, then our state will flounder in a quagmire of failure and despair." [14]

Though the acts of 1964 authorized and instructed the State Board of Education to develop minimum standards for public schools, they were not applied statewide until the 1966-67 school year. The state board appointed a committee on standards in 1965 to study needs and develop practical standards. Some of the leading educators in the state served on this committee, chaired by Dr. W. H. Shaw, superintendent of Muscogee County schools. After several schools participated in a pilot program in 1966, the standards were revised, then implemented by the State Department of Education. Dr. Clyde Pearce, standards coordinator in the State Department of Education, has worked closely with the Standards Council to upgrade the program annually.

The United States Congress boosted education in 1965 by enacting Public Law 89-10, commonly known as the Elementary and Secondary Education Act (ESEA). Most significantly, Title I of the bill assured increased financial support to students in deprived areas. Local school districts devoted energy to improving instruction in districts or areas where the economic level had been historically low. Titles II, III, IV and V of the bill supplemented support for textbooks, libraries, and other instructional materials; research and experimentation; strengthening and improving state departments of education and for improvements in auditing and accounting services.

Under Title III of ESEA, a Shared Services Project begun in 1966 permitted several school systems to share educational services which they might otherwise be financially unable to provide individually. With the first project's extraordinary success, the idea quickly spread throughout the state. The original project was in the Ninth Congressional District with headquarters in Cleveland, Georgia. The second Shared Services Project was in the First Congressional District with headquarters in Statesboro, Georgia. As the plan spread throughout the state, legislation was enacted and state financial support became a reality. An act in 1972 provided the legal status for these projects, their organizational pattern, methods of financial support and powers and duties of a board of control.[15] The name was changed under the act to Cooperative Educational Service Agencies (CESA). The program trained staff specialists to work with local personnel in instruction as well as testing and psychological services. Some districts also used cooperative buying to save local funds.

Under the 1974 APEG Act, the CESA program was again strengthened and broadened. Every school system in the state has access to membership in one of the CESA projects. Some larger systems have elected not to participate in CESA, mainly because they have sufficient resources to provide services on an individual school system basis.

Under the Elementary and Secondary Education Act the State Department of Education expanded its services to local school districts, especially in the fields of instruction and accounting services. Title I and Title V funds permitted the State Department of Education to extend its services to children who were handicapped and visually impaired. Other federal funds for special education were provided under Public Law 85-926. Title IV of ESEA in 1967 extended services to the handicapped from ages three through 21 years.

A very broad program of education for all exceptional children by 1976 was mandated by the General Assembly in 1968.[16] This bill prescribed a state and local advisory council on exceptional children, as well as obligated the state to more support and services on state and local levels. Subsequent progress can be attributed to the passage of this act, H. B. 453 of 1968. Many goals sought by the State Board of Education for special education were accomplished by this mandatory legislation.

The Professional Teachers Practices Act, passed by the General Assembly in 1967, was activated in 1968.[17] By declaring teaching a profession, this legislation accorded to teachers and administrators all rights and privileges extended to other legally recognized professions in the state. Educators received authority to develop codes of ethics and professional performance. The act also established a Professional Practices Commission with power to hold hearings for members of the profession whose ethics had been questioned. Financing of the commission's operations was detailed in the law. Subsequent work of the Professional Practices Commission has proven to be an asset to members of the teaching profession.

Two bills enacted in 1968 strengthened the vocational education program and also provided industry with much needed talent. The Quick Start Training Program authorized the State Board of Education to provide training programs for new and expanding industries.[18] A companion bill created an Industries Services Advisory Committee to work with local boards of education, vocational-technical schools, federal and other agencies which provided skilled and semi-skilled training for industry. These training programs, each lasting less than one year, included basic academic education whenever required to insure trainees success in their respective occupations.[19] Broad powers were given to the State Board of Education in the operation of this program. Its success has been outstanding.

Other than Social Security, non-teaching school employees usually received little or no retirement benefits. A constitutional amendment in 1968 authorized a state retirement plan for non-teaching school employees.[20] This amendment was ratified by the voters and soon became law. Bus drivers, maintenance workers and school food service personnel were covered under this act. As contributions and appropriations increase from year to year, benefits have become more salutary.

Many Georgia school systems had paid very little local taxes for the support of education until the enactment of required local effort factors in the two foundation programs (1951 and 1964). When they started paying taxes for school operation, many taxpayers experienced a shock. With the adjusted tax digest of the 1964 foundation law, local systems were charged for their wealth whether they collected taxes on it or not. Thus, local systems began tax re-evaluation in earnest. But required local effort became anathema in several circles. Education was often cited as the cause for all increases in local taxes. Studies for the years of 1966 through 1971, however, showed that the county boards of commissioners collected more taxes in the aggregate during those years than did county boards of education. In 1968 the Association County Commissioners of Georgia sponsored legislation to reduce the maximum local tax levy from 20 mills to 5 mills, to raise the sales tax from three percent to four percent and distribute the additional sales tax revenue on an average daily attendance basis. The General Assembly immediately recognized two fallacies in this proposal. (1) There would be a local loss in school revenue of $28,600,000 and (2) distribution of funds on an average daily attendance basis would completely eliminate the one equalization factor by giving the poorer districts (based on taxable wealth per student) $41 millon less than their then current funds, while wealthier districts (based on taxable wealth per student) would receive $13 million more than their current receipts. The act failed. However, in 1969 by legislative act the cost of educational television was deleted from the local effort formula and was thereafter paid entirely from state funds.[21]

In 1970, the Association County Commissioners proposed legislation to remove property tax as a source of revenue for schools.[22] Without a design to revise the state tax structure, this plan also faltered. The county commissioners were not alone in their desire to reduce taxes or to eliminate required local effort from the school law. In successive sessions of the General Assembly, legislation has been repeatedly introduced which, if passed, would seriously hamper educational financing. Some of the proposals have suggested a rollback feature which in effect would automatically reduce local taxes by an amount equal to the increase in state funds. This plan was tried in Florida but was ruled unconstitutional in 1970 by a federal court.[23] In 1969, the Georgia Municipal Association presented a plan of distribution of extra state funds to include municipalities as well as counties and school systems.[24] The report did preface its proposed allotments with the statement: ". . . . These figures should be considered estimates only to be used for comparison and study. They do not represent official figures." [25] Accuracy was not a factor in the distributed report, as some legislators detected immediately a series of errors for each school system in the state. Some reports were recovered immediately and the municipal association plan did not get a hearing in 1969.

In order to simplify and more nearly equalize the required local effort feature of the foundation law, Superintendent Nix advocated a bill in 1971 which changed the method of calculating the required local effort to read in effect, "the amount of such funds to be raised by each local unit of administration shall be calculated by multiplying the formula of .29 of one percent times the total equalized adjusted school property tax digest." [26] The bill passed with no major opposition.

The law significantly eliminated rapid escalation of required local effort due to increases in the cost of education. Consequently, school systems' required local effort increased only when there was an increase in the local system's adjusted property tax digest. The simplicity of this formula allowed local boards and superintendents to determine their required local effort months in advance of the upcoming fiscal year.

The following year the General Assembly froze the state total required local effort at an amount not to exceed $78,600,000.[27] This did not freeze the required local effort for each system, which was still determined by the 1971 act. A slight variation could occur, but no sudden increase would be possible without a sudden surge in the adjusted property tax digest.

From 1968 through 1972 a number of court cases throughout the nation challenged the methods of financing public schools. Unlike in Georgia, where a majority of school funds comes from state taxes, these cases surfaced in states whose school districts were financed primarily by property taxes. The most significant cases were in Illinois [28] in 1968, four 1971 cases in Texas,[29] California,[30] Minnesota [31] and Wyoming [32] and the New Jersey [33] case in 1972. The California state court determined that its statewide public school financing system, with its substantial dependence on local property taxes and resulting wide disparities in school revenue, was discriminatory and violated the equal protection clause of the 14th amendment by making the quality of a child's education dependent on the wealth of parents and neighbors. Because the California court was reviewing the propriety of a demurrer and remanded the case to the trial court, the decision has not been appealed to the United States Supreme Court.

In the Texas case, commonly referred to as *Rodriguez*, a federal court opinion was appealed to the United States Supreme Court. Though the appeal was not sustained, the major question again was whether the Texas system of financing public education discriminated on the basis of wealth when it permitted citizens of affluent districts to provide higher quality education for their children while paying lower taxes.

The Texas and California cases were similar in impact throughout the country. The effect of these and other cases caused some concern in Georgia. A federal court in Atlanta heard a case brought by the Whitfield County Board of Education based on similar questions.[34] Before a decision was rendered in the Whitfield case, the U. S. Supreme Court ruled on the Texas case and therefore nullified the contentions of the Whitfield County plaintiffs. Since that time Whitfield County Board of Education has brought a case in the Polk County Georgia Superior Court [35] against the State Board of Education which is similar to other such cases pertaining to tax structure and methods of school support. By July 1976, this case had not been heard. Other cases filed in Georgia have not found favor for pursuit in the courts. Similar cases have been filed in about 30 other U. S. states.

Georgia's position in 1971 was less vulnerable than that of other states dependent on local property taxes rather than state funds. A comparison of sources in selected states is shown below.

Percent of Educational Support by Sources [36]

	State Funds	Local Funds	Federal Funds
Georgia	59%	28%	13%
California	34%	58%	8%
Minnesota	49%	55%	6%
New Jersey	14%	82%	4%

	State Funds	Local Funds	Federal Funds
Texas	39%	52%	9%
Delaware	70%	26%	4%
New Mexico	65%	14%	21%
Nort Carolina	64%	21%	15%
New Hampshire	10%	86%	4%
Nation as a whole	41%	52%	7%

Greatly concerned with the prospect of even slight variations in local support per student, Nix advocated a bill to equalize the per pupil support for education up to at least the fiftieth percentile of property values. This bill had not been financed by July 1976. The mechanics for equalizing a minimum educational support per student are now contingent on appropriations to finance this section of the law. The urgency for financing an equalization measure has been acute since 1966. With the pending court actions facing all states, the need to equalize educational opportunities in all school systems has sharpened. Many of Georgia's low-cost systems are in that position because of electing low millage when they could collect more taxes with their current digests. The students pay the price for low quality education.

During his 1966 gubernatorial campaign, Lester Maddox championed increased appropriations for teachers' salaries and local boards of education maintenance and operational costs. He also advocated a tax study committee to revise the state tax structure. During his term as governor, teachers' annual salaries were raised an average of $1783. The increments came in average annual increases of $700, $558 and $525. Beginning teachers' salaries were raised $1400 during the Maddox administration. Also during his term, January 1967 through December 1970, state funds for maintenance and operations increased $202 per allotment unit.

At the request of Governor Maddox, the General Assembly approved a study committee to review Georgia's tax structure and recommend improvements. The committee, commonly known as the Papke Committee, was named for tax expert Dr. James Papke of Indiana, who directed the study. Several members of the General Assembly and many civic and professional leaders served on the committee. As far as can be ascertained, no member of the education profession was ever invited to appear before the group, nor were any educational data requested. Following the conclusion of the study committee, Governor Maddox conducted several hearings throughout the state on a proposal to increase the state sales tax in order to expand services in all areas of state government. Staff of the State Department of Education were assigned to the team which was composed of leaders in each major state agency. This contingent of governmental administrators accompanied Governor Maddox to each of the hearings and presented a brief discussion of what the additional funds could provide in expanded state services. Subsequent sessions of the General Assembly failed to comply with Governor Maddox's request to increase the sales tax.

For many years prior to 1972, Georgians had been concerned about the lack of regulations governing proprietary schools. The problems became more acute as veterans applied for aid to attend school in order to learn a trade or occupation. Nonveterans were also interested in this training, but in many instances schools were abusing normal standard practices in advertising, recruitment, fees, staffs, facilities and caliber of instruction. Taking an intense interest in ths problem, the General Assembly enacted laws in 1972 to establish regulations relating to certain non-tax-supported vocational educational institutions.[37] The bill clarified legal relationships and provided adequate protection for students, educational institutions and the general public. Power was given to the State Board of Education to set up rules and regulations by which a Proprietary School Advisory Commission should govern these schools. The law established criteria for rating the schools. Operating bonds, hearing appeals and certification were prescribed in the law. The act was amended in 1973 [38] and again in 1974 [39] to clarify and strengthen certain sections. At least five of the advisory commission's nine members owned or taught at accredited proprietary schools. Funds for operating this unit within the State Department of Education were appropriated by the General Assembly.

As many previous governors had done, James Earl (Jimmy) Carter campaigned for office on a platform of "improving education." He had served on the Sumter County Board of Education and succeeded his father as its chairman for many years. He had also been on the Governor's Commission to Improve

Education in 1963 when he was a member of the Georgia Senate. During his term of office from January 1971 through December of 1974, many pieces of educational legislation were enacted as administration measures. Early in his term he began working to improve education.

Governor Carter expressed concern about "conflict of interest" tactics used by some members of county boards of education when dealing with schools in their respective districts. After consulting with educational leaders, he supported an administration bill to correct the problems. In 1972 the General Assembly set the qualifications of county board of education members.[40] With no opposition, this bill disqualified as members of county boards of education all persons serving on other school boards, including the State Board of Education, and also disqualified persons employed by other school boards and the State Board of Education. This section did not apply to institutions above the high school level.

Another act initiated early in the Carter administration was the Early Childhood Development Act of 1972,[41] which allowed local school systems and other state agencies to plan and implement early childhood development programs. The programs met the recognized needs of children whose parents voluntarily sought testing, diagnosis and treatment of physical or mental handicaps of children from one to three years of age; education programs for children five years of age and for children three to five years of age who have physical or mental handicaps. The State Board of Education was charged by law to evaluate the objectivity, scope and procedures of early childhood education programs within local school systems.

Among the many federal programs initiated and funded from 1965 through 1972, the important Right to Read program sought to insure literacy to all Georgians by 1980. Programs originating under ESEA as experimental have become a way of life in many areas of the state because of their effectiveness in improving instruction.

Highlights of the 1965-72 curricular accomplishments include career education programs, the quarter system plans, special education, instructional materials, statewide testing and high school holding power.[42] In 1966 the enrollment in grades 9-12 was 251,394; by 1972 this number had grown to

297,662. The number of high school graduates increased from 51,842 in 1966-67 to 56,982 in 1972. Seven percent more graduates entered college in 1972 than in 1967. Fewer students entered private colleges in 1972, but more students entered junior colleges that year. In 1965, there were 1,944 public schools in the state; in 1973 there were 1,803.

In 1965-66 there were 6.9 library books per child; in 1971-72 there were 13 per child. Other materials had grown proportionately in all libraries. Libraries existed in 93 percent of all schools in 1965-66. By the 1972-73 school year, only five schools were without libraries. Employment of full-time librarians increased from 910 schools in 1965-66 to 1,504 in 1972-73. Certified librarians had increased from 72 percent to 96 percent of the total. All other media increased substantially as well.

The goal of reaching the total population has caused a dramatic increase in special education services within local schools. Psychoeducational centers have been added across the state. Special facilities have been provided for the multiply handicapped at the Georgia Academy for the Blind in Macon.

The declining enrollment in city schools and the proportionate increase in county systems are revealed by the increase in transported students (506,955 in 1965-66; 599,216 in 1971-72) even though the total number of students in the state has remained relatively stable (1,114,309 in 1964-65 to a high of 1,147,957 in 1972-73). The decline in birth rate has affected the original high growth projections.

There were 51,708 high school graduates in 1965 and 57,755 in 1973. Three comprehensive high schools operated in 1965 and 80 in 1974. General Education Development (GED) tests administered increased from 3,535 in 1964 to 9,143 in 1973.

The following data show how high school students' course selection changed considerably from 1965 to 1972.

The 1972 enrollment for grades 9-12 increased 20 percent over 1966.

(a) The number taking English increased nearly 33 percent.

(b) Reading enrollment doubled.

(c) There were 33 percent to 100 percent increases in numbers of students taking mathematics. Enrollment in second year algebra increased by 20 percent. Consumer and applied mathematics courses grew from 2,500 to 7,300 students. Calculus courses grew from 258 to 836 students.

(d) Specialized courses in general science increased enrollment by 40 percent. Biology course enrollment grew 12 percent, even though it was no longer required. Enrollment in chemistry courses remained approximately the same while physics decreased 50 percent.

(e) In social studies there had been normal growth in enrollment, but in world history, world geography, sociology, international relations, introduction to law, contemporary affairs, Biblical history, there was a growth of 33 percent and more.

(f) Latin and French enrollment decreased; Spanish and German increased slightly and Russian enrollment remained the same.

(g) Physical education, driver education and ROTC showed a 30 to 50 percent increase. Health education decreased 30 percent.

(h) All vocational areas generally increased beyond normal growth. Many courses were added and enrollment grew rapidly.

(i) Industrial arts increased slightly in high schools and rapidly in the junior high-middle schools.

(j) Art education grew from an enrollment of 13,000 to 35,000.

(k) Music education grew normally.

The most valid long-range test comparisons cover a period from 1962 to 1974 and are shown in brief form below.

Statewide Test Scores: Reading Research Report, 1962.
Analysis

A study published in 1962, "Analysis of the Reading Achievement of White and Negro Pupils in Certain Public Schools of Georgia" reported lags in achievement increasing from the fourth to the twelfth grade.

. . . 5. At the twelfth grade level, the lag between achievement and the mid-year point of reference was considerably less for white pupils than for Negro pupils. The lag for white pupils was 1.5 grade levels in vocabulary, 2.2 grade levels in comprehension, and 2.0 grade levels in total reading achievement. For Negro pupils, the lag was 5.1 grade levels in vocabulary, 5.3 grade levels in comprehension, and 5.3 grade levels in total reading achievement.

In 1973-74, statewide scores for the total student population in Georgia indicated a reading score at the twelfth grade of 45.9, assuming 50 is the nationally standardized median score. ". . . The average increase per year varies somewhat among tests and among different levels of achievement within a given test, but an increase of 2 to 4 points should be regarded as within the normal range of progress."

During the period of 1965-1975 the following steps were taken to remedy the situation.

1. Three consultants statewide and varying numbers in local school systems and CESAs were employed to specifically handle the skills problem in reading.
2. The Model English and Model Reading Programs were developed.
3. Instructional materials used for teaching reading skills and informational and pleasure reading doubled in all schools and more than doubled in schools serving economically deprived students.

Comparison of scores from the two testing periods cited above strongly indicates overall reading improvement, though average scores remain slightly below the national norm.

Pupil Personnel Services improved in staff and quality during the period. School psychologists increased from 10 in 1966 to 185 in 1974-75. School counselors increased from 678 in 1966 to 1,025 in 1974-75. Certified visiting teachers increased from 240 in 1966 to 255 in 1974-75.

Special education also improved considerably. As special education services in schools developed, the state increased its numbers of psychological, psychometric and guidance personnel. Visiting teachers have redirected their efforts toward social work and contact rather than serving strictly as attendance workers.

The quarter system of operation was initiated in the late 1960s, primarily to expedite flexible scheduling. As study continued, however, numerous advantages became apparent for school systems making curriculum adjustments to meet individual student needs. With assistance from the Instructional Division of the State Department of Education and some state colleges, many school systems became intensely involved in the transition to the quarter system. By 1975, there were 108 school systems participating in the operation or planning stages. Eight other systems intended to begin transition in 1976.

Other practices have developed concurrent with the quarter system, particularly in the high schools. Joint enrollment with nearby colleges has aided students who wisely scheduled their high school courses. Such students may attend two high school classes daily while spending the remainder of the day in college classes. Some students have been able to begin college before completion of the twelfth grade because of careful course selection. A few colleges with declining enrollments have actively recruited students who have not completed high school, a practice discouraged by school officials.

Work-study programs approved by the State Board of Education are becoming more popular among parents and students in quarter-organized high schools as well as those operating on the year-long basis. In another program students work almost full-time while taking at least two high school courses per quarter. On the senior plan a student may complete the senior year at a nearby college, vocational-technical school or junior college. Full-time attendance at schools outside high school does not qualify the high school for allotment credits for the respective students.

As school systems became more aware of advantages in wider course offerings, more flexibility in scheduling and greater demands for skilled and semi-skilled talent in the industrial fields, parents, students and guidance counselors became more critical of student choices in course selection. In the post-Sputnik era from 1959 to 1971-73 and after a full school course of 12 years, the college freshmen test scores at the University of Georgia showed a tremendous increase, though the freshmen enrollment had more than doubled. This seemed to indicate students entering the University of Georgia freshman class had a broader background. Records of median freshmen test scores are shown.[43]

Year	Number Entering	Verbal Scores	Mathematics Scores
1959	1461	402	422
1971	2265	505	534
1972	2953	486	517
1973	2588	488	523

Other colleges in the university system showed similar test score increases. Statewide tests administered in the public schools in grades four, eight and 11 reveal skills achievements. While still below national norms in statewide averages, the more recent scores have shown marked improvement. Even more important, the statewide tests help educators plan and develop methods and materials to meet the future needs of education.

The State Department of Education has begun promoting a curriculum comprehensive in scope as well as in sequential difficulty. There are six types of course selections in the quarter system, all based on common skills, knowledge and attitudes. Elective courses increasingly offered in high schools include advanced science, advanced mathematics, world literature, advanced electronics, refrigeration, transportation, office practices, government, economics, societal problems, health services, food services, drafting, metalwork, home engineering areas, life oriented topics and individual study. Adequate buildings, sufficient instructional materials, specialized staff and extensive planning have become educational necessities. Work-study and career experiences have been developed for high school seniors in nearly all subject areas. Educators have learned that minimal training for utility is insufficient in American society. Parents, teachers, counselors and administrators have become more aware of the student's need for specialized studies after he or she has fulfilled the general education required for all citizens.[44]

Reorganization of state government was among the major planks in Governor Carter's campaign platform. Under a 1972 act the General Assembly reorganized state government, reducing to 25 the number of state agencies in the executive branch.[45]

Each major state agency furnished one leading administrator to work with the Governor's Commission on Reorganization. From the State Department of Education Nix assigned Dr. Clyde Pearce, a former county school superintendent who was serving as director of the Proprietary School Unit and as the standards coordinator. His experience in these fields served the Commission on Reorganization advantageously. Raymond O. Herman, vice president of the Citizens and Southern Bank of Atlanta, headed the group studying the State Department of Education. The study continued for several months while professional and management teams carefully examined every agency in state government.

Under the adopted plan two newly created governmental agencies, the State Department of Human Resources and the State Department of Administrative Services, acquired many of the services formerly performed by many other agencies of state government. The Office of Vocational Rehabilitation was transferred from the State Department of Education to the new Department of Human Resources; State Department of Education data processing services and printing services were transferred to the Department of Administrative Services. Under the reorganization act the Industry Services Advisory Committee created in 1968 was transferred to the State Department of Education.

A New Education Law

The Adequate Program for Education in Georgia (APEG) must be labeled as the most constructive piece of educational legislation to be enacted in any single decade of Georgia education history. Exactly ten years after authorizing Governor Sanders' Commission to Improve Education, the General Assembly in 1973 again authorized a blue ribbon committee to study and recommend improvements in the educational system of Georgia.[46] Two sections of the 1964 law were never funded during its existence, sections 32-615 and 32-628, (consumable instructional materials and contingency funds, respectively).

Before Governor Carter officially announced his candidacy for the office in 1969, he told about 900 delegates to a governor's conference, "There is an urgent need to acquaint our people with the fact that we have an abysmally poor academic program." [47] His comments were in part based on his experience and that of his father as chairmen of the Sumter County Board of Education.[48] Some smaller school systems, including Sumter County, commonly refused state and federal funds to support comprehensive high schools and instead maintained small high school units. As governor, Carter was responsive to the interests of many Sumter County residents in transferring to the county from his emergency funds $10,000 to reroof the basketball court at Plains High School.[49] In 1974 he transferred another $10,000 to repair the gymnasium at Union (Leslie) High School.[50]

The APEG committee was composed of 10 legislators, the governor, the state school superintendent, chairman of the State Board of Education and presidents of Georgia School Boards Association, League of Women Voters, Classroom Teachers, Georgia Congress of Parents and Teachers and the University System. Dr. Edmund C. Martin, executive director of the Georgia Educational Improvement Council, led the staff of 15 professionals whose activities originated from his office. The study concentrated on 37 subjects under three major divisions.

Governor Carter chaired the division dealing with the instructional program. Again the services of Raymond Herman, vice president of C & S Bank, were solicited to head the Division of Supportive Services. Representative Hugh Jordan, a long-time member of the House Education Committee, served as chairman of the Financial Foundations Division, while Senator Terrell Starr and Representative Robert Farrar, chairmen of the Senate and House Education Committees, respectively, co-chaired the entire study.

The various groups studied data and scores of position papers. Public hearings were held throughout the state to receive input from hundreds of Georgia's citizens. Though all areas of education were studied and thorough research was given to each, it was apparent that recommendations could not be forthcoming on each subject discussed. After analyzing all available data and ventilating all of the issues, the committee made feasible, practical recommendations of highest priority. Of great significance in the introduction to the report is one paragraph stating,

> All of the issues presented in this report are building blocks for a quality program of education; if any piece is removed, the whole structure will be weakened. Whether we are talking about a supportive service, the instructional program, or financial foundations, each issue is an interlocking piece of the total picture of an adequate program of education in Georgia.[51]

The following sections briefly explain and summarize recommendations submitted by the APEG committee.

Section I. INSTRUCTIONAL PROGRAM

Chaired by Governor Carter, this subcommittee consisted of a task force and the following official members who explored basic, developmental, career and vocational education for all ages. Its members were: Peyton S. Hawes Jr., vice-chairman; A. T. Mauldin, Margie Britt, Anna Trimble, Don Ballard, William Breeding, Jim Langford, Grant Venn.

Recommendations

1. In order to provide greater flexibility to the local system, fund allocations should be made on the basis of instructional units rather than number of teachers, and each school should be able to use up to one-third of such units for "licensed" personnel. The State Board should be authorized to supplement the salaries of qualified "permitted" teachers.

2. The State Board of Education should provide incentive allotments to local school systems which initiate comprehensive program improvements at the 6-8 and the 9-12 grade levels. These systems would receive funds for initial and continuing costs for 6-8 grade level programs which emphasize career exploration and 9-12 grade level programs which provide comprehensive plans for occupational development and work experience. This state funding plan would provide additional teachers to the systems participating more fully in these programs. Local systems should be free to make

funding allocations within grades 6-8 and 9-12 in support of these programs, thereby generating a greater degree of individualized instruction for students. Placing teachers where needed would effectively reduce the pupil-teacher ratio; however, at no time should actions by the local system result in a pupil-teacher ratio higher than 1:25.

3. Instructional media should be provided at a rate per instructional unit which promotes individualized instruction.

4. The State Board of Education should provide career education to all students in grades K-12.

5. Local school systems should be provided with state funds to purchase and replace instructional laboratory equipment.

6. The General Education Program should facilitate the student's entry into employment or advanced training by providing adequate guidance, placement and follow-up services.

7. A director of job placement should be allocated to local school systems or CESAs for every 5000 ADA in grades 7-12, to assist systems in advising students and coordinating services with the Georgia Department of Labor.

8. In order to use the whole community as a learning laboratory, schools and communities should establish cooperative relationships which will foster responsible adulthood and integrate students into functional community roles.

9. Funds should be made available to local school teachers to supervise community work experiences of students after school and during the summers.

10. Funds should be provided to reimburse school systems for transporting students to and from authorized job sites during school hours and for field trips connected with career programs.

11. The State Board of Education, in conjunction with the State Labor Department, should investigate labor laws and recommend ways in which employment restrictions can be modified to promote work experiences for

youth who are properly enrolled and supervised in secondary school vocational programs.

12. Legislation or State Board of Education policy should be adopted to entitle teenagers who are married, pregnant, or parents, to an educational instruction program equal to that provided other students.

13. The judicious, properly supervised use of qualified students for teaching at the lower level in all areas (such as general education, special education, compensatory education, physical education and pre-school education) should be encouraged.

Special Education

Under Special Education the subcommittee discussed thoroughly the areas of mental retardation, learning disabilities, behavioral disorders, physical impairments, hospital/homebound and gifted. After assessing the state's current efforts in these fields the committee made recommendations 14-23.

14. After taking educational, psychological and medical tests, every exceptional student in Georgia should receive an educational program which will develop his maximum potential for participating in family and community life.

15. The educational program should serve to integrate exceptional children into the regular class program as early as possible, even if only on a part-time basis.

16. The state should be responsible for providing adequate educational services for the institutionalized or severely handicapped who are unable to attend public schools.

17. The state should provide special opportunities for advanced achievement, experimentation and creativity for gifted students.

18. One instructional unit should be provided for every 12 exceptional students with special needs. Appropriate funds for instructional media, maintenance and operation should also be provided.

19. One instructional unit should be provided for every 37 students who need the services of an itinerant special education teacher. Associated operating expenses

should also be provided, including travel costs but excluding maintenance and operation except when special resource rooms are used.

20. One leadership position should be provided for every 40 special education instructional units.

21. Funds and services for exceptional children should be provided on the basis of accurately established needs of each subpopulation and comprehensive plans developed to meet those needs.

22. The State Board of Education and the Human Resources Board should establish a coordinating committee to develop and execute effective educational programs for institutionalized children and adults.

23. The Legislature, the State Board of Education, the Board of Regents, and the Scholarship Commission should make every effort to meet the personnel needs for special education programs by FY 1976.

Compensatory Education

Compensatory education studies indicated the drastic need for upgrading instruction for students who scored below the national norms. Recommendations 24-26 are based on the success of Title I programs under federal ESEA funds, which have demonstrated the effectiveness of compensatory education in the basic skills.

24. Compensatory education should be made available to all students in grades three through 12 who are sufficiently behind in their basic skills (reading, math and use of the English language) and to children in grades one and two who score significantly below average on a readiness test. A child is considered sufficiently behind when scoring at least one year behind the national norm in grades three and four, one and one-half years behind in grades five and six, and two years behind in grades seven through 12.

25. All students in grades three through 12 in need of a compensatory education program in the basic skills should be identified by an achievement test and administered a comprehensive evaluation which includes physical, psychological and educational components.

Children in grades one and two in need of compensatory education will be identified through a readiness test.

26. After determining the number of children in need of compensatory education who are not being served by existing federal programs, the State Board of Education should fund needed services for these children, subject to federal legislation, rules, regulations and policies.

Preschool Education

Preschool education discussions included handicapped children, perceptually and linguistically deficient children and an additional 70,000 preschool children who needed a program focusing on the developmental skills to prepare them for first grade. Only two or three school systems provided education for preschoolers before federal funds were available. In 1973, the legislature made an appropriation of $6,700,000 for beginning a kindergarten program with state funds. Feeling the need for expansions in all areas, the subcommittee made recommendations 27-32.

27. Kindergarten should be provided for all five-year-old children in Georgia who reach age five on or before September 1 of the school year.

(a) The program will include at least the equivalent of one-half day at school, five days a week.

(b) This program can be most efficiently implemented in steps. Although ideally kindergarten should be available immediately, the realities of capital outlay needs, recruitment of qualified teachers, and curriculum development necessitate that this program be implemented over the next several years.

28. The state should provide early childhood education for three- and four-year-olds who are either physically, mentally or emotionally handicapped or perceptually or linguistically deficient. As with kindergarten, this program can be most effectively implemented in steps.

29. The Department of Human Resources should provide services for those preschool children not covered under this program.

30. The State Board of Education should establish and uniformly administer policies and procedures for identifying and placing the handicapped.

31. Instructional units should be provided on the basis of one teacher to certain ratios of students as follows.

    40 ADA—nonhandicapped, age 5
    27 ADA—deficient, age 5
    23 ADM—handicapped, age 5
    25 ADA—deficient, ages 3 and 4
    21 ADM—handicapped, ages 3 and 4
    (For one-half day, these ratios would be cut in half.)

32. One leadership position should be provided for every 50 teachers.

Adult Education

Since the passage of the Adult Education Act in 1966, Georgia has been forced to recognize the economic, industrial and ethical needs of Georgia's adult citizens. Closely allied with basic adult education is the need for vocational training of citizens over 16 years of age. Working with local boards of education, the subcommittee agreed that state financed facilities, staff and administrators should be utilized to the fullest. Recommendations 33-38 reflect that attitude.

33. The state should provide that all persons age 16 and over be given the opportunity to develop competence in the basic skills equivalent to an eighth grade education and to develop skills necessary to benefit from vocational training. Funding priority should be provided first to those adults with less than an 8th grade education, second to those adults who have acquired between an 8th and 12th grade education level, and last to those with more than a 12th grade education.

34. All unemployed or underemployed persons age 16 and over, who possess basic educational skills, should be given the opportunity to develop occupational skills for job entry, job upgrading or advanced technical training required for satisfactory employment.

35. Participants in adult education programs should receive sufficient vocational counseling.

36. The State Board of Education should be the central funding and coordinating agency for all adult education and adult vocational programs in the state.
37. All aspects of adult education—basic, vocational, developmental, avocational, and recreational—should be integrated as soon as possible into a comprehensive educational program which contributes to the development of the whole individual.
   (a) Every comprehensive high school in the state should be designated as an Educational Community Center which operates 365 days a year and offers the following types of programs:
   Recreational programs
   Avocational courses such as arts and crafts
   Adult education
   Vocational education
   Service organization meeting rooms
   Programs for senior citizens
   Driver training
   (b) A community education specialist should be provided for each CESA. Each school system should provide leadership positions for coordinating community school programs.
38. Every effort should be made to secure federal funds in the area of adult education.

Fine Arts

Fine arts should be an important part of all educational programs. Recommendations 39-43 advise the inclusion of music, visual arts, dance and drama in a comprehensive educational program.

39. A music specialist and a visual arts specialist should each be available on the basis of 1 to every 15 instructional classroom units in the elementary grades.
40. All students in grades seven through nine should be provided with at least 90 class hours of fine arts per year. This should be considered one of the state's minimum requirements.
41. The State Board of Education should adopt as minimum graduation requirement one course credit in the fine arts or in aesthetics and humanities.

42. Adequate facilities for both the visual and performing arts should be available to every public school.

43. Funds should be made available to bring professional artists and their works into the schools.

Physical Education

The subcommittee on instruction realized that physical education in Georgia schools suffered. Recommendations 44-48 are prefaced with a warning against placing excessive attention on competitive sports at the expense of overall development.

Research indicates a high correlation between academic achievement (particularly reading skills) and motor performance. Yet Georgia's policies concerning physical education, while recognizing its importance within the overall instructional program, are not specific enough to assure adequate quality. In most elementary schools physical education is taught by classroom teachers, with no training in the fundamental skills of movement. Physical education courses are offered to some degree in all public high schools, but the emphasis is on coaching highly competitive sports rather than on developing lifetime habits of physical fitness.

Georgia lacks an overall physical education philosophy. Physical education must be perceived not as an end in itself, but as a means of preparing students for a total lifestyle. School administrators in Georgia generally have not encouraged a series of planned, sequential and comprehensive physical education programs for all students, both girls and boys, in enforcing state standards, in hiring qualified staff and in providing instructional equipment. Programs should be based on personal competence, so each child may progress at an individual pace. Teacher certification for physical education instructors is not flexible enough and teacher preparation is generally for the secondary level. Teacher training programs offer insufficient preparation in health and physical education for prospective teachers. In addition, teacher training programs should be broadened in compliance with State Law 32-1903 (1971 Acts) requiring colleges and universities to have separate courses in health and in physical education. Teacher certification should be based upon both elementary and secondary levels of physical education instruction. Recommendations 44-48 address these problems.

44. Physical education specialists should be made available in the elementary grades at the ratio of 1 to every 25 instructional classroom units.

45. All students in grades one through nine should be required to complete at least 150 minutes of organized physical education activities spread over three or more days per week.

46. All students in grades 10 through 12 should be given at least 150 minutes per week of organized physical education activities, spread over three or more days, which will provide course credit for graduation.

47. The State Board of Education should adopt teacher certification criteria for at least two separate levels of physical education instruction—preschool through eighth grade and sixth grade through twelfth grade.

48. Adequate indoor and outdoor facilities for physical education should be available to every public school student.

Driver Education

At the time of the APEG studies Georgia was the only state in the Southeast not funding driver education as such. Some schools borrowed teachers from their regular courses to teach intermittent driver education classes, thereby reducing the number of regular courses offered, while other schools relied on the help of local automobile dealers, local agencies and civic groups to teach driver education. Recommendations 49-51 attempt to correct the situation.

49. Each public high school should make a driver education course available to all students. This course should be part of the regular academic curriculum and include both classroom and behind-the-wheel instruction.

50. State or federal funds should assist local systems with the operation of the driver education program. The reimbursement, however, should not exceed $50 per student who successfully completes the driver education course.

51. The driver education staff and facilities should be made available to adults, especially those who are referred to the course by a court or governmental agency, insofar as funds and facilities are available.

Health Education

In order to meet the health education requirement, Georgia public schools have offered everything from "crash" courses to well coordinated sequential programs. The subcommittee based recommendations 52-56 on the opinion that health education should be closely coordinated with other agencies seeking to improve the physical and mental health of the entire community and should be integrated within the framework of all school health services.

52. Every school should offer a comprehensive program of health education, including instruction in physical and mental health. Special courses should prepare secondary students for adult responsibilities in the areas of personal, family, and community health care.
53. The health education program should be reinforced by a healthful and safe school environment and by services to help students function at maximum effectiveness throughout their school years and into adulthood.
54. Teachers of health education should have comprehensive training in the specific field of health education.
55. A health specialist/consultant should be provided for each CESA, to provide regional leadership in establishing comprehensive health programs in local school systems.
56. State funds should be provided for a task force to study and identify plans and implementation mechanisms for providing family life, health and nutrition education in the public school systems.

Year-Round School

The year-round school concept in Georgia is not new. It was authorized in previous laws, with actual recommendations in the 1964 Foundation Act. More Georgians were becoming concerned with the vast waste in facilities during long periods of nonuse, especially during the three summer months. The agrarian-based school year became obsolete years ago as

Georgia became more and more urban. Many school systems had already reorganized their programs on the quarter or trimester systems. The committee studied the merits of each and suggested plans for implementation. At the time of the study only Atlanta schools offered a tuition-free fourth quarter or summer school. Recommendations 57-59 reaffirmed previous laws.

57. All school districts should immediately institute a system which provides maximum year-round use of educational facilities, equipment, and media. The State Board of Education should modify the grants procedure to make this possible and should develop criteria for establishing alternative operational plans for year-round schools.

58. The state should provide funds to local systems for students voluntarily enrolled in public schools longer than the 180 official attendance days. Those in grade 12 should receive priority, with each lower grade receiving funds as they become available.

59. The State Board of Education should be authorized to adjust the school year schedule in the event of national emergency.

Program Assessment

Program assessment became necessary when the committee determined that Georgians demand more than an equal opportunity; they demand an equity of results. Children should be expected to achieve at a level commensurate with their abilities. An assessment program must provide means to diagnose individual students' needs and place priorities on critical educational needs when planning instructional programs and budgets. Based on this, the subcommittee recommended the following:

60. The current Statewide Testing Program is the only statewide effort to assess the effectiveness of our school programs. This program should be expanded to include a readiness test to be administered early during a child's first year in school.

61. The State Board of Education should maintain permanent records for each child entering school.

62. The confidentiality of all student records, including results of health and academic tests, should be maintained. Student records should be made available for program evaluation and assessment. Even then, however, confidentiality should be assured. If existing laws and State Board of Education policies violate such confidentiality, appropriate legislation should be developed for the student's protection.

63. Schools must improve techniques of assessing test results. Each CESA should employ at least one professional with sufficient expertise to assist local programs in this effort.

64. The State Board of Education should develop goals and objectives (describing the expected student behavior) for all skills required by Georgia students.

65. Whenever the State Board of Education adopts an objective, it should systematically measure the results of that objective.

66. The State Board of Education should develop a program cost accounting procedure in order that local systems may determine the cost of bringing students to the mastery level for each objective or series of objectives.

67. Each local system should be required to adopt an assessment program and be given adequate technical assistance.

68. Funds should be provided for operating a program cost accounting system.

69. The State Board of Education should use the results of local assessment programs as basis for requesting funds from the General Assembly to meet the critical needs that have been identified.

Program Improvement

Program improvement naturally follows program assessment. Educational improvement has been the objective of Georgia educators for generations. The subcommittee studied various avenues of the improvement process. Placing increased responsibility on the State Board of Education, the State Department of Education, the local school administrators, the local boards of education and the teacher training institutions the group arrived at recommendations 70-76.

70. The State Board of Education should provide in-service training and appropriate release time for local school administrators to participate in a staff development program designed to increase their knowledge and skill in implementing a systematic improvement program.

71. The State Board of Education should be provided with funds to identify and test improved practices and curriculum.

72. The State Board of Education should adopt certification alternatives which are based on demonstrated competency.

73. Each system should develop a three-year plan for the systematic improvement of its program. The State Board will utilize these plans in making improvement grants to local systems.

74. Each system should provide a staff development program designed to improve the performance of all personnel. The State Board should regularly authorize teacher release time for in-service training.

75. Each system should adopt improved instructional techniques and curriculum content designed to meet both individual student needs and the overall needs of society.

76. The State Board of Education should be allowed to modify foundation act requirements and regulations applying to local school systems to the extent necessary to allow implementation of State Board approved local system improvement plans.

Non-Public Schools

The state has historically assumed little responsibility for non-public schools. Although a 1945 bill required non-public schools to report school attendance to local boards of education, they were not required to meet any State Board of Education standards regarding curriculum, courses of study, teacher qualifications, minimum school term, sanitation, health, safety or length of school day. The subcommittee recommendations 77-78 were not supported by legislation.

77. In order to insure the well-being of every student in Georgia, the state should immediately require that private secondary and elementary schools meet the same mimimum legal standards as public schools.
78. Every non-public school should annually report monthly enrollment and average daily attendance data to the State Board of Education.

Local Leadership

Although subcommittee members perceived a need for improved commitment to the public education program among local communities and leadership, recommendations 79-80 failed to receive legislative support.

79. No parent of a school-aged child shall be appointed or elected to serve as a member of a state or local board of education while that child is enrolled in a non-public elementary or secondary school, unless the child meets the criteria of the State Board of Education for being categorized as an exceptional child.
80. Each local board of education should establish at least one advisory council which is broadly representative of the school system and hold joint meetings with this council at least quarterly. This should be a requirement for state school standards.

Section II. SUPPORTIVE SERVICES

Chaired by Raymond O. Herman, vice-president of Citizens & Southern Bank, this subcommittee consisted of a task force and official members, Paul Broun, Mitchell Conner, L. L. Phillips, E. G. Summers, Roy A. Hendricks, Genevieve Hill and Virginia Stringer.

Supportive Services provide the operations and programs that support the instructional needs of a school system. Though some of the areas studied may have appeared to be a bit remote from support, or may have been considered to be a financial need rather than a supportive program, the subcommittee studied services as they related directly to the improvement of instruction. Physical facilities, pupil transportation, food services, plant maintenance, administrative and supervisory services, student personnel services, educational television, Cooperative Educational Service Agencies, school standards, health services, clerical assistance and other services included in this study needed expansion and improvement.

Physical Facilities

Physical facilities are an essential tool in any school's instructional program. The subcommittee specifically studied planning, financing, renovating and replacing buildings and materials. Particular attention was given to public library and vocational/technical school construction. The subcommittee felt that as in previous state building programs, some local financial participation should be required. Recommendations 81-83 follow.

81. A permanent planning process should be established to assess the current and future facility needs of each school system.

82. The state should adopt a policy of financing 80 percent of the four-year projected capital outlay needs for each school system with each system having sufficient funds available annually to develop the same proportion of physical facility needs. The local school systems should provide the local school site plus an amount of revenue generated by a millage rate established by the State Board of Education and applied to all systems in the same manner.

83. Separate provision should be made for the construction of both library facilities and vocational-technical schools. In each case recommendations should include assessing professionals, on-site needs, establishing common construction and renovation criteria, generating sufficient funds through the issue of general obligation bonds and establishing a classification system for ranking construction needs in priority order.

Transportation Services

Pupil transportation services in Georgia have long been a responsibility of the state and local boards of education. Georgia has the framework for operating an efficient system of pupil transportation; however, as in other phases of the school program, a lack of funding has limited the rapidity of growth. In order to improve the services the group urged recommendations 84-87.

84. The state should provide transportation for all students attending public schools who live more than 1½ miles from school.

85. Each CESA should be authorized to provide economical and efficient transportation services and maintenance for all member systems.

86. At least twice during each school year, each pupil who is transported in a school vehicle and each school bus driver should be instructed in safe riding practices and participate in emergency evacuation drills.

87. Special transportation services, including the use of minibuses, should be provided for eligible vocational, special education, compensatory education students and handicapped children attending kindergarten in the public schools.

School Food Services

Recommendations 88-93 addressed the need for continued financial expansion of school food services to provide adequate nutritional programs.

88. Nutritionally adequate and reasonably priced lunches should be made available to all Georgia's public school students. Full student participation in the program should be encouraged.

89. Breakfast should be provided for those public school students who are eligible under federal guidelines.

90. The State Board of Education should develop and implement a plan for nutrition education.

91. The State Board of Education should set certification standards for school food service directors and managers. Minimum salary schedules should also be developed for these personnel with consideration given to a 12-month salary schedule.

92. School systems should be encouraged to join with other systems in centralizing purchasing, storing, accounting and management functions.

93. Additional state funds will be needed to support the operating costs of food service programs to meet the goal of a nutritious food service for all students.

Plant Maintenance

When the state became a partner in schoolhouse construction the State Board of Education and the State School Building Authority improved school plant maintenance by developing consultative services to local school systems. Recommendations 94-98 addressed the need for further custodial services.

94. The State Department of Education should encourage the design and selection of equipment which will minimize required servicing, encourage preventive maintenance and improve efficiency.

95. The State Board of Education should recommend that school systems maintain a standard custodial staff at the ratio of one custodian to every eight teachers.

96. All schools should be air conditioned except in cases where building condition or age does not justify the additional investment.

97. Sick leave expenses should be separated by law from the allocations for maintenance and operations.

98. Maintenance and operating funds should be provided at a level in line with actual expenditures as reflected in management reports.

Administrative and Supervisory Services

With an increased complexity of operations it became apparent that administrative and supervisory services provided by the 1964 MFPE Law needed updating. New teaching strategies, new and different administrative problems and greater need for staff development would require more administration and supervision in the public schools. With these increasing demands in mind the subcommittee made recommendations 99 and 100.

99. Each school should be provided with support personnel for administration and supervision based on the ratio of one per 190 students in average daily attendance.

100. Sufficient central administration personnel should maintain plant operations, transportation, food services, instructional supervision, finance and business services and planning and evaluation.

Student Personnel Services

The demands and requirements by law have necessitated employment of more school counselors, psychologists and social workers. These professionals should have reasonable and practical work loads. When working with the full staff of a school system, the required specialists can render untold benefits; therefore, the subcommittee made recommendations 101 and 102.

101. On the basis of data derived from current pilot programs, the State Board of Education should adopt criteria allowing student personnel service programs to be included in the School Standards Program.

102. The allocation of professional service personnel should be considered as a separate category within the law. Personnel from this category would be allocated on the basis of one to every 400 students in average daily attendance. Local boards of education should determine which professionals are needed in their school systems.

Library Services

Library services have been included in other school funding programs. While school libraries function mainly to augment the school program, the public libraries must serve the broader needs of the entire community. Recommendations 103-107 expanded services for both school and public libraries.

103. School libraries should be encouraged to emphasize audio-visual instructional media as a library service. They should also provide assistance for students who wish to use such media.

104. Local boards of education and principals should provide more flexibility in the hours the library is open, particularly before and after regular school hours.

105. The State Board of Education should continue as the agency channeling state financial support to public library systems in Georgia.

106. All libraries should make adequate provisions for the blind and other individuals with special media needs.

107. Where no public libraries exist, school libraries should be expanded to accommodate public patrons. The architectural design should provide outside access to the library.

Educational Television

The committee realized that educational television potential had not been maximized. Calling attention to the need for further use on the high school level, the committee felt that more study should be given to flexible scheduling. Recommendations 108 and 109 included

108. An intensive study of educational television should be made to determine its future course of development.

109. This study should be completed before any other major funds or commitments are made for new directions.

Cooperative Educational Service Agencies

Through the CESA Act of 1972 and other actions, the effectiveness of educational programs in local systems improved when personnel served several neighboring school systems. Prior to the CESA Act local boards of education were caught between providing a needed school service and maintaining a fiscal position acceptable to local taxpayers. The CESA units now available to all school systems in the state which elect to affiliate, provide smaller units with resource specialists which they would not have otherwise. The subcommittee improved the provisions with recommendations 110-113.

110. The basic grant of $90,000 in state funds provided in FY 1974 should be continued.

111. The State Board of Education should be provided with an additional $2 million annual appropriation to be equitably reallocated to the 16 CESAs on the basis of need.

112. Approved automated systems should be available to CESAs in order to provide services such as student accounting, test scoring and scheduling to the participating school systems.

113. In order to improve the effectiveness of the CESA services to participating school systems, the local board of control should assume strong leadership.

School Standards

School Standards authorized and prescribed by the 1964 school law were applied beginning in 1967. Schools were evaluated by their success in achieving the educational goals established by the State Board of Education. Accreditation is voluntary; meeting State Board of Education Standards is mandatory. The law authorizes the State Board of Education to withhold state funds for noncompliance with certain minimum standards. At the time of this study, the state had experienced seven years in the application of standards with unfavorable results; therefore, the committee felt an essential improvement factor was inherent in recommendations 114-117.

Level 1—Minimum Requirements—Certification

114. There should be common minimum requirements which each school and school system must meet in order to be certified.

   (a) Each school and school system must be certified each school year. The deficiencies of those schools failing to be certified must be evaluated by a "visiting team" who will assist the local school system in developing a plan of action to remediate the deficiencies. The State Board of Education shall publish annually a list of those schools and school systems failing certification. The board will also send news releases to local newspapers listing schools and school systems which have qualified for certification and those schools and systems failing certification.

   (b) The visiting team's recommendations shall be submitted to the State Board of Education. The State Board of Education shall assist those systems financially unable to remediate deficiencies. If a local system is unwilling to implement the plan of action to remediate such deficiencies, the State Board of Education should withhold funds.

Level II—Instructional Program Standards

115. Common or statewide performance-based criteria should be established to evaluate the instructional program in Georgia's public schools.

116. In addition to the common standards criteria, the visiting team, local school officials, teachers and local citizens jointly shall develop local standards against which the local system/school will also be evaluated. Local standards should reflect situations and needs distinctive to that particular school or community.

117. The school standards program shall reflect various levels of attainment such as

(a) *Standard*—earned by a school/school system which has satisfied all required criteria.

(b) *Conditionally Standard*—awarded to a new school or school system which has made acceptable beginnings but does not meet all required standards.

(c) *Probationary Standard*—given to a school system which has deviated from the minimum standards criteria to the extent that it is failing to maintain an adequate educational program. Probationary standard is a warning that the school must make certain improvements before either the *Standard* or *Conditionally Standard* classificafication may be awarded.

(d) *Non-Standard status*—given to a school or school system which fails to meet minimum standards. A school system shall be classified as *Non-Standard* for a given school year if 25 percent or more of the schools within the system are classified as *Non-Standard*.

(e) Until a school achieves *Standard* status, it shall be evaluated each year by a visiting team. Standard schools should be visited every three years.

(f) Policies and procedures for enforcement of standards in each school system should be adopted by the State Board of Education effective for the 1975-76 school year. Enforcement policies should be effective for the 1976-77 school year.

School Health Services

Several school systems have combined efforts with their local health departments whenever time and personnel would permit. The subcommittee became more concerned with all phases of school health which included, but were not limited to, healthy school environment, disease control and illnesses caused by physical, mental and emotional disorders. In the absence of legal requirements, the committee studied organizational patterns, funding, personnel and legalities for a statewide comprehensive program of health services within the schools. Recommendations 118-123 encouraged close cooperation with local health units of the State Department of Human Resources.

118. The Foundation Law for Education shall unequivocally recognize school health services as an integral part of the total educational process and establish local policies which are conducive to the achievement of the goals and objectives of the school health services program.

119. Sufficient nursing services should be available within each system.

120. A full-time position within the Child Health Unit of the Department of Human Resources' Physical Health Division should be established to coordinate planning and implementation of school health services. To fulfill these responsibilities, this individual should chair a joint committee of personnel from both the Department of Human Resources and the Department of Education. This committee should attempt to establish and maintain channels of communication between the two departments to insure a joint cooperative effort in the formulation of a statewide health services plan.

121. The Department of Human Resources should implement statewide the present Dental Education and Prevention Program and the Dental Care Program in a manner consistent with DHR board policy.

122. Emergency services and treatment policy and procedures should be established as soon as possible.

123. A health screening examination should be given to every child entering public school and a complete health record maintained throughout the school career.

Local DHR health units should coordinate all health data collection and maintain central informational files.

Clerical Assistance

Increased clerical work has taken a great deal of time from the professional personnel which should have been used for instructional and administrative duties. The expense of this service has traditionally been paid for through local funds. Accrediting commissions have required certain clerical assistance, but this voluntary requirement often suffers. Recommendation 124 attempts to remedy this situation.

124. A sufficient number of clerical personnel, including supervised high school students, should be provided to relieve teachers and other professional personnel of routine clerical activities so they may use their time more effectively in the instructional program.

Section III. FINANCIAL FOUNDATIONS

The Financial Foundations Subcommittee studied issues relating to the economic base for public education. In addition to the specific issues cited in this report, many related issues received study and committee consideration. Such areas as equity of taxation, level of state funding, new revenue sources and a weighted pupil method of distributing state funds were studied, and the information gathered was used as background for the specific recommendations made by the subcommittee.

Representative Hugh Jordan chaired the subcommittee studying this area, and Lamar Plunkett served as vice chairman. Other members were Jerry Dickson, Senator Ebb Duncan, Representative Grace T. Hamilton, Dr. Jack P. Nix, Asbury Stembridge and Ann Woodward. Senator Terrell Starr and Representative Robert Farrar served as ex-officio members.

Federal Funding

Federal funds have always played an important role in state school financing. At the time of this study they amounted to about 13 percent of the total school cost in the state, with no assurance that any of the funds and programs will be continued for any given length of time. The following chart lists major federal programs in Georgia schools.

Title	1971 Funds* 1972 Funds+	Services
ESEA of 1964	$50,380,000*	For educationally deprived and handicapped
MDTA of 1962	34,020,000*	Occupational training and re-training
Nat. Sch. Lunch	27,460,000*	Nutritional, breakfast and milk programs
Vocational	13,570,000*	Vocational training for eligible citizens
Voc. Rehabilitation	3,660,000*	Training handicapped adults
Handicapped Act	1,560,000+	Education of handicapped children
Adult Ed. Act	1,700,000+	Teacher training and demonstration
EDA of 1964	1,700,000+	Pre-school training for low-income groups
Library Construction	116,400+	Library construction and services to physically handicapped

Recommendation 125 is based on the subcommittee's attitude that all worthwhile programs should be continued if federal funds are not available.

125. The state should utilize federal funds, wherever permitted by federal law, to supplement an adequate program of education in Georgia. If federal funds are curtailed, critical foundation programs should be continued with state funds.

Local Funding

Required local effort has been a source, however meager, of public school financing in Georgia since 1919. The 1949 Foundation Law provided a more detailed formula for local funding through the property tax, while major sources of state funding have been the sales tax and the income tax. The three taxes have maintained a rather delicate balance among all taxpayers. Although there have been numerous efforts to reduce or even abolish local support for public schools, the members felt that any effort to modify the property tax should be thoroughly examined in terms of required local effort. This is essential to finance an adequate educational program and to encourage local involvement and efficiency. Per-pupil expenditure for education in local funds in 1971 ranged from $23 to $182. The great difference was due to the willingness of local boards of education to levy enough taxes to support the desired school program. Indifference often plagued local schools as drastically as low taxable wealth. During the 1971-72 school year local support accounted for about 28 percent of all educational funds, while state and federal funds were 57 percent and 13 percent respectively. At that time Georgia ranked forty-fourth in the nation in the percent of school revenue derived from local funds. To relieve local property taxpayers of school support would require the equivalent of an increase of two and a half to three cents in sales taxes. The subcommittee, therefore, made recommendations 126 and 127.

126. The state should retain the concept of Required Local Effort.

127. Because Georgia has an excellent collective mix of taxes, and since the state constitution preempts the use of the sales or income tax at the local level, no changes are recommended in the local revenue structure.

Supplemental or Enrichment Funds

Supplemental or enrichment funds have provided some revenues to local systems above the required amount. Although "enrichment" implies improvements in student services beyond the basic program, these small local funds barely supplement an already inadequate educational budget. During 1971-72 the required local effort was approximately 4.91 mills on 40 percent of the equalized property tax digest. Tax levies for enrichment ranged from a low of one-half mill to a high of 23 mills, with a one-mill levy generating a range from $3.92 to $37.19 per student, depending on the wealth of the school system. The committee believed that equitable financing is a major component of an adequate educational program and, therefore, proposed a District Power Equalizing method. An alternative proposal would have been full state funding, but as pointed out earlier, that would require an additional $350 million in state funds just to maintain the status quo. Both plans are based on the doctrine of fiscal neutrality, which means that the quality of a child's education is a function of the wealth of the state as a whole and not merely of the wealth of the district in which the student lives.

Georgia's plan of school financing prior to the 1974 study was enacted in the 1964 MFPE Law. The 1964 plan ranked high nationwide in providing equality of educational opportunity. The extremely high range of assessed valuation and expenditure levels, common to many states, did not exist in Georgia. Required Local Effort, based on wealth, offset many disparities. However, the committee found that some disparities still existed in wealth per student. The wealthier systems therefore could and did raise more revenue for schools with less effort (lower millage) than poorer systems could with higher millage.

Under the District Power Equalizing plan every school system would have the revenue-producing capacity of a system at a selected level of assessed valuation per student. All systems below the selected level would be guaranteed the amount of revenue which a system at a selected level would produce. The difference between the system's selected expenditure level and the actual revenue produced would be supplied by the state. This state commitment establishes a relationship between effort and expenditure levels of each system, regardless of wealth, and provides that the local unit or school board will determine the effort or millage. Therefore, the subcommittee made recommendation 128.

128. In order to develop an adequate educational program and more equitably distribute the tax burden, a form of District Power Equalizing should be adopted.

Teacher Benefits

Teacher recruitment and benefits have been in the forefront of education for generations. With year-round schools and other strong innovations, teacher roles have become increasingly more complex. Although salaries and other benefits have progressed, recommendations 129-133 would further expand professional services.

129. Teachers should be granted an annual salary increase equal to or greater than the increase in cost of living until such time as Georgia teacher salaries reach the national average.

130. Adequate funding should be provided to insure sick and personal leave time at a level no less than $125 per instructional unit.

131. After 35 or more years of service, teachers should be allowed retirement without penalty. This retirement benefit should also be extended to eligible teachers who have already retired.

132. A competency-based tenure system should be established for teachers.

133. All teachers should serve a 180-day internship with pay, under qualified supervision, before receiving certification.

School District Reorganization

The size of the district and the size of the school serve as major factors in educational costs, efficiency in operation, supportive services and comprehensiveness of the instructional program. Recommendations 134-137 note the need for more effective uses of facilities and staff in larger systems which could maintain a higher degree of flexibility.

134. The state constitution should be amended to remove all barriers to school district consolidation, including the provisions that each county must constitute a district, and a majority of 51% of the registered voters must approve any change.

135. A statewide plan for the reorganization of school systems should be developed and approved by the General Assembly and presented in the form of a referendum to the voters of each recommended district. Only that portion of the plan approved by referendum would be implemented.

136. School systems in Georgia should be consolidated, with preferably no less than 10,000 students in each new district. In order to effectively accomplish this the following incentives should be offered.

    (a) Superintendents and other system-wide personnel with at least 25 years of service, whose jobs are abolished as a result of consolidation, shall be permitted early retirement with full annuity.

    (b) The state shall assume for 5 years all increased capital outlay caused by consolidation.

137. School systems that reach a size too large to provide optimum programs should be reorganized into administrative subdistricts for instructional purposes only.

Isolated Schools

Isolated schools were created and identified in the 1964 MFPE Law. One additional teacher was allotted to each school that was hindered by natural or artificial barriers from consolidating with another school. The subcommittee felt that four of the five remaining schools were within commuting distance with other schools and therefore recommended that all but the school on Sapelo Island be abolished. Recommendation 138 follows.

138. The State Board of Education should eliminate the classification "Isolated Schools" with the request that the General Assembly make special provision within the law for students on Sapelo Island.

Student Accounting

Student accounting is the process of counting students and utilizing the results to make decisions concerning allocations. With a more complex system of education emerging, the subcommittee based recommendations 139-140 on a need for refined accounting methods.

139. A uniform statewide numbering system should be developed which would assign a unique identification number to each student.

140. The State Board of Education should research methods of student accounting by using one CESA as test case to determine the most efficient and effective accounting method, which will in turn be adopted by all 16 CESAs.

Allotment Formula

The allotment formula follows a recommendation on student accounting. The major concern of members was projection of enrollments and average daily attendance to predict more accurately future increases and decreases in the number of students. The statement of the group follows.

141. The allotment formula should be modified in the following ways to make the adjustment process more efficient.

(a) First four months' ADA figures should be used consistently throughout the formula.

(b) Changing trends in enrollment should result in the development of variations in the allotment formula to provide more efficiently for the allocation of funds.

Program Accounting

The committee felt that the planning process in education had proceeded more or less at random with very little assessment of how effectively resources were being utilized. Legislative bodies are requesting greater accountability of how educational funds are being spent. Factors augmenting this study emphasized an increased demand to broaden the scope of the educational program, the burst of new ideas and technology, the schools' place in solving social problems and the greater competition for the tax dollar. The subcommittee recommended the following.

142. The State Board of Education should develop and implement a program accounting system for selected programs. The State Board should then evaluate the impact of these programs and, based upon the results, develop an action plan for the implementation of a full scale program accounting system.

Cash Flow

Flow of cash grants to local school systems has insufficiently met financial obligations during critical periods of the year. During the 1973-74 school year local boards of education paid out over $1 million in interest on loans, mostly as a result of cash flow problems. Recommendations 143-146 advised the following concrete actions.

143. The Department of Education should be authorized to increase the financial management assistance to local systems by adding three specialists to the staff of the State Department of Education.

144. Legislation should be implemented for collection of educational taxes without penalty to the educational funds.

145. The House Ways and Means Committee should develop a method for collecting all local revenues from the property tax on a quarterly basis.
146. The State Department of Education should provide cash advances to systems with approved tax digests.

Review of Educational Laws

Georgia law requires the systematic and periodic review of educational laws. The updating process is usually slow; however, with rapid changes in the state's economic, cultural and educational structure, a regular review of the laws is essential to maintaining an adequate educational program. Recommendation 147 provides the following solution.

147. In order to provide for systematic and periodic review of Georgia's educational requirements and laws, the education committees of both the House and the Senate shall review these recommendations and make an annual progress report which is a matter of public record. The State Board of Education shall meet jointly with these committees at least once a year.

The 147 recommendations resulted from more than 1,000 pages of data and position statements. This committee report generated legislation commonly known as APEG (Adequate Program for Education in Georgia).[52] Covering 52 pages in the Georgia Laws, Acts of 1974, the bill's 72 major sections included many but not all of the committee recommendations. The committee leaders stated firmly and clearly the attitudes of previous governmental officials and members of the General Assembly when they said,

". . . public education in Georgia can only be as good as the people of this state want it to be . . . Our goal is an adequate program of education for all Georgians, but it can be attained only with the help and encouragement of all our citizens." [53]

This bill poses even broader framework around which a good educational system can be built. When fully financed, additional services will include such major items as increases in classroom teachers and special education teachers, vocational education specialists, elementary education specialists, student service support personnel, job placement directors, administrative and supervisory personnel, preschool and special education specialists, school food service specialists, pupil transportation specialists and clerical assistance. Programs to be enlarged or initiated included preschool, health services, driver training, public libraries, capital outlay, district power equalizing, honors program, educational research, instructional materials and media, instructional equipment, adult education and administrative training. Most of the increases in state appropriations in subsequent years have financed certain items in the APEG law. By FY 76, full funding was far from complete; the actual proof of the product is in the funding, as has been the case for generations.

Some financial achievements were gained during the early 1970s. In the four-year period 1971-74, inclusive, teachers recevied three increments in salaries totaling $1,379 for beginning teachers, with the average increase for all teachers totaling $1,793 for the four years. Maintenance, operation and sick leave funds had increased tremendously at the local level. Average spending by local boards exceeded $2,000 per teaching unit. The state appropriations increased in 1974 from $1,250 per teaching unit to $1,350 per unit. In 1973, the legislature appropriated $6,700,000 for the initiation of a preschool program with state funds. This was the beginning of state support for preschool education.

CHAPTER VI

1. George R. Gilmer, *Sketches of Some of the First Settlers of Upper Georgia, of the Cherokees, and the Author.* (Baltimore: Genealogical Publishing Co., 1965), p. 405.
2. From interview with Z. B. Rogers in Elberton, Georgia, in October 1941.
3. From interview with Hershel H. Elders and County School Superintendent Jerry Holland in Reidsville, Georgia, in February 1943.
4. National Education Association, Research Report R1, *Rankings of the States* (Washington, D. C., 1961), p. 27.
5. *Georgia Laws,* 1963, pp. 394-396.
6. Governor's Commission to Improve Education, *Educating Georgia's People—Investment in the Future,* 1964, pp. 17, 64, 67.
7. *Georgia Laws,* 1964, pp. 3-47.
8. National Education Association, Research Report, *Rankings of the States* (Washington, D. C., 1973), p. 48.
9. *Georgia Laws,* 1964, pp. 706-711.
10. *Georgia Laws,* 1969, pp. 248-249.
11. R. L. Johns, ed., *Alternative Programs for Financing Education,* (Gainesville, Florida: National Educational Finance Project, 5, 1971), p. 250.

12. W. C. McClurkin, ed., *Organization of School Systems in Georgia* (Nashville: George Peabody College for Teachers, 1965), p. 13.
13. William H. Schabacker, Russell S. Clark and Homer C. Cooper, eds., *Focus On the Future of Georgia, 1970-1985* (papers prepared for use by Advisory Commission on Educational Goals of the Georgia Board of Education), 1970.
14. Carl E. Sanders (paper read at the dedication of educational television station), Wrens, Georgia, October 11, 1966.
15. *Georgia Laws*, 1972, pp. 550-551.
16. *Georgia Laws*, 1968, pp. 120-124.
17. *Georgia Laws*, 1967, pp. 840-844.
18. *Georgia Laws*, 1968, p. 1138.
19. *Ibid.*, pp. 1138-1141.
20. *Ibid.*, pp. 1595-1597.
21. *Georgia Laws*, 1969, pp. 248-249.
22. Association of County Commissioners of Georgia, Report, *Surging Ahead in the '70's. Proposals for Further Advancements of County Governments of Georgia*, (Atlanta, 1970).
23. Hargrave v. Kirk—Citation 313/F. Supp., p. 933, Northern District of Florida, 1970. Vacated 401 U. S. 476 (1971).
24. Georgia Municipal Association, *An Analysis of Current and Proposed Grants to Municipalities, Counties, and School Systems*, (Atlanta, January 27, 1969).
25. *Ibid.*
26. *Georgia Laws*, 1971, pp. 574-576.
27. *Georgia Laws*, 1972, pp. 406-408.
28. McInnis v. Shapiro, 293 F. Supp. 327 (n.d. 111. 1968) aff'd sub nom.
29. Rodriguez v. San Antonio Independent School District, et al., 337 F. Supp. 280. Western District of Texas, 1971. Appealed to U. S. Supreme Court, October Term, 1972 No. 71-1332.
30. Serrano v. Priest, 5 Cal. 3d 584, 487 p. 2d 1241 (1971).
31. Van Dusartz v. Hatfield, 334 F. Supp. 870 (D. Minnesota 1971).
32. Sweetwater County Planning Committee v. Hinkle, 491 P. (2d) 1234 (Wyoming 1971).
33. Robinson v. Cahill, 297 A. 2d 187 (New Jersey 1972).
34. Whitfield County Board of Education v. Georgia State Board of Education, et al., Polk County Georgia Superior Court, Civil Action No. 8275.
35. *Ibid.*
36. National Education Association, Research Report R1, *Rankings of the States, 1971* (Washington, D. C.: 1971), pp. 48, 50.
37. *Georgia Laws*, 1972, pp. 156-173.
38. *Georgia Laws*, 1973, pp. 613-614.
39. *Georgia Laws*, 1974, pp. 1418-1422.
40. *Georgia Laws*, 1972, p. 236.
41. *Ibid.*, pp. 722-26.
42. Information pertaining to curriculum from 1965 through 1975 received from Dr. Claude Ivie, director, Division of Curriculum Development and Pupil Personnel Services, Georgia Department of Education, 1976.
43. Regents of University System of Georgia, *Normative Data for the 1974-75 Freshman Class, University System of Georgia*, (Atlanta, 1975).
44. Curriculum Framework Revision Committee, *Planning for Education in Georgia*, (Atlanta: Georgia Department of Education, 1976), pp. 16-17.
45. *Georgia Laws*, 1972, pp. 1015-1067.
46. *Georgia Laws*, 1973, pp. 1476-1478.
47. *The Atlanta Constitution*, October 10, 1969, p. 1C.

48. *Comprehensive Study of Schools in Sumter County*, Georgia Department of Education, May 3-5, 1971, p. 3.
49. Georgia Board of Education, *Minutes* (March 8, 1973).
50. Georgia Board of Education, *Minutes* (April 11, 1974).
51. *Report of the Minimum Foundation Program for Education Study Committee*, (Atlanta: Georgia Educational Improvement Council, December, 1973), p. 9.
52. *Georgia Laws*, 1974, pp. 1045-1098.
53. *Report of the Minimum Foundation Program for Education Study Committee*, p. 3.

Epilogue

Public Schools Belong to the Public

Throughout history Georgia public schools have struggled for excellence. The charter of 1732, granted by King George II of Great Britain, specified that the Georgia colony would offer a new beginning for indigent persons in Great Britain. Since then, whether from pure poverty, indifference or other reasons, Georgians have never assumed national leadership in financing support for government services. According to various national rankings, financial support for public education in Georgia has left much to be desired. Thus the heritage of indigent persons has prevailed for many generations.

In spite of the state's early problems, colleges, schools for the deaf and blind and private academies were developed. Although public school education for the masses was delayed until the twentieth century, Georgia is proud of its records in equalization of school support, school consolidation, reduction of sub-tax districts, schoolhouse construction, pupil transportation, school food service, special education, area vocational and technical schools, cooperative educational service agencies, public libraries, educational television, staff development, Governor's Honors Program, Teacher Education Council, state minimum salary, consultative curriculum staff, vocational education and educational media services. Unfortunately, Georgia has enacted more educational laws than it has appropriated funds to support. Through the years, more financial support could have increased the potential impact of many authorized programs.

By 1976 Georgia had established a legal framework for providing a good educational system for its citizens. Nothing more was needed except funds to implement the authorized programs in their entirety. Much of the constructive legislation in the 40-year period prior to 1976 was the result of studies conducted by legislative committees. The APEG laws enacted in 1974 were primarily recommendations of the 1973 study committee. Similarly, the MFPE Act of 1964 was the result of the committee created by the 1963 session of the General Assembly; concurrent with the MFPE Committee was the Governor's Commission for Efficiency and Improvement in Government, which recommended changes discussed in chapter six. Four legislative committees created in 1954 provided the impetus for numerous laws from 1954 through 1961. The Georgia Commission on Education in 1956 studied and recommended measures for the retention of state control over education. In 1960 the General Assembly Commission on Education, known as the Sibley Committee, recommended alternatives for operating the public schools in accordance with recent federal court decisions. The recommendations of the 1961 Joint Committee on Education to Study Fiscal Affairs of the Georgia Public School System, enacted by the General Assembly, included the following.

1. Establishment of a budget officer to supervise agency budgeting.
2. Standardization of budgeting and bookkeeping forms.
3. Presentation of biennial school budget to the General Assembly by December 1.
4. Initiation of new programs only with legislative authority.
5. Elimination of funds transfers from item to item.

The first extensive draft of educational legislation resulted from the 1947 study committee, which recommended the first Minimum Foundation Program in 1949. Though a large number of professional and lay members participated in the study, the results came about through legislative authorization and participation.

The Constitution of 1945 had a tremendous impact on educational organization and administration. The Constitutional Committee was established by legislative action and was composed of legislators, professional educators and professional leaders in the state.

During the 1938-39 school year a crisis developed in the operation of the schools. Not enough money had been initially appropriated to complete the school term, and the legislature did not appropriate additional funds to complete the school term. The schools had three choices—to close down when funds were exhausted, to ask the teachers to work free or at reduced salaries or to raise money locally to operate the full term. Some teachers with bachelor's and master's degrees were working for an annual salary of $490 ($70 per month for seven months). Many schools were forced to close early and consequently lost their accreditation. Through House Resolutions 9 and 206, the legislature created a Legislative Committee on Economy and Efficiency to study every department of state government. On June 3, 1939, the committee reported several recommendations pertaining to the operation of the schools for the 1939-40 school term. Noting on page 25 of its report that teachers had received only three and one-half months' salary for the state seven-months school term, the committee urged cutbacks in allocations, reductions in personnel, reduction of transportation costs, elimination of small schools through consolidation and elimination of overstaffing in some schools. Some positions within the State Department of Education were abolished, including a supervisor of supervisors and some positions in the Division of Curriculum Development. The committee noted that the State Board of Education and the State Department of Education cooperated 100 percent in the study and in executing the recommendations. The impact of that year's activities remained with public education for more than a decade.

There were at least 25 additional legislative committees on education during the same period 1950-1970. Though important in acquainting the General Assembly with matters pertaining to public education, these 25 studies carried less impact as far as subsequent legislation was concerned. Briefly, the legislative resolutions covered the following topics or purposes.

1. 1953, a joint House and Senate committee to study the salaries of teachers, the administration of the schools and the use of MFPE funds.

2. 1958, a House committee to study college book store operations.

3. 1959, a joint Senate and House Committee on education to study the preparation of students for college and the availability of colleges.

4. 1960, a joint committee on teacher education; also to study any other educational problems deemed necessary.

5. 1962, a joint committee on public schools and the University System of Georgia; a continuation of the 1961

Joint Committee on Fiscal Affairs. (Recommended establishment of community colleges.)

6. 1962, House committee to study educational television. (Recommended that ETV remain in State Department of Education and not become a separate commission.)

7. 1964, House committee to study admissions, policies and practices in the University System of Georgia.

8. 1964, Joint Senate and House committee to study school bus transportation.

9. 1965, House committee to study 12 month school year.

10. 1965, House committee to study private financing of dormitories in the University System of Georgia.

11. 1966, House committee to study public school personnel retirement.

12. 1966, House committee to study uniform transcripts for high school students.

13. 1966, House committee to study teacher tenure.

14. 1966, House committee to study school district organization and criteria.

15. 1967, House committee to study care and training of preschool children.

16. 1967, House education subcommittee to study property evaluation.

17. 1967, Joint House and Senate committee to study the Teachers' Retirement System of Georgia.

18. 1967, House education subcommittee to study vocational education.

19. 1967, House committee to study teacher certification policies. (Report made January 1968.)

20. 1968, House committee to study the performance of high school graduates in college.

21. 1968, House committee to study driver education. (Report made January 1969.)

22. 1968, House committee to study teacher retirement and compensation. (Report made January 1969.)

23. 1969, House education subcommittee to study vocational education. (Report made January 1970.)

24. 1970, House education subcommittee to study school dropout rate computation.

25. 1970, House education subcommittee to study state standards and regulations for public schools. (Report made January 1971.)

26. 1970, House education subcommittee to study special education. (Report made January 1971.) [1]

Although legislative study committees have contributed greatly to the growth and progress of public education within recent years, their influence has not always been effectively used. For many of the early years the education profession and key legislators carried the burden of pushing bills through the General Assembly. Edward McMichael is said to have lobbied 12 or 15 years before persuading the 1905 legislature to pass the McMichael Bill permitting local taxes for schools. C. R. McCrory of Schley County presented his bill on uniform textbooks many times before it was finally enacted into law in the early 1900s. Governor E. D. Rivers worked for four years to get the Seven Months School Act passed and signed into law. The professional organizations and the college leaders recognized the great need for free public education in the early years. In 1919, such legislative leaders as Z. B. Rogers, William Barrett, Herschel Elders and George Carswell worked with State School Commissioner M. L. Brittain and the professional educators in getting Governor Hugh Dorsey's approval on the voluminous educational legislation of that year.

Throughout Georgia history lack of financial support has been the greatest obstacle to educational progress. In a taped interview Dr. James S. Peters, chairman of the State Board of Education, stated in 1971 that in his 86 years' experience "Taxation, of course, was always the trouble. Money, schools have always been expensive, and that is what prevented us from making progress . . ." [2] In 1959, speaking to the Georgia Teacher Education Council on the "Purposes of Education in the Modern World," Dr. Jordan C. Ward, vice president and dean of faculties at Emory University and a noted historian said,

The major questions in the controversy over public education today emerge from the idealism in our system. Some persons, of course, do not really believe in universal public education. There have always been opponents. They still persist. They oppose because they do not want to pay the bill. Some fear widespread enlightenment among all classes. Some see education as impractical and materially worthless. Others oppose the methods and philosophy of schools as presently administered. The segregation issue has given these opponents a new fortress from which to carry on the ancient attacks under new flags . . .

The second problem arises from the fact that the public schools belong to the public. It may be true that not all educators have exercised the touch and aggressive leadership for quality that might have been expected of them. Nevertheless the softness in the public schools is little more than a reflection of the softness in our society. If there has been a question of how much homework was to be assigned, if any; if there has been a question of whether Johnny was to register for physics or journalism, or whether Mary was to take foreign language or social adjustment; if there has been a question as to whether recognition was to be given for athletic prowess or intellectual achievement, or whether it was more important to attend classes or ride in a float in the downtown parade— the decisions have usually reflected public desire. Public control is both the blessing and the curse of the public schools. In the final analysis, however, the public has gotten what the public wanted.[3]

Two very pertinent points emerge from Ward's speech. The first is that many of the opponents of public education are against schools because they do not want to pay the bill; second, the schools belong to the public, and the public has got what it wanted. When a program has been passed and signed into law and has been financed, the schools have gone forward. When interest has lagged and funding has diminished, the growth toward quality education has slowed. Senator Terrell Starr and the late Representative Robert Farrar said jointly in the foreword to the 1973 Report of the MFPE Study Committee, ". . . Public education in Georgia can only be as good as the people of the state want it to be . . . Our goal is an adequate program of education for all Georgians, but it can be attained only with the help and encouragement of all our citizens."

Government leaders cannot always be consistent. Some of the most severe critics of public education have often been the leaders who exert the least effort to help improve education. When money which could have financed unfunded, approved programs is diverted to areas not related to education, the leaders responsible for the transfer sometimes become the leading critics of education, as was the case in the 1973 tax rebate action.[4]

Politicians and would-be politicians have often mentioned the shortcomings of education. Professional educators have often failed to accent the positive. Progress is made by overcoming adverse circumstances confronting the schools, but society needs some definite and confident assurance that the schools are serving the public in a manner desired by the public. State School Superintendents Collins, Purcell and Nix have consistently emphasized the state's progress in educational programs. And these points were numerous. Consider, for example, the fact that for 127 years, from 1785 to 1912, there was a breach in state support between the elementary school and the college level. A new generation of high school educated citizens did not suddenly emerge ten years after state funds were allocated to high schools in 1912. By contrast, in 1976 any school system that did not have access to a comprehensive high school was in that position by choice; state funds had been made available to any school system in the state electing to qualify.

When Governor George Busbee adjourned the 1976 Governor's Conference on Education, he charged the participants to go back to their respective systems, and with as much citizen participation as possible, establish local educational goals for their systems, to assess their present status in relation to those goals, to set priorities on their goals and to place a price tag on objectives requiring additional funding. His anxiousness for civic participation is based on the theory that the schools belong to the public, and the public gets for its schools what the public wants for its schools. He promised to base his recommended program to the forthcoming legislature on the results of his charge.

Too often the cry has been made that the schools are getting more money than they have ever received; the reply might be, so have other agencies of state and local governments. Among the 36 legislative study or investigative committees cited earlier, many referred to "WHEREAS, the state expends over 50 percent of its tax funds in the field of education; and . . ." This is certainly an error, in that at no time during the period cited were the public schools the recipient of 50 percent of state funds. In some years the public schools and the university system combined received in excess of 50 percent of state funds. In 1942 the public schools and the university system together received 42.5 percent of the total state appropriations.[5] In subsequent years, after the enactment of the Teacher Retirement Act, the percentage surged, but not to a point as high as 50 percent. Still on the law books in 1976 was a statute passed in 1919 which reads,

> 32-935 School Fund. Fifty percent of all revenue received by the State from all sources of income or taxation shall be used and expended for the support and maintenance of the common schools for the year in which said income or taxes are due and payable.[6]

Since the state has not complied with this law in recent years, and the law has not been repealed, there may be some basis for the assumption by many legislators and others that schools do receive half of the state's appropriations. Not only is the assumption erroneous, but from 1966 to 1976 this percentage has declined, as shown by the following chart. The amounts shown in the chart reflect education and teacher retirement appropriations combined.

Fiscal Year	Total State Appropriations	Education Dept. and Teacher Retirement	Per-cent	Net State Surplus Funds
1952	.. $ 217,110,507	$ 90,777,393	41.8	$ 30,214,586
1962	.. 419,988,535	195,443,414	46.5	35,098,511
1966	.. 591,624,550	281,972,635	47.5	105,954,934
1967	.. 658,762,157	293,612,449	44.5	119,598,252
1968	.. 774,001,216	345,937,114	44.6	86,125,551
1969	.. 864,045,034	381,317,396	44.1	59,153,077
1970	.. 935,151,802	382,642,587	40.9	92,270,719
1971	.. 1,071,163,947	420,407,837	39.2	36,327,273
1972	.. 1,165,264,374	437,685,595	37.5	90,950,097
1973	.. 1,318,323,996	481,727,709	36.5	122,144,639
1974	.. 1,664,168,762	586,302,208	35.2	100,985,177
1975	.. 1,666,876,714	598,146,374	35.4	47,606,488
1976	.. 1,841,125,219	658,671,754	35.8	N.A.[7]

Evidence has existed for years that Georgia could support its schools in a manner more in line with its ability to pay. For example, Georgia was tied for 49th place in the nation (with only one state in less favorable position), in public school revenue receipts in 1971-1972 as a percent of personal income in 1971.[8]

Continued efforts at improvement are being made by the public school teachers and administrators, the State Board of Education and the State Department of Education. Teacher training institutions have been working with public school personnel in developing competency-based preparation of teachers and also performance-based certification of teachers. Greater emphasis is being placed on program planning, graduate requirements, special education, vocational training, guidance, compensatory education and flexibility to permit changes with the rapid growth of knowledge.

The public schools also have responded to the need for maintaining high academic standards and levels of instruction. True, skilled workers will always be needed, but a democratic society will also need professional men and women, a citizenry trained for business, as well as teachers, writers, dramatists, musicians, poets and philosophers to envision the future. The public schools of Georgia have the potential of supplying society's needs if the public is willing to provide the resources.

EPILOGUE

1. Legislative Study Committee (or Investigative Committee) Reports may be found in the respective legislative committee offices.
2. H. S. Shearouse, interview with Dr. James S. Peters, Manchester, Georgia, July 7, 1971.
3. Judson C. Ward, speech given at the Teacher Education Council Meeting at the Georgia Center for Continuing Education, University of Georgia, January 22, 1959.
4. *Georgia Laws*, 1973, pp. 1372.
5. State Auditor's Report: Summary Statement of Financial Condition June 30, 1975, and Statements of Receipts and Allotments Fiscal Years Ended June 30, 1942, 1952, 1962 and 1966-75. pp. 9-11.
6. *Georgia Laws*, 1919, pp. 288-331.
7. Auditor's Report: Summary Statement, pp. 9-11, and State of Georgia Budget Document for FY 76, pp. 33, 47, 166.
8. National Education Association, Research Report R1, *Rankings of the States* (Washington, D. C.: 1973), p. 48.

Appendix I: *Resolutions and Acts of the General Assembly of Georgia*

Academies Which Have Not Purchased F1000 Confiscated Property, Senate Resolution, 1817.

"Be it further resolved, That the commissioners of academies, in the several counties in this State, who have not received the sum of one thousand pounds, out of the sales of confiscated property, for the use and benefit of their several academies, on their or any of them finding any land or lands, subject to be sold under the act of confiscation and banishment, to make return of the same to the sheriff of the county in which such land lies, and whose duty it shall be, to advertise as is customary for sheriffs' sales, and sell the same at public outcry, at the court-house of said county, to the highest bidder, payably in three annual installments; and the proceeds of such sale shall to the use of the academies of the county to which such commissioner or commissioners belong, until such county or counties shall have received the full sum of which, together with what they may have previously received, will amount to one thousand pounds, and the balance, after paying all costs, to be equally divided amongst the other counties in this state, who may not have received the said sum for their several academies; and the commissioners of confiscated property, be, and they are hereby authorized and required to make titles to all and any lands thus sold, to the purchasers or their order, or to the order of the sheriff.

Approved, 20th December, 1817." [1]

Free Schools, Senate Resolution 1819. "In Senate, 17th December, 1819.

The committee on public education and free schools, Report —That it being ascertained that only a small portion of the free school fund has been made active, it is evidently altogether impracticable, at this moment, to put in operation the free school institution. It therefore only remains to recommend to the consideration of succeeding legislatures, and of the citizens of this state, the system best adapted to the circumstances of the country. That most suitable system appears to your com-

521

mittee to be the system of South Carolina. As the imprac-
ticability of giving effect to the institution results from the
reserved fund not having been active, it is recommended that
the executive be advised of the expediency of vesting the fund,
as speedily as advantageously can be done, in some profitable
stock. Your committee therefore submit the following resolutions:

Resolved, That the law of the state of South Carolina
establishing free schools in that state, be published in one of
the public gazettes for this state for the consideration of its
citizens.

Resolved, That his excellency the Governor be requested to
carry into effect, as speedily as advantageously can be done,
the second section of an act passed 18th December, 1817, entitled An act to create and establish a fund for the support
of free schools throughout this state, and also to invest in
profitable stock, such sums as may have accrued on interest,
or may hereafter accrue from stock belonging to this fund.

Approved, 20th December, 1819." [2]

House Resolution #36, 1820. Free Schools Committee.
"[No. 36] In The House of Representatives, November 28th,
    1820.

The joint committee appointed by both branches of the
General Assembly, to take into consideration all subjects in
relation to literature, public education, and free schools, re-
spectfully submit to the following report, to wit:

There has been submitted for the inspection and consideration of your committee, reports, exhibiting the present state
and condition of the University of this State. Also, of twenty
Academies, the principal part of which are legally branches
of the University.

From the report of the Treasurer of this State, it appears
that from the fund of $250,000 set apart for free schools,
$150,000 has been vested in Bank Stock; $50,000 in stock of
the Bank of Augusta, and $100,000 in Darien Bank Stock—
and that the whole amount of interest yielded upon the above
stock, up to the 5th of June 1820, (since when no dividend
has been declared), amounted to the sum of $18,566.66 cents.

After the most diligent research, your committee have not been able to ascertain with precision what sum has actually been received by each county, for the use of the county academies, under the different acts of the Legislature, but it is obvious that the proportion received has been very unequal, many of the counties not yet having received one cent. Hence your committee have been considerable embarrassed in the discharge of their duty as pointed out by a resolution from the House of Representatives, directing them to inquire into the expediency of making an appropriation for the benefit of such county academies, as have not received their proportion of the appropriation, authorized by the act passed in the year 1792. Nevertheless they have deemed it expedient to report a bill, calculated as they conceive, in some degree, to remedy the inequality complained of by many of the counties of this State, to which bill your committee beg leave to refer.

The most pleasing reflections are excited while we witness the advancement of many public and private academies in this State. The advancement of those institutions present a prospect of literature highly honorable to individual exertion and patriotism, and which amounts to an imperious call on the Legislature for the extension of a fostering hand, by a simultaneous exertion and co-operation.

If it, be admitted that the will of the people deliberately expressed should at all times have due weight and influence on a Legislature who are their immediate representatives, we are led to the conclusion that the present Legislature are under the strongest obligations to patronize, and encourage by a liberal policy, the advancement of education in this State. That it is the wish of the people is incontrovertible, when we take into view the individual exertion exercised in the establishment of so great a number of respectable schools in different parts of the State, without the smallest aid or patronage from the government. The example set by the citizens of some of the counties of this State, to promote schools, are in the opinion of your committee worthy of the imitation of all, whether in public or private situations.

That the general diffusion of knowledge, through the medium of a well organized system of education, is an object of vital and primary importance in a government like ours, where the most important portion of our political system is and ought to be retained in the hands of the people themselves, is a proposition which has long since been demonstrated, and must consequently command the attention of an enlightened Legislature. There can be no objects in the circle of political institutions the utility of which are more universally ascertained and acknowledged—none that do more honor to the governments whose wise and enlarged patriotism duly appreciate them.

Therefore your committee beg leave to offer the following resolutions:

Resolved by the Senate and House of Representatives of the State of Georgia, in General Assembly met, That the fund of $250,000, set apart by a former Legislature, as a free school fund, and the interest yielded thereon, from time to time—together with lots of land, Nos. 10 and 100, set apart by an act of the Legislature of 1818, for the education of poor children, shall not under any authority or pretence whatever, be applied to any other object than that of free schools, in such mode and manner as may hereafter be prescribed by the Legislature.

And be it further resolved, That a committee be appointed, vested with authority to propose, arrange, and digest a system of Education best calculated to provide for the objects intended to be promoted by the provisions of the foregoing resolution, and report the same to the House of Representatives, on or before the tenth day of November next.

Approved, December 12th, 1920." [3]

County Academies Endowment

[No. 15] AN ACT for the permanent endowment of County Academies, and to increase the funds heretofore set apart for the encouragement and support of Free Schools, and for the internal improvement of the State.

§1. Be it enacted by the Senate and House of Representatives of the State of Georgia, in General Assembly met, and it is hereby enacted by the authority of the same, That the sum of five hundred thousand dollars, be and the same is hereby set apart, the one half for the support and encouragement of free schools, and the other half for the permanent endowment of county academies; and the further sum of five hundred thousand dollars be and the same is hereby set apart for the internal improvement of the State.

§2. And be it further enacted by the authority aforesaid, That the said sum of five hundred thousand dollars, first above named, shall be denominated the School Fund, and shall be composed of two hundred thousand dollars of the stock of the Bank of Darien, two hundred thousand dollars of the stock of the State Bank, and one hundred thousand dollars of the Bank of Augusta. The fund to be denominated the Internal Improvement Fund shall be composed of one hundred thousand dollars heretofore vested in stock of the Steamboat Company, one hundred and twenty-five thousand dollars in the stock of the Bank of Darien, two hundred thousand dollars in stock of the State Bank, and seventy-five thousand dollars in stock of the Planters' Bank.

§3. And be it further enacted by the authority aforesaid, that the principal sums set apart as aforesaid shall at no time, or for any purpose, be appropriated or used: but the interest arising thereon shall be applied to the purposes herein before mentioned, as the legislature may from time to time direct.

§4. And be it further enacted by the authority aforesaid, That it shall be the duty of the Treasurer, Comptroller-general, Trustees of Commissioners or county academies, and the Inferior Courts of the several counties within this State, together with the Senators of said counties, to examine and make full and accurate report to the next Legislature of the amount received by said counties respectively, in confiscated property or other endowment; and when such returns are made, and information obtained, the dividends yielded by the one half of the school fund aforesaid, shall be apportioned and paid semi-annually to the several counties, as a future legislature may direct.

§5. And be it further enacted by the authority aforesaid, That it shall be the duty of all Trustees, Commissioners, Courts or Agents, receiving any portion of the funds aforesaid, to keep regular statements and entries of the manner in which the same may be disbursed, and make an annual return thereof to the Senatus Academicus on the second Monday in November.

§6. And be it further enacted by the authority aforesaid, That nothing in this act contained shall be so construed as to prevent any future General Assembly from altering or repealing this act, or any part thereof.

DAVID ADAMS,
Speaker of the House of Representatives.

MATTHEW TALBOT,
President of the Senate.

Assented to, 21st December, 1821.[4]

JOHN CLARK, *Governor.*

Report of Joint Committee and Resolution — December 22, 1821 on appropriation of public lands by the Congress of the U. S. for the purpose of Education — concerning Northwest Ordinance of 1785.

"It is believed that no nation has produced as many testimonials of a desire for the universal diffusion of knowledge as the United States. This has been evinced in every way by the States individually, and by their Representatives in Congress; and it is with grateful pride we can say, that is the United States have not reared the temple of knowledge to an unexampled height and splendor, she has laid its foundation on a base broad as humanity, and durable, it is hoped, as any of the works of men. A system of education, having for its object the instruction of every individual in a great nation, was reserved as an achievement for the United States of America.

Be it resolved by the Senate and House of Representatives of the State of Georgia, in General Assembly met, That each of the United States has an equal right to participate in all the advantages arising from the public lands, the common property of the Union; and that his excellency the Governor is hereby requested to transmit to our Senators and Representatives copies of this preamble and resolution.

Approved, December 22d, 1821." [5]

Academies Make Report to Senatus Academicus—House Resolution, 1824.

"The Committee on Public Education and Free Schools, to whom was referred a resolution from Senate directing an inquiry into the propriety for amending, or explaining the several laws now in force in relation to the Senatus Academicus, and the accountability or county academies to the same, and a uniform method of their reports, have had the same under consideration, and take leave to offer the following remarks:

In the fourteenth section of the charter it is declared that all public schools, instituted or to be supported by funds or public moneys in this state, shall be considered as parts or members of the University, and shall be under the foregoing regulations.

Resolved, That hereafter it shall be the duty of the trustees of all academies in this State which derive a part or the whole of their support from the State funds, to make an annual report to the Senators of the county in which such academy may be, of the following form:

1. The number and salaries of instructors.
2. The number of scholars.
3. The annual income.
4. Branches of learning taught in each, together with any material change which may have taken place since the last report.

Resolved further, That if any academy shall fail to make such report in time for it to be laid before the Senatus Academicus, such academy shall be debarred from any further aid from the funds, which now or hereafter, set apart for that purpose, until such report shall be made as herein contemplated.

Approved, December 18th, 1924." [6]

Committee-County Academics Report: (1825)

"The Committee to whom was referred the reports of the several county academies, have had the same under consideration, and report:

With the view of classical learning, it is a source of melancholy regret that so little care should be bestowed by the patrons of our academies, on this important part of juvenile education. More deplorable is the apparent want of munificence on the part of the Legislature, the assumed guardians of the literary character of the State. With an extent of territory equalled by but few or none of our sister States; with sources of revenue none other can possess; with a climate mild, though varied, and congenial to the expansion of human intellect, the Legislature hitherto has refused even a temporary endowment for a professorship of modern languages, and also moral and mental philosophy for the University.

When we compare the literary character of Georgia now, with what it might have been—when we contrast it with many of our sister States, the votary to science will blush, indeed, at the apathy and indifference to intellectual advancement which have hitherto obscured it. When we see our sister States of the North and East so wonderfully and efficiently uniting capital and intellect for our humiliation and ruin, will Georgia scorn the means which can avert and arrest the approaching triumph and consequent dependence? Will she longer remain supine and in cold-hearted indifference, and see these means wrested from her, which can not only insure her preservation, but raise her to pre-eminence and distinction? These truth, obvious and incontrovertible, it is hoped, will awaken the guardians of the literature of the State to a sense of our literary degradation, and induce a future appropriation from the funds arising from the sale of public lands, for the permanent endowment of the different professorships which may enable us to sustain, protect, and advance our literary and scientific character.

The committee recommend the following resolutions:

Resolved, That the Justices of the Inferior Court, and the Trustees of the Poor School Fund of each county, make to the grand juries in the ensuing year, returns of the disbursements of the funds since December, 1825, together with a particular statement of the number of children instructed, their ages, sex, and mode of instruction pursued, and the persons employed as teachers; and that the said returns to be forwarded by the clerk of the Superior Court to the Governor, to be laid before the Senatus Academicus and General Assembly.

Resolved, That the annexed be the form of a return of the several academies and free schools in this state."

*Resolution—Committee on Public Education and Free Schools
—1826.*

"The Committee on Public Education and Free Schools have had their attention drawn to a variety of subjects connected with the literary concerns of the State . . . The sale of the college lands amounted to the sum of one hundred and twenty-seven thousand dollars . . . The Legislature of that year placed the institution beyond the fluctuations of commerce and of bank dividends, by providing a permanent endowment of eight thousand dollars.

The funds heretofore set apart for the endowment of county academies, and for the encouragement and support of free schools, the manner in which these funds have been applied, and the effects produced next demand the examination of your committee.

The school fund consists of five hundred thousand dollars, and is made up of

Stock of the Bank of Darien $200,000
State Bank 200,000
Bank of Augusta 100,000

$500,000

The several acts which have been passed upon the subject of county academies, commencing with the charter of the University in 1785, and terminating in 1824. With this view, that charter made each county academy a branch of the University, and subjected them to supervision accordingly. In furtherance of this view also was the act of confiscation and amercement in 1792, authorizing commissioners from each county to purchase in confiscated property to the amount of one thousand pounds . . . For the last political year, ending on the first day of November, the distributive share amounted to the sum of $215.38. This is receivable at the treasury upon the joint application of the trustees of the incorporated academies in each county, and to be divided between them in proportion to the number of scholars usually taught in each." [7]

Committee on Education—1828.

[No. 574.] In Senate, December 19th, 1828.

The joint committee on Education and Free-schools, to whom was referred the reports of the academies and free-schools in the counties of this State, beg leave to report:

That such has been the irregular manner in which these reports have been made, that they find it impossible to give such a condensed view of them as can lead to any correct conclusion as to the real state and condition of these institutions; but so far as we have examined we find out one fact, that there has been great waste and misapplication of the funds to those purposes. But although we are obliged to say this is generally the case, we are happy to state there are some few honourable exceptions. In order that the public may know what the real situation of these institutions is, and what has been their management, we recommend the adoption of the following resolution:

Resolved, That the condensed report on academies and free-schools, together with the Governor's communication giving a list of the moneys drawn by the several counties for the purposes of education, be published in pamphlet form, and distributed in the several counties in the proportion of ten to each county, and that the act passed the present session be appended to said pamphlet.

Approved, December 20th, 1828." [8]

Resolution #635—House of Representatives—Saturday, December 12th, 1829.

Poor School Fund—1829.

"*Whereas*, doubts are entertained by the present Trustees of the Poor-school Fund of the several counties of this State, in relation to the payments of accounts due to teachers prior to the appointment of said Trustees, and which have not been paid by their predecessors; therefore,

Resolved, That the Trustees of the Poor-school Fund to said counties be, and they are hereby authorized and required to accept and pay off all accounts due for the tuition of poor children prior to their acceptance of the appointment of trustees (and which have not been paid by their predecessors), in order the same become due; *Provided*, the persons claiming such accounts shall render the same under oath.

And be it further resolved, That his excellency the Governor be, and he is hereby authorized and required to pay over the amount of the Poor-school Fund set apart for this State.

Approved, December 18th, 1829." [9]

Education Committee—House Resolution #643—1829.
[No. 643.] In Senate, December 16th, 1829.

The joint Committee on Public Education and free schools, to whom was referred a resolution of Senate, instructing them to inquire into the expediency of appointing one or more competent persons to collect information on the subject of free schools, and to digest and arrange a system for the free schools of Georgia, to be submitted to the next Legislature beg leave to report:

That they have the subject under serious consideration, and are duly impressed with the importance thereof. That the present free-school system of Georgia is miserably defective, your committee have had but too mortifying testimony in the returns of the several counties, submitted to their inspection during the present session. The fund set apart for free schools, although entirely inadequate to effect the important desideratum of furnishing the means for a plain and substantial education to every family in the State, under a more regular and economical administration, has, it is feared, been dissipated comparatively little benefit.

Your committee have no hesitation in saying, that Georgia is yet possessed of ample means to consummate the most sanguine wishes of the philanthropist in regard to universal education, so far as her own population is concerned. To apply these means effectually to the object seems then to be the only difficulty which presents itself to your committee. They, therefore, have thought it expedient to offer the following resolution:

Resolved, That his excellency the Governor be authorized (if in his discretion it be deemed necessary) to appoint one or more fit and proper persons to digest and arrange a system for the free schools of Georgia, to be submitted to the consideration of the next Legislature; and that the Governor, together with the person or persons so appointed, be instructed to correspond with such distinguished and intelligent persons in any part of the world as they may deem necessary, to afford practical information on this very interesting subject.

Approved, December 19th, 1829.[10]

The report adopted by the legislature in December 1831, [Pam. 284].

"In our country every man ought to prepare himself for taking part in her public business. Should he never aspire to a seat in her state or national councils, he yet owes it as a duty to himself and his posterity, to let any talent he may possess appear at least in her primary assemblies.

If this view of our duty be correct, and it is believed it cannot be controverted, the committee feel warranted in considering the subject of education, the noblest and most important that can engage the attention of the lawgiver, it lies, in truth, at the basis of the whole social system. It affects not only the individual happiness, the character and the usefulness of those who are its objects, but it exerts a most powerful and irresistible influence upon the government, the laws, and the liberties of communities. No nation when the majority of the people is well educated, can remain enslaved; no nation when the great mass is ignorant can retain its freedom. In proportion to the general intelligence will be the force, the wealth, and the influence of a State, and it will be respected in the exact ratio of the instructed talent it can bring into its negotiations." [11]

1. Lamar, Lucius O. C., Esq., *A Compilation of the Laws of the State of Georgia, passed by the Legislature Since the Year 1810 to the Year 1819, Inclusive.* (Augusta: T. S. Shannon, 1821), 1182 and 1183.
2. *Ibid.*, 1221.
3. Dawson, William C., *A Compilation of the Laws of the State of Georgia, passed by the General Assembly, since the year 1819 to the year 1829, inclusive.* (Milledgeville: Grantland and Orme, 1831), 6, 7.
4. *Ibid.*, 9.
5. *Ibid.*, 13, 14.
6. *Ibid.*, 40, 41.
7. *Ibid.*, 92, 93.
8. *Ibid.*, 79.
9. *Ibid.*, 116.
10. *Ibid.*, 138.
11. *Ibid.*, 148.

Appendix II: *Four Early School Systems*

Several communities in the state claimed to have established the first free public school in the state. As has been noted above in the text earlier, the school established for the Salzburger community at Ebenezer was free to the children of the Salzburgers. The schools organized in Savannah did become a free school. These two situations did continue under both the trustees and the royal governors.

Soon after the state came into being as a part of the United States, the development of education continued. It seems appropriate at this time to mention four counties with a brief summary of certain educational developments within these counties, namely Bibb, Chatham, Glynn, and Richmond. These counties are unique in that they finally developed a county system and have been able to maintain it throughout the history of the educational changes in the state up to the present time.

Bibb County was not established as a county until 1822. The Academy was chartered in 1823. The first Board of Commissioners of the Bibb County Academy were Oliver H. Prince, Charles J. McDonald, Mathew Robinson, James Frierson, and Rice Durett. The Board of Trustees in 1858 agreed to open the school as a free school. The Board of Trustees had some investments which produced some revenue and they paid half of the expenses and the Merit Council of the city of Macon paid the other half. Although it had been agreed to open the school as a free school, nevertheless, some tuition was charged for the next three years to some pupils. Persons who took Latin and Greek had to pay $30 a year. In 1861, the Board of Trustees did make the school "strictly a free school." After the Civil War, they opened the Macon Free School again after receiving some "Yankee" money from the American Indian Commission. The Macon Free School was already in operation when the state finally was able to set up a public school system and Bibb County was able to move into the statewide system.[1]

The Chatham Academy was chartered by the Legislature in 1788. The original Trustees were John Houston, John Habersham, William Gibbons, Sr., William Stephens, Richard Wylly, James Houston, Samuel Elbert, Seth John Cuthbert, and Joseph Clay, Jr.[2] It seems difficult to say for a certainty when the Chatham Academy was opened. The first building occupied by the Academy was opened January 5, 1813, with 219 pupils.[3] It is suggested by Bowden that the Academy may have been in operation prior to this time when he quotes an editorial in *The Gazette* of March 28, 1793, to the effect that a public examination was held in the Academy in the presence of the Trustees and a number of citizens. He also quotes from minutes, "Meeting Trustees of Chatham Academy the 20th of March, 1793." [4] A group of citizens in Chatham County organized the Savannah Free School Society. This Society was incorporated by the Legislature in 1818.[5] The city of Savannah gave financial support to the school. The school undertook to give an education in the elementary branches to the poor children of Savannah. The Massey School was organized and put into operation by the City Council of Savannah. One Peter Massey of Glynn County had left a bequest of $5,000 for the education of poor children in Savannah. By the time the City Council put this school into operation, the $5,000 through investment had increased to $8,750.46.[6] The Legislature of 1866 established the Board of Education for the City of Savannah and the County of Chatham.[7] All of the public schools in Savannah and Chatham County were organized under this Board of Education into a public school system for Savannah and Chatham County.[8]

Glynn Academy was authorized by the Legislature in 1788. In the One Hundred Eighteenth Annual Report of the Public Schools of Glynn County, Georgia for the Year 1905-1906, the superintendent, N. H. Ballard, says that although Chatham and Richmond Academies were chartered prior to the Glynn Academy that for quite a period of time their jurisdiction was local. He says that the Glynn Academy had jurisdiction and maintained public schools throughout the county from the beginning, 1788. "It is perhaps the only county system whose schools for more than 117 years had been maintained without tuition but entirely and completely public schools." [9] If Glynn County had been operating a public school system for 117 years without tuition in 1905-06, then last year, the school year 1973-74, they finished their 185th year.

In 1833, the Legislature authorized the Commissioners of Glynn Academy to establish free schools in the county. Robert

Hazelhurst and James Hamilton Couper were appointed as Commissioners to the Glynn County Academy in addition to the persons who were already in office. One school was to be established in the 27th District at a proper place. They were authorized to employ one teacher for each school. Section 2 of the act reads as follows, "And be it enacted by the Academy aforesaid, that no child or children shall receive their tuition gratuitously, whose parents pay $2.00 as their state tax; and any money which may arise from the tuition of children sent to these schools, shall go to the support of said schools." [10]

Richmond Academy was chartered by the state Legislature in 1783. The Richmond Academy opened in 1785. The first Trustees were William Glascock, George Walton, Joseph Pannel, Andrew Burns, and Samuel Jack.[11] Jones says the Richmond Academy is the oldest seat of learning in the United States with the exception of Yale, Harvard, and Princeton.[12] The Augusta Free School Society was incorporated by the Legislature in 1821. The Directors, under the Act of Incorporation, were Reverend William T. Brantley, Reverend William Moderwall, Augustus Moore, William J. Hobby, Ralph Ketchum, Samuel Hale, Hugh Nesbit, Joel Katlin, Abiel Cramfield, Robert A. Reid, Carlos Tracey, John Campbell, and Thomas McDowell. According to the act, the Augusta Free Society was already in operation for the education of indigent children.[13] Jones says that Richard Tubman was one of the generous benefactors of the school and that Thomas Snowdon was for a long time the principal and one of the most successful teachers ever known in Augusta. Also he says Martin V. Calvin at one time was principal of this school.[14]

Another important institution in Augusta was the Houghton Institute. A Mr. Houghton, a merchant in Augusta, left an endowment for a school to bear his name to be free to all the children of Augusta.[15] Jones says that under a local law passed in 1872 public instruction in the city and county was put under one board to have entire charge of the program.[16]

The Richmond Academy was authorized by the Legislature of 1783 and opened its doors April 12, 1785. The Academy was closed in 1798 and reopened in 1802.[17] The Academy was not in operation during the Civil War; but with these two exceptions, Richmond Academy has been in operation since 1785.

It is interesting to note that these four systems were organized prior to the Constitution of 1877: Chatham, 1866; Bibb, 1872; Richmond, 1872; and Glynn, 1873. The Constitution of 1866 and 1868 did not limit the taxing power which the General Assembly might delegate for school purposes for the scope of public education. However, the Constitution of 1877 had two serious limitations; (1) state support of public education was limited to a grammar school education and (2) local taxation was dependent upon local referendum. The Constitution of 1877 stipulated that existing local school systems shall not be affected by this Constitution. This came to be known as the "protective clause," also, the Constitution of 1945 stipulated that systems existing prior to the Constitution of 1877 would not be affected by that Constitution.[18]

1. Minutes of Trustees of Bibb Academy. Manuscript filed in Office of Bibb County Board of Education.
2. William Harden, *A History of Savannah and South Georgia*. (Atlanta, 1969) I, 265-266.
3. Marie Margaretta Furrer, *Development of the Public School System in Savannah and Chatham County*. (Athens, 1933.) Unpublished Masters Thesis.
4. Haygood S. Bowden, *Two Hundred Years of Education*. (Richmond, Va., 1932), 85.
5. *Lamar Digest*, 844-1848.
6. Bowden, *Two Hundred Years of Education*.
7. *Acts of the General Assembly—Annual Session—December 1865, and January, February and March, 1866*. (Milledgeville, 1866), 78-80.
8. Bowden, *Two Hundred Years of Education*, 249.
9. *One Hundred Eighteenth Annual Report of the Public Schools of Glynn County, Georgia, 1905-1906*—N. H. Ballard, Superintendent (Emory Library), 9.
10. *Dawson's Digest*, 17.
11. Charles C. Jones, *Memorial History of Augusta Georgia* (Syracuse, New York), 157.
12. *Ibid.*, 157.
13. *Dawson's Index*, 191.
14. Jones, *Memorial History of Augusta*, 319.
15. *Ibid.*, 318.
16. *Ibid.*, 324.
17. Charles Guy Cordle, *An Ante-Bellum Academy, The Academy of Richmond County*. Unpublished Masters Thesis, University of Georgia (Athens, 1935), 19-20.
18. Marion Jennings Rice, *Georgia School Law: a case study Based on the Decisions of the Georgia Supreme Court and the Court of Appeals*. Unpublished Dissertation, University of Georgia (Athens, 1960), 48-53.

APPENDIX III: *Department of Human Resources: Number Rehabilitated by Division of Vocational Rehabilitation 1921 - 1974*

Year	Number Rehabilitated	Cumulative Total	Year	Number Rehabilitated	Cumulative Total
1921	... 5	5	1948	... 2,490	18,228
1922	... 14	19	1949	... 3,075	21,303
1923	... 16	35	1950	... 2,859	24,162
1924	... 64	99	1951	... 2,982	27,144
1925	... 59	158	1952	... 3,194	30,338
1926	... 51	209	1953	... 3,914	34,252
1927	... 69	278	1954	... 3,954	38,206
1928	... 86	364	1955	... 4,552	42,758
1929	... 85	449	1956	... 5,093	47,851
1930	... 114	563	1957	... 5,326	53,177
1931	... 126	689	1958	... 5,518	58,695
1932	... 167	856	1959	... 5,628	64,323
1933	... 132	988	1960	... 5,914	70,237
1934	... 200	1,188	1961	... 6,014	76,251
1935	... 201	1,389	1962	... 6,105	82,356
1936	... 238	1,627	1963	... 6,503	88,859
1937	... 270	1,897	1964	... 6,803	95,662
1938	... 234	2,131	1965	... 7,221	102,883
1939	... 248	2,379	1966	... 8,010	110,893
1940	... 260	2,639	1967	... 8,751	119,644
1941	... 290	2,929	1968	... 9,031	128,675
1942	... 413	3,342	1969	...10,215	138,890
1943	... 2,109	5,451	1970	...11,142	150,032
1944	... 2,771	8,222	1971	...11,512	161,544
1945	... 2,361	10,583	1972	...12,592	174,136
1946	... 2,400	12,983	1973	...12,686	186,822
1947	... 2,755	15,738	1974	...11,786	198,608

APPENDIX IV: *State Board of Education Policies and Procedures*

40-2600   LOCAL SCHOOL SYSTEM MERGER,
           SCHOOL CONSOLIDATION

40-2610   Policy

Adopted June, 1975

The State of Georgia, State Board of Education recognizes that each school system, to be effective, must be sufficiently large to have an adequate financial base so that it can offer education programs and services of acceptable scope and depth. The Board believes that each individual school should be sufficiently large to have an adequate staff to provide comprehensive programs and services to meet the various needs of children and youth. To encourage the consolidation of small schools within a county or independent system boundaries, or both, specific allotments of capital outlay funds to finance the construction of buildings shall be made in accordance with the following conditions.

1. The local system board of education shall, by official resolution spread upon the minutes of the board, vote to consolidate the schools under consideration and pledge that the consolidation will be effected immediately upon completion and acceptance of the facilities.

2. The local system must, with the assistance of the State Superintendent of Schools, complete a comprehensive study within two years preceding an application for capital outlay funds for consolidation.

3. Application for funds shall be made to the State Board on forms provided by the State Board; the application shall follow the recommendations of the comprehensive study team. In case a local board applies for consolidation construction funds which are not recommended by a study team, the board shall appear before the State Board to justify exceptions.

4. When two or more system boards of education enter into long-term contracts to consolidate schools across county

538

or independent system lines, or both, the State Board shall set up allotments of capital outlay funds to provide facilities for these consolidated schools when, in the opinion of the State Board, the best interests of the children of the systems will be served. These contracts must be for periods of not less than 25 years.

5. The criteria for determining needs shall be those currently in effect as provided by policies of the State Board.

6. A system must acquire funds from some source other than the State of Georgia and have the same on deposit and reserved for expenditure on the proposed project or projects or have outstanding bonds equal to or exceeding an amount which equals 14 percent of the system's total bonding capacity on the most recent certified digest or an adequate combination of both methods of producing local funds.

7. The local system shall assume responsibility for the construction of facilities for which state aid is not available (such as gymnasiums, auditoriums, stadiums, site development, etc.).

8. The capitalized allotment of capital outlay funds available to the system under the current building program shall be applied to any proposed project under this program unless, in the judgment of the State Board, these funds should be used for projects having a higher priority (for example, projects needed to house children presently in sub-standard facilities).

9. The State Board shall accept and file applications in the order received. When applications are approved, the State Board shall set up allotments of capital outlay funds as funds are available for implementation of this program.

10. When two or more units are joined across county or independent system lines, it shall, insofar as possible, be the policy of the State Board to guarantee that neither system be penalized in operating funds.

11. In submitting programs of school consolidation as the basis for application for allotment of capital outlay funds, a local system may present plans for consolidation of high school grades and plans for consolidation of elementary grades as separate proposals to be considered by the State Board independently of each other.

12. All programs of consolidation presented to the State Board must provide for schools which meet the minimum standards of the State Board for allocation of capital outlay funds. (An average daily attendance of 500 in grades nine-12 and 200 in grades one-seven is the current requirement.)

The State Board encourages and promotes the consolidation of elementary schools to achieve minimum enrollments of 500 children in grades K-seven and of 1,000 students in grades eight-12, if organized on that basis.

The State Board encourages and promotes legislation and a constitutional amendment that would provide for the merger of school systems into units with minimum enrollments of 10,000 students.

Legal Authorization

Georgia Code: 2-5901(d), 2-7201, 2-7202, 32-641a (1974), 32-648a (1974, 1975), 32-663a (1974), 32-915 (1919, 1946), 32-1201 (1926), 32-1203 (1926), 32-1404 (1923), 32-1405 (1923), 32-1406 (1923).

40-2620   Executive Procedure

The Office of School Administrative Services shall prepare the procedures and forms to be used by local system boards in making application for capital outlay funds for school consolidation and shall provide assistance to local system superintendents in completing the forms.

The Office of School Administrative Services shall conduct a comprehensive study of local school systems within two years preceding a system's application for capital outlay funds for consolidation. Staff from within the department shall serve on the study team. Final approval of comprehensive studies shall be made jointly by the Office of School Administrative Services, the Office of Instructional Services and the Office of Adult and Vocational Education.

40-3200   LOCAL SCHOOL SYSTEMS'
              ELIGIBILITY FOR RECEIVING STATE
              CAPITAL OUTLAY FUNDS

40-3210   Policy

                   Adopted May, 1975

The State of Georgia, State Board of Education has the responsibility for determining the local systems eligible to receive capital outlay funds. State law directs the State Board of Education to consider the financial ability of local school systems to furnish local capital outlay funds from existing unused bonding capacities of local systems and the willingness of the local system to provide such local capital outlay funds. The State Board of Education considers local school systems that meet the following conditions as being eligible for capital outlay provided they have earnings from increased attendance, consolidation, obsolescence or renovation.

1. A system must acquire funds from some source other than the state of Georgia and have the same on deposit and reserved for expenditure on the proposed project or projects or have outstanding bonds equal to or exceeding an amount which equals 14 percent of the system's total bonding capacity on the most recent certified digest or an adequate combination of both methods of producing local funds.

2. All school systems shall have a comprehensive study at least every five years and within two years preceding an application for capital outlay funds or upon the request of the system board of education. This study shall consist of curriculum needs, utilization of school staff, utilization of time schedule (daily, monthly and annually), curricula offerings, graduation requirements and special instructional facilities. This study shall also include building needs and financial resources.

    The State of Georgia, State Department of Education, with the assistance of the local school systems, shall assume responsibility for organizing the study teams which shall be composed of State Department of Education personnel, college personnel and the local school superintendents. The superintendent, or a person appointed by the superintendent, shall be used by the study team as a consultant or resource person to the study team. Local boards of education, in making application for state capital outlay funds and the use of annual grants on new projects, shall follow the recommendations of the study team. In cases where local boards of education apply for funds for the construction of projects not recommended by the study team, said boards shall appear before the State Board in order to justify exceptions. The local system superintendent and the board of education shall have an opportunity to consult with the study team prior to the draft being finalized.

3. A local school system's capital outlay allocation must be based on students residing within the school system and students from adjoining systems covered by a 25-year contract. This contract must begin or be renewed within five years preceding the date of application.

Legal Authorization

Georgia Code: 32-641a (1974), 32-648a (1974, 1975).

40-3220   Executive Procedure

The Office of School Administrative Services shall prepare information concerning the bonding status of local school systems and the required amount of bonds necessary to receive capital outlay funds. This office shall also develop a file containing copies of all 25-year contract agreements between local school systems.

The Office of School Administrative Services shall conduct a comprehensive study of local school systems within two years preceding a system's application for capital outlay funds. Staff from within the Department of Education shall serve on the study team. Final approval of comprehensive studies shall be made jointly by the Office of School Administrative Services, the Office of Instructional Services and the Office of Adult and Vocational Education.

The Office of Staff Services shall furnish the Office of School Administrative Services the necessary basic data from local school systems' annual reports on outstanding bonds.

40-3300   STATE CAPITAL OUTLAY
                       FORMULAS

40-3310   Policy

Adopted May, 1975

The State of Georgia, State Board of Education has the responsibility for devising a formula for the allocation of state capital outlay funds.

1. Allocations per square foot shall be $20.00 plus six percent for architect fees and four percent for contingencies, making a total allocation per square foot of $22.00.
2. The increased attendance allotments will be 78 square feet for each pupil increase in average daily attendance.
3. Other capital outlay allotments will be based on the following tables.

Elementary Schools

1 to 500 students	@ 73 Sq. Ft.
501 to 750 students	@ 58 Sq. Ft.
751 to 1000 students	@ 52 Sq. Ft.
1001 to 1500 students	@ 46 Sq. Ft.
Above 1500 students	@ 41 Sq. Ft.

High Schools

1 to 500 students	@ 93 Sq. Ft.
501 to 750 students	@ 73 Sq. Ft.
751 to 1000 students	@ 66 Sq. Ft.
1001 to 1500 students	@ 59 Sq. Ft.
Above 1500 students	@ 54 Sq. Ft.

Legal Authorization

Georgia Code: 32-641a (1974), 32-648a (1974, 1975).

40-3320   Executive Procedure

The Office of School Administrative Services shall develop procedures for allocating space requirements to local school systems for increased attendance, consolidation, obsolescence and renovation.

The office of Staff Services shall furnish the Office of School Administrative Services the necessary basic data for making allocations.

40-3400   PRIORITIES FOR STATE CAPITAL
OUTLAY FUNDS

40-3410   Policy

Adopted May, 1975

The State of Georgia, State Board of Education has the responsibility for determining the priorities to be used in approving applications for the allotment of state capital outlay funds. In determining priorities, the State Board of Education must consider the availability of standard classrooms and the most efficient and economical use of state capital outlay funds in assisting local systems in providing additional classroom space.

Capital outlay entitlements will be made on the basis of increased attendance, consolidation, obsolescence and renovations combined with exhibited local financial support for the system. First priority shall be given to systems which qualify for increased attendance earnings. Capital outlay funds remaining after all eligible systems with increased attendance earnings have been funded may be used for consolidation, obsolete buildings in use at the time of the allocation and/or recommended by the comprehensive study team and renovating buildings to house the program as recommended by the comprehensive study team—second, third and fourth priorities respectively. (Priority for increased attendance earnings shall be given first to the system which qualifies for increased attendance earnings and which has obligated itself to the greatest extent in levying taxes to support the system and to retire outstanding bonds.)

In determining entitlements, the State Board of Education will give priority to entitlements of $100,000 or more. Entitlements of less than $100,000 will not be funded except in cases of extreme hardship. Entitlements of less than $100,-000 will be established to the credit of the local system to be added to subsequent entitlements until such a time as the system has entitlements totaling $100,000 or more, at which time the entitlements will be funded as funds are available.

Capital outlay applications shall be restricted to such projects as will provide the children of Georgia the needed additional classrooms, libraries, sanitary facilities, lunchrooms, mechanical improvements, school sites and equipment necessary for the projects. All construction shall be of noncombustible materials. The approval of plans for school buildings, additions to buildings and major changes in buildings and renovations for which state capital outlay funds are to be used must be secured from the State of Georgia, State Department of Education.

In approving the expenditure of capital outlay funds, priorities will be established in the following order.

1. Payment of lease rentals to the Georgia Education Authority (Schools) and any other authority that may be established by law.
2. Expenditures in erecting new buildings or additions to old buildings which have been designated as permanent school centers. (The construction of classrooms, sanitary facilities, lunchrooms, libraries and administration facilities must be provided for all children in the system before state captal outlay funds are spent for other needs.)
3. Expenditures for equipment for new buildings and additions to buildings. (Some examples of equipment are desks, chairs, tables, bookcases, shop machinery, fixed science equipment. Those items not considered as equipment for capital outlay purposes include musical instruments, typewriters, business machines, microscopes, tape recorders, library books and projectors.)
4. Expenditures for major improvements to bring existing facilities up to satisfactory standards, such as central heating to replace room-fired heaters (not replacement of worn-out boilers) and adequate lighting systems.
5. Expenditures for completion of buildings constructed where items such as tile, interior painting of concrete blocks (not repainting), installing acoustical tile or additional lights are needed to complete a project.
6. Expenditure on a 50-50 basis (state and local) for construction of gymnasiums, auditoriums or both when adequate and standard classroom facilities have been provided for all of the school children of a system.
7. For payment of principal and interest of new local bond issues if and when adequate and standard facilities have been provided for all of the school children of a system.

8. For acquisition of school sites provided the appropriations bill for the fiscal year allows for expenditure of funds for that purpose.

State funds are not available for replacement of buildings destroyed by fire or other causes. Local units of administration shall provide adequate insurance for buildings not covered by the Georgia Education Authority (Schools) or any other building authorities that may be established by law.

Legal Authorization
Georgia Code: 32-641a (1974), 32-648a (1974, 1975).

40-3420   Executive Procedure
The Office of School Administrative Services shall develop the procedures for determining the local systems meeting the priorities established by the State Board of Education.

The Office of Staff Services shall furnish the Office of School Administrative Services the necessary basic data for determining priorities. The additional data necessary shall be compiled by the Office of School Administrative Services from comprehensive studies and reports from local school systems.

40-3500   ALLOCATION OF STATE CAPITAL
OUTLAY FUNDS FOR INCREASED
ATTENDANCE

40-3510   Policy

Adopted June, 1975

The State of Georgia, State Board of Education has the responsibility for determining current and future capital outlay needs of local systems and allotting capital outlay funds for increased attendance. The State Board defines increased attendance, for this purpose, as growth or projected growth in average daily attendance experienced by a school system with the base ADA being the largest ADA figure used in making a past allocation of state capital outlay funds.

The State Superintendent of Schools shall determine the amount of capital outlay funds for which the system shall be eligible according to the following criteria.

1. The local system must, with the assistance of the State Superintendent, complete a comprehensive study within two years preceding an application for capital outlay funds for increased attendance.

2. Application for funds shall be made to the State Board on forms provided by the State Board; the application shall follow the recommendations of the comprehensive study team. In case a local board applies for increased attendance construction funds which are not recommended by a study team, the board shall appear before the State Board to justify exceptions.

3. A system must acquire funds from some source other than the State of Georgia and have the same on deposit and reserved for expenditure on the proposed project or projects or have outstanding bonds equal to or exceeding an amount which equals 14 percent of the system's total bonding capacity on the most recent certified digest or an adequate combination of both methods of producing local funds.

4. The local system shall assume responsibility for the construction of facilities for which state aid is not available (such as gymnasiums, auditoriums, stadiums, site development, etc.).

5. In computing increased attendance earnings, a system's allocation must be based on students residing within the school system and students from adjacent systems covered by a 25-year contract which has been signed within the past five years.

6. All applications for increased attendance funds presented to the State Board must provide for schools which meet the minimum standards of the State Board for allocation of capital outlay funds. (An average daily attendance of 500 in grades nine-12 and 200 in grades one-seven is the current requirement.)

The State Board encourages and promotes the construction of elementary schools to achieve minimum enrollments of 500 children in grades K-seven and of 1,000 students in grades eight-12.

Legal Authorization
Georgia Code: 32-641a (1974), 32-648a (1974, 1975).

40-3520   Executive Procedure

The Office of School Administrative Services shall prepare the procedures and forms to be used by local system boards in making application for capital outlay funds for increased attendance and shall provide assistance to local system superintendents in completing the forms.

The Office of School Administrative Services shall conduct a comprehensive study of local school systems within two years preceding a system's application for capital outlay funds for increased attendance. Staff from within the Department of Education shall serve on the study team. Final approval of comprehensive studies shall be made jointly by the Office of School Administrative Services, the Office of Instructional Services and the Office of Adult and Vocational Education.

40-3600   ALLOCATION OF STATE
                 CAPITAL OUTLAY FUNDS FOR
                REPLACING OBSOLETE BUILDINGS

30-3610   Policy

Adopted May, 1975

The State of Georgia, State Board of Education has the responsibility for determining current and future capital outlay funds for replacing obsolete buildings. The State Board defines obsolescence, for this purpose, as the state or condition of a school building that renders it unsuitable for continued educational use for reasons of age, construction characteristics and safety factors which cannot be corrected according to established criteria without the expenditure of funds exceeding established limits of economy.

A building is considered obsolete if the total cost of placing the building in acceptable condition to serve adequately the children of the school and its program exceeds 40 percent of the cost of a new building to replace the old one, provided the local board of education shall concur with the study team that the building is obsolete.

When a Comprehensive Study Committee determines that an existing school building or part of an existing school building presently in use and necessary to house the system's ADA is obsolete, the system shall be eligible to receive capital outlay funds for replacement of the obsolete building.

The State Superintendent of Schools shall determine the amount of capital outlay funds for which the system shall be eligible according to the following criteria.

1. Earnings for obsolescence shall be based upon the established State Board of Education earnings on average daily attendance. The ADA to be housed at the site shall be recommended by the Comprehensive Study Committee. Only the ADA which will be required to be housed in the obsolete facilities shall be considered for earnings.

2. To be eligible for a grant to replace obsolete buildings a local school system must be bonded to the same amount as required by the State Board of Education for any other capital outlay grant.

3. Earnings shall be computed on the basis of buildings in use at the time of the effective comprehensive study. No retroactive allocations will be made.

Legal Authorization

Georgia Code: 32-641a (1974), 32-648a (1974, 1975).

40-3620 Executive Procedure

The Office of School Administrative Services shall develop procedures for allotting capital outlay funds to local school systems for the replacement of obsolete buildings in local school systems.

The Office of Staff Services shall furnish the Office of School Administrative Services the necessary basic data for calculating allocations.

40-3700 PRIORITIES FOR STATE CAPITAL OUTLAY ANNUAL PAYMENTS UNDER THE FIRST AND SECOND BUILDING PROGRAMS ALLOTTED PRIOR TO 1963-64

40-3710 Policy

Adopted May, 1975

The State of Georgia, State Board of Education has the responsibility for determining the priorities to be used in approved applications for the expenditure of state capital outlay funds for annual payments under the first and second building programs.

Local boards of education, in making application for the use of annual grants, shall follow the recommendations of the most recent comprehensive study.

In approving the expenditure of the annual payment funds, priorities will be established in the following order.

1. Expenditures in erecting new buildings or additions to old buildings which have been designated as permanent school centers. (The construction of classrooms, sanitary facilities, lunchrooms, libraries and administration facilities must be provided for all children in the system before state capital outlay funds are spent for other needs.)

2. Expenditures for equipment for new buildings and additions to buildings. (Some examples of equipment are desks, chairs, tables, bookcases, shop machinery and fixed science equipment. Those items not considered as equipment for capital outlay purposes include musical instruments, typewriters, business machines, microscopes, tape recorders, library books and projectors.)

3. Expenditures for major improvements to bring existing facilities up to satisfactory standards, such as central heating to replace room-fired heaters (not replacement of worn out boilers) and adequate lighting systems.

4. Expenditures for completion of buildings constructed where items such as tile, interior painting of concrete blocks (not repainting), installation of acoustical tile or additional lights are needed to complete a project.

5. Expenditures to modernize and improve facilities including general renovation and painting of old buildings which have been designated as permanent school centers.

Legal Authorization
Georgia Code: 32-641a (1974), 32-648a (1974, 1975).

40-3720   Executive Procedure

The Office of School Administrative Services shall prepare the procedures and forms to be used by local system boards of education in making application for the expenditure of state capital outlay annual payment funds.

The Office of School Administrative Services shall conduct a comprehensive study of local school systems within two years preceding a system's application for the expenditure of state capital outlay annual payment funds. Exceptions to the above procedures can be made upon the recommendation of School Plant Services and the Director of Regional Services for systems with small annual payments, provided the funds be expended for improvements to permanent centers constructed since 1959 or for equipment.

40-3800 COMPREHENSIVE HIGH SCHOOL VOCATIONAL CONSTRUCTION, RENOVATION AND EQUIPMENT GRANTS

40-3810 Policy

Adopted May, 1975

The State of Georgia, State Board of Education recognizes the need to assist local boards of education throughout the state to establish comprehensive high schools in their school systems. State and federal funds available to the State Board may be allotted to local school systems for construction, renovation and equipment for the vocational component of comprehensive high schools in keeping with the following provisions.

1. State and federal vocational funds may be allotted to local school systems for construction, renovation and equipment for the vocational component of comprehensive high schools which have been recommended by a State of Georgia, State Department of Education comprehensive survey made within the past two years and accepted by the local board of education.

2. The number and types of occupational courses may vary provided, however, that a minimum of five, two of which are laboratory centered, must be established to qualify for construction, renovation and equipment grants. For high schools with enrollments of 1,000 or more, at least seven courses must be made available, four of which are laboratory centered.

3. Two or more school systems may join together by long-term contractual agreement to qualify for larger grants to provide a more adequate vocational program through an area vocational high school.

4. Capital outlay grants to local school systems for construction, renovation and equipment shall be based on the ADA of the school or schools. The allotment per ADA shall be determined annually on the basis of the estimated current cost of construction, renovation and equipment and the availability of state and federal funds.

5. Local matching requirements also shall be determined annually. Relative need and the local system's ability to provide funds may be considered in determining matching requirements.

6. The system must agree to use its earned state capital outlay funds or have funds available and on hand to match the state and federal vocational funds.

7. The system must file a grant application on a Georgia Department of Education form provided for this purpose. Applications will be reviewed and ranked annually, or more frequently if necessary, to allocate the funds available. The State Plan for Vocational Education (Part I—Administrative Provisions, Item 3.27) criteria and formulas will be used to determine the relative priority of applications. The formula allocation is determined by assigning point values to the following factors in each school system.

   a. Manpower needs and job opportunities
   b. Vocational needs of the group to be served
   c. Relative ability to provide resources
   d. Excess cost

   Approved applicants will retain their rank order until they are funded or have withdrawn their application.

The State Superintendent of Schools shall develop regulations and procedures whereby local school systems may apply for comprehensive high school vocational construction, renovation and equipment grants.

40-3800 COMPREHENSIVE HIGH SCHOOL
VOCATIONAL CONSTRUCTION, RENOVATION
AND EQUIPMENT GRANTS

Legal Authorization

Georgia Code: 32-2208 (1953), 32-2301a (1953), 32-2303a (1953), 32-2305a (1953).

40-3820 Executive Procedure

The Office of Adult and Vocational Education shall develop procedures for applying for capital outlay grants. These procedures shall include, but not be limited to the following.

1. Periods of filing grant applications.
2. Submission of request on an approved Georgia Department of Education application form.
3. Appropriate supporting documents including, but not limited to an architect's agreement and an agreement between the State Board and the local board of education to include.

a. A statement of fund limitations.
b. Programs to be offered.
c. Statement that the local board of education will provide a suitable construction site and proof of clear title.
d. List of proposed instructional equipment with costs.
e. Statement of compliance with Civil Rights Act.
f. Statement of compliance with regulations governing federally assisted construction projects, if applicable.
g. Statement of accessibility to physically handicapped.
h. Statement of continued use as a vocational facility and the state equity if discontinued.
i. Statement of assuring local support.
j. Statement of state equity and maintenance of inventory.
k. Environmental clearances, if applicable.
l. Statement that the contract for construction will be awarded by the lump sum contract method, that adequate methods of obtaining the competitive bidding will be employed prior to awarding the construction contract, by public advertising, and that the award of the contract will be made to the responsible bidder submitting the lowest acceptable bid.

The Office of Adult and Vocational Education shall review completed capital outlay applications in the order in which they are received and make recommendations to the State Superintendent. Established priorities shall be used in recommending projects to the State Superintendent for approval.

The Office of Adult and Vocational Education shall develop guidelines and procedures for insuring that construction projects will proceed in an orderly fashion and for making capital outlay payments to local school boards. These guidelines and procedures shall make provision for the following.

1. A systematic scheme for completing construction projects.
2. A schedule of proposed payment requests filed by the local board of education with the Office of Adult and Vocational Education.
3. Review of requests for grant payments by the Office of Adult and Vocational Education.
4. Payment of grant requests providing that construction begins within the period specified in the State Plan for Administration of Vocational Education unless an extension is granted by the State Board.
5. Making grants on the basis of cost estimated in the approved application.

The Office of Adult and Vocational Education shall provide technical assistance in all phases of capital outlay project development. Procedures shall be developed for coordinating and supervising the vocational construction projects. On-site visits during the project will be made by the local board of education and the Office of Adult and Vocational Education.

40-4000   ALLOCATION OF STATE CAPITAL
OUTLAY FUNDS FOR RENOVATING
EXISTING BUILDINGS

40-4010   Policy

Adopted May, 1975

The State of Georgia, State Board of Education has the responsibility for determining current and future capital outlay needs of local school systems and allotting capital outlay funds for renovating existing buildings. The State Board of

Education defines renovation, for this purpose, as the construction necessary to modify or upgrade existing buildings as to make them suitable to house the program recommended by the comprehensive study required under policy number 40-3200 and approved by the State Board of Education.

A system shall be eligible to receive capital outlay funds for renovation provided the comprehensive study committee determines that an existing school building, or a part of an existing school building, needs renovation, and the building is necessary to house the system's ADA and provide adequate space for the recommended program.

The State Superintendent of Schools shall determine the amount of capital outlay funds for which the system shall be eligible according to the following criteria.

1. Earnings for renovation shall be based upon the estimate of the local system's architect and approved by the State of Georgia, State Department of Education. The ADA and the program to be housed at the site shall be recommended by the comprehensive study committee. Only the renovation necessary to house the recommended program shall be considered for state capital outlay earnings.

2. To be eligible for a grant to renovate buildings, a local school system must be bonded to the same level as required by the State Board of Education for any other capital outlay grant.

Legal Authorization

Georgia Code: 32-641a (1974), 32-648a (1974, 1975).

40-4020 Executive Procedure

The Office of School Administrative Services shall develop procedures for allotting capital outlay funds to local school systems for the renovation of buildings in local school systems.

Appendix V: *Department of Education Capital Outlay Funds Since 1951*

Year	Amount	Source of Funds	Number of School Systems Receiving Fun Growth	Consolidati
1951	$10,333,800	State Appropriations (1) 28		
1952	32,097,000	S.S.B.A. Bond Revenue 29		
1953	63,300,000	S.S.B.A. Bond Revenue 74		
1954	20,949,600	State Appropriations (2) 22		
	32,512,000	S.S.B.A. Bond Revenue 50		
1955	29,238,000	S.S.B.A. Bond Revenue 38		
1961	31,452,000	S.S.B.A. Bond Revenue 31		
	3,810,400	State Appropriation (3) 61		
	12,484,860	State Appropriations (4) 65		
1962	26,600,000	S.S.B.A. Bond Revenue 50		
1964	27,905,000	S.S.B.A. Bond Revenue 35	6	
1965	27,030,000	S.S.B.A. Bond Revenue 34	22	
1966	32,125,000	S.S.B.A. Bond Revenue 16		
1967	28,020,000	S.S.B.A. Bond Revenue 38	12	
	32,120,000	S.S.B.A. Bond Revenue 37	12	
	732,000	S.S.B.A. Bond Revenue	1	
	1,247,000	S.S.B.A. Bond Revenue	1	
	866,000	S.S.B.A. Bond Revenue	1	
1968	21,800,000	S.S.B.A. Bond Revenue 21	10	
	5,200,000	S.S.B.A. Bond Revenue 8		
1969	13,245,000	S.S.B.A. Bond Revenue 17	7	
1970	11,500,000	S.S.B.A. Bond Revenue 7	2	
	24,715,000	S.S.B.A. Bond Revenue 18	9	
	1,656,340	State Appropriation (5) 8	3	

(1) These funds were accrued annually over a 20-year period from FY 1952-1971. T annual appropriation by the General Assembly to provide these funds amount to $516,690.

(2) These funds were accrued annually over a 20-year period from FY 1954-1973. T annual appropriation by the General Assembly to provide these funds amount to $1,047,480.

(3) These funds were a cash grant handled through the SSBA exactly as the 19 bond sale, i.e., Authority lease rental agreements providing for repayment over 20-year period were signed although no bonds were actually issued.

(4) These funds are accruing annually over a 20-year period from FY 1961-1980. T annual appropriation by the General Assembly to provide these funds amounts $624,242.

(5) These funds were surplus Authority Lease Rental funds which were allocated direct cash grants.

ear	Amount	Source of Funds	Number of School Systems Receiving Funds Growth	Consolidation
971	14,700,000	S.S.B.A. Bond Revenue	17	11
	15,700,000	S.S.B.A. Bond Revenue	7	6
	346,500	State Appropriation (6)	2	
972	10,200,000	S.S.B.A. Bond Revenue	10	8
	170,190	State Appropriation (6)	1	
	19,580,000	S.S.B.A. Bond Revenue	15	5
973	8,040,000	S.S.B.A. Bond Revenue	3	6
	5,000,000	S.S.B.A. Bond Revenue	3	5
	23,000,000	Federal Revenue Sharing	10	15
974	12,229,876	General Obligation Bond Revenue	7	4
975	5,878,750	General Obligation Bond Revenue	3	3
	10,057,574	General Obligation Bond Revenue	3	5
976	18,001,914	General Obligation Bond Revenue (7)	14	4
	1,400,000	State Appropriation (6) (8)	1	
	390,000	General Obligation Bond Revenue (9)	1	
977	9,296,611	General Obligation Bond Revenue	4	8

6) These funds were appropriated by the General Assembly for direct cash grants.

7) $6,462,914 of this amount is included in a bond issue for March, 1976.

8) $431,000 not previously encumbered was deferred from allocation by the Governor and is not included in the total. This amount is proposed to be eliminated from the budget for fiscal year 1976.

9) Due to excellent bond sales, additional $390,600 became available enabling systems to receive total amount appropriated in General Obligation Bonds (FY 1976).

APPENDIX VI: *Georgia Public Schools School Bond Elections 1959-60—1975-76*

Year	Amount Passed		Amount Failed	
1959-60	$ 15,422,000	(12)	$ 598,000	(2)
1960-61	20,610,000	(29)	2,200,000	(6)
1961-62	15,863,000	(31)	2,338,000	(6)
1962-63	45,496,000	(27)	27,948,000	(7)
1963-64	18,586,600	(23)	2,900,000	(3)
1964-65	16,852,000	(35)	2,094,000	(6)
1965-66	46,025,000	(25)	3,680,000	(4)
1966-67	18,550,000	(18)	8,450,000	(7)
1967-68	29,150,000	(18)	7,891,000	(8)
1968-69	84,240,000	(15)	18,728,367	(6)
1969-70	41,500,000	(11)	14,380,000	(12)
1970-71	22,620,000	(11)	9,670,000	(8)
1971-72	8,995,000	(11)	15,000,000	(5)
1972-73	104,925,000	(17)	12,750,000	(6)
1973-74	51,515,000	(16)	24,495,000	(10)
1974-75	14,080,000	(8)	19,470,000	(8)
1975-76	23,900,000	(4)	12,300,000	(4)
TOTAL	$578,329,600	(311)	$184,892,367	(108)

APPENDIX VII: *Average Cost Per Square Foot Of School Buildings*

Year	Statewide Average (Without Metro Atlanta)	Metro Atlanta Average	Combined Average
1963-64	$10.95	$13.69	$12.32
1964-65	11.46	13.94	12.70
1965-66	12.37	15.73	14.05
1966-67	12.60	18.43	15.51
1967-68	14.20	16.86	15.53
1968-69	15.74	20.03	17.88
1969-70	16.31	21.28	18.79
1970-71	17.93	25.66	21.97
1971-72	18.50	22.21	20.35
1972-73	19.66	24.17	21.91
1973-74	25.87	28.21	26.39
1974-75	22.78	25.93	23.52

Bibliography

BOOKS

Abbot, W. W. *The Royal Governors in Georgia 1754-1755.* Chapel Hill: University of North Carolina Press, 1959.

Arthur, T. S., and Carpenter, W. H. *The History of Georgia from its Earliest Settlement to the Present Time.* Philadelphia: Lippincott, Grambo & Co., 1852.

Association of Colleges and Preparatory Schools of the Southern States. *Proceedings of the Annual Meeting, 1904.* Chattanooga: Southern Educational Review, 1905.

Avery, I. W. *The History of the State of Georgia from 1850-1881.* New York: Brown & Derby, 1881.

Bonner, James C. *The Educational History of Carroll County.* Milledgeville: Georgia College Duplicating Department, 1968.

—————————. *The Georgia Story.*

—————————. *A History of Georgia Agriculture 1732-1860.* Athens: University of Georgia Press, 1964.

————————— and Roberts, Lucien E., eds. *Studies in Georgia History and Government.* Athens: University of Georgia Press, 1940.

Boogher, Elbert W. G. *Secondary Education in Georgia 1732-1858.* Camden: I. F. Huntzinger, 1933.

Bowden, Haygood S. *The Building of the Empire State.* Savannah: Braid and Hutton, 1925.

—————————. *Two Hundred Years of Education Bicentennial 1733-1933 Savannah, Chatham County, Georgia.* Richmond, Virginia: Press of the Dietz Printing Co., 1932.

Bowen, Eliza A. *The Story of Wilkes County Georgia.* Marietta: Continental Book Company, 1950.

Brittain, M. L. *Georgia School Laws and Decisions.* Atlanta, 1911.

Brown, Ira L. *The Georgia Colony.* New York: Macmillan, 1970.

Bryan, T. Conn. *Confederate Georgia.* Athens: University of Georgia Press, 1964.

Butler, John G. *Origin and History of the Georgia Academy for the Blind.* Macon: F. W. Burke, 1887.

Candler, Allen D., and Knight, Lucian Lamar, eds. *The Colonial Records of the State of Georgia, 1904-1916,* I-XXIX. Atlanta: Franklin Turner Co. (Note: Volumes 27-39 in manuscript at the Georgia Department of Archives and History.)

Candler, Allen D., and Evans, General Clement A., eds. *Cyclopedia of Georgia.* Atlanta: State Historical Association, 1906.

Chalker, Fussell M. *Pioneer Days Along the Ocmulgee.* Carrollton: Thomasson Printing and Office Equipment Company, 1970.

Clark, Thomas D., and Kirwan, Albert D. *The South Since Appomattox. A Century of Regional Change.* New York: Oxford University Press, 1967.

561

Clayton, Augustin Smith. *A Compilation of the Laws of the State of Georgia, passed by the Legislature since the political year 1800 to the year 1810, inclusive.* Augusta: Adams & Duyckinck, 1812.

Cobb, Thomas R. R. *A Digest of the Statute Laws of the State of Georgia, in Force Prior to the Session of the General Assembly of 1851, I, II.* Athens: Christy, Kelsea & Burke, 1851.

Coleman, Kenneth. *The American Revolution in Georgia 1763-1789.* Athens: University of Georgia Press, 1958.

Coleman, Leadel. *Statesboro—A Century of Progress 1866-1966.* Statesboro: Bulloch Herald, 1969.

Coulter, E. Merton. *Auraria, The Story of a Georgia Gold-Mining Town.* Athens: University of Georgia Press, 1956.

——————. *College Life in the Old South.* Athens: University of Georgia Press, 1951.

——————. *Georgia's Disputed Ruins.* Chapel Hill: University of North Carolina Press, 1937.

——————. *Joseph Vallence Bevan, Georgia's First Official Historian.* Athens: University of Georgia Press, 1964.

——————, and Saye, Albert B., eds. *A List of the Early Settlers of Georgia.* Athens: University of Georgia Press, 1967.

——————. *Old Petersburg and the Broad River Valley of Georgia, Their Rise and Decline.* Athens: University of Georgia Press, 1965.

——————. *A Short History of Georgia.* Chapel Hill: University of North Carolina Press, 1933.

Cubberly, Ellwood P. *The History of Education.* Boston: Houghton Mifflin, 1948.

——————. *Public School Administration.* Boston: Houghton Mifflin, 1922.

Cuthbert, J. A. *A Digest of All the Laws and Resolutions now in Force in the State of Georgia on the Subject of Public Education and Free Schools Prepared under a Resolution of the Legislature.* Milledgeville: Polhill & Cuthbert, 1832.

Dabney, Charles William. *Universal Education in the South from the Beginning to 1900, I.* Chapel Hill: University of North Carolina Press, 1936.

Davidson, Victor. *The History of Wilkinson County.* Macon: J. W. Burke, 1930.

Dawson, William C. *A Compilation of the Laws of the State of Georgia Passed by the General Assembly, since the Year 1819 to the Year 1829, inclusive.* Milledgeville: Grantland and Orme, 1831.

Dean, Russell J. N. *New Life for Millions: Rehabilitation for America's Disabled.* New York: Hastings House, 1972.

Ethridge, Willie Snow. *Strange Fires. The True Story of John Wesley's Love Affair in Georgia.* New York: The Vanguard Press, 1971.

Evans, Lawton B. A. M. *First Lessons in Georgia History.* New York: American Book Company, 1922.

——————. *A History of Georgia for Use in Schools.* New York: American Book Company, 1908.

Flanders, Ralph Betts. *Plantation Slavery in Georgia.* Chapel Hill: University of North Carolina Press, 1967.

Foster, Arthur. *A Digest of the Laws of the State of Georgia.* Philadelphia: Towar and Hogan, 1831.

Fries, Adelaide L. *The Moravians in Georgia 1735-1740.* Baltimore: Genealogical Publishing Company, 1967.

Fuller, Edgar, and Pearson, Jim B., eds. *Education in the United States: Nationwide Development Since 1900, I, II.* Washington, D. C.: National Education Association of the United States, 1969.

Garrett, Franklin M. *Atlanta and Environs, A Chronicle of Its People and Events, I.* Athens: University of Georgia Press, 1954.

Georgia Scenes, Characters, Incidents, etc. in the First Half-Century of the Republic, by a Georgia native. New York: Harper & Brothers, 1840.

Gillies, John D. D. *Memoirs of Rev. George Whitefield.* Middletown: Hunt & Noyes, 1837.

Gilmer, George R. *Sketches of Some of the First Settlers of Upper Georgia, of the Cherokees, and the Author.* Baltimore: Genealogical Publishing Company, 1970.

Good, Harry Gehman. *A History of American Education.* New York: Macmillan, 1962.

Good, Carter, V. *The Dictionary of Education.* New York: McGraw-Hill, 1959.

Goswell, Cullen B., and Anderson, C. David. *Government and Administration of Georgia.* New York: Thomas Y. Crowell.

Harden, William. *A History of Savannah and South Carolina, I.* Atlanta: Cherokee Publishing Company, 1969.

Harper, Francis, ed. *The Travels of William Bartram.* New Haven: Yale University Press, 1958.

Harris, Joel Chandler, ed. *Joel Chandler Harris' Life of Henry W. Grady including His Writings and Speeches.* New York: Cassell Publishing Company, 1890.

Johns, Roe L., ed. *Alternative Programs for Financing Education, I-VI.* Gainesville, Florida, 1971.

Johnson, Amanda. *Georgia As Colony and State.* Atlanta: Cherokee Publishing Company, 1970.

Johnston, Richard Malcolm. *Old Times in Middle Georgia.* New York: The Macmillan Company, 1897.

Jones, Charles C., Jr. *The Dead Towns of Georgia.* Savannah: Morning News Steam Printing House, 1878.

————————. *The History of Georgia, I, II.* Boston: Houghton, Mifflin and Company, 1883.

————————, and Dutcher, Salem. *Memorial History of Augusta, Georgia. From Its Settlement in 1735 to the Close of the Eighteenth Century and From the Close of the Eighteenth Century to the Present Time.* Syracuse, New York: D. Mason & Co., 1890.

Jones, Charles Edgeworth. *Education in Georgia.* (Circular of Information, 4.) Washington, D. C.: Government Printing Office, 1889.

Jones, George Fenwick, ed. *Henry Newman's Salzburger Letterbooks.* Athens: University of Georgia Press, 1966.

Jones, George Penwick, and Urlsperger, Samuel, eds. *Detailed Reports on the Salzburger Emigrants who Settled America.* (Wormsloe Foundations Reports, 9. I, II.) Athens: University of Georgia Press, 1968-69.

The Journals of Henry Melchior Muhlenberg, translated by Theodore G. Tappert and John W. Doberstein. Philadelphia: Muhlenberg Press, 1963.

Kemble, Francis Anne. *Journal of a Residence on A Plantation in 1838-1839.* New York: Harper & Brothers, 1863.

King, Spencer B., Jr. Georgia Voices. *A Documentary History to 1872.* Athens: University of Georgia Press, 1966.

Knight, Lucian Lamar. *Georgia's Landmarks, Memorials and Legends, I, II.* Atlanta: The Byrd Printing Company, 1914.

Knight, Lucian Lamar. *Reminiscences of Famous Georgians, I.* Atlanta: Franklin-Turner Company, 1907.

Knight, Lucian Lamar. *A Standard History of Georgia and Georgians, I-VI.* Chicago: Lewis Publishing, 1917.

Lamar, Lucius Q. C. *A Compilation of the Laws of the State of Georgia, Passed by the Legislature Since the Year 1819, Inclusive.* Augusta: T. S. Hannon, 1821.

Lane, Mills. *"War Is Hell," William T. Sherman's Personal Narrative of His March Through Georgia.* Savannah: Beehive Press, 1974.

McCain, James Ross. *Georgia As A Proprietary Province.* Boston: Richard G. Badger, 1917.

McCall, Hugh. *The History of Georgia Containing Brief Sketches of the Most Remarkable Events Up to the Present Day (1784).* Atlanta: Cherokee Publishing Company, 1969.

McPherson, John H. T. *The Government of the People of the State of Georgia.* New York: Hinds, Noble and Eldredge, 1908.

Mann, Harold W. *Atticus Green Haygood—Methodist Bishop, Editor, and Educator.* Athens: University of Georgia Press, 1965.

Marbury, H., and Crawford, W. H. *A Digest of the Laws of the State of Georgia from its Settlement as a British Province in 1755, to the Session of the General Assembly in 1800, Inclusive. Compiled, arranged and digested from original records and under the special authority of the State.* Savannah: Seymour, Woolhopter & Stebbens, 1802.

Mauelshagen, Carl. *Salzburg Lutheran Expulsion and Its Impact.* New York: Vantage Press, 1962.

Meyer, Adolph E. *An Educational History of the American People.* New York, 1957. Mitchell, Mary Edward. *Memories of James Mitchell.* N.P., N.D.

Morphet, Edgar L., et. al. *Educational Administration.* Englewood Cliffs, N. J.: Prentice Hall, 1959.

Morse, Joseph Laffan, ed. *The Universal Standard Encyclopedia.* New York, 1954.

Nixon, Raymond B. *Henry W. Grady, Spokesman of the New South.*
New York: Alfred A. Knopf, 1943.

Oberman, C. Esco. *A History of Vocational Rehabilitation in America.*
Minneapolis: T. S. Denison, 1968.

Orr, Dorothy. *A History of Education in Georgia.* Chapel Hill: University of North Carolina Press, 1950.

Owsley, Frank Lawrence. *The South: Old and New Frontiers.* Harriett
Chappell Owsley, ed. Athens: University of Georgia Press, 1969.

Parker, Percy L., ed., *The Journal of John Wesley.* Chicago: Moody
Press, 1951.

Prince, Oliver H. *A Digest of the Laws of the State of Georgia.* Athens:
Oliver H. Prince, 1837.

Reese, Trevor Richard. *Colonial Georgia.* Athens: University of Georgia
Press, 1963.

Saye, Albert B. *A Constitutional History of Georgia, 1832-1945.* Athens:
University of Georgia Press, 1948.

Schofield, Orrin. *Travels and Labors of Lorenzo Dow, in Europe and
America.* Rochester: Printed for Publisher, 1842.

Sherwood, Adiel. *A Gazetteer of the State of Georgia.* Athens: University of Georgia Press, 1929.

Smith, George G., Jr. *The History of Methodism in Georgia and Florida,
From 1785 to 1865.* Macon: J. W. Burke & Company, 1881.

——————. *The Life and Letters of James Osgood Andrew.* Nashville: Southern Methodist Publishing House, 1883.

——————. *The Life and Times of George Foster Pierce, D.D., LL.D.*
Sparta: Hancock, 1888.

——————. *The Story of Georgia and The Georgia People, 1732-
1860.* Atlanta: The Franklin Printing and Publishing Co., 1900.

Stevens, William Bacon. *A History of Georgia.* Revised edition I, II.
Philadelphia: E. H. Butler, 1859.

Strobel, P. A. *The Salzburgers and Their Descendants.* Athens: University of Georgia Press, 1953.

Temple, Sarah B. Gober, and Coleman, Kenneth, eds. *Georgia Journeys.
Being an Account of the Lives of Georgia's Original Settlers and
Many Other Early Settlers from the Founding of the Colony in 1732
until the Institution of Royal Government in 1754.* Athens: University of Georgia Press, 1961.

Thompson, C. Mildred. *Reconstruction in Georgia. Economic, Social,
Political 1865-1872.* Atlanta: Cherokee Publishing Company, 1971.

Vanstory, Burnette. *Georgia's Land of the Golden Isles.* Athens: University of Georgia Press, 1956.

Voight, A. G. *Ebenezer Record Book.* Savannah: Evangelical Lutheran
Synod of Georgia and Adjacent States, 1929.

Wade, John Donald. *Augustus Baldwin Longstreet. A Study of the
Development of Culture in the South.* Athens: University of Georgia
Press, 1969.

Watkins, Robert, and Watkins, George. *A Digest of the Laws of the
State of Georgia from Its First Establishment as a British Province*

Down to the Year 1798, Inclusive, and the Principal Acts of 1799.
Philadelphia: R. Aiken, 1800.

Wheeler, John T. *Two Hundred Years of Agricultural Education in Georgia.* Danville, Illinois: The Interstate Company, 1948.

White, George. *Historical Collections of Georgia.* New York: Pudney & Russell, 1854.

—————————. *Statistics of the State of Georgia.* Savannah: W. Thorne Williams, 1849.

Wiley, Bill Irvin, and Milhollen, Hirst D. *Embattled Confederates, an Illustrated History of Southerners at War.* New York: Bonanza Books, 1964.

Willingham, Robert Marion, Jr. *We Have This Heritage. The History of Wilkes County, Georgia Beginnings to 1860.* Wilkes Publishing Company, 1969.

Wylly, Charles Spalding. *The Seed That Was Sown in the Colony of Georgia. The Harvest and The Aftermath 1740-1870.* New York: The Neale Publishing Co., 1910.

Young, Ida, Gholson, Julius, and Hargrove, Clara Nell. *The History of Macon, Georgia, 1823-1949.* Macon: Lyon, Marshall and Brooks, 1950.

Zettler, B. M. *War Stories and School Day Incidents.* New York: The Neale Publishing Co., 1912.

PERIODICALS

Accredited Elementary Schools Bulletin, 6, 1929.

The Atlanta Constitution, February 10, 1900; June 27, July 3, July 18, 1919; January 11, January 12, March 4, March 29, 1935; September 29, 1954; October 10, 1969.

The Atlanta Journal, October 22, November 1, 1954.

The Atlanta Journal and *The Atlanta Constitution.* May 27, 1951; May 9, 1954; November 14, 1954.

Bulletin I. Victory Corps Series. U. S. Office of Education. Washington, D. C., 1942.

Bulloch Times and Statesboro Herald. 1931, 1940 (48, 49).

Carroll Free Press. September 13, 20, 1889; January 3, 1890; July 7, 1893; August 11, 1893; April 12, 1895; January 1, 1932; February 2, 1933.

Carswell, Kathleen Jones, ed. *Collections of Twiggs County—Here and There,* 1973. Reprinted from the *Georgia Genealogical Magazine,* IV, October 1954.

Collections of the Georgia Historical Society, VI, Habersham to Rev. Thomas Broughton, Secretary to the Society for Promoting Christian Knowledge, December 1, 1770, *Savannah Morning News Print,* 1904.

The Columbus Enquirer and Ledger. May 22, 1976.

Coulter, E. Merton. "The Ante-Bellum Academy Movement in Georgia," *Georgia Historical Quarterly,* V, 4, 1921.

—————————. "A Georgia Educational Movement During the Eighteen Hundred Fifties," *Georgia Historical Quarterly,* IX, 1925.

Ellison, Paul. "The Legal Growth of the Common School System of Georgia," *Georgia State School Items*, VIII (2), 1931.
The Federal Union, July 10, 1872.
Georgia Education Journal.
March 1936, November 1938, December 1938, February 1942, December 1942, February 1943, May 1943, October 1943, November 1943, December 1943, May 1944, January 1945, December 1946.
Georgia Education Journal. Advertisement for General Extension. November 1937.

GEORGIA EDUCATION JOURNAL ARTICLES

"The ABC of the School Situation in Georgia," May 1939.
Aderhold, O. C. "Pass the Ammunition," December 1942.
——————. "Georgia High Schools Organize Victory Corps," June 1943.
——————. "Georgia Victory School Program," January 1944.
Allman, J. I. "Financing a Minimum Term and a Minimum Salary," XXIX, 1936.
——————. "President's Message," August 1940.
"Audio-Visual Conference," November 1937.
Burgess, J. R. "Composition of Boards of Education of Independent City Districts of Georgia," March 1936.
Collins, M. D. "Message from the Superintendent," September 1947.
——————. "What the Legislature Did for Georgia Schools," September 1937.
"Curriculum Page," March 1938.
"Editorial," April 1939.
"Education in the New Constitution," May 1945.
"Education Panel," May 1947.
"Facts About Teacher Retirement," November 1943.
"The 15-mill Tax Amendment," October 1936.
"From the Editor's Desk," October 1938.
"Georgia Teacher Retirement Law," October 1943.
"Georgia Wartime Education Commission," September 1942.
Greene, J. H. "Plans for Teacher Retirement," December 1938.
"Headlines and Highlights of District Meetings," December 1946.
"Here They Stand," August 1940.
Lester, L. M. "Curriculum Revision in Georgia Summer Schools," April 1935.
"The Light Must Not Fail," February 1939.
McDonough, Thomas E. "Physical Fitness War Time Program for High School Victory Corps," February 1943.
"Our Legislative Program," February 1937.
"Outstanding Educational Events of 1942," February 1943.
"Personalities," January 1946.
Purcell, Claude. "The Compulsory Attendance Law," October 1945.
"Questions and Answers," December 1942.

Ramsey, Ralph. "Teacher Retirement," May 1942.
"Report of Representative Assembly," XLI, March 1948.
"Resolutions," May 1947.
"Resolutions by Bulloch Teachers," March 1939.
"Resolutions of the G.E.A. Representative Assembly," March 1939.
"Resolutions of the Georgia Education Association," September 1938.
"Resolutions of the 1934 Representative Assembly of the Georgia Education Association," XXVI, May 1934.
"Resolutions of the Representative Assembly, Georgia Education Association," May 1939.
Saxon, J. Harold. "President's Message," September 1936.
Shearouse, H. S. "Need to Professionalize the County School Superintendent," November 1945.
Smith, Mark. "Retirement System for Georgia Teachers," December 1935.
"Statement of Policy," April 1940.
"Taxes," September 1935.
Georgia Gazette, June 16, 1763.
The Georgia Historical Quarterly, IV, V, LIV.
Georgia State School Items.
November 5, 1923; February 1, June 1, July 1, 1924; February, July 1, 1925, II; February 1931.
Gibbons, Nell A. "A Short History from the Life of the Georgia School for the Deaf. Centennial Celebration, 1848-1948," *The School Helper.* Cave Spring: GSD Press, 1948.
Graham, Fannie Blitch. "Those were the Days," The Peabody *Reflector,* XLV. Nashville, 1972.
High School Quarterly, XIII. January 1915, 1921, IX(2); October 1923.
Jackson, Lena Sewell. "Memories," *Carroll Free Press.* March 1, 1928.
Kilpatrick, William H. "The Beginnings of the Public School System in Georgia," *Georgia Historical Quarterly,* V, 3, 1921.
Milledgeville Union Recorder, March 20, 1939.
Morgan, David T. "The Consequences of George Whitefield's Ministry in the Carolinas and Georgia," *Georgia Historical Quarterly,* LV, 1971.
Muse, Helen E. "The Georgia School for the Deaf at Cave Spring," *The Deaf American.* October 1966, XIX.
Reed, T. W. "Life of Joseph S. Stewart," *High School Quarterly,* XXII.
Saxon, J. Harold. "The Accredited High Schools of Georgia," University of Georgia *Bulletin,* XXXIX, 1938.
Snavely, Guy. "A Short History of the Southern Association," *Southern Association Quarterly,* IX, 1938.
Stewart, J. S. "High School Development in Georgia Before the Civil War," *Georgia Historical Quarterly,* IV, 1913.
Union and Recorder, August 6, 1873.
University of Georgia *Bulletin,* 1903-1904, 1938, 1939, 1940-1941.
Western Herald. Auraria. December 14, 1833.
Wilkins, Barratt. "A View of Savannah on the Eve of the Revolution," *Georgia Historical Quarterly,* LIV, Winter 1970.

ANNUAL REPORTS OF
THE GEORGIA DEPARTMENT OF EDUCATION

1871 Annual Report of State School Commissioner of the State of Georgia to his Excellency the Governor, July 1872.

1872 Report of State School Commissioner submitted to the General Assembly of the State of Georgia, January 1873.

1873 Third Report of State School Commissioner submitted to the General Assembly of the State of Georgia, January 1874.

1874 Fourth Annual Report of State School Commissioner submitted to the General Assembly of the State of Georgia, January 1875.

1875 Fifth Annual Report of State School Commissioner submitted to the General Assembly of the State of Georgia, January 1876.

1876 Sixth Annual Report of State School Commissioner submitted to the General Assembly of the State of Georgia, January 1877.

1877 Seventh Annual Report of State School Commissioner submitted to the General Assembly of the State of Georgia, November 1878.

1878 Eighth Annual Report of State School Commissioner submitted to the General Assembly of the State of Georgia, January 1879.

1879– Operations Report of State School Commissioner of Georgia to
1880 the General Assembly.

1881– Report of the State School Commissioner of Georgia to the
1882 General Assembly, 1882.

1883– Report of the State School Commissioner of Georgia to the
1884 General Assembly, 1884.

1885– Report of the State School Commissioner of Georgia to the
1886 General Assembly, 1886.

1887– Report of the State School Commissioner of Georgia to the
1888 General Assembly, 1888.

1889– Report of the State School Commissioner of Georgia to the
1890 General Assembly, 1890.

1891 Report of the State School Commissioner of Georgia to the General Assembly, 1891.

1892 Report of the State School Commissioner of Georgia to the General Assembly for 1892.

1893 Report of the State School Commissioner of Georgia to the General Assembly for 1893.

1894 Report of the State School Commissioner of Georgia to the General Assembly for 1894.

1895 Report of the State School Commissioner of Georgia to the General Assembly for 1895.

1896 Report of the State School Commissioner of Georgia to the General Assembly for 1896.

1897 Report of the State School Commissioner of Georgia to the General Assembly for 1897.

1898 Twenty-Seventh Annual Report from the Department of Education to the General Assembly of the State of Georgia.

1899 Twenty-Eighth Annual Report from the Department of Education to the General Assembly of the State of Georgia.

1900   Twenty-Ninth Annual Report from the Department of Education to the General Assembly of the State of Georgia.

1901   Thirtieth Annual Report from the Department of Education to the General Assembly of the State of Georgia.

1902   Thirty-First Annual Report from the Department of Education to the General Assembly of the State of Georgia.

1903   Thirty-Second Annual Report from the Department of Education to the General Assembly of the State of Georgia.

1904   Thirty-Third Annual Report from the Department of Education to the General Assembly of the State of Georgia.

1905   Thirty-Fourth Annual Report from the Department of Education to the General Assembly of the State of Georgia.

1906   Thirty-Fifth Annual Report from the Department of Education to the General Assembly of the State of Georgia.

1907   Thirty-Sixth Annual Report from the Department of Education to the General Assembly of the State of Georgia.

1908   Thirty-Seventh Annual Report from the Department of Education to the General Assembly of the State of Georgia.

1909   Thirty-Eighth Annual Report from the Department of Education to the General Assembly of the State of Georgia.

1910   Thirty-Ninth Annual Report from the Department of Education to the General Assembly of the State of Georgia.

1911   Fortieth Annual Report from the Department of Education to the General Assembly of the State of Georgia.

1912   Forty-First Annual Report from the Department of Education to the General Assembly of the State of Georgia.

1913   Forty-Second Annual Report from the Department of Education to the General Assembly of the State of Georgia.

1914   Forty-Third Annual Report from the Department of Education to the General Assembly of the State of Georgia.

1915   Forty-Fourth Annual Report from the Department of Education to the General Assembly of the State of Georgia.

1916   Forty-Fifth Annual Report from the Department of Education to the General Assembly of the State of Georgia.

1917   Forty-Sixth Annual Report of the State Department of Education to the General Assembly of the State of Georgia for 1917.

1918   Forty-Seventh Annual Report of the State Department of Education to the General Assembly.

1919   Forty-Eighth Annual Report of the State Department of Education to the General Assembly of the State of Georgia for 1919.

1920   Forty-Ninth Annual Report of the State Department of Education to the General Assembly of the State of Georgia for 1920.

1921   Fiftieth Annual Report of the State Department of Education to the General Assembly of the State of Georgia for 1921.

1922   Fifty-First Annual Report of the State Department of Education to the General Assembly of the State of Georgia for 1922.

1923   Fifty-Second Annual Report of the State Department of Education to the General Assembly of the State of Georgia for 1923.

1924 Fifty-Third Annual Report of the State Department of Education to the General Assembly of the State of Georgia for 1924.

1925– Fifty-Fourth and Fifty-Fifth Annual Report of the State De-
1926 partment of Education to the General Assembly of the State of Georgia for 1925-26.

1927– Fifty-Sixth and Fifty-Seventh Annual Report of the State De-
1928 partment of Education to the General Assembly of the State of Georgia for 1927-28.

1929– Fifty-Eighth and Fifty-Ninth Annual Report of the State De-
1930 partment of Education to the General Assembly of the State of Georgia for 1929-30.

1931– Sixtieth and Sixty-First Annual Report of the State Department
1932 of Education to the General Assembly of the State of Georgia for 1931-32.

1933– Sixty-Second and Sixty-Third Annual Report of the State De-
1934 partment of Education to the General Assembly of the State of Georgia for 1933-34.

1935– Sixty-Fourth and Sixty-Fifth Annual Report of the State De-
1936 partment of Education to the General Assembly of the State of Georgia for 1935-36.

1937– Sixty-Sixth and Sixty-Seventh Annual Report of the State De-
1938 partment of Education to the General Assembly of the State of Georgia for 1937-38.

1939– Sixty-Eighth and Sixty-Ninth Annual Report of the State De-
1940 partment of Education to the General Assembly of the State of Georgia for 1939-40.

1941– Seventieth and Seventy-First Annual Report of the State De-
1942 partment of Education to the General Assembly of the State of Georgia for 1941-42.

1943– Seventy-Second and Seventy-Third Annual Report of the State
1944 Department of Education to the General Assembly of the State of Georgia for 1943-44.

1945– Seventy-Fourth and Seventy-Fifth Annual Report of the State
1946 Department of Education to the General Assembly of the State of Georgia for 1945-46.

1947– Seventy-Sixth and Seventy-Seventh Annual Report of the State
1948 Department of Education to the General Assembly of the State of Georgia for 1947-48.

1949– Seventy-Eighth and Seventy-Ninth Annual Report of the State
1950 Department of Education to the General Assembly of the State of Georgia for 1949-50.

1951– Eightieth and Eighty-First Annual Report of the State Depart-
1952 ment of Education to the General Assembly of the State of Georgia for 1951-52.

1953– Eighty-Second and Eighty-Third Annual Report of the State
1954 Department of Education to the General Assembly of the State of Georgia for 1953-54.

1955– Eighty-Fourth and Eighty-Fifth Annual Report of the State

1956 Department of Education to the General Assembly of the State
of Georgia for 1955-56.

1957– Eighty-Sixth and Eighty-Seventh Annual Report of the State
1958 Department of Education to the General Assembly of the State
of Georgia for 1957-58.

1959– Eighty-Eighth and Eighty-Ninth Annual Report of the State
1960 Department of Education to the General Assembly of the State
of Georgia for 1959-60.

1961– Ninetieth and Ninety-First Annual Report of the State Depart-
1962 ment of Education to the General Assembly of the State of
Georgia for 1961-62.

1963– Ninety-Second and Ninety-Third Annual Report of the State
1964 Department of Education to the General Assembly of the State
of Georgia for 1963-64.

1965– Ninety-Fourth and Ninety-Fifth Annual Report of the State De-
1966 partment of Education to the General Assembly of the State of
Georgia for 1965-66.

1967– Ninety-Sixth and Ninety-Seventh Annual Reports for Biennium
1968 Ending June 30, 1968.

FEDERAL AND STATE PUBLICATIONS AND OFFICIAL
PUBLICATIONS OF EDUCATIONAL AND OTHER
ORGANIZATIONS

*Achieving Quality in School Library Service; a Report of the Committee
of the Southern States Work Conference.* Daytona Beach, 1961.

Aderhold, O. C. *School Leaders Manual, Program of Educational Development for Georgia.* Atlanta: State Department of Education,
1947.

Aderhold, O. C., ed. *A Survey of Public Education of Less than College
Grade in Georgia.* General Assembly Special Committee on Education. Atlanta, 1947.

*An Analysis of Current and Proposed Grants to Municipalities, Counties,
and School Systems.* Georgia Municipal Association. Atlanta, 1969.

Annual Descriptive Report. Division of Vocational Education, State
Department of Education, 1970.

Annual Reports, Georgia Association Future Business Leaders of
America. Atlanta, 1960, 1961.

Bodenhamer, R. E. *A History of the Development of Area Vocational
Technical Schools in Georgia.* Athens, 1968.

Brinson, Phelps. "A History of Camp John Hope," *Activities at Camp
John Hope.* Fort Valley, Georgia.

Brittain, M. L. "The Administration of the Smith-Hughes Vocational
Act in Georgia, for the Second Year, July 1, 1918, to July 1, 1919, 9."
——————. "Georgia State Plan for Vocational Education Under
the Smith-Hughes Law, 1918, 4."

Brittain, M. L., ed. *Survey of Rabun County Schools.* 1914.
——————. *Survey of Wayne County Schools.* 1916.

Building a Better South Through Education; Improving Education in the Southern States. Florida Department of Education (Bulletin 3), 1943.

Certification of Teachers, 1937. Bulletin, Georgia Department of Education, 1937.

Chapter Guides, Facts and Figures. National Office of Future Homemakers of America. Washington, D. C., 1974.

Comprehensive Study of Schools in Sumter County. Georgia Department of Education. Atlanta, 1971.

Criteria for Programs of Library Media Specialists. Atlanta: State Department of Education.

Duggan, M. L. *Educational Survey of Tift County, Georgia.* (Bulletin 23) State Department of Education, 1918.

Economy and Efficiency Committee, Report.

Educating Georgia's People; Investment in the Future. Governor's Commission to Improve Education. 1964.

Education in the Forty-Eight States. U. S. Advisory Committee on Education. Washington, D. C.: Government Printing Office, 1939.

Education Supervision: A Leadership Service. Proceedings of the Southern States Work Conference on Educational Problems. Florida Department of Education, 1954.

Educational Exhibits and Conventions at the World's Industrial and Cotton Centennial Exposition, New Orleans, 1884-85, part 1. U. S. Bureau of Education. Washington, D. C.: Government Printing Office.

Elementary Principles and Standards. Atlanta: Southern Association of Colleges and Schools, Commission on Elementary Schools, 1970.

Evaluating the Elementary School Library Program. Atlanta: Southern Association of Colleges and Schools, 1964.

Every Elementary School Can Have a Library. Report of the Elementary School Library Work Conference, Emory University, 1954. Atlanta: Georgia Department of Education Division of Instructional Materials and Library Services, 1954.

Flanagan. *School Food Services.* 1969.

Forty-Eighth Annual Report of the Trustees of the Georgia Academy for the Blind to the Governor of Georgia, 1898-99. Macon: Press of Smith and Watson, 1899.

Forty-Seventh Annual Report of Trustees of the Georgia Academy for the Blind to the Governor of Georgia, 1897-98. Macon: Press of Smith and Watson, 1899.

"The Georgia Accrediting Commission and Its Role in the Accreditation of Elementary Schools." *Bulletin* of the Georgia Association of Elementary School Principals, 1975.

Georgia Board of Education *Minutes.* 1884 to the present.

The Georgia Education Advocate. Georgia Department of Education, 1969-70.

Georgia General Assembly *House Journal.*

Georgia General Assembly *Senate Journal.*

General Policies Adopted by the Georgia Board of Education for the Operation of the Public Schools Under the Minimum Foundation Program Law. January 1, 1957.

Guide to Curriculum Improvement, Bulletin No. 2. Program for the Improvement of Instruction, Georgia Department of Education, January 1942.

Guide to the Evaluation and Accreditation of Elementary Schools. Committee on Elementary Education. Atlanta: Southern Association of Colleges and Schools, 1970.

Haskew, L. D. *The Educational Clinic.* American Council on Education. Washington, D. C. 1949.

History of Home Economics in Georgia. Standards Committee, Georgia Home Economics Association, 1933.

How Georgia Operates its Schools. Georgia Department of Education, Division of Public Information, 1961.

Imagination at Work. Georgia Department of Education, Division of Public Information, 1962.

Jarrell, A. P. *Report of the Division of Vocational Rehabilitation.* Georgia Department of Education, 1965.

Johnson, Richard Malcolm. "Early Educational Life in Middle Georgia." *Report of the Commissioner of Education for the Year 1894-95,* II. Washington: Government Printing Office, 1896.

Joiner, Oscar H. *Education in the States: Historical Development and Outlook.* 1969.

Jones, R. L., ed. *Alternative Programs for Financing Education.* National Educational Finance Project. Gainesville, Florida, 1971.

Journal of the Proceedings of the Constitutional Convention of the People of Georgia, 1867-1868. Augusta, 1868.

Legislative Study Committee and Investigative Committee Reports.

Look at Our Schools. Georgia Department of Education, Administration Division, 1949.

Loyless, Thomas W., ed. *Georgia's Public Men.* Atlanta: Byrd Printing Co., 1903.

McClurkin, W. C. *Organization of School Systems in Georgia.* George Peabody College for Teachers, Nashville, 1965.

McMichael, Anne Hixon. *Supplement to History of Certification.* 1961.

Maher, Mary Helen. *Statistics of Public High School Libraries, 1960-61.* U. S. Office of Education, 1964.

Mayo, A. D. *Report of the Commissioner of Education for the Year 1895-96.* Washington: Government Printing Office.

————————. *Report of the United States Commissioner of Education, 1899-1900.* Washington: Government Printing Office.

Media Centered Library. Georgia Department of Education, School Library Services Unit, 1969.

Monroe, Paul. "City District Superintendents." *Cyclopedia of Education.* New York: Macmillan, 1925.

Morrison, B. G. "The Bell and Lancaster System—What is in it for the Schools of the South." *Report of the Commissioner of Education for the Year 1894-95*, II. Washington: Government Printing Office, 1896.

Mort, Paul R. *State Support of Public Education.* American Council on Education. Washington, D. C., 1933.

Nolan, Nathan. *Chronology of Rehabilitation History,* 1970.

Normative Data for the 1974-75 Freshman Class, University System of Georgia. Regents of University System of Georgia. Atlanta, 1975.

Pearson, Jim B., and Fuller, Edgar, eds. *Education in the States: Historical Development and Outlook.* Washington: National Education Association, 1969.

Planning for Education in Georgia. Curriculum Framework Revision Committee. Georgia Department of Education. Atlanta, 1976.

A Practice Book for Observation and Teaching in Small Rural Schools. Bulletin No. 3A. Division of Negro Education, Georgia Department of Education, November 1938.

Prickett, John S., Jr. *Report of the Office of Vocational Rehabilitation.* Georgia Department of Education, 1970.

Proceedings of the Georgia Teachers' Association. 1869, 1871-1936.

Proceedings. 39th Annual Meeting of the Southern Association of Colleges and Secondary Schools, 1934.

Proceedings and Addresses. Georgia Education Association. 59th annual meeting, 1924.

A Progress Report with Facts and Figures. Georgia School Building Authority, 1957.

Proll, Charles E. *State Programs for the Improvement of Teacher Education.* American Council on Education. Washington, D. C., 1946.

Rankings of the States. National Education Association Reseach Reports, 1955-1969.

Regulations for Administering the Seven Months School Law, Georgia Board of Education, 1937.

Report of the Minimum Foundation of Education Study Committee. Georgia Educational Improvement Council. Atlanta, 1973.

Report on Leadership Conferences for Improving School Library Service in Georgia. School Library Services Unit files, Georgia Department of Education, 1961.

Report on School Library Clinics, 1941. School Library Services Unit files, Georgia Department of Education.

Report on the System of Public Schools for the State of Georgia. Adopted by the State Teachers' Association. Macon, 1869.

Reports. Georgia State School Commissioner. 1888, 1897, 1902-07, 1909-13, 1916-17, 1922.

Reports. Georgia State School Superintendent. 1924-1938.

Schabacker, William H., et. al., eds. *Focus on the Future of Georgia, 1970-1985,* 1970.

School Leaders Manual. Education Panel. Georgia Department of Education, 1945.

School Library Media Center Statistics, 1970-71. School Library Services Unit, Georgia Department of Education.

Schoolhouse Story. Georgia Department of Education, Administration Division, 1955.

Second Annual Report, Fiscal Year 1967, Title II, Elementary and Secondary Education Act of 1965. U. S. Department of Health, Education, and Welfare, Office of Education, 1967.

Short History of Certification. Georgia Department of Education, 1958-60.

"Specific Suggestions Concerning the Development of the 12-year Program." Georgia Department of Education, 1947.

Srygley, Sara K. *Study of Selected Elementary School Libraries in the Southern Region.* Cooperative Program in Elementary Education, Southern Association of Colleges and Schools, Atlanta, 1964.

Standard for Public Schools of Georgia. Georgia Department of Education, 1971.

Standards for School Library Programs. American Association of School Librarians. Chicago: American Library Association, 1960.

Standards for School Media Programs. American Association of School Librarians, Division of Audio-Visual Instruction. Chicago: American Library Association and National Education Association, 1969.

State Auditor's Reports. Summary Statement of Financial Condition, 1975. Statements of Receipts and Allotments, 1942, 1952, 1962, 1966-75.

Statistical Report. 1969-1970.

"Study Guide for the Transition to a 12-year Program." Georgia Department of Education, 1947.

Surging Ahead in the '70s. Proposals for Further Advancements of County Governments of Georgia. Association of County Commissioners of Georgia. Atlanta, 1970.

Thorpe, Francis Newton, ed. *The Federal and State Constitutions, Colonial Charters, and other Organic Laws, etc.* 7 volumes. Washington: Government Printing Office, 1909.

A Survey of Public Education of Less Than College Grade in Georgia. Report of the Bureau of Educational Research and Field Service. University of Georgia College of Education, Athens, 1947.

Time for a New Breakthrough in Education in Georgia. Georgia Department of Education, Administration Division, 1963.

Twenty-Ninth Annual Report of the Trustees of the Georgia Academy for the Blind to the Governor of Georgia, 1880. Macon: J. W. Burke, 1880.

Vocational Education in Georgia. Georgia Nuclear Advisory Commission Task Force on Vocational Education, 1960.

Wheeler, John T. "Apprenticeship Practice in Training Teachers of Vocational Agriculture," *Georgia State College of Agriculture Bulletin,* 378.

Woofter, T. J. "Report of Committee on Betterment of Education in Georgia." *Proceedings and Addresses of the Forty-Second Annual Meeting of the Georgia Educational Association.* Valdosta: Times Publishing Co., 1908.

UNPUBLISHED PAPERS, LETTERS, SPEECHES, INTERVIEWS
AND MISCELLANEOUS SOURCES

Authors' Interview with Hershel H. Elders and Supt. Jerry Holland. Reidsville, 1943.

Author's Interview, H. S. Shearouse with James S. Peters. Manchester, 1971.

Authors' Interview with Mark Davis.

Authors' Interviews with the State Superintendent of Schools and Division Directors of the Georgia Department of Education. December 1965 and February 1971.

Authors' Interview with Z. B. Rogers. October, 1941.

Barber, Janet McGarity. *The History and Development of the Georgia Association, Future Homemakers of America, 1944-1965.* Unpublished master's thesis, University of Georgia, Athens, 1966.

Bonner, James C. *The Gubernatorial Career of William J. Northern.* Unpublished master's thesis. Athens, University of Georgia.

Bryant, J. G. *Vocational Education in Georgia.* Unpublished manuscript.

Burgess, John Evans. *Development and Present Status of Public Education in Glynn County, Georgia.* Unpublished master's thesis, Duke University, Durham, N. C., 1939.

Calvin, Marvin. "Recent Progress of Public Education in the South." A paper read before the Georgia Teachers' Association at Savannah, May 5, 1870. Augusta: Chronicle & Sentinel Steam Printing Establishment, 1870.

Paul Cobb to James C. Bonner, August 20, 1965. In private possession.

Cook, John. "The History and Development of the Chattooga County School System." Unpublished manuscript.

Cordle, G. *An Ante-Bellum Academy of Richmond County, 1783-1863.* Unpublished master's thesis. University of Georgia, Athens, 1944.

Dickerson, I. A. "A Study of Vocational and Technical Education in Georgia." Unpublished term paper. University of Georgia.

Heard, Janie. *History of Certification in Georgia.* Unpublished manuscript, 1944.

Hightower, Grace. *Growth of Libraries in the Public Schools of Georgia.* Unpublished doctoral dissertation. Peabody Library School, Nashville, 1955.

"Important Decisions by Captain Bradwell." Manuscript in private possession.

Information received from Dr. Claude Ivie, Director, Division of Curriculum Development and Pupil Personnel Services, Georgia Department of Education, 1976.

Ingram, I. S. *History and Significance of the A. and M. Schools of Georgia.* Unpublished master's thesis. Emory University, Atlanta.

Joiner, Oscar Hardy. *A Comparison of Local and Non-Local Teachers as to Their Training and Salaries.* Unpublished master's thesis. Duke University, Durham, N. C., 1939.

Jones, Mamie Jo. *History of Program for Exceptional Children, State Department of Education, 1951-1970.* Unpublished manuscript.

Jones, Sara. "School Libraries." Unpublished manuscript. Georgia Department of Education, Atlanta, 1972.

Letter from Attorney General M. J. Yeomans to Dr. M. D. Collins, State Superintendent of Schools. Department of Archives and History, June 21, 1937.

Letter from Superintendent Jack P. Nix to Representative John Carlisle, November 6, 1973.

Letters

McCaul, Robert L. *A Documentary History of Education in Colonial Georgia.* Unpublished doctoral dissertation. University of Chicago, 1953.

Renfroe, Carl G. *The Growth and Development of Teacher Certification in Georgia.* Unpublished doctoral dissertation. University of Georgia, Athens, 1964.

Rice, Marion Jennings. *Georgia School Law: A Case Study Based on the Decisions of the Georgia Supreme Court and Court of Appeals.* Unpublished doctoral dissertation. University of Georgia, Athens, 1960.

Carl E. Sanders. Speech at dedication of Wrens ETV Station, 1966.

Shearouse, H. S. *Historical Statement of the Teacher Standards Movement in Georgia.* Unpublished manuscript, Georgia Department of Education.

Singleton, Gordon G. *State Responsibility for the Support of Education in Georgia.* (Contributions to Education No. 181). New York: Teachers College, Columbia University, 1925.

Smith, Allen C. *The Quiet Revolution.* Paper read at Georgia Department of Education Staff Conference, Lake Jackson. September 1969.

Steelmon, Peggy S. *Growth and Development of the Georgia Education Association.* Unpublished doctoral dissertation. University of Georgia, Athens, 1966.

Usher, George Ephraim. *Development of the Georgia Education Association.* Unpublished master's thesis, Duke University, Durham, N. C., 1935.

Judson S. Ward. Speech at Teacher Education Council. Athens, 1959.

Williams, Joseph A. *A Proposed Method of Distributing State Funds for Public Education of Less Than College Grade for the Purpose of More Nearly Equalizing Educational Opportunity in Georgia.* Unpublished doctoral dissertation. University of Georgia, Athens, 1948.

STATE AND FEDERAL LAWS, PROCEEDINGS AND
LEGAL REPORTS

Acts of the Legislature, 1834, 1937, 1840, 1843, 1947.

Acts of the General Assembly. 1934, 1858, 1866, 1870.

Constitutional Amendment ratified October 5, 1904.

Georgia *Civil Codes.* Secs. 32-2901, 32-2932.

Georgia Laws. 1833, 1839, 1847, 1851, 1852, 1866, Special Session, 1868, 1870-72, 1874, 1876, 1877, 1878, 1879-80, 1880-81, 1884-85, 1886, 1887, 1888, 1890-93, 1896, 1897, 1903, 1905, 1909, 1911-12, 1916, 1919, 1929, 1931, 1937, 1943, 1949, 1951, 1964.

Georgia Reports of Cases Decided in Supreme Court of the State of Georgia. CCIV

Georgia School Laws, 1971.

Hargrave vs. Kirk. Citation 313/F. Supp. Northern District of Florida, 1970.

Hopkins, John L. *The Code of the State of Georgia, Adopted August 15, 1910.* Atlanta, 1911.

McInnis vs. Shapiro, 293 F. Supp. 327, 1968.

Minimum Foundation Program of Education Act No. 523, Section 16. 1964.

Rodriguez vs. San Antonio Independent School District, 337 F. Supp. 280. Western District of Texas, 1971.

Report of a Constitutional Convention, Constitution of 1877.

Serrano vs. Priest. 5 Cal. 3d 584, 487. California, 1971.

State of Georgia, *Constitution of 1945.*

Sweetwater County Planning Committee vs. Hinkle. 491 P. 2d 1234. Wyoming, 1971.

U. S. Congress, Public Laws 88-452, 1964; 89-750, 1960; 91-230, 1969.

Van Dusarty vs. Hatfield. 334 F. Supp. 870. Minnesota, 1971.

Whitfield County Board of Education vs. Georgia State Board of Education, et. al. Polk County Superior Court, Civil Action No. 8275.

LOCAL SCHOOL REPORTS, PUBLICATIONS AND COUNTY HISTORICAL NOTES

Charlton County Historical Notes, 1972.

Childs, E. W. *Annual Report of Randolph County Public Schools.* Cuthbert: The Leader Print, 1905.

Elrod, Frary. *Historical Notes on Jackson County, Georgia.* Jefferson, 1967.

Faulk, Lanette O'Neal, and Jones, Billy Walker. *History of Twiggs County, Georgia.* Jeffersonville: D.A.R.

First Annual Report of the Public Schools of Thomasville, Georgia, 1901-02. Thomasville, 1902.

Garrett, William T. *Dublin Public Schools.* Dublin, 1916.

Harris, John. *Charlton County, Georgia Historical Notes.* Jesup: Jesup Sentinel Press, 1972.

Hart, Bertha Sheppard. *The Official History of Laurens County, Georgia, 1807-1941.* Atlanta: Cherokee Publishing Co., 1972.

Minutes of the Mt. Zion Seminary Association. Carroll County, 1878-1895.

Minutes of Pulaski County Board of Education. Hawkinsville, 1895-1925.

Minutes of Screven County Board of Education. Sylvania, 1897-1929.

Minutes of the Troup County Board of Education, November, 1927.

Mount Zion Methodist Centennial, 1875-1965. Carrollton, 1965.

Report of the Bibb County Board of Education and Orphanage, 1908.

Report on Current Practices. Office of Superintendent, Baldwin County Schools.

Rome Public Schools, Eighth Annual Report, 1901-02. Rome, 1902.

MISCELLANEOUS

The Alstonian. Alston, Georgia: Alston Consolidated School, November 1, 1934.

Current Employment Form.

Goodwill's Story. Document of Goodwill Industries of America, Inc. Washington, D. C., 1972.

Proceedings of the Teachers' Society, Milledgeville, 1832.

Program of the 1896 Georgia Teachers' Association Annual Meeting. Notation made by Joseph S. Stewart.

ACTS AND RESOLUTIONS
OF THE
GENERAL ASSEMBLY
OF THE
STATE OF GEORGIA

SESSION OF 1870

The following is a reproduction of the law passed by the General Assembly of the State of Georgia on October 13, 1870 establishing public schools in the State.

TITLE VI

EDUCATION.

(No. 53.)

An Act to Establish a System of Public Instruction.

SECTION 1. *Be it enacted by the General Assembly of the State of Georgia,* That the Governor, the Attorney-General, the Secretary of State, the Comptroller-General and the State School Commissioner shall constitute a board to be denominated "The Georgia State Board of Education." Of this board the State School Commissioner shall be the chief executive officer. The clerk of the State School Commissioner, as hereinafter provided for, shall be the clerk of the State Board of

State Board of Education—how organized.

Name and style.

583

Education. He shall have the custody of its records, papers and effects, and keep minutes of its proceedings: *Provided,* That such records, papers and effects, and minutes, shall be kept at the office of the Commissioner, and shall be open for inspection.

Proviso.

SEC. 2. *And be it further enacted,* That the said board shall meet upon the call of its president, or a majority of its members, who shall constitute a quorum, at the office of the State School Commissioner, at the capital, or at such other places as may be designated in the call.

Meeting of board–when and where held.

SEC. 3. *And be it further enacted,* That the board may take and hold, to it and its successors, in trust for the State, any grant or devise of lands, and donation or bequest of moneys or other personal property, made to it for educational purposes, and shall, forthwith, pay over to the Treasurer of the State for safe keeping all money and personal property so received, taking therefor a receipt from said officer. The General Assembly may, from time to time, invest such money in the name of the State: *Provided,* That all money so obtained for educational purposes, with the profits accruing from its investments, shall be subject for final use only for educational purposes in the State. The State Treasurer shall pay to the order of the board the income and principal thereof, as it from time to time may require, consistent with law; but no disposition of any devised donation or bequest shall be made inconsistent with the condition or terms thereof. For the faithful keeping of all property so received by the Treasurer, he shall be responsible, upon his bond, to the State, as for other funds received by him in his official capacity.

Powers.

Proviso.

SEC. 4. *And be it further enacted,* That the State Board of Education shall devise, adopt and procure a seal, on the face of which shall be the words, "Department of Education, State of Georgia," and such other device or motto as the board may direct, an impression and written description of which shall be recorded in the minutes of this board, and filed in the office of the Secretary of State, which seal shall be used for the authentication of the acts of the board, and the important acts of the State School Commissioner.

Seal.

Description o f seal.

SEC. 5. *And be it further enacted,* That the State Board of Education shall prescribe, from time to time, what text-books and books of reference shall be used in the common schools of the State: *Provided,* That the Bible shall not be excluded from the public schools of this State.

Books for use of schools.

SEC. 6. *And be it further enacted,* That the State Board of Education shall, within five days after the meeting of each and every annual session of the Legislature, lay before that body an account in detail of all the doings of said board, with such observations upon the condition and efficiency of the system of popular education, and such suggestions as to the most practicable means of extending and improving it, as the experience and reflection of the board may dictate.

Annual report to Legislature.

State School Commissioner — by whom appointed. Duties.

SEC. 7. *And be it further enacted,* That the State School Commissioner shall be appointed by the Governor and confirmed by the Senate. He shall be charged with the administration of the system of public instruction and a general superintendence of the business relating to the common schools of the State, and of the school funds and school revenues set apart and appropriated to their support. A suitable office shall be furnished him at the seat of government, at which the books, papers and effects relating to the business of said office shall be kept, and there he shall give reasonable attendance

Must give opinion in writing.

in writing to any school officer asking the same, touching the administration or construction of the school law.

Oath of office.

SEC. 8. *And be it further enacted,* That before entering upon the exercise of his official duties, the said Commissioner shall take and subscribe to the same oath required of other officers of this State.

SEC. 9. *And be it further enacted,* That he shall prescribe suitable forms and regulations for making all reports and conducting all

School Commissioner shall make rules.

necessary proceedings under this act, and shall cause the same, with such institutions as he may deem necessary and proper for the organization and government of schools, to be transmitted to the local school officers, who shall be governed in accordance therewith: *Provided,* That appeals may be made from the State School Commissioner to the State Board of Education, whose decision on all matters relating to the schools shall be final.

School Commissioner shall visit Senatorial Districts — for what purpose.

SEC. 10. *And be it further enacted,* That it shall be the duty of the Commissioner to visit as often as possible the several Senatorial Districts, to examine into the administration of the school law in said districts, and to counsel with the school officers, and do such other acts as may be deemed best to subserve the interest of popular education.

Apportionment of School fund.

SEC. 11. *And be it further enacted,* That it shall be the duty of said Commissioner to apportion equitably the revenue to be raised as hereinafter provided, to the different school districts of the State, upon the basis of the aggregate of youths between six and twenty-one years of age in each district; and he shall draw his warrant upon the Treasurer of the State for the sum belonging to each county according to said apportionment. He shall see that the money to be used for the purposes of education is not misapplied, and that the proper actions provided by law are brought against all officers and agents of the system who are liable to the same.

Annual report to the General Assembly.

SEC. 12. *And be it further enacted,* That it shall be the duty of said Commissioner to, at the same time with the State Board of Education, make an annual report in each and every year to the General Assembly, and he shall have power to require of local boards of education, trustees or other school officers, and of clerks and treasurers of counties, recorders and treasurers of cities and villages, copies of all reports by them required to be made, and all such other information in relation to the fund and condition of schools, and the management thereof, as he may deem inportant.

SEC. 13. *And be it further enacted,* That the State Commissioner, in the annual report of his labors and observations, shall present a statement of the condition and amount of all funds and property appropriated to the purposes of education; a statement of the number of common schools of the various grades in the State; the number of scholars attending such schools, their sex, color and the branches taught; a statement of the number of select and private schools in the State, so far as can be ascertained, and number of scholars attending such schools, their sex and the branches taught; the total number of children of school age in the State, so near as can be ascertained; a statement of the estimates and accounts of the expenditures of the public fund of every description; a statement of plans for the management and improvement of common schools, and such other information relative to the educational interest of the State as he may think important.

Shall report amount and state of School fund.

Number of schools and scholars, etc.

Estimate of expenditures.

SEC. 14. *And be it further enacted,* That the said Commissioner shall be entitled to receive for his services the sum of $2,500 annually, in quarterly installments, from the School Fund of the State; and all his necessary traveling expenses, incurred in the performance of his official duties, and all postage and other expenses, absolutely necessary, arising in his office; shall be paid out of the School Fund. He shall keep an itemized account of all expenses connected with his department, which account shall be audited by the State Board of Education. He shall be allowed one clerk, at a salary not to exceed $1,200, to be paid out of the School Fund.

Salary of Commissioner.

Account of expenses.

Clerk— salary of.

COUNTY BOARD OF EDUCATION

SEC. 15. *And be it further enacted,* That hereafter each and every county in the State shall compose but one school district for all purposes connected with the general interest of education in the county, and shall be confided to the management and control of a board of education, and the several school districts or fractional parts thereof, which now are, or may be hereafter, established in the several counties of the State, shall be regarded as sub-districts and be confided to the management and control of local directors as hereinafter provided.

School districts.

Sub-districts.

SEC. 16. *And be it further enacted,* That the county board of education shall consist of one person from each militia district, and one person from each ward in any city in the county, and one from each incorporated town, who shall be elected by the legal voters of said district, ward or incorporated town, at some suitable place designated therein; and the term of office of said board shall be two years, or until successors are elected, the first election for which shall be on the first Saturday in January, 1871, and on the same day every second year thereafter.

County board of education — how organized.

By whom elected.

Term of office.

Election — when held.

Meeting of co. board.

SEC. 17. *And be it further enacted,* That they shall meet on the first Tuesday of the month succeeding that of their election, at the court-house of their respective counties, which place shall be thereafter the regular place of meeting of said board, and organize by electing one of their members president, and a secretary, which last mentioned officer shall also, by said election of the board, become the county school commissioner. A majority of the board shall constitute a quorum for the transaction of business. It shall be the duty of said secretary to be present at the meeting of the board, and to record in a book to be provided for the purpose all their official proceedings, which shall be a public record, open to the inspection of any person interested therein; and all such proceedings, when so recorded, shall be signed by the president and secretary.

President and secretary elected. Secretary is county commissioner.

Duties of Secretary.

Regular sessions of co. boards— when held.

SEC. 18. *And be it further enacted,* That it shall be the duty of the county board of education to hold regular sessions on the first Tuesday of the month succeeding their election, and regularly thereafter each three months at the court-house of the county, for the transaction of business which may be necessary in relation to the subject of either the primary or graded schools of the county, with power to adjourn from time to time. In case of the absense of the secretary, they may appoint one of their own number to serve temporarily as clerk.

Absence of Secretary.

County boards shall lay out sub-districts.

SEC. 19. *And be it further enacted,* That the county board of education first constituted under this act shall, at their first meeting, proceed to carefully lay out and describe sub-districts, as hereinafter mentioned, throughout their respective counties. The said board and their successors in office shall prepare, or cause to be prepared, a map of their district as often as they may deem necessary, on which shall be designated the sub-districts of their districts, which they may change or alter at any regular session, and the number of scholars assigned to each, but no sub-district shall contain within its limits less than thirty pupils resident, by enumeration, except where, in the opinion of the board, it is necessary to reduce the number, as in cases hereafter provided for in ambulatory schools; and it shall be the duty of the board to establish a school in each sub-district, of such grade as the public good, in their opinion, may require; and in the location of primary schools, or schools of higher grade, the board shall have reference to population and neighborhood, paying due regard to any school-house already built, or site procured, as well as to all other circumstances proper to be considered, so as to promote the best interest of the schools.

Shall prepare map of districts.

Number of pupils to a sub-district.

Location of primary schools.

Name and style— may sue and be sued.

SEC. 20. *And be it further enacted,* That the said boards of education, in their respective counties, shall be a body politic and corporate in law, and as such may contract and be contracted with, sue and be sued, plead and be impleaded in any court of the State having competent jurisdiction, and receive any gift, grant, donation or devise made for the use of schools within their jurisdiction; and, moreover, they shall be, and they are hereby, invested in their corporate capacity with title, care and custody of all school-houses, sites, school libraries, apparatus or other property belonging to the district as now organized, or which may hereafter be organized, within the limits of their jurisdiction, with all power to control the same in such manner as they may think will best subserve the interest of common schools and the cause of education; and when, in the opinion of the board, any schoolhouse site has become unnecessary, they may sell and convey the same in the name of the county board of education of the proper district, such conveyance to be executed by the chairman and secretary of said board, and all conveyances of real estate which may be made to said board shall be to said board in their corporate name and to their successors in office.

> Control of schoolhouses, libraries, etc.

> May sell schoolhouse site.

SEC. 21. *And be it further enacted,* That the county board of education may establish such graded schools in their respective counties as they may think proper, with full power, in respect to such schools, to employ, pay and dismiss teachers; to build, repair and furnish the necessary school-houses, purchase or lease sites therefor, or rent suitable rooms, and make all other necessary provisions relative to such schools as they may deem proper; and it shall be the duty of said board of education to exercise all the powers conferred on local trustees in respect to sub-district schools, whenever such local trustees shall neglect to discharge their duties in any sub-district, as required by this act; and it shall also be the further duty of said board to prescribe rules and regulations for the government of the schools within their jurisdiction, consistent with the regulations prescribed by the State Commissioner for the management of the same.

> General power.

> Board shall prescribe rules.

SEC. 22. *And be it further enacted,* That it shall be the duty of the county commissioners to hold public examinations of all applicants for license to teach within their respective counties, and before their respective county board of education, at each regular time of meeting of said board at the county-site. Said commissioner shall be allowed to invite to assist in the examination of teachers any persons they may deem proper. If, from the ratio of correct answers, and other evidences disclosed by the examination, the applicant is found to possess knowledge which is sufficient, in the estimation of the board, to enable said applicant to successfully teach in a common school of the State, orthography, reading, writing, arithmetic, English grammar and geography, and to govern such a school, said commissioners shall give to said applicant a license of the first, second or third grade, according to the ratio of correct answers and other evidences of qualification given upon said examination. The standard of which grade of license shall be fixed by the State Commissioner, and said license shall be good for one, two or three years, according to its grade. And all applicants, before being licensed, shall produce to the Commissioner satisfactory evidence of good moral character.

> Examination of teachers.

> Grade of teachers' license in accordance with the ratio of correct answers.

SEC. 23. *And be it further enacted,* That the county commissioner shall have power, and it shall be his duty, to revoke licenses granted by him or his predecessors for incompetency, immorality, cruelty, or general neglect of the business of the school; and the revocation of the license of any teacher shall terminate the connection of said teacher with any school which said teacher may have been employed to teach; but any teacher so dismissed shall have the right to appeal to the county board of education, whose decision shall be final, unless appeal is made by said teacher within ten days after said dismissal, to the State School Commissioner.

SEC. 24. *And be it further enacted,* That the county commissioner shall provide a blank book, in which he shall keep minutes of his proceedings, and shall deliver said record and all the books, papers and property appertaining to his office to his successor. He shall report annually to the State School Commissioner the names of all persons to whom he has granted licenses, with the grade of such licenses, giving number of males and females, the number, but not the names of all applicants for license who have been rejected, and the names of those whose licenses have been revoked.

SEC. 25. *And be it further enacted,* That said county commissioners shall constitute the medium of communication between the State School Commissioner and subordinate school officers and the schools. They shall decide all points of differences between trustees of any school district, subject to appeal to the county board of education. They shall visit the schools of their respective districts as often as they may deem it necessary during each term, but they shall visit each school in their respective districts at least once each year, for the purpose of increasing their usefulness; elevating, as far as practicable, the poorer schools to the standard of the best; advising and securing, as far as practicable, uniformity in their organization and management, and their conformity to the law and the regulations and instructions of the State School Commissioner. They shall receive from the trustees their reports of enumeration and their regular school and other reports which are required by law to be made to them, and otherwise gather the necessary data and information, including that in relation to private schools, high schools, colleges, and other institutions of learning within their respective districts, so as to present a view of the educational facilities, and enable them to make full and complete reports to the State School Commissioner. They shall advise the trustees as to the most approved school furniture, apparatus, and educational agencies, and shall furnish the trustees and teachers with regular forms, blanks, instructions, regulations and reports issued from the Department of Education which relate to the respective branches of the school service.

SEC. 26. *And be it further enacted,* That the county commissioner shall, on or before the first day of November in each year, make out and forward to the State School Commissioner the enumeration of his district, with the same particular discrimination required of trustees. He shall also furnish the statistical information which trustees are required to report to him, in such form as may be prescribed by the State School Commissioner.

SEC. 27. *And be it further enacted,* That the said county commissioner shall receive three dollars for each day actually employed in the discharge of the duties required by this act, the same to be paid out of the Educational Fund furnished the county. His claim for services shall be filed in a bill of accounts against the county board of education, and be verified by affidavit to the effect that the said account is just and true; that the service therein named was honestly and faithfully rendered, and that the account therein claimed is rightly due and remains unpaid. When said account shall have been duly audited by the county board of education, the County Treasurer shall pay the said commissioner out of the revenue aforesaid: *Provided, however,* That the county board of education shall have power to determine the number of days in each year in which said county commissioner may labor in the performance of the duties required of him.

Compensation county commm sioner.

Account swc to.

Provis

SCHOOL DIRECTORS, OR TRUSTEES.

SEC. 28. *And be it further enacted,* That the legal voters of each sub-district shall, upon the first Saturday in January in each year, elect three school trustees, one for a term of three years, one for a term of two years, and one for a term of one year; and annually thereafter said legal voters shall, on the first Saturday in January, elect one school trustee for the term of three years.

School trustee when elected.

Ter

SEC. 29. *And be it further enacted,* That the said trustees, within five days after their election, shall take an oath or affirmation faithfully and impartially to discharge the duties of their office, which said oath the trustees are authorized to administer to each other. And in case a vacancy shall occur in the office of trustee, either by death, resignation, refusal to serve or otherwise, it shall be the duty of the remaining trustees to fill such vacancy within ten days after such vacancy may occur, by appointment of some suitable person residing in said district, who shall hold the office until the time of the annual election, when a trustee shall be elected for the remainder, if any, of the unexpired term, in the manner prescribed in the preceding section.

Oa

Vacancies – h(filled.

SEC. 30. *And be it further enacted,* That it shall be the duty of the trustees in each sub-district to take the management and control of its local interest and affairs; to employ teachers; to certify the amounts due them to the county commissioners; to, at any time, for reasons deemed sufficient, report them for dismissal to the county board of education, and to visit the school of their district at least twice during each term, by one or more of their members, with such other person or persons, competent to examine pupils in their studies, as they may choose to invite:. *Provided,* If any person shall be employed by the trustees aforesaid who has not received a certificate of his or her competency from the county commissioner, said person shall not be allowed any compensation for his or her services; and any person

Duties trustees.

desiring to teach in any county other than that in which they have obtained license, shall, before doing so, have said license countersigned by the school commissioner of the county in which they may design to teach.

SEC. 31. *And be it further enacted,* That it shall be the duty of the trustees, in their respective districts, to negotiate and make, under such rules and regulations as the county board of education may prescribe, all necessary contracts in relation to providing fuel for schools, repairing, building or furnishing school-houses, purchasing or leasing school-house sites, renting school-houses, and making all other provisions necessary for the convenience and prosperity of the schools within their districts; and the funds for all such expenditures shall be raised by a tax levied upon the taxable property of said district, and by assessment on the labor of the qualified voters of the same, as may be determined by the county board of education; and wherever an assessment is made on the labor of any voter, said assessment may be discharged by labor.

SEC. 32. *And be it further enacted,* That it shall be the duty of the trustees, in their respective districts, to make all necessary arrangements for the instruction of the white and colored youth of the district in separate schools. They shall provide the same facilities for each, both as regards school-houses and fixtures, and the attainments and abilities of teachers, length of term-time, etc.; but the children of the white and colored races shall not be taught together in any sub-district of the State.

SEC. 33. *And be it further enacted,* That it shall be the duty of the trustees in each school district to take, or cause to be taken, annually, between the first and fifteenth of October in each year, an enumeration of all the unmarried white and colored youths, noting them separately, between the ages of five and twenty-one years, residents within the said school district, and not temporarily there, designating between male and female, and return a certified copy thereof to the county commissioner; and in case the trustees in any school district, shall fail to take and return said enumeration, it shall be the duty of the county commissioner to employ a competent person to take the same, and allow him a reasonable compensation for his services from the School Fund, and shall proceed to recover the amount for such service, in a civil action before any court having jurisdiction, in the name of the State of Georgia, against said trustees in their individual capacity; and in such suit said county commissioner shall be a competent witness, and the money collected shall be applied to the use of the common school in said sub-districts. The county commissioner shall make an abstract of the enumeration so returned to him, designating the number of youths in each district, and transmit such abstract, duly certified, to the State Commissioner on or before the first day of November in each year.

SEC. 34. *And be it further enacted,* That it shall be the duty of said trustees to record their proceedings in a book provided for the purpose, together with the minutes of the proceedings of all school meetings held in such district by the qualified voters thereof, which shall be a public record, and all such proceedings, when so recorded, shall be signed by the majority of said trustees. The trustees may meet as frequently as they may think necessary for the transaction of business, but shall receive for their services as trustees no compensation or endowments of any kind whatever.

Trustees mu keep minutes (their proceeding

Shall receive compensation.

TEACHERS.

SEC. 35. *And be it further enacted,* That it shall be the duty of the teachers to make and file with the county commissioner, at the expiration of each term of school, a full and complete report of the whole number of scholars admitted to the school during such term, distinguishing between male and female, colored and white, the average attendance, the books used, the branches taught, the number of pupils engaged in the study of each of said branches, and such other statistics as he or she may be required to make by the trustees of said sub-district or by the State School Commissioner, and until such report shall have been certified and filed by said teacher as aforesaid, it shall not be lawful for said trustees to audit the account of said teacher for his or her services.

Teachers mu make report i county commi sioner — whe

Teacher accounts n o audited until r port is made.

SEC. 36. *And be it further enacted,* That each and every lot, or parcel of land which heretofore has been or hereafter shall be appropriated for the use of common schools in this State on which there has been or shall be a school-house erected, and which has been or shall be occupied for the purpose of accommodating the common school, of whatever grade, in the usual manner, from time to time, howsoever or by whomsoever the legal title to the same may be held and vested, shall be and is hereby exempted from sale on any execution or other writ or order in the nature of an execution, and all taxes, State or county: *Provided,* That the lot of land so exempted shall not exceed four acres, and if there be any excess, that portion most convenient for school purposes shall remain exempt, as aforesaid, to be determined by the proper school trustees or other officers having charge of schools: *Provided further,* That nothing in this act shall be so construed as to interfere in any way with private schools or private school property.

School estat exempt fro levy, sale ar taxation.

Provis

Private scho property.

SEC. 37. *And be it further enacted,* That whenever and wherever not less than thirty-five youths between five and twenty-one years of age may be found not already provided for, the territory containing said children shall be, so soon as practicable after the passage of this act, constituted by the county board of education in whose purview it is found, a sub-district, and provided with buildings and other appliances for school purposes.

Sub-districts how organized

SEC. 38. *And be it further enacted,* That admissions to schools of higher grades than primary shall be gratuitous to the children, wards, and apprentices of all actual residents in the districts possessing said schools who may be entitled to the privileges of the public schools,

Admission to high schools gratuitous t whom.

roviso.

under the general laws of this State: *Provided,* That said board shall have power to admit to said schools other pupils, upon such terms or upon the payment of such tuition as they may prescribe.

vening schools.

SEC. 39. *And be it further enacted,* That the board of education of any county may, at their discretion, upon their respective fields, provide a suitable number of evening schools, for the instruction of such youth, over fourteen years of age, as are prevented by their daily avocation from attending day schools, subject to such regulations as said board from time to time may adopt for the government thereof.

Term of con-
nuing schools
operation
nually.

SEC. 40. *And be it further enacted,* That the board of education of any county, including the county commissioner and local trustees of any sub-district, shall, according to regulations hereinbefore prescribed for schools, make the necessary provisions for continuing in operation the schools over which they have jurisdiction, for the term of three months in each year, except as hereinafter allowed in case of ambulatory schools; and in case the board of education of any county, or the local officers of any sub-district, shall fail to make the necessary provisions

Upon failure,
rfeit school
nd.

for continuing the schools in operation the length of time herein required, such graded or high schools, and primary schools, as the case may be, shall not be entitled to any portion of the School Fund arising from the State tax during the next succeeding school year, and such forfeited State school funds shall be distributed to the other several sub-districts of the county, in proportion to the enumeration of youth; and such of the officers above referred to as shall neglect or refuse to comply with the provisions of this section, shall be individually responsible for all losses sustained by any district or sub-district by reason of such neglect or refusal to comply with the provisions of this

Neglecting
'ficers i n d i-
dually responsi-
le.

section, and shall be severally and jointly liable for the same in a civil action, to be brought by the county commissioner in·the name of the State of Georgia; and the amount so recovered shall be apportioned to the several sub-districts in the same manner as the school funds would have been.

ounty school
nd to be de-
osited with Co.
reasurers.

SEC. 41. *And be it further enacted,* That the quota of the general school fund found belonging to each county in the State shall be, at the close of each fiscal school year, upon an order of the State Commissioner on the Treasurer, sent to and deposited with the respective County Treasurers, who shall be holden for such amount upon their

isbursement.

official bonds as Treasurers, who shall disburse the same to the various school districts in his county, upon order of the trustees, countersigned by the county commissioner or county board of education.

AMBULATORY SCHOOLS.

Ambula-
ry schools.

SEC. 42. *And be it further enacted,* That whenever and wherever there shall be found three militia districts contiguous, or in near proximity to each other, containing each not.less than 15 children of school age, provisions shall be made whereby schools may be kept in each two months annually. The place of holding the school shall be in locations most convenient to the larger number of the children, and the school terms so arranged that any one teacher may supply at least three schools. The districts referred to in this section shall be under the control of trustees, whose elective duties shall be the same as those in the more populous sub-districts; and the maintenance of a school in each militia district described in this section, for two months in each year, shall be held as compliance with terms contained in section 40 of this act, regulating the time entitling to the apportionment of school funds.

COMMON SCHOOL FUND.

SEC. 43. *And be it further enacted,* That for the support and maintenance of the common schools of this State, the poll-tax, special tax on shows and exhibitions, on the sale of spirituous and malt liquors, the proceeds arising from the commutation of military services, all endowments, devises, gifts and bequests made, or hereafter to be made, to the State, or State Board of Education, any and all educational funds and incomes not belonging to and due the State University, and one-half of the net earnings of the Western & Atlantic Railroad, are hereby appropriated to the State Common School Fund; and it shall be the duty of the State Board of Education to determine the amount which, in addition to the foregoing, should be raised annually by taxation upon all the taxable property of the State, and to report annually to the General Assembly the estimate which they may find necessary to support a school in every school district in the State, of at least three months in each year, in the manner provided in this act, the same to be apportioned with other funds, as hereinafter directed. *[Common schoo fund–ho made up. State Board Education mu determine ad tional am'ts be raised taxation.]*

SEC. 44. *And be it further enacted,* That the county board of education shall have power to organize in each county one or more manual labor schools, on such plans as will be self-sustaining: *Provided,* The same be approved by the State Board of Education. *[Manual lab schools. Provis]*

SEC. 45. *And be it further enacted,* That nothing contained in this act shall prevent the collection of any accounts rendered from a private school, or the teacher thereof, for the education of beneficiaries of the common school fund, in localities where the common school may not have been organized: *Provided,* That such accounts shall have been first duly audited by the board, whose duty it is to audit all school accounts. *[This act shall n prevent c lection of priva school accounts]*

SEC. 46. *And be it further enacted,* That the State Board of Education shall not be permitted to introduce into the schools any text or miscellaneous books of a sectarian or sectional character. *[Sectarian boo]*

SEC. 47. *And be it further enacted,* That the Secretary of State shall, as soon as practicable, make, or cause to be made, a digest of all the laws of force in this State relating to schools and education. *[Secretary State to ma digest of scho laws.]*

SEC. 48. Repeals conflicting laws.

Approved October 13, 1870.

Index

595